character &
characters

character & characters
The Spirit of Alaska Airlines

ROBERT J. SERLING

Documentary Media LLC
Seattle, Washington

BIRTHPLACE

There's the land. (Have you seen it?)
It's the cussedest land that I know,
From the big, dizzy mountains that screen it
To the deep, deathlike valleys below.
Some say God was tired when He made it;
Some say it's a fine land to shun;
Maybe; but there's some as would trade it
For no land on earth — and I'm one. . . .

I've stood in some mighty-mouthed hollow
That's plumb-full of hush to the brim;
I've watched the big, husky sun wallow
In crimson and gold, and grow dim,
Till the moon set the pearly peaks gleaming,
And the stars tumbled out, neck and crop;
And I've thought that I surely was dreaming,
With the peace o' the world piled on top. . . .

There's a land where the mountains are nameless,
And the rivers all run God knows where;
There are lives that are erring and aimless,
And deaths that just hang by a hair;
There are hardships that nobody reckons;
There are valleys unpeopled and still;
There's a land — oh, it beckons and beckons,
And I want to go back — and I will.

Robert W. Service (from "The Spell of the Yukon")

DEDICATION

To the men and women of Alaska Air Group —
past, present, and future. The people of an airline are
the real historians, not authors.
You are a very special people who have written, and
are still writing, a very special history.

And

To the memory of
Bruce R. Kennedy
1938 – 2007

Bob Serling

Character & Characters: The Spirit of Alaska Airlines

First edition 2008

Printed in Canada
Printed on recycled paper—100 percent PCW.

Documentary Media LLC
3250 41st Avenue S.W.
Seattle, Washington 98116
206 935-9292
www.documentarymedia.com

Managing Editor: Petyr Beck
Copy Editor: Judy Gouldthorpe
Designer: Sancho Design
Publisher: Barry Provorse

Library of Congress Cataloging-in-Publication Data

Serling, Robert J., 1918-

Character & characters : the spirit of Alaska Airlines / Robert J. Serling.
p. cm.

Includes bibliographical references and index.

ISBN 978-1-933245-11-9 (alk. paper)

1. Alaska Airlines—History. I. Title. II. Title: Character and characters.

HE9803.A94S74 2008
387.7065'73—dc22

2008007708

CONTENTS

FOREWORD

Representing Alaska in the United States Senate for more than 38 years has meant hundreds of trips between the Last Frontier and our nation's capital. It has also meant countless visits to constituents in communities all across our state. Most of this travel has been on Alaska Airlines. As a pilot and a frequent flier, I have long admired "our" little airline, which has now grown to be one of the nation's largest.

Alaska Airlines has been a part of my life since I arrived in Alaska in 1953, six years before the Territory of Alaska would achieve statehood. Among the first people I came to know in our state were pilots who worked for this airline. Some were returning veterans like me, and others were old-timers with gripping stories about flying canvas-winged Stinsons for the companies that eventually formed Alaska Airlines.

Those pilots flew through blinding snowstorms, passed between mountaintops, and often landed on gravel bars. They braved Alaska's harsh conditions to deliver basic goods such as flour, condensed milk, and even eggs to miners, trappers, and other hardworking characters scratching at Alaska's vast geography in search of a living.

Over the years, it has been my privilege to know many of the chief officers of Alaska Airlines — men such as Ray Marshall, Ron Cosgrave, Bruce Kennedy, Ray Vecci, John Kelly, and Bill Ayer — all remarkable individuals who chiseled Alaska Airlines' strong character and expanded their company when Congress deregulated airlines in 1978. They successfully entered new markets, financed new equipment, and overcame changes in the price of jet fuel. Alaska Airlines now employs more than 10,000 people and operates one of the most modern fleets in the sky.

Bob Serling's story of Alaska Airlines is a great addition to the historical books about Alaska, and it underscores the significance of aviation to our state. Nowhere in the world is air transportation more important than in Alaska. For thousands of Alaskans, aviation is truly a lifeline — more than 70 percent of our cities, towns, and villages cannot be reached by road.

Alaska Airlines has helped meet the transportation needs of countless Alaskans for more than 75 years. Today, they operate over 100 planes and offer service to more than 58 cities throughout North America. We can even fly Alaska Airlines from Anchorage to Washington, D.C., on the same plane. When I think back, I know why this pioneering airline has been able to come so far: it was Alaskans who made their dreams come true.

My advice to Alaska Airlines? Keep up the great work — and be sure the company remains Alaskan!

Best wishes,

U.S. Senator Ted Stevens

INTRODUCTION

This is the biography of an airline. I suppose it would be more politically correct to call it a corporate history, but after writing about U.S. civil aviation since 1947, I am unable to regard any American air carrier as a typical corporation.

Yes, they all have the usual trappings of every publicly held corporate entity, with boards of directors, listings on stock exchanges, requisite annual reports, chief executive officers, platoons of vice presidents arranged in precise pecking order, managers, supervisors, and of course an army of rank-and-file employees.

Add up the sum of all those individual parts and you have a quintessential corporation. Add them up at an airline, and the corporate entity turns out to be something different — an entity that's alive, infused with the personalities, dreams, courage, and resilience of very special human beings.

They are special because they work in an environment where superb technology still requires the human touch. And the latter is generated by an individual's attitude toward company and job. Call it pride, a word that covers a lot of territory. Pride is not exclusive to the airline industry, but its importance to air carriers is enormous.

Other industries seek employee pride, but for airlines it is vital. It provides a protective armor in a cyclical industry so terribly vulnerable to so many negative influences, most of them beyond the control of those who have to deal with their impact. Theirs is a constant battle for survival that became unusually acute in 1978, when the airline industry was deregulated, worsened following the first Gulf War, and turned into a bloodbath after the carnage of 9/11.

The body count of major and regional airlines that no longer exist is brutal, and it includes carriers that were more like national institutions than mere companies. Consider the fates of Pan American, TWA, and Eastern. Add the names Braniff, Western, National, Capital, Flying Tiger, and Northeast. Don't forget PSA, Air Florida, Republic, Hughes Airwest, People Express, and Air California. And that's only a partial casualty list.

The Alaska Airlines story is a saga of survival, and a key factor is that pride has become part of the company's culture. But there are two other reasons, both rather unusual:

One – The airline has had an uncanny knack for picking the right leader at precisely the right time, and conversely, each leader has been succeeded by the right new leader.

Two – It has never forgotten where its real roots lie, in the state of Alaska itself.

The first is a practical explanation. The second, strange as it may seem, is an almost intangible yet very real state of mind that permeates the entire company, from senior officers down through the ranks. In effect, the airline has taken on the personality, psyche, values, ethics, courage, determination, and resilience of the rugged land whose name it bears.

I have written the histories of six airlines (North Central, Western, Continental, Eastern, TWA, and American) and two aerospace companies (Boeing and Learjet). I greatly respected and admired each of them. But I have never encountered anything in aviation quite as unusual as an airline that technically, economically, operationally, and geographically has outgrown its name — and yet refuses to change it.

It makes absolutely no difference that Alaska Airlines has matured into a transcontinental and international carrier whose routes now stretch coast-to-coast and extend into Florida and Mexico. Its aircraft pull into gates at Phoenix, Miami, Orlando, Chicago, Newark, Boston, Washington, Dallas/Fort Worth, and at this writing 10 destinations in Mexico, including Mexico City and La Paz. Yet the tail of each jetliner still proudly displays the airline's famous logo, which some consider incongruous: an Eskimo with a hint of a kindly smile on his face. And on the forward fuselage, in bold blue script, is the name *Alaska*. The combination seems almost defiant.

The very uniqueness of that tail insignia has helped set the airline apart from other carriers. It symbolizes the company's heritage, traditions, and commitment to being a little different from and often a little better than anyone else.

Even in its direst times, its worst moments of crisis, Alaska has always been blessed with customer loyalty unsurpassed by that of any other airline. The core of that loyalty rests within the state of Alaska, and by the same token the airline has remained loyal to the people of Alaska. It has to be that way, for if this air carrier is unique, it is because so too is the land in which it was born. Alaska itself has known adversity — a devastating earthquake, volcanic eruptions, hostile weather, and in World War II, a Japanese invasion.

What eventually would become the 49th state was purchased from Russia in 1867 for $7.2 million, a deal engineered by Secretary of State William H. Seward that narrowly escaped rejection by a dubious Congress. Before Alaska acquired its modern moniker The Last Frontier, its unofficial nickname was Seward's Folly. Most Americans thought that Russia had pulled off a swindle akin to selling residential lots in the middle of the Florida Everglades.

It turned out to be not a swindle but a steal. The United States had acquired, for what a single jet airliner would cost in the late 1970s, a land with enormous natural resources, from gold to oil to priceless scenery and magnificent wildlife. The word *Alaska* comes from the Aleut word meaning "Great Land," and it fits. The state is more than twice the size of Texas, larger than the combined area of France, Germany, and Spain. It is one-fifth the size of the other 49 states combined. Yet it has fewer roads than tiny Rhode Island and only two-thirds its population.

Washington's King County, which includes the city of Seattle, has a million more people than the entire state of Alaska. The combined population of Anchorage, Fairbanks, and Juneau — Alaska's three largest cities, in that order — is less than that of Long Beach, California.

Fairbanks, which used to be bigger than Anchorage, has always been a little sensitive about its second-place population ranking. A favorite local saying goes: "The best thing about Anchorage is that it's only five minutes away from Alaska."

Alaska is America's most northern state, and Nome, which became a boomtown during the Gold Rush of 1897, geographically lies farther west than Honolulu. The discovery of gold, incidentally, brought some 30,000 migrants into Alaska, most of them hopeful prospectors who turned the Klondike region and towns such as Nome, Sitka, and Ketchikan into replicas of the old Wild West, complete with noisy saloons, gunfights, and prostitutes.

The Gold Rush era was the seediest period in Alaska's history, yet it also had an upside. These indomitable new settlers brought with them the kind of toughness they needed to survive in an unfriendly wilderness. They were a hardy can-do breed, determined to overcome adversity, refusing to give up no matter what the odds. Most Alaskans of today seem to have inherited that strength.

Symbols of strength and the ability to survive, the first people who migrated to Alaska came from Siberia around 3000 BC, a rough trek over ice despite the fact that Alaska is closer to Russia than to the rest of the United States. An example is Alaska's Little Diomede Island, only two miles from Russian soil.

Native Alaskans are skilled hunters, trappers, fishermen, and artisans who for generations depended on sled dogs for transportation, a mode that the white settlers later adopted. But dogs and sleds obviously couldn't handle the needs of this vast expanding territory. The forbidding terrain and adverse weather limited both the laying of railroad tracks and road-building, so it was the airplane that really took Alaska into the 20th century. In effect, aviation and Alaska have become practically synonymous.

Thus was born the legend of the bush pilots, and it must be remembered that these hard-drinking, hard-living characters were angels of mercy to scores of isolated villages, whose residents learned to depend on them in any situation requiring emergency food, medicine, or medical care. They flew in even the worst weather, often under visibility conditions that would ground the average airman.

Eskimos and Alaskans in general are a resourceful, proud people. So it is entirely possible that the little smile on the face adorning the tails of more than 100 modern jetliners is one of pride. After all, the flying Eskimo symbolizes a very proud and resourceful airline that happens to be grateful for its ancestral roots.

Robert J. Serling
Tucson, Arizona

PROLOGUE

1932 . . .

It was the coldest winter on record in Fairbanks, Alaska, and the worst year of the worst depression in American history. There are no definitive figures on how many adult Americans were unemployed, the estimates ranging from slightly under 9 million to as high as 17 million. Most historians accept 12 to 13 million out of 1932's total U.S. population of 125 million as probably the most accurate.

It was no different in Alaska. Its colonial economy prospered for a while after the stock market crash in 1929, for its wealth was based on its natural resources. When the price of copper and fish values were halved, however, Alaskans joined the rest of North America in widespread poverty. Kennecott Copper collapsed before the end of the Depression, and its failure put about 600 miners out of work. Countless others suffered indirectly from the closure.

The federal government was Alaska's largest employer, and where the bureaucrats lived, local economies survived. At one point, 52 federal government agencies ruled the Territory. Alaska's 60,000 or so residents benefited little from FDR's New Deal, but thanks to federal funds 1,000 Swedish-emigrant farmers from Michigan, Wisconsin, and Minnesota were relocated north to settle and farm the Matanuska Valley floor, about 190 miles northeast of Anchorage. In theory it was to make Alaska's agriculture self-sustaining, but the plan fizzled like cheap fireworks.

Even with the allure of the Alaska Railroad, tourism dropped from 30,000 visitors in 1929 to less than 15,000 by 1932. A trip to Alaska could cost as much as $600 at a time when $350 would buy travelers six weeks in Europe.

Air travel had developed in Alaska after World War I, and the Territory's early pilots were made of strong stuff. Pilots were heroes, especially after Charles Lindbergh's trans-Atlantic flight in 1927. Alaska's pilots were no different, just colder.

In the Lower 48 it was the battered economy, not the troubles of a few bush pilots, that dominated the headlines. For these were the days of breadlines, soup kitchens, ramshackle camps for the homeless derisively called Hoovervilles, and migrants in the thousands riding illegally on whatever freight trains they could sneak onto that were heading west. That's where at least the weather, if not the job market, was warmer.

Los Angeles was a magnet for these desperate wanderers, although Southern California's healthiest industry — the motion picture studios — had very few help-wanted signs posted at the gate. In fact, one of them, RKO Pictures, was gambling on a single film that it hoped might save it from bankruptcy.

It had been in secret production during most of 1932, filmed under tight security because its bizarre story required the creation of what were then the most challenging special effects in film history. Its "chief technician," that era's nomenclature for a special-effects director, was an inventive genius named Willis O'Brien. He spent the year constructing and then animating, with a technique called stop-motion animation, miniature dinosaurs with rubber skins and jointed metal skeletons. His major task, however, was to create the film's star: a 30-foot-tall gorilla. What O'Brien fashioned was only 18 inches high, with articulated limbs like those of the tiny dinosaurs, and covered with dyed rabbit fur.

The ape, of course, was the immortal King Kong. The film of the same name cost RKO an estimated $670,000 to make, which might be compared to the $207 million the 2005 remake cost. But it was worth every penny to RKO because *King Kong* probably saved the studio.

Willis O'Brien's work earned a special niche in aviation history as well as film history. In 1924, eight years before *King Kong* was made, O'Brien had used animated rubber dinosaurs in the first movie adaptation of Arthur Conan Doyle's novel *The Lost World*. In April 1925, passengers on an Imperial Airways Handley Page biplane, flying from London to Paris, watched the movie in its entirety, the first in-flight motion picture in commercial aviation history.

It figured that a foreign carrier had pioneered something like in-flight entertainment. In 1932, U.S. civil aviation was just beginning to catch up with Europe's. Scheduled air service had been commonplace there since the early 1920s, and that included modern aircraft with enclosed cabins, lava-tories, upholstered seats, and uniformed stewards serving beverages and in-flight food. In contrast, some of the early American carriers inaugurated service in one-passenger open biplanes, and if the mail load was heavy, the customer sat on top of the mail bags that had been dumped where he was supposed to sit.

In 1932 this country's airline industry was only six years old, its birth coming in 1926, when Congress forced the Post Office Department to turn over its airmail routes to private operators. During those six years, considerable progress had been made from the days when carrying the mail was most airlines' prime revenue source and developing passenger traffic was not only ignored but in some cases even discouraged. Mail contracts ruled the commercial skies, and "Fly with the U.S. Mail" was a favorite airline advertising slogan that was supposed to attract passenger business.

When airmail started as an experiment in Alaska in 1924, it was not a financial success for the postal service or for the territory's bush pilots. There were only 26 landing strips scattered over the territory's 570, 833-square-mile landmass. Mail service in the far north was more of a patchwork solution than a system. Most intraterritorial mail moved in the bellies of riverboats when rivers were ice-free, or was packed over Alaska's 5,000 miles of flagged, overland trails. Not until 1938 did Pan American begin carrying the mail between Seattle and Alaska.

Overall, the nation's airline industry had a lot of growing-up to accomplish and countless hurdles to overcome, not the least of which was the Depression itself. Even in the boom years of the 1920s, air travel in the United States was about as popular as head colds. It is one of history's greatest ironies that the nation where heavier-than-air flight was first achieved was the last major industrialized country to realize the commercial potential of the airplane.

Most Americans thought of airplanes in terms of World War I aerial dogfights — in 1927 the very first Academy Award for Best Picture went to Paramount's *Wings* — and postwar barnstorming pilots who toured county fairs in old biplanes, entertained with wing-walking and other aerial stunts, and offered rides for five dollars to anyone brave enough to climb into the front seat of an ancient Jenny biplane.

Fear was the infant airline industry's biggest problem, and not without considerable justification. In 1932, U.S. scheduled air carriers suffered 108 accidents, 16 of them fatal. Virtually every crash was blamed on pilot error, yet given the limited technical tools available to 1932 airmen, a dismal safety record was inevitable. The airlines, for example, had just begun equipping their fleets with a newfangled gadget: the two-way radio. Before that, radio communications in Alaska had been transmitted mostly in Morse code by widely scattered Army Signal Corps stations, and some ships at sea when high mountain peaks didn't block the signal.

Maps in Alaska were no better than radio communications. Pilots simply had to know where they were, and what altitude was necessary to clear mountain passes.

For airlines in Alaska and the Lower 48, it took salesmanship to fill seats. Safety was weighed against necessity before booking a flight. Most life insurance policies were automatically voided for the duration of any air trip; not until 1938, thanks largely to the increasing use of the new DC-3s and their reputation for safety, could flight insurance be purchased at airports. A $5,000 policy cost 25 cents.

As 1932 was coming to a close, one safety measure caused great consternation among veterans of the old airmail days, men used to flying by the seat of their pants. The federal government announced that effective January 1, 1933, all airline pilots had to be qualified to fly on instruments whenever necessary. Uncle Sam might as well have questioned their manhood.

Excluding Pan American Airways, then the nation's only international carrier, there were 24 scheduled domestic U.S. airlines in 1932, operating 700 daily flights with a fleet of about 450 aircraft, a whopping 80 percent of them single-engine planes that usually needed only a single pilot. The queens of the domestic airways were the noisy but sturdy all-metal Ford Tri-Motor, the Boeing Model 80 tri-motor biplane, and the relatively luxurious but woefully slow Curtiss Condor, a big twin-engine biplane whose forest of wing struts and guy wires literally created their own headwinds.

In 1932, however, a revolutionary airliner was taking shape in Seattle: Boeing's all-metal, twin-engine 247, with the first retractable landing gear ever installed on a commercial transport. The 247 turned out to be a technological triumph, winning the 1932 Collier Trophy for the year's most outstanding aeronautical achievement. But it was an economic failure. Even larger and better airliners were coming off the drawing boards that would make the 247 obsolete almost overnight. These included the new Douglas DC-2, which in turn begot the immortal DC-3.

United, TWA, American, and Eastern were known then as the Big Four of the nation's domestic carriers, and Pan Am made it an unofficial Big Five. This quintet truly dominated an air transportation system whose 25 airlines carried a record half-million passengers in 1932. Their schedules took up

most of the space in the 1932 *Official Aviation Guide*, but also included were
the schedules of such familiar names as Northwest, Braniff, and Western,
and such unfamiliar ones as Martz, Bowen, Mamer, Reed, Rapid, Wyoming,
Hunter, Ludington, Coast, and Hanford Tri-State.

That same 1932 *Guide* made no mention of any scheduled passenger or
airmail service to or from Alaska, nor even within the Territory. Ships carried
all the incoming and outgoing mail, much of it via major seaports such as
Anchorage and Valdez. Most air operations at that time were either chartered
or impromptu flights.

In retrospect, one has to wonder how the airlines ever found some 500,000
people willing to fly. Even discounting the industry's horrendous safety record, a trip by air was not synonymous with joy, pleasure, or comfort. A 1932
advertisement extolling the virtues of the Ford Tri-Motor boasted that the
airplane was "swift as the wind, smooth as a yacht." The ad failed to mention
that the Tin Goose was also noisier than a boilerplate factory.

One out of every two passengers riding on *any* airplane in the 1930s
was almost certain to get airsick. In fact, the prevalence of airsickness was
the major reason why the early flight attendants had to be registered nurses,
and this requirement lasted on the majority of carriers until World War II.
Maximum height was five feet three inches because aircraft cabins of the late
1920s and early 1930s weren't high enough for anyone taller.

On long trips, passengers frequently deplaned to eat at airport restaurants during refueling stops, and there were quite a few if you were traveling
any distance by air. The famous Harvey restaurant chain, so familiar to railroad passengers, had eating facilities at several airports along one carrier's
transcontinental route.

The average commercial transport plane could fly only 300 miles before
having to land for refueling. Weather delays and cancellations were so frequent that pilots often carried vouchers for railroad tickets in case a flight had
to be grounded for a great length of time. In winter months the airlines were
often the railroads' best customers. A cruising altitude exceeding 5,000 feet
was a rare occurrence, and few flights went higher than 8,000 feet, which of
course meant there was little or no chance of flying above bad weather.

If weather was the number one operational enemy of 1932 air travel,
engine reliability was number two. Engine inspections had to be made after
every 25 hours of flight, and that was because any engine that went more
than 50 hours without some kind of inspection or preventive maintenance

— usually checking spark plugs and cylinder heads — was guaranteed to develop some form of mechanical malfunction.

Schedule unreliability led inevitably to massive red ink. So desperate were the airlines for additional revenue that in 1932, seven of them resorted to selling card advertisements placed on the cabin walls of their aircraft, similar to those on city streetcars and buses. The card ads lasted about a year before it was decided they were too undignified for airline customers, who in 1932 were, for the most part, relatively substantial businessmen.

It might also be noted that with only 700 daily flights, the airlines in 1932 were running their own air traffic control system. Not for another four years would the federal government's Bureau of Air Commerce take over the task of controlling traffic on the nation's airways.

Air travel was still considered such a novelty in the early 1930s that the airplane even became a political weapon for a presidential candidate, namely Franklin D. Roosevelt, the polio-crippled governor of New York, who had just been nominated by the 1932 Democratic convention in Chicago. He insisted on flying from Albany to the Windy City to accept the nomination.

Competing with the 1932 presidential election as the year's biggest news story was the kidnapping and murder of Charles Lindbergh's infant son, a crime that some mystery buffs still believe was never fully solved. The New Jersey datelines of Hopewell, where the Lindberghs lived, and Flemington, where Bruno Richard Hauptmann was tried and convicted, were branded into the memories of countless Americans who temporarily forgot their economic problems to sympathize with the Lone Eagle and his wife, Anne Morrow Lindbergh.

There was little drama in the presidential election, which brought no surprises. Incumbent Herbert Hoover, in truth a caring and capable man, stood no chance against the dynamic FDR, but history has been unkind to the Quaker from California, who at least deserved some gratitude from the aviation community. Hoover had been Secretary of Commerce in the Coolidge administration, and in 1926 was instrumental in creating the new Aeronautics Branch within the Commerce Department.

The Aeronautics Branch was the first federal agency to oversee the young, undisciplined airline industry, taking on such regulatory responsibilities as establishing new standards for pilot qualifications and investigating accidents, plus improving the airways. By 1932, the government had established some 18,000 miles of lighted airways, dramatically increasing night flying. In that respect at least, the United States was ahead of Europe.

Come the 1932 election, however, achievements so important to civil aviation made little difference at a time when a demoralized nation associated Hoover with jobless millions. FDR carried 42 of the 48 states, winning 472 electoral votes to Hoover's 59.

Of course, there were no electoral college votes to be counted in America's largest chunk of real estate: the 586,400 square miles that constituted what was then the Territory of Alaska. It wouldn't achieve statehood for another 27 years.

It would have been rare to find even mildly interesting headlines coming out of that vast wilderness in 1932, certainly not any concerning an unknown 35-year-old adventurer from Indiana and Montana who had arrived in Anchorage three years earlier, as ambitious as he was broke. Yet that is where the story of Alaska Airlines began — seven and a half decades ago.

CHAPTER ONE

A Midwife Named McGee

His name was Linious McGee, and he was more entrepreneur than pilot. He didn't learn to fly until after he came to Alaska, and never achieved the fame nor the flying skills of such legendary Alaskan bush pilots as Noel Wien, Bob Reeve, Merle "Mudhole" Smith, and Bob Ellis. But he did share their stubborn resolve and aspirations.

Contrary to what most aviation buffs believe, bush flying did not originate only in Alaska. It seems to have sprung up in at least four countries almost simultaneously after World War I, when hundreds of former military pilots began looking for flying jobs, the only trade they knew and loved.

Airlines were scarcely out of the womb and offered employment to only a fraction of this army of frustrated airmen. So they gravitated toward remote areas where settlements were hundreds of miles apart, almost totally isolated except where terrain permitted such primitive means of transportation as animal-drawn carts, wagons, or sleds, or human feet.

Four areas were early targets for the pilots: Alaska, Northern Canada, the scrublands of Australia, and the South African interior. But bush flying also spread to the Amazon rain forests, New Guinea, and Mexico's Sierra Madre. South Africa, in fact, might be the logical nominee as its birthplace.

But to most Americans, bush pilot flying is associated almost entirely with Alaska and, to some extent, Canada.

Linious "Mac" McGee was an unlikely candidate for membership in this exclusive fraternity. He was a native of Francesville, Indiana, who then moved to Montana. Like many other restless and unemployed young men of the Depression era, McGee was attracted by Alaska's unlimited if still theoretical potential. He was ambitious, a hard worker, and without strong family ties, and like Alaska itself, he had potential.

So in 1929, he stowed away on the steamship *Aleutian* and landed in Anchorage virtually broke. Time has blurred his exact financial status upon arrival, but McGee himself once told an interviewer that all he had in his pocket was $1.65. He was a real-life Horatio Alger character, willing to work at anything for anybody, provided it would further his ultimate goal: to be the boss of his own company.

Over the next three years, he was a dishwasher, miner, and truck driver for Standard Oil, living as simply and frugally as possible while building up a modest cash reserve. In his spare time, he made friends with several bush pilots. There were always plenty of these rugged and sometimes rowdy characters around.

It seemed as if anyone who owned an airplane was running some kind of bush operation and calling it an airline, even if he had only one airplane. In the earliest days, the bush pilots flew a motley collection of secondhand airplanes, many of them surplus noncombat aircraft from the war. Low price tags were their major virtue.

Pilots do not necessarily make good businessmen, but there were a few who built up respectable air carriers from scratch. Art Woodley, whose Woodley Airways became Pacific Northern Airlines, was one, and so were Noel Wien, Bob Reeve, Bob Ellis, and S. B. "Shell" Simmons. As it turned out, so was Mac McGee.

The best description of Alaska's pioneering bush pilots came from the dean of aviation historians, R. E. G. Davies, who wrote this paragraph in his classic *Airlines of the United States Since 1914*:

"They operated on a financial shoestring. The owner flew the aircraft, his wife kept the books. He sold tickets through friends and by the application of low cunning beat his rivals. His business ethics were born of the Klondike saloon and were hardly genteel. He would cheerfully risk his life and his assets (i.e., his aircraft) in a foolhardy gamble perhaps to make a quick dollar, perhaps to rescue a competitor in trouble. The men who contributed to the saga of Alaskan airline development belong to a distinguished company."

McGee established a close relationship with one pilot in particular, an ex-barnstormer with a reputation for some screwball antics, such as taking off from a dry gravel road in a plane equipped with snow skis. He was Harvey Barnhill, nicknamed "Barney," and while a bit flaky, he was also a brilliant pilot, the kind who could have flown an iron bathtub if it had wings and an engine. By 1931, McGee had saved enough to start his own fur-trading business and decided he needed an airplane. Trappers and trading posts were scattered all over Alaska. Quite naturally, he turned to Barnhill for advice, and this mismatched pair formed a partnership.

McGee was a workaholic, serious, and scrupulously honest. Barnhill was unpredictable, a marginal alcoholic with a devious streak. McGee once wryly observed, "Barney's pretty fast on his feet." It was a comment made after their first joint business transaction.

They purchased an airplane from Walter Varney, an aviation pioneer himself who in 1926 had started an airline bearing his own name, one that eventually became Continental Airlines, a carrier, incidentally, that decades later was to provide Alaska Airlines with some of its finest talent. The negotiations were held in San Francisco, and the airplane Varney wanted to sell was a three-seat Stinson monoplane, a smaller version of the popular Stinson Detroiter. The aircraft was only two years old and reasonably priced at $5,000, but according to McGee's later account, Barnhill almost blew the deal.

It seems that what Barnhill tried to give Varney for his $2,500 share of the airplane were bonds from the city of Kelso, Washington. Varney checked with his broker and was told the bonds weren't worth anywhere near $2,500, so Barnhill had to rush to Seattle to raise the amount in cash. Where and how he got it is unknown.

The partners flew the airplane from San Francisco to Seattle, then had it crated up and sent to the Alaskan port of Valdez by boat. For a brief time, the lettering on the fuselage read "McGee-Barnhill Airways," and the airplane initially was used solely to support McGee's fur business. But with the dawn of 1932, McGee apparently was bitten by the aviation bug and decided to offer charter service between Anchorage and Bristol Bay.

McGee even took the drastic step of learning to fly, just to relieve Barnhill, who was flying the Stinson to every remote trading post and village within range. Then McGee got a break when some businessmen in Seward talked him into providing charter flights to new prospectors and other fresh arrivals who wanted fast transportation from Seward to various

Alaskan locations.

With the aid of a bank loan, the partners bought a second Stinson, painted black and silver like the first. The plane was delivered to them by none other than McGee's half-brother, Estes Call, a pilot himself who decided to stay in Alaska and work with Mac. Now McGee and Barnhill had a real airline, in a land where even just two airplanes constituted a fleet. But this turned out to be their last joint venture.

Late in the spring of 1932, the McGee-Barnhill partnership was dissolved. McGee never explained exactly why they ended not only their business relationship but apparently their friendship as well. Barnhill had somehow wound up owning the second Stinson, probably as a payback for his share of the deteriorating partnership, tried in vain to sell it in the lower 48 states, and finally sold it back to McGee at a nice profit.

At that point, Barnhill seems to have faded from McGee's life. Years later he was a passenger in a fatal automobile accident, thus defying the predictions that he was destined to die in an airplane crash while drunk. Mac hired two experienced employees — Oscar Winchell, a veteran bush pilot, and a full-time mechanic named Earl Woods — and it was now McGee Airways. So Alaska's bush carriers had a new boy on the block.

Curiously, Linious McGee's name isn't even mentioned in most of the books written about Alaska's bush-flying era, probably because although he became a fairly good pilot, absorbing flying knowledge from airmen such as Barnhill and Winchell, his real talent was in management. In that area, he displayed not only instinctive executive ability but also surprising farsightedness for an airline neophyte. By the time his company merged with Star Air Service in 1935, McGee's fleet included seven Stinson Model S Junior aircraft.

The only author to thoroughly research McGee's life was Archie Satterfield, a freelance journalist who wrote *The Alaska Airlines Story*, a history published in 1981 to mark the airline's 50th anniversary. Satterfield described McGee as "a compulsive worker."

"He never walked," Satterfield wrote. "He ran or jogged everywhere. He did not know how to play . . . even on vacation. He worked every day of the week under the assumption, one friend said, 'that since there are seven days a week, you might as well work them all.' He expected his employees to work equally hard."

Yet McGee seems to have been a fair boss, and he may have invented the first version of a profit-sharing plan. Instead of a salary, Oscar Winchell, his pilot after Barnhill left, received 12.5 percent of the airline's gross revenues, and McGee later raised the percentage to 15. He made the same arrangement with other pilots he subsequently hired.

McGee is also credited with being one of the first, if not *the* first, airline officials to adopt the policy of fleet standardization, operating identical aircraft so that parts were interchangeable and maintenance costs reduced. This was an eye-opener for many bush operators, whose fleets might include four or five different types of aircraft.

As McGee expanded his air service, he ended up with a fleet of seven identical Stinsons. He hired full-time mechanics who worked in a well-equipped hangar, and the Lycoming engines that powered the Stinsons were shipped to the Lycoming factory for regularly scheduled major overhauls after every 750 hours of service.

Not all the bush airlines operated with such regimented maintenance. It was more common to wait for an engine to get terminally ill before doing anything about it. McGee extended his better-to-be-safe-than-sorry philosophy to his pilots as well. He tried to give them better weather information, either deliberately or accidentally borrowing a technique believed to have been originated by French pilots flying airmail trips through Andes mountain passes in South America. Weather observers were stationed in strategic locations overlooking the passes and would report current visibility conditions by radio or telephone. The 1939 film *Only Angels Have Wings*, starring Cary Grant, Jean Arthur, and Rita Hayworth, depicted just such an operation.

A U.S. airline, Western Air Express, put a variation of this safety measure into operation as early as 1928 on its Los Angeles-San Francisco route. The carrier hired special weather observers who radioed up-to-date weather reports to the flights as they proceeded along the airway.

It's unlikely that Mac McGee had ever heard of Western's so-called "Model Airway." Nor was safety his only motive for unwittingly imitating the weather-observing stations. While he was fully aware that inadequate weather information was probably the leading cause of Alaskan plane crashes, his other motive was economic. It was a way to beat competitors vying for the same charter service out of Anchorage to outlying fur-trading villages.

The shortest air route between Anchorage and those villages was through a mountain gap known as Rainy Pass. McGee built two cabins, one on each side of the pass, stocked them with food and beverages, and added something that few if any Alaskan bush carriers had at the time: two-way radios. The radios were installed for the weather observer that McGee parked in each cabin, and in the Stinsons as well.

If the visibility at Rainy Pass was bad, McGee's pilots would land near one of the cabins, leave their passengers there to eat and relax, and then fly back to Anchorage. When the weather observers reported improving visibility, the pilots would pick up another load, fly through the pass to wherever the passengers were heading, then fly back to the pass, pick up the stranded passengers, and take them to their destinations.

Those two trips provided air service for about the same number of customers as McGee's competitors were carrying in one of their larger aircraft. It was not only cheaper than buying bigger airplanes, but also safer. McGee's standing rule for every man who flew for him was simple: "If you have any doubt about the weather, stay home."

From all accounts, McGee was a well-liked figure around Anchorage, and his friends included some of his competitors. He even had an amicable relationship with the one who gave his airline the most trouble, the irascible Art Woodley, whose explosive temper was legendary. Woodley once got so mad at his secretary for misspelling a word in a business letter that he threw her typewriter out of a second-story window.

But in truth, all of McGee's popularity, ingenuity, and dedication to both safety and efficiency were mere stopgap measures that temporarily staved off the inevitable. There were just too many bush companies competing for the same business in a relatively limited market.

Larger, better-financed carriers were gradually squeezing the smaller ones into oblivion, either through bankruptcy or mergers. Linious McGee's brave little upstart was one of the latter, and so was a company that could have been its twin. It was called Star Air Service, and like McGee Airways, it was launched in 1932 with a single airplane.

Star's midwives were Stephen "Steve" Mills and Jack Waterworth, a pair of flight instructors from Seattle, and a young Canadian pilot named Charlie Ruttan who had migrated to Anchorage, learned to fly, and become friends with Mills. Ruttan had something the other two lacked — a little cash — and Mills talked him into becoming the third partner in starting up a one-plane airline.

All three were young; Ruttan and Waterworth were only 22, and Mills at 36 wasn't exactly a senior citizen. What they shared besides the enthusiastic confidence of youth — and what they also shared with Linious McGee — was ambition so strong that it turned dreams into reality.

But reality also took the form of accepting limitations. The aircraft they finally bought, with money that Ruttan loaned to the new partnership, was an open-cockpit, one-passenger Fleet biplane, considerably inferior in every respect to McGee's first Stinson monoplane, which at least had an enclosed cockpit and a cabin with three seats. Anyone who saw pictures of the Fleet was reminded of the flimsy relics flown by the early airmail pilots. But it was all that these embryonic airline moguls could afford, and typical of the equipment that launched so many of the early bush operations.

The first name they chose for their minuscule airline was Northern Air Service, but this was discarded when they realized there were too many bush airplanes flying around with the word "Northern" somewhere on the fuselage. Their second choice was North Star Airlines (although calling the lone Fleet an airline was decidedly pretentious), and this was shortened to the name they finally settled on: Star Air Service.

All three, however, were still a bit enamored with "North Star," so they christened their single airplane *North Star* and painted the name on its nose. Formal partnership papers were drawn up, and the new venture began with a modest capitalization of $4,000 that Ruttan provided. Today, $4,000 would just about cover the cost of jet fuel consumed on a 737-800 flight from Seattle to Anchorage.

The partnership agreement also called for Mills, as senior partner and chief pilot, to be paid $200 a month, with Waterworth and Ruttan getting $150. Ruttan was named business manager, and Waterworth was at the bottom of the management totem pole as a mere flight instructor. But as Ruttan commented years later, when writer Satterfield interviewed him for his golden-anniversary book, those salary scales remained imaginary for some time because "there wasn't any money to divide."

Star Air Service got off the ground in April 1932, but not as a real airline. For several months there was little demand for charter flights, so Star operated almost exclusively as a flight school, and in this air-minded land there were enough Alaskans who wanted to take flying lessons to bring in some revenue. This, plus the earlier formation of a legal if temporarily impoverished partnership, attracted a few investors, the principal one being Earl Dunkle, a wealthy Alaskan mining engineer and a good friend of Mills and Waterworth.

In fact, before Ruttan entered the picture, Dunkle had loaned Mills and Waterworth enough money to buy a two-place Davis monoplane so they could start a flying school in Anchorage. Unfortunately, Waterworth crashed while on a test flight, damaging it beyond repair. Mills and Waterworth not only lost the airplane, but Dunkle soured on helping them again until he heard about the legally organized partnership that already had an airplane.

The flying school got some customers, but there wasn't enough revenue to pay all the bills, and things were so tight that Ruttan joined the Anchorage Fire Department so he'd have a free place to sleep. Then, only three months after its founding, Star Air Service went out of business temporarily when Al Monson, another local bush pilot, borrowed the Fleet and then cracked it up landing at Anchorage's Merrill Field.

The partners had to get jobs shoveling gravel for a construction company so they could raise enough money to pay for the Fleet's repairs. They did the work themselves, at night, after they had finished their temporary manual-labor jobs.

With Star back in business, they got Earl Dunkle to provide fresh financial help and raised additional cash from other investors. This enabled them not only to purchase a second airplane — a three-seat Curtiss Robin cabin monoplane — but also to gradually acquire 13 more aircraft of varying types.

Yet profits in the fiercely competitive atmosphere of bush operations were harder to find than palm trees in Alaska. McGee Airways, like Star, could barely stay afloat. By early 1935, Star, McGee, and Woodley Airways were the only three airlines operating out of Anchorage. At best, there was room for only two, and one of them had to be Woodley.

Art Woodley may have been one of the most foul-tempered characters in the entire Territory, but he was a good airline man and fiercely competitive. He, too, had started his airline in 1932, but he had begun with a small yet relatively modern fleet of six-passenger Travel Air cabin monoplanes, far superior to what McGee and Star were using.

A brief flashback to 1932 illustrates why small bush carriers were at such a disadvantage facing competitors like Woodley. This was the year of an event that sounded a for-whom-the-bell-tolls warning: mighty Pan American Airways' invasion of Alaska. As part of its formation of a Great Circle route to the Far East, Pan Am had established a fully owned, well-financed Alaskan subsidiary called Pacific Alaska Airways.

In that same year, Pacific Alaska quickly improved its competitive position even further by acquiring two other carriers: Alaskan Airways, owned by giant Avco (the holding-company conglomerate that also included American Airways), and a small charter operator with the impressive but overblown name Pacific International Airways.

Unlike his counterparts, Mac McGee apparently had never made serious efforts to obtain funding from outside investors. He had begun to acquire, on a small scale, a few promising mining investments, but he kept this business venture separate from his ailing airline. And McGee Airways itself was not only sick but also approaching the terminal stage.

Early in 1935, McGee and the three Star partners began to discuss a possible merger. Mills, Waterworth, and Ruttan initiated the talks. One positive merger result, albeit a superficial one, was that combining McGee's well-maintained seven Stinsons with Star's hodgepodge assortment of 15 aircraft would create the largest airline in Alaska.

Size itself, of course, did not guarantee a profitable operation. One major problem was the difference in the management styles of the two carriers. The 1935 merger agreement they drew up called for McGee to sell the Stinsons to Star for $50,000, which would make Star the surviving carrier and pretty much eliminate Mac McGee as a contributor to the new alliance.

McGee seems to have had some concerns about dropping out of the picture entirely. He liked the three men who owned Star, but he obviously had some doubts about the way they ran their airline. So he insisted on a provision that would protect not only his interests but also those of the few McGee Airways employees who would be joining Star. It stipulated that if Star failed to pay the $50,000 it owed for the seven Stinsons within a specified length of time, McGee would take over command of the airline himself until the money was paid.

The merged carrier continued to operate as Star Air Service, but the name played second fiddle to a new insignia that appeared on all the airplanes: a huge white star on each side of the fuselage, loosely resembling the one that would be used by U.S. military aircraft during most of World War II. Yet while the very size of the newly formed airline gave it some dominance, numerical fleet superiority was an empty honor.

Star continued to bleed from every pore, starting with the winter of 1935, when extremely bad weather led to several nonfatal crashes, requiring expensive repairs to the airplanes. It didn't take long for the partners to default on that $50,000 they owed on the Stinsons. Yet it was fate, not poor management, that doomed the partnership and brought McGee back into the picture.

In August 1936, Steve Mills was killed in a crash while piloting a fishing-charter flight with five passengers aboard, all five perishing along with Mills. At the time, it was the worst air accident in Alaska's history, and it gave

Star a black eye, for the cause was obvious pilot error.

The crash occurred near the Russian River, a favorite fishing location on the Kenai Peninsula. Mills was supposed to fly a fisherman and two married couples to the river early in the morning for a full day of fishing, then return to Anchorage the same evening. The Bellanca cabin monoplane never returned, and a search party found its wreckage the next day on a slope that was 2,000 feet above Skilak Lake, a ridge familiar to Star pilots, who often flew over it so that passengers could enjoy the area's attractive scenery. From the air, however, that slope appeared deceptively gradual and lower than it actually was. Mills apparently had misjudged his altitude and flew into the ground. When searchers located the airplane, they found that the Bellanca's engine had been driven back into the cabin, and it was obvious that everyone had died instantly.

With Mills's death, the partnership began to unravel, a process that speeded up when McGee, who still hadn't been paid for his airplanes, came back to run Star. Jack Waterworth, who had studied pharmacy in college, bailed out, opened a drugstore, and sold his share of the airline to McGee after a loud argument over some undisclosed issue.

Ruttan eventually was to follow Waterworth out the door, but he stayed on at Star as office manager long enough to help McGee run the airline. In fact, Ruttan was in charge more often than Mac, who was busy looking after his budding mining interests. The Canadian was not only admirably loyal but also a pretty good executive, for Star began a modest recovery, and Ruttan decided it was a good time to leave. He bought himself an oil dealership in Anchorage and never returned to the airline business.

McGee put Kenny Neese, who had become chief pilot when Steve Mills was killed, in charge of the airline. By this time, McGee was totally disenchanted with the airline business and the proliferation of government-imposed rules and regulations. He put Star Air Service on the market, found some interested buyers, and in 1937, after only five turbulent years, sold the airline.

Exit Linious McGee, an unheralded figure in America's aviation history and Alaska's as well. In addition to his mining investments, he opened a very successful liquor store in Anchorage, far more prosperous than any of his other business ventures. McGee eventually retired, living first in Vancouver, Washington, and finally settling in Reno, Nevada, where he died in 1988 at the age of 91.

A corporation, put together in 1937 by one of McGee's former pilots and investors from a wealthy Alaskan mining family, now owned Star Air Service. Seven years later, with World War II still in progress, a junk dealer named Raymond W. Marshall would be running the company under its new name: Alaska Airlines.

CHAPTER TWO

Mayhem
by Marshall

How did a junk dealer wind up owning an airline? The somewhat convoluted story began with that 1937 change of command at Star. It produced another new name and competent new leadership, but balance sheets still written in red ink. And red ink eventually smells like blood to business predators ready to pounce on weakened prey.

Star Air Service had been incorporated under the name Star Air Lines. The major stockholders in the takeover corporation were Don Goodman, one of Star's most reliable and intelligent pilots, and the Strandberg mining family — David Strandberg and his sons.

One of the sons, Harold, became Star's president, with David Strandberg as vice president and Goodman serving as secretary/treasurer. But it was Goodman who really ran the airline, along with Kenny Neese, who continued as chief pilot. Despite this influx of new blood, however, finances still were so shaky that when an opportunity arose to buy a new airplane at a good price, it was Neese who furnished the cash, the company agreeing to repay him in installments.

Actually, "new" is not the right adjective. The airplane, Star's first multi-engine transport, was a used Ford Tri-Motor purchased from Noel Wien for

$9,000. This model of the Tin Goose sold for $50,000 brand-new, so not only was the price a good deal, but a 10-passenger airplane was evidence that Star, though hard-pressed as usual, was trying to improve its fleet.

That Star was acquiring some respectability was due to Don Goodman as much as anyone else. Unlike McGee, he did not resent the intrusion of new federal authority into Alaska's hit-or-miss bush operations. Men like Goodman, Wien, Reeve, and Woodley realized that the undisciplined bush operators had to reform or perish.

The executioner's ax fell in 1938 with the passage of legislation known as the Civil Aeronautics Act, which transferred responsibilities from the Commerce Department to a new independent agency, the Civil Aeronautics Authority. In 1940, it was divided into two new agencies: the Civil Aeronautics Administration (CAA), which operated the air-traffic-control system and had jurisdiction over pilot and aircraft certification, and the Civil Aeronautics Board (CAB), which decided what routes carriers could fly and what fares they could charge, and also investigated airline accidents.

Thanks mainly to Goodman, Star had already begun operating on at least a partially scheduled basis with a 15-aircraft fleet, and had established uniform passenger and freight tariffs. This was enough to earn federal certification and take Star out of the bush status forever. Unfortunately, this did not take it out of the financial woods.

One problem was the lack of decent equipment. By 1938, major U.S. carriers had already begun to operate newer twin-engine airliners such as the DC-2, the immortal DC-3, and Lockheed's twins, the L-14 Super Electra, which became World War II's Hudson bomber, and the even bigger L-18 Lodestar. The Ford Tri-Motor that Star had purchased, for example, was already hopelessly antiquated, as were virtually all the aircraft then being flown in Alaska. The Territory had always been a dumping ground for airplanes that nobody else wanted. Aging airplanes were cheap to buy but expensive to maintain.

Stockholder Harold Strandberg seems to have been something of a figurehead president during his tenure of less than four years. During that period, Don Goodman was running the airline and was trying manfully to keep it competitive. One of his first moves was to scrap Mac McGee's system of paying pilots by giving them a percentage of gross revenues. By the late 1930s there were too many airmen on Star's roster to do that, and Goodman began paying them regular salaries.

His biggest goal was to break out of Star's limited role as strictly an intraterritorial carrier. He wanted a route from Anchorage to Seattle. But this dream collided head-on with Star's Achilles' heel: the airline, like the Territory itself, had no political clout in Washington, D.C.

This fact of life was in stark contrast to the welcome mats laid down in Washington State for a couple of major carriers already casting covetous eyes on Alaska: Pan American and Northwest. Both of their presidents, Pan Am's Juan Trippe and Northwest's Croil Hunter, enjoyed strong political connections in the nation's capital, and Trippe's extended all the way into the White House.

Goodman charged ahead anyway, filing an application with the Civil Aeronautics Board in 1940 for authority to operate scheduled air service between Anchorage and Seattle. A football team from Slippery Rock College would have been given better odds against Notre Dame than those Goodman faced at the CAB. Yet he almost pulled it off. Pan Am, to no one's surprise, opposed the application but was so overconfident that it sent the equivalent of fourth-string lawyers to Washington to argue its case, and they blew it.

In March 1941, the CAB granted Star's application, but Goodman's joy was short-lived. The route award still had to be approved by the White House, and Trippe happened to be a good friend of President Roosevelt, who, without really knowing much if anything about the case, overturned the CAB's decision.

This was the major flaw in the CAB's route-award procedures. Many of the board's own decisions became political footballs, finalized not on merit but on who had the most clout at the White House. Presidential veto power stayed in effect until 1978's deregulation law abolished the CAB entirely.

Stymied by this setback, Goodman tried again by forming an alliance with Star's old nemesis, none other than Art Woodley, who also was frustrated and angered by all the political shenanigans. In 1942, shortly after the attack on Pearl Harbor, they applied jointly to the CAB for permission to merge Star Air Lines and Woodley Airways, contingent on the board's granting the merged carrier — to be called Alaska Air Lines — a Seattle-Anchorage route.

Goodman and Woodley attended the subsequent CAB hearings, but the board turned them down. Woodley, whose airline had prospered in contrast to Star's continuing struggles, had stockpiled considerable cash. He offered to buy Star but discovered he was too late. The Strandbergs and other disillusioned stockholders already had decided to sell out to someone else in a deal that, to Art, smelled unkosher.

Hell hath no fury like an Art Woodley who believed — quite justifiably —

that he'd been double-crossed. He had been using, as a negotiating go-between, a firm called Aero Exchange that specialized in buying and selling aviation properties. Woodley's direct contact with Aero Exchange was through its top representative, Homer Robinson, and it was Robinson who was supposed to make Star's owners an offer.

Robinson showed up at Woodley's office and Art asked him if he had bought Star as instructed. Robinson nodded. "Yes," he replied, "but we decided to keep it ourselves."

Woodley exploded, threw Robinson out, and swore eternal vengeance against anything or anyone connected with Star Air Lines or, as it turned out some years later, anything or anyone connected with Alaska Airlines. What Robinson hadn't told him was that the new owner of Star Air Lines, namely Ray Marshall, also owned a chunk of Aero Exchange.

Woodley already knew the gentleman and already disliked him. Raymond Marshall had tried to sell him some used aircraft parts until Art noticed they all carried the red "rejected" stamp of a federal inspector, the equivalent of a "condemned as junk" label.

It was Marshall who changed the name to Alaska Airlines, two years after he bought the airline, although for a brief time it operated as Alaska Star. The final name change was another blow to Art Woodley. While the airline he had attempted to buy was called Alaska Star, he had tried to incorporate his own airline as Alaska Airlines, but his lawyer forgot to pay a $15 filing fee and Art didn't find out about it until the deadline had passed. He subsequently changed Woodley Airways to Pacific Northern, but what Woodley said to the attorney who goofed could have curdled fresh cream.

Marshall acquired his new possession sometime in 1942 — the exact date is uncertain — but it was after Woodley had made one last effort to block the planned acquisition. The CAB banned any acquisition of a carrier if the buyer was also an officer in another transportation company, whether airline, bus, or railroad.

Woodley had learned that Marshall owned stock in some obscure railroad and petitioned the CAB to void his purchase of Star. The board did investigate, found that the railroad existed only on paper, and rejected Woodley's request. So Ray Marshall now had a clear field to run the airline. Run it he did, brooking no interference from his rubber-stamp board of directors. The airline was mismanaged right from the start of his regime and would be for the next 15 years. But during the war, at least, Alaskans couldn't have cared less. Too much was happening in their own backyard.

The United States had been slow to recognize Alaska's strategic importance, and this indifference extended to the War and Navy Departments. One exception, however, was a maverick, whistle-blowing brigadier general in the Army Air Forces named William "Billy" Mitchell.

In 1921, Mitchell's young army pilots, among them such future World War II air commanders as Hap Arnold and Tooey Spaatz, sank the former German battleship *Ostfriesland* to demonstrate that airplanes could sink any warship afloat. Mitchell deliberately used 2,000-pound bombs instead of the 1,000-pound ordnance he had been ordered to drop.

Three years later and still in hot water with his superiors, Mitchell published a voluminous and highly controversial study of Pacific defense strategy in which he named Japan as not just a potential enemy but a probable one. That he predicted the sneak Pearl Harbor attack almost as accurately as if he had planned it himself is a well-known historical fact. Not so well known was his uncanny prediction that Alaska in general, and the Aleutian island chain specifically, would be of tremendous strategic importance in the event of a Pacific war: an ideal place from which to launch long-range bombing against Japan, but also an inviting target for Japan.

The Japanese government angrily denounced Mitchell as a warmonger, but it is safe to say that its naval command read Mitchell's study with great interest. Six months after Pearl Harbor, a Japanese task force led by two carriers invaded the Aleutian chain, landed troops on the islands of Kiska and Attu, and occupied them for about a year. Meanwhile, the Territory became a bustling base for wartime air traffic, including armament bound for Soviet Russia. Some logistical air support was also needed during the wartime construction of the Alaska Highway (nicknamed the Alcan Highway), which stretched 1,422 miles from Dawson Creek, British Columbia, to Delta Junction, Alaska.

At the same time, Alaska experienced another kind of invasion, a large-scale peaceful one by major carriers participating in history's first military airlift. Pan Am, American, United, Northwest, and Western led the way, sending hundreds of flights northward and exposing crews and aircraft to weather and terrain they had never faced before. These airlift flights were prompted by the Japanese occupation of Attu and Kiska, which the War and Navy Departments feared might be used as staging areas for invading Dutch Harbor, where the U.S. Navy had a large base. From there the Japanese might have launched an offensive against mainland Alaska. So the earlier airline flights into the Territory were jammed with troops, ammunition, vehicles, and field artillery as reinforcements to protect Dutch Harbor.

Alaska's airports, at least in the early stages of the war, were mostly dirt and gravel strips, and navigation aids were nonexistent. Navigation charts were largely the product of guesswork because much of the Territory had never been accurately mapped.

The airlines were operating the majority of airlift flights in and out of Alaska as part of the Army Air Forces' Air Transport Command (ATC). For most of those assigned to the Alaskan airlift, the average flight between any two points within the Territory was 500 miles, and the majority of that distance had to be flown on instruments. One captain flew a trip that, including fuel stops, took 23 hours, and he was flying "blind" on instruments for 17 of those hours.

All things considered, including their inexperience with Alaskan flying conditions, the airline crews compiled a pretty decent safety record during the war. That there were comparatively few accidents was a blessing, because when a plane did go down, it often was extremely difficult to find the crash site.

Alaska's winter of 1942-43 turned out to be one of the coldest on record, the worst since 1898. Temperatures through much of the Territory dropped to as low as 65 degrees below zero and stayed that way for weeks.

It was especially hard on airplanes and aircraft maintenance. Rubber fittings crystallized to the point where the slightest touch would shatter them like fragile glass. Oil took on the consistency of thick mud, and grease simply froze in wheel bearings. Fuel hoses became so brittle that they would snap even in a modest wind. Altimeters, their air intakes often clogged by ice and heavy snow, could be a thousand feet off in either direction, a deadly booby trap for pilots already daunted by the mountainous terrain and frequent poor visibility.

The latter included many from airlines that normally operated in much friendlier climates. Western's pilots, for example, were mostly Los Angeles-based and regarded Alaska as the equivalent of flying routes on the moon. A group of nervous newcomers made a point of asking a veteran bush pilot for advice.

"What's the best technique for flying from Fairbanks to Anchorage?" one inquired hopefully.

"Well, you just put your airplane into a steep climb as soon as you take off," the bush pilot informed his rapt audience. "Don't level off till your props are churning stardust. Then you just hope you're at the spot in that Alaskan mountain range where Mount McKinley ain't."

There is no evidence that Ray Marshall's Alaska Star, the airline's name at the time of Pearl Harbor, played any role whatsoever in the emergency airlift, but neither did most of Alaska's other airlines. They lacked the resources to contribute to any great extent, especially adequate flight equipment like the modern, larger aircraft the major carriers and military were bringing in: DC-3s, C-47s, the new Lockheed twins, and the massive, fat-bellied C-46 air freighters, which at the time were the largest twin-engine transports flying.

There were two exceptions to this nonparticipation: Art Woodley and Bob Reeve. Woodley hauled a few military supplies over his route between Kodiak and the Alaska Peninsula, although he did so without an ATC contract. The only veteran bush pilot who had a formal military contract was Bob Reeve, whose Reeve Airways eventually became Reeve Aleutian. He had started his little company in Valdez, Alaska, with a rented Eaglerock biplane shortly after his 1932 arrival, fresh from a job flying the airmail over the Andes in South America.

Reeve had a self-deprecating sense of humor, as demonstrated by the sign he put over his first hangar at Valdez. It carried the most negative message in aviation history, and read:

> ALWAYS USE REEVE AIRWAYS.
> Slow Unreliable Unfair and Crooked.
> Scared Unlicensed and Nuts.
> Reeve Airways — the Best.

Reeve drove to work in a Model T Ford on whose side he had painted *AIRLINE OFFICIAL.* He became a legend to virtually every airline and military crew that took part in the Alaskan airlift, and he also contributed more to it than any other former bush pilot.

Reeve assigned to the job a pair of airplanes that probably qualified for residence in an air museum. One was a 14-year-old single-engine Fairchild monoplane, the other a Boeing Model 80 trimotor biplane whose design dated back to 1927. The Boeing was painted bright yellow and became known throughout the Territory as "The Yellow Peril."

In those two relics, Reeve completed such missions as flying in 1,100 tons of cargo to help build a strategic military air base at Northway, Alaska. He ferried more than a thousand troops between various Alaskan bases, and tons of priority freight. He was a welcome sight at every military installation in the Territory, even though the Army never could get him to follow the correct approach procedures required at all military fields.

Reeve bestowed most of his affection on the little Fairchild, and it was the kind of love affair that only a bush pilot could understand. He landed the airplane once at some military base and found a young Air Corps major staring at it.

"Say, old man," the major inquired, "what kind of airplane is that?"

"Fairchild DGA," Reeve growled. "DGA stands for Damned Good Airplane, and if you call me old man again, I'll take you over my knee."

Sadly, Ray Marshall's airline could have used a Bob Reeve, or even an Art Woodley. The company that became Alaska Airlines in 1944 seems to have spent the war years in a lackadaisical, almost moribund state that reflected Marshall's uninspired leadership.

He not only spent an inordinate amount of time in his New York office, but also surrounded himself with sycophants at the airline. His entire board of directors consisted of business associates whose combined knowledge of airline operations could charitably be classed as limited. Meanwhile, Marshall lost his most capable, experienced officer, Kenny Neese, who left early in the war to fly for the Air Transport Command.

His exodus was one of many that would plague the airline for years. In the official chain of command, Marshall listed himself as only a vice president, but there was no doubt who was boss, no matter who happened to be president. The first one he hired was Warren Cuddy, an Anchorage banker who had been one of Star's directors.

Cuddy was succeeded in the spring of 1943 by Theodore Law, whose family was in the oil business and who had invested $250,000 in Marshall's airline. This not only made Law the airline's major stockholder, ahead of R.W. himself, but also may have forced Marshall into naming him president. Law had the clout to challenge Marshall but not the will, and served for less than a year. But he did make a major contribution during his brief tenure by authorizing the purchase of the first brand-new airplane in the airline's history.

It was a Lockheed Lodestar, delivered to Alaska Star at Merrill Field in 1943. Normally a 14-passenger aircraft, it could be configured to carry 26. It not only had excellent cargo capacity, but also ranked as the fastest twin-engine airliner in the world, with a cruising speed of more than 250 miles per hour. The airline assigned it almost exclusively to its tri-weekly Anchorage-Juneau route, which was its longest at the time and produced fairly heavy passenger traffic.

(Lockheed envisioned the Lodestar as the successor to the DC-3, but in that respect it struck out. Only 125 Lodestars were built, compared to the more than 10,000 DC-3s and C-47s that Douglas turned out.)

If anyone wondered how Law got that new airplane purchase past the penurious Marshall, the explanation was simple: Law paid for part of it himself, which meant he didn't have to confront the "vice president" who outranked him.

Raymond W. Marshall was interested in making money, not spending it, even for legitimate and worthwhile purposes. His relationships with the men who flew and maintained his airplanes were thorny at best. It reached the point where every pilot and mechanic who had ever worked for him simply despised him.

The anything-goes philosophy that had enabled Marshall to prosper in the junk business was carried over to his venture into commercial aviation, where slipshod practices could have more serious consequences than inefficiency. That Alaska Airlines never had an accident that was directly attributed to Marshall's shoddy *modus operandi* was simply incredible luck.

Even after the war ended, when the supply of new spare parts improved considerably, Alaska Airlines was still relying on the cheap, worn-out junk that Marshall gave his mechanics. Asking for new engines was like asking for a 300 percent wage increase, and many of the spare parts he bought were as bad as the condemned stuff he had tried to palm off on Art Woodley. When it came to buying anything new, Marshall either flatly refused the request or resorted to delaying tactics.

One veteran mechanic, Cecil Higgins, asked Marshall for some badly needed new wing covers. When they failed to show up, Higgins inquired why, and Marshall told him he had put the request up for bids but hadn't received any yet. Higgins informed Marshall that there wasn't time for bids. He needed the wing covers immediately. Marshall refused to authorize the purchase, so Higgins quit, as did many other disgruntled employees.

Those who stayed created a kind of family atmosphere of their own, largely in self-defense against Marshall's little dictatorship. The seeds of that sense of being family, which became part of the airline's culture, may have been planted during the years when employee self-pride and loyalty were all that kept the airline alive, no matter what the owner did to hurt it.

Alaska's pilots ranked Marshall somewhere in the vicinity of engine failures, in-flight fires, and flying blind into towering mountain ranges. One of the airmen was Warren Metzger, a captain who was to become chief pilot as well as vice president of flight operations, and a legend in his own right at Alaska Airlines.

As a young four-striper, he was exposed to the airline's in-the-basement credit standing with oil companies. Marshall often refused to pay fuel bills, which forced the pilots to pay for gas out of their own pockets and then submit the expenses for reimbursement. True, they always got back their money, so promptly that they naturally wondered why Marshall hadn't paid for the fuel in the first place, instead of putting employees in the embarrassing position of being told their company had no credit.

Metzger decided to rebel. He had flown a trip from Anchorage to Ketchikan, where he needed to refuel for the return flight. He was told that Alaska Airlines no longer had any credit, but Metzger wasn't about to pay for the gas out of his own pocket again.

"I was determined to sit in Ketchikan until the company sent me the money," he related, "but my copilot was dating a girl in Anchorage and wanted to get home. He bought the gas out of his own pocket as usual."

Trivial? Perhaps, but like the steady, unending little drips associated with water torture, the trivialities began adding up to overall inefficiency, low employee morale, and a terrible but unfortunately deserved reputation for the airline. Thus did Alaska Airlines acquire its first unflattering nickname, in the form of a sarcastic slogan composed by Captain Bill Lund, one of the many pilots disgusted with Marshall's mismanagement. Widely circulated throughout the company, it referred to the L-18's three weekly flights between Anchorage and Juneau, and read:

Tri-Weekly. Try Weakly. Try Woodley.

Ted Law, who had more influence as a major stockholder than as president, might have saved Alaska Airlines from Marshall's mismanagement if he had stayed longer. But like so many employees, he ran out of patience with Marshall's brand of leadership, sold his stock, and early in 1944 quit the airline, leaving Marshall as the majority stockholder.

His replacement was Marshall Hoppin, a former CAA official who had been serving in Alaska. He knew the Territory and something about aviation, but he knew nothing about running an airline and had no stomach for confronting Marshall, who by now had named himself board chairman.

Hoppin served as president long enough to add a couple of war-surplus DC-4s to the fleet, which led to the hiring of the airline's first stewardesses. But the acquisition also cost Hoppin his job. Marshall blasted him for spending what R.W. considered too much money training Alaska's pilots to fly the big four-engine DC-4s, and fired him.

His replacement turned out to be a temporary respite from Marshall's despotic rule, but in the end, not the right choice. Hired in June 1947 as the new president of Alaska Airlines was an aggressive man with a fervent desire to run his own airline the way he wanted it run.

His name was James A. Wooten, and he came to Alaska Airlines with blue-ribbon credentials. He had been head of American Airlines' cargo division and, in fact, had created that carrier's first department devoted exclusively to airfreight.

Wooten had introduced the concept of a centralized hub that would receive freight shipments from throughout American's system and redistribute them to their final destinations. It was the forerunner of the technique that was to make Federal Express successful with its Memphis hub. The hub location that Wooten chose for American was St. Joseph, Missouri, and the new cargo division was launched early in 1946 using six DC-4 passenger planes converted to an all-cargo configuration.

It was a concept ahead of its time. American lost nearly a quarter of a million dollars in the first year of its operation, and its president, C. R. Smith, abolished the new division. Wooten and other officers tried to talk Smith into accepting another idea: modifying the DC-4s into convertible aircraft, with quickly removable seats being used for daytime passenger service and then removed at night to create an all-cargo configuration. (Alaska Airlines would · adopt this concept with great success some years later.)

When C.R. balked at this new plan, Wooten figured he wasn't going anywhere at American and was in a receptive mood for any attractive offers. The one he accepted was from Alaska's board of directors. Whether hiring Wooten was Marshall's idea, or whether the board decided to put its rubber stamp into a drawer long enough to hire a strong president, is unknown. At any rate, the airline got a new leader with both experience and ingenuity, adjectives that certainly applied to Jim Wooten.

There was no question that Jim Wooten was a genius at generating new business, and he accomplished this by simultaneously increasing the size of Alaska's fleet. The War Assets Administration (WAA), a postwar government agency responsible for disposing of surplus aircraft, was running aviation's greatest bargain sale, and Wooten took advantage of it. "Alaska Airlines" began appearing on the fuselages of used DC-3s, C-47s, DC-4s, and C-46s — all of them a bit war-weary but still very serviceable.

A brand-new DC-3, for example, had cost $125,000 before the war; the WAA was offering war-surplus DC-3s in mint condition for only $25,000 each, and even less if an airplane was beat-up. And thanks to Wooten's ability to obtain new charter and freight business, the DC-4s and C-46s began appearing all over the world, including Japan and China. He considered these revenues absolutely essential to the airline's survival. At the time he joined Alaska, it owed about $350,000 in unpaid bills.

He got the airline involved in the 1948 Berlin Airlift, using DC-4s converted into freighters to carry priority cargo into Munich, Frankfurt, and Wiesbaden — a total of 87 trips — and filled some of the return flights with German war brides who had married American GIs and needed transportation to the United States.

Wooten also landed an unusual contract that resulted in one of the most memorable missions of the early postwar era. Dubbed "Operation Magic Carpet," it involved transporting Jewish refugees from the seaport city of Aden, in Yemen, to the newly established state of Israel. The airlift had been contracted by the American Jewish Joint Distribution Committee, an organization set up to facilitate the relocation of refugees to the new Jewish homeland. The Yemenite Jews had a special historical distinction: they were one of the fabled Lost Tribes of Israel.

(More than 50 years later, Aden itself would become the focus of world attention in a different way. This was the port where suicide bombers blew a hole in the hull of the destroyer USS *Cole*, killing 17 American sailors.)

The Magic Carpet airlift began early in 1949 and lasted until early 1950. By the time it ended, Alaska had flown some 40,000 Yemenite Jews to their new home, and Wooten, who was no longer around by then, could have laughed in Ray Marshall's face.

R.W. had opposed the entire deal as a waste of the airline's time and money. He claimed it would cost at least $50,000 to set up the Yemen charter and insisted that Wooten provide the funds himself because the airline didn't have the money. Wooten raised the $50,000 by borrowing it from a travel agency associated with the Joint Committee.

He assigned two DC-4s and a C-46 to the operation. Captain Warren Metzger, who had also participated in the Berlin Airlift, flew the first trip in a DC-4 originally designed to carry 50 passengers. By replacing regular airliner seats with long benches, however, it could now carry as many as 120. The benches had seat belts, but this had to have been a very uncomfortable way to fly 3,000 miles; it was like traveling that distance on a park bench.

"I had no idea what I was getting into," Metzger recalled years later. "Arabs were shooting at the planes every chance they got, and the airport at Tel Aviv was getting bombed all the time. Navigation was either by dead reckoning or just by our eyeballs. We had to carry extra fuel tanks, and they were fastened down in the cabin along with a hundred or so passengers, so there wasn't much room to move around or go to the lavatory."

There wasn't much publicity given the venture until long after it ended, and that recognition came in the form of a lengthy episode devoted to Operation Magic Carpet in Leon Uris's best-selling novel *Exodus*. Wooten didn't care about publicity; he was too busy drumming up other missions for the airline even while Magic Carpet was in progress.

He wrangled a contract with the Navy that involved flying supplies to a geological and seismographic expedition working close to the North Pole. The scientists were based on a frozen strip of Arctic real estate known as Ice Island. It was a challenge to the Alaska pilots assigned to the project, one of them being Warren Metzger. "The island kept moving," he recounted, "which made navigation interesting."

Wooten was engineering so much charter business, in fact, that to handle the overflow, he bought a couple of war-surplus airplanes and started his own charter airline, which he called Near East Air Transport (NEAT). This turned out to be a wise decision because Alaska's burgeoning charter operations had drawn the unwelcome attention of the Civil Aeronautics Board.

The prelude to Wooten's eventual downfall can be traced to what had happened in the airline industry after Japan's surrender in August 1945. Like the original bush pilots in Alaska, everyone wanted to start an airline, usually on undercapitalized shoestrings, to take advantage of the pent-up demand for air travel and airfreight's potential. More than 2,700 applications to launch nonscheduled airlines poured into the CAB within a few months of the war's end, and the successful applicants would wind up operating a fleet of some 5,000 aircraft. The board authorized them to conduct chartered passenger and freight service, but with limited frequency between any two points, including those on a route served by a certificated carrier.

Alaska, of course, was a certificated scheduled carrier, not a so-called "non-sked," but Wooten began acting as if it were. As the airline began to acquire larger aircraft, it outgrew Anchorage's Merrill Field, and Wooten decided he needed a bigger base for his mushrooming charters. First, he negotiated a lease for a hangar at the Elmendorf Air Force Base, outside Anchorage, then decided that still wasn't enough.

Somehow he talked local officials in Everett, Washington, into building Alaska Airlines a hangar at Paine Field, and followed this drastic step by temporarily moving the airline's corporate offices and maintenance facilities to Paine. Anchorage, the airline's birthplace, became what it is today: its major regional base in Alaska, headed by a senior vice president to reflect the state's importance.

Wooten followed this move by running a slew of regulatory red lights. He would start a charter service between two points not on Alaska's route system and then operate so many flights that it became a route the airline wasn't even authorized to serve. Wooten defined this practice as "frequent nonscheduled flights."

Among his "frequent nonscheduled flights" were a daily service from Chicago and Minneapolis to Seattle and Alaska, and illegal service from Paine Field to Anchorage. Including all these operations within his straight-faced "frequent nonscheduled flights" definition was like trying to hide an elephant under Saran Wrap. And suddenly, everything fell apart on the energetic president of Alaska Airlines.

The CAB did more than merely disagree with that definition. It lowered the boom. Alaska was fined $34,000 for operating illegal scheduled flights and, even more serious, for using pilots unqualified to fly certain types of aircraft on some of the charters and also for running several engines beyond their mandatory deadlines for complete overhaul. It was a stiff penalty in those days, especially for a company already deeply in debt, and Wooten was socked with a $1,000 personal fine.

On October 14, 1949, Jim Wooten resigned as president. Two months later, Marshall selected as his successor Stanley McCutcheon, a well-known and well-liked attorney and politician who was speaker of the Alaska State House of Representatives. He was exactly what Marshall wanted: an aviation neophyte with no particular desire to cross swords with him, yet an Alaskan with good political connections, thus making the airline's absentee ownership a little more palatable. And at least on the surface, McCutcheon's presidency appeared to be successful. The Korean War was raging, and

Alaska won new and lucrative contracts with the newly created Military Air
Transport Service (MATS).

Alaska's DC-4s began hauling tons of military freight and hundreds of
passengers between Anchorage and Japan, earning the airline more than $2
million a year during the war. Not until later was it disclosed that the government's checks were going not to the airline but to Marshall's New York office.
His explanation was that the money was used to repay him for personal loans
he had made to the airline.

This apparently satisfied the CAB, which in 1951 tried to help the airline
by granting it temporary authority to operate a Portland-Seattle-Fairbanks-
Anchorage route. But the board was still concerned about Alaska Airlines'
ability to continue as a financially responsible carrier. One result was
McCutcheon's resignation in July 1952, not through any fault of his own but
indirectly because of the CAB's dwindling confidence in Marshall, almost a
case of "guilt by association."

The CAB also ordered Marshall to put his stock into a three-year voting
trust, which in effect hung a restraining bit in his mouth and a harness over
his head. And to his further displeasure, McCutcheon's replacement wasn't
anyone of his own choosing. Alaska's new president had been recommended
by none other than CAB member Donald Nyrop, who would become the
CAB's chairman a short time later and subsequently take over as president of
Northwest Airlines.

The man that Nyrop had practically shoved down Marshall's throat
was Nelson (Nels) David, and he was far more than just a personal friend of
Nyrop's. David had been a major with the Air Transport Command in World
War II, had considerable postwar airline experience at both United and
American Overseas Airlines, and knew the Territory.

David was not only well qualified but also tough. He became president
on July 15, 1952, and one of his first actions was to instigate an investigation by a Seattle bank official into the airline's accounting practices. What
the bank's expert uncovered was like peeling layers from a spoiled artichoke.
In addition to discovering that revenues from military-contract charters
and government subsidies had been siphoned off to Marshall instead of the
airline, he found that Marshall had ignored requests by both the CAB and the
Internal Revenue Service to reform Alaska's accounting system.

R.W.'s sleight-of-hand financial manipulations had resulted in the
airline being far more deeply in debt than anyone had suspected — owing, for
example, more than $500,000 in back payments to the Workmen's Com-

pensation Fund. When the accounting sleuth asked Marshall why he hadn't
made the payments, he claimed it was because the government owed Alaska
Airlines at least that much.

Nels David first went to work on the airline's maintenance department.
As chief of maintenance he hired Tom Campobasso, who had been vice president of Pan American's flight operations in Frankfurt, Germany. Campobasso started out by investigating the spare-parts situation and was horrified
to find that Marshall had been buying worn-out war-surplus engines and
engine parts and selling this junk *back* to the airline.

The Seattle airport had been built during the war, when the military
fields in the area were closed to civilian traffic. On July 9, 1949, with the com-
pletion of a new terminal and control tower, it became the Seattle-Tacoma
International Airport (Sea-Tac). David engineered another momentous event
in the airline's history when he made Jim Wooten's transfer of corporate
headquarters out of Anchorage permanent. On June 5, 1953, the directors
approved his recommendation that corporate headquarters be established at
2320 Sixth Avenue, Seattle, Washington.

David and Campobasso, not to mention the airline's other loyal employees, tried their best to keep the airline afloat during the five years that
David served as president. The problem was not a lack of zeal and ability,
but Raymond Marshall's continuing presence and the power he still wielded.
Nor did the three crashes the airline suffered between 1954 and 1957, with 12
total fatalities, help David's sagging morale.

On May 15, 1957, he threw in the proverbial towel. So did Raymond W.
Marshall, albeit under duress. But Marshall realized that he was permanently
persona non grata at the fed-up CAB, which would never do anything for
Alaska Airlines as long as he controlled it. So he agreed to sell a huge chunk
of his majority stock — about 200,000 shares — to someone he knew the CAB
would love to have running the airline: a decorated World War II Navy pilot
with an excellent reputation at both the White House and on Capitol Hill.

The airline's 378 employees viewed the choice with a cautious wait-
and-see attitude. They had no inkling that their airline was getting a colorful, dynamic, but tragically flawed new leader. On the same day that Nelson
David officially resigned, Alaska's board of directors elected, as the airline's
president and its very first chief executive officer, Charles F. Willis Jr.

CHAPTER THREE

Life with Charlie

It has been said that history is composed of factual events spiced with occasional myths, most of them more interesting than the facts. And the most persistent myth at Alaska Airlines, still believed by many of the older employees and passed on to the younger ones, is that in 1957, Charlie Willis rode in like the U.S. Cavalry to save their airline from the foul clutches of the villainous Raymond Marshall.

Many myths have an element of truth, and so does this one. Willis didn't really save the airline from Marshall. After all, R.W. was the one who got him the job. But Charlie did save Alaska from something else: its image of dull, uninspired service, its lowly status as an unimaginative nonentity in the postwar explosion of air travel, and above all, its failure — despite its name — to be the dominant air carrier within Alaska itself.

The jet age was only one year away when Willis took command, at a time when every carrier was trying to establish itself as different, special, better, and more innovative than its competitors. American Airlines was an industry leader in that respect, pioneering airline VIP clubs at airports, for example, and TWA's public relations staff was especially skilled in courting the media with slick publicity gimmicks.

That Willis was able to achieve at least some distinction for Alaska was a remarkable feat. For one thing, the airline was virtually unknown outside Alaska. Nor was there anything in Charlie's own background to suggest a flair for marketing and promotion. Willis appeared to be just a likeable, gregarious, reasonably competent young man whose outstanding talents were his knowledge of aviation and ability to fly airplanes. He had been a genuine, much decorated hero in World War II, serving as a Navy patrol bomber pilot. He flew 250 combat missions in the Pacific, plus 35 more in the European theater.

Willis was assigned to a PBY patrol squadron just before Pearl Harbor, and by war's end he had been credited with helping to sink a Japanese destroyer and a German submarine, as well as flying a number of successful patrol and rescue missions. (The PBY amphibian, built by Consolidated Aircraft, was the DC-3 of seaplanes, a well-designed, versatile workhorse for the Navy and Coast Guard. It was never intended to serve as an airliner, but it was to play an interesting peacetime role in Alaska's history even in its makeshift civilian garb.)

Hollywood's central casting office couldn't have made a better choice to play a handsome young airline president. Willis was only 38 when he took the Alaska job. Admittedly, there were a few dark shadows-of-things-to-come as he started his career at Alaska, a heavy drinking problem being the darkest.

Willis, like many other borderline alcoholics, never tried to hide this weakness, insisted that his drinking wasn't really serious, and even told self-deprecating jokes about it. He liked to admit that his going into the military was fueled by whiskey, not patriotism. After graduating from college in 1940, he and a buddy went out on a nonstop binge, and when they woke up the next day, they both managed to remember that they had enlisted in the U.S. Navy.

The story got even better after that. Willis was cleaning bilges as an apprentice seaman on a submarine when an officer who had spotted his status as a college graduate suggested that he apply for flight school, which Willis did. Nor did it ever bother Charlie that his eventual nickname in the PBY squadron was Whiskey Willis; characteristically, he thought it was funny.

After the war, incurably infected with the aviation bug, Willis became one of the 2,700 would-be airline entrepreneurs filing applications with the Civil Aeronautics Board for authority to operate as nonscheduled air carriers. His proposed venture, called Willis Air Service, was thinly capitalized with about $13,000 he had saved up in military pay and money borrowed from friends.

Willis Air Service was strictly an airfreight operation, first within the United States and later expanding into an international air cargo operation.

It was no Flying Tiger in size or scope, but Willis milked the freight market more effectively than most other small cargo carriers. He shipped designer dresses from New York's Seventh Avenue to Dallas, shrimp out of New Orleans, and cattle from American ranches to Bogotá.

Willis and another ex-Navy pilot associate founded the Citizens for Eisenhower organization, which was instrumental in getting General Dwight D. Eisenhower the 1952 Republican presidential nomination. Charlie, in fact, has been credited with originating the very effective "I Like Ike" slogan that became the GOP's campaign battle cry.

As far as the White House was concerned, Charlie Willis could do no wrong. It was "Ike Likes Charlie" at 1600 Pennsylvania Avenue, and this popularity couldn't have come at a better time. Willis Air Service had folded before Eisenhower's nomination, and Charlie was unemployed.

The reasons for his cargo airline's failure remain somewhat fuzzy. According to one account, the CAB shut it down for operating too many charter flights on a regularly scheduled basis (à la Jim Wooten). Willis always insisted that the airline was put out of business after it applied unsuccessfully for a crucial certificated route — from East Coast cities to the Caribbean and South America — that it already had been flying on a regular basis. He claimed he lost the case because the winning applicant had connections with the Truman administration.

There seems to be some truth to both versions. Willis had indeed run afoul of the CAB's regulations and applied for the certificated route because it was the only way he could stay in business. That he lost because of White House interference with the route-awards process also was entirely possible; it wouldn't have been the first time, or the last. It is just as likely, however, that having been caught operating that contested route illegally, he stood no chance of winning the case anyway.

More important is the fact that Charlie Willis didn't remain unemployed for very long. When Eisenhower succeeded Truman, Willis took on a number of aviation-oriented tasks for the new administration, as well as being a special assistant to the president in charge of appointments and patronage — he had more connections than the White House telephone system. He became skilled in Washington's major industry, politics, but the airline industry remained his real love.

Willis resigned from his White House job to join W.R. Grace & Company, whose properties included Panagra Airlines. But he was disappointed to find that the job had nothing to do with the airline subsidiary. He admitted later he was getting paid for doing practically nothing, and when Raymond Marshall sounded him out on Alaska Airlines, through intermediaries, Willis reacted like a discouraged spinster getting an unexpected marriage proposal.

Willis was no dummy. He knew that Alaska was a sick company with an antiquated fleet serving a feeble route system, but that didn't matter to a man who, for all his faults, truly loved challenges.

Years later, he told an interviewer that buying out 200,000 shares of Ray Marshall's common stock had cost him $2.5 million, most of which he raised from friends, which included the family of his wife, Elizabeth Firestone Willis, and that the whole deal was contingent on Alaska getting a seven-year renewal of its temporary authority to operate an Anchorage-Fairbanks-Seattle route. Charlie won that route certificate renewal by going to Congress personally even before Alaska's board had named him president and chief executive officer.

Certainly no stranger to lobbying on Capitol Hill, he knew all the right people. The renewal legislation sailed through Congress, and was signed by President Eisenhower without even getting deposited on the CAB's doorstep. It proved, however, to be a Pyrrhic victory. Alaska was at a competitive disadvantage because it was required to operate an Anchorage-Fairbanks-Seattle service, not the Anchorage-Seattle nonstop authority already enjoyed by both Pan American and Pacific Northern. A few months after the renewal, in fact, the CAB made matters worse by giving Anchorage-Seattle nonstop authority to Northwest Airlines.

During the war, Anchorage had overtaken Fairbanks as Alaska's largest city. By 1957, Fairbanks was only half the size of Anchorage, and the demand for nonstop service between Fairbanks and Seattle was minuscule compared to what it was for Anchorage-Seattle.

Willis probably didn't realize the full significance of this disadvantage when he took over, nor was he aware at first that one of Alaska's major competitors in the overcrowded Alaska-Seattle market, namely Pacific Northern, was headed by a man who couldn't even say "Alaska Airlines" out loud without turning purple.

Inevitably, Willis and Art Woodley had to meet, and while there was no particular animosity on Charlie's part, it seems that Woodley took an instant, intense dislike to the new arrival on Alaska's aviation scene. No one knows why, but there aren't enough synonyms for *hate* in any thesaurus to adequately cover Woodley's feelings toward his Alaska Airlines counterpart.

Woodley was waxing eloquent one day on Charlie's perceived

shortcomings. His listener was one of his officers at Pacific Northern, and Art's oration was being delivered with the zeal of an impassioned evangelist surrounded by atheists, a lengthy tirade denouncing Willis's business ethics, the questionable legitimacy of his parentage, his morals, personal appearance, intelligence, and on and on. The longer that Woodley talked, the louder his voice and the more florid his complexion became, until the crimson turned to a deep lavender and his worried listener thought Art was going to have a stroke.

"You shouldn't get that upset about Willis," he cautioned. "After all, Charlie's his own worst enemy."

"NOT WHILE *I'M* ALIVE!" Woodley roared.

Part of the reason for Woodley's apoplectic enmity, of course, was Willis's emergence as a more formidable competitor than he had expected. Art was a solid, capable airline man, but he didn't have Charlie's flair for aggressive promotion. Yet in truth, the Alaska Airlines official that Woodley should have feared even more than Willis was an unknown public relations and marketing genius from tiny Northern Consolidated Airlines. His name, forever carved into the annals of Alaska Airlines, was Bob Giersdorf.

Willis and Giersdorf. Their names would always be linked, an inseparable team. A lot of people around the airline thought that Willis often took credit for some great ideas that actually were spawned in Giersdorf's fertile mind, and that may have been true at times. But that's an unfair rap on Willis. The two simply worked well together, feeding off each other's strengths while compensating for each other's weaknesses.

Giersdorf, a slender man with a boyish face and a flattop haircut, found out quite soon in their relationship that his boss was a Jekyll and Hyde — a funny, warm-hearted, reasonably capable executive when he was sober, but unpredictable and irrational when he'd had too much to drink.

On more than one occasion, Willis would be on, say, a United flight and after several drinks become unduly impressed with the job that a UAL flight attendant was doing. He would offer her a better-paying job at Alaska, then completely forget about the offer. The woman would show up at corporate headquarters a few days later, and Giersdorf or some other embarrassed officer would have to tell her it was all a mistake.

On another occasion, however, Willis actually did a nice job of talent-scouting. He had taken several guests to a Seattle restaurant and was impressed by the way the hostess handled his party, combining amused tolerance with just enough discipline to keep things in order. Before they left the restaurant, he gave her his business card, and she ended up flying for Alaska as one of its best flight attendants.

Charlie's "hiring by whim" habits occasionally backfired. He had a gardener, a friendly young man who could hardly speak English, but Willis decided he would make a great ticket agent and insisted on getting him a job at the Fairbanks Airport. His supervisor was Tom Dezutter, who never forgot what happened when the former gardener was boarding his first flight.

"The kid kept looking over his shoulder toward the gate to see how things were going," Tom recalled, "but he never checked his coupons for a passenger count. When he figured the airplane must be full, he closed the gate and Lord knows how many passengers were left standing there, holding confirmed reservations on an airplane that took off with a cabin full of empty seats."

Bob Giersdorf always called Willis "Skipper," which may have reflected the fact that Charlie took nearly as much pride in having been a Navy aircraft commander as in being an airline president and CEO. Not a few people around Alaska Airlines suspected that Willis subconsciously yearned to be an airline captain himself. He loved to sit in the cockpit on flights and usually was welcome, provided he was sober.

This was hard on pilots, who naturally were reluctant to evict their own boss from the flight deck. At least one captain got rid of Willis by telling him there was a nosy and very strict FAA inspector on board.

On one occasion, a stewardess named Patty Huey refused to let Willis into the cockpit because he was drunk, and Charlie threatened to fire her. As usual, the next day he had to be reminded of the incident and took Giersdorf's advice to drop the matter.

So there were times when people like Giersdorf had to protect Willis from himself, something that Bob hadn't expected when he joined Alaska. Giersdorf was Northern Consolidated's station manager in Fairbanks when Charlie met him. Jim Johnson, who came to Alaska Airlines from Alaska Coastal and eventually became senior vice president of public affairs, recalled being told that Giersdorf actually sold himself to Willis. "I don't know what Charlie was doing in Giersdorf's office in Fairbanks at the time," Johnson reminisced, "but the story I heard was that Bob started right off by telling Willis, 'You need me at Alaska' and that when Charlie left, in effect he took Giersdorf with him."

This was early in 1958, a time when Willis really needed someone like Giersdorf to help add some whipped cream and hot fudge sauce to the airline's bland vanilla image. Pan Am, Northwest, and Pacific Northern were operating 300-mph, pressurized DC-6s and Constellations between Seattle and Anchorage; Alaska was competing with slow, unpressurized DC-4s whose Seattle-Fairbanks-Anchorage flights took eight hours or even longer.

So Willis bought a used DC-6A, the cargo version of the original DC-6 airliner, and installed passenger seats on removable pallets. He hired an artist to decorate the cabin walls, then installed a piano and lounge seats in the rear of the airplane to create a small piano bar. Around this time, Willis and Giersdorf settled on a name for the airline's fresh image: "Golden Nugget Service."

With that name came a dramatic upgrading of in-flight food and beverage service on DC-6 flights — assorted cocktails, hot entrées with baked potatoes, vegetables, desserts, and as a finishing touch, hot towels. Alaska Airlines inaugurated DC-6 service on the Seattle-Fairbanks-Anchorage route on April 25, 1958. Charlie's wife, Elizabeth Firestone Willis, an accomplished musician, played the piano while her husband — in all his gregarious glory — tended bar. That one flight just about wiped out the airline's staid image, but Willis wasn't finished with his "we'll compete with gimmicks" strategy.

He installed a movie projector in the front of the DC-6 cabin and in 1958 began showing feature films on Seattle-Fairbanks-Anchorage flights. The Willis-Giersdorf publicity machine cranked out news releases announcing that Alaska Airlines was the first airline in the world to show in-flight movies.

Their zeal was admirable and understandable; their historical accuracy was off by 33 years. They couldn't even claim to be the first U.S. carrier to show in-flight films because TAT (Transcontinental Air Transport, predecessor of TWA) showed a newsreel and a cartoon on a Ford Tri-Motor flying from Columbus, Ohio, to Waynoka, Oklahoma, in 1929.

For that matter, the first movie shown on the DC-6 was a Jerry Lewis comedy that turned out to be something of an embarrassment and had to be withdrawn prematurely. No one had previewed the movie before it went into the projector, so neither Giersdorf nor Willis realized that the film opens with a close-up of large headlines on the front page of a 1935 newspaper:

WILL ROGERS, WILEY POST
DIE IN ALASKA AIR CRASH

But the Jerry Lewis movie and the false historical boast were small potholes on the Willis-Giersdorf road to enhanced recognition and reputation for Alaska Airlines. Winning recognition, of course, was only half the battle because reputation was a two-sided coin. All the publicity in the world can't provide a far-higher passenger priority: reliability.

Charlie's own number-one priority quite naturally involved putting passengers on his airplanes, before he could start worrying about such factors as reliability. Competing against Pan American's and Northwest's forthcoming jet service on Seattle-Anchorage flights was alarming enough, but then Pacific Northern ordered two new Boeing 720s (a smaller edition of the 707), in addition to buying a third one from Braniff, and announced nonstop jet service on the same route.

Willis realized that the word *compete* was now spelled j-e-t. His dilemma was simple: a new Boeing, Douglas, or Convair four-engine jet transport cost around $5 million in 1960, and Willis couldn't afford even the minimum down payment of only 10 percent. (This was a rock-bottom figure in the 1960s; a more typical advance payment on a $5 million jetliner was about $1.5 million.)

While wrestling with the problem of how to finance the stiff entry fee into the jet age, Willis and Giersdorf did their best with the airline's outmoded piston-engine planes. Alaska acquired two more DC-6s, each configured to carry 88 passengers, and one of them was operated under a lease arrangement, which angered a certain stockholder, none other than the redoubtable Raymond Marshall. Like the bad penny that keeps turning up, Marshall still owned enough Alaska Airlines stock to complain about how the company was being run. And complain he did, angrily informing Willis that leasing a DC-6 was an unnecessary expense that cost the airline more than $1 million.

Willis ignored him and continued to wage war against 600-mph jets with 300-mph DC-6s and 250-mph DC-4s. It was like sending World War I Spads and Sopwith Camels up against modern F-86 jet fighters. While improved food service and in-flight movies were good competitive weapons, both Willis and Giersdorf knew this was an inadequate response to the fact that it took only three hours to fly from Seattle to Anchorage on a jet, compared to six to eight hours on a DC-6.

Bob Handley, who worked for North Central Airlines before joining Alaska in 1960, recalled another little Willis-Giersdorf competitive touch, minor yet wistfully typical. "There were always current newspapers and fresh flowers in the DC-6 boarding lounges," he said. "I was a ticket agent in Seattle at the time, and we really were trying hard."

It would have been difficult to find a stewardess from those early Willis years who disliked Charlie, his drinking notwithstanding. Many flight attendants, in fact, never saw his "Mr. Hyde" side and remembered Willis as invariably respectful, courteous, and charming.

The flight attendants, more than any other group of employees, including even the pilots, who really admired Charlie, were cognizant and appreciative of his competitive efforts. After all, their attitude toward their jobs and the level of service they provided were a vital part of those efforts. It was a lot easier to keep passengers happy on a three-hour flight than on one that might take eight hours.

Marcia Broyles, one of the earliest stewardesses from the DC-4 era, remembered that even the pilots got bored on such long flights and resorted to playing tricks on the flight attendants. On one Fairbanks-Seattle trip, she was summoned to the cockpit by Captain Eddie Courtemanche, a huge man with the fearsome build of a Kodiak bear and the disposition of a friendly puppy.

He said he wanted a cup of hot chocolate. Broyles was fairly new on the job and thought airline captains ranked with U.S. senators and state governors. So she entered the cockpit carrying the hot chocolate, took one look at the occupant in the left seat, and almost dropped the cup. There was her dignified captain, resplendent in his silver-braided uniform hat, white shirt with four epaulets, regulation black tie, and nothing else except a pair of fake leopard-skin shorts.

Broyles also liked to fly with Captain Art Clune, who always brought a deck of cards along on lengthy DC-4 trips. But one night, after his copilot had beaten him about six consecutive times at gin rummy, Clune lost his cool, opened the cockpit window, and tossed the deck out. A few minutes later, Broyles came into the cockpit and found the shamefaced captain laboriously cutting out 52 pieces of blank paper, trying to fashion a makeshift deck of cards.

Broyles, who was based in Anchorage for 18 years, was luckier than many of the younger stewardesses in that she had been trained at the McConnell Airline Training School, which sent its graduates to airlines such as Alaska and other small airlines that lacked credible training programs. At a time when carriers such as American, United, and TWA were expanding training facilities in preparation for the transition to jets, turning their training centers into miniature colleges with detailed cabin and galley mockups, a flight-attendant classroom at Alaska was often a supervisor's office. Well into the mid-1960s, training at Alaska lasted only three weeks, compared to five to six weeks at major airlines, and many stewardesses who already were working trips had never had much formal training, and in a few cases none.

Alaska's policies for hiring new stewardesses at the time of the 880's introduction generally followed industry standards of that era. Age: minimum 20, maximum 26. Height: five feet two inches minimum, five feet nine inches maximum. Weight: no minimum, 135 pounds maximum. A woman had to be single when hired but could stay on the line if she married while employed. This was changed later to mandatory resignation if a flight attendant married or became pregnant. At least two years of college was a preference but not a requirement.

The starting pay after three weeks of training was $370 a month, increasing to $470 at the end of three years, a pay scale based on flying at least 78 hours a month, with extra incentive pay for flying more than the 78-hour minimum. The women were represented by the Air Line Stewards and Stewardesses Association (ALSSA), a division of the Air Line Pilots Association.

One rather startling example was Barbara "Barb" Foster, a native of Seattle who had always wanted to be a stewardess and at age 21 sent applications to four carriers: United, TWA, Pan Am, and Alaska. She was accepted by all of them and picked Alaska.

"This was in 1958," she recounted, "about a year after Charlie Willis became president. The day I reported for what I assumed was initial training, they told me to go out and buy a skirt, a white blouse, and a pair of high-heel shoes. There was no training. When I got back with the skirt, blouse, and shoes, they said that was my temporary uniform, put me on one of our DC-4s, and we took off for Fairbanks — two pilots, three passengers, and me.

"About all I did most of the trip was walk up and down the aisle asking the three passengers if they were comfortable. I didn't know I was supposed to turn on the galley ovens right after takeoff, and I didn't introduce myself to the pilots because I thought they were so important I wasn't allowed to talk to them unless they spoke first.

"I didn't serve any meals until the copilot came out to see how I was doing and discovered that the ovens hadn't been turned on yet. The DC-4 galleys were small, and so were the ovens, so the food took about four hours to heat, and we were halfway to Fairbanks before anyone ate. I did manage to find the liquor kit, so I served one round of drinks, then put the kit away."

The captain came back to check on Foster's progress, discovered she had closed the liquor kit after a single serving, and told her to open the kit again. "You trying to hoard the stuff?" he demanded.

Foster's second trip was a bit smoother because there was another stewardess aboard who had flown for United and was able to give her a quick course. Such instructional training became more of a supplemental "post-graduate" way to learn as the airline grew and training got more sophisticated, but on-the-job training was not an infrequent occurrence until well into the era of jet operations.

Admittedly, not a few new stewardesses came from unsophisticated family backgrounds, and Alaska's earlier training curriculum did not include bartending. Barb Foster was one of these innocent souls, and on one of her first flights, a male passenger politely asked for a screwdriver.

"Be right back," she assured him. She went to the cockpit and told the captain, "I've got a passenger who needs a screwdriver."

"What for?"

"I don't know. I guess his seat tray must be loose or something."

The captain reached into a small tool kit, fished out a screwdriver, and handed it to Foster. "Be sure and get it back when he's finished," he cautioned.

She returned to the cabin and put the screwdriver on the mystified passenger's tray. "Let me know when you're finished with it," she said cheerfully. "Meanwhile, what can I get you to drink before lunch?"

"Well," he said solemnly, "bring me some vodka and a glass of orange juice."

The screwdriver was returned before they landed, and later that night, Foster was telling her father about "this nutty passenger" who had asked for a screwdriver he apparently never used, and then ordered this "absolutely weird concoction" for a cocktail.

Her more worldly father shook his head. "Barbara," he explained gently, "when you put vodka into a glass of orange juice, it's called a screwdriver."

Eventually — in other words after a few short months of flying — Foster became a relative veteran, used to difficult passengers and pilot pranks. For some unknown reason, no flight-attendant course for any airline in the world has ever warned naive beginners about the practical jokers inhabiting airliner cockpits. And if a flight attendant dared to retaliate, she usually came to regret it.

Alaska had one captain — he shall remain nameless — who used to irritate the rest of the crew because he always was the first one off the airplane at the end of a trip, and those he left behind included the passengers. Barb Foster decided to retaliate.

DC-4 pilots invariably stored their overnight bags in a small cargo compartment behind the cockpit. Within seconds after the engines were turned off, this captain would rush to the compartment, pick up his bag, and flee the airplane. So on the last leg of one trip, Foster sneaked up behind the cockpit and tied the four-striper's bag to a cargo tie-down ring.

The DC-4 came to a stop in front of the terminal. The boarding stairs were pushed to the rear cabin door. The captain came out of the cockpit in his usual hurry and picked up his bag.

Or tried to. As the famous song goes, he flew through the air with the greatest of ease, but with no class whatsoever. He landed on his back, considerably bruised and extremely angry.

Barb figured she had gotten away with justified revenge, but someone snitched. When she went out to her car later, all four tires were flat.

On another occasion, Foster drew a brand-new stewardess working her first trip, a DC-6, and the woman disappeared from view a few minutes after takeoff. Foster finally located her as she emerged from a lavatory, out of breath as if she had just run a fast hundred-yard dash.

"Where have you been?" Foster demanded.

"Flushing toilets," the rookie panted. "Right after we took off, the captain told me they were having trouble raising the landing gear, so I had to recharge the hydraulic system, you know, by flushing the toilets." She had fallen for one of aviation's oldest practical jokes.

Foster herself was unwittingly responsible for one brand-new stewardess resigning after her first trip. Barb had slipped on some spilled ice on the galley floor, and to keep from falling had instinctively grabbed an oven door handle. The "handle" screamed. What Foster had grabbed was the rookie flight attendant's blouse, tearing it completely off. The newcomer resigned two days later, explaining to her supervisor that "flying is too dangerous."

Which it could be at times, far more frequently in the piston-engine days than in the jet age. Foster's worst experience didn't involve the usual hazards of flight, however. Hers occurred during a natural disaster. She was a flight attendant on the last aircraft to leave the Anchorage airport before the city was hit by a monster earthquake on Good Friday, March 27, 1964.

"It was a DC-6 trip," she recalled. "We were just taking off, and I was in a rear-facing jump seat when I looked out the window and saw the runway buckling underneath us. Then I saw a house fall into the sea, followed by another building which fell into a crevasse that had opened up — it just disappeared."

Ten years later, the Universal film *Earthquake* duplicated that airport-takeoff scene, using LAX as the airport instead of Anchorage. That 1964 earthquake, incidentally, was the worst in U.S. recorded history. Measuring 8.5 on the Richter scale, and revised to 9.2 on a new magnitude scale developed later, it was stronger than the 1906 quake that devastated San Francisco. It originated at the northern end of Prince William Sound, 80 miles east of Anchorage, striking the city itself at 5:36 p.m.

The shock waves rolled down Alaska's south-central coast, flooding scores of coastal towns. Valdez, Cordova, and Seward were among the cities hit especially hard. Tidal waves were generated all the way to Japan and as far south as the Antarctic, and in the United States, the quake was felt all the way to Houston, Texas. The death toll of 125 Alaskans was mercifully low, considering the quake's magnitude and all the damage it caused, but thousands of square miles of Alaska's coastline simply vanished.

Inasmuch as Alaska was forced to operate an all-piston fleet before it could afford its first jet, the airline packed as many seats as possible into some of its older aircraft. Some DC-3s had as many as 35 seats, although the cabin originally was designed to carry not more than 28. The DC-4 was a 50-passenger aircraft, but Alaska added 15 seats. Simple demand was the reason for this "sardine seating" policy.

In the meantime, Charlie Willis finally arrived at a strategy to acquire a new jetliner without a down payment — not from the two leading aircraft manufacturers, Boeing and Douglas, but from the Convair division of General Dynamics, a company desperate to grab a bigger share of the jetliner market. Convair was convinced that it had a winner in its fast new CV-880 (the 880 designation was based on its projected top speed of 600 mph, which translated into 880 feet per second). Convair had sold the 880 to TWA, Delta, and Capital, but when United merged with Capital, it canceled the latter's 880 order, and in doing so opened the door for the bargain-hunting Mr. Willis.

Charlie's approach to Convair was almost entirely psychological, inasmuch as he was negotiating with an empty checking account. His trump card was the knowledge that the 880 program was in trouble. Convair had the right-size airplane for a number of carriers, one that was smaller than the big 707 and DC-8, but Boeing had trumped that by developing a truncated version of the 707, the 720, which United and other carriers had already ordered. The 720 had a significant advantage over the 880. Cabin width was identical to the 707's, with the same six-abreast seating in coach; the 880's narrower cabin had three-and-two seating in coach, and fewer seats meant less payload.

Loosely yet accurately paraphrased, Willis's pitch went this way: "We need a new jet but can't afford the down payment right now. You need to sell more 880s but can't find enough customers because you're butting heads against Boeing and its 720. Yet suppose you sold Alaska Airlines an 880? You'd have a Seattle-based airline, right in Boeing's own backyard, flying around in a Convair 880 built in California. That's the greatest testimonial you could have for your airplane and the worst kind of publicity for Boeing."

In retrospect, Willis's scenario probably had about as much validity as the plot of a B-grade horror movie, but Convair officials bought it. The $4.5 million airplane, delivered in mid-August of 1961, was an 880-M, slightly faster and longer-ranged than the standard 880. It was one of the 880s that Capital had ordered, and Alaska was given its original assembly-line and delivery positions.

Willis decided to operate the 880 with an all-coach configuration, while still providing the equivalent of first-class in-flight service. This made the jet a 110-passenger airplane, but because of the narrow cabin, Willis had to retain the aircraft's original coach configuration of two-and-three seating. Giersdorf made a point, however, of emphasizing in publicity releases and advertising that two-and-three seating was preferable to the more crowded six-abreast on Boeings and DC-8s.

More than 20 years later, the airline's sales and marketing department would justify Alaska's choosing the MD-80 over the Boeing 737 by emphasizing that its two-and-three coach seating provided more passenger comfort and fewer center seats than the Boeing's six-abreast seating.

Giersdorf's valiant efforts to offset the airline's numerous competitive disadvantages could have been graded A for their ingenuity. Typical was his strategy for overcoming that mandatory stop at Fairbanks on the Seattle-Anchorage route. He created a unique cover for the airline's new timetable. Dick Garvin, who joined Alaska as a salesman in 1954, had known Giersdorf when Bob was a salesman for Northern Consolidated in Fairbanks and Garvin was managing a radio station there. "The map was deliberately distorted," Garvin recalled. "It showed Fairbanks and Anchorage both being equal distances from Seattle."

On August 30, 1961, the airline inaugurated jet service between Seattle, Fairbanks, and Anchorage, one day before PNA put its first 720 into service between Seattle and Anchorage. The new 880, carrying a full load of 110 passengers, proceeded to set a speed record between Seattle and Fairbanks of two hours and 22 minutes, and both Giersdorf and Willis were in a publicity seventh heaven.

Before the return flight arrived in Seattle, Giersdorf was at the airport armed with a brief script describing the new jet's virtues, which he took to the Alaska Airlines ticket counter. Bob Handley was the agent on duty. "When our 880 comes in," Giersdorf told him, "I want you to read this over our PA system so everyone at the airport will hear it."

Handley scanned the script doubtfully. "Look, Mr. Giersdorf," he protested. "We're not supposed to use our PA system for stuff like this."

"Do what I said," Giersdorf ordered. "Here comes our airplane, so start reading."

Handley dutifully began reciting what Giersdorf had composed. As he came to the line "The 880 is virtually a smokeless jet," he happened to glance outside and saw Alaska's new jetliner on final approach. It was spewing thick black smoke out of all four engines in such mammoth proportions that, as Handley recalled, "the damned thing looked like it was on fire." From that day on, for as long as Alaska operated that 880, the airplane was known as Old Smoky.

Coincidental with the inauguration of the airline's first jet service was the erection of a huge billboard near the airport. Giersdorf was responsible for the message it conveyed. It went down as one of the most misleading advertisements in commercial aviation history. It announced: FOUR JETS DAILY TO ALASKA.

Giersdorf did it with malice aforethought, as the saying goes. Pan Am and PNA were each operating four daily Seattle-Anchorage flights, so Giersdorf decided to counter this disadvantage even though his "four jets daily" referred to the number of engines on that lone 880. Most people thought it was more of a tongue-in-cheek gag than a deliberate attempt to deceive, but nevertheless, Pan Am would cite that ad and Alaska's sumptuous 880 in-flight coach service as examples of unfair competitive practices and haul Charlie before the CAB.

A one-airplane jet fleet obviously raised questions about downtime when that single jetliner had to be taken out of service for mandatory maintenance work. The solution was to do the maintenance in gradual stages, instead of waiting for the usual periodic major work that would take the airplane out of service for several days.

When the FAA approved the schedule, Willis proudly proclaimed it the first such plan in the entire industry. Like insisting that Alaska Airlines had pioneered in-flight movies, however, this was another inaccurate boast. Continental Airlines had introduced what it called "progressive maintenance" on its first four 707s in 1959, two years earlier.

The 880 proved to be an instant success, grabbing 64 percent of the Seattle-Anchorage market in the first year of its operation, even with the mandatory Fairbanks stop. The bloom came off the rose, of course, when PNA began operating all three of its 720s over the route.

Even as Alaska entered the jet age, Raymond Marshall's association with the airline was coming to an end. The Civil Aeronautics Board had been investigating Marshall's continuing influence, much to the delight of Charlie Willis, who had already had an unpleasant experience with his business practices. R.W., apparently thinking he had found an unsuspecting sucker, had tried to sell him some spare parts that already had been condemned.

The CAB eventually found that Marshall had an illegal interlocking relationship with several Alaska directors and ordered them removed from the board. This gave Willis a chance to nominate several of his own choices for directors, giving him a board majority. After a bitter proxy fight, in which Charlie had the active support of every employee, Marshall was ousted permanently.

With that burr under the saddle removed, the Willis-Giersdorf team continued its campaign to polish the airline's image with the Golden Nugget Service theme. On the DC-6, it had been more of a gimmick than a legitimate revolution in service. But acquisition of the 880 really brought it to life, and the original Golden Nugget theme was remodeled into a Gay '90s motif featuring new stewardess outfits that were more like costumes than uniforms.

Jo Coughlin, whose flying career with Alaska began on the first 880 flights, remembered the uniforms switch as something of a revolutionary changeover. "My first uniform on the 880," she related, "consisted of beige high heels, a green skirt and jacket with a yellow blouse, white gloves, and a cute little hat. We looked like we were selling Girl Scout cookies. Then came the Gay '90s summer outfit: split velvet skirts, velvet hats, and black mesh nylon stockings.

"Two of the girls almost got arrested in Anchorage. They were walking around downtown in those new uniforms, and a cop thought they were hookers. When they told him they were airline stewardesses, the cop didn't believe them at first."

By and large, the flight attendants loved the Gay '90s uniforms because they were so different from what flight attendants on other airlines were wearing. It is believed that Giersdorf came up with the idea of applying the theme to flight-attendant uniforms, but there's no doubt he had Charlie's enthusiastic support.

Even the ticket counters and city ticket offices were dressed up with the Gay '90s look, using special wallpaper and lighting fixtures disguised as 19th-century gas lamps.

Willis loved "theme" decor. Walking into his office in Seattle was like entering a time machine — visitors suddenly found themselves in a Klondike saloon during the Gold Rush days. Over the entrance was a sign that read: Charlie's Saloon. The office had swinging barroom doors, cold beer on tap, red velvet drapes, a player piano featuring honky-tonk tunes, an antique rolltop desk, and a stuffed moose head mounted on a wall.

Giersdorf, however, definitely was the one who conceived the idea of sprucing up the pre-takeoff public-address safety announcements required by the newly created Federal Aviation Agency (later renamed the Federal Aviation Administration) along with increased emphasis on cabin safety during training. Giersdorf agreed with the vast majority of flight attendants, on Alaska and all other carriers, who complained that as passengers became accustomed to jet travel, no one listened to the "canned" briefings they had heard so many times before.

A flight attendant on one carrier proved the point when she advised everyone: "When the oxygen mask drops, attach it to your navel and breathe normally." Not a single passenger looked up from a book or newspaper.

Giersdorf decided to do something about this indifference. Borrowing in some measure from famed Canadian poet Robert Service, he composed a series of PA safety announcements in rhyme. One sample will suffice:

> *Our best to you from the Gold Rush crew*
> *Of the Golden Nugget jet.*
> *We welcome you to a rendezvous*
> *Where the old and new are met.*

> *A life vest neat is beneath your seat*
> *They're stored so we won't lose 'em.*
> *Now fix your eyes on the flight attendants*
> *They'll show you how to use 'em.*

There were additional stanzas covering oxygen masks and in-flight service, but when Giersdorf proposed using them on the 880, several officers warned him that the FAA would never approve such a lighthearted approach to a subject as serious as what-if safety advice. Giersdorf didn't agree, and much to the surprise of a lot of people, the FAA approved the unique little announcements.

Thus did Bob Giersdorf set a precedent for unconventional safety PAs that years later would make Southwest Airlines famous, and also inspire several future Alaska Airlines flight attendants. Bambi Coons and Tanya Roberts often composed their own safety messages, and Marty Calhoun became the airline's own Rich Little, an impressionist of remarkable professional skill.

On Alaska's lone 880, the opulence of Golden Nugget service, the new Gay '90s stewardess uniforms, and the lighthearted cabin PAs were actually a bit of slick legerdemain. It was illusionary, like the Wizard of Oz appearing as a monstrous talking head while the real "wizard," a mild-mannered little fraud and con man, was manipulating it from behind a screen. The truth was that Alaska wobbled rather than flew into the jet age, a financially sick airline that was so broke it couldn't even afford enough dinner plates for the elaborate food service. It had fewer than 90 plates, and the 880 carried 110 passengers.

Ken Skidds, who eventually would become one of Alaska's highest-ranking officers, started out in fleet service about the time the 880 was introduced and witnessed the airline's financial troubles from a front-row seat. "The flight attendants on the 880 would serve the first meals to about 80 passengers," he related, "then take about 30 of the used plates back to the galley, where they'd hurriedly wash them so they could serve the rest of the passengers."

Continued Skidds: "Ostensibly, fleet service was supposed to involve just cleaning airplanes, but even though there were only two of us, we did everything such as loading and unloading the in-flight meals and beverages. We were so poor that when an airplane came in, one of our jobs was to take off all the unused salt and pepper shakers, sugar packages, and plastic utensils. These we'd rush over to Host, our caterer at Sea-Tac at the time, so they could be put back on the next airplane. When the Host trucks delivered meals, we had to unload them ourselves because Alaska couldn't pay Host's unloading fees.

"We had a baggage tug that was so old, the Port Authority finally condemned it. So for a while, we had to pull the baggage carts by hand. Fortunately, we had a ramp man in Anchorage, Jerry Smith, who leased secondhand ground equipment to the airline, because it couldn't afford to buy its own. At the Seattle airport, we borrowed anything we could from anyone who would loan us what we needed. And if we couldn't borrow something, like biffy juice (lavatory cleaning fluid), we'd appropriate it."

That was a firsthand report on life with Charlie, who really did resemble the flimflam Wizard of Oz when it came to drawing curtains over the airline's poverty status. Yet he also was getting maximum mileage out of pitifully small resources, and the kind of scrounging and improvising that Ken Skidds described was not just a way of life at Alaska at the dawn of the jet age; it was a way to survive.

Even when things got so bad that paychecks were limited to a maximum of $100, there were no employee demands for Charlie Willis's scalp. He had employee loyalty even when he didn't really deserve it, and that included the pilots. Especially the pilots. How could they get angry at a guy who, when informed there was a $100,000 shortage in the pilots' pension fund, mortgaged his house for that amount and put the money into the fund? Even his detractors had to admire his competitive spirit, so sorely tried in those early days of jet service.

Not having nonstop Seattle-Anchorage authority was a handicap competitively, and so was the airline's diminutive jet fleet, which in 1967 actually doubled — to two jets — with the acquisition of a Convair 990 from the Brazilian airline Varig. The 990 was a larger version of the 880 and supposedly faster (with a top speed of 990 feet per second), but the airplane never lived up to all its advertised performance promises, including top speed, and was a disappointment to the carriers that bought it.

When it first joined the fleet, the 990 was used to fly cargo into South America and was based for a brief time in Miami, of all places, along with a full flight crew. Mobil and Texaco were drilling for oil in the jungles of Ecuador, and Willis had signed a contract to fly oil-drilling rigs and pipelines into the country. The crew consisted of Captain Sam Silver — one of Alaska's most colorful airmen — a copilot, a flight engineer, and two mechanics, one of whom served as loadmaster. The cargo deal was a concession to Willis's longtime but never-realized ambition: to operate scheduled passenger service between the United States and South America, even though this would have pitted him against such formidable competitors as Pan Am and Braniff.

Alaska's 990 earned the unflattering nickname "hangar queen" because it was afflicted with so many mechanical malfunctions that its downtime seemed longer than its logged flight time. Willis never intended it to be more than a stopgap, however. He really wanted the new Boeing 727, a jetliner with three aft-engines, and he already had been talking to a Boeing salesman named Clancy Wilde.

Wilde, contrary to Charlie's hopes, couldn't have cared less whether Convair had one of its jets flying around Seattle. Boeing already was pulling ahead of both Convair and Douglas in jet orders, yet like any good salesman, Clancy hated to lose a single prospect and still considered any airline, even Alaska, a potential customer.

Clancy Wilde wasn't just any Boeing salesman when he became directly involved with Willis and Alaska Airlines. Wilde was something of a legend at the big aerospace company. In the early 1960s he was manager of domestic sales, which included the United States and Canada, and later he would be promoted to vice president of international sales.

Wilde also happened to be the elected mayor of Bellevue, Washington, a post that, as it turned out, probably saved Charlie from a DUI conviction. As Wilde remembered that memorable evening sometime in late 1962 or early '63, it began when he invited Willis and a couple of Charlie's officers over to his apartment for cocktails. Wilde had made dinner reservations at the Crabapple restaurant in Bellevue, but Willis's two companions had made other plans and took a cab home. Charlie decided to drive to the restaurant by himself, while Wilde and a Bellevue attorney named Mike Donovan drove there in Clancy's car.

They were still waiting at the Crabapple for Willis to show up when Wilde got a phone call from a Bellevue police department patrol car. "Mr. Mayor, we've got a guy named Willis who says he's president of Alaska Airlines and that he's a friend of yours. His car's in a ditch and he's had a few, to put it mildly. We'll drive him to the Crabapple if you'll vouch for him."

"Yeah," Wilde sighed, "I'll vouch for him. Drive him over to the Crabapple and I'll get him home."

"Mr. Mayor, are *you* sober?"

"Completely," Wilde assured the officer.

"Good, because this guy's in no shape to drive a car farther than 10 feet."

So Willis arrived at the restaurant in the backseat of a police car, unfazed by the experience. From the Crabapple after dinner, the trio proceeded to Donovan's apartment for more drinks, and that's when Wilde and Willis began discussing business.

"We're trying to sell Charlie some airplanes," Wilde explained to the attorney.

"Yeah," Willis agreed. "I wanna buy a few 727s, but Boeing won't sell me any."

This, Wilde knew, was only too true. Hal Haynes, Boeing's very conservative vice president of finance, took a dim view of selling airplanes to airlines that couldn't afford to pay for them.

"And at the time," Wilde recalled, "Alaska Airlines had a debt-to-equity ratio of about 10 to 1. Its credit standing was only a few notches above that of a homeless derelict."

There was a brief silence in Mike Donovan's apartment, and then Willis suddenly blurted, "Clancy, I wanna sign a contract right now. Mike, you got any paper around?"

"No," Donovan replied, "but I've got a white T-shirt under my regular shirt. I'll take it off and you can write something on that, sort of a letter of intent. It'll be legal, by the way."

Donovan handed Charlie his T-shirt. Willis scribbled a few lines on it — Wilde remembered something like "Alaska Airlines agrees to buy three or four 727s from Boeing" — and then signed his name.

The next day, Wilde showed the "contract" to a Boeing lawyer, who shook his head. "You guys must have had one hell of a party last night," he commented sourly. Willis and Boeing then negotiated a more formal agreement, in 1964, for two 727-100s, and later increased the order to three.

All three 727-100 jets were C models, meaning they were built primarily for cargo operations. But Willis wanted the first one, anyway, to have a passenger compartment whose interior reflected his Golden Nugget/Gay '90s theme. He proceeded to order it delivered with red and black seats, the epitome of incongruity in a jetliner model actually designed more for cargo than passengers.

Yet the fact that the airline's first three Boeings were cargo aircraft reflected Willis's long-standing belief in air cargo's viability. Remember, his very first aviation venture was a cargo airline. Airfreight bypassed the shackles of CAB-regulated routes; all you needed was a contract and suitable airplanes, and you could fly just about anyplace in the world.

Willis had considerable help in all these cargo ventures from a man he trusted as implicitly as he did Bob Giersdorf, and that was saying a lot. LeRoy Peterson had handled cargo for the Air Force in World War II, first as an enlisted man and later as an officer. He had worked for Willis at Willis Air Service, and soon after Charlie took over Alaska Airlines, he called Peterson and asked him to come out and help him run the airline.

"When I saw what was happening there," Peterson recalled, "I said to myself, this isn't even an airline. I think we had only one DC-4 and a DC-3 at the time. In most of the 18 years I was there, we had more income from freight and charters than passenger business."

Willis named him vice president of sales, but two years later gave him the more realistic title of vice president of services, which involved leasing, buying, and selling airplanes, and dealing with the FAA and CAB. He worked at least 60 hours a week and spent as much time away on business trips as he did at home. But it was mainly LeRoy Peterson, as quietly efficient as Willis was flamboyant, who among a myriad of other tasks, engineered the expansion of the airline's cargo fleet.

Even before the 727 contract, Willis and Peterson had added several all-cargo aircraft to the fleet: two Lockheed 1649 Constellations, the longest-ranged piston airliners ever built, and a smaller 1049 Super Constellation. All three were former TWA airplanes originally designed solely for passenger service but modified into freighters because there was no longer a profitable market for piston-engine airliners. Even the small regional, or so-called local-service, airlines were ordering jets.

The L-1649 was a superb airliner, but it had gone into service when the jet age was just around the corner, and TWA, which had ordered 25 of them, found itself saddled with an airplane already obsolete the first day it flew. TWA's nimble public relations staff tried to recoup by calling the 1649 The Jetstream, implying that it was jet-powered, but that didn't save the 1649 from being considered, through no fault of its own, one of commercial aviation's flops. The cargo version served Alaska well if briefly, however, and the airline eventually bought a third one from TWA. These planes also made it necessary for Alaska to hire its first navigators for the long overseas flights to distant countries.

In the mid-1960s, Willis won new government contracts to fly cargo to underdeveloped nations and used these to finance the acquisition of new Lockheed C-130 freighters, which gradually replaced the Constellations in cargo service and became one of the most important airplanes in the airline's history. They, too, often required navigators as part of the cockpit crew, and two of them — Dave Zehrung and Pat Glenn — were to play major roles at Alaska. Zehrung was the first one hired for L-1649 missions, and he in turn hired Glenn. At the height of these far-flung cargo operations, the airline had 11 navigators on its payroll.

Appropriately dubbed the Hercules, the C-130 was a four-engine turbo-prop. Its jet engines were hitched to conventional propellers. Most military C-130s had three-bladed propellers, but Alaska ordered them equipped with four-bladed props to give it more short takeoff and landing capability.

Lockheed's choice of the name Hercules for the C-130 was derived not from the legendary strong man of Greek mythology but from a northern constellation. At Alaska, the airplane was fondly called the Herc by everyone associated with loading, maintaining, or flying the big freighter. It originally was designed for the Air Force, first flew in 1952, only three years after the Berlin Airlift ended, and was put into service by the Military Air Transport Service (MATS) in 1962.

The Herc — at this writing still on active military duty after more than 50 years of service — was versatile, fast, long-legged, and rugged. It cruised at well over 320 mph with a full load, could fly more than 3,600 statute miles without refueling, carried up to 35,000 pounds of cargo (about double what a 727C could haul), and could land virtually anyplace where the ground was level, such as the dirt and gravel runways so prevalent in Alaska and on the state's frozen strips in the far north. (The Navy, in fact, some years ago landed a ski-equipped Herc at the South Pole.)

Alaska Airlines was the first commercial air carrier to operate the C-130. And it needed such an airplane because Charlie Willis, like Jim Wooten before him, was sending Alaska's planes all over the world on various contracted cargo assignments: South America, New Guinea, Japan, Vietnam, and Australia.

Ken Skidds had been a loadmaster on Hercs in the Air Force before joining Alaska in 1965, just when the airline was deciding whether to order the big turbo-prop. "So help me, they actually were studying the possibility of using them to haul all of Seattle's garbage out of the area," Skidds remembered. "It would have taken a hell of a lot of C-130s."

A retired and much-respected mechanic named "Smokey" Schnee recalled the Australian mission in particular. Schnee, a native of Alberta, Canada, joined Alaska in 1955. His first job was washing engine parts for $1.15 an hour, and four years later, Schnee got his airframe and powerplant (A & P) license as a full-fledged mechanic, "plus a big raise — to $1.35 an hour," he laughed.

France was operating a rocket-testing facility in Australia, and Willis had finagled a contract with the French government to fly some test equipment from Paris to Australia via Iran. The contract called for a total of three trips, and Schnee went on the first one as the mechanic assigned to the flight. On all the long-haul cargo flights to other countries, a mechanic and a loadmaster always went along as crew members, and Smokey was riding the Herc's cockpit jump seat when they landed in Australia for the first time.

"There was a big crowd at the airport," Schnee recounted. "I looked out the window, and everyone was looking at the Herc and laughing their heads off. So the captain told me to find out what was so funny."

Schnee deplaned and asked the first Australian who approached him what everyone was laughing at. The Aussie pointed to the C-130's big tail, with its proud insignia: "Golden Nugget Freighter."

"What the hell's so funny about that?" Schnee demanded.

The Aussie burst out laughing again. "Mate," he finally managed to explain, "in Australia, 'nugget' means *turd*."

The Berlin blockade and the Korean War could be classed as dress rehearsals for the far greater airlift demands of the Vietnam conflict. Alaska's participation was limited to the few long-range cargo aircraft it was operating, and until the Hercs joined the fleet, the L-1649s shouldered most of the load. The airline's L-1049 Super Constellations also flew a few military contract flights, but most mechanics, including Smokey Schnee, took a dim view of the smaller Connies.

"They had electric props that were always giving us fits," Schnee said. "The 1649s had regular props and were a pretty good airplane. But of all the freighters, the Hercs were the most reliable. The C-46 could carry a hell of a load for a twin-engine airplane, but if you lost an engine on takeoff, the crew had better start singing 'Nearer My God to Thee.' "

The C-130 had the lowest operating costs of any aircraft employed in the Vietnam airlift — better than any piston, propjet, or pure jet that flew in or out of that war theater. Yet neither equipment economy nor reliability could save Alaska Airlines from the embarrassment of having one of its Herc crews arrested upon arrival at the Saigon airport.

It seemed that Willis or some subordinate had neglected to obtain the necessary diplomatic authority to land in Vietnam, and the fact that Alaska had a MATS contract made no difference. The first Herc flight landed in Saigon, unloaded, and took off again before any of the Vietnamese authorities could check on landing authorization.

But the hasty departure aroused suspicion, and when the second C-130 landed a few days later, police were waiting and hauled the crew off to jail. They were released thanks to intervention by George Knuckey, the Saigon station manager for Flying Tiger, who had witnessed the arrest. Knuckey later ended up working for Alaska as one of its best-liked, most versatile managers, and he recalled the incident as typical of the way all the airlines participating in the Vietnam airlift cooperated with each other.

"We were really one airline over there," he reminisced. "Borrowing spare parts from another carrier was an accepted and necessary practice because it took so long to get parts from the U.S. Even Pan Am, which wasn't exactly noted for its generosity, would loan another airline a spare part in an emergency. And when some top airline official like Bob Six of Continental or Bob Prescott of Flying Tiger would come into Saigon, all the other airlines would get together and throw him a party."

Another future Alaska executive who worked for the airline's Vietnam airlift was Pat Glenn, whose career was one of those Horatio Alger stories so typical of the airline industry in its years of unlimited opportunity. Glenn was a youngster fresh out of the Air Force when the airline hired him. He had been a navigator on military C-130s and was assigned to Hercs as a navigator as his first job with the airline.

"I'll never forget those Vietnam experiences," Glenn mused. "Nobody liked to land at night because you could see the tracer fire below so plainly. Of course they were shooting in the daytime, too, but at least then you couldn't see the tracers."

Alaska's Vietnam return flights always stopped in Japan, where the Hercs were loaded up with hibachis and Honda motorcycles. Alaska was one of the few airlines that didn't carry passengers in or out of Saigon, so the C-130s had plenty of available cargo space when flying home.

Continued Glenn: "It got to the point where we wouldn't take off from Japan without a full load of hibachis and motorcycles, especially the pots. I think at one time there wasn't an Alaska Airlines employee who didn't own one of those hibachis."

Alaska's Hercs would go on to significant new adventures after the Vietnam conflict ended. And Charlie Willis likewise was flying high. In March 1965, he finally persuaded the CAB to give Alaska Airlines direct Seattle-Anchorage nonstop authority, eliminating the mandatory Fairbanks-Anchorage leg, and three years later he embarked on a new course that would change the company's future.

Willis was determined to make the airline Alaska's dominant air carrier. His strategy was a simple six-letter word . . .

Merger.

CHAPTER FOUR

Three
Scrappy Airlines

Alaska Coastal Airlines. Ellis Air Lines. Cordova Airlines. These were just three of the 11 intrastate carriers operating scheduled service within Alaska about the time the Territory became America's 49th state.

Most had been founded by former bush pilots and were not too far removed from the old bush carriers in the kind of obsolete airplanes they flew and unsophisticated operating procedures they used. But they also still possessed the resilience, adaptability, and fierce loyalties that had marked bush-era fliers, founders, officers, and employees alike. Two of them — Reeve Aleutian and Wien Alaska — clung stubbornly to their founders' names and their independence for as long as possible.

Most of those 11 bush-era survivors had long ago erased the belief that bush pilots flew airplanes better than they ran their airlines, and this also was true of the three that finally found themselves hovering on the precipice of merger. They were professionally operated, despite their limited resources and restricted operational areas, and they were not blind to the realities facing their little companies. They were battling to exist in a period of increasing inroads by larger carriers, just when Alaska's economy was promising to reach boom proportions.

In the mid-1960s, rich oil deposits were discovered on the North Slope in the Prudhoe Bay area. Oil was known as "black gold," an appropriate appellation, for Alaska was suddenly facing a modern re-enactment of the Gold Rush days, with a surge of new jobs, large-scale worker migration from the Lower 48, and demands on air transportation for logistical support that were reminiscent of World War II's massive airlifts.

Inevitably, most of the tiny Alaskan regional carriers were threatened with extinction. They were too small to compete successfully, except in communities so tiny or so isolated that the larger airlines weren't interested in serving them. Yet at the same time, some of these little regional carriers were so strategically located that they were inviting targets for acquisition because they could feed traffic into the state's more heavily traveled air routes.

Alaska Coastal, Ellis, and Cordova were the carriers serving Southeast Alaska's vast expanses, and belonged in that category. They also offered another enticing rationale for merger: all three had a history of being well-run, getting the most mileage out of their small-scale resources, and being blessed with a dedicated little army of skilled and resourceful employees.

Beyond that, however, were two equally strong incentives for Willis to add them to the Alaska Airlines family. First, they offered the opportunity for a single airline to penetrate all of Southeast Alaska for the first time, moving into a market with great potential. Second, the airline's oldest competitor suddenly decided to bail out, and this was to change the course of Alaska Airlines' destiny. In the fall of 1966, Art Woodley unexpectedly sold Pacific Northern to Western Airlines. "I just figured the day of the small carrier was over" was Woodley's explanation for his surprise decision.

This was a logical and in some respects accurate reason, but it wasn't the whole story. Charlie Willis may have been his own worst enemy, but the same label could have been pasted on Woodley as well. His temper had dipped him into hot water more than a few times, and his almost irrational hatred of Willis didn't help.

PNA had lost virtually every route case it had brought before the Civil Aeronautics Board, especially the major ones, and at one point, PNA's Washington, D.C., representative, a feisty little Irishman named Gerald O'Grady, decided it was time to mend some fences. He arranged for Woodley to meet the powerful chairman of the CAB, James Landis, and warned Art to behave himself.

"Don't say anything to upset him," he cautioned. "He's up for reappointment, and he's naturally a bit sensitive to the slightest criticism."

They entered Landis's office and O'Grady introduced Woodley to the chairman, who extended his hand and said cordially, "It's a pleasure to meet you, Mr. Woodley."

Woodley, pointedly ignoring his outstretched hand, shouted, "Landis, I think you're crooked! You're in bed with that goddamned Alaska Airlines!"

Landis, who also had a temper, responded with a few expletives of his own, and O'Grady hurriedly ushered Woodley out before the two came to blows. Once outside the building, Woodley was grinning with satisfaction.

"Well, I guess we told that bastard off," he chuckled. "Where do we go now?"

O'Grady, a devout Roman Catholic like Woodley himself, shook his head sadly. "To church," he sighed. "We need to say a few Hail Marys to make sure Landis won't get reappointed."

O'Grady shouldn't have been surprised. Woodley's career was studded with examples of his distaste for government authority. Art's most defiant act came early in PNA's history when the old CAA ordered all Alaskan carriers to equip their aircraft with rubber de-icing boots on the leading edges of the wings. Woodley decided this would be too expensive, so he merely painted all the leading edges black and got away with the ruse.

The Landis incident wasn't really more than a relatively minor contributing factor in Woodley's pulling out of what he believed had become just a rat race he couldn't win. True, he was frustrated by his long losing streak in route cases and knew this wasn't likely to change. He actually had turned down an earlier offer from Pan Am's Juan Trippe to buy PNA's Alaskan routes, after Trippe spent two full days wooing him. But at the time, Woodley honestly had believed that Pacific Northern could go it alone. He no longer thought so.

On the surface, PNA was doing a lot better financially than Alaska. In 1965, it netted a $2 million profit on a record gross of $30 million, and carried more passengers between Seattle and Alaska than Pan Am, Northwest, and Alaska Airlines combined.

Nevertheless, Woodley became increasingly convinced that his airline's future was grim. The decisive development came that same year when he ordered four new 727s from Boeing, then had to cancel the contract because he couldn't raise the financing. And that was when he entered serious negotiations with Western's president, Terry Drinkwater, who offered him a lucrative stock-exchange deal, a position on Western's board of directors, and a job with the title of vice president-Alaska.

Woodley insisted on a provision guaranteeing that none of PNA's 830 employees (about twice the 417 on Alaska's 1965 workforce) would lose their jobs because of the merger. He had always professed great cynicism about his employees. A reporter once asked him how many people he had working for him, and Woodley replied, "Oh, about half of 'em." But he really did care about them, and as it turned out, most of them were a lot happier after the merger than he was.

Woodley's title of "vice president-Alaska" proved to be meaningless, and his influence on Western's board minimal. The truth was that Drinkwater simply ignored a man who had written so much of Alaska's aviation history.

Art was naturally bitter. He went to a Los Angeles barbershop one day, fed up with inactivity, and the barber asked him what he did for a living.

"I'm with Western Airlines," Woodley said.

"Oh? What capacity?"

"About a fifth a day," Art grunted.

Woodley, more deeply hurt than he let on, resigned from both posts in 1971, yet he continued to harbor more ill feelings for Charlie Willis and Alaska Airlines than he did for Drinkwater. When Western eventually sold the three Boeing 720s it had inherited in the PNA merger to Alaska Airlines, of all buyers, someone told Woodley about the deal, expecting a megaton explosion. His reaction was a relatively mild "Why the hell couldn't they have sold it to some other airline?"

Alaska Airlines' bitterest competitor spent his last years in New York City, where he died in 1990 at the age of 84. In one respect, he had finally beaten the younger Willis at something. Charlie would die three years after Woodley, but Art had lived 10 years longer.

PNA's sale to Western removed a major hurdle on Willis's expansion march within the state, and it occurred at a time when other mergers were sweeping through Alaska's airline industry. Wien absorbed Northern Consolidated. Alaska Coastal and Ellis merged to become a single carrier, and Willis was successfully courting Cordova. Now, by absorbing these three small regional carriers, Alaska Airlines could control all local service operations in Southeast Alaska with one exception: the Juneau-Ketchikan-Seattle route that Pacific Northern was flying and Western assumed after the PNA merger.

Both Ken Skidds and Pat Glenn were junior managers during the flurry of mergers in the 1960s. Looking back, they felt that over the years, Willis's later troubles blurred appreciation of his significant achievements, not the least of which was forging Alaska Airlines into the state's flagship air carrier, an unofficial status it was never to relinquish.

"I think it's safe to say that Willis wasn't a good businessman," Glenn admitted. "He didn't know how to run an airline on a day-to-day basis. Yet he had a good reputation in Alaska itself. His political connections in Washington were awesome, and he had some clout within the CAB, which in those days was subject to a lot of political pressure in route cases."

Skidds agreed. "One important factor in the initial merger with Alaska Coastal," he pointed out, "was that it got us into Sitka for the first time. All we had then was that Fairbanks-Anchorage-Seattle route. Sitka was a real plum because that gave us a Sitka-Anchorage-Nome-Kotzebue route. It may not seem important now, but at the time it was damned important because that was our first step into Southeast Alaska.

"For one thing, it gave us a mail route from Southeast Alaska to Nome, and we flew the mail at the so-called 'bush rate,' which was a whopping dollar a pound, much higher than the so-called 'mainline' rates.

"I remember when we decided to build a brick hotel in Nome, and one plan we considered was mailing a few hundred bricks at a time up there. Eventually we did build the Nome Nugget Hotel, which was constructed with materials we flew in on our Hercs. We also owned another hotel in Nome, and we ended up flying in all their food, liquor, and other supplies as mail, while getting paid a dollar for every pound we carried."

Expanding into the hotel business was strictly Willis's idea. He believed that owning hotels would increase passenger business. The airline also bought a hotel in Fairbanks and another one in Sitka, although there was some opposition within the company to serving Sitka at all because its airport, located on an adjacent island, had a fairly short gravel runway. Willis scoffed at objections that it was not an inviting facility for Alaska's 727s.

"Hell, we don't need a 10-thousand-foot runway there," he insisted. "The runway's long enough for a 727. It's the gravel that's the problem."

The temporary answer was to acquire a Convair 340, a twin-engine piston airplane that wasn't vulnerable to ingesting gravel. Meanwhile, the real solution came from a joint committee from Boeing and Alaska Airlines, the latter represented by two relatively new executives: LeRoy Peterson, vice president of services, and Gus Robinson, vice president of maintenance, a tough ex-Marine who had put gravel deflectors on Hercs operated by the Marine Corps.

The committee devised a system that modified the 727's forward wing flaps, and put gravel deflectors on the nose gear. Thus did Sitka get its first jet service, despite the primitive state of its tiny airport. Robinson was especially proud of the deflector system. They were called "Third World deflectors" because they could be used on runways in undeveloped countries. Later they were adapted for the Boeing 737.

Ken Skidds was stationed in Sitka for nine months when the terminal was a 10-by-10-foot wooden shack. During the war, the Navy had operated a base at Sitka and built a small torpedo shed there that Alaska used for freight. The shed was next to a creek, and as Skidds recalled, "We had to walk through the creek to get to the terminal."

The 340 was used mostly to get Alaska Airlines people into Sitka so they could open the station there. Later the 727 provided passenger and freight service that almost came to grief because of an only too familiar handicap: Willis's ambitious ventures, such as plunging into the hotel business, had depleted the airline's thin cash reserves. Just when 727 flights began, the refuelers at the island airport refused to accept the company's credit card, and Alaska was back to the days when the pilots had to pay for the gas with their own cards and pray they'd eventually be reimbursed by the airline.

Once again, Charlie was in his Jekyll-Hyde mode, performing good deeds with one hand and tempting bankruptcy with the other. Yet the "triple play" that made Alaska Coastal, Cordova, and Ellis important additions to Alaska Airlines' routes certainly qualified as one of his better deeds.

Alaska Coastal was the first airline that fell into the willing arms of Charlie Willis — a proud little company founded in 1935 by Sheldon Bruce "Shell" Simmons, a bush pilot of incomparable skill with a reputation as a good businessman. Like so many of his colleagues, he never went to college and was largely self-taught, with real-life experience serving as his classroom. A native of Yakima, Washington, he quit school at 16, got his first job as a deckhand on a freighter, and spent three years driving a delivery truck in Ketchikan, Alaska. After studying electrical engineering in Los Angeles, he returned to Alaska to work in a Juneau mine as an electrical engineer.

In 1929, Simmons returned to Yakima long enough to take flying lessons and obtain a pilot's license. From then on, he was hooked on aviation as a career and Alaska as the place to practice it. In 1934, he bought a wrecked airplane in Juneau for one dollar, raised enough money from a few local investors to rebuild it, and launched a one-aircraft carrier he called Alaska

Air Transport. Its slender financial underpinnings notwithstanding, the tiny airline did well enough to attract Marine Airways as a merger partner, which in 1939 led to the creation of Alaska Coastal Airlines.

Simmons was only 26 when he founded Alaska Air Transport and still a young 31 when the airline began operating as Alaska Coastal. Yet he demonstrated business acumen and a level of professionalism far beyond his years.

He was not a trained aeronautical engineer, but he had the instincts of one. He played an active role in modifying and modernizing the ex-Navy PBY amphibians that the airline was operating. He insisted on improving the PBY instrumentation so his pilots could make instrument landings at Sitka and operate at night at Juneau. He often flew 16 hours a day, and he was the first commercial pilot in Southeast Alaska to fly year-round.

If anything, Shell had more of a scientific mind than a business one. He even tinkered with a primitive form of airborne radar years before it became standard equipment on all airliners. He was fond of all his 200 or so employees, but there was no doubt that his favorites were pilots and mechanics. They talked his language and shared his technical interests, especially his drumbeat of ideas for transforming the PBYs into 24-passenger airplanes. Some Alaska Coastal veterans think that Shell may have gotten credit for some innovations and improvisations that actually came from subordinates, but even if true, no one ever questioned his inspirational qualities as a natural leader.

One of his favorite mechanics was Art Peterson, a native Alaskan whose grandfather operated a trading post in a tiny village 90 miles east of Nome where Peterson was born. The grandfather and two uncles had been partners with Wyatt Earp in a Nome saloon during the Gold Rush days. "That was my one claim to fame," Peterson laughed in recollection.

Not quite. Art Peterson eventually became a highly respected expert in engineering and maintenance at Alaska Airlines. He earned the company's highest award and greatest honor: designation as an "Alaska Airlines Legend."

Yet for Peterson, like so many other alumni of Alaska Coastal, some of his fondest memories were those of the pre-merger days, especially the way Shell Simmons and his mechanics rebuilt the "fleet queens" — the PBY Catalina patrol bombers — into 24-passenger airliners. "They were all ex-Navy planes," Peterson said, "and when we bought them, all but one still had their Plexiglas blisters used by the side gunners. We replaced the blisters with flush doors. The military version also had a water rudder, which had to be removed because of the structural changes we were making. It was mostly Shell himself who devised an ingenious system that used the landing gear to steer the airplane while it was taxiing on water."

The PBY-rebuilding process included replacing the war-weary engines, and Simmons hit a jackpot when he located a number of overhauled Wright R-2600s, powerful engines used on B-25 medium bombers, which he bought for $150 to $200 apiece. And if the PBY was the queen of Alaska Coastal's fleet, the prince was the Grumman Goose, a much smaller twin-engine amphib carrying only eight passengers.

Peterson also had warm memories of some of his fellow mechanics at Alaska Coastal, one in particular being Roy Connors, a six-foot-four-inch lead mechanic built like a steel bridge girder who, luckily for his associates, never got mad at anybody.

"Like so many big guys," Peterson related, "Roy was a very gentle person. But if you didn't know him, Connors could scare the hell out of you. We had a young mechanic's helper named Alex Makowsky who didn't speak English very well and was terrified of Connors. Well, one day Alex was repainting the fuselage of a Goose that had just come out of overhaul.

"Roy was in the airplane tidying up the interior and stuck his head out a side window to say something just as Alex's paintbrush swept across his face. Connors didn't say a word, but he gave Makowsky a look that must have implied imminent assault and battery.

"The kid just threw down the brush, fled out of the hangar, and we didn't see him for the rest of the day."

Peterson added: "My mentor at Alaska Coastal was Jack Bracelen, the chief engineer and inspector, who personified the can-do spirit that made both Alaska Coastal and Alaska Airlines so special — it's the spirit of the state itself. Jack loved to quote a slogan so old that it's more of a cliché now than a slogan: 'We do the difficult every day; the impossible just takes a little longer.'

"Like Gus Robinson, Bracelen was an ex-Marine. Even though I was a civilian, every time I walked into the office of either one of them, I felt like saluting, and I did always call them sir.

"Shell Simmons was an interesting man to work for. When he wanted something done, he might not have any idea of how it should be done, and sometimes what he wanted done would be wrong. Occasionally you could show him there was a better way to do it, but he was an opinionated cuss, and it was hard to argue with a guy who was paying the bills. Like almost all bush pilots, Shell was a jack-of-all-trades."

Peterson went to high school in Sitka with another illustrious graduate of the Sheldon B. Simmons Airline College. That was James A. Johnson, who was raised in Petersburg, Alaska, and who began his aviation career at Alaska Coastal when he was still in high school, loading baggage aboard the PBYs and Grummans. That was in 1951. On June 30, 1993, after 42 years with the company, he retired as senior vice president of public affairs.

Jim Johnson became the airline's "Mr. Alaska," the equivalent of an ambassador to another country. So popular was he that near the end of his career, his hometown of Petersburg named its airport after him. If he had ever harbored political ambitions, he probably could have been elected as the state's governor or one of its senators. Everyone liked him, and that was because he was — and at this writing still is — the kind of person who genuinely likes people and treats them equally, whether it's a top airline or government official, or a brand-new ramp-service worker.

As a youngster with Alaska Coastal, Johnson was brash, perpetually curious, and not afraid to ask questions. He had been with the airline for two years when he was transferred from Petersburg to operations in Juneau. A Teletype came in one day advising that "a Herman Nelson" was arriving on the next flight. Must be some big-shot officer, he was thinking, so he approached his supervisor. "I've been with this airline for two years and I thought I knew everybody," Johnson said, "but who in the hell is Herman Nelson?"

The supervisor gave him one of those "how dumb can these kids get?" looks that are a supervisor's trademark. "A Herman Nelson is the heater they use to warm up the engines on a PBY," he explained.

"I was pretty naive in those days," Johnson admitted. "Another time, I was working in communications and we got a Teletype advising that a flight was arriving with a plugged-up pitot tube. I thought it was some kind of tube used in a radio until someone told me it was a device on the wing that measured airspeed by the amount of air being blown into the tube."

A few years later, while working for Alaska Airlines, Johnson was assigned to community relations in the state of Alaska, and one of his jobs was dealing with local issues in the small communities the airline served. "If you don't catch hell in the first five minutes," he admitted, "it's not a successful trip." But he was good at his job. One city official told him, "There's one thing I like about you, Jimmy. You come to town, you talk to me, you never answer any of my questions, but I feel better because at least I got to tell you."

The supreme compliment Johnson received came after he retired. At a meeting in Seattle, the officers were discussing an angry letter of complaint that had come in from a customer in Petersburg and what to do about it. Someone asked, "How do you think Jim Johnson would have handled this?"

Ken Skidds supplied the answer. "If Jim were still here," he growled, "there wouldn't have been any letter."

Ten years after Johnson retired, he could not visit an Alaska Airlines station or ride on an Alaska Airlines airplane without having some veteran employee or employees recognize him, invariably greeting him like everyone's favorite uncle, always with a "Hi, Jimmy!"

In a sense, Johnson was following in Bob Giersdorf's footsteps when it came to winning popularity among Alaskans. In his younger days, Giersdorf served a term in the state assembly and then was elected to the state senate, only to have his victory invalidated when it was discovered he was too young to have run for that office in the first place.

Jimmy Johnson, of course, was also too young to have made much of an impression on anyone when he first came to Alaska Coastal, and it took a while for Shell Simmons to realize he had a future dynamo in his employ — a kid with an incredible work ethic and the personality of a born politician.

Shell often was too busy trying to solve engineering problems to pay much attention to the youngsters on his payroll. He tended to leave the day-to-day running of the airline to his chief lieutenant, a meticulous Alaska Coastal veteran named O. F. "Ben" Benecke, hired by Simmons just before World War II as office manager and bookkeeper. Benecke served in the Navy during the war and returned to Alaska Coastal as Shell's chief assistant.

But Simmons did not ignore the difficulties facing every small Alaskan regional carrier: how to survive in a geographically limited area with a makeshift kind of operation. Still, Simmons was perhaps the most successful of them all. Alaska Coastal had paid dividends for six consecutive years.

Yet, just like Art Woodley, Shell worried about the uncertain future. More in self-defense than zeal, he decided to join forces with a Southeast Alaska rival, a fellow ex-bush pilot suffering from the same misgivings about the future. And that was another legend of Alaskan aviation: Robert E. Ellis.

Bob Ellis and Shell Simmons were brothers-in-arms, Siamese twins joined at the hip by love of flying and Alaska in equal proportions. Yet in background, they were far from mirror images.

Ellis, an Easterner by birth, had spent two years at the Naval Academy in Annapolis, Maryland, and might have gone on to a naval career if the Academy hadn't been downsized after World War I. During those two years, however, Ellis had received flight training, and eventually he gravitated toward Alaska, that "Great Land" holding out the only available welcome mat for any unemployed airman crazy enough to want to fly for a living.

Unlike Simmons, who was always pretty much his own boss, Ellis worked for a number of Alaskan bush carriers before forming his own company in 1936. He called it Ellis Air Transport, and as was usual in those days, the name was a lot fancier than the flying equipment. He started with a single-engine Waco floatplane. Ellis based his infant company in Ketchikan, and against astronomical odds was successful enough to become incorporated in 1940 as Ellis Air Lines.

The name change didn't hide the fact that Ellis remained a bush airline, but to the citizens of Ketchikan and scores of tiny Southeast Alaska villages, Bob Ellis was the world's greatest airline president. He would fly to the villages, take orders for groceries, fill them in Ketchikan, and deliver them no later than the next day. Bad weather never seemed to daunt him, and his record for reliability was remarkable.

He lived, breathed, and bled customer service, although by more modern standards he had little with which to serve other than getting a charter, freight assignment, or mercy flight from A to B safely, and as soon as humanly possible. On special occasions he went above and beyond the call of duty; at Christmas time, for example, he would don a Santa Claus costume and fly over villages dropping candy to excited children below.

He was a gentle, unassuming man with a quick wit and the kind of natural personality that made people like him immediately. And the people of Ketchikan liked him well enough to elect him their mayor, and later a Territorial senator.

No, he was not a mirror image of Shell Simmons, although the airlines they founded were operating primarily seaplane fleets with similar efficiency and dedication. In 1961, the year before they merged, Alaska Coastal and Ellis Air Lines carried more than 110,000 passengers between them. This would have been small potatoes for one of the big major airlines, but it reflected the highest ratio of passengers to population in the world.

Each carrier brought to the merger a "dowry" in the form of its aircraft fleet. The new airline, at first called Alaska Coastal-Ellis, wound up with 17 Grumman Goose amphibs, four Catalina amphibs, and a combined workforce of some 400.

Bob Ellis was asked later why he agreed to merge with Shell Simmons's slightly larger company. He sang the same tune that Art Woodley did when he sold PNA: all the fun had gone out of the airline business, he was tired of fighting government red tape, and like most of his breed, he didn't understand why employees needed unions if they were treated well without them.

Ketchikan remained Ellis's home for the rest of his life, and he died there in 1994 at the age of 91. But, as did Shell Simmons with Alaska Coastal, he lived long enough to see his beloved Ellis Air Lines live on as part of Alaska Airlines.

And so would the third of these unforgettable bush pilots, perhaps the most colorful of them all, "Mudhole" Smith.

Merle "Mudhole" Smith didn't found Cordova, but he ran it for most of the three and a half decades of its existence. The airline, initially named Cordova Air Service after the seaport town of Cordova, was launched in 1934 by a group of businessmen and successful miners. One of the stockholders, M. D. "Kirk" Kirkpatrick, was a bush pilot and took over as its first president.

Kirkpatrick hired Merle Smith, who, like so many other youngsters of the post-World War I era, had taught himself how to fly, when he was a teenager in Kansas. Smith cut his pilot's teeth working mostly for the Inman Brothers Flying Circus, which toured county fairs in Kansas, Oklahoma, and Nebraska during the Depression.

It was a precarious occupation financially as well as professionally, and as the barnstorming days faded into history, Smith moved to that mecca for unemployed airmen — Alaska — and went to work for Cordova in 1937. He hadn't been with the airline very long before he acquired the nickname that would plague him for the rest of his life.

He was flying a Stearman biplane in the Chugach mountains to a gold mine called the Yellow Band Mine. He landed on a muddy strip, his wheels hit a hole, and the Stearman nosed over, breaking the propeller. Smith radioed Cordova asking for a replacement prop, and his transmission was overheard by the only bush pilot in Alaska who was overjoyed to have anything happen to a Cordova Air Service airplane, short of a fatal crash. That was Bob Reeve.

Cordova had forced Reeve out of his original home base of Valdez, and Smith's minor mishap provided Reeve with some inexpensive revenge. From that day on, he always called Merle Smith "Mudhole," and the name stuck.

In April 1939, Kirk Kirkpatrick was killed when his Bellanca got caught in a snowstorm going into Cordova and crashed. The stockholders asked Smith to take over the airline, and he ran it successfully for the next three decades, until the merger with Alaska.

As a boss, he could be warm-hearted, generous, and an incurable sentimentalist. He used to fly Cordova school kids to Anchorage once a year — absolutely free — to see a circus, and he was a soft touch to any employee with a hard-luck story. He was "Smitty" to everyone. No one dared call him Mudhole.

But he had a tough, ill-tempered side, too, and one of the best eyewitnesses to his management style was Susan Bramstedt, a native of Alaska who got a summer job with Cordova when she was only 16. Bramstedt, like Jim Johnson before her, became a walking chamber of commerce, unofficial historian, and goodwill ambassador for Alaska Airlines throughout the 49th state.

Her mother worked for a bush airline and her father was in the broadcasting business before he became chairman of the state's Republican party. So Susan was both an airline brat and a political brat. By the time she got a full-time job at Cordova, the airline had moved its company headquarters to Anchorage, and that was where she became Smith's personal secretary.

"I was scared to death," she remembered, "because while he could be the sweetest guy in the world, he had a terrible temper. About the first day I started working for him as his secretary, I was walking down the hallway toward his office and I heard him yelling. He was using every four-letter word in the English language.

"He was rather short and stubby, and when he was screaming with all those expletives, you could almost see his blood pressure going up. But he calmed down as fast as he exploded."

Once, after one of his worst temper tantrums, he called Bramstedt in and snapped, "Take a letter."

"Yes, sir," she said, wondering who was going to be the target of his vitriolic rage. "To whom?"

"My aunt in Kansas. I'll give you her name and address when we're finished."

"Then," Bramstedt related, "he proceeded to dictate the sweetest note I could imagine — loving, thoughtful, and sentimental."

Smitty shared with Bob Ellis an inability to understand the unionization of pilots. Perhaps this was an inevitable prejudice on the part of men who as bush pilots could never afford to limit the number of hours they flew, nor turn down trips because of threatening weather. Staying on the ground meant they wouldn't get paid, and in the bush days, if you didn't fly, you might starve.

Cordova, like most of Alaska's other small regional airlines, operated a hodgepodge fleet: floatplanes, biplanes, single-engine monoplanes, and eventually used DC-3s. Smith himself, however, had a love-hate relationship with an old Boeing 80A, the trimotor biplane that was the queen of United's fleet when that airline was known as Boeing Air Transport, back in the late 1920s and early '30s. It was a pretty reliable airplane, and unlike most biplanes, which were made largely of wood and coated fabric, it had a metal structure with an aluminum tubing fuselage and duralumin wings. The 80A that Cordova acquired had been modified to carry cargo by cutting a large hole in one side of the fuselage and installing a big cargo door. This had weakened the fuselage, but it was beefed up with additional metal tubing so it could carry several thousand pounds of freight.

Like all Boeing 80As, this one — ship number 515 — had two major flaws: it was woefully slow, and its brakes, which were the same mechanical drum types used on cars of that era, were terrible. The latter deficiency betrayed Smith one day when he was taking off from Merrill Field in Anchorage. One engine failed, and Smitty aborted the takeoff. But then the airplane began drifting off the runway when the brakes started fading, and finally failed entirely. The 80A headed straight for a hangar owned by Art Woodley, who had several Travel Air biplanes parked outside an open hangar door. The runaway Boeing hit two of the Travel Airs, the impact tearing off one of its own wings and the center engine, then went headfirst into the hangar, where it finally lost its momentum and came to a stop. Miraculously, Smitty wasn't hurt, but Woodley was out two planes.

Smith flew 515 again after it was repaired, mostly to make it more attractive to some buyer because of its unique cargo door. On another flight, said Ken Smith, Merle's son, the old Boeing actually hauled a 12,000-pound boiler. The 80A's official maximum payload in passenger configuration was only 1,000 pounds.

The same airplane, 515, eventually was restored as a passenger aircraft minus the big door, was repainted in its original United livery, and is now one of the outstanding vintage aircraft on display at the Seattle Museum of Flight.

Ken Smith and his brother both became pilots, the latter running an air taxi company and Ken flying for Cordova and later Alaska Airlines. Merle insisted that Ken work in the general offices during the slow winter months, to gain overall airline experience. And Smith took Ken with him to Washington, D.C., where he was privy to the negotiations that led to the merger with Alaska.

"It was some time after the Western-PNA merger," recalled Ken, "and it was pretty clear that one wasn't going to be the last. The CAB was making noise about ending federal subsidies to regional airlines, and it was obvious the remaining Alaskan regional carriers couldn't exist without subsidies. Cordova was a little better off, but by 1968, we all were feeling the pinch. So the atmosphere was ripe for mergers when we met with Charlie Willis in his Washington office on Connecticut Avenue. Dad and I had been in Washington previously, trying to put a deal through with Northern Consolidated, but that had fallen through when they merged with Wien. So Dad phoned Willis.

"We had talked to Alaska Airlines in '65, three years earlier, but Dad was always nervous about Willis. He thought Charlie was a little squirrely. At the time, Cordova had just gotten into Juneau with an Anchorage-Cordova-Yakutat-Juneau route, and was an attractive candidate for a merger. But nothing came out of those '65 contacts.

"This time it was different. Willis was so impulsive, he wanted to announce the merger even before we had a chance to talk to the CAB, but Dad talked him out of it. Instead, we first met with the airline's board of directors. They were delighted, and the merger was a done deal."

Willis asked Merle Smith to serve on Alaska Airlines' board of directors, but he also invited Ken Smith to attend board meetings "to calm Dad down if he lost his temper."

"Dad was loyal to Charlie," Ken said, "but he was pissed off at him all the time for buying stuff the airline didn't need. My father was real outspoken."

Merle "Mudhole" Smith was an active Alaska Airlines director — so active that Charlie Willis seemed a little afraid of him. Contrast Smith's status on the board with the way Art Woodley was treated at Western. Note the post-merger experiences of Shell Simmons and Bob Ellis. Both were treated with dignity and respect. They, too, became active Alaska Airlines directors and later were named directors emeriti. Today, Richard Wien, Noel Wien's son, is a member of Alaska's board. Likewise, many employees of the pioneering carriers went on to make their mark at Alaska Airlines.

Alaska Coastal, Ellis, and Cordova: they're still flying through Alaska's skies, fueled by the immortal memories and traditions that have so enriched Alaska Airlines. In many ways, their acquisitions were Charlie Willis's finest contributions. Whether he ever realized this is anyone's guess. He seldom if ever looked back, for he was too busy looking ahead to further ventures and adventures, in which he had the full support and loyalty of Bob Giersdorf.

For better or for worse, and there were generous portions of both, they were armed with their usual enthusiasm, their champagne tastes, and their cheerful indifference toward a budget that had trouble meeting the price of a beer.

CHAPTER FIVE

More Life with Charlie

With a foothold in Southeast Alaska firmly secured, the Willis-Giersdorf juggling act seemed to have a dozen balls in the air simultaneously. Major changes in the composition of the fleet . . . a clash with Pan Am over in-flight service that was more humorous than serious . . . generating national headlines by opening the first charter-air service between the United States and the Soviet Union . . . acquiring more hotel properties . . . and, of course, more Giersdorf promotion stunts.

Willis and Giersdorf had one negative trait in common: neither paid much attention to what a promotion idea might cost. It was style over substance. Gimmicks had a higher priority than budgets. Typical was their decision to install a stand-up beer bar in the rear of the 880 to go with the Gay '90s theme. To make room in the aft cabin for that unique lounge, it was necessary to remove nine seats. The obvious fact that nine fewer seats in the 880's narrow cabin reduced the revenue potential of every flight mattered little.

Giersdorf could develop tunnel vision when he was promoting or publicizing something, and Dick Garvin, who worked for him in sales, remembered one occasion that got both of them into trouble. Giersdorf had committed Alaska Airlines to be a sponsor at the Alaska Visitors Association annual convention — another instance, Garvin noted, "of taking on big tasks with no money to pay for them."

For the 1969 convention, Giersdorf dreamed up a fancy outing he called "The Great Alaska Experience," which involved a "mystery trip" for AVA members. Their annual meetings were always raucous affairs, and Giersdorf was not one to be easily outdone. What began in Ketchikan ended up at Totem Bight State Historical Park, about 10 miles north of town. Garvin never forgot what ensued.

"We rented school buses for the drive, then we began the hike into the lake. We were serving Cold Duck wine in plastic glasses all along the trail, and by the time the mob reached the lake, everything was in shambles."

Garvin remembered that Giersdorf tried to restore order, but was handicapped by the fact that he wasn't feeling any pain himself. There was a rumor that some of the Cold Duck had been spiked with grain alcohol. Giersdorf had hired the King Island Eskimo dancers, whose specialty was a three-day "Wolf Dance" routine, and he choreographed it down to a seven-minute act. However, by the time the dancers started, nobody was paying much attention.

"At this point," Garvin related, "Bob decided it was time to deliver a speech in what everyone assumed was Inupiaq, a real Eskimo language. Actually, he didn't know Inupiaq from Hebrew, but he had a knack for mimicking foreign dialects, something like Sid Caesar imitating a German professor without uttering a single legitimate word of German.

"Unfortunately for both of us, Giersdorf told me to translate his remarks into English for our guests. The problem was that I couldn't hear a word he was saying, and even if I could, I wouldn't have been able to understand his gibberish. So I ad-libbed the translation as he talked, an extemporaneous interpretation of his remarks. It laid an egg of a size only a brontosaurus could have hatched."

Garvin tried to avoid him for the rest of the day, but when he later went back to their hotel, he had the misfortune to run into Giersdorf, who chewed him out royally. The egg-laying translation wasn't the only mishap of the day, however. Giersdorf had arranged for a huge Alaska king salmon to be placed on ice inside a large wooden box as big as a kitchen table. Fascinated by the fish, and drunk, two of the guests wound up in the box alongside the salmon.

Even though the airline couldn't really afford to throw such parties in the late 1960s, they did generate goodwill in Alaska. And the relationship that Willis and Giersdorf established with the Alaska Visitors Association was to prove extremely beneficial in the future when officers such as Jim Johnson were very active in the development of Alaskan tourism. Over the course of his long career with the airline, Johnson served on 21 local committees and boards dealing with tourism, airport matters, and various civic projects in both Alaska and Seattle.

The state had ended up with three tourism agencies: AVA, which became an advocacy organization; the Alaska Tourism Marketing Council, which promoted Alaska tourism in North America; and the Division of Tourism, which concentrated on international marketing for the state. The former two had separate directors but eventually were combined into a single unit: the Alaska Travel Industry Association. (Its president, Ron Peck, later played a leading role in creating tour-package programs for Alaska Airlines, especially with the Disney organization.)

Operating as if the airline had unlimited financial resources, Willis never lost his obsession for hotel acquisitions, adding first the North Star Hotel, in Nome, and then the new, still relatively undeveloped Alyeska Ski Resort, near Anchorage. It was small, with only one lift, but it had great potential. At the same time, Willis hired Chris Von Imhoff, a veteran of the hotel business in both Europe and the United States.

Von Imhoff discovered later that Willis had bought Alyeska by trading Alaska Airlines stock for the necessary down payment because, as usual, he had no cash. Yet in the first two years, Von Imhoff had a firm construct a new 32-room lodge and restaurant called the Alyeska Nugget Inn, which he leased back from the firm that had built it. Later he added a 45-room unit and expanded the ski facilities with new lifts. Under his direction, it became the state's premier ski resort, with an international reputation and year-round facilities. Yet all the glitz and glamour of this magnificent, successful ski resort merely demonstrated that Von Imhoff was running a hotel more efficiently than Willis was running the airline.

Willis made a big splash in the summer of 1967, when he announced that Alaska Airlines was going to buy a Boeing 747 jumbo jet, the new giant airliner still undergoing flight tests prior to its introduction into airline service by Pan Am in 1970. The company newspaper, called the "Talking Totem" at the time, featured an artist's rendition of a 747 in the airline's livery, including the Golden Nugget tail logo, plus a drawing of the airplane's spacious upper lounge, decorated like a Klondike saloon with two huge chandeliers. The announcement added that the airline was taking out an option to buy this airplane, which was priced at more than $20 million.

The employees knew that Alaska couldn't afford to buy one of the 747's engines, let alone a plane. When Willis quietly dropped the option, a gag ran through the company that he canceled the deal because Boeing was asking $100 for an initial payment, and Charlie couldn't raise the cash.

Employee cynicism was only too natural, for during this period the airline was earning the nickname Elastic Airlines, thanks to the worst schedule-reliability performance in the industry. The frontline troops — the employees who had to deal face-to-face with disgruntled customers — were the ones whose morale was most sorely tested by the airline's sorry reputation.

Typical was Danna Maros-Siverts, who was a young schoolteacher in Fairbanks when she joined the airline as a ticket agent in 1969. Along with Susan Bramstedt, Maros-Siverts was to become a trusted member of the airline's management corps. When she started, however, she was just one of the many rank and file who viewed "life with Charlie" with both affection and misgivings.

"Back then it was such a bad airline, it was embarrassing," she admitted. "Our on-time performance in Fairbanks alone went as low as 34 percent. Passengers would come up to the counter and ask sarcastically, 'What time is your scheduled flight getting in today?' I remember once having a flight that came in at 11 o'clock at night with only one passenger — and we had lost his bag.

"We didn't always get paid, and when we did, sometimes it was only a hundred dollars. The bank in Fairbanks used to keep track of how many tickets we sold each day, and if there hadn't been enough sold to cover the paychecks, you couldn't cash them. So we had to go back to the bank the next day after we had sold more tickets."

Yet Maros-Siverts was one more employee who kept seeing Willis's transformations from Jekyll to Hyde. "He was a very charming man," she conceded. "Handsome, always friendly, and never aloof with any of us. He liked to park himself at the reservations desk and just shoot the breeze, and sometimes when we were very busy he'd answer the phones himself and do the booking.

"He loved to come to Fairbanks and drink, and if he'd had a few, you never knew what he might do. I remember one night he had borrowed a local travel agent's car, got drunk, and drove the car into a river."

Shortly after Maros-Siverts went to work for Alaska, Fairbanks suffered a major flood and the airport's runway was one of the few places in the city not under water. Willis committed the airline to rescue operations, mostly

flying evacuees out of the stricken city. With flights still arriving and departing, employees had to get to the airport in boats and lived in the waterlogged
terminal for about six weeks. When Willis discovered that they were existing
on cold military C rations, he ordered the flight attendants on every incoming Alaska flight to prepare hot meals in the galley for his Fairbanks airport
personnel.

"Thanks to his thoughtfulness," Maros-Siverts said, "for a while we were
getting the only hot food in Fairbanks."

She also remembered the fun-loving Willis. He usually arrived in
Fairbanks accompanied by Giersdorf, when the two of them were launching
one of their promotion schemes. "They were so creative," she explained, "so
lively and so compelling and full of fun that we would have done anything for
them and this crazy little airline, even when we didn't get paid. They seemed
to have a fresh idea every minute.

"When Alaska was celebrating its centennial year, they had a field day
with their promotions. One was dressing a stilt dancer named Bonnie Pikert
in a flight attendant's uniform, only the skirt had to be about eight feet long
to cover up the stilts. The crowning touch was a red velvet teardrop hat three
feet tall that Charlie and Bob had someone make up for her.

"Bonnie would meet all our incoming flights. She'd stand outside the
airplane, look through the cabin windows, and wave at the startled passengers. When we didn't have an arriving flight, she'd stride through the
terminal on those stilts. But one day I saw her doing her terminal bit and
thought she was walking kind of funny. When she stopped in front of our
ticket counter, the slit in her skirt opened up and out stepped Charlie Willis,
laughing his head off."

There was another and rather rare side to Charlie's many-faceted
personality, however, and this one could only be labeled as cheap. After
the Cordova acquisition put Alaska into Juneau, Maros-Siverts was sent
to open the station there. This was not an easy assignment, by the way,
because she found that people in Juneau were still fiercely loyal to PNA and
welcomed Alaska Airlines with the enthusiasm they might have shown to
an invading army.

Willis knew that her parents lived in nearby Douglas, Alaska, and that
she could stay with them instead of in a Juneau hotel while she was getting
the station operations started. She did just that, but she also submitted an
expense account for the bus fare between Douglas and Juneau. Willis phoned
her to complain about the bus fare item. "Why couldn't your dad drive you?"

he grumbled. This from a man who would cheerfully spend thousands of dollars on promotion schemes, while ducking creditors who were baying at his heels like wolves closing in on a crippled moose.

Willis did try to do something about the on-time performance debacle, aware that much of it was due to maintenance problems. He hired a new vice president of maintenance in the person of Gus Robinson, who had spent 25 years in the Marine Corps as a pilot and maintenance expert. He had retired in 1967 as a lieutenant colonel, serving as commander of a Marine transportation squadron that operated Hercs and helicopters.

Robinson bore more than a slight resemblance to Vince Lombardi, although he did not have the legendary football coach's stocky build. But they shared a fierce temperament that demanded perfection and did not suffer fools lightly.

Robinson's predecessor as vice president of maintenance was LeRoy Peterson, who was totally miscast in that role through no fault of his own. Peterson was an operations man, and why Willis saddled him with the maintenance job was a mystery. Jim Johnson, who knew both Peterson and Robinson well, thought Willis originally assigned Peterson to maintenance because he wanted someone in there he could control.

"Charlie Willis ran everything," Johnson said, "and Peterson didn't have much say. You went along with Charlie, or else."

Robinson was with Alaska only two months before Willis, apparently out of desperation, named him vice president of maintenance. He couldn't have made a better choice, for the airline's maintenance department was in disarray and ex-leatherneck Robinson was a no-nonsense boss with the hide of a rhino and the determination of a pit bull.

Being an ex-Marine with *Semper Fidelis* engraved on his heart, he had a built-in bias against unions. He liked his mechanics, and learned to live with their local union officers, but come contract-renewal time, he had no use for their national negotiators.

His appointment solved some problems, but not the ones stemming from Willis's lack of fiscal responsibility. This was how Robinson described the Pandora's box of headaches he opened as the new honcho of maintenance:

"The first thing I saw was a thick catalog of violations the FAA had filed against the airline. I spent my first six months trying to get us off the hook with the feds. One thing we needed badly was spare parts. I just went out and ordered them, and let Willis worry about how we were gonna pay for them.

"I went through all the violation notices and found that less than half

— 40 percent at the most — were legitimate complaints. Yet I couldn't blame the FAA. Alaska had screwed up so much in the past, the feds were nit-picking at everything. I finally got us to the point where the FAA would at least talk to us. Their chief inspector came over so often he'd invariably tell his office, 'If anyone calls me, tell 'em I'm over at Alaska again.'

"Charlie Willis was smart. He couldn't tell a bolt from a screw, but at least he knew it and he left me alone. So did Bob Giersdorf, who also didn't know beans about maintenance.

"Looking back, it's hard to realize we had so many maintenance problems with so small a fleet. When I came in, we had only three 727-100s, a few Connies, a few Hercs, and in the beginning three 720s, two from Western and one surplused by United. Alaska later traded its 720s in on five 727-100s from Pan Am's internal German air fleet. Alaska didn't get its first 727-200 until 1978."

But at least the airline had a real maintenance chief who was beginning to create a professional maintenance organization. Gone were the days when some of Alaska's pilots had to serve as emergency mechanics themselves, one of the most skilled being Captain Bob Long, whose nickname was Mr. Fixit. His most famous feat occurred one bitterly cold winter day when he was flying a DC-3 from Nome to Gambell, a Siberian Yupik Eskimo village located on St. Lawrence Island.

After landing, Long discovered there was a tear in the fabric that covered one of the elevators, the horizontal stabilizers on the tail section. Neither the DC-3s nor the later DC-4s were truly all-metal aircraft; like the old biplanes, their tail control surfaces were fabric-covered.

Long's repair job was a classic of improvised ingenuity. He dipped a piece of cloth into a pail of water. The cloth immediately froze in the subzero temperature, and Long then simply sealed the tear with the solidly frozen cloth. The patch job held until they returned to Nome for permanent repairs.

One of Robinson's other jobs was maintaining the big ex-Navy F6F Hellcat fighter that Willis had acquired and kept in Alaska's hangar. Willis christened it *Little Nugget* and had it painted in the airline's colors.

"He was a good pilot," Robinson admitted, "but I was always afraid he was going to kill himself. There were times I'd see him so drunk he could hardly walk. Yet as far as I knew, he always stayed sober when he was flying that Hellcat."

Willis once did a "wheelie" at Sea-Tac, retracting his landing gear during a takeoff when he was still on the ground. Navy carrier pilots used the technique if they lost an engine on takeoff. If they hit the water with the wheels down, the airplane would cartwheel, but with the gear retracted, the aircraft would "skip" along the water until it came to a safe stop.

According to Bob Gray, a Navy air traffic controller during the Korean War, who was hired by Alaska Airlines in 1961 to handle labor relations, the FAA cited Willis for doing the maneuver at a commercial airport, and also filed charges against him for buzzing a few buildings in the airport area. "It was widely suspected he'd been drinking," Gray said, "and he was extremely fortunate the feds didn't charge for flying under the influence."

Reportedly, the airline was paying for the Hellcat's maintenance and fuel. In addition, Robinson was charged with maintaining Willis's 38-foot cabin cruiser. All of this may not have amounted to much, yet some thought it was an ill-advised extravagance at a time when Alaska was bleeding red ink.

Robinson, perhaps because of his Marine background and training, stayed loyal to Willis for as long as the two worked together. But his patience must have been sorely tried at times, as it was when Boeing refused to give the airline further credit for some needed 727 parts until Willis paid something on what Alaska already owed. Wes Laubscher, a now-retired mechanic who was a maintenance planner at the time, never forgot an incident that occurred shortly after Boeing lowered the boom.

It was a Friday evening, as Laubscher remembered it, when Robinson came into the hangar and made the following announcement: "I'm giving you guys a thousand dollars in cash [to pay for emergency spare parts] to keep the airline running over the weekend. But just in case this isn't enough, you'll have to go to the ticket counter and grab whatever is in the till."

"And that's exactly what we did," Laubscher recounted. "Monday morning found us broke as usual, but the airplanes were flying on time."

"Broke as usual" was the airline's theme song in those days. Looking back, it's hard to believe that mighty Pan Am found it necessary to haul Alaska Airlines before the CAB, claiming unfair competition, something akin to Goliath accusing David of using an illegal slingshot. Pan Am had taken a dim view of the Willis-Giersdorf in-flight movies gimmick. But after the Alaska Coastal-Cordova merger, Alaska added an in-flight music system, and the Pan Am camel's back apparently collapsed under the weight of that little straw.

The subsequent CAB hearing turned out to be something of a farce in which Juan Trippe's world-girdling airline wound up with egg on its haughty corporate face. When Charlie Willis was sober, he had an instinct for puncturing stuffed shirts. He insisted that Alaska's attorney call him to testify, and he personally choreographed the script, which came out exactly as he had hoped.

"Be sure and ask me about who caters Pan Am's food service and then about ours," he instructed his attorney.

Willis was sworn in. The lawyer dutifully followed Charlie's script by bringing up the subject of comparative in-flight food service.

"Mr. Willis, to the best of your knowledge, who caters for Pan American?"

"Maxim's of Paris," Charlie answered promptly. It was unnecessary for him to add that Maxim's was and still is one of the most prestigious restaurants in the world.

"And who caters for Alaska Airlines?"

"Sally's Box Lunches of Fairbanks," Willis replied.

The laughter, in effect, ended the hearing. The "Sally's Box Lunches" line ended up as one of the most frequently quoted passages of dialogue in the airline's history, although in the interest of accuracy it must be pointed out that there was no such catering establishment in Fairbanks. The real name was Sally's Catering, but Willis had deliberately and cleverly misstated the firm's name because "Box Lunches" was such a perfect contrast to "Maxim's of Paris."

Sally's Catering was named for one of its owners, Sally Rand, who ran the business with her husband, Fred. Because she had the same name as the fan dancer who won fame at the 1933 Chicago World's Fair, a lot of people in Fairbanks firmly believed that their own Sally had once been a fan dancer, supposedly in Fairbanks, during her younger days. This appears to have been unfounded gossip, but Sally herself, an uninhibited soul, reportedly was delighted with the story and refused to deny it even if it wasn't true.

She was well past middle age when she began catering the airline's flights out of Fairbanks. Willis liked her personally as much as the passengers liked her food, and she adored Charlie, though only up to a point, as we shall see. She also catered the parties that Willis often threw for employees when he came to Fairbanks, always providing plenty of food and numerous cases of beer.

During one of these shindigs, Charlie decided it was time to pay her a public tribute. He rose, got everyone's attention, thanked her for everything she had done for the airline, and then concluded with an unflattering and untrue remark about her virtue.

Sally herself led the laughter. They were great friends until Willis stopped paying the bills she submitted for her catering service. He ran up such a huge tab, amounting to several thousand dollars, that she got a lawyer to draw up papers repossessing one of the airline's Twin Otters.

The papers were served on Bob Handley, Alaska's station manager in Juneau at the time. Handley, knowing that the airline couldn't afford to lose that Twin Otter, resorted to an ingenious delaying action that, if filmed, would have earned him an Academy Award.

As Sally's attorney was about to present him with the repossession notice, Handley slapped a hand to his chest, moaned "I'm having a heart attack," and was rushed to the hospital for three days of tests. By the time the tests showed that his heart was perfectly sound, he had given Willis enough time to get his own lawyer to stave off the confiscation. Exactly how Willis pulled it off, Handley never found out. But he did confirm that the episode definitely ended Charlie's friendship with Sally.

Through all the airline's trials and tribulations, Willis continued to rely heavily on Bob Giersdorf, who by 1970 was a one-man management squadron. He later admitted that he personally had restructured the executive TO — Table of Organization — putting himself in command of sales, advertising and promotion, public relations, in-flight services, flight attendants, tariffs, and scheduling.

Finance might as well have been located on the moon. Giersdorf would submit budget requests, which Willis automatically approved, both knowing that the airline didn't have the funds to cover such expenditures. There were times when Giersdorf probably welcomed Charlie's binges because when he was sauced, Willis would give him anything he asked for and the next day wonder when or why he did it.

With Giersdorf calling so many shots, the airline's only independent departments were maintenance, flight operations, and legal. LeRoy Peterson, although considered a logical heir-apparent should Willis ever step down, didn't have the clout to challenge the Willis-Giersdorf "dynamic duo." Neither did Ben Benecke, Shell Simmons's chief lieutenant at Alaska Coastal, who had just begun to exert some influence at Alaska Airlines. And Gus Robinson was swamped with his own problems in maintenance.

It was a blueprint for financial disaster, but Wizard of Oz Willis once again temporarily diverted attention from the airline's "Elastic" stigma. This time he did it with the inauguration of commercial flights to the Soviet Union.

True, the authority permitted only chartered flights, not a regularly scheduled operation. Yet Willis made it happen, using his Washington connections and also making a few preliminary trips to the Soviet Union. There he made progress with a combination of perseverance and personality, and possibly because the Russians he dealt with were impressed by the way he matched their vodka consumption, drink for drink. From all reports, they liked this breezy, personable American.

He did run into a hassle when he was negotiating the fees to pay for servicing and provisioning the return charter flights. Willis thought $500 per turnaround was reasonable, but the Russians were holding out for $700, which was what Pan Am had charged Aeroflot when the Soviet carrier began flying into New York. Things were at an impasse and tempers were getting a bit short when Bob Dodd, who was on the team accompanying Willis, pulled him to one side. "Charlie," he advised, "let's face it. Their price is seven hundred and they're not gonna budge."

Once that was settled, Willis had achieved quite a coup for one of America's smallest airlines. So small, it turned out, that Alaska had to lease a Pan American 707 for the summer of 1970, and the same jet for the next two summers. The authorized route for the chartered service was from Anchorage in Alaska to Khabarovsk in the Soviet Far East, 3,800 miles, which was beyond the range of Alaska's 727s. From Khabarovsk, Aeroflot flew the passengers to various destinations in the Soviet Union.

To coincide with planning for the Russian charters, the Golden Nugget/ Gay '90s theme was jettisoned and replaced by "Golden Samovar Service," which was named for the traditional large Russian beverage urns. Willis and Giersdorf added the definitive touch: new flight-attendant outfits styled after Cossack uniforms that included high-necked blouses in red with black trim and matching red-and-black short skirts. Black mesh stockings and artificial bearskin hats completed the eye-catching ensemble.

The historic inaugural flight, which took off from Anchorage early in June 1970, displayed Charlie Willis at his best and also at his worst. The leased 707 was loaded with such celebrities and dignitaries as Mr. and Mrs. Eddie Bauer and CAB chairman Secor Browne, plus a number of prominent Alaskan civic leaders and businessmen.

Whatever their stature and reputation, however, all the inaugural guests occupied coach seats because the airline reserved the entire first-class section for relief crew members: two extra pilots and copilots, a second flight engineer, and a relief navigator. Also aboard were a Russian navigator and an interpreter, both provided by the Soviets to facilitate communication with Russian air-traffic controllers, who, unlike their counterparts in Western and Asian countries, were not noted for their mastery of the English language.

Captain Bill "Dark Cloud" Lund was in command of the flight. He was a big, corncob-tough, somewhat intimidating character, but a brilliant airman who always had an unlit cigar in his mouth. Two widely accepted versions of how he acquired his nickname circulated. One was that he had a pessimistic approach to weather forecasts; the other was that it was derived from a character in Al Capp's *Li'l Abner* cartoon series who walked around with a perpetual thundercloud over his head.

Despite his nickname, Lund was well liked throughout the airline, and his selection as commander of the inaugural flight was a deserved tribute to his airmanship. Ditto the navigators assigned to the mission: senior navigator Dave Zehrung with Pat Glenn.

Jo Coughlin was one of the flight attendants working the inaugural, and she watched with some dismay as Charlie Willis predictably began taking on more fuel than the airplane. "We were pouring drinks for the passengers as fast as we could, and Charlie was keeping up with everybody," she reminisced. "He kept trying to get into the cockpit, but the crew wouldn't let him, until we ran into trouble."

After the 707 entered Soviet airspace, the Russian navigator told Lund that Moscow had failed to advise the Soviet military's air-defense command that the jet had been authorized to fly into Siberia and land at Khabarovsk. Lund decided to divert to Japan, where they could refuel and wait for Moscow to deliver its promised clearance. Before he could change course, two Russian MiG fighters suddenly appeared off their left wing, signaling them to turn around.

When Lund complied, Willis noticed the turn and charged into the cockpit, accompanied by Giersdorf and one of the VIP guests. Because of all the confusion and the passage of time, three and a half decades later, no one who was in that cockpit could remember for sure who the VIP was. The best guess is that it was CAB chairman Browne.

After Lund briefed Willis on what was happening, Charlie went into orbit and ordered him to keep flying toward Khabarovsk. By this time the flight deck was crowded with curious crew members, including navigators Zehrung and Glenn. They saw the two Soviet fighters still escorting them out of Russian airspace, and Glenn, listening out of one ear to Willis yelling "turn around" at Lund, asked the Russian navigator, "What would happen if we turned around?"

The Russian formed one hand into the shape of a pistol. "Rat-tat-tat-tat," he said, imitating a machine gun.

Dave Zehrung had had enough. Knowing that Bob Giersdorf was possibly the only one who could calm down the infuriated Willis, he said bluntly, "Mr. Giersdorf, if you don't get Mr. Willis and that other guy out of this cockpit, Pat and I are going to walk off this plane in Japan and you won't have any navigators to get you back into Russia."

Giersdorf nodded, but before he could act, Charlie exploded. "For the last time, Lund," he shouted, "are you gonna turn this airplane around?"

"No," Lund said quietly.

"Then you're fired and so is everybody else in this crew!"

Lund ignored him and kept on course to Japan. When they landed at the Tokyo airport, they discovered that Captain Lund's nickname might very well have applied to this apparently jinxed inaugural flight. The terminal was temporarily closed because of some pollution problem, so no one was allowed to deplane except the Russian navigator and the interpreter. They went into the terminal to phone Moscow. Everyone else stayed on the 707, sweating.

"The temperature was 104 outside," Jo Coughlin recalled, "and there was no APU [auxiliary power unit] available to provide air-conditioning."

Meanwhile, Willis had sobered up enough to talk his own way off the airplane. He spotted an Aeroflot aircraft parked nearby and eventually returned to announce that he had persuaded the Aeroflot crew to let him use their radio to contact Moscow.

It is unclear whether it was his efforts or those of the two Russians using a terminal phone that resolved the situation. The latter is a better bet because as far as anyone knows, Charlie Willis couldn't speak Russian.

The delayed clearance finally came through several hours later. Jo Coughlin thought they were on the ground for about two hours; others remembered it as being at least four or five hours.

When the airplane was refueled and they were finally ready to leave, Willis — his good humor restored — told Lund to take off.

"I can't," he replied. "Remember? You fired me and the rest of the crew."

"Aw, Bill," Charlie said sheepishly, "you know I was just kidding."

Thus, the troubled inaugural flight had a happy ending. But the firing episode exposed a side of Willis's personality that could be likened to the temper tantrums of a child. And a later charter to Russia exposed another unpleasant trait: he could be cruelly, unreasonably vindictive.

One of Giersdorf's best friends was veteran reporter and writer Stan Patty, who throughout his career was always fair to Alaska Airlines. But for whatever reason, Willis disliked him, and after one story that Patty wrote,

Charlie phoned and called him a few unprintable names. Meanwhile, Giersdorf had invited Stan and his wife as guests on one of the Russian charters, but as they were about to board, Willis spotted them and yelled, "You're not going, Patty, you son of a bitch."

Giersdorf heard him, walked over to Willis, and said in a voice that could have cut through five inches of steel, "Charlie, if he's not going, I quit!"

Willis mumbled, "Aw, hell, get on the goddamned airplane."

The Russian charter flights lasted for three years but failed to generate the hoped-for passenger loads. George Knuckey — the same Knuckey who had bailed an Alaska crew out of a Saigon jail in Vietnam — was responsible for obtaining the subsequent necessary clearances and coordinating the charter operations with the Soviet government.

"At the peak of the charters," Knuckey said, "we operated eight or nine trips during the summer, usually on weekends, and we were carrying specific groups: businessmen, missionaries, and a lot of Eskimo families reuniting with their relatives in Siberia.

"Then the Russian economy went south and the charter traffic dwindled. In the end, we were carrying hardly anybody, and the emotional excitement of boasting that Alaska Airlines was flying into Russia had lost its luster. Personally, I don't think the operation was worth all the effort that went into it."

In 1964, Alaska hired a customer-service agent (CSA) named Dave Palmer, a former Boeing salesman. In 1964, going from a company like Boeing to an airline like Alaska was *really* going from the sublime to the ridiculous. A native of Seattle (his father had also been a Boeing salesman), Palmer began his stint at Sea-Tac at a time when Alaska's tiny squad of airport personnel spent an inordinate amount of time playing practical jokes on their counterparts at much busier airlines.

"In those days the people at other carriers were more like friends than enemies," Palmer reminisced, "but I'm quite sure there were times when they wanted to kill us. We were always trying to appear bigger than we were, and we took advantage of not being busy while everyone else was.

"One of our favorite games was announcing the arrivals and departures of imaginary Alaska flights. We'd get on the PA with 'Alaska Airlines announces the arrival of Flight 410 from Anchorage,' although we didn't have any Flight 410; the incoming airplane would be one of our pilots practicing touch-and-go landings at Sea-Tac.

"Our usual targets were Pan Am and PNA, our biggest competitors. We'd sneak over to the PNA ticket counter when it wasn't being manned and spray shaving cream on the phone they kept under the counter. Then we'd wait until they had passengers checking in and dial their counter number."

Palmer modestly disclaimed any credit for being the chief instigator of such shenanigans, but he did prove to be a crackerjack ticket agent whose sense of humor and puckish personality seems to have drawn the attention of Bob Giersdorf, who transferred him into sales and marketing. There he became something of a Giersdorf disciple, yet realizing that Bob, like Charlie, was extremely effective but also extremely undisciplined.

Giersdorf had a special genius for promotion — big, flamboyant ideas, getting the airline recognition way out of proportion to its size. Yes, he was undisciplined, yet he knew how to get attention and keep the airline in front of people.

"I learned a lot from Giersdorf. I learned that you can create lots of noise with the right idea. I also learned you can spend too much money on a wrong idea.

"Bob, with his enthusiasm and entrepreneurial spirit, would jump from one new promotion to another, and that's when cost became a problem. It was highly entertaining but sometimes confusing to employees and customers alike."

In 1967, Giersdorf involved Palmer in one of his most offbeat promotion stunts. He dispatched him on a cross-country tour plugging Alaska as a tourist attraction. Palmer drove a big improvised van with an interior fashioned into a facsimile of an airplane cabin, right down to real airline seats and overhead bins.

The term *van*, as we define that type of vehicle today, didn't really apply to this contraption. The "cabin" actually was a huge box, mounted on the bed of a Ford pickup truck. Built by the airline's mechanics in the maintenance shop, it was about 8 feet wide, 14 feet long, and 10 feet tall.

Palmer was on the road for more than a year and a half, following an itinerary that took him throughout the Lower 48 visiting travel agents, newspapers, radio and TV stations, even county fairs, "anyplace that seemed like a good stop to put on our show, which featured a film travelogue on Alaska," said Palmer. "It was basically missionary work for the state. We felt if we could get people interested in flying to Alaskan destinations, we'd grab a lion's share of the business because we were developing close relationships with the major tour operators and cruise lines. They were pretty small at the time, but Giersdorf in particular saw their potential."

Different Alaska Airlines uniformed flight attendants were assigned to various legs of the tour. Jo Coughlin, for instance, accompanied Palmer on a West Coast trip to San Francisco, Los Angeles, and Las Vegas, and later on an East Coast tour with stops at Buffalo and other cities in New York State. She remarked later that overnight accommodations were not always, say, of Marriott, Sheraton, or Hilton caliber.

"I remember staying in one motel I'd never want to see again," she said. "I think it was in or near Buffalo and looked exactly like the Bates Motel in the movie *Psycho*. After we checked in, I called Dave's room and told him not to take a shower."

At the start of the promotion safari, Palmer figured he was getting a pretty good deal. He had given up his Seattle apartment, eliminating months of rent payments, and put his clothes in storage, and he was submitting bi-monthly expense reports covering all meals, laundry, and hotel charges. With these basic essentials supposedly covered by expense reimbursements, he expected to save a chunk of money by being away.

Mark well that word *supposedly*. The airline's coffers, as might be expected, varied between almost empty and completely empty. His reim-bursements were delayed so long that his car was repossessed because of late payments.

"I had to sell some expensive stereo equipment to get my car back," he related. "I can laugh about it now, but at the time it wasn't at all funny."

The problem with successful promotional jaunts such as Palmer's ingeniously conceived van tour was that while it did get people throughout the Lower 48 to be aware of this upstart little airline, it did nothing to alter its image in Alaska itself. The nickname "Elastic Airlines" degenerated even further to "Spastic-Elastic," and it would take more than a few cute stunts to change *that* image.

Coinciding with the various promotions in this period was the transforma-tion of the fleet. Gone was Old Smoky, the Convair 880 that had taken the airline into the jet age. It was sold to Cathay Pacific in 1966 and was finally scrapped in 1984. The 990 suffered a more ignominious fate: Alaska leased it to AREA of Ecuador in 1968, and two years later sold the airplane to Modern Air Transport, which operated it for less than a year before it was destroyed in a landing accident. The three former TWA L-1649s were sold to an oil company, and all the Super Constellations were long gone.

By the start of the 1970s, except for a few leased Hercs and smaller aircraft such as the de Havilland Twin Otters, so well suited for serving the small Southeast Alaskan communities, Alaska's aircraft had been pruned down to an all-Boeing jetliner fleet — six 727-100Cs.

The airline, like its fleet, was still so small that the camaraderie that had always existed among the pilots and flight attendants took a lot longer to dissipate than it did at much larger carriers. The fly-by-the-book demands of unforgiving swept-wing aircraft plus heavier workloads on flight attendants serving twice as many passengers on a jet as on a prop-driven airliner seemed to leave no time for the traditional crew horseplay and practical jokes.

Alaska's pilots flew jets by the book, like everyone else, and because they were so used to operating in unfavorable weather, there weren't any more professional airmen at any carrier. It just took a lot longer for crew deportment to become less informal.

Marcia Broyles, a flight attendant from the days of those eight-hour DC-4 flights between Seattle and Fairbanks, could quickly confirm this. "We had a flight attendant, Madge Janey, who waged a constant bloodless war with a captain named Phil Watts," Broyles related. "He used to toss his uniform cap into his flight bag instead of hanging it on a cockpit hook like everyone else did. So before one trip, Madge sneaked a cake with gooey chocolate frosting into his bag and Phil put his cap right on top of it.

"But the jets really changed things in the cabin. In the old DC-4 days, we served only snacks and we seldom had more than 20 passengers on a 50-passenger airplane, so we had lots of time to talk to passengers and even play with kids, which I loved because I was a teacher before I became a flight attendant."

Broyles liked to recall the personality of Don Fox, one of several captains with a devilish sense of humor that refused to be diminished by the jets. "His favorite copilot was Ken Clark, and they usually flew together," she remembered. "They were close friends, but that didn't stop Don from playing tricks on him."

As a four-striper who had transitioned well into turbine aircraft, Fox still adhered to the unwritten rule that captains make the cabin announcements. Now, it is a fact that since cockpit-to-cabin PAs were introduced on DC-3s back in the late 1930s, most young copilots have harbored a yearning ambition to deliver them, and Ken Clark was no exception.

One day, just after leaving the gate, Fox unexpectedly invited him to make the departure announcement. Clark was ecstatic. To him, welcoming everyone on board the 727 by providing the en-route and destination weather, the route they'd be flying, and its scenic highlights was the equivalent of Lincoln delivering the Gettysburg Address.

Nervously yet proudly, Clark began his spiel without realizing that Fox had surreptitiously disconnected the PA system. His copilot was talking into a dead microphone. Clark rambled on for several minutes before concluding his maiden oration. The captain summoned Broyles, who was in on the gag.

"How did Ken's PA sound?" Fox inquired.

"What PA, Don? I didn't hear any."

"Sorry, Ken," the captain apologized with feigned regret, "but you'd better repeat that PA."

Poor Clark dutifully went through his whole routine again, not noticing that Fox had reconnected the mike. Broyles laughed, "Don must have pulled that stunt on him several times before Ken found out he was being sabotaged."

Then there was the ultimate "stewardess-gets-her-revenge" story that became part of Alaska's flight-attendant lore. This one involved Captain Charlie Dwight, a four-striper with the kind of appetite that demanded being served meals with prompt efficiency. That hadn't happened on this particular morning flight, when Charlie didn't get his breakfast served soon enough, at least not by his standards of punctuality.

He griped and growled and grumbled to the stewardess, who thought that serving the passengers first was a higher priority than the cockpit. Dwight finally stopped complaining long enough to go to the lavatory. He was still sitting on the john when the stewardess opened the door and shoved a breakfast tray in his lap.

The jets also brought a new nomenclature for stewardesses: they, along with male stewards, became simply flight attendants. Alaska's diminutive size in the first half of the 1970s precluded any large-scale hiring of males for its cabin crews, although the airline had actually had them as far back as the early 1950s.

Bob Dodd, whose long airline career included not only Alaska but also Northwest, Cordova, Ryan Air, and Wien, joined Alaska as a ticket agent and then became one of the airline's first males assigned to in-flight cabin duties. Most of them, Dodd pointed out, were recruited from ramp-service jobs and were known as "flying ramp boys."

As late as 1970, the airline was down to only three passenger jets, and Willis was still scrounging for charter business. One little-publicized plum fell into his lap when Eastern dropped its authority to fly charters out of Charleston, South Carolina, to the Navy's Caribbean bases in Guantánamo Bay, Panama City, and Puerto Rico. Willis assigned a 727 to the charters, along with nine pilots and 12 flight attendants who were temporarily based in Charleston.

One of the flight attendants was Gail Spaeth, who began flying for Alaska in 1970 and had many vivid memories of those days of poverty spiced with pizzazz. Spaeth practically memorized the letter that accompanied the $100 paycheck she got on May 20, 1971.

"It began 'Dear Family,' " she recalled, "and went on to say, 'There is just so much money in the company coffers. I can either meet the payroll or the creditors. If I meet the creditors, we can fly for 30 more days. If I meet the payroll, they'll shut us down.' "

One has to put the text of that letter side by side with her memories of the food service on the Seattle nonstops of the same period. "We had gold utensils and even gold salt-and-pepper shakers in first class," she reminisced. "We'd top Caesar salads with caviar and large slices of hard-boiled eggs. The food in coach wasn't quite that fancy, but the wine was complimentary, and we had the Russian samovars and the Cossack uniforms with the bear hats.

"We had to either wear short-hair wigs or keep our own hair curled up under the hats because no hair was allowed to show. Charlie Willis knew that most of us were wearing wigs under the hats, and when he got drunk on one of our flights, he'd knock the Cossack hat off your head, then pull off the wig. He thought it was funny."

Spaeth was hired by Jean Sherwood, a supervisor with an unusual background. She had been a Rockette at Radio City Music Hall in New York. Spaeth remembered her not only as "a class act," but also for some of the non-flying assignments she handed out. Spaeth, for instance, had to serve as a hostess at Charlie Willis's third wedding, to the daughter of a wealthy banker. Considerably more painful was a meeting of the International Air Transport Association that convened in Seattle one year. "My job was to run around the meeting hall waving a banner that read Miss Alaska," Spaeth recounted.

There also were times when an Alaska Airlines flight would land with one more passenger than had been aboard when the airplane took off. Rushing pregnant mothers from remote Alaskan villages to communities with modern maternity wards was not an infrequent occurrence. Unscheduled landings because of medical emergencies are not uncommon, but Alaska Airlines has had more than its share because it has served so many remote areas.

The airline established a reputation for being willing to make medical-emergency landings regardless of the cost involved. In the event that a mother went into labor with no chance to make it to a hospital, Alaska's 727s carried an incubator attached to the bulkhead in Row Six to handle a premature birth.

Spaeth was among the less inhibited of Alaska's flight attendants and enjoyed having the freedom to inject a little humor into the usual canned cabin announcements. What no one enjoyed was the rare grouchy passenger with no sense of humor.

"We'd have 150 people aboard," she commented, "and while you might get laughs from 149, the 150th would be offended and complain to the airline. During the holidays I still wish everyone a Merry Christmas, even though it's not supposed to be politically correct."

A few laughs were welcome around the airline as the decade of the seventies began. The expected financial bonanzas from the mergers and the elimination of formidable competitor PNA had yet to really materialize. The only potential bright spot was the pending construction of the Alaska oil pipeline, whose origin would be Prudhoe Bay in the North Slope area, with Fairbanks as the marshaling point for airlift logistical support.

Oil drilling was in progress, but pipeline construction was still pending, awaiting congressional approval and funding, and resolution of Alaska Native land claims. Until pipeline construction became definite and full-scale, airlift support would fill only preliminary needs.

George Knuckey, because of his extensive air cargo experience with Flying Tiger, took an active role in Alaska's North Slope operations. He had represented Alaska Airlines in Vietnam after leaving Flying Tiger, and LeRoy Peterson summoned him to Fairbanks when the airline won a contract to fly supplies up to the Distant Early Warning installation, called the DEW Line. This was prior to the award of any North Slope contract, and when Knuckey reported for duty in Fairbanks, he received his first culture shock.

"I've seen some skimpy airline operations," he related, "but Fairbanks was the epitome. When I started working on the freight ramp, my so-called office was in a flimsy, unheated trailer, and I was trying to make out flight plans wearing a thick parka and gloves. Then the whole station ran out of heating oil, so we had to walk about a mile to a latrine."

When the North Slope operation began, Knuckey got a taste of what Gus Robinson was going through in his underfunded maintenance department. The airline's 727s had maintenance priority because they flew passengers as well as freight. The Hercs, even when they needed major overhauls, had to wait until the shop could accommodate them.

Originally, three Hercs were assigned to the North Slope operation. But Knuckey too often found himself with one of the three grounded indefinitely, awaiting a mandatory overhaul, so a fourth C-130 had to be assigned, increasing operating costs and almost negating the contract's thin profit margin.

A Herc maintenance problem led to one of the funniest snafus in the history of the North Slope operations. A C-130 was grounded in Fairbanks because of a cracked cockpit windshield. Fairbanks called Seattle and requested a new C-130 windshield ASAP. It was obtained out of stores (the maintenance parts department) and sent over to Western's freight center to be shipped to Fairbanks.

But Western refused to send it because Alaska hadn't paid several overdue bills. So someone got LeRoy Peterson out of bed, and he went to Western's freight center and paid the back bills personally. The replacement windshield arrived in Fairbanks, where its shipping box was opened. Inside was a framed picture of a 727 that had been hanging in Charlie Willis's office. No new windshield.

It seems that Willis hated the picture and ordered it removed from his office. It ended up in stores and put into an empty shipping box labeled "C-130 windshield."

The Hercs were the only airplanes around that could carry the big, heavy drilling rigs, and what they didn't haul, the ubiquitous, versatile 727-100 combis did. It was a Herc, however, that flew the most hazardous mission of the first pipeline airlift: 25,000 pounds of dynamite from Sea-Tac to the North Slope. The air trip on this flying keg of explosives was bad enough, but even worse was the unloading when the airplane arrived in Fairbanks.

"The Herc's cargo doors were operated electrically," Pat Glenn pointed out, "so all we could do was pray that there wouldn't be an accidental spark when we opened the door. We also brought heating oil to the camps, and we would load some 20,000 gallons of fuel into a Herc for the ground vehicles and heaters. I kept thinking that if one of those Hercs crashed, we'd blow up half the North Slope."

While the Hercs were feverishly flying in and out of Fairbanks, Alaska Airlines earned a profit, the first in several years. Expanding oil activity on the North Slope gave every indication that the prospects for the future were brilliant. During the summer of 1969, Willis sold Parker Drilling Company 150,000 shares of the airline's stock, and he had entered into negotiations with First California Company of San Francisco for a $5 million underwriting of 930,000 shares.

Native land claims and environmental concerns smacked the state of Alaska hard, forcing its robust economy into a stall. The airline's first-half losses in 1970 were staggering. First California advised Willis of its intent to withdraw from the agreement, but as a concession the venture-capital firm agreed to broker the airline's shares. During the offering period of June, the price for Alaska's stock on the open market fell below its offering price. The result was tragic. Less than $500,000 was realized from the sale of Alaska Airlines stock. Losses exceeded $5.5 million, shareholder equity declined more than $3 million, and Willis had become desperate.

In the context of the 1970-71 economic climate, a collection of small problems could mushroom into a crisis. Recession was the synonym for crisis in this time frame, and what was happening to Boeing was painfully symbolic. In those two years, the aerospace giant's workforce plummeted from about 100,000 to 32,000. Alaska and the state of Washington shared an unemployment rate in excess of 10 percent.

A sign appeared on a Seattle billboard reading: "Will the last person leaving Seattle please turn out the lights?" It brought some smiles, more rueful than humorous. Like a quake-generated shock wave, the recession's effects were felt throughout the airline industry and especially at a vulnerable airline such as Alaska, already staggering economically.

At long last, Charlie Willis seemed to acknowledge that he had a punch-drunk airline on his hands and he had to do something before it went down for the full count.

Willis never had a more loyal subordinate than Dennis Kelley, who came to Alaska Airlines in 1967 as LeRoy Peterson's executive assistant. Kelley was no green rookie. He had spent 14 years at Northwest and another six at West Coast Airlines, acquiring a reputation as a financial troubleshooter.

He found plenty of troubled targets at Alaska, where he was surprised to discover that no one had any idea how much money was coming in and how much was going out. "I asked LeRoy Peterson about it," Kelley remembered. "He said, 'We used to have a revenue and expenditures forecast years ago, but nobody paid any attention to it, so we just gave up.' "

Kelley told Willis that the airline badly needed those incoming and outgoing forecasts, adding that he had 20 years of experience doing just that at two other carriers and would be happy to do the same for Alaska. Willis agreed, so Kelley set up what he hoped would be a realistic revenue forecast and expense budget, based on estimates from the various departments.

"Shortly after this," Kelley recounted, "the mergers with Alaska Coastal and later Cordova took place. Everyone thought that was going to solve all our problems and that we were going to finally make money overnight.

"I kept track of our revenues from Southeast Alaska traffic for the first seven months after the Cordova merger, and it showed we were missing our revenue forecasts every month. We simply weren't taking in as much money as everyone assumed."

In 1970, just before the summer traffic boom began, Kelley made a final analysis of revenues versus expenses for January to April, and the outlook for the next seven months. He passed the word to all the officers that Alaska theoretically should be making a half-million-dollar profit in each of those seven months, but instead was going to be losing the same amount every month.

"Charlie wasn't happy with that gloomy report. In fact, he was pissed off," Kelley continued. "But just as I had feared, he passed the buck to his chief ally, Bob Giersdorf, and I never saw eye-to-eye with Giersdorf. He was a terrific promoter, but he couldn't care less about how much his promotions cost."

Kelley balked when Willis told him to "go see Giersdorf and tell him this thing has to be straightened out."

"Charlie," Kelley pleaded, "don't send me in to see Giersdorf. I've been there before, and I always come back with my hat in my hand."

"You just go in there and tell him what you want done," Willis persisted.

"So I went and saw Bob," Kelley continued. "It was about 11 o'clock in the morning, and Giersdorf said he was too busy to discuss budgets with me and to come back at two that afternoon. I knew what was going to happen at two. Giersdorf was going to put on one of his dog-and-pony shows and cover it all up. And that's exactly what happened at the two o'clock meeting."

Furious, Kelley returned to Willis's office and unloaded his frustration. "Here I am back, Charlie, with my hat in my hand, just as I predicted," he stormed. "The guy won't do a damned thing."

At that moment, Giersdorf was walking by Willis's office and stuck his head in the door with his usual greeting of "Hi, Skipper."

Willis invited him in. "Dennis and I have been talking about the forecast," he said, "and I think we'd better do something about it."

According to Kelley, Giersdorf's response was to argue that the forecast was too pessimistic and that with good promotional efforts, traffic was going to increase dramatically and so would profits. Then, Kelley added, "Charlie said, 'Well, you're my chief salesman, Bob, and I have to believe you. So go out and do it.' "

Yet Willis himself subsequently provided the first indication that Giersdorf had been wrong and Kelley right. Charlie had to face up to the fact of the airline's precarious financial state. Whether he should have faced it a lot sooner would always be a subject for debate among his defenders and detractors. His continuing inability to obtain badly needed financing for badly needed new airplanes, not to mention the airline's anemic credit standing, raised red flags. And the blame was being placed directly on his shoulders. To turn down the heat on himself, he engineered the election of Preston Blatter, who was with the Civil Aeronautics Board when Willis lured him to Alaska, as the airline's president.

Blatter was well liked — "a super guy" was how Jim Johnson described him. But Blatter might as well have been hired as a ticket agent. Charles F. Willis was still calling all the shots, including one that came as a surprise.

On New Year's Day of 1971, Willis called a special meeting of all officers, including assistant vice presidents as well as senior executives. Kelley, who had been promoted to assistant vice president under Peterson, was a pleased attendee and said later that Willis appeared to have finally gotten the message.

"He told us the company was close to going out of existence," Kelley related. "That we had to work harder, and that he wanted some ideas on how to reduce expenses immediately. What surprised me, however, was that when Willis asked for our input, only two people spoke up: me and Ed Lang, another assistant vice president, who had come over to Alaska from West Coast and eventually left to join Braniff.

"After Ed and I made a few cost-cutting suggestions, and no one else said anything, Charlie announced he was appointing what he called a cost-control committee of about a half-dozen assistant vice presidents. I guess because of my big mouth he named me chairman.

"We met weekly for six months and came up with suggestions that would reduce annual costs by about a million dollars, which was big money in those days. But the company's elected officers rejected every one of our proposals. In fact, I was led to believe that Charlie, who was supposed to be relying on his top officers to discuss our suggestions with him, actually never saw any of them. That's hard to swallow, but that is what I was told."

In late June of 1971, Willis called another meeting and announced that the cost-control committee had been totally ineffective, and as a result he had hired the prestigious management consulting firm Alexander Proudfoot. "I've told this outfit to go through the airline with a fine-tooth comb, and each of you is going to cooperate with them to the nth degree," Kelley quoted him as saying.

The Proudfoot firm was given one year to analyze the goals and performance of every Alaska Airlines department, then recommend solutions to the company's financial woes. At the end of the first six months, the consultant was to select an employee from the airline itself and train him to implement its recommended management program to achieve greater efficiency at the lowest possible cost.

The consulting firm brought in a team of about 25 who began extensive questioning of department heads, supervisors, and rank-and-file employees. They even used stopwatches to time people performing various tasks; one primary goal of any management study, of course, is to determine whether more efficiency can be achieved with less manpower.

By September, the Proudfoot study was still four months short of its first six-month deadline when the entire airline temporarily forgot all about efficiency studies, oil pipeline contracts, promotion stunts, deficits, unpaid bills, and paychecks that threatened to bounce like tennis balls.

On September 4, 1971, an Alaska Airlines 727 on final approach into Juneau crashed into a mountain and exploded, killing all 111 aboard — 104 passengers and seven crew members. At the time, it was the worst single-aircraft accident in U.S. civil aviation history. Initially suspected to be pilot error, the cause would not be determined for another four years. That long search for the truth would involve dogged detective work by Alaska's own pilots and technicians, and would even delve into the supernatural.

Yet despite all evidence to the contrary, this was an accident that to this day the government still lists as unsolved.

CHAPTER SIX

A Jinxed Beam
at Juneau

On September 4, 1971, contact with Flight 1866 was lost. The 727, commanded by Captain Dick Adams, was a southbound, multi-stop trip from Anchorage to Seattle via Cordova, Yakutat, Juneau, and Sitka. Aboard was a typical cross-section of passengers from every walk of life, every age group, every economic stratum. What the majority had in common was residence: 67 of the 104 passengers were Alaskans.

Death didn't respect geography. The other 37 passengers came from places as far away as Japan and Hawaii, as well as Ohio, Missouri, Arizona, and California. Thirteen of the dead were students from all parts of Alaska: nine freshmen heading for orientation at Sheldon Jackson College and four bound for Mount Edgecumbe boarding school.

To Jim Johnson, the normally jovial "Mr. Alaska," the disaster brought not merely grief but also a sense of guilt. A Western Airlines ticket agent he knew in Cordova had wanted to take his wife and two children to Seattle, but hadn't been able to get passes on his own airline. Johnson, who never could resist helping out anyone who worked for an airline, whether his own or someone else's, got them Alaska Airlines passes — on Flight 1866.

Flight attendant Gail Spaeth had a different reaction, one of shuddering relief. She was supposed to board the flight at Anchorage but was pulled off at the last minute because a nonstop to Seattle was short one flight attendant. The pilot she would later marry, Chuck Spaeth, who retired in 1996, was one of the first two men to reach the crash site.

Gail knew everyone in 1866's crew, and one of the stewardesses had been a classmate. "I didn't cry," she recalled, "but when I got home the next morning, the door to my apartment was open. I walked in and there were my parents staring at me. They thought I had been on the Juneau flight and didn't know I had been pulled off. We starting hugging each other, and that's when the tears began to flow."

Charlie Willis flew immediately to Juneau as soon as word came that the flight had crashed, and later he was especially considerate to the families of crew members who had perished. Because the accident occurred late on a Saturday afternoon, there were virtually no people around company headquarters to answer the avalanche of phone calls that started after the plane was reported missing. Two officers, LeRoy Peterson and assistant vice president of interline sales Frank Feeman, came in to take on much of that unpleasant chore. They were joined by Bill Burke, who owned a Seattle public relations firm that Bob Giersdorf used from time to time. Burke was very close to both Willis and Giersdorf, and Charlie had put him on the board of directors.

Burke also handled calls from the media, not the easiest job after an accident, but in this case it wasn't as bad as an experience that Bob Dodd had. Dodd, an assistant vice president, had flown to Juneau the night of the accident to help put a passenger list together. He was working out of the Juneau city ticket office when he got a call from some reporter who asked, "Was it crew error or the fault of aircraft maintenance?"

Dodd, exhausted from hours of work on the passenger list, didn't realize he had been blindsided. Without thinking, he replied, "I don't know; it's too early to tell."

The story the reporter wrote called him "a high airline spokesman" and quoted him as saying that "he didn't know whether the accident was caused by pilot error or aircraft maintenance."

"Our lawyers went crazy," Dodd said. "Even though the reporter had deliberately twisted my words, I felt so bad that I resigned. Fortunately, I was told to withdraw my resignation."

Dodd always swore that the fatalities totaled 113, not 111. "We were using an old copying machine in the CTO to print out the list," he recalled, "and it didn't always work perfectly. The list we ran off left out two names at the bottom of the paper, a doctor and his wife. We sent out a corrected total later, but 111 is still the figure most often used."

Kay Adams — Dick Adams's wife and a former Alaska Airlines stewardess — had spent part of the afternoon of September 4 shopping in a Seattle suburb with her two young sons, ages two and four. She was on her way home around an hour or so after the 727 crashed. The car radio was usually on, but for some reason it wasn't this time, and Adams was grateful she didn't hear about the accident that way.

When she got home, she put the boys down for a nap and was writing a letter when the doorbell rang. In her own words, this is how she found out that she no longer had a husband, and their sons no longer had a father:

"The doorbell rang. It was Ken Zaretske, one of our pilots, and his wife, who lived down the street from us. They lived nearby, so the airline had asked them to tell us to prepare for the worst. I thought they were there for a social visit, which would have been odd because they had never been to our house before.

"Kenny told me, very gently, that Dick's plane was overdue and reported missing, that radio contact with the flight had been lost, and that search parties were looking for the airplane. They didn't find the 727 until later that evening, and until then we didn't know anything.

"I was fortunate that my older sister, Lynn O'Dell, who became an Alaska Airlines stewardess the year after I did and still works for Alaska Airlines to this day, was on a layover in Seattle and spending the night with us. She had been napping in a back bedroom, woke up when she heard the doorbell, and was standing right behind me when Kenny broke the news.

"Lynn stayed with me, night and day, for the next month, helping me cope with grief and helping me with the two boys."

Kay Adams, who later remarried and is now Kay Reeves, had become a flight attendant during the mid-1960s, when there was still no real formal training. "The course lasted three weeks," she reminisced, "but there were only three of us in the class, and in 1965, I don't think we had more than a dozen flight attendants in the whole airline. There were no cabin mockups to practice in, so we sat around the instructor's desk and listened to her lecture for the whole three weeks."

She had met Dick Adams in 1966, when she was the only flight attendant on a military charter from Fairbanks to the Aleutian Chain. It was an inauspicious beginning to a romance. After taking off for the L-1649's return ferry trip to Fairbanks, the Connie's electrical power failed and the airplane was without heat.

"I kept walking up and down the aisle just to keep warm," Kay recalled. "In those days we all wore parkas and ski pants on winter flights, but two winter uniforms couldn't have kept me warm on that Connie."

Kay Adams's story is a poignant reminder that airline families are affected by air disasters just as much as the families of passengers, something the public and the media tend to forget in the rush to attach blame. And the fate of Flight 1866 truly stunned this tiny airline because it was Alaska's first catastrophic accident and because the airline was a family within itself. Everyone knew everyone else.

It would have been difficult to find a pilot or flight attendant at Alaska Airlines who hadn't flown with or at least known 1866's seven Seattle-based crew members. And there was a husband-wife team in that crew: copilot Leon "Red" Beach, known as a fun-loving, happy-go-lucky extrovert, was married to Cathy Beach, one of the four flight attendants on 1866.

Dick Adams was the quintessential Alaska Airlines captain. Conscientious, a veteran weaned on foul weather flying, he loved his job as much as he loved his family. He had been with Alaska for some 20 years at the time of the accident, and had flown just about every type of four-engine equipment Alaska operated, including the 1649 Constellations and C-130s in the Vietnam airlift.

Neither Adams nor Beach, who was flying the 727 into Juneau that day, was a stranger to the tricky approach to the Juneau airport. The final descent path led incoming flights through a valley between two rugged mountains. The approach wasn't hazardous in clear weather, but in poor visibility it could be a potentially deadly obstacle course.

Ordinary ILS (instrument landing system) approaches did not work at Juneau because the terrain doesn't allow the ILS beam to travel uninterrupted for any distance. The normal ILS signal is projected from a ground transmitter to a glide slope indicator, an instrument showing the course and descent path to the runway. But Juneau's terrain would cause the ILS beam to bounce off mountains and break up into more than one path; an analogy would be the "ghost" images that used to appear on old television sets.

So to guide planes safely through this mountainous terrain, the Federal Aviation Administration had installed a different navigation aid called a VOR (visual omni-directional range), an electronic guidance beam that provides the correct bearing toward the assigned runway. Adams and Beach were known to be using that VOR on their final approach because visibility was so poor. Within a few hours of the crash, the FAA tested the VOR signal and found it to be accurate, so the words "pilot error" hung in the air, unanswered, like a frozen jet contrail.

No one in Alaska's flight operations wanted to believe that for one minute, yet there was no other immediate explanation. The taped communications between Flight 1866 and the FAA's Juneau Approach Control didn't reveal anything out of the ordinary. The flight had transmitted nothing indicating some problem that required a different heading. The 727, for reasons unknown, had simply flown into a mountain on a course that represented a 45-degree deviation from the normal VOR heading that should have been displayed on its instrument panel.

The National Transportation Safety Board hung its investigative hat on the conviction that whatever the cause, it could not have been a faulty VOR signal because the post-crash FAA test showed that it was working perfectly. The NTSB suggested two possible explanations for the crew not following the course prescribed by the VOR: the pilots may have accidentally tuned to the wrong VOR frequency, or they may have been distracted by an improperly cleared light plane in the area, apparently uncertain of its position, that presented a potential collision hazard.

In other words, what the NTSB was saying implied that yes, the accident probably was caused by misleading navigational information on the flight's VOR display. Yet there was absolutely no evidence that the signal itself may have been wrong, so it was possible that the crew did something that resulted in the plane taking the wrong flight path.

Alaska's flight operations department, led by Warren Metzger, who had become chief pilot during the Willis regime, tried its best to establish the FAA's supposedly accurate VOR as the culprit. It had considerable help from Captain Chuck Davis of Western Airlines, a former PNA pilot who had flown that Juneau approach many times.

Like many Alaska Airlines and PNA crews familiar with the Cordova-Juneau route, Davis, too, suspected that somehow, possibly because of rare and freakish atmospheric conditions combined with the daunting terrain, the Juneau localizer could "bend" just long enough to lead an approaching flight into disaster, yet still test perfectly a few hours later. There had been previous cases of pilots reporting false VOR signals, but in each instance FAA tests showed that the VOR signal was normal. Neither belief nor suspicion offered proof, of course, and the pilots were faced with an inescapable fact: there seemed to be no logical reason why the VOR installation at Juneau should fail intermittently.

The pilots thought the NTSB itself admitted that the crew seemed to have received what it called "misleading navigational information." This at least suggested a faulty localizer beam, a possibility that warranted further investigation. But instead, the NTSB was implying that the crew itself might have been responsible for displaying the wrong heading, either through carelessness or from distraction.

About a month after the crash, the FAA did install a second navigation aid on the approach path, a distance measuring equipment (DME) transmitter, which sends a radio signal that gives flights the exact distance to the assigned runway. Alaska's jets already had DME receiving units on their instrument panels, but they still relied on that more precise VOR beam as the primary nav aid. At best, DME information was helpful but not a foolproof substitute for VOR. Nor did DME quell pilot complaints about the Juneau VOR.

Chief pilot Metzger, acknowledging that few if any pilots are electronics experts, welcomed the input from just such an expert: ex-navigator Dave Zehrung. When the Hercs stopped flying overseas, navigators were no longer needed, and only Zehrung, Pat Glenn, and Sid Johnson — who had staff jobs — stayed on at Alaska. At the time of the Juneau accident, Zehrung had become director of communications.

Zehrung actually was involved in the accident investigation right from the start. The day after the crash, LeRoy Peterson put him on the NTSB human factors team, but Dave was later transferred to the systems team, where he really belonged.

As part of its investigative process, the NTSB assembles teams of experts to help in determining the cause or causes of a crash. These include electronics, flight controls, engines, operational, structures, and human factors teams. The NTSB relies on these teams for technical help from appropriate experts from the airline, airframe and engine manufacturers, and the Air Line Pilots Association, the pilots' union. The teams provide specific areas of expertise, but have no say in determining the final probable cause.

Sometime after the Juneau tragedy — the exact time is uncertain, but it may have been about a month — during the course of the ongoing investigation, a letter arrived at flight operations and was turned over to Warren Metzger as the chief pilot. It was from someone both he and his wife, Marian, had known casually. Metzger read it in disbelief, yet thought it was intriguing enough and perhaps even important enough to show to someone else: Kay Adams, the grieving widow of Captain Dick Adams.

And that was when the mystery of Flight 1866 veered into a kind of Twilight Zone of its own.

The letter was from a spiritual medium named Mary Ann Elko, who had once lived in Seattle and knew several Alaska Airlines families, including the Metzgers and, coincidentally, someone else who saw the letter, Dave Zehrung. Elko had conducted a number of séance demonstrations in the Seattle area before moving to Pennsylvania, from where the mystifying letter had been mailed.

It included what Elko said was Dick Adams's signature. To those who attended her séances, she always explained that she transcribed messages from her spiritual contacts in the handwriting of the deceased person and that she was merely relaying what Adams had dictated.

Metzger sent someone from flight operations to the Adams home — nearly 40 years later, he could not remember specifically who — to see if Kay could verify the letter's handwriting. Kay said she was shocked when she saw the handwriting. "As far as I could tell, it was Dick's," she recalled. "I don't see how anyone could have faked it. Dick had signed the letter. He had very flowery, almost feminine handwriting, and there was nothing about it that told me it wasn't his. I remember it didn't mention me or the kids at all; it just tried to relate what they were doing in the cockpit prior to hitting the mountain."

Yet Dave Zehrung, who also saw the letter, believed that Kay might have been victimized by a very natural form of wishful thinking. Perhaps she *wanted* it to be from Dick, and in his own handwriting, so badly that her memory betrayed her. "I remember the letter being very brief," Zehrung said. "It just said they [the crew] had no idea what happened, that everything seemed normal and then all of a sudden it was all over. It added that they [Adams and Elko] would be in touch with us later.

"We took the letter to a handwriting expert, along with samples of Dick Adams's signature on his training records. The expert told us the signatures on the training records were written by a male, and the handwriting on the medium's letter was that of a female — they were not from the same person. He said the handwriting in the letter appeared to have been written by a son who was copying his mother's handwriting."

Did that eliminate the supernatural factor? Not entirely. For one thing, there are two kinds of legitimate handwriting experts. First, there are graphologists, like the one the airline consulted, who can determine certain personality traits from someone's handwriting. The other accepted experts are called "certified forensic document examiners," employed by the FBI to determine whether signatures are genuine. But fairly recent FBI studies have shown *there is no foolproof way of determining a person's sex from handwriting*, and the courts no longer will accept testimony even from established handwriting authorities as to whether handwriting is male or female.

So not only does that discount what a graphologist told Alaska's inquisitive investigators, but according to Dave Zehrung, a second letter came from the medium, Mary Ann Elko. Zehrung thought there might have been a third letter, but it was the second one that really rang some bells.

Again, the same feminine handwriting and Adams's signature, yet with one huge difference. It carried some information that would help substantiate the pilots' conviction that there was something wrong with the Juneau VOR signal. The pilots, not the NTSB, would zero in on the reason that the VOR could go haywire without warning, then self-correct its own error with improbable quickness. The answer lay in where the FAA had installed this particular VOR station: not only a vulnerable location, but also one that violated the agency's own technical standards.

The second letter arrived in the flight operations department around January 3, 1972, about four months after the Juneau crash. In it, he (Adams) noted that he now had a partner helping him look for the cause of the accident.

Zehrung described its content: "The partner was a captain from Spain's Iberia Airlines named Carlos, who had crashed in a Caravelle that hit a large hill near a lake on an approach path leading to a Spanish airport. Carlos told him the weather was clear enough for him to have seen the hill, but that he had pulled up too late." (The Caravelle was a French-designed, French-built twin-engine jetliner and the first aft-engine jet in the world. It carried up to 80 passengers.)

"By itself this wasn't much of a clue," said Zehrung. "The letter didn't mention any magnetic interference with a radio navigational signal in the Iberia accident, and all VOR stations emit electromagnetic signals. Yet there was an implication that the Iberia aircraft was relying on the same mechanism that lured Flight 1866 into a mountain.

"We were working with an accident-investigation specialist at the University of Southern California's accident investigation school. I called him about this report out of Spain, although I didn't tell him that the information came from a medium's letter. I asked him if he could check out that reported

Iberia accident, and he contacted an associate in the Netherlands who for-
warded our inquiry to Spanish aviation authorities.

"The information we got back confirmed the circumstances of the
Spanish crash," said Zehrung, "including that the captain was named Carlos
something. But there was a lot more. The flight *was* using a VOR station, just
like Flight 1866. The Spanish VOR station was located on the shore of a lake;
the one for Juneau was located on the small, rocky Sisters Island, in the cold
salt waters of Lynn Canal off the Gulf of Alaska. That was all the information
we got on the Iberia crash, but it was enough to show us it could have been,
and probably was, a mirror image of the Juneau accident."

Armed with this remarkable coincidence, Alaska's own investigative
team still would need another three and a half years of solid detective work
to prove its case. Zehrung especially appreciated the help he got from Joann
Osterud, the airline's first female pilot, who also was one of the few airline
pilots in the world — perhaps the only one — to hold a degree in nuclear
physics. She also had several technical degrees, and her flying skills included
aerobatics. She was a role model for every female pilot who followed her at
the airline.

Alaska gave her permission to work with Zehrung, whose knowledge of
electronics made him something of an unofficial team leader. The first piece
of solid evidence the team unearthed pointed directly at the FAA's choice of
the Sisters Island site for the VOR station installation. For Zehrung, it was
like Sherlock Holmes suddenly discovering an unexpected clue.

"The problem stemmed from how the FAA had sited on the island," he
pointed out. "First, you needed a 300-foot diameter of level land surrounding
the central VOR antenna to keep the signal stable. That was the minimum
diameter the FAA's own technical standards required. But the diameter of
Sisters Island's land mass was less than 150 feet. It was not much more than
a big rock."

This flaw led the airline's "crash detectives" into the second causal factor: the inadequate level land around the antenna ended at a 60-foot ledge
that dropped abruptly into the water.

"The fact that the station was located on an abbreviated parcel of level
land generated an erroneous signal down to the cold salt waters toward the
northwest," Zehrung explained. "When the water was very calm, that erroneous signal would be reflected upward to combine with the correct signal,
moving the radio pattern counterclockwise.

"And on the afternoon of September 4, 1971, the water around Sisters

Island was glassy-smooth, which is very rare in the Juneau area. Another possible contributing factor was that the tide was unusually high that afternoon, so the false signal didn't have to bounce very high. In other words, it was an accident being invited to happen."

Obviously, this explained why the FAA could test the VOR signal within hours of a reported malfunction and insist there was nothing wrong with the signal. That "glassy smooth" water could become choppy at any time, and the waves didn't have to be very high to negate the effects of the erroneous signal.

But it wasn't until the summer of 1975 that Zehrung and Osterud finally had a chance to prove or disprove the evidence pointing to their unusual suspect: the rare but deadly combination of site location and water-surface conditions. They fashioned some homemade testing instruments relating to electro-magnetic signals and borrowed one of the airline's Twin Otters, which Osterud was flying out of Juneau at the time. Basically, they were trying to determine the accuracy of what the FAA had testified at the original NTSB accident hearing — that they had run a thorough malfunction predictability analysis on the Sisters Island VOR site's signal and found it to be well within acceptable limits.

That was not what the Zehrung-Osterud test flights showed, conducted under varying water-surface conditions, from completely calm to extremely choppy. "We found evidence that the reflected signal from that Doppler VOR station didn't behave the way the FAA's predictability analysis said it should," Zehrung recounted. "And this was because the technical criteria the FAA had used to establish the VOR station site had been wrong."

Their test flights in the Twin Otter also pinpointed the exact VOR signal error. It had given Flight 1866 a heading precisely 45 degrees different from the one that would have taken the 727 safely into Juneau.

"Joann took the data we had collected from our test flights," Zehrung added, "and flew down to Los Angeles to show them to a UCLA physicist who had done extensive studies on microwave reflections. He supported our findings."

By now it was the fall of 1975. Zehrung was invited to testify on the test flights at a special master's hearing in Los Angeles, a proceeding to establish liability in the various lawsuits that had been filed after the Juneau crash. The government attorney representing the FAA objected to Zehrung's testifying at all, on the grounds that he and Osterud had used "Mickey Mouse" equipment in their test flights. The hearing master then ordered the FAA itself to repeat the tests, using "properly equipped aircraft," and to take

Zehrung and Osterud along.

"We fooled around Sisters Island for almost a week but never saw water calm enough to repeat the tests," Zehrung related. "At the end of the week, the FAA told us we were all going back to LA. But after Joann and I got to the Juneau airport, I got a call informing me the waters had finally calmed.

"I immediately told this to the FAA people and asked them to go back to Sisters Island so we could run the new tests. It was only noon on that Friday, and there was plenty of time. No way. They refused and said they were returning to LA anyway, with or without us."

Osterud and Zehrung were furious, but the next development nearly gave them apoplexy. It was late Friday afternoon before Zehrung finally reached the lawyer they had been working with at the master's hearing, and told him what had happened to the scheduled Juneau tests. He wanted badly to go back to LA as soon as possible and testify on the FAA's refusal.

That desire was immediately drenched in ice water. The attorney informed Zehrung that the government — in other words, the FAA — had reached an out-of-court settlement with Alaska under which the airline was to receive $15 million.

"There won't be any further tests," the lawyer added. "The records in the case have already been sealed."

Most of the $15 million, incidentally, went to plaintiffs who had sued the airline.

The Zehrung-Osterud test flights never became part of the official investigation. However, in what might be interpreted as a tacit admission of possible VOR inadequacy, the FAA subsequently imposed stricter ceiling minimums on the approach to Juneau that remained in effect until improved navigation aids, which provided precise, safe approaches and were developed in part by Alaska Airlines, were adopted in the mid-1990s.

In 1994, the story of Flight 1866 surfaced again when the NTSB conducted a study of then-existing safety conditions at Juneau. It included a review of the 1971 accident report, and the board's fresh analysis concluded that the navigational readings that Captain Adams had received were wrong. But the review also concluded that "the origin of the erroneous information could not be determined by the NTSB." The board apparently reached this conclusion because the Zehrung-Osterud evidence never became part of the official record. So officially, the mystery of the crash remains unsolved.

Dave Zehrung eventually left Alaska to work briefly for Boeing, and later started his own electronics firm. Of all the contributions he made to the

airline, he was proudest of having invented the first "hot line" radio communications network along the West Coast from Seattle to Fairbanks. It enabled
dispatchers to talk to each other instead of having to rely on the much slower
Teletype system, and it also enabled dispatchers to communicate directly
with flights. Because funding wasn't immediately available, the hot line
wasn't activated until after Zehrung had left the company. But it was to prove
its worth in 1989, when the Mount Redoubt volcano, south of Anchorage,
erupted — a story to be related later.

Joann Osterud left Alaska to fly for United and eventually retired as a
737 captain.

How much of a role those letters from the medium actually played in solving
the mystery of that tragic flight, and whether they really came from a dead
pilot, must always be fodder for speculation. Unfortunately, the letters
themselves no longer exist. They were inadvertently thrown away a few years
ago during a periodic "housecleaning" of flight-operations files, and no one
recognized their historical significance. This wasn't surprising, as the
improbable yet tantalizing supernatural aspects of the crash's aftermath were
not common knowledge.

Dave Zehrung, whose opinion may be the most objective of anyone's,
said only that while the séance-inspired letters didn't solve the mystery of the
crash, "they did keep us looking."

Mary Ann Elko, who never married, died a few years before research
began on this history. She might have been able to answer a few nagging
questions that remain in the wake of that jinxed beam at Juneau. If she faked
the alleged contact with Dick Adams, how did she know about that "mirror
image" Iberia accident? How did she know that Carlos was the first name
of the Iberia captain? From a newspaper or news broadcast account? While
the U.S. news media does report on accidents involving foreign carriers, its
coverage, including crew member names, is limited at best.

Perhaps the only answers to these and other questions lie in the words
that William Shakespeare wrote for his character Hamlet:

*"There are more things in heaven and earth, Horatio, than are dreamt
of in your philosophy."*

CHAPTER SEVEN

Palace Coup

It was an event that drew very little attention from anyone, officers and employees alike. It occurred long before the Juneau crash, and involved merely the naming of a relatively obscure real estate developer to Alaska's board of directors and bestowing on him what literally was the honorary title of executive vice president, a post carrying no specific duties or authority whatsoever. Yet it was to change the airline's course forever because if it hadn't happened, Alaska Airlines most likely would have had to choose between bankruptcy and accepting Wien Consolidated's terms for a merger.

The turbulence that immediately followed the Juneau accident came at a time when the airline's finances were spiraling downward. Alaska had yet to build the kind of customer loyalty base it would enjoy in later years, and the state was stifled by delays in the construction of the trans-Alaska pipeline. Nationally, a recession was in full bloom.

The CAB devised a balancing act meant to shore up weakened carriers. It revoked Western's historic Seattle-Ketchikan-Juneau route, which had come to Western with its purchase of Pacific Northern, and conveyed the authority to Alaska Airlines. It was a huge plum. The CAB decision also withdrew the Anchorage, Yakutat, Nome, and Kotzebue route from Alaska's schedule and gave the northern loop to Wien to help stabilize its business. Compared to the Seattle-Ketchikan-Juneau route, it was a small loss for Alaska, and years later it would regain the route.

Charlie Willis offset this opportunity with an ill-advised purchase of the Voyager Hotel in Anchorage. This move was a clear indication to senior management that his vision of the airline was becoming distorted.

The atmosphere of near desperation at just one station, Sitka, was symbolic of an airline bleeding to death from a ruptured main artery while trying to stop the flow with a Band-Aid. Bob Dodd, who was in Sitka during the nosedive, remembered what it was like:

"Even those hundred-dollar paychecks looked better than not getting paid at all. We'd get back-pay in driblets, so late that I used to walk employee wives down to relief offices for money to tide them over.

"I made a deal with a local Coca-Cola distributor, who agreed to put a Coke machine in our terminal lobby with no money down. We eventually paid him out of petty cash, and meanwhile we used the dough from the Coke machine to buy basic office supplies, like pens and pencils.

"We began to build up a little cash reserve so we could buy other needed office supplies, like an adding machine for the freight office. We had tried to open a charge account at a Sitka office-supply firm but were turned down because the airline had no credit. And no wonder — it took months for passengers to get refunds on unused tickets, and creditors were put off even longer."

Such gallant improvisation was standard operating procedure in a company whose pillars of security were crumbling like stale crackers. Life with Charlie had become a case of battling demoralization with defiance. Bob Gray, labor relations vice president, also had grim memories of those near-bankruptcy days:

"I'll never forget how bad Alaska Airlines was in the early 1970s. I had come from a company that had all modern equipment, including computers; we thought Teletypes belonged in the Middle Ages. One day I had to go over to our hangar at Sea-Tac and went up to Alaska's reservations facility on the second floor. It was about the size of the average corporate executive's office, staffed by a couple of women with noisy, outmoded Teletype machines. They kept all their reservations records on three-by-five cards and filed them — I kid you not — in old Florsheim shoe boxes. This was at a time when the rest of the airline industry already was operating with computers."

A shoe box full of reservations and Coke machine revenue could simply not offset Alaska's mounting debt with Chevron for jet fuel, which by 1971 amounted to hundreds of thousands of dollars. Chevron threatened to shut off the airline's fuel supply until its bill was paid.

With the dawn of 1972 came the end of the Proudfoot consultants' first six months of dissecting Alaska Airlines, its officers, and its workforce. A representative from the firm informed Dennis Kelley that he was their choice to coordinate their recommendations, which Kelley knew had to involve wholesale workforce reductions and some high-level head-chopping.

"No way," Kelley said firmly. "I will not be the company's hatchet man."

The Proudfoot team kept after him, and Kelley kept refusing. "There isn't enough bourbon in the entire city of Seattle to make me take that job," he told them.

Proudfoot advised Willis that they had run into a brick wall. Willis summoned Kelley and informed him that he now had a new job as assistant to the chairman of the board and was to work with Proudfoot to put its recommendations into effect. But this command was accompanied by Willis's again suggesting that Kelley work with Giersdorf, something akin to asking the Hatfields to invite the McCoys over for dinner. As it turned out, neither Kelley nor Giersdorf had much chance to do anything, and Proudfoot's association with Alaska Airlines would come to an end with virtually none of its recommendations being adopted except for a few reductions affecting about 200 employees.

For all the probing, interviewing, and analyzing accomplished by Willis's consultants, they missed what three of the airline's key officers sincerely believed to be the main reason why Alaska was in a fatal tailspin: mismanagement at the very top. That meant Willis, with Giersdorf sharing at least some of the blame. Those three officers were Pres Blatter, LeRoy Peterson, and Ben Benecke.

This trio of potential rebels needed a leader. Benecke and Blatter were good men, but nonconfrontational types, and Peterson not only didn't have enough influence among the directors to challenge the "dynamic duo," but he was also cursed with ambivalence. He knew that the airline was in trouble, but more than anyone else, he still felt tremendous loyalty toward Willis.

What the three of them needed — and what they were convinced the airline *desperately* needed — was fresh leadership. Someone, most likely from the outside, even if not an experienced airline executive, who had the toughness, the business acumen, and enough clout with the airline's board of directors to engineer a coup against Willis.

They found their man, or rather — with delicious irony — Willis himself found him. He was a stark contrast to Willis, a no-nonsense, soft-spoken, self-assured, and highly intelligent ex-Marine named Ronald F. Cosgrave. Without realizing it, Charlie had invited a fox into his henhouse. And this was the ostensibly minor event that sowed the seeds of rebellion.

Ron Cosgrave was a native of Albany, New York, where his father was a postal worker who sired 11 children for his mother to raise. Psychologists have long believed that kids who come from large families generally tend to be more self-reliant, more ambitious, and tougher because all through childhood and well into their teens they've had to compete against their siblings. Thus they tend to have a stronger work ethic. During the 1950s and 1960s, for example, airline recruiters looking for promising flight attendants often gave preference to women from large families.

Cosgrave became one of the many young men from the Lower 48 who migrated to Alaska and stayed there because they loved the challenges, opportunities, and potential of the young state. He had enlisted in the Marine Corps at the outset of the Korean War. His unit was engaged in some of the bloodiest battles of that conflict, and because of heavy casualties suffered by higher-ranking Marines, Cosgrave was soon an acting platoon leader. He was awarded the Bronze Star for valor before he was discharged as a staff sergeant in 1952.

After briefly running a pool hall back in Albany, he piled into an old Ford with three friends and drove to the West Coast. From there, two of them turned north, and in due time found themselves in Valdez, where they secured work unloading pipe for a military pipeline.

It was in Valdez that Cosgrave had a chance encounter with Dr. Charles Bunnell, the founding president of the University of Alaska. Bunnell challenged him to move north to Fairbanks and enroll at the university. Cosgrave accepted the challenge and four years later became the institution's first chemical engineering graduate.

In November 1957, Northern Alaska Development Corporation (NADCO) was incorporated by Cosgrave and seven University of Alaska students, some of them attending school on the GI Bill. Payment for stock came in over the summer from subscribers working on road-construction crews or other projects in the bush. NADCO's tentative plans included acquiring acreage near the campus from the estate of Dr. Bunnell and building a mobile-home park to address the shortage of affordable housing near the university. The young entrepreneurs also bought mobile homes in the Lower 48 and transported them to Alaska for sale, subdivided some of the Bunnell property, and built a few houses to sell.

For a brief time, Cosgrave pursued a teaching fellowship at the Massachusetts Institute of Technology (MIT), but he was quickly drawn back to Fairbanks when it became apparent that NADCO would go nowhere without his direct involvement.

Then Cosgrave met Bruce Kennedy. A native of Denver, Kennedy was a slim, handsome man with a perpetually youthful face that could be deceptive. He was to prove a lot tougher and more decisive than he looked. He became Ron Cosgrave's protégé, and almost from the day they met, their friendship ran the gamut from businesslike to stormy.

Kennedy's father was a civil engineer with the Bureau of Reclamation who had moved his family frequently as projects were completed. Bruce attended eight schools in four states before he reached college age. One of his father's assignments was the Eklutna Hydroelectric Project, in the Matanuska Valley of Alaska, where Bruce attended Palmer High School.

In 1959, Kennedy was studying civil engineering in California and had become an experienced land surveyor. He was only 20, having just finished his second year at Sacramento Junior College in California, when he responded to his brother Charles's urging to return to Alaska to find summer work. Chuck had stayed in Alaska when the family moved away and was attending the University of Alaska. Bruce flew to Juneau and shopped around federal and state offices for a job. The Department of Highways needed surveyors in Fairbanks, so he flew north. He squatted in his brother's dorm room while Chuck completed his final exams before leaving for a summer job in the bush. NADCO's temporary office was located in the same dorm, and Bruce became acquainted with Ron Cosgrave in the student lounge.

Kennedy had a promise of a surveying job, but Cosgrave offered him immediate employment in a job that defied description. The agreement included Kennedy's acceptance of NADCO stock in lieu of cash. It would turn out to be the best investment he ever made.

NADCO fascinated Kennedy. "With little more than determination, NADCO seemed on a path to survival, if not prosperity," he recalled. "Paydays were irregular, and cash was available only on an individual-need basis. I even loaned NADCO $300 some weeks before I received my first $100 paycheck, around the Fourth of July."

Kennedy became acting corporate secretary before he turned 21. Cosgrave was not yet 30. Titles meant nothing, and NADCO's total assets

were less than $100,000 at the time. Kennedy was also NADCO's office man-
ager, which during the summer building season meant dispatching supplies
and in the cold dark of winter meant strapping on snowshoes and reading
electric meters in the mobile-home park. In a nostalgic yet sober assessment
of this early career with NADCO, Kennedy said, "Thawing frozen water lines,
snaking out steaming blocked sewers, collecting overdue rent, or staving off
creditors was all in a day's work.

"NADCO kept going, another month, another season. We all had in
common a sense of ownership, and hope for a more prosperous future," said
Kennedy. And before the end of the decade, the company's seeds took root.
Eventually, NADCO built a motel out of mobile units, and still later a 36-unit
apartment complex, a post office, and a bank.

Cosgrave's company experienced setbacks, among them a major fire, a
massive flood, and even reversals of fortune caused by the company's own
poorly conceived plans. NADCO began to diversify, with investments outside
Alaska that included education-oriented daycare facilities in Oregon and
even a resort development in Fiji. To reflect its widened horizon, its corporate name was changed to Alaska Continental Development Corporation
(ALCO). By 1969, ALCO would have about 150 stakeholders.

In 1968, the anemic Alaskan economy received a transfusion when
Atlantic Richfield Company, using a drill rig that had been transported on an
Alaska Airlines C-130 Hercules (Herc), made its epic oil discovery at Prudhoe
Bay. By the following summer, Herc freighters operated by Alaska Airlines
and others were flying seismic equipment, tons of supplies, and personnel
from Fairbanks to the North Slope around the clock. Alaska Airlines found
itself paying $1,000 a day to house its crews at the best place in Fairbanks,
The Golden Nugget Motel (a property later acquired by Charlie Willis).

Alaska negotiated with ALCO for land on which to locate crew-housing
units and housekeeping services. "We struck a deal with the airline," recalled
Cosgrave. "Alaska would pay only utility expenses, and after three years title
to the units would revert to ALCO." He remembered that the park's first
water supply was "rich in iron and turned bright orange when heated." However, as part of the Alaska agreement, the airline built a new water-treatment
plant to make potable water that served the entire ALCO mobile-home park.

By 1969, Kennedy had graduated from the University of Alaska with a business degree and put in two years of active duty as an artillery officer at Fort
Wainwright, outside Fairbanks. And he had married the young woman he

was dating in California before coming to Alaska.

When the company expanded outside the state, Kennedy was put in charge of the entire Fairbanks operation, and it was in that capacity that he flew down to Seattle and forged a crew-housing agreement with Ben Benecke of Alaska Airlines. Part of the deal included stock in lieu of rent. Without realizing it, Kennedy had stepped across the threshold of a new career; the crew-housing contract was his introduction to an airline with all the longevity prospects of ice under the midnight sun.

Ron Cosgrave had already crossed the same threshold, by getting involved with Charles F. Willis. "First time I met Charlie," Cosgrave recalled, "was when I happened to be in Seattle meeting with a lawyer from Springfield, Oregon — Henry Camarot — who knew both Willis and Bob Giersdorf pretty well. Henry had been invited over to Willis's house, and I went along with him.

"Charlie was entertaining some Russian official in connection with the charter flights to the Soviet Union. Willis and I hit it off pretty good. He was charming, colorful, and likeable. Over time, our relationship blossomed. He'd call me and say, 'I need you to do this,' or 'I need you to do that.' "

The Cosgrave-Willis relationship was at first mutually beneficial. Willis was struck by ALCO's ability to manage real property, and he wanted the airline's Alyeska Resort and its other properties managed on a profitable basis. By the end of summer 1970, Cosgrave and Willis had agreed that Alaska Airlines would transfer all of its real property in Alaska to ALCO in exchange for ALCO stock. The airline's board stopped the transaction, however, because it feared that the transfer of sellable assets out of the company might weaken its borrowing ability, although by then it was clear that even with its assets, it could not obtain loans or attract new investors.

Cosgrave had been particularly valuable in helping Willis close a lucrative deal for some land that he owned in Maryland. It was the site of a small college for students from wealthy families. Willis had installed his own man as the school's president, someone he had known in the Navy. But it didn't work out. The college was closed and the property was sold to the National Maritime Union for its new national headquarters, a sale brokered by Cosgrave.

In gratitude, Willis named Cosgrave executive vice president of Alaska Airlines. But Cosgrave was an officer without portfolio, whose only real duty consisted of being handy when Willis needed something done — usually to pull him out of some new financial hole he had dug for himself and/or the airline.

Yet giving an exceptionally smart businessman like Ron Cosgrave an inside look at what was transpiring at Alaska Airlines was the biggest mistake Charlie Willis ever made, insofar as his personal future was concerned. That supposedly honorary title of executive vice president led Cosgrave to friendly contacts with such deeply concerned officers as Ben Benecke, LeRoy Peterson, Pres Blatter, and practically everyone else with the exception of Bob Giersdorf and the ever-loyal, though equally concerned, Dennis Kelley.

Willis was not blind to the dangers of letting Cosgrave get too chummy with officers such as Benecke and Peterson. In fact, he began to perceive Cosgrave as a potential threat to his authority. Several officers told Cosgrave that Willis was advising everyone, "If you've got problems, come see me and stop going to Ron Cosgrave."

Such admonitions came too late. In June 1971, the pot of discontent boiled over. Peterson was their spokesman. "Ron," he said with a frankness born of desperation, "we have to save this company, and you're the only one who can do it. If you have to sacrifice me, I'm willing to go, but somehow you gotta get Charlie and Bob Giersdorf out of there."

Cosgrave kept remembering that visit, and Peterson's plea, as he became increasingly involved in the airline's fortunes and misfortunes. And Willis, the man Cosgrave had admired and liked so much at the start of their relationship, steadily began growing a collection of ugly warts.

Alaska Airlines desperately needed cash, or hard assets for use as collateral to secure bank loans. Its overdue liabilities had topped $16 million. In early 1972, Willis entered into an agreement with ALCO to exchange 574,328 shares of airline stock for Alaska General Properties, Inc., and 203,968 shares for the Golden Nugget Motel, Inc. According to the CAB filing, the swap would provide the airline with "saleable assets having a fair market value in excess of $2.6 million." ALCO now owned 23 percent of Alaska Airlines. Willis also agreed to options and warrants in exchange for guaranteeing loans for the benefit of the airline, which if exercised would increase ALCO's ownership to 46 percent.

In March of that year, Charlie Willis was not only cold sober but also scared to death of the day when his biggest creditor would finally get fed up with his endless procrastination and empty promises of "Don't worry — you'll get paid." In February 1972, Chevron had threatened to cut off the airline's fuel supplies because the unpaid bills had reached a staggering $600,000. To make matters even worse, Chevron had also notified Alaska governor Bill

Egan, Senator Ted Stevens, and the Civil Aeronautics Board of its intentions. It was an impending disaster that would have put Alaska Airlines out of business, and Willis called Cosgrave to his office in a state of panic.

"You gotta do something about this, Ron," Willis pleaded, "because Chevron's about to shut us off."

Cosgrave charitably refrained from telling Willis that his chickens had finally come home to roost. The first thing he did was to make a personal telephone call to Bill Roberts, president of the airline's fuel supplier, Chevron International Oil Company, Inc. "We've got some new blood coming in here, and we should be able to work everything out," he assured Roberts, who still would make no promises.

Cosgrave then called in someone whose judgment and skills he had learned to respect: attorney Henry Camarot, whom Willis, at Ron's urging, had made the airline's assistant general counsel and who later was given the top legal rank of general counsel. Camarot contacted someone at Chevron. Cosgrave couldn't remember who he talked to, but it must have been someone not too far removed from Bill Roberts himself because whatever Camarot said helped stave off the Chevron wolf howling at Alaska's door.

Cosgrave, however, did remember what Camarot told this oil company executive. "You're looking at a big lawsuit if you shut us off," he warned. "You've been selling us fuel for 40 years, and you've been overcharging us during all of those years. That's why we're in this financial situation."

Whether there was any validity to these accusations, Cosgrave couldn't say, and he suspected that Camarot may have been resorting to pure bluff and bluster, a tactic not unknown to the legal profession and one at which Henry Camarot was exceptionally adept. The bottom line was that it seems to have given Chevron pause, resulting in a five-month grace period. In the meantime, Cosgrave secured loans in excess of $1.6 million just to keep Alaska Airlines flying.

But something still had to be done about Charlie Willis. There was a keg of dissident dynamite sitting in the Alaska Airlines boardroom. And a lit match was touching the fuse.

The dynamite exploded on Friday, May 12, 1972, just three days short of Charlie Willis's 15th anniversary as the top dog of Alaska Airlines. Ron Cosgrave had engineered a special meeting of the board, ostensibly to correct an error in the annual financial statement that had been submitted to the Securities and Exchange Commission. The directors had to approve the corrected figure, a purely technical matter, which in this case was like treating a hangnail before brain surgery.

Dennis Kelley, as special assistant to the chairman, had been invited to attend, along with Bob Giersdorf. Kelley thought it would be a waste of his time and asked Willis, "Do you see any reason why I should go?"

Willis shrugged, "Not unless you want to."

Kelley hesitated, but at the last minute decided that such a routine session wasn't going to last very long, so he went into the boardroom and sat down in one of the chairs reserved for invited guests. Giersdorf came in, too, along with Henry Camarot, now the airline's general counsel. Unlike Kelley and Giersdorf, he knew that this was not going to be a routine board meeting.

A dozen directors plus Chairman Willis were present. Five of the 12, including Willis, were so-called "inside" directors — men who were current officers (Ben Benecke, LeRoy Peterson, Pres Blatter, and Ron Cosgrave). Then there were the former heads of carriers that had been merged into Alaska (Shell Simmons and Bob Ellis; Merle Smith was en route but arrived after adjournment; he was present for the second special meeting that would be called for the next day).

Willis called the meeting to order, acknowledging the presence of a quorum.

"Charlie," Dennis Kelley pointed out, "ran a very loose, very casual directors' meeting and paid no attention to *Robert's Rules of Order.*"

On this particular occasion, perhaps tipped off to Cosgrave's intentions, Willis came with his own agenda. He had a statement he wanted to read concerning a big loan he said he had arranged with LaSalle National Bank in Chicago. It was a $3 million secured revolving line of credit, of which $1.6 million would be used to pay off the Chevron debt and other immediate obligations. He began by reading a proposed press release announcing that $5 million of the airline's debt had been converted into deferred notes ranging from a term of 13 months to three years.

The details rolled glibly off his tongue — as one might expect from a snake-oil pitchman, Cosgrave was thinking. The airline's receivables would be pledged against the LaSalle loan, which Willis had obtained at 8.5 percent interest.

Willis next read into the record the text of a telegram from a LaSalle official confirming that this financial transfusion had been approved "subject to certain conditions."

"This loan will pull us out of our financial problems," Willis asserted confidently. Such confidence was woefully premature. It took just one quick call to Chicago to check out Charlie Willis's story with LaSalle.

"It was typical Charlie," Cosgrave related. "The telegram wasn't even signed by a top bank official. We soon found out it was some minor loan officer Willis had been talking to. Charlie had pledged *all* the airline's assets against that loan, and then made the mistake of signing the agreement as 'president and chief executive officer of Alaska Airlines,' which he wasn't."

In fact, while Willis was still reciting further details of the tremendous deal he had made with LaSalle, several cynical directors already were shaking their heads in open disbelief and murmuring, "Charlie, Charlie . . ."

One director, C. R. "Kay" Stewart, finally became exasperated with Willis's smoke screens. "Enough of this bullshit, Charlie," he snapped. "We've got a resolution we'd like to read."

Stewart's open antagonism told Willis he was in real trouble. Stewart was one of two directors — W. E. Bullington was the other — who were officials of the Parker Drilling Company, the nation's biggest oil-field exploration and development company at the time, and also Alaska Airlines' second-largest stockholder. Only ALCO held more shares. Willis had put them on the board, along with a couple of other men he thought he could trust, specifically to quell any threats to his reign.

What Willis hadn't counted on was that Ron Cosgrave had already gone to Tulsa, Oklahoma, to meet with Bob Parker, president of the big drilling company. Cosgrave knew that if the directors from Parker aligned themselves with Willis loyalists, any vote to oust Charlie would likely fail.

So during that Tulsa meeting, Cosgrave had convinced Bob Parker that Willis had to leave, if only to protect ALCO's and Parker's holdings in Alaska Airlines. He also reminded the pragmatic Parker that Cosgrave's own company, ALCO, had even more at stake in this fight than Parker Drilling's 150,000 shares. ALCO owned more than 775,000 shares, and it had warrants and options that could entitle Cosgrave's company to 1.5 million more over the next five years in exchange for additional loans, or at a price of $4 per share. During the negotiations between Cosgrave and Willis, Alaska Airlines' stock price had ranged between $7⅝ and $8⅝, but at the time, outside interests had offered no more than $2.50 a share.

Cosgrave had then suggested that when the battle for control was over, Parker's son Robert Jr. could replace Kay Stewart on the Alaska board. Willis's carefully constructed strategy of packing the board in his favor had already collapsed without his realizing it. Cosgrave, anticipating almost every Willis move, had beaten him at his own game, and at least one officer who wasn't surprised was Bob Gray, Willis's chief labor-relations man.

"Ron Cosgrave was the most intelligent man you could ever meet," Gray said. "If you didn't think so, you were making a mistake."

Which is exactly what Willis did. He had underestimated Cosgrave, and he was about to find that out in a boardroom that had suddenly turned into a courtroom.

It was Kay Stewart who nodded in the direction of Ben Benecke. Benecke rose and addressed Willis. "Mr. Chairman," he said in his soft voice, "I'd like to make a motion."

Willis, a little annoyed, asked, "Is this old business or new business?"

"This is new business."

"We've got an agenda," Willis complained. "If you've got new business, we'll take it up at the end of the agenda."

"No," Benecke said firmly. "We can't do that. It has to be now."

There were audible murmurs of agreement among the directors, and Willis finally gave in. "Oh shit, Ben," he grumbled. "Go ahead and read your goddamned motion."

Benecke rose and began reading:

The undersigned directors hereby move and second the adoption of the following resolution:

WHEREAS, over a period of years Charles F. Willis, Jr., has served as the Chairman of the Board, the Chief Executive Officer, and/or the President of the Company, and . . .

Benecke paused to clear his throat. Willis smiled slightly, expecting that the rest of the motion would pay him homage on the occasion of his 15 years as head of the airline. So were Kelley and Giersdorf.

Benecke resumed in his dry, pedantic voice:

WHEREAS, Alaska Airlines has sustained extensive accumulative losses over this period of years, and the annual report for 1971 shows a continuation of the losses,

WHEREAS, serious financial and other problems exist in the company, and the undersigned Directors have come to the firm and irrevocable belief that it is in the best interests of the Company, its stockholders, and employees, to remove Mr. Willis from his present positions in the Company . . .

The dynamite had exploded. Willis's face turned chalk-white, then took on the appropriate hue of freshly spilled blood, in this case his own.

Benecke read the final two paragraphs of the motion:

NOW, THEREFORE, BE IT RESOLVED that Mr. Willis be

removed as Chairman of the Board, Chief Executive Officer, and/or President, and the duties of the Chairman of the Board be immediately assumed by the present executive vice president, Ronald F. Cosgrave, and he is hereby elected chairman, and

FURTHER RESOLVED that the voting be by secret written ballot and be supervised, counted, and recorded in the minutes of the meeting by the Secretary, Henry Bierds, and the General Counsel, Henry Camarot.

The proposed resolution had been seconded and signed by nine of the 12 directors present, already a majority and pointedly including the names of LeRoy Peterson, Pres Blatter, and Benecke himself, plus outside director Bill Burke, whom Willis himself had put on the board. Willis's top three officers and several of his trusted directors had deserted him — or, in his eyes, betrayed him.

Dennis Kelley, sitting off in a corner of the boardroom, was stunned. Torn between his loyalty to Willis and painful awareness of his leadership flaws, Kelley kept his eyes on him as the drama unfolded. "Charlie's reaction was that of an angry bull," he recalled.

First Willis yelled that he was firing everybody. Then he declared the meeting adjourned and was promptly overruled by the directors. Both he and Henry Camarot went back to their respective offices. Then all hell broke loose.

A listening device with a tiny FM transmitter had been taped to the underside of the coffee table in Charlie's "Klondike" office. No one ever admitted being the one who ordered the bugging, but the bizarre episode demonstrated how much the directors mistrusted Willis. After Willis discovered that the listening device had been planted in his office, which was next to the boardroom, he and Kelley went to Camarot's office to complain about the bug and, Kelley remembered, "they [Willis and Camarot] began screaming at each other and finally started throwing punches. After I got them separated, I was the one who called the Seattle cops, something Charlie got blamed for later. I don't honestly know why I did it, except that I was afraid the situation was getting out of control. By the time the police arrived, things had settled down a bit, and I went back to the boardroom with Charlie, where the directors hadn't begun voting yet."

A grim-faced Willis told the directors, "I'm reconvening this meeting in my office in five minutes. Those of you who are still with me should be there."

He looked around the room, already sensing defeat, and shouted, "You're all a bunch of shits!" Then he gave attorney Camarot a final glare and yelled, "And Henry, you're the biggest shit of all!"

Willis strode out of the boardroom and waited in his office for the "loyalists" to show up. After he stalked out, the directors voted 11-1 for the resolution to oust Willis and make Cosgrave the new board chairman.

The lone dissenting vote was cast by Robert Reeves, a banker from Anchorage and a longtime friend of Willis. It had been Bob Reeves who arranged the financing for the acquisition of the Hercs that were to prove so valuable. He had put his own relatively small bank on the line when he vouched for Willis's integrity and reliability.

The emergency meeting that Willis had called died on the vine. There was no sign of Bob Reeves or, for that matter, Bob Giersdorf or the two directors from Parker Drilling, whom Charlie thought he had in his hip pocket. The only one who showed up was Dennis Kelley, whose presence really moved Willis.

"Dennis," he said, "we gotta do something to keep this airline together. I'm making you executive vice president, effective immediately. Here's what I want you to do. First, prepare some messages we'll send by Teletype to employees all over our system, advising them of what's happened and so on. Then cut off telephone service to all the officers, including Peterson, Blatter, Benecke . . . "

Willis went down a long list of everyone he was firing for disloyalty, then gave Kelley the names of their replacements. His choice as the new president was something of a surprise to a lot of people — Gus Robinson. It shouldn't have been that much of a surprise, not if you knew that with the exception of Bob Giersdorf, Robinson carried more weight with Charlie Willis than anyone else in the company.

One incident was indicative of Robinson's influence. During one of the charter flights to Russia, the leased 707 broke down in Anchorage. The 707, as well as the 727, required a flight engineer in addition to two pilots, and that third crew member was supposed to be a Mr. Fixit in case there was a mechanical problem and no regular mechanic was available.

The flight engineer in this case was Dave Archambeau, who notified Seattle of the delay. Willis fired him, and when Gus Robinson called Dave to see how the repairs were going, Archambeau told him he couldn't work on the airplane because he had been fired.

"Go ahead and fix that airplane," Robinson told him, and then phoned Willis.

"Charlie," he said angrily, "if that flight engineer's fired, so am I."

The airplane got fixed, Archambeau kept his job, and he eventually became an Alaska Airlines captain.

Kelley carried out Willis's orders for the phone cutoffs and Teletype messages, using Giersdorf's work space. His desk was empty. Kelley had no idea where Bob had disappeared to and never did find out. At the time, Willis's "Charlie's Saloon" was at the southwest corner of the airline's hangar at Sea-Tac, and Giersdorf worked in the opposite corner.

Because there was not a lot of room in the hangar for regular offices, even vice presidents were relegated to just a desk, usually parked along the wall. There weren't even cubicles to provide a little privacy. The only exceptions to these sadly inadequate accommodations for corporate headquarters were Willis's garish "saloon" and a small office for the airline's legal department. Gus Robinson had his own small office, but that was on the main hangar floor.

"I used Bob's desk," Kelley explained, "because I couldn't use mine. There were too many secretaries and other employees around who could have heard me cutting off communication to almost every officer in the company."

Kelley found some scratch paper in Giersdorf's wastebasket, scribbled out the message Willis wanted to send, and began transmitting Charlie's "war bulletin." Its gist was that there had been an attempted coup, all the disloyal officers had been fired and already replaced, and Charlie Willis was still in complete charge. Each Teletype message concluded with the names of the new officers.

While all this was going on, Cosgrave had reconvened the afternoon session, at which he proceeded to dissect, demolish, and dismember Willis's claim to having arranged a life-saving loan with the Chicago bank. Cosgrave obviously had been in contact with LaSalle officials, and exposed Willis's rosy assurances as mostly pure fiction.

"Charlie had a gift for outlining the most outrageous tales," Cosgrave recounted, "and actually believed what he was saying."

The board meeting also produced evidence that Willis may have sensed there was real trouble brewing. Cosgrave learned that weeks before the board met, Willis had talked several directors into signing open letters of resignation, meaning that he could accept them at his discretion. The directors who had signed were Benecke, Blatter, and outside directors Shell Simmons and Ralph Bailey, the latter an officer of a bank in Fairbanks.

That Willis had singled out this quartet for his "hit list" hardly seems coincidental. All four were perceived as obvious potential enemies, and they had confirmed his apparent suspicions on May 12. But Cosgrave was aware of the trap Willis had laid, and by the time the board met on that fateful Friday, all four had withdrawn their resignations.

At the afternoon session, Cosgrave drove another nail into the Willis coffin. He noted that Charlie's dismissal had left a vacancy on the board and introduced Bruce Kennedy as his nominee to fill the vacancy. He also nominated as a new director John Dees, another official from the Parker Drilling Company.

He asked that the two nominees be allowed to attend the rest of the special sessions, although no vote on the nominations would be taken until a later board meeting. In fact, both nominations would be resubmitted at that later board session, but with a huge difference: the next time they would be opponents competing to fill a single vacancy.

The immediate bottom line, however, was that Willis's end run, to remove four known hostile directors, had been stuffed at the line of scrimmage. Cosgrave, in turn, had achieved two goals: first, in Kennedy he had a future leader for the airline; and second, he had effectively blocked any further Willis attempt to regain control of the board through the Parker organization.

Cosgrave didn't miss a trick. Among the precautionary measures he took before the board met that Friday was hiring a parliamentary expert from the University of Washington, just to make sure the directors' actions followed established parliamentary rules and were in accordance with the company's by-laws. He also took this precaution to make sure that Willis, as chairman, didn't try anything illegal. It turned out that the expert wasn't needed. Willis was too infuriated to make any calmly considered parliamentary challenges.

In the midst of all the boardroom action, Dennis Kelley was still at Giersdorf's desk trying to collect his thoughts when a delegation showed up from "the enemy camp" — Cosgrave, Benecke, and two of the outside directors. Kelley remembered that one of them, public relations consultant and outside director Bill Burke, said they all sympathized with him and appreciated what he was going through.

"It has been a bad day, a black day at Alaska Airlines," Burke said, "and we don't like it any more than you do. But what we've done is perfectly legal and in accordance with our by-laws. Charlie is no longer with the company, and we think the best thing you can do is take the rest of the day off."

Kelley, emotionally drained, lost his temper and was about to tell them where they could stick their sympathy when they departed the scene. He returned to Willis's office, where Charlie told him to go home. Instead, Kelley went to a nearby bar, ordered a double martini, and then decided this was no time to get drunk. He suddenly had an idea that might save the day for Charlie Willis.

Meanwhile, Cosgrave made one final attempt to push Willis out the front door with a minimum of humiliation for a man who had done so much *for,* as well as *to,* the airline. All around were signs of a company in a state of quiet chaos. Bewildered employees, supervisors, and lower-echelon officers were asking, "Who's in charge?"

And this wasn't happening just at corporate headquarters and the Seattle base. Cosgrave was aware of the messages that had gone to all stations, and he dispatched Teletype instructions to disregard all previous communications and ignore Willis's claim of still being in command. His hoped-for solution was to give Willis a face-saving alternative that would end all the uncertainty.

Cosgrave appointed a three-man committee to present his peace pro-posal. He thought Willis would at least listen to Bill Burke, LeRoy Peterson, and Bob Giersdorf, especially Giersdorf, who honestly considered Cosgrave's offer reasonable under the circumstances. Cosgrave and the board itself were willing to let Willis stay on as chairman, but without decision-making authority, while Cosgrave would become president and chief executive officer without the chairmanship. In addition to continuing as chairman, Willis would have a small private office and full pass privileges.

The answer came back swiftly. In effect, it was "Go to hell."

By Friday night, it was only too evident that the war hadn't ended. Charlie Willis had made it clear he was not going to bow out peacefully, and another emergency board meeting was scheduled for the following day. The directors hired their own private security force, apparently fearing either violence or some kind of retaliation for the bug planted in Willis's office. To anyone asking "Who's in charge?" the only truthful answer was "Confusion reigns."

Uncertainty described the feelings of many lower-level officers as word spread that Willis had been fired. Not a few were wondering whether past allegiance to Willis would jeopardize their own jobs. Ron Cosgrave was something of an unknown quantity. Jim Johnson was one of those facing a "What's going to happen to me?" dilemma. Since 1958 he had been working for Bob Giersdorf, first as assistant vice president of sales for Southeast Alaska, and then in Seattle as assistant vice president and general sales manager.

McGee Airways in Bristol Bay.

Legendary bush pilot Oscar Winchell, on left, and fur trader
Leo Koslosky with a valuable load of native fur destined for
world markets in 1932.

Star Air Service was founded in 1932. Its first aircraft was *North Star*, a Fleet B-5, shown with pilot Jack Waterworth. By 1934, with the financial assistance of several partners, Star had a fleet of 15 aircraft that varied in type, size, capacity, and condition.

(Top) Larry Flahard, an Alaska Airlines chief pilot, is shown in the 1940s with a Stinson Model A trimotor in the background. (Above) With a loan from pilot Kenny Neese, Star Air purchased a Ford trimotor from Noel Wien for $9,000. Shown is a Star Ford trimotor, circa 1942.

Fairchild Pilgrims with reinforced struts were Star Air Service pack mules, rated to carry a 3,000-pound payload. However, that payload was frequently doubled.

(Top) Alaska Star Airlines purchased its first new airplane, a Lockheed Lodestar, in 1943. (Above) Congratulating each other upon delivery of the Lockheed Lodestar are, from left, Alaska Star Airlines majority owner and successful junk dealer Raymond W. Marshall; his principal operating officer, Homer Robinson; and the company's Anchorage Station manager, Eddie Orr.

A refurbished surplus DC-3, a post-World War II mainstay, is unloaded in Anchorage. Alaska Airlines was the first commercial operator to take off and land a DC-3 on skis.

A Marshall-era DC-4 flight crew, circa 1950, consisted of a pilot, copilot, navigator, radio operator, and two flight attendants.

Alaska flew surplus World War II Curtiss C-46 aircraft, configured to haul both cargo and passengers, between 1948 and the early 1960s.

In 1949, Alaska Airlines transported Yemenite Jews between Aden and Israel as part of the fabled "Operation Magic Carpet." By the time the company's planes were reassigned, they had carried more than 40,000 refugees.

Alaska Airlines mechanics Johnson, Steward, and McCoy (from left) work on an engine at Asmara, Eritrea, in January 1949.

Charles F. Willis was a decorated war hero, an Eisenhower appointee, and an entrepreneur who in 1957 was hired by Ray Marshall to run Alaska Airlines.

Willis wanted air travel to be fun, really fun, and he hired the promotionally gifted Bob Giersdorf to direct Alaska Airlines' sales and marketing. Shown is Giersdorf behind the ticket counter in Fairbanks, 1960.

After unproductive negotiations with Boeing and Douglas, Willis was able to buy a Convair 880. It was configured to carry 96 passengers; it flew faster, quieter, and higher than a DC-6; and it cut the flying time between Seattle and Fairbanks from six to less than three hours.

Willis had his airline's Convair 880 equipped with a bar. Free beer was served to all military personnel.

One of Giersdorf's promotional ideas was the "Stilt Lady."
Perched on eight-foot stilts and dressed in Gay '90s attire,
she was able to look eye-to-eye at passengers inside an
arriving airplane.

Willis not only increased the airline's speed and comfort for passengers, but he also enhanced Alaska's heavy-lifting capacity when he acquired a fleet of Lockheed C-130 Hercules for charter service around the world, including Vietnam and later Prudhoe Bay, on Alaska's North Slope.

Willis took delivery of Alaska's first two Boeing 727 combis in 1966 and sold the fuel-sucking Convair 880.

Alaska Airlines acquired Alaska Coastal-Ellis Airlines in 1968. Alaska Coastal-Ellis represented 32 years of Alaska aviation history, including legendary bush pilots Bob Ellis (left) and Shell Simmons (middle). Cordova Airlines, also acquired that year, came with Merle "Mudhole" Smith (right), a veteran pilot who began flying in Alaska in 1937.

Flight-attendant uniforms were likely never more dramatic
than when Alaska Airlines introduced "Golden Samovar Service."
Long coats, short tunics, and tall hats set Alaska Airlines' flight
attendants apart from their peers.

Ronald F. Cosgrave engineered a palace coup in 1972 that ousted
Charlie Willis and saved the airline from its creditors.

Since its introduction in the early 1970s, the Alaska Airlines Eskimo has
become one of the most recognizable airline logos in the world.

"I was loyal to Charlie because I've been loyal to every person I ever worked for," Johnson explained. "So when the coup was pulled off, I couldn't see how Giersdorf could survive after Charlie left, so I didn't know where I stood." But Johnson, along with other concerned officers, didn't know that Cosgrave understood that capable people like Johnson were victims of inevitable ambivalence, torn between emotional loyalty and pragmatic judgment.

For officers such as Ben Benecke and LeRoy Peterson, who had been with Willis for years, voting against him was one of the most difficult decisions of their lives. "I had to choose doing the right thing over personal friendship," Peterson confessed.

Late Friday night, after Willis learned exactly which officers had deserted him, he phoned Peterson. "That call ended our friendship," Pete related. "He told me I was a Benedict Arnold, although he used a lot stronger language than that. But I felt I had to support all those people working for the airline, even though when I made that decision I knew I might be going, too. I never talked to Charlie Willis again."

The officer with the most right to feel ambivalent about choosing between loyalty and defection, since Willis had defiantly anointed him as the new president of Alaska Airlines, was Gus Robinson. He had spent all night Friday standing guard in front of Willis's office because Charlie was afraid the Cosgrave "conspirators" would try to raid his personal files.

"I didn't know what had happened at the board meeting until Willis told me," Gus recalled. "After he asked me to stand guard, he went home, and when I got to his office, sitting in a chair in front of the door was one of the security guards the directors already had hired. He was sound asleep and didn't wake up all night long.

"I didn't know Willis had named me president until I saw the Teletype message he sent to all employees. But I was president for only about 24 hours. And I have to say this about Willis: if he could have laid off the booze, he would have made a fine leader."

"If he could have laid off the booze . . ." That seemed to be Charlie's epitaph at Alaska Airlines, reflecting a strange mixture of regret but also relief felt by virtually everyone throughout the company. Danna Maros-Siverts's reaction was typical. She was a ticket agent in Seattle when the coup exploded. As she put it, "I think most people wanted the airline to go forward and knew that something drastic had to be done — that we needed businessmen like Cosgrave and Benecke, and later Bruce Kennedy. I don't think most of us knew how close we were to being liquidated."

After Willis was fired, Maros-Siverts was talking to a mechanic who said he missed him. "Don't you like getting your paycheck on time, every two weeks?" she asked.

"Yeah," he replied, "but Charlie used to come in and talk to us."

And that, too, was another kind of epitaph for Charlie. A great many employees from the Willis era remembered his good deeds, his charisma and breezy informality, as well as his heedless disregard of fiscal responsibility. Susan Bramstedt, for example, recalled the painful adjustment from tiny, close-knit Cordova Airlines to Alaska and how both Charlie and Mudhole Smith had tried to make the transition easier.

"The worst moment came when I took the first call after the merger," she recalled, "and I had to answer 'Alaska Airlines' instead of 'Cordova.' Like everyone else, I was concerned about my future.

"But Charlie, and Smitty too, sold us on the idea that this was a golden opportunity for us, that by merging we were expanding our horizons, and that everything was being done to protect our old positions. And Charlie kept his word. I was Smitty's secretary at Cordova, and the merger agreement specified that I would continue in that job when he came over to Alaska."

At the time of the coup, Bob Handley was in Sitka, where the reaction was typical of the stations throughout Alaska. "The Teletypes began coming," he related, "first from Willis firing all the officers and naming new ones, then from Cosgrave countermanding everything Willis had sent. No one in the field knew what the hell was going on in Seattle. For a long time we couldn't get through to the Seattle switchboard, so we couldn't find out who was running the airline. We couldn't find anybody to talk to, and it was as if the inmates had taken over the nuthouse."

Pat Glenn, then a rising star in flight operations, had a different perspective. "I was a little distant from the turmoil that Friday, being in dispatch," he said, "and then I got the first word from Ken Skidds, who alerted me to call the airport police. Then came the Teletype messages and frantic phone calls systemwide.

"But while there was a lot of confusion, what amazed me, and still does even today, was that there was not one single hiccup in flight operations — not one slowdown, delayed flight, or canceled flight despite all the upheaval around us. Everyone did their job while waiting to find out what was really going on."

According to Glenn, the pilots were the most dubious about the change of command. "They knew Charlie, they trusted him, and they didn't know Cosgrave or any of their other new bosses," he pointed out. "On the other hand, some of the names on Charlie's list of new officers were actually weird choices. He made some guy a vice president who was the biggest loser I ever saw.

"Like almost everyone else, I was a little shocked when Willis got the gate. Yet I knew it had to be done. I remember when Charlie was still in power, I happened to make a call one day to see how much dough I had in my retirement fund. I was told it was none of my business."

A few veterans such as Ken Skidds, whose sense of humor often was applied with a large needle, managed to dredge a little humor out of the tense atmosphere. Which was natural, because airline humor is like military humor — it often emerges in times of adversity as a kind of armor plate against gloom.

Skidds watched in disbelief as uniformed police began appearing on the premises, practically every one of them wondering what all the fuss was about. "At one time," he remembered, "there were four different police forces called in. They were from the Seattle PD, airport police, private security guards, and even military police, all running around like the Keystone Kops from a Mack Sennett silent comedy."

Right after the vote was taken on Friday, Dennis Kelley accosted Skidds. "Rush down to the accounting department," he ordered, "and protect the file cabinets. We don't want anyone stealing the records."

So Ken headed for Accounting, which happened to be next to Gus Robinson's office. Skidds knew about the Teletypes that had gone out, including the surprise selection of Robinson as president, and poked his head into his office.

"Hey, Gus," he chirped, "I've got a pay raise coming, and seeing that you're in charge, I figured you can give it to me right now."

"Goddammit," Robinson growled, "this ain't funny. I've been sitting on both sides of the fence so long, my scrotum's gone."

Both men started laughing, and at that point Dennis Kelley came in, shook his head at all the merriment, and said sternly, "You both should realize we're all gonna be fired along with Charlie, so you might as well go home."

It was understandable why Kelley saw no reason for laughter. He was about to take off for Tulsa on his long-shot mission to save Charlie Willis's job.

Willis already had gone home, and it was there that Kelley headed first. Like Cosgrave, Kelley had concluded that Parker Drilling held the key to the success or failure of the coup, and the man he wanted to talk to was Bob Parker, who headed that company. When Willis let him into his house, Kelley immediately asked him, "Charlie, have you talked to Bob Parker yet?"

"I called him twice," Willis replied, "but he either wasn't home or didn't want to talk to me."

"How about my flying down to Tulsa? I'll talk to him and see if I can swing him over to our side. If he does, his people on the board would change their votes, and I think other directors might follow."

"If you can do that, Dennis, I'll really appreciate it," Willis said gratefully.

Kelley left, arranged for a pass on Continental Airlines, and flew to Tulsa late Friday night. He checked in at a hotel, grabbed a few hours' sleep, and early Saturday morning phoned Bob Parker at home. Parker told him he was a pallbearer at a funeral that morning but would see him at his home around noon. When Dennis got there, he found that Parker had invited the company's treasurer, Bill Jackson, to be present.

Both Parker and Jackson listened courteously to Kelley's impassioned defense of Willis, but then Parker went into a long dissertation on his responsibility to his own stockholders. He couldn't see any chance of the airline recovering as long as Willis was in charge.

"Do you mind if I report this conversation to Charlie?" Kelley asked, and Parker told him, "I think you should, by all means."

When Kelley returned to his hotel to check out, there was a message waiting for him to call Bill Jackson. He did, and the Parker official informed him that he had just finished talking to Ron Cosgrave, and added ominously, "I have a message for you."

Kelley's heart sank, and he was thinking, *This is it. I'm about to join the ranks of the unemployed.* Aloud, he asked Jackson to give him the message, and the Parker treasurer repeated it verbatim: "Dennis: I know you're in Tulsa. I know why you went there, and I know that you failed in your mission. Come back to Seattle as fast as you can. We have a lot of work to do and a big job for you. There are no hard feelings."

Dennis Kelley, Willis's last ally, finally raised his own white flag. In an honorable surrender, Kelley returned to Seattle as instructed, and as soon as possible met with Cosgrave. Kelley made it clear that he was not going to apologize for backing Willis. "I want you to understand that I worked for Charlie, he needed help, and I tried to help him," Kelley explained. "I know my helping him caused you some problems, and if they did, I'm sorry. But I did it, and I don't regret it. I figure if the shoe was on the other foot, I'd do the same for you."

Cosgrave smiled. "Dennis," he said, "I want you to take some time off. Go home and just relax for a full week. Then come back and we'll decide what you can do around here."

Kelley did just that, but first he went to every officer in the company and told them exactly what he had told Cosgrave, that he was not going to make excuses for backing Willis because he considered that part of his job. When he returned after a brief rest, his job as assistant to the chairman had been abolished, but over the next 16 years he was to hold several responsible management positions with the airline. He retired in 1988 as assistant vice president of ground operations.

"I saw Charlie a few times after the coup, and he still was bitter as hell," Kelley related. "Eventually, he turned against me, partially because I went over to the other side. But what really ended our friendship was when he tried to start a new cargo airline and I refused to join him."

This occurred about seven months after the coup. Willis phoned Kelley to tell him about his proposed airfreight company, which would fly fresh fruits and vegetables from California to Alaska, where such commodities were almost always in great demand and short supply.

"I'd have you run the whole operation," Willis promised. "You'd be the head honcho."

"Charlie, I really appreciate the offer, but how about financing?" Kelley inquired.

He had asked the wrong question. Willis hemmed and hawed for several minutes without really answering, and Kelley finally told him he wasn't interested. Willis hung up in a huff and never spoke to him again.

When Kelley started working for Alaska Airlines, he had made a list of 65 things he wanted to accomplish before retiring. As it came time to leave, he took stock of the past 41 years and discovered he had accomplished all 65 goals. Not included in that 65-item agenda, however, was to leave Alaska Airlines with a reputation for loyalty and dignity under the most trying circumstances. Perhaps that could have been his 66th goal, and if so, he achieved it as he had all the others.

Dennis Kelley passed away in April 2006. He was genuinely mourned by every Alaska Airlines officer and employee who had ever known him.

The Saturday directors' meeting was supposed to be almost an anticlimax, more of a mopping-up exercise than continued combat, but it didn't start out that way.

Late arrivals swelled the attendance to 15 directors, and listed in the official minutes as "also present" were a glowering and unhappy Charlie Willis and Henry Margolis, president of the Elgin Watch Company of New York, an old friend whom Willis had put on the board. Except that one of the last actions the board had taken on Friday was to accept Margolis's resignation, tendered at Cosgrave's request. Cosgrave had already eliminated this diehard Willis supporter, or thought he had.

After Cosgrave called the meeting to order, Margolis rose and announced he had a statement to make.

"Henry, what are you doing here anyway?" Cosgrave demanded. "You're no longer a director and you're out of order."

"This meeting itself is out of order," Margolis retorted. "The notice I received simply said that a special meeting had been called without stating its purpose. Under SEC rules, no special meeting can be called unless the directors are advised of its reason or reasons. The notice I received merely stated that the meeting was to establish a new date for the annual shareholders' meeting."

Willis was nodding vigorously in triumphant agreement. Margolis continued: "If I had been advised that a management change was to be part of this special meeting, I would have been here for yesterday's session. This board of directors can do anything it wants to, but it must be done legally."

Cosgrave smiled wryly. He hadn't expected this last-minute attempt to throw overalls in his carefully cooked chowder, but he recognized the maneuver as nothing more than a final, desperate delaying action. He decided to defuse it.

"I'll give you the courtesy of the floor for another five minutes, Henry," he said graciously.

Margolis launched into an impassioned if truncated defense of Willis's leadership and the injustice of his removal. Then he and Willis left the room. The whole exchange had taken only 15 minutes, and when Cosgrave adjourned the meeting 20 minutes later, the war was over and the rebels had won. Cosgrave had all the votes needed to separate Willis from Alaska Airlines.

Now the airline was holding its collective breath, wondering whether the revolt's mastermind was going to move through the management ranks with an executioner's ax.

Dennis Kelley already knew that Cosgrave had no desire to treat Willis loyalists as corporate lepers. Cosgrave even extended an olive branch to the executive

whose head everyone assumed would be first on the chopping block: Bob
Giersdorf. After it became clear that Willis had suffered total defeat, Giersdorf
frankly asked Cosgrave, "Where do I stand, with Charlie gone?"

"I don't know," Cosgrave answered with equal frankness. "It looks like
there's a move on to replace you, too. But I think you rate a chance to defend
yourself."

Cosgrave did better than that. He had decided that like Kelley and other
Willis supporters, Giersdorf deserved to start off under the new regime with
a clean slate. Giersdorf was retained as vice president of marketing and sales,
although his authority and jurisdiction stopped at the borders of that one
department. He was no longer running several shows.

Giersdorf was still in that position when Cosgrave came to him with
another offer. Cosgrave was aware that Benecke and Giersdorf had never
really gotten along, and their relationship hadn't improved since the coup.
Cosgrave, trying to keep the airline out of insolvency, saw a way to settle their
differences gracefully without having to fire either of them. He wanted no
part of one of those "either he goes or I go" ultimatums.

He called Giersdorf in and asked him to take over the company's tour
business, one of the Willis subsidiaries that, like the hotels, Cosgrave wanted
to ditch. "I know you and Ben can't get along, and I can't afford to keep both
of you," he said bluntly. "But if you agree to step down as marketing vice
president and run our tour operations, we'll finance it for you so you can buy
it back from us."

Giersdorf jumped at the offer. He eventually bought the tour subsidiary from Alaska and called it Alaska Tours and Marketing. Then he created
Exploration Cruise Lines, which had seven ships but too few passengers. The
cruise line went bankrupt, and Giersdorf sold it and other business interests
to Anheuser-Busch, makers of Budweiser beer. Then, still refusing to stay
down, he started another cruise line based on a ship of his own design, the
Empress of the North, a 100-passenger vessel with hinged bows, like the
landing craft of World War II.

At this writing, the *Empress* is still in service, but Giersdorf never got
to see his new cruise line started. He died at age 67 in February 2003, only
three weeks after his beloved wife, Laurie, passed away. His oldest and best
friend, travel writer Stan Patty, delivered the eulogy and certainly knew this
unusual man as well as anyone.

"I loved the guy," Patty said. "He could be mean and nasty, but more
often he was a saint. I never met a marketing genius like Giersdorf, but he

couldn't handle money. He stayed loyal to Willis until the end, but they stopped being good friends after Charlie got the gate. Willis was dating Giersdorf's sister, and I think Bob finally got fed up with his drinking."

Patty was the source of the most poignant post-coup story, centered on Giersdorf and his popularity among Alaska's employees, especially the flight attendants. He was taking a business trip on Alaska Airlines shortly after his cruise line went bankrupt, so he was flying coach to save money.

The senior flight attendant spotted him in coach and came over to his seat. "Mr. Giersdorf," she said, "there's an empty seat in first class, so why don't you move up front?"

"I don't have a first-class ticket," Giersdorf said.

"Mr. Giersdorf," she said softly, "you *always* have a first-class ticket when I'm working a flight."

"I heard that story from Bob himself," Patty said, "and he sobbed as he was telling it."

Another relatively early departure was that of LeRoy Peterson. Of all the inside directors who had voted to oust Willis, Peterson suffered the most from pangs of regret bordering on guilt. "Charlie trusted me," he reminisced, "but I never tried to advise or warn him that we were getting into real serious trouble financially. I didn't have to because he already knew it, and tragically, he just didn't do anything about it.

"I always got along with him fine, but I recognized that he had troubles up to his ears. I thought that basically he was a decent guy who wanted to keep his job, but his credit was gone and I knew damned well that if the airline was going to survive, somebody else was going to have to do it."

"Pete" Peterson left Alaska Airlines shortly after Willis departed. But he left voluntarily, not because Cosgrave fired him. He had kept the promise he made to Cosgrave a year before the coup, when he told him that Willis had to go even "if you have to sacrifice me."

For some 15 years after he resigned from Alaska, Peterson operated a couple of car washes he had started when he thought the airline was going under. But he also became involved — and at this writing still is — with a Small Business Administration project called SCORE, Service Corps of Retired Executives, which recruits former top management officials to help people trying to start up small businesses. Peterson headed the SCORE program in the state of Washington for almost six years.

Peterson and Giersdorf, at least, ended their careers at Alaska with some class and dignity. Willis ended his by refusing to admit defeat, and his bitterness fed his continuing resistance. Ron Cosgrave found himself combating Willis's "rear-guard" actions as soon as the directors had voted to fire him. One of Cosgrave's first moves was to change the door locks in Charlie's office. He didn't want Willis barricading himself in his beloved ersatz saloon, issuing more contradictory orders.

The new corporate slate consisted of:

Kay Stewart – vice chairman of the board

Pres Blatter – president

Ben Benecke – senior vice president of corporate services

R. A. Bergman – assistant corporate secretary

It was mostly a temporary list, and everyone knew it. Stewart eventually would be replaced on the board by Robert Parker Jr., and Stewart would serve only briefly as a nominal vice chairman with no particular duties or authority, although, as we shall see, he assumed that the position carried more authority than it really did.

Blatter, too, had no great desire to continue serving as president, and Cosgrave would shortly replace him with Benecke. Cosgrave also intended to name Bruce Kennedy vice president of properties, while grooming him as his own eventual successor.

Cosgrave himself was a somewhat reluctant new leader as chairman. "Actually, I knew nothing about running an airline," he admitted, "and all of a sudden I found myself running one."

His obvious priority was to dig Alaska out of the financial swamp that Willis had bequeathed to the company's new leaders. One of the last things Ron Cosgrave did to ease Charlie Willis's pain over his dismissal was to cut a deal with him. Willis received a half-million dollars in severance pay, on the condition that he resign from the board as a director; he had already been fired as chairman. The vacancy created was the one that Cosgrave would fill with Bruce Kennedy, who by then had been named the airline's vice president of properties.

In May 1972, after Willis's ouster, Cosgrave, as chairman and chief executive officer, described the airline's reorganization in a document filed with the CAB, in which he said: "In all honesty, our situation is a crisis a minute. We have serious financial problems. At this time of year, because of the increased cash flow with the summer traffic, we are able to pay our day-to-day operations. However, we are carrying $16 million in cumulative losses . . . with actually a negative stockholder equity of $4 million. While the interest of these banks and underwriters has risen sharply (since the accession of new management on May 14, 1972), there are no commitments forthcoming.

"The creditors, on the other hand, are encouraged, but still apprehensive. They are looking to October 1, when the cash flow goes negative, and the Company has a real juggling job to do to rearrange or renegotiate deferrals of payments on the $16 million in overdue liabilities."

With annual revenues of less than $34 million, it would take a financial magic act to save Alaska Airlines.

Cosgrave and Kennedy were in some ways an odd couple: a tough, largely introverted ex-Marine and a young, deeply religious, Bible-reading aviation neophyte who had more experience thawing pipes than running an airline. Yet it was this incongruous pair that would pilot the carrier known so derisively as Elastic Airlines to unfamiliar altitudes of achievement — those of economic stability and a reputation for excellence in every phase of commercial air travel.

Charlie Willis took the severance pay, but he also took with him his never-ending anger and resentment. "He never stopped believing that the airline had been stolen from him," Cosgrave noted. "And he could always find some lawyer to listen to his version, believe him, and agree to sue us."

On one occasion, however, Willis swallowed his pride and made one final attempt to return to the airline. He showed up in Cosgrave's office and told him he was willing to accept his offer to serve as merely a titular chairman with no voting power, but with such perks as a private office and full pass privileges. When Cosgrave turned him down, Willis resumed his futile legal war against the airline.

Willis's last aviation venture was a brief association as an adviser with LOT, the Polish airline. He never got his proposed California-Alaska air-cargo airline off the ground. He died at age 74 in a Washington, D.C., hospital on March 16, 1993. The headline over his obituary in the *New York Times* called him an "innovator in aviation," and merely reported that he had once headed Alaska Airlines. There was no mention of his having been fired.

The tragedy of the Charles F. Willis Jr. story is that he had the intelligence and charisma to achieve what his successors at Alaska did — and blew it. Any objective historian could sum up his 15-year career at Alaska Airlines with the two saddest words in the English language: *If only* . . .

CHAPTER EIGHT

The New Broom

Almost as soon as the dust of internecine war had settled, Ron Cosgrave called another kind of meeting, this one with as many of the Seattle-based employees as possible. No one took a head count, but there must have been around 300 people in attendance, filling most of the hangar and ranging from ship cleaners to supervisors.

"This is the situation," Cosgrave began. "We have no credibility. Our performance is lousy. We're losing our customers because, among other complaints, passengers are not getting their refunds in a timely manner.

"Our stockholders haven't gotten anything back on the investments they've made, and we can't raise the capital to buy the better equipment we need. And I also know you've missed more than one paycheck.

"Some of you have been with Alaska for 20 or 25 years, and you have the most to lose if we go under. To survive, we have to learn to do our jobs better, and I give you my word I'll work with you to make that happen."

A flurry of questions came from his audience, but none were antagonistic or cynical. There were no loud cries of "We want Charlie back" either, something that Cosgrave had half-expected. Indeed, he thought his management team needed a heart-to-heart talk just as much as and maybe more than the rank and file.

Cosgrave thought he had a chance of stitching enough money together to carry the airline through its financial turbulence, but he wasn't sure Alaska knew enough to become a good airline. And its spirit was flagging.

Only a few weeks after the coup, he began taking management groups to Murrieta Hot Springs, California, away from the office for talks. He also arranged for a series of meetings with key officials from Continental Airlines — in effect, a "faculty" of experts who would teach them how to run their own airline better.

"We picked Continental," Cosgrave explained frankly, "because at the time they were the industry's class act."

He could not have picked a better corporate role model, although Continental's revenue stream in 1972 was something like 25 times larger than Alaska's. Led by the colorful and dynamic Bob Six, Continental was a profitable and competitive carrier known for providing superior service. Six had a gut feeling for passengers and employees alike; the latter may have been scared to death of him at times, yet they adored him. Continental's slogan, "The Proud Bird with the Golden Tail," reflected the sense of pride that permeated the entire company. That's why Six could give absolute fits to competitors five times Continental's size.

Ron Cosgrave never claimed that he wanted to remake Alaska Airlines into a mirror image of Continental. For one thing, the carriers had entirely different route structures and market requirements, not to mention that one was prosperous and the other almost broke. But Cosgrave did believe that Six's airline had consistently demonstrated how a relatively small carrier could not only compete against the industry's entrenched giants but also actually outperform them.

Over a period of three weeks, Cosgrave sent three mixed groups composed of directors, elected officers, and managers to what might be dubbed the "Bob Six College of Competition." Ben Benecke and Pres Blatter were among those present, and participant Bruce Kennedy wryly commented, "They were the only ones wearing ties."

Kennedy remembered that they also seemed to be the only ones who were somewhat defensive about their own airline's failings. "When other officers got up to list our shortcomings, they'd get up and insist that things weren't that way at all," he said. "Our guys were still digging in against any changes."

Ron Cosgrave encouraged change and was particularly impressed with Continental's recommendation: that Alaska do only one thing at a time and do that one thing well. "They opened our eyes to a lot of things we hadn't realized," he admitted, "because we were all so scattered and not doing any one thing very well. The biggest lesson we learned was that we had to become a *passenger* airline and do that job well because that was the long-range future of the company.

"Taking a good, hard look at the things we had been doing wrong really helped. Like having to lease airplanes for the heavy summer traffic and not having any use for them during the winter. Like leasing 707s, an airplane that required additional pilot training and was unfamiliar to our mechanics."

It was a soul-searching experience for the Alaska officers, and for the most part, they took the "concentrate on one thing and do it well" advice to heart.

Cosgrave quickly put one recommendation into effect. He began the process of selling off the hotel properties, which had been more of a bust than a boon, with the notable exception of the Alyeska Ski Resort, near Anchorage. Alyeska, however, would be later sold to a Japanese conglomerate and at a decent price, but with the stipulation that Chris Von Imhoff continue as the resort's manager.

With new leadership and strict financial management, Alaska's chances of survival improved. It was still bleeding, but the massive hemorrhaging stopped. In 1972, the company reported a loss of something over $2.5 million, but by 1973, Cosgrave's first full year in office, the red ink had finally turned black with a net profit of $440,000, passenger boardings had jumped nearly 40 percent, and on-time performance kept pace with that improvement. In fact, 1973 marked the beginning of what was to be 19 consecutive years of profits.

Before this dramatic turnaround, however, Cosgrave had to beat back an attempt by a rebellious director to unseat him as chairman. About three months after the coup and just before the Continental training sessions, vice chairman Kay Stewart tried to oust Cosgrave at a special board meeting. Stewart's insurrection surprised some people. He had openly supported Cosgrave's fight to oust Charlie Willis and, in fact, had been the one to snap, "Enough of this bullshit, Charlie" when Willis was expounding on the supposed loan from a Chicago bank.

Cosgrave wasn't surprised, however. He knew that Stewart's anti-Willis stance carried a price tag. Stewart assumed that by supporting Cosgrave, he would be rewarded with a high executive post at the airline, apparently something he preferred to his job as a Parker Drilling vice president.

But Cosgrave wanted Stewart off Alaska's board. The vice chairmanship was just a meaningless title designed to stroke Stewart's ego long enough for Cosgrave to get rid of him. Cosgrave already had told Bob Parker Sr. that when the coup smoke cleared, he intended to replace Stewart with Bob Parker Jr. as one of Alaska's directors.

"Once Kay became our vice chairman," Cosgrave said, "he started going all over our system throwing his weight around. It was destructive."

Stewart let it be known that he thought ALCO had too much power over decisions affecting the airline and that Cosgrave and heir-apparent Kennedy were just real estate men who knew nothing about running an airline. Of course, neither did anyone from Stewart's own company, Parker Drilling.

Cosgrave admitted years later that he was more concerned about Stewart's defiance than Willis's. Stewart showed up at the special meeting surrounded by a phalanx of lawyers from Parker Drilling along with Bill Cheek, former general counsel under Willis at Alaska. They were armed with documents purporting to show that Cosgrave's close association with ALCO was harmful to Alaska Airlines.

Cosgrave immediately challenged the legality of having any lawyers present. "This is a directors' meeting, and only directors can attend," he declared.

Stewart called for a vote on Cosgrave's motion to evict the lawyers. The result among the 14 directors present was a 7-7 deadlock, and the motion, which required a majority vote to overturn the chairman's ruling, failed.

The 15th director, Shell Simmons, was en route from Juneau. "I didn't know what the hell to do except stall for time," Cosgrave said. "The meeting had started at 10, it was now 11:30, and I needed Shell there to break that tie. He arrived around noon. Following our return from lunch, confident of an 8-to-7 majority, I nominated Bruce Kennedy to fill the vacancy left on the board by Willis's departure."

Kay Stewart nominated John Dees of Parker Drilling and argued strenuously against Kennedy, saying that his election would merely increase ALCO's influence on the board's actions.

Cosgrave retorted that inasmuch as ALCO held far more stock in the airline than Parker Drilling, ALCO had every right to majority representation.

Cosgrave expected Kennedy to be elected by that narrow 8-7 margin, but the actual vote was 9-5 for Kennedy, with one abstention. It took the irrepressible Merle "Mudhole" Smith to swing the tide heavily in Kennedy's favor.

In the course of the debate, someone asked Mudhole why he was going to vote for Kennedy despite his youth and lack of airline experience. "Well," Mudhole drawled, "Kennedy went to school with my son Kenny, and Ken told me Bruce was a nice guy. That's good enough for me."

Thus ended the last challenge to Ron Cosgrave's leadership. He now had the solid mandate he needed to continue leading the airline out of the jungle of insolvency and disrepute. And the timing couldn't have been better for doing something about the airline's corporate facilities, which were not only inadequate, but also second-rate.

Alaska was the only airline of its size in the United States whose corporate offices were still in a hangar. The last major trunk carrier so housed was Capital Airlines, quartered on the second floor of a hangar at Washington National Airport until 1961, when that carrier merged with United. But at Capital, there were at least conventional offices and cubicles.

Cosgrave winced every time he walked into the hangar that housed the majority of what passed for corporate "offices." There was a total lack of privacy, with not even cubicles as buffer zones, and the noise level rivaled that of a city room at a metropolitan daily newspaper.

The hangar's exterior looked better than the interior. The section devoted to offices had an attractive facade with a lot of glass windows, and the location, just southwest of Sea-Tac's main terminal, was certainly convenient.

Presiding over its cluttered scene of interior poverty was the incongruously jarring sight of Willis's gaudy former office. One of Cosgrave's first acts after Willis departed was to tear down the sign "Charlie's Saloon" and then strip the room itself. Out came the swinging doors, the beer cooler, the rolltop desk, the brothel-styled drapes, and everything else except whatever conventional furniture could be salvaged when the room was refurnished in more conventional decor.

Cosgrave considered Alaska's hangar-headquarters totally inefficient, despite its convenient close-to-the-action location. There was some sentiment among the directors that it would be preferable to lease better office space than to spend millions on a new building. But Cosgrave was not buying that idea. While he was still new to the airline business, he was not a rookie in the world of real estate. "We needed space," he emphasized, "and it made economic sense to own the property instead of leasing a building."

Mobile Towns of America, Inc., an ALCO affiliate, had purchased on speculation a site near Angle Lake, south of Sea-Tac International Airport, in the early 1970s. When it later appeared that the site would be an excellent location for a new Alaska Airlines headquarters, the land was acquired by the airline at its appraised value. Mobile Towns' acquisition price was about $250,000, and the sale price to Alaska Airlines was about $350,000.

Nearly a year passed before construction could begin. Most of the land where corporate headquarters now stands was heavily forested. There was a little 1940s-style motel and a small trailer court on the site. Getting rid of the motel was no problem, but getting rid of the trailer court was. The airline ran into a thicket of state laws dealing with the relocation of the trailer court residents. Alaska gave the residents a year's notice, which seemed reasonable, but not to most of them, who had lived in the trailer court for a number of years and didn't want to move at all. It took several months to work out acceptable deadlines for vacating.

While that hurdle was being cleared, the construction contractor was bringing the basic architectural design to life. As practical as it was beautiful, the design allowed for future expansion that would not interfere with the original concept.

One of the new building's greatest admirers was the man largely responsible for its later enlargement. Cliff Argue, who had graduated from Cornell University with a degree in civil engineering, joined Alaska in 1983, after construction of the first wing was completed. Later he would hold Bruce Kennedy's old job as vice president of properties and facilities, and he always praised Cosgrave's foresight in the early planning.

"In designing a corporate headquarters building or any company office facility," Argue said, "the key is to have a good space plan: how many people have to be accommodated and what we call 'adjacencies' — who needs to be next to whom in the building. The groups that work closely need to be next to each other to foster communication. You can design great-looking brick and mortar on the exterior, but getting the right layout inside is really critical."

One of the smartest things Cosgrave did was to promise all residents of the area not to remove any more trees than absolutely necessary, and he went a few steps beyond that. Knowing that a lot of homeowners in the neighborhood were concerned about the visual impact of a large corporate building in what was then a largely residential area adjacent to the waterfront neighborhood around Angle Lake, he circulated architectural drawings of the planned structure. When the first wing was finished, he invited everyone to inspect the new headquarters, served punch and cookies, and proved that Alaska Airlines could be a good and caring neighbor.

"It was very important that Cosgrave was a real estate man," Argue explained. "He had the background and the vision to know that we should always acquire enough land so we'd never get hemmed in when we needed to expand. Then, when we eventually outgrew the first wing, the company was smart enough to hire the same architects to design the second wing. The result is a seamless look to the entire complex."

Alaska's new headquarters was opened in 1976 at a cost of about $5 million. When the airline moved out of the hangar, its annual revenue was about $60 million. By the time the west wing was added to the complex in 1989, Alaska Airlines' revenues had increased to nearly $800 million.

Erasing the "Elastic Airlines" stigma wasn't accomplished with mirrors or the power of prayer. The airline's resurrection was based on a plan devised by Gus Robinson and Ben Benecke. The latter may have been dragging his heels a bit during the Continental sessions, but not when Cosgrave issued what amounted to an "improve or else" order.

"Gus and Ben led the charge," Cosgrave declared. "They tackled on-time performance as a key initiative to right the airline. They started with our infamous 'noon balloon' from Seattle to Fairbanks, a single daily flight that had a terrible on-time record. They investigated and dissected the reasons for every delay, day in and day out. Actually, they studied all of our routes. They created a system for identifying flight-delay problems and fixing them, appropriately dubbed Operation Bootstrap.

"No one excuse dominated, just a number of supposedly small problems that should have been easy to correct — like a small light bulb that needed replacement or some other little gadget that had malfunctioned, the sort of thing the airline had grown to accept while flying old equipment, when a new fleet was still only a dream."

Preston Blatter briefly served as the company's president while Alaska Airlines sorted itself out, and he retired in 1973. He knew that the presidency was an interim position for him. He had been named mostly to show the Civil Aeronautics Board, for which he had once worked, that the airline finally had responsible leadership.

Ben Benecke took over as president. He was a quiet achiever who a year later paid a heavy personal price. He suffered a massive heart attack, but true to his character, Benecke returned to the job within weeks and continued to serve as president until 1976. By then the airline had attained one of Cosgrave's first objectives: the "Elastic Airlines" stigma had been replaced with an enviable record for on-time service.

Those who worked for Benecke had fond memories of this rather prim but pleasant-faced man who looked like everyone's good-hearted favorite grandfather. He had a nice, rather shy smile that endeared him to everyone, yet in many ways he may have been the airline's most underrated president. In his own quiet way, he got things done.

"Ben was a typical but likeable bean-counter," Jim Johnson recalled. "His forte was writing business letters, and his responses to complaint letters from passengers were classics. I think he would have stayed active at the airline a lot longer if he hadn't developed a heart condition."

Because the heart condition eventually sidelined him, Benecke served as Alaska's president for only three years. He remained on the board until 1990, when he finally retired after a 49-year career in the airline industry. He died four years later at age 75, a highly respected icon at Alaska Airlines who also contributed much to the rich aviation traditions of the state itself.

As on-time performance improved, so did morale, to the point where the marketing department felt it appropriate to do a little bragging. Alaska's advertising had included the slogan "Nobody knows Alaska like Alaska knows Alaska," and it later was changed to "LATE is a four-letter word" to reflect its improved on-time record.

Eventually the airline felt confident enough to challenge Western Airlines' boast of being "The On-Time Airline to Alaska." It took a little while, but the first time the CAB's monthly on-time statistics came out listing Alaska's performance as better than Western's, up went new billboards proclaiming a new champion.

"It was a big deal and it was successful, which made bettering Western that much more satisfying," remembered Cosgrave. "We had finally understood what contributed to what had been our deplorable on-time results. We analyzed the delays to every flight on our schedule, and fortunately, we didn't have many flights in those days. Eventually, competition developed among the station managers and nobody shrugged off delays anymore; they fretted over them instead."

Benecke was succeeded by another bean-counter in the presidency, Ross Anderson, who had joined the airline a year after the coup as vice president of finance. He had been an executive with a Pacific Northwest telephone company, and he was uncharacteristically hired by Cosgrave from the outside to shore up Alaska's financial management. Anderson was creative, but mercurial and demanding.

He was credited with developing Alaska's Community Advisory Boards, which began on a modest scale in Southeast Alaska, then spread to Anchorage, Fairbanks, and other communities that the airline was serving in the state. The boards critiqued the airline's service and provided helpful feedback. Whether Anderson was the first to come up with the idea is uncertain; some sources credit Susan Bramstedt's father and his Alaskan radio station network with originating the basic concept. Yet no matter who deserves the credit, much of their success can be attributed to Jim Johnson and later Bill MacKay, who worked closely with the boards after they were shifted from the airline's marketing department to public affairs.

Anderson himself served as president only a little over a year before he lost a battle with Cosgrave over policy differences that the latter thought could compromise the character of Alaska Airlines. His departure led Cosgrave to appoint Bruce Kennedy as president in February 1978. This is getting a bit ahead of our story, however, for it was during the 1970s that the airline's most interesting and controversial corporate face began adorning the tails of its aircraft.

Perhaps the longest debate within Alaska Airlines was about what appeared at first to be airplane cosmetics but through the years would become far more significant than anyone thought at the time. It began in 1970, when Willis and Giersdorf were experimenting with four different logos to replace the airline's aging Golden Nugget insignia.

From all the available evidence, it appears that neither Giersdorf nor Willis actually conceived any of the logos that were considered. Giersdorf had turned to Bert Nordby, who was an account executive with the now defunct ad agency that created what Nordby called "The Four Culture" concept.

Four aspects of Alaskan history were depicted: Russian Alaska (church spires outlined in purple), the culture of Southeast Alaska (totem pole in green), Gold Rush Alaska (a red drawing of a sourdough miner with a pick), and the face of a typical Alaskan Eskimo (outlined in green and peeking out from under a blue parka). With each logo went different fuselage livery — white with stripes matching the colors of the tail logo. On a few airplanes, even the seat upholstery matched the color scheme of the fuselage and logo.

But they were never actually tried out on the entire fleet until about a year after Willis was ousted. After an outside marketing consultant pointed out the possible confusion of using four logos with only six jets, Cosgrave decided to use only one, and the company settled on the eye-catching fourth logo: the rugged, weather-beaten visage of an Eskimo wearing a traditional parka. Overall, it symbolized the airline's heritage and represented the state's tradition of hospitality better than the other three logos combined.

Years later there remained an unresolved question surrounding all four logos and the Eskimo face in particular. Namely, who first thought them up and when were they introduced? In my research, a long list of names claim to have created the Eskimo.

Ron Cosgrave himself gave the credit to Willis and Giersdorf. "They were the ones who conceived the idea of using the Eskimo on the tail, along with the other three experimental logos," he insisted. "But the Eskimo face wasn't chosen as our exclusive logo until several years later."

Bruce Kennedy agreed with that recollection, as did Jim Johnson, who remembered Bob Giersdorf showing him sketches of the four logos with their individual color schemes in the very early 1970s.

Yet other veterans don't recall seeing the logos until long after the coup. In Archie Satterfield's history of Alaska Airlines, which covered all the years of the Willis regime, there is no mention of either Willis or Giersdorf conceiving the face of an Eskimo as a tail logo, nor for that matter the other three proposed logos.

Contemporary newspaper feature stories on the famous face, which shares with American Airlines' eagle the reputation of being among the most easily recognizable airline logos in the world, merely reported that the Eskimo first appeared in the early or mid 1970s, without pinpointing a specific year.

The first appearance of the Eskimo logo was not without heated speculation and even controversy. No one knew for sure whether the face was an enlargement of an artist's original drawing or an enlarged photographic reproduction of a real person. Once freshly painted 727s began flying all over the state, there were loud claims of supposed recognition such as "That face is definitely my Uncle Louis."

The dispute over whether the Eskimo was a painting or a photograph was a question not of aesthetic merit but of legality. There were claims that the airline had used the face of some real-life person without permission. Friends and relatives of a gentleman from northwest Alaska, Chester Sevak, insisted that he was the Eskimo on the tail. Cosgrave acknowledged that Sevak "really did look like our Eskimo, although both Willis and Giersdorf firmly denied using him as a model."

Not so, according to veteran travel writer Stan Patty, who gave sole credit to Giersdorf for all four tail logos but said Chester actually was "the original prototype for the face, although the final version was a conglomeration of several faces."

Sevak's casting as a logical "suspect" was only too natural because he and his wife loved to maintain the tradition of Eskimo dances, helped promote the airline, and occasionally came down to Seattle and had dinner with the Giersdorfs and Pattys. And Cosgrave admitted that Sevak's name was the most frequently mentioned when all the speculation on the face's origin began.

"We got a number of letters from various Eskimo families insisting the face was that of their relative," Cosgrave reported. "On the other hand, some people thought we had used the faces of celebrities. Johnny Cash was the first guess that came after a demo flight in Montana during the airline's push for the Northern Tier route between Seattle and Minneapolis/St. Paul." Others mentioned were Jimi Hendrix and Soviet president Leonid Brezhnev.

The initial face was serious and rather dour, but it was altered to support Alaska's "Fly with a happy face" marketing campaign. The Eskimo image was changed to a darker shade of blue, and a gentle smile was added to the facial expression. The Eskimo would become a permanent fixture and remain unchanged until Alaska began expanding its routes into Southern California, when the airline's new ad agency, Chiat/Day, suggested that the Eskimo temporarily don Mylar-decaled sunglasses.

Admittedly, at first these symbols *were* merely a cosmetic improvement, yet they also represented an airline recommitting itself to be *Alaska's* airline, a carrier that the state and its people could be proud of. That was Willis's goal, too, but he had tried to achieve it with flashy promotional gimmicks while letting service deteriorate. Under the new regime there was a competitive spirit based on improving service, and it helped that two of the airline's biggest rivals — Pan Am and Western — were both suffering from a stagnating disease known as overconfidence bordering on arrogance.

Pan Am was the worst because it also was guilty of incredible inefficiency. Jeff Cacy, who started working for Alaska Airlines in 1975 as its campus representative at the University of Alaska in Fairbanks and later rose to become one of the airline's managing directors in the marketing department, saw how Pan Am operated in Alaska during the 1970s.

"I had been promoted from campus rep to ticket agent," he recounted, "and our ticket counter in Fairbanks was next to Pan Am's. They had only one flight a day, and for some time they were using a Boeing 707 on the route, a plane too large for the market's traffic. But then they put a 747 on the route, and that was ludicrous.

"They had 83 employees in Fairbanks for that one flight; we had 26 people handling five flights. Pan Am's flight arrived in Fairbanks at 11:30 a.m. and didn't go back to Seattle until the next morning. So they had all these people sitting around the airport waiting for that one flight.

"They kept their ticket counter open 24 hours a day, but their agents weren't allowed to make phone reservations because Pan Am also had a downtown ticket office plus a call center in Fairbanks for handling phone reservations."

Pan Am eventually put its Fairbanks-Seattle route on the market with a fire-sale price tag of $1 million. Western was interested but backed off because it thought the price was still too high. In fact, Western never developed into the competitor it could have been, certainly not in comparison to Pacific Northern under the belligerent Art Woodley.

Cacy thought that Western, like Pan Am, was too complacent for its own good. "In 1972, after Willis left, we still were the little guy in the state," he said. "Western had everything going for it. They were serving a lot of Alaskan towns they had inherited from the PNA merger. They had three or four daily nonstops to Seattle, they had ordered a bunch of new DC-10s [a three-engine jumbo jetliner], they had an in-flight service product that people liked, and they had a long tradition that dated back to 1926."

At the time, Western was the oldest carrier in the United States still operating independently under its original name. It has long since been swallowed up by Delta Airlines and almost forgotten.

"In '72," continued Cacy, "we were Podunk playing Florida Gators, but we were scrappy while Western got arrogant. We were building an airline, it was going to be run well, and we went after the business."

"We went after the business." Flash-forward a few years to 1978, when Western was no longer a competitive factor in Alaska and, in fact, had furloughed many of its employees in the state. Two of them, one of whom was Western's former sales manager for the entire state of Alaska, opened a small travel agency in Anchorage. And Jeff Cacy, a brand-new, full-time, full-fledged Alaska Airlines sales representative, called on them to solicit their business. He walked in the door and introduced himself. "I'm Jeff Cacy from Alaska Airlines."

The two travel agents stared at him. "You gotta be kidding," one of them said. "Did you know we both came from Western Airlines?"

"Sure. I knew that when I walked in."

"So what the hell are you doing here?"

"Well, we've now got three flights a day to Seattle, and we'd like your business."

They laughed, and one of them said, "You really think you're gonna sell us on Alaska Airlines?"

"Yep. And for starters I brought you guys a bottle."

They shared a round of drinks, and the ex-Western men became good customers. One of them told Cacy later, "You know, Jeff, you guys came in here as soon as we opened and *asked* for our business. Do you know how long it took Western, our own airline, to do that? A very, very long time. They just assumed we'd give them our business because we were former employees."

Their company expanded into the largest travel agency in Anchorage. And, Cacy recalled with great satisfaction, "they even ended up telling us what new prospects we might see and tipping us off to possible new corporate accounts."

That one experience was a perfect example of how Alaska Airlines was changing its entire personality in the steady march toward respectability. Beating Western was vital. It was the one large carrier that could have offered real competition.

Northwest Orient Airlines served Alaska through Minneapolis/St. Paul and Detroit. For a time it expanded service with southern West Coast service through Seattle to Anchorage, and this pressured Alaska Airlines into entering into a code-sharing arrangement with Northwest. Only after the agreement was in place did Northwest drop its Midwest service to and from Anchorage. For a time, Anchorage remained an important hub for Northwest and served as a refueling stop for its Far East flights before the route was dropped from its schedule.

As Cosgrave and his team were turning Alaska around, the major roadblock to dominating Alaskan air travel appeared to be Wien Consolidated Airlines. Founder Noel Wien had long since retired, although his two sons, Merrill and Richard, had become Wien pilots. Richard, who left Wien in 1969 to become president of a helicopter and air taxi company, later was elected to the board of directors at Alaska Airlines.

Cosgrave put his concerns about Wien on the back burner, a battle yet to be fought. The continued recovery and improvement of the airline's image were his immediate priorities. But in 1974, while attending the Paris Air

Show, he ran into Ray Peterson, a former bush pilot who was Noel Wien's successor at Wien Consolidated. The chance encounter took place in a Paris restaurant.

"Ray brought up the subject of a merger," Cosgrave related, "and insisted the only problem was just a matter of who was going to be the stud duck, as Ray styled it, when the merger took place. But it would be another couple of years before we actually got serious about merging with Wien. That's when Peterson brought around a guy named Jim Flood, who had become Wien's chairman and CEO.

"By that time, the airline had gotten into a war with its pilots over their demand that Wien's new Boeing 737s had to be flown by a three-man crew. Wien refused at first, and its pilots went on strike. The airline finally gave in, started losing its shirt, and became a vulnerable target for acquisition. That was when we got into a bidding war with the other contestant, the well-heeled Household Finance Corporation [HFC]."

Cosgrave was referring to the "third man" issue, the airline industry's most controversial labor dispute during the 1970s. The Air Line Pilots Association (ALPA) was insisting that twin-engine jets, like the bigger three- and four-engine jet aircraft (DC-8s and Boeing 707s and 727s), could only be flown safely by three-person crews. This was in spite of the fact that every twin-engine turbine-powered transport, including the French Caravelle, British BAC-111, Douglas DC-9, and Boeing 737, had been designed for two pilots, not three. There wasn't even room for a third man unless he occupied a small jump seat behind the captain and first officer.

Technically true, ALPA responded, but it argued that all jets were unforgiving beasts, operating at unprecedented altitudes and speeds, and a third pilot provided an extra measure of safety such as looking out for conflicting high-speed traffic that presented potential collision hazards. The problem was that Delta's pilots, also ALPA members, had already bolted from the union's three-man-crew policy and agreed to fly Delta's DC-9s with two pilots. But United and Western caved in and agreed to use three pilots in their 737 cockpits.

FAA administrator Najeeb Halaby had gotten into the act by declaring that the 737 was perfectly safe with two pilots and that putting a third one into the cockpit, with virtually nothing to do except look out the window, was just union "featherbedding." When the controversy was at its height, Halaby used that expression at every opportunity. The media ate it up, and ALPA officials winced because some of them privately admitted that the third man really did nothing to enhance safety.

It is hard for any organization — union or company — to admit being wrong, but by the time Alaska began operating its own 737-200Cs, the three-pilot issue was moot. After the order with Boeing was announced, Alaska's ALPA unit pressed for a three-pilot cockpit configuration. Bruce Kennedy reiterated the airline's staunch position regarding what it viewed as feather-bedding, stating that the airline would not take delivery until the issue was resolved and would sell the planes unused if necessary.

"Isn't that cutting off your nose to spite your face?" a union official asked Kennedy.

"Maybe," Kennedy snapped, "but that's the way it will be."

Humor helped reduce the three-man dispute to a non-issue because it's almost impossible to defend a policy that everyone else is laughing at. Western had been calling the third man a "Gib," for Guy in Back, until some pilot happened to run across the word *gib* in a dictionary and discovered that it was a castrated tomcat.

Then came an incident after Alaska's pilots had agreed to operate the 737 as a two-man airplane. Two Wien pilots began picketing in front of Alaska's hangar, whereupon a maintenance supervisor asked them in a tone of innocent curiosity, "Say, guys, how come it takes three of you to fly a 737 and only two to picket?" The pickets disappeared a few minutes later.

No Alaska-Wien merger was ever to take place, but the story must be told in proper chronological order. That very brief preliminary merger dis-cussion that Cosgrave had with Ray Peterson in 1974 paled in comparison to another event of that same year. It was not only a landmark in the history of the 49th state, but also a significant development for the airline bearing the state's name.

This was the start of construction of the trans-Alaska pipeline.

CHAPTER NINE

The Pipeline, the Playmate, and Prudhoe Bay

Obviously, improved passenger service was a key factor in the airline's recovery in the post-Willis era. Yet looking back at that period, it is also clear that winning a logistical-support contract for the pipeline was a tremendously important proposal, one that would buttress the turnaround. There are veterans of that era who are convinced that rejuvenation of the long-dormant project was vital to Alaska Airlines, making recovery certain.

After the 1968 discovery of vast oil deposits in Prudhoe Bay on the North Slope, everything skidded to a halt while the entire state waited for the congressional traffic light to turn green. It took almost seven years for supporters of the pipeline project to fight their way through legislative delays, red tape, and legal wrangling.

The first breakthrough came in 1971, when Congress passed the Alaska Native Claims Settlement Act. That important legislation authorized that 44 million acres of land plus nearly $1 billion be provided to Alaska Natives in exchange mostly for relinquishment of aboriginal rights to land crossing the pipeline corridor. Two years later came congressional passage, by a paper-thin margin, of the Trans-Alaska Pipeline Authorization Act. It took Vice

President Spiro Agnew's vote to break a 49-49 tie in the Senate, and President Nixon signed the bill into law.

That narrow victory put the Alyeska Pipeline Service Company in business. This was the firm that designed, built, and would operate the pipeline. But before construction could begin, the company would have to obtain 515 federal and 832 state permits, and regulators buzzed around the state like clouds of mosquitoes. Construction of Alyeska's 800-mile metal artery stretching from Prudhoe Bay to the seaport of Valdez would be an engineering feat that invited comparison to the building of the Panama Canal, and at $8 billion it was the most expensive private project in the history of the world. And today about three quarters of a million barrels of crude oil a day still flow through the trans-Alaska pipeline on its way to Lower 48 refineries.

Once President Nixon had signed the authorization bill in 1973, the Alyeska Pipeline Service Company wasted no time before issuing invitations for bids to provide airlift logistical support. The winner was Alaska Airlines.

Incredibly, there was no real competition from much larger and stronger carriers. Alaska won the contract for two reasons: First, no other airline submitted anything to match its formal, highly detailed bid. Second, even before Alaska bid on the contract, a special task force from its operations department had completed a thorough study of specific airlift needs for the massive and remote construction project.

Pat Glenn participated in that study group. So did pilot representative Captain Don Fox; the versatile Ron Suttell, who had experience in cargo, maintenance, and facilities; and others from various departments. Glenn always believed it was this voluminous study that really tipped the scales in Alaska's favor.

"A California consulting firm had put such a study up for bid on behalf of Alyeska," he recalled, "and I think we won it because we knew the state so well, plus the fact that we already had operated an airlift to the North Slope in the initial stages of Prudhoe's oil exploration and development.

"We worked up our analysis at a hotel across the street from Sea-Tac. Our final report emerged in three thick volumes of data. We looked at everything: what airports could be used; what type of aircraft would best provide logistical support; how much aircraft capacity would be needed and for how long; what long-range weather patterns could be expected; what kind of terrain would likely be encountered; and how many gallons of fuel oil would be needed during the winter months at the camps constructed to house the pipeline workers. We had every base covered."

What determined the type of aircraft Alaska Airlines would use was dictated almost entirely by an interchange agreement signed with Braniff International in 1974. Unlike the earlier Prudhoe Bay airlift, primarily a job of moving heavy drilling equipment, the new airlift task involved a mass movement of passengers. Building the pipeline would eventually require some 28,000 workers, the vast majority of them from the oil-producing states of Texas and Oklahoma, "pointy toes," as the locals called them.

They would have to be flown back and forth between these southwestern states — which Alaska Airlines didn't serve — and Fairbanks/Anchorage, which Braniff didn't serve. So under the interchange agreement, Braniff would carry the workers from cities such as Houston and Tulsa to Seattle, where Alaska crews would take over and complete the trip to Fairbanks and Anchorage.

The two-carrier airlift was dubbed "The Pipeline Express." The airlines would alternate in providing the flight equipment, which of course had to be the same type of jet. Braniff was assigning its Boeing 727-200s to the interchange, while Alaska would fly 727-100s.

Alaska needed more planes. Used-aircraft prices being quoted by Boeing to its very small customer were too high, and even with a certain amount of hometown patriotism, Alaska could not afford Boeing's second-hand planes.

Acquiring used airplanes that didn't have to be completely rebuilt and were reasonably priced was one of Gus Robinson's specialties. But it was not easy to find readily available 727-200s, rated throughout the aviation community as one of the best transports Boeing ever built. Powered with three engines mounted aft, the 100s and 200s were affectionately known as "three-holers."

Robinson was a skilled tire-kicker and he didn't care how badly Alaska needed the equipment. If it wasn't in reasonably good condition, he either went elsewhere or insisted that the seller correct every flaw and fault.

Ken Skidds accompanied Robinson on a buying expedition to Miami, where Eastern was readying some 727-100s for delivery to Alaska. "Gus insisted on overseeing the overhauls before he'd accept delivery," Skidds recalled. "Boy, he put those Eastern guys through a wringer. He caught them charging us for things they hadn't done and not doing things they were supposed to have done."

Yet despite all his precautions, those former Eastern 727s were aging faster than Robinson or anyone else expected, probably because of Florida's high humidity and proximity to salt air, which invited metal corrosion. One airplane in particular had been giving Alaska one problem after another. It wasn't due for a D-check (the stiffest major overhaul, which took several weeks to complete) for at least another 18 months. But Robinson ordered one immediately, and D-checks cost upwards of a million dollars.

"Gus Robinson," Skidds emphasized, "could wink at some minor maintenance infraction, but never at anything that might jeopardize safety." This was in about 1975, when Alaska began upgrading its fleet, acquiring five 727-100s, a step viewed as a great advance toward fleet standardization and modernization.

The first 727-100s had proved so popular and efficient that Ron Cosgrave decided it was an opportune time to dump the three fuel-guzzling former PNA 720s purchased from Western. So they were swapped for Pan Am's well-maintained 727-100s along with a little cash. Pan Am had been operating three-holers within Europe to provide connecting service with its international flights.

"It was a great deal," Cosgrave recalled. "The trade-in allowance Pan Am gave us on those 720s was more than we paid Western for them in the first place."

Preceding the Pipeline Express inaugural was a big promotional party hosted by Braniff at the Houston Yacht Club. Jim Johnson arranged for a husband-and-wife team of Eskimo dancers from the Ahmaogak family to provide the airline's share of the entertainment. But when he saw the entertainers that Braniff had flown in, his heart sank. Braniff's contribution was a group of attractive Hawaiian hula dancers wearing grass skirts and little else except bright smiles.

"I figured we were going to be upstaged big-time," Johnson said. "But the opposite happened. Our two Alaskans stole the show, and not just with their dances. They also talked about their long history, their life in Alaska, and their Eskimo culture. And they had brought along some artifacts that really displayed their handicraft skills."

Alaska Airlines threw its own inaugural reception at the other end of the Pipeline Express, a huge barbecue at the Anchorage home of Bob Atwood, then publisher of the *Anchorage Times*. Many of Alaska's civic, political, and business luminaries attended the event.

Braniff's role as an interchange partner lasted through much of the pipeline years, although during the later stages of construction, new interchange alliances were formed — first with American and then briefly with Continental. They sparked other promotional activities. Such events provided fun and fellowship, but the bottom line of the Pipeline Express and the entire trans-Alaska pipeline project was its significance to Alaska Airlines. Beyond the obvious financial rewards, it brought a realization by the state, its people, and the airline industry that this battered, often-maligned, and frequently inept carrier had changed.

Even in the glory years of the Willis era, with all the glitzy, publicity-generating gimmicks, it had been an airline with a lot of style but very little substance. But in the few years immediately preceding the pipeline project and during its actual construction, Alaska Airlines completely changed its image. It acquired its own special, unique brand of professionalism.

Professionalism. It's a word that can have several shades of meaning. At Alaska, it came to mean combining smooth efficiency with human under-standing. It meant striving for technical superiority without losing the human touch. It meant learning to change and accepting change without ever forget-ting there are some things that should never change.

Perhaps the best observer of what Alaska Airlines was like during those critical transformation years was an airline cockpit crew member who took part in the Pipeline Express, flying not for Alaska but for Braniff. His name was John Nance. In years to come, he was to earn fame and prestige, first as a best-selling airline pilot/author in the tradition of Air France's Antoine de Saint-Exupéry, American's Ernest Gann, and British Airways' David Beaty, and then later as a respected aviation commentator for the ABC-TV network. In that latter role he never sensationalized, never second-guessed, and never offered premature conclusions based on speculation and rumor. In other words, he was a straight-shooting rarity among the many "talking heads" billed as aviation experts.

When the interchange flights began in 1974, Nance was a 727-200 flight engineer who tended to look down his nose at Alaska's much older flight equipment. The instrumentation was different, and the airplanes were shabby looking in comparison to Braniff's much newer 727s. Nance, like virtually every other Braniff airman, thought the quality of Alaska's crews matched that of their airplanes.

By the time the Braniff-Alaska interchange ended, however, Nance's perception of Alaska Airlines had done a one-eighty. "I began seeing changes in their old three-holers," Nance remembered. "I had left the interchange in

1977 to bid DC-8 and 747 trips, but when I came back to the interchange a year later, the differences from what I had seen in '77 were astounding."

In the spring of 1982, Nance decided to fly for Alaska. Braniff by then had folded, a classic example of an airline that overexpanded when the airline industry was deregulated in 1978. "I figured my airline career was over," Nance said, "but I had some friends from Alaska Airlines in an Air Force Reserve transportation squadron based at McChord Air Force Base in Washington that I had been flying with, and they urged me to apply to Alaska."

By this time, Bruce Kennedy had taken over as chairman and CEO. Nance summed up the new Alaska Airlines through the eyes of an airman who found himself suddenly exposed to an environment he hadn't known at Braniff.

"I was momentarily concerned that Alaska might be even worse than Braniff, where cockpit discipline and standardized procedures were often ignored," Nance recalled. "At Braniff the captain was God. I knew four-stripers who refused to read a checklist; they let the copilot or flight engineer perform that duty.

"We had some real cowboys at Braniff, like one captain who was only 40, looked 75, and was a terrible alcoholic. He came out of an overcast one day and found himself at a 35-degree angle to the runway and only 200 feet off the ground. If the copilot hadn't taken over, they would have crashed. People had been covering up for that guy for years.

"But after I was accepted at Alaska and went through their training course, I was really impressed. This wasn't Braniff at all. This was a professional, highly polished operation with great emphasis on safety and disciplined procedures. At Alaska, no one would tolerate a captain not reading a checklist. That kind of discipline really sets the tone. I began to realize that these people had their act together as far as safety was concerned."

Nance's view of the pipeline operation was brief and rather limited, yet it was significant because by coming in just at the start and then not returning until after its finish, he could better appreciate what the people of Alaska Airlines had accomplished, officers and employees alike.

From a historical standpoint, the pipeline years were among the most colorful in the airline's existence, in some ways almost a reincarnation of the 49th state's rowdy Gold Rush days.

Fairbanks was affected by the pipeline project more than any other city in Alaska. Because it was the closest major city to Prudhoe Bay, it served as the main staging area for the massive movement of manpower and materials to the North Slope. The Fairbanks airport rivaled Anchorage as the busiest in the state, and at one point, there were more people working at Prudhoe and along the pipeline than there were in Juneau, Alaska's third-largest city.

Pipeline construction was demanding. Most people employed on the line worked nine straight weeks before getting a two-week break. When hundreds of workers rotated back to Texas and Oklahoma for a few weeks' vacation time, the same number of replacements would be flown in. It seemed as if every Alaska Airlines flight between Seattle and the Fairbanks/Anchorage airports was full during the years of the pipeline project.

Not all the passengers, however, were pipeline workers, Alaskans, and tourists. As opportunity swelled the city, Fairbanks' prostitute population expanded, though the actual numbers must be left to social science studies. Tom Dezutter, who became station manager in Fairbanks during the pipeline days, witnessed as many as 15 or 20 prostitutes arriving on some flights from Seattle.

"The town was hookers' heaven," he observed wryly. "Most of them came in on a red-eye we were operating from Seattle."

Fairbanks hotels were so crowded that some rented out rooms in three daily shifts. A guest would get a room from 8 a.m. to 4 p.m., then would have to leave so the next guest could use it from 5 p.m. to 1 a.m., followed by the third shift, which ran from 2 a.m. to 7 a.m.

Many of the southbound workers would arrive in Fairbanks on a Wien flight that landed about four hours before the next interchange trip left for Seattle. They'd check their luggage at the Alaska Airlines ticket counter, then head either for the airport bar or into town — and the latter choice often led to trouble.

"If they went into town or even just to the airport bar," Jeff Cacy said, "we might not see them for another two days. One guy showed up, and after I checked his bag I didn't see him until the next day. He had been picked up by a hooker who got him drunk and took all his money. On top of everything else, he had lost his ticket.

"He told me his wife would pay for another ticket and gave me her phone number in some town in Louisiana. He got on the phone and gave her some cock-and-bull story about having his pocket picked. So we arranged a prepaid ticket for him and sent him on his way."

Many pipeline workers came to Alaska with their own tools, and when they went home on rotation they'd take the tools with them. With a hundred or so of them checking in for each interchange flight, weighing luggage was almost impossible. Cacy solved that by becoming his own scales, literally.

He was then a pretty husky 21-year-old, so when a worker plunked down one of those heavy toolboxes, Cacy would say, "If I can lift it, there's no overweight charge." He never tried to cheat in these improvised weighing procedures, nor were his decisions ever challenged.

"Fairbanks before the pipeline was built," Cacy recalled nostalgically, "used to be a kind of colorful yet quiet Western town. And then came this huge influx of transients who weren't from Alaska. It wasn't that they were all that tough and unruly, but all of their camps were dry, and in a predominantly male environment to boot.

"So when the guys had worked for weeks living like an army of Trappist monks, they'd come into Fairbanks, booze it up, and get pretty wild. It was impossible to find apartments, and hotel rooms were at a premium. It was a typical supply-and-demand problem: all demand and no supply. Yes, it was the atmosphere of the Gold Rush days."

Intoxicated passengers were a nightmare for every agent. The FAA had instituted a rule forbidding airlines to board anyone who was "obviously drunk," a determination that often was in the eye of the beholder and could be a difficult judgment call. This made it especially challenging for agents handling the interchange flights out of Fairbanks because the intoxicated homeward-bound pipeline workers often outnumbered the sober ones by a sizable margin.

One of Dezutter's rookie counter agents was a newcomer named Ed White, a native of Glacier Bay, Alaska, whose burly six-foot-four-inch frame was so intimidating that he admitted later he probably was hired more as a bouncer than a ticket agent. His daunting physique, however, was misleading. Like many other big men, White was mild-mannered, gentle, and extremely sensitive to the feelings of others, a quality that was to serve him and the airline well years later in one of its worst crisis periods. But during the rowdy pipeline days, when the counters were staffed mostly by women, White's presence had a calming effect on even the most belligerent customers, including pipeline workers.

If female agents ran into a drunk they couldn't handle, White would talk to the inebriate as politely as possible and tell him if he didn't behave, he wouldn't be allowed to board his flight. The diplomacy along with the no-boarding threat usually worked, but one night there was a male customer who was a mean drunk spoiling for a fight. He approached the counter with a glass of whiskey in his hand, and when White told him to behave himself if he wanted to board his flight, the passenger smashed the glass on the counter and waved a jagged shard in White's face. If the counter had not been in the way, White might have been badly cut. He was still trying to calm down the berserk drunk when airport security arrived, handcuffed him, and hauled him off to jail.

When metal detectors were introduced at the Fairbanks airport in the mid-1970s, it sometimes was possible to make that difficult board-or-don't-board decision according to how a passenger behaved while going through the detector screening.

Carrying guns aboard the airplanes presented another problem. Guns were routine during the early bush days, when hunters were frequent passengers. But during the pipeline days, airport-security rules had stiffened. A lot of the workers loved to go hunting on their off-days and wanted to take their rifles home with them, so the airline installed special gun racks in the front of the airplanes that were locked up on takeoff.

One unexpected downside to the pipeline boom, as far as the airline was concerned, was the lure of the higher-paying jobs being offered by Alyeska and its contractors. The project needed lots of construction workers, but it also required a small army of office personnel to handle the mountain of paperwork. Payrolls, requisitions, records, status reports, and general correspondence were generated in such volume that if paper were asphalt, there would have been enough to pave the 360-mile Haul Road.

The increased demand for office help had a severe impact on Alaska Airlines, especially in such a strategic location as Fairbanks. "A lot of our people who lived in Fairbanks and worked for us in cargo, on the ramp, or on the ticket counters went to work for the pipeline," Tom Dezutter recounted. "We were hiring replacements as soon as our employees walked out the door. The first year I was there, we had a 300 percent turnover rate."

All of the drawbacks and difficulties of the pipeline, however, were dwarfed by the economic bonanza it brought to the recovering but still struggling airline. Alaska's entire fleet consisted of 727-100 passenger and combi models, and until the summer of 1977 and the end of pipeline construction, they flew most of the time with unprecedented 100 percent load factors. And the revenues were almost entirely in pure cash.

Jeff Cacy remembered that it was not unusual to have more than $20,000 in cash in the Fairbanks ticket-counter drawer at the end of the day. And this was a company that was "bankrupt and didn't know it," as one veteran officer put it, only two years before the pipeline contract was awarded.

Easily the most colorful and best-remembered event of the later pipeline years came after construction had been completed and oil had started flowing through the pipeline. It had nothing to do with construction, airplanes, oil, revenues, load factors, roads, or boarding problems with passengers feeling no pain. It had a lot to do with what was becoming one of the airline's proudest traditions: the knack of promoting goodwill. This event was the wingding that Alaska Airlines threw to show its appreciation to the permanent oil-field workers confined to their camps on the North Slope, a camp on each side of Prudhoe Bay, one operated by BP-Sohio and the other by ARCO.

The party was held a short time after Bruce Kennedy had succeeded Ron Cosgrave. There was momentary concern among the handful of party planners that the deeply devout new chairman of the board and CEO might take a dim view of two events on the proposed agenda. The first involved the importation of beer into the no-alcohol environment of the North Slope. Of equal concern was their new boss's possible negative reaction to the event's potential star attraction: one of *Playboy* magazine publisher Hugh Hefner's Playmates of the Month.

Much of the advance planning for the event was in the hands of a relative newcomer who had joined the airline's public affairs staff in 1977. Dave Marriott, a young Washington native, was hired at Alaska after a brief stint in radio and television news. Marriott, born to be a PR man, was gregarious, personable, and resourceful. He also possessed absolutely essential traits for working in airline public relations — a thick skin and a sense of humor.

All of Marriott's experiences prior to the challenges of planning the Prudhoe Bay blast seemed inadequate for what loomed as a daunting assignment. Marriott began by addressing the protocol of getting about 400 cases of Lone Star beer, a favorite brew in Texas, into the bone-dry jurisdiction of Prudhoe Bay without having to smuggle them. He talked to Dave Bean, a public relations consultant in Anchorage, who was helpful though not very hopeful.

"First, you have to get approval from the state liquor board," Bean informed him. "Then you need permission from both camp directors — a guy from ARCO runs one camp, and a guy from Sohio is in charge of the other camp."

The three green lights for importing the beer were obtained without too much hassle, and Marriott then turned to a pair of security problems: (1) preventing a beer stampede resembling an enraged buffalo herd and

(2) protecting the pulchritudinous *Playboy* import. The planners already had arranged to hire a few security guards, but they knew this small force would be inadequate.

The most obvious course, Marriott reasoned, would be to hire the entire First Marine Division. Instead, he settled for a couple of former pro football players from the Oakland Raiders who would have scared the skin off a 600-pound gorilla. One was defensive tackle Tom Keating, six feet four inches and 250 pounds. The second was even bigger: defensive end Big Ben Davidson, who was a fearsome six feet eight inches and weighed 270 pounds.

Of course, not even this pair of giants could have held off a horde of several thousand thirsty oil workers heading for 400 cases of Lone Star beer. So Marriott and his cohorts devised a reasonably practical distribution plan. First, they planned to hold the beer party in the big Alaska Airlines cargo hangar at Prudhoe Bay. That provided plenty of enclosed space and protection from the cold.

"Then there were several things we did besides the Lone Star, and we combined them with distributing the beer," Marriott explained. "We brought along hundreds and hundreds of baseball hats with 'Alaska Airlines – Prudhoe Bay' printed on the crown. We decided we'd give a hat to every man who showed up for the beer. With each hat came two tickets, each good for a bottle of beer, and that put a lid on anyone guzzling too much brew. Alaska Airlines' staff was adorned with Texas-style cowboy hats that were so prized that by the end of the day those, too, had been given away. Still, if someone got out of control, we were prepared with the security cops and the two monsters from the Raiders to keep order. We also invited one camp to attend the first night, and the other for the second night.

"One of our objectives wasn't really altruistic. We wanted to get as much information as we could about the workers up there, each of them a potential customer. The camp directors wouldn't give us their individual mailing addresses at the camps themselves, and that's when someone — I think it was Dave Bean — came up with the idea of getting some girl from *Playboy* up to the North Slope.

"The idea was to have a photographer at the beer party for anyone who wanted his picture taken standing next to a gorgeous Playmate. We knew he wouldn't want that snapshot mailed to his home address where a wife or his kids might see it, but they gladly gave us their camp addresses. The result was a hell of a mailing list, one that Wien, our competitor at Prudhoe Bay, didn't have."

All this planning took about three months, and Marriott thought everything was in place until he was summoned to Bruce Kennedy's office. Present were Kennedy, Bob Gray, Gus Robinson, and Jim Johnson, the latter Marriott's boss. "They looked like a hanging committee from the Spanish Inquisition," he recalled morosely.

Kennedy got to the point quickly. "Are you planning to serve beer on the North Slope?" he asked sternly.

"Yes, sir."

"Don't you know that's illegal?"

Marriott was so stunned and angry that he couldn't even reply. He wanted to tell them he was young, not stupid, but anger smothered his vocal cords. He had kept Jim Johnson informed of how he was obtaining permission to serve beer, or thought he had. Apparently there had been a breakdown in communication, what with Johnson traveling so much, and no one in the room knew that all the proper arrangements had been made legally.

Still so furious he couldn't talk, Marriott got up to leave when Gus Robinson put one muscular hand on his shoulder. "Sit down, son," Robinson said with menacing softness.

Marriott sat down, and found his voice. "Do you guys think I'd ever put this airline into that kind of position?" he demanded. "I can furnish you with signed copies of letters from the state liquor board and the directors of both North Slope camps authorizing us to serve beer at our party."

Kennedy offered his apologies, and Marriott was off the hook. The *Playboy* organization agreed to send a Playmate to the North Slope, provided she was properly escorted. And that was how Kelly Ann Tough, Miss October of 1981, became part of the airline's lore.

Public Affairs discreetly assigned a female escort to Miss Tough, namely the competent Jill Childs, a member of Jim Johnson's staff. Actually, Kelly probably didn't need an escort. "Boy," Dave Marriott recalled, "she was as tough as her name."

When Miss October deplaned at Prudhoe Bay and was escorted into the cargo hangar, the epidemic of popping eyeballs must have registered on every seismograph in Alaska. A jittery Bob Handley met the flight and sighed later: "She was wearing a knit dress about the thickness of onion skin, and it clung to her like Saran Wrap. Every guy in the ramp and hangar area was drooling like a toothless infant."

Miss Tough had a problem, and it was Handley who rushed gallantly to the rescue. Well, at least Handley considered himself gallant; everyone else thought he was a scene-stealing s.o.b. trying to hog Miss October's arrival spotlight.

Such opinions were not only unfair but obviously stemmed from petulant envy and despicable jealousy. It seems there was a tremendous amount of static electricity in the cold, dry Arctic air, and Tough's dress was picking it up, much to her obvious discomfort. Sir Robert sprang to the rescue.

He had a can of anti-static spray in his office, and managed to race there without tripping over his tongue. He returned to apply the spray to the knit dress and her nylon stockings as well, receiving in return a look of gratitude that would have melted through the armor plate on the hull of the battleship *Missouri*.

Let us cut quickly to the opening night of the party. Alaska had flown in a country-western band for the entertainment. Miss October was a huge success and so was the beer. Even Bruce Kennedy joined the party. Everyone was having such a good time that nobody wanted to leave, and there were more workers clamoring to get in.

Ken Skidds, then superintendent of stations, who had flown in for the event, solved this crisis by opening the hangar doors. It was December, about 60 below outside, and when that cold air swept into the hangar, the earlier arrivals fled back to their camp and a new group was admitted.

By every standard, the Prudhoe Bay beer bash was a huge success. Ninety percent of the workers in the two camps had attended, and Kelly Tough's posing for pictures was a marketing gold mine. By offering to mail the photographs to the camps, the airline got the mailing list it wanted. It was spending $3.7 million to improve facilities at the Deadhorse Airport and intended to end Wien's domination at Prudhoe Bay.

Those two nights in Prudhoe Bay were the most eventful of Marriott's five years at Alaska Airlines, but his most vivid recollection was not of Miss October or the beer and the country music, or of being unfairly accused of planning to serve beer illegally. No, none of the above. What was most memorable was the sight of Bruce Kennedy demonstrating his rare quality of leadership during the two-night party.

He wasn't the kind of man who honestly enjoyed raucous beer parties. But he knew how important the entire oil and pipeline venture had been to the people of Alaska and the people of Alaska Airlines, and how hard the airline's planners had worked to make those two evenings so enjoyable to the thousands of workers. So he not only supported the Prudhoe Bay festivities but also extended the highest level of courtesy to all in attendance.

When Bruce Kennedy took over the leadership reins from Ron Cosgrave in 1979, not a few people at the airline wondered whether they were getting more of an evangelist than an executive. Such concerns were unfounded.

Among the many past and present officers and employees interviewed for this book, there was universal appreciation and admiration for the way Kennedy kept his own strong religious convictions completely divorced from the job of running the airline during the 12 fruitful and eventful years he served as chairman and CEO — and this included key personnel decisions as well as his relations with fellow officers. He never tried to force religion on anyone, nor did he proselytize. Every man and woman at the airline knew exactly where Kennedy stood in his private beliefs. All he ever asked was that they respect his convictions as he respected theirs.

But it would be the inexperienced Kennedy who harbored doubt.

CHAPTER TEN

"The Kid" Takes Over

Bruce Kennedy assumed top command of Alaska Airlines in 1979. He was young for an airline chief, but not exactly in rompers, and he certainly wasn't the youngest man ever to become president of a U.S. scheduled airline. That distinction belonged to Hal Carr of North Central Airlines, who became NCA's president and general manager in 1954 at age 33. Carr, however, wasn't elected North Central's chairman and CEO until 1969, when he was 48. Kennedy became Alaska's chief at age 39.

Kennedy's youthful appearance was an early handicap. He looked about 20 years younger than his chronological age. Although this could be a blessing in that people tended to underestimate him, he also had to overcome the frequent assumption that anyone looking *that* young was likely to be impulsive, immature, and unwilling to accept advice from older, more experienced subordinates.

In actuality, these characteristics did not apply to Kennedy. It was not his youth but rather his inexperience that contributed to his early lack of confidence as president and COO. Instead of displaying the arrogance of youth, he went in the other direction. He was unsure of himself and afraid of the awesome responsibility that went with corporate command, something he frankly admitted years later.

He had become president and chief operating officer early in 1978, after Ross Anderson was fired. "I was way over my head in that position," Kennedy conceded. "I hadn't a clue as to what I was doing or was supposed to do for most of the first year I held that office." And if he felt ill prepared to be the airline's president, what happened next would be a real test of his mettle.

In August 1979, just when Kennedy was beginning to feel more comfortable as president, he unexpectedly replaced Cosgrave as Alaska Airlines' chairman and chief executive officer. Cosgrave and Kennedy had discussed the probability of his succeeding Cosgrave, but the succession came much sooner than Kennedy had planned. The timing was so unexpected that when Cosgrave informed Kennedy of his election, he blurted incredulously, "You mean *me*?" Ironically, an attempt to acquire Wien forced Cosgrave to relinquish the helm of Alaska.

Sometime before his abrupt exit, Cosgrave had imparted to his senior officers what he believed should be the airline's strategy for competing in the unfamiliar climate of a deregulated industry. At that time a deregulation bill was still before Congress, and despite the almost unanimous opposition of the major airlines (United was the exception), all the political weather vanes were pointing in the direction of passage.

Cosgrave's formula called for judicious expansion into markets needing new or additional service; he did not want the airline acting like an undisciplined child let loose in a candy store, which is precisely what would later destroy Braniff. But the second part of Cosgrave's game plan, proposed with some hesitation, called for a merger with a troubled Wien in which Alaska would be the surviving partner.

Wien, Reeve Aleutian, and Alaska Airlines were the three remaining Alaska-born carriers whose roots went back to the bush-pilot days. But although Wien was the largest, with a 15,000-mile intrastate route system stretching from Ketchikan to Nome, it had fallen on hard times. Its crippling pilots' strike over the 737 crew-complement issue, followed by a costly settlement that gave in to the union's third-pilot demands, had almost drained the lifeblood from Noel Wien's proud airline, leaving it vulnerable to either a takeover or a merger.

The pragmatic Cosgrave wasn't interested in sentimental loyalty to Wien's past; it was his own airline's future that concerned him when he began considering a merger — considering, not committing, it must be emphasized. The legislative battle over deregulation was still raging in Congress, and the outcome was uncertain because of the fierce opposition of most of the airline industry. In no way was Cosgrave ready to take a merger plunge at a time of so much uncertainty for all carriers.

The issue came to a head at a management meeting in San Diego, where Alaska's officers had gathered to discuss a possible merger with Wien. When it was Cosgrave's turn to comment, he said flatly, "We don't need it, we don't want it, and I'm not gonna do it."

But it was pointed out to Cosgrave that Household Finance Corporation (HFC) had already made a tender offer of $6 a share for Wien stock. Obviously, it was gunning to obtain majority control at what almost everyone at the San Diego meeting regarded as a ridiculously low price. The prevailing opinion among Alaska's officers was that Wien stock was worth at least twice what HFC was offering.

Cosgrave's strategy called for acquiring Wien shares through Alaska Northwest Properties, Inc. (ANPI), Alaska's real estate holding subsidiary originally established to enhance the airline's stockholders' investment. For the company's effort to acquire the majority interest in Wien, ANPI was richly endowed with cash and real estate, including the Alyeska Ski Resort. Its assets exceeded $20.7 million after it was spun off in August 1979. Alaska's analysis rated Wien stock as worth between $11 and $14 a share, but ANPI upped the ante over HFC's bid by only $.50 a share.

Complicating the prospects for a merger at this stage was the fact that deregulation hadn't yet become law. The Civil Aeronautics Board still existed, and so did a CAB regulation stating that if a carrier's non-airline subsidiary acquired more than 9.9 percent of another airline's stock, the subsidiary's chairman (in this case Cosgrave) could not also serve as chairman of the parent airline (also Cosgrave). If, however, the subsidiary chairman severed all relations with the airline's board, both as a director and chairman, the 9.9 percent limit no longer applied. So to make a merger with Wien possible, Cosgrave resigned from Alaska Airlines, and the board elected Kennedy as his replacement.

Over a period of three days, ANPI proceeded to buy up 35 percent of Wien's shares. It still needed another 16 percent to gain majority control when HFC obtained an injunction against the purchase of any additional Wien stock by ANPI. HFC's grievance filed with the court claimed that ANPI was nothing but a dummy corporation whose officers and stockholders were the same as Alaska's.

The CAB agreed. Before the board went out of existence, it fined the airline, Cosgrave, and several other individuals a total of $300,000 for violating the 9.9 percent limit. HFC went on to acquire 58 percent of Wien's stock.

ANPI's plan failed, and the deal was dead. The CAB ordered ANPI to divest itself of its entire interest in Wien, and Cosgrave went to Chicago to meet with HFC's chairman, Gilbert Ellis. By then, HFC had acquired a 56 percent stake in Wien at a cost of $6 per share, and it offered Cosgrave even less for ANPI's Wien stock.

Ellis thought he had Cosgrave over a barrel, but Cosgrave countered the offer by threatening to distribute ANPI's Wien stock to ANPI's 10,000 stockholders, which would have greatly complicated HFC's attempt to acquire additional Wien stock. Ellis raised his offer and Cosgrave accepted his enhanced bid, although in the end ANPI sold its Wien interest at a loss.

Probably the least-disappointed figure in Alaska's failed merger attempt was Ron Cosgrave himself. He made no secret of his belief that HFC knew little about running an airline and that an ailing carrier such as Wien had too many problems to cope with absentee ownership.

"It's going to die a natural death," he predicted, and he was right. Wien hung on until 1985, when it finally was forced to fold its wings. In a sense, as far as Alaska Airlines was concerned, so had Ronald F. Cosgrave. His seven years as its dominant guiding force had been some of the most significant and productive in the airline's history. Just as Charlie Willis had saved the airline from Raymond Marshall and oblivion, Cosgrave had saved it from Willis and bankruptcy.

He certainly had left a brighter legacy than the shambles Willis had bequeathed, thanks to a record of major progress and a well-mapped course for the airline's future. From an airline teetering on the edge of collapse, Cosgrave had built a very profitable company with assets of more than $92 million. Its fleet consisted of eight modern Boeing jets, and thanks in large part to the pipeline-fueled economy, Alaska's 1978 income amounted to more than $7 million. Cosgrave's legacy included a strong management team and an invigorated workforce that would prove key to Kennedy's future success. But Cosgrave also left to his young successor some serious and unexpected problems.

Bruce Kennedy discovered that to finance ANPI, Cosgrave's strategic creation, most of the airline's wealth had been stripped, including $16 million of Alaska's $27 million in shareholder equity, and virtually all of its cash. Kennedy had been the company's COO, and he put much of the blame on

Alaska's chief financial officer, Bill Allen, feeling that the CFO should have become alarmed at what was transpiring. "I was oblivious to the proportion of the airline's assets being transferred to ANPI," Kennedy asserted. "The company's solvency was the province of its chief financial officer."

It was bad enough that the merger had been blown out of the water. But now brand-new chairman and CEO Kennedy was dealing with a black eye administered by Wall Street. As of the end of 1979, the book value of Alaska Airlines' stock had dropped from $6.40 a share to $2.58. The company's balance sheet was so anemic that at the dawn of a new decade, Alaska had to sell one of its airplanes just to make ends meet.

Kennedy had always been Cosgrave's choice to succeed him, although there were times during their long association that their friendship was sorely tested; they once got into a verbal argument that escalated into a brief fistfight. Yet it was to Cosgrave's credit that despite Kennedy's sputtering, ineffectual performance at the start of his regime, he never lost faith in his appointed successor.

Kennedy acknowledged the inadequacy of his initial performance as the company's president. While he hadn't received much airline training, Cosgrave always had made sure that he was part of "the inner circle," as Kennedy put it. "Ron gave me a firm background in management," he emphasized. "Thanks to him, I spent seven years on the board of directors' executive committee."

Being only human, Cosgrave enjoyed being asked for advice after his official role at Alaska ended. He was always regarded as a much admired and respected elder statesman even though he was only 48 when he resigned from Alaska. He later returned to serve the airline for 25 more years as a member of the board of directors and the airline's chairman emeritus.

Kennedy's first priority as CEO was acquainting himself with the personalities, abilities, and objectives of his fellow officers. He frankly wanted to form his own team, not necessarily Cosgrave loyalists, and he didn't want to make any decisions about individuals until he'd had a chance to judge them objectively himself.

One monstrous hurdle was winning the respect and confidence of veterans such as Ken Skidds, Bob Gray, and Gus Robinson. They really missed Cosgrave and had serious doubts about his successor. In their minds, a high-school coach had replaced Vince Lombardi.

The irreverent Skidds regarded Ron Cosgrave with near reverence. He liked to recall an incident that took place shortly after Charlie Willis

left. Skidds was superintendent of stations and had attended a meeting at
which Cosgrave was determining what the stations needed in the way of new
ground equipment, especially in the winter, when on-time performance was
horrendous.

"At places like Cordova and Yakutat," Skidds said, "our de-icing equipment consisted of a rope. We'd drag it over the wings, fuselage, and tail
surfaces and hope that was enough to scrape off most of the ice and snow."

Cosgrave had asked him to prepare a cost estimate before the meeting,
and Skidds submitted a specific figure: $349,000, an amount that horrified
Ross Anderson, who was then Alaska Airlines' irascible treasurer. "I should
fire your ass," Anderson growled, as they were about to enter the meeting
room. "You'd better get that report of yours off the table."

"Ross, I just did what Cosgrave asked me to do," Skidds replied.

At the meeting, Cosgrave read the report carefully, was quiet for a long
time — a habit of his at almost every staff or board meeting — and finally
said, "Ken, you go get whatever ground equipment you need."

Then he gave Anderson a look that could have punctured armor plate.
"And *you*, Ross," Cosgrave snapped, "go find the money to pay for it."

It took time for the airline's capable veterans, who respected toughness
and decisiveness, to get used to Kennedy's rather shy, quiet personality.
It says a lot for officers and employees alike that they showed Kennedy
patience, understanding, and loyalty instead of behind-the-back sneers and
ridicule. And it paid off.

Skidds, who regarded the airline's stations and their employees with
the pride and affection of a father for his children, was always grateful that
Bruce Kennedy considered Prudhoe Bay or Sitka or Wrangell or Barrow just
as important in its own way as Anchorage or Seattle.

"Every time we opened a new station," Skidds marveled, "Bruce would
show up. Believe me, the people at that station appreciated it."

Bob Gray continued as senior vice president responsible for the airline's
industrial relations on the new Kennedy team. Like Skidds, Gray was a hold-
over from the Willis regime, and thought the world of Cosgrave. And he was
typical of virtually all such veterans in his gradual acceptance of Kennedy and
acknowledgment of how much he grew in stature and ability over a relatively
short time.

Gray's appraisal when Kennedy was promoted to president and chief
operating officer was brutally frank. "When he succeeded Ross Anderson as
president and COO, the first position of real significance he had at the airline,

he did a very poor job," Gray said. "He was competent as vice president of properties, but that wasn't enough to prepare him to run an airline. He was running scared and had a difficult time making decisions. He had no airline background whatever. He had a huge inferiority complex, and he was too meek and quiet because he didn't recognize his own potential. He didn't realize he was 10 times better than he thought he was."

Gray came to regard Kennedy as a superb executive, and he spoke for a lot of employees and officers when he expressed gratitude that Kennedy refrained from elevating his religious faith to the status of executive policy. "I wouldn't have been surprised if there were some officers who expected Bruce to open staff and board meetings with a prayer, but this never happened," he said.

"Kennedy really grew in the job, that's for damn sure," Gray added. "In the final analysis, he became an excellent chairman and CEO. He stepped back a few paces, used his God-given good judgment, and did a good job by anyone's standards. He was smart enough to let Gus Robinson run the day-to-day operations while he made the long-range decisions. Conversely, Gus would have been out of his league as chairman, but he was a damned fine operations man."

Kennedy himself agreed with Gray's assessment of his early leadership inadequacies. "I was terrified at the thought of taking the top job," he confessed. "I couldn't conceive of the board confirming me as chairman and CEO. I not only had no confidence in myself, but I was convinced the company was going to fail."

After becoming chairman and CEO, he held on to the president and chief operating officer positions, but Kennedy soon promoted Gus Robinson from vice president of maintenance and engineering to executive vice president of operations.

In 1980, Kennedy promoted Robinson to executive vice president and chief operating officer, a position he held nearly until his retirement. Kennedy retained the president's title in the belief that this position had primarily an external focus. "Gus was at his best when he concentrated his attentions inside the company's operations," Kennedy explained. But early in 1985, six months before Gus was scheduled to retire, the board elected Robinson president as an acknowledgment of his contributions to the company and the airline's gratitude for his strong leadership as second-in-command.

Kennedy had inherited two promising young officers who had been hired by Cosgrave, both of them enormously talented. One was an exceptionally talented planner, and the other a gifted marketeer.

Raymond J. Vecci was an airline industry veteran who had been with United Airlines and the International Air Transport Association (IATA). Cosgrave had lured him to Alaska to become its assistant vice president of planning and regulatory affairs.

The other noteworthy manager was Mike Ryan, recruited from Continental to become Alaska's vice president of marketing and sales, and who could have been cloned from the immortal Bob Giersdorf. Mike, like Giersdorf, was brilliant promotionally but allergic to budgets.

Ryan quickly made an impression on his new fellow officers. It happened during an officers' luncheon, a tradition at Alaska inherited from Cosgrave. Officers regularly gathered for lunch to exchange views and discuss current problems. Under Kennedy, the agenda was broadened and the Officers' Lunch became not only a frank forum for airing views, but also a chance to try out new ideas for improved service, including the airline's food service.

His fellow officers learned quickly that Ryan considered doing anything that wasn't first class the equivalent of slumming. At his first lunch he showed up with a bottle of 100-year-old French wine from his personal stock that he shared with everyone, pouring it with a flourish that would have drawn an admiring salute from any New York sommelier. Everyone was duly impressed, with the exception of Bruce Kennedy, who appreciated the gesture more than the wine.

"It wasn't that great," Kennedy remembered, "but it was an experience worthy of Mike's showmanship."

The Officers' Lunch, especially after it had been moved from its original location, just down the street at the Red Lion Hotel, to Alaska's newly completed corporate dining room, developed traditions, including the chairman's seat at the table. "If a visitor arrived before the chairman and unknowingly took that place, the tension was palpable," recalled Kennedy.

At Alaska, Ryan demonstrated a Giersdorf-like talent for marketing. One of the first things he did after joining the airline was to stump throughout the 49th state introducing himself to sales personnel at every station, large and small. It was a traveling crash-course aimed at creating a rejuvenated, professional sales staff. (It must be hastily added that circumventing or ignoring budgets was not part of the curriculum.)

What Ryan was seeking was a team of enthusiastic sales and marketing people unafraid to try something new, unique, and attention-grabbing.

Underline *team*. Mike believed that the most effective marketing ideas seldom, if ever, came from any single individual, but rather from the entire staff.

John Kelly, the most successful graduate of Ryan University, attested to that philosophy. "Mike encouraged discussion and debate," Kelly explained. "One guy might come up with an idea or concept, but I never saw a real blockbuster that wasn't the result of a lot of people kicking the idea around until we all agreed on a final product. And that was certainly true of the most successful in-house campaigns we created without help from an ad agency."

It was inevitable that as Kennedy gained confidence in decisions of his own making, he needed Cosgrave's reassurance less. Cosgrave resented being left out of the loop, and never one to mince words, he called Kennedy down to his ANPI Angle Lake office one day and vented his feelings.

"You know, Bruce," he began, "I never made a major decision in the past 15 years without hearing your opinion. Then you took over, and you haven't asked for my opinion once. Why?"

More than two decades later, Kennedy admitted it was one of the most painfully poignant questions he'd ever had to answer. He was only too well aware of how much he owed Ron Cosgrave.

"I told him I had to do it my own way," Kennedy explained. "I said I appreciated his counsel, but his way of doing things was different from mine. I had been part of his inner circle, but now I had to form my own inner circle with people who worked for me, people I knew well and trusted, people like Gus Robinson, Jim Johnson, and Bob Gray."

One of Kennedy's first major personnel decisions, on the other hand, was to expose his inexperience and even naïveté. He admitted right from the start that he knew little if anything about finance, except as it related to real estate. Shortly after he became CEO, Stan Patty of the *Seattle Times* interviewed him and asked, "Bruce, what's your long-term debt?"

"I don't have any idea," Kennedy answered truthfully.

As chief operating officer, he hadn't had to worry about such things as long-term debt and balance sheets. When he became CEO, he knew that he needed an experienced financial officer, one he could trust, to guide him until he became more proficient, but his relationship with CFO Willard Allen was dysfunctional.

Allen had succeeded Ross Anderson as CFO, and had served effectively under Cosgrave for several years. He had been posted overseas with the U.S. Foreign Service, spoke numerous languages, and was obviously very intelligent. When he was hired by Alaska, Allen had been serving as treasurer of a NYSE-listed company. His considerable charm clashed with his open disdain for anyone he viewed as his intellectual inferior, which covered a large chunk of the airline's executive corps, including Bruce Kennedy.

An appropriate analogy would be his close resemblance to Major Charles Emerson Winchester, the snobbish Boston-bred, Harvard-educated surgeon on the television series *M*A*S*H*. Their relationship was shaky while Kennedy was president, and worsened after Cosgrave left the company. His personal feelings toward Allen aside, Kennedy at first still regarded him as a legitimate financial guru, but that was before the ANPI drain that siphoned off Alaska's cash resources.

At that point, Kennedy's inexperience led him to make a mistake he was never to repeat. He replaced Allen with a man he met at church, a self-styled financial expert who talked a better game than he played. He didn't last very long, and for more than seven months Kennedy served as his own chief financial officer.

Fortunately for the airline, he was a fast learner in the mysteries of corporate finance. His goals were (1) to restore Alaska's reputation on Wall Street, and (2) to replenish the company's depleted coffers. He hit both objectives.

Mike Ryan will always be remembered at Alaska for his instinctive promotional skills. Both Cosgrave and Kennedy credited him with choosing the Eskimo logo over the three competing designs, and then recommending that it be adopted as the airline's official aircraft symbol. In the same year Cosgrave recruited him, two men who had been Ryan's associates at Continental joined him at his new airline. Both were to make their mark at Alaska, one as its chairman and CEO and the other following in Jim Johnson's footsteps as the 49th state's second Mr. Alaska.

They were John Kelly and Bill MacKay. Ryan had become acquainted with both men during his time at Continental. He found that Kelly had left Continental to join the Ziff Davis publishing empire. Ryan talked him into being interviewed by Bob Gray, always a unique experience. Gray's mysterious yardstick for judging applicants on the basis of automobile preference was still in effect. Although Kelly was driving an Audi at the time, he declared his preference for a certain Mercedes-Benz model. This pushed the right button, and he was offered a job as assistant vice president of sales.

It was Kelly who then recruited Bill MacKay after learning that he wanted to leave Continental. MacKay joined Kelly in the sales department, and eventually both became members of Ryan's little army.

Kelly and MacKay had an unusual friendship. They had met years before, but neither remembered the occasion until sometime after their initial association at Continental.

In 1968, MacKay was in Korea doing a two-year stint in the Air Force. While on leave, he and a roommate hitched a ride on a MAC (Military Airlift Command) flight to Sea-Tac. Their final destination was Albuquerque, where they both had gone to the University of New Mexico on athletic scholarships while working part-time for Continental in the summer.

They approached the Continental ticket counter at Sea-Tac and identified themselves as former part-time employees who had worked for the airline on the Albuquerque ramp.

"Some kid was manning the counter," MacKay remembered, "and when he told us what the fare would be, our faces fell. We had only 15 bucks between us."

They turned to leave, wondering what to do next, when the young agent stopped them. "Wait a minute, guys," he called out. "I remember seeing something in our company policy manual about employees coming home on military leave. Lemme look it up."

He thumbed through the manual and nodded. "Yeah, here it is. If you're on military leave, you get free passes. I'll call my supervisor and get it all okayed."

MacKay realized too late that he should have made a point of looking at the agent's name tag, but in the excitement of catching the flight home, he forgot. Years later, he was telling that story to some other employees at Continental, including Kelly, who kept staring at him until he suddenly blurted, "That's it!"

"That's what?" Bill asked.

"That agent was me," Kelly laughed. "I've thought a thousand times I've seen you somewhere before, but until you told that story, I couldn't remember where it was."

The team that Mike Ryan eventually formed at Alaska Airlines was talent-packed. It included the two newcomers, Kelly and MacKay, plus such experienced holdovers as Dave Palmer and Craig Battison.

One of the Ryan team's promotional efforts in the early 1980s was aimed at repairing the still-visible damage done to the airline's image during the Willis regime. Despite all the reforms and improvements achieved by Cosgrave, the residue of ill will from the "Elastic Airlines" days had never completely faded. The resentment came from (1) those unable to forget or forgive the Juneau crash — pilot error was still believed to have been the cause by many Alaskans who didn't know the real story — and (2) businessmen, primarily in Anchorage, whom Charlie Willis had offended in one way or another.

When Jeff Cacy was transferred from Fairbanks to Anchorage long after the Willis ouster, one of his first sales calls was at a local company where he asked to see the owner, identifying himself as an Alaska Airlines sales rep. The owner came charging out of his office like an enraged rhino. "I'm not seeing any son of a bitch from Alaska Airlines!" he screamed. "That bastard Charlie Willis almost ruined my business!"

Cacy didn't wait around to hear the details. He reported the aborted mission to Susan Bramstedt, who was then a secretary in the Anchorage sales office.

"I wish you would warn me who in Anchorage is still mad at Charlie Willis," he suggested plaintively.

"It might take too long," she sighed.

Ryan came up with a sequel to the old Golden Nugget Service theme, based on a successful promotion he had created while at Continental called AutumnFest. "He liked it so well that he just changed the name to AlaskaFest," recalled Kelly. Basically, it was an upgrading of in-flight food service.

"There were lavish meals served in both first class and coach," Cacy recalled. "The first-class service included oversized trays loaded with larger-than-usual entrée portions, a fresh flower, and a split of fine wine on each tray.

"Ryan had us doing food-tasting promotions for the Alaska media, featuring the first-class meals. When the food preparers brought in those big trays, a lot of the reporters thought they were a smaller version of buffet tables. That's when I knew we were winning the battle."

Western responded to AlaskaFest with its own upgraded meals. It introduced Pacific Northern Service, trying to capitalize on the nostalgic loyalty that so many Alaskans felt toward Art Woodley's old airline. It was a game but futile try.

Ryan had observant and unbiased (he hoped) Alaska employees riding Western flights incognito as regular passengers. This was the airline version of retail comparison-shopping, designed to see how the competition's service stacked up against Alaska's. The verdict was unanimous: Pacific Northern Service was pretty good, but not as good as AlaskaFest — no such touches as fresh flowers or wine splits, for example.

Before deregulation of the industry and the cutthroat competition that followed, the cost of fine food and service was accepted as part of the price paid to attract passengers and engender loyalty. Alaska, with its promotions, food, flowers, and fine wine, became a high-priced carrier, but that would all change when the price wars began in earnest a decade later.

Historically speaking, promotions such as AlaskaFest went far beyond the immediate goals of generating goodwill in places such as Anchorage, or getting the airline's foot in the door when expanding in later years to cities in the Lower 48. They marked the emergence of an airline that was maturing without getting stuffy. An airline striving to be not merely cute or different, but better. An airline with new ideas and fresh approaches to making air travel more enjoyable and also safer.

But those days would soon be over, and to compete against the new, low-cost airlines spawned by deregulation with the same plush service of the past was suicidal. Airline operating costs are determined by a standard called cost per seat-mile: what the carrier must spend to fly one passenger one mile. Factored in to that equation are such costs as fuel, taxes, airport fees, insurance, crews' salaries, and in-flight service amenities. The problem that Alaska faced was its own improved reputation for superior service. Alaska's seat-mile cost during the early 1980s, when low-cost carriers had begun moving into its markets, was a relatively high 11 cents, compared to only 7 cents for a typical low-cost competitor.

Both Cosgrave and Kennedy had done much to change the "Elastic Airlines" stigma that Willis had bequeathed to them. Charlie, too, had tried to give the airline a better reputation, but he did it with flashy promotional gimmicks it couldn't afford, thus creating an image that looked great at first and then turned ugly.

Ron Cosgrave began planning a cautious expansion strategy in 1977, at a time when Congress was only debating deregulation and the Civil Aeronautics Board still influenced the direction the political winds were blowing. This legislative uncertainty complicated Cosgrave's blueprint for Alaska's future. Should the airline apply now for new market penetration and take its chances that Congress would reject deregulation?

Cosgrave, according to John Kelly, developed a participative management style that became a hallmark of Alaska Airlines. "Perhaps the best example of Ron's management style," explained Kelly, "was during the buildup to deregulation. We had competing factions. Mike Ryan argued for a route to Minneapolis, Ray Vecci was in favor of San Francisco, and the marketing department wanted to go to Reno. Ron was absolutely masterful in making everyone feel as if their favorite selection for the new route was worthwhile."

Management pondered whether it would be safer to wait for deregulation, which would eliminate the time and expense required by the highly bureaucratic route-application process, or push for a new route before the act went into effect. After what sometimes seemed like endless discussion, there was unanimous agreement among the officers to immediately apply for the so-called Northern Tier route, a market then dominated totally by Northwest Airlines. It had exclusive authority to operate between Seattle, Minneapolis, and stops along the way in Spokane, Missoula, Great Falls, and Billings.

Expanding south into California was set aside because it would mean competing with the big dogs, Western and United Airlines, for business. The general view among Alaska's officers was that routes farther south than Seattle would be immediately challenged by giant territorial competitors.

So in 1977, Alaska filed for authority to serve the Northern Tier. The decision to invade the Northern Tier was based on a political and economic feasibility study that showed it to be the largest market in the United States without competitive service, a ripe plum waiting to be plucked.

Alaska worked quickly along the Northern Tier to build support for its application before deregulation went into effect. Jim Johnson and Alaska's young and inexperienced president, Bruce Kennedy, met with community and state officials in Montana. They flew to Helena, the state's capital, where they met with the governor and with the head of the Montana Aeronautics Division.

Alaska's team presented the airline's interest to local officials, civic leaders, and influential businesspeople in Missoula, Billings, and Great Falls. All three communities had been complaining about what they considered Northwest's indifferent service. Alaska especially worked the Big Sky State, hoping that when it came time for the CAB to begin weighing the respective merits of its case, community preference would tip the scales in the airline's favor.

Bruce Kennedy injudiciously commented to a trade-publication reporter in 1978 that "Northwest's record of poor service" across the Northern Tier was enabling Alaska to develop enthusiasm for its competitive initiative. This infuriated Donald Nyrop, Northwest's bristly chief. The day after Kennedy's comments were published, a senior Northwest sales official showed up in Seattle to collect Kennedy's courtesy pass — never to be returned.

Meanwhile, Boeing had just delivered Alaska's first new 727-200. Cosgrave, Johnson, and a few others thought it could be used before it was put into scheduled service as a flying showpiece. They reasoned that it might help to change a few minds across the country that thought Alaska was, at best, a cowboy airline flying used-up equipment. The assignment was handed to Mike Ryan, and that was akin to asking Cecil B. DeMille if he wanted to direct a biblical epic. *Epic*, as a matter of fact, described the blitz that Ryan unleashed across the Northern Tier.

Montanans loved the show and appreciated the attention, but to nobody's surprise, the Minneapolis party, in Northwest's hometown, was a bust. In the end it was Jim Johnson's personal initiative that garnered enough regional political support to move the CAB to grant the expansion route to Alaska Airlines. However, the decision was bittersweet.

This was the impending dawn of deregulation, and along with announcing the approval of Alaska's application to serve the Northern Tier, the CAB announced a new policy it called "Multiple Permissive" route awards. In granting route authority to Alaska, the CAB also indicated to other airlines that it would grant the same authority to any other carrier desiring to compete along the Northern Tier without the customary requirement that new-route authority be exercised by any specific date.

Four new competitors showed interest in the Northern Tier route, and it appeared there could be as many as five carriers to challenge Northwest, Alaska being the smallest. It brought to mind the adage "When elephants make love, grass gets trampled," and Alaska didn't want to be the grass. Messing up the Northern Tier case was one of the CAB's last hurrahs before deregulation entombed the agency forever.

In essence, Alaska's hopes for success were dashed at the gate. "We could not invest the capital and assume the start-up losses for developing the market knowing that at any time, one or more of the other, larger, stronger airlines could step in and consume the route," lamented Kennedy 20 years later. "It was an unacceptable risk."

Kennedy assigned a reluctant Jim Johnson the task of retracing his steps across the Northern Tier to inform all the friends he had made on behalf of the airline that Alaska would be unable to provide them with competitive service. This route had been nearly a personal effort on the part of Johnson, and to further rub salt in his wounds, he had to fly Northwest to deliver the news.

None of the other airlines granted authority at that time ever exercised it.

For Alaska, it was back to square one again.

Ray Vecci had argued against Alaska's foray to Minneapolis. He thought that Alaska should expand south into California, starting with Seattle-San Francisco service. After the CAB's ruling, Vecci was again arguing vociferously for the Golden State, while Ryan's marketing group backed Seattle-Reno as the best expansion target.

The decision? California, here we come!

Getting into San Francisco proved quite a bit harder than getting out of the Northern Tier. It was preceded by a cautious step across the border between Seattle and Portland, Oregon, in May 1979. A month later, Alaska inaugurated Seattle-San Francisco service, but that month included a few days of temporary panic.

There were no "Welcome to SFO" signs anywhere in sight at San Francisco International Airport. Airport officials didn't get personal, but what they did do was far worse. In effect, Alaska was told it simply couldn't operate out of SFO.

The decision to expand into California had brought on a new headache of migraine proportions: finding a gate in SFO's main terminal, which became Mike Ryan's problem. His solution was to dispatch two reliable veteran troubleshooters to SFO with instructions to find just one gate — any gate — in that terminal.

Ken Skidds accompanied Dennis Kelley to San Francisco International and met with the airport manager. They got nowhere. "He took us to a window overlooking one of the gate areas in the main terminal," Skidds recalled. "Then he said, 'Take a good look at those gates from here because you'll never get down there to use them.'"

Skidds and Kelley flew back to Seattle a few hours later, after prowling all over SFO looking for anything that seemed even faintly promising, and reported back to Mike Ryan. "We let you down, Mike," Skidds said. "We've looked at everything except the airport broom closets, and there just isn't a gate available. And what the hell are you grinning at?"

"You've been saved," Ryan chuckled. "Take a look at this telegram I just got."

The wire was from Pat Sullivan, Canadian Pacific Airlines' manager in San Francisco. It read: "We will accommodate you at our international terminal."

Skidds was only half-relieved. "Mike," he pointed out, "CPA's facility there is substandard. Dennis and I saw it."

"I don't care," Ryan replied. "It's a foot in the door, and we can go on from there."

The Canadian Pacific gate that Alaska acquired was at the far end of the concourse, with no visibility, where nobody wanted to go. Yet Ryan was right. It was a foot in the door, and Alaska Airlines was in San Francisco to stay. Later, Alaska moved over to the main terminal when the airport commission had a change of heart.

Alaska originally was assigned only one gate in the main terminal, and later added a second. When Delta merged with Western a few years later, Alaska traded its two SFO gates for three that Western had been using.

Ken Skidds always remembered the whole SFO gate experience as typifying Mike Ryan's ability to turn oatmeal into a T-bone steak.

"Ryan was a great performer," said his understudy John Kelly. "He could be just as flamboyant as Giersdorf, maybe even more so. At Continental, he'd hire a brass band to show up at annual management meetings, and he did that once at Alaska, too."

He also had pianos installed in Continental's 747 lounges, complete with singers, *Playboy* bunnies, and the early electronic game Pong. In addition to drinks in the back of the plane, passengers could purchase Nathan's hotdogs, potato chips, and a beer for $1.50.

Perhaps John Kelly's description of Ryan's contributions to AlaskaFest illustrated the intangibles that such a person could contribute. Kelly recalled, "Mike's AlaskaFest service concept truly offered up the best food and drink in the business. He ran full-page ads and beat every drum he could find, and Alaska really got noticed. The downside? Huge, huge expenditures for all the in-flight food, new uniforms for the flight attendants, and all the advertising and promotion. But Mike's enthusiasm was contagious, and everyone on the ground and in the air was having fun again."

It was the airline's entrance into the Golden Gate City that gave Dave Palmer, Craig Battison, Jerry Johnson, John Kelly, and Bill MacKay a chance to display their promotional creativity. During a planning session in San Francisco, they conceived a doozy of a stunt that's still remembered for its enormous success, although to this day no one seems to know exactly how much it eventually cost.

In anticipation of Alaska's expansion south from Seattle, Kelly returned to Seattle and presented the idea of promoting a new San Francisco route with gold. Ryan loved the idea and he rebranded the in-flight product "Gold Coast Service." The promotional scheme was to present every passenger who boarded a Seattle-San Francisco flight during the first month of service with a five-gram Credit Suisse pure gold ingot as a souvenir, reminding them of this new airline from the old Gold Rush country that was now serving the Bay Area. Over the years those ingots have become keepsakes treasured by hundreds of customers. Many of the miniature gold bars now adorn gold necklace chains or charm bracelets.

The price of gold in 1979 was a little over $300 an ounce, and the cost of the five-gram ingot was about the same as for a one-way coach ticket between Seattle and San Francisco. The ingot promotion also reduced the threat of a price war with San Francisco's largest carrier, United Airlines. The entire marketing group shared Cosgrave's sour opinion of fare wars, namely that nobody wins. But free gold ingots for flying between two former Gold Rush cities? Why, that was simply brilliant marketing that had a dramatic impact.

Ken Skidds, who opened the San Francisco station, couldn't believe the impact of the ingot campaign. "I saw some people flying two or three flights a day between San Francisco and Seattle just to get those ingots."

In truth, it really didn't matter how much the promotion cost. Measured against the attention, goodwill, and instant recognition factor it generated, the ingots were worth every penny. Alaska not only successfully invaded a United fortress, but also competed with Western's strong Bay Area presence.

Admittedly, it also didn't hurt that United was hit by a mechanics' strike about the time Alaska inaugurated service. But the Seattle/San Francisco market had been well served by United and Western exclusively for some 30 years. Alaska reduced service from four to three flights a day, and eventually found that it could sustain only two daily flights.

"It's worth noting," Bruce Kennedy said, "that after our initial experience in the Seattle-San Francisco market, where it took a long time before we became a real competitor, we decided to challenge airlines that were more our own size, in markets we had served before. So in 1980, we went up against the struggling Wien Air Alaska on the Anchorage to Nome and Kotzebue route."

In the fall of that year, Alaska also rather gingerly dipped its toe into the untested pool of another California destination by extending its Seattle-San Francisco service to Palm Springs. Ed White, the former Fairbanks peacekeeper/customer-service agent, was tagged as Palm Springs' first station manager.

White was thrilled because, as he put it, "I had never been to Florida before." In his excitement at being promoted to station manager and getting out of the Pacific Northwest for the first time in his life, it never occurred to him to wonder why Alaska Airlines was suddenly flying to a small city not only on the East Coast, but also in southern Florida.

"Ken gave me my ticket, which was for an Air California flight," Ed related, "and it didn't dawn on me that Air California's routes didn't come within 2,000 miles of Florida."

Reality failed to set in even when he got to the Air Cal gate and saw his flight's posted itinerary: Portland-Sacramento-Palm Springs. "I still thought I was going to Florida," he confessed. "My only excuse is that I was a true Washingtonian who had never been to California and already disliked the place even though I had never been there. Anyway, this all happened in November, and Palm Springs is a lovely place to be in November. I got to love it, and I met my future wife there."

For nearly six decades, Alaska's fleet had consisted primarily of bargain-basement, secondhand airplanes flown by so many pilots for so many years that their rudder pedals were worn to the smoothness of glass. The fleet was updated with profits that came with the trans-Alaska pipeline. In 1978, Alaska took delivery of its first new airplane in many years, a Boeing 727-200. The 200 was ranked by many as one of the finest airplanes Boeing ever built. It was larger than the 100 it replaced, with a greater payload, increased range, and more powerful engines.

Two years later, Wall Street acknowledged the airline's improved financial status when its stock began trading on the prestigious New York Stock Exchange under the symbol ALK. Previously its stock had been listed on the smaller American Stock Exchange.

In 1981, Alaska netted a profit of almost $8 million, small by today's inflated standards but a tremendous performance for that era. It was the highest profit the airline had posted in its first 50 years.

The red-ink-to-black-ink turnaround was also reflected in steady fleet growth. In the three-year period of 1980 through 1982, the airline acquired nine additional Boeing jetliners: four new and one used 727-200; one used 727-100C; and three new 737-200Cs, the latter being the versatile passenger/freight combis and Alaska's first 737s. They were ideal for Alaska, where isolated towns were dependent on good air-cargo service. These would be the last new Boeing airplanes Alaska Airlines would acquire until the delivery of its first 737-400, leased from ILFC, in 1991. Until then, however, Boeing's pricing of its new models to Alaska and other small airlines was prohibitive, and instead of stretching its budget to the breaking point, Alaska scoured the world for good used aircraft, a search that continued even after its new MD-83s began to arrive in 1985.

It was Gus Robinson who took the lead, and from Asia to Africa and throughout Europe, he found suitable aircraft. "And somehow," recounted Kennedy, "they would arrive and be put into service just in time for the new summer schedule. The only problem was that no two were quite alike, and that caused ongoing maintenance headaches."

Robinson's purchases sometimes presented unexpected problems, like Nigerian cockroaches. After mysteriously protracted third-party negotiations to acquire two 727-200s from Nigeria, Gus Robinson and Irv Bertram flew to London along with two flight crews, one captained by John Powis, to accept delivery of the used aircraft. Before acceptance, the planes were sealed and fumigated.

En route to Seattle, flying somewhere over Winnipeg, Canada, Captain Powis laid a sandwich down near his seat. A few minutes later, he looked down to see his half-eaten sandwich crawling with giant cockroaches. This was in November, and a decision was hastily made to fly north and park both airplanes in Fairbanks.

The subzero temperatures there quickly killed the tropical cockroaches, but not the story. For years after the incident, the Nigerian 727s were better known by their nickname than their tail numbers, the "Roach Coaches." As the story was retold over the years, the cockroaches grew in size to the dimensions of a tour bus.

By 1982, Alaska had begun serving the California cities of Ontario and Burbank. Only the mighty citadel of Los Angeles remained to be stormed, a tougher nut to crack than San Francisco.

The first few post-deregulation years were turbulent and devastating for many carriers, old and new alike. It was a period of tortuous readjustment, and Alaska was no exception. Kennedy would later describe it as "pretty much a perpetual state of crisis. During the early years of deregulation, Alaska, as one of the smallest and weakest airlines in the country, with some of the highest costs, expanded its system while under continuous assault by legacy giants and low-cost upstarts. The odds that someone at that time would have given on our survival over the next few years would have been heavily against us," said Kennedy. "West Coast carriers such as PSA, AirCal,

Western, and giant United Airlines fought furiously for market share. And Alaska managed to survive suicidal attacks by Wien Alaska, MarkAir, and Republic (Hughes Airwest), as well as several unsolicited takeover attempts, including one from Marvin Davis. And in the economic turbulence of this era, more than 30 airlines, large and small, new and old, that tried to operate in the new climate of deregulation, ended in bankruptcies or being sold to bottom feeders." Deregulation was no panacea.

Yet as it had been for so many years, Alaska was a survivor, and even managed to position itself for growth, as its steadily increased penetration into California and later to international destinations demonstrated.

By 1980, one familiar face absent from Alaska's senior ranks was Mike Ryan. His flamboyant, free-spending habits and run-amok budgets had posed too many challenging adjustments for the airline. CEO Bruce Kennedy passed the word to Bob Gray that he wasn't happy with Ryan's foibles. But Ryan had already been looking for a new opportunity and found one as president of Air Florida. He resigned before Kennedy had to take any further action.

Ryan's farewell party at Alaska was spectacular, so good in fact that for years it was assumed that Mike had staged it himself. Not true. John Kelly scripted the going-away bash. Ryan arrived at the Longacres racetrack in a helicopter, and the whole event came as a complete surprise to Mike. Alaska picked up the bill thanks to Bruce Kennedy, the same man who had decided that Ryan had overstayed his welcome at Alaska.

"It was a class act by Bruce," Kelly reminisced.

Ryan served for a very short time as president of Air Florida, and while he was there he tried to talk Kelly and MacKay into joining him. They turned him down, but it was typical of Mike that he didn't resent their rejections. Ryan dabbled in the restaurant business before joining Reno Air. When that two-hub air carrier was acquired by American Airlines in 1999, he worked for American in sales before retiring.

Mike Ryan shared something else with Bob Giersdorf besides a talent for promotion, and that was the genuine affection that each man's Alaska cohorts felt toward him, flaws notwithstanding. In Mike's case that affection was underscored by the standing ovation he got when his 'copter landed at the racetrack.

And no one who knew him could ever forget his never-ending kindness and thoughtfulness toward anyone who worked for him, a quality he demonstrated even after he left Alaska. When John Kelly was promoted to vice

president of sales as his replacement, Kelly received a warm note of congratulations from his former mentor.

The demands of the growing route system fed the need for new aircraft
acquisitions, and two relative newcomers were to play important roles in
negotiating what at the time was the airline's largest new-airplane contract in
its history.

One turned out to be the man Bruce Kennedy needed to replace Willard
Allen as Alaska's top financial officer. His name was Ray Vingo, recommended to Alaska Airlines by a headhunting firm. When Kennedy interviewed him,
Vingo was treasurer of a large San Francisco direct-marketing firm, but what
impressed Kennedy was not only his finance and accounting background, but
also the fact that he had spent eight years in Los Angeles as treasurer of Flying
Tiger, a carrier with something of the same can-do tradition as Alaska.

The other newcomer was Irv Bertram, a young attorney who had earned
his law degree at the University of California and joined the airline in 1976.
At this writing, Bertram's career has spanned more than three decades and
has earned him a reputation as one of the best airplane-contract negotiators
in the industry.

After passing the California bar, Bertram wound up with a small law
firm in Anchorage, and was reasonably happy and doing well until Cupid
torpedoed him. The woman Irv fell in love with refused to marry him unless
they could live in Seattle. On such geographical biases are career futures
often determined.

He already had formed a jaundiced opinion of the airline when he saw
its "lawyer wanted" advertisement. "Previously I had been in private practice
with an Anchorage law firm," Bertram said, "and I told my secretary at the
firm that if she ever booked me on an Alaska flight, she was fired. Those were
the Charlie Willis days."

Bertram had only one aviation client in Anchorage and very little
knowledge of airlines. But he had handled a number of litigation cases in
Anchorage and knew the state well. One of the fascinating anomalies about
Alaska Airlines is that it often has based its hiring decisions on an applicant's
familiarity with Alaska. In some cases that has carried as much or more
weight than extensive aviation experience.

Bertram's first major assignment at Alaska was to accompany then-
CFO Willard Allen to New York, where Allen was negotiating financing for
the purchase of a 727-200. It was Bertram's introduction to aircraft financ-

ing, and such a fascinating new experience that his enthusiasm fogged his judgment. He began suggesting changes in provisions that had already been approved. With each new suggestion, Allen's displeasure was signaled by a firm under-the-table kick on the shin.

After the third or fourth kick, Bertram mumbled that he had to talk something over with Allen, and the two of them went outside, where Allen chewed him out unmercifully. "From now on, I don't want you questioning anything but punctuation!" he stormed. "We really need this loan, so just shut up!"

It was a demoralizing incident for Bertram, but as he gained more experience, he also acquired more confidence in his judgment. For one thing, he learned that Willard Allen actually disliked the negotiating process. "It was because he was so impatient," Bertram recalled. "He just took care of whatever price had been decided, then he'd handle the financing. But if there was any negotiating involved, especially when it came to leasing aircraft, Gus Robinson took over. Gus loved to wheel and deal."

On one of Bertram's other early assignments, before the rather humiliating New York trip, he got acquainted with Robinson, launching a business association that became a close friendship. Bertram had been told to help Robinson sell the airline's Twin Otters, with Gus finding buyers and Irv helping with the formal sale agreements. They formed an unlikely duo — the eager but very green young lawyer and the extremely blunt then-maintenance chief — yet somehow their personalities clicked.

"I really liked Gus," Bertram said. "He taught me a lot about airplanes, and I taught him something about law. We got along great."

Bertram got along far better with Robinson, in fact, than with Willard Allen, who simply refused to listen to anyone once he had made up his mind about something. Allen announced one day that he had arranged for Greyhound Finance, a leasing company, to buy a new airplane from Alaska and then lease it back to the airline. He already had sent Greyhound a good-faith deposit of $50,000 along with a letter of intent.

Bertram begged him not to do it, but Allen waved his objections aside. "Forget it," he advised. "We're going to do it, and there won't be any problem."

But it turned out that there was a very large problem. When the lease agreement came back to Alaska's legal department, Bertram looked it over and went straight to Allen's office. "This lease is so bloody one-sided, there's no way we can get it to work," he informed the chief financial officer. "And I don't think we can get Greyhound to give us any lease that's at all favorable to the airline."

Without approval from the legal department, Willard Allen's deal with Greyhound was dead. When Bertram tried to get Greyhound to return the $50,000 good-faith payment, the leasing firm refused.

This was Bertram's second unhappy experience with an airplane-leasing company. He and Robinson had gone down to Los Angeles with Allen to negotiate a lease agreement for a 737-200 combi previously leased to Federal Express. The company that owned the airplane was the newly founded International Lease Finance Corporation (ILFC). At the time, it had only eight people in the entire organization: three Hungarian-born partners and five employees. Bertram remembered that dealing with the partners was like running an obstacle course. "At first we could never get the three of them together at the same time," he said. "And when we did, they'd all start talking in Hungarian, and we didn't know what the hell was going on."

As might be expected, the perpetually impatient Allen soon got fed up and went back to Seattle. It took a full week to negotiate a lease agreement for one airplane, ship number 741, which was still in Alaska Airlines' fleet 22 years later.

It must be emphasized, however, that this frustrating experience occurred when ILFC was in its infancy. Under the leadership of its most influential founding partner, Steven Udvar-Hazy, the company was to grow into one of the largest and probably the most successful and sophisticated aircraft-leasing companies in the world, one with which Alaska Airlines was to enjoy a long, mutually friendly relationship.

Selling Otters and acquiring an occasional Boeing jet were minuscule tasks compared to a far more important and difficult assignment. In 1983, the airline formed a legal and technical team to help senior management decide which new jetliner would best serve as the queen of the Eskimo fleet.

The competing candidates were the McDonnell Douglas MD-80 and the Boeing 737-300. Both were twin-engine airplanes; the MD-80's engines were aft-mounted and the 737's were in pods under each wing. Each jet had its vociferous supporters, resulting in an internal civil war that pitted the airline's technical staff against its marketing and sales force.

The pro-Boeing contingent was headed by Gus Robinson, whose chief ally was Ken Skidds. Ray Vecci, supported by the entire sales organization, went down to the McDonnell Douglas factory in Long Beach, California, to inspect the MD-80, a stretched and vastly improved version of the veteran

DC-9 series. He returned to Seattle singing its praises.

To be technically correct, the McDonnell Douglas airplane that Alaska initially was interested in was the MD-83, almost identical to the original MD-80 but with more powerful engines and larger fuel tanks for greater range. And to call either version a "stretched" design was an understatement. The MD-80 fuselage measured just under 148 feet from nose to tail. That was a whopping 15 feet longer than the original DC-9 (the MD-80 originally was called the DC-9 Super 80). It was only two feet, five inches shy of the 150-foot fuselage of a DC-8, Douglas's first four-engine jetliner, which in turn was about equal in size to the Boeing 707.

Furthermore, the MD-80 cabin itself was narrow, wide enough for only three-and-two seating in coach, compared to six abreast in the rival Boeing. Alaska's marketeers considered this a positive rather than a negative factor, as it meant fewer middle seats, the bane of every coach passenger's existence.

Yet to officers such as Robinson and Skidds, that narrow fuselage meant drastically reduced cargo space. This, in turn, would severely restrict the MD-80's utilization in the state of Alaska, where cargo capacity was as important as passenger accommodations.

Ray Vecci urged Bruce Kennedy to buy the MD-80, citing its passenger-oriented main cabin, good seat-mile costs, large passenger capacity, and adaptability to Alaska's expanding route system south of Seattle.

"The important thing to remember," John Kelly explained, "is that the MD-80 was ideal for our new expansion into California. Admittedly the airplane would have been a disaster in Alaska, where cargo is so important, but that's why we also were acquiring more Boeing combis at the same time."

Gus Robinson investigated the MD-80, studying its design features and examining the performance and operating-cost figures that had so impressed Vecci. In Robinson's case, however, all the manufacturer's claims in the world couldn't influence a man who was biased against the MD-80 even before seeing the actual airplane. He was well aware of an incident involving the MD-80 prototype, the first test airplane. It was undergoing precertification test flights, and the FAA test pilot made an exceptionally hard landing, so hard that the long fuselage buckled and almost broke in two. McDonnell Douglas beefed up the fuselage structure to prevent any similar occurrence, but the incident was enough to further sour Robinson's opinion of that elongated fuselage.

After Kennedy quoted Vecci's fulsome praise of the MD-80, Robinson's input was decidedly negative. "Bruce," he snorted, "if all those things were true, I'd buy the airplane myself. But for starters, it's nothing but a long, narrow tube, and I never did like to ride in one of them."

There were other factors involved in Alaska's eventual choice of the MD-80 over the 737-300. First and foremost, the latter fell short of Alaska's strong preference for a 140-passenger airplane. The MD-80 met that requirement, while the 737-300 was about 20 seats shy of Alaska's desired capacity. The "long tube" design to which Gus Robinson had objected utilized its greater length to achieve greater passenger capacity.

Boeing was planning to build a 737-400 series with at least 140 seats, but that project was still in the preproduction phase and the McDonnell Douglas entry promised far earlier delivery dates. So delivery time was the second factor in Alaska's final choice.

The third factor was price and financing terms. The Long Beach company had long since fallen far behind Boeing in jetliner sales, a decline that began when the 707 eclipsed the late-starting DC-8 and then really went into a nosedive because Douglas had no jet to compete against the popular 727. With MD-80 sales sluggish, McDonnell Douglas was extremely anxious to get a Seattle-based customer — shades of Charlie Willis conning General Dynamics into discounting the 880 with the same argument.

So Alaska's negotiators were holding some high cards. The initial team that went down to Long Beach to work out a deal consisted of Robinson, Bertram, and Bob Gray, with Ray Vingo ready in the wings to handle the financing for whatever deal was worked out.

This was Gray's first experience in aircraft purchasing. He was assigned to the negotiating team largely because he was a respected member of Kennedy's own "inner circle" of veteran officers that the CEO had come to trust and rely on.

The team's strategy was to take advantage of McDonnell Douglas's strong desire to sell the MD-80 to an airline based in Boeing's own backyard, first enticing them with a tentative order and then playing a trump card to get the deal they hoped to make.

"We knew McDonnell Douglas was coming out with an improved MD-80 model, the MD-83," Bertram related, "and that was the airplane we really wanted."

McDonnell Douglas asked the negotiating team to sign a letter of intent to buy six MD-82s. This basically was identical to the original MD-80 and was an airplane that Alaska *didn't* want. When the team was asked to sign the letter, the airline's negotiators played their trump card. "We told them,"

Bertram said, "that we'd sign only if they gave us six MD-83s instead of the 82s, and for the same price. They agreed and we struck a deal."

The MD-83s that Alaska ordered were not standard models; in fact, they really were hybrids. They had the MD-83's larger and more powerful engines, but to obtain at least a little more cargo space, the MD-82's smaller fuel tanks were substituted. In addition, a new heavier landing gear replaced the MD-83's standard gear to compensate for the slightly increased cargo capacity.

Even with a price break, Ray Vingo didn't think the company had sufficient cash reserves for what amounted to a nine-aircraft order, including its commitment to Boeing. So he worked out a leasing deal with a Japanese company for the first two airplanes that reduced the substantial required down payment.

With a few contractual issues still up in the air, Kennedy sent Vecci, Robinson, and Gray down to Long Beach to close the deal. Then he faced the unpleasant chore of phoning Thornton Wilson, Boeing's short-tempered CEO, whom everyone called T, and telling him that Alaska was going to buy the MD-80.

"Damn it, Bruce," Wilson grumbled, "you *know* we build better airplanes than they do."

"The decision was based mostly on price," Kennedy explained. "They were very aggressive on price. The MD-83 matched the seating capacity of the Boeing 727-200s it would replace, while the 737-300 would not."

T cooled off quickly. "Well," he said philosophically, "Bill Allen [Boeing's former CEO] told me years ago never to regret losing a sale on which you would have lost money."

It was sportsmanship that Kennedy was not to forget.

Deliveries began early in 1985, and the first delivery flight turned into a nightmare for both McDonnell Douglas and Alaska Airlines. The only exception to the general embarrassment was Gus Robinson, who, without a doubt, was justified in thinking, "*I told you so.*"

Alaska had invited a planeload of various dignitaries to ride on the airline's first MD-83 from Long Beach to Seattle. The new jet then would be flown to Anchorage for the formal delivery, thus avoiding the stiff sales tax that would be levied if delivery took place in Seattle.

Problem 1: The first airplane was temporarily fitted with older, less powerful engines. The bigger power plants that Alaska had ordered hadn't yet been certificated by the FAA. Because the airplane was underpowered, it was slower than Alaska's old Boeings. (In truth, even when the larger engines were installed, the MD-83 was still slower than the old 727s.)

Problem 2: Because of a mechanical glitch, the airplane was late taking off from Long Beach.

Problem 3: The water system failed as soon as the plane was airborne, so it was impossible to flush any of the toilets.

The only thing that went right on the Long Beach-Seattle leg was the meal service, which was so good that most of the guests weren't aware that a brand-new jetliner was being delivered in a condition no air carrier could tolerate. Irv Bertram used a yellow legal pad to list the airplane's more obvious flaws and defects.

Bertram's list, however, wasn't as long as the one Gus Robinson compiled mostly on the leg between Seattle and Anchorage, which took four hours because of headwinds and the temporary engines. There was a McDonnell Douglas vice president aboard, and it must have been a long four hours listening to both Robinson's and Bertram's complaints.

Robinson was furious. He and Ken Skidds were fervent believers in a saying that had been quoted throughout the aviation community since the jet age began: "If it ain't Boeing, I ain't going!" And in truth, no Boeing jetliner would ever have left the delivery flight line in the condition of Alaska's first MD-83.

"The airplane had been through two prior shakedown flights, the first by the manufacturer and the second by the airline," Bertram recalled, "and we shouldn't have had all these deficiencies show up on the delivery flight. What we didn't know was that McDonnell Douglas had been having a lot of production problems because of major management upheavals. In addition to sloppy work on the assembly line, it took forever to get the bigger engines we had ordered, so we wound up having to use leased engines on four of the airplanes. But in the long run, we saved more money that way than if the airplanes had been delivered with the bigger engines."

One rather significant aspect of choosing the MD-83 over the 737-300 was that Bruce Kennedy went along not only with Vecci, but also with younger management people such as John Kelly in marketing, while rejecting the advice of older officers such as Robinson and Skidds. Robinson at the time was executive vice president and chief operating officer, the second-highest position in the company. It wasn't a case of Kennedy disregarding the opinions of experienced veterans and listening instead to youthful go-getters. Rather, it was an indication that Kennedy had become his own man. He had honestly weighed the merits and faults of both airplanes, listened to their detractors and supporters alike, and then made up his own mind. He was being completely honest when he told T Wilson that the decision to go with the MD-83 was based primarily on price.

One of Kennedy's most surprising strengths was in an area that had been among his weakest: finance. Lou Cancelmi, who joined Alaska in 1985 as its public relations chief, observed Kennedy from the fresh standpoint of someone who was new to the airline industry but no stranger to corporate America. He had come from the giant Atlantic Richfield Company, where he worked in Alaska after a stint with Alyeska Pipeline Service Company during the pipeline years.

"Bruce seemed always to have his finger on the financial pulse of the business in addition to having great instincts," Cancelmi commented. "He was in control, but was always willing to let his operational people do what they needed to do. He realized it wasn't all about him and that he needed veterans like Robinson, Jim Johnson, Pat Glenn, Ken Skidds, and Bob Gray to make the airline work. And he gave all points of view a hearing before making a final decision."

Pat Glenn's appraisal of Kennedy as a CEO was unique and illuminating. "What fascinated me about Bruce," he recalled, "was the way he'd run the officers' planning sessions. At times you'd think he was preoccupied with something we weren't even discussing. I agree that this was probably because he didn't have an airline background and didn't want to get involved with details. Yet he always managed to ask not only the right questions, but the big questions."

It was evident that Kennedy had done more than merely inherit Cosgrave's leadership mantle. He had learned how to wear it. And this was important because in Kennedy's eighth year as CEO and president, his generally sunny skies suddenly darkened as Alaska was hit with a mechanics' strike. The clouds first appeared at a December 1984 planning session. "Continental was low-balling our fares," recalled Kelly, "and we determined that we had to move quickly to cut costs or we wouldn't be competitive." Alaska's mechanics and flight attendants wanted no part of any compromise, and they balked.

It was more than just another labor dispute. The walkout was the longest experienced by any airline since the industry was deregulated in 1978, and for Alaska the ill will that it generated continued to be felt more than 15 years after it ended.

CHAPTER ELEVEN

State of the Unions

A traumatic three-month strike occurred in 1985 and primarily involved 650 mechanics, ramp workers, and some clerical personnel represented by the International Association of Machinists and Aerospace Workers (IAM). Compounding the IAM bolt, however, was a sympathy walkout by a few flight attendants who refused to cross the IAM picket lines. This, in a sense, was even more of a problem than having the mechanics walk out. These actions festered into bitterness between labor and management. To counter the immediate threat of not having enough attendants for its flights — something that could have grounded the airline — Alaska requested permission from the FAA to modify its flight-attendant training course. At the same time, it identified and hired a number of former Wien flight attendants. The combination of an experienced labor pool and the FAA's approval of Alaska's shortened training program allowed the airline to keep flying.

Like the flight attendants, the airline's clerical, office, and passenger service (COPS) personnel — whose contract was still in effect and whose members belonged to another IAM bargaining unit — initially honored the mechanics' picket line. However, as the strike continued to grind along, the vast majority of COPS employees crossed the picket line and returned to their posts. This contributed to some internal hard feelings, at least temporarily.

Yet despite all the labor turmoil that marked 1985, the airline somehow continued to grow during that hectic year, initiating service to Phoenix, Tucson, and Las Vegas, and continuing its fleet expansion. By 1985, Alaska had a 34-aircraft roster, consisting of six MD-83s, twenty 727-200s, six 737-200Cs, and two 727-100s — the latter the oldest jets in the airline's fleet.

The management team confronting the rebellious union had changed, too. Gus Robinson was the airline's chief operating officer and president. Ray Vecci was vice president of planning, and John Kelly had replaced Mike Ryan, first as staff vice president of sales and then as vice president of marketing following Ryan's resignation.

Bill MacKay was regional vice president in Alaska and later replaced Jim Johnson as "Mr. Alaska." How he inherited that title is a story in itself. Mike Ryan had asked John Kelly if he wanted to become the company's regional vice president for Alaska, which would have been a demotion inasmuch as Kelly already was vice president of sales for the entire company. Kelly declined, but recommended MacKay for the job in Anchorage.

MacKay balked too, ranking service in Alaska as the equivalent of a prison sentence in Siberia. He finally agreed to go, provided that he could return to Seattle as soon as possible. By the time that opportunity arose, however, MacKay had fallen in love with the Great Land and was reluctant to return to the Lower 48.

Another legendary character in the airline's history was the unflappable Bob Gray, senior vice president of industrial relations and the company's point man in hiring, firing, and dealing with the double-barreled 1985 strike. No one in management envied Gray his job. The IAM had a reputation for playing hardball with airlines, employing an "us against them" philosophy. The union's national officers in Washington, D.C., governed one of the country's most powerful labor organizations, and while its local affiliates were allowed some autonomy in contract negotiations, many believed that no contract could violate what its Washington headquarters had established as an IAM national policy.

Bea Knott began her career with Alaska in management working for Bob Gray, but she later chose to become a reservations agent, customer-service agent, and union official. She challenged that assertion of undue influence of the national over the local union. According to Knott, Charles Easley, the general chairman of Alaska's local, was autonomous. "Charlie would have to make a presentation to people from time to time, it is true, but he directed and made the decisions with regard to our strategy during 1985."

The mechanics' union had demonstrated its clout in the summer of 1966, when it simultaneously shut down five major U.S. carriers for 43 days: United, TWA, Eastern, Northwest, and National. The IAM strategy was aimed not so much at the carriers as at the ceiling of 3.2 percent that President Lyndon Johnson had placed on all wage increases.

The IAM strategy was brilliant. It picked the vulnerable airline industry as a test case and initiated the five-carrier strike in the heart of the heavy summer travel season. LBJ urged the airlines to hold out as a regulated industry. The industry had to comply, even though all were willing to negotiate wage increases higher than the White House guidelines.

The unaffected carriers sagged under the extra traffic loads. American, the only transcontinental carrier still flying, was operating its coast-to-coast flights with 100 percent load factors and averaging 30 standbys on every flight. Even Alaska, with its then-tiny route system, picked up a little of United's and Northwest's traffic.

But the strike was no bonanza for the airlines still operating. With the exception of Delta, the carriers had signed a profit-sharing agreement, called a Mutual Aid Pact, under which they had to share their extra profits with their competitors that were being struck. So only Delta really profited from the strike.

The grounded carriers finally defied White House pressure, granting wage boosts that broke the 3.2 percent limit. As for the IAM, its leaders could be forgiven for strutting a bit; they had successfully confronted not only five strong air carriers, but the president of the United States as well.

And this was the union about to confront Bob Gray.

(Historical footnote: The 1966 strike also produced one of the industry's funniest incidents. American's reservations agents were swamped with customers clamoring to get space on its transcontinental flights, and the most common ploy was to claim a personal friendship with C. R. Smith, American's legendary president, who had recently retired and been replaced by a soft-spoken Southern gentleman named Marion Sadler. One of American's agents became fed up, having heard this fabrication once too often. "I suppose you're also a personal friend of Marion Sadler," the agent responded sarcastically. "I certainly am," the customer chirped. "As a matter of fact, I've been dating her for two years.")

For an airline that was 53 years old in 1985, Alaska had been relatively free of the labor strife that comes with such a unionized industry. There had been a 21-day walkout by flight attendants in 1976 that was a dispute over wages and hours. Gray himself wasn't surprised at that walkout. Flight attendants had just broken away from the Air Line Stewards and Stewardesses Association (ALSSA), for years an ALPA subsidiary, and formed the independent Association of Flight Attendants (AFA).

Though the flight attendants believed they won a victory in the 1976 strike, flight operations returned to normal fairly quickly after the company began hiring replacement flight attendants. However, replacements aside, Bea Knott, by then an IAM member, thought the flight attendants earned a solid victory in 1976 primarily because they and the entire Alaska workforce were unified. "The corporate office was practically a ghost town," said Knott. "All of management was out on the front lines struggling to keep the airline operating. That gets old fast."

To be sure, the strike probably would have fizzled out sooner if a number of pilots hadn't refused to cross the AFA picket lines. All airlines fear a strike by their pilots more than anything else because the replacement strategy won't work.

In fact, in the next pilots' contract talks, Gray negotiated a new deal with ALPA in which both the union and company agreed to submit a maximum of five major issues in any contract dispute to arbitration. In return, the pilots pledged not to honor another union's picket lines, or to strike.

Like all good company officers handling labor relations, Bob Gray walked a precarious tightrope. He had to be fair and objective about what employees wanted and might well deserve, but he also had to never forget that he represented the interests of the company and its stockholders as well. In plain language, he couldn't give away the company store merely to achieve labor peace.

This dichotomy has always been a high-wire balancing act, but Gray was a master at the game. One of the best observers of his virtuoso performances was his longtime assistant Gail Neufeld, who joined the airline in 1977. She was working as a sales and marketing coordinator for a Seattle wholesale food distributing company when Ed Schnebele, a former associate who had become Alaska's personnel manager, phoned her.

He told Neufeld there were three job openings at the airline: she could work for Bruce Kennedy, Ray Vecci, or Bob Gray. She chose Gray because she had always been interested in industrial relations and personnel matters. She went to work for him just at the time that he was engaged in contract talks with the union representing the airline's COPS employees.

Neufeld worked for Gray until he retired in 1989, a span of 12 and a half years, and no one at Alaska knew him as well as she did. To some of his fellow officers, Gray was something of an enigma, rather austere and remote. Not to Neufeld, however, nor to many of the union officials Gray faced across a bargaining table.

Tom Gibbs, at one time IAM's chief negotiator and the union's spokesman at Alaska, respected him as a worthy opponent who had unimpeachable integrity. Shortly after Gray retired, Neufeld asked Gibbs what he honestly thought of Gray. "Well, I'll tell you this, Gail," Gibbs replied. "We may not have liked what he said, but we knew when he said it he wasn't going to change his mind every 10 minutes."

Added Neufeld: "Bob really did have integrity, and he tried to protect the employees within the limits of his responsibility to the company. During the '85 strike, I was outside the boardroom one day and heard him arguing the union's position *against* some other officers.

"One thing I learned from Bob Gray was never to take the labor-relations job personally because it'll either kill you or you'll simply have to get out of it. He warned me there were going to be days when I would get upset and angry because the union guys would attack me personally, and that I had to realize they were just trying to get me to lose my cool."

Not that Gray himself didn't indulge in occasional histrionics, feigning bursts of rage when he thought the union negotiators were getting too cocky, insulting, or unreasonable. He never really walked out of a bargaining session, but he sometimes threatened to, and he was so convincing that the union reps often backed off.

Only Neufeld knew that Gray was following a script he had written himself. He'd tell her, "Now let's not spread everything out on the table at once, because at some point I'm going to announce I'm walking out because we're not getting anywhere." In reality he was very even-tempered and rarely got mad.

Neufeld was fascinated by Gray's habit of sitting in his office and just staring out the window, giving everyone the impression he was either daydreaming or merely loafing. "What he was doing," she related, "was planning the strategy he'd use at the next bargaining session. But he never had a plan so rigid that he'd wind up painting himself into a corner. He'd be thinking, 'Now if I went this way and they went that way, then what would I do?' He was a chess master — that's the best description I could give of the way he negotiated."

Yet not even the bargaining skills of Bob Gray and his fast-learning disciple could prevent the 1985 strike, and this was largely because the company's most controversial new-contract proposal collided with the intractable opposition of the IAM's national leadership, or "the international," as it was called. Alaska Airlines wanted to cut labor costs by establishing so-called B-scale wages for newly hired mechanics and ramp workers. The whole idea was anathema to the IAM and had been the union's major target since American Airlines established a B-scale, or "two-tier," wage plan in 1982 that reduced the starting-salary scale for new employees by as much as 50 percent. After it won union acceptance in exchange for greater job security, American went from a $19.6 million loss in 1981 to a healthy profit the following year.

American, however, had been dealing mostly with the Transport Workers Union (TWU), not the IAM. The TWU was no pushover labor group, but it did not have IAM's more militant reputation.

So it was a different situation at Alaska, where the IAM represented not only mechanics and ramp workers but also COPS employees. It was not pleasant to contemplate trying to operate an airline without maintenance workers, ground personnel, or customer-service representatives.

Bea Knott, originally on Gray's staff when she began her career with Alaska, was now working on the Seattle ticket counter and had become involved in union activity. A member of the COPS employee group, she had never been on strike, but she had no problem honoring the picket line. "These were people I respected. They were war veterans. They were blue-collar workers. They were employees who were proud of who they were and what they had contributed to the company. I felt at home with them."

Gray emphasized that the B-scale controversy wasn't the only reason for the strike, but it constituted a huge stumbling block to a peaceful settlement. Knott said that another major concern of the mechanics centered on Alaska's desire to lower costs by transferring the mechanics' authority for pushing back airplanes from the gate to ramp-service agents. Up to that point, me-chanics had used tugs and maintenance personnel to move the planes clear of the gate area. For the union, it was about jobs and safety. For the airline, it was about costs. The carrier thought it should be able to either "power back," that is, back the planes out on their own power, or have lower-waged ramp-service workers do the job, and either would be just as safe.

"The two-tier scale was only part of the problem," Gray recounted. "I think you have to remember that 1984 was not a very good year financially, and competition from low-cost carriers was getting fierce.

"At an officers' planning session in Tucson, there was total agreement that we had to cut labor costs. So we decided to propose the B-scale structure to our unions. In return we'd offer a profit-sharing plan similar to what salaried, nonunion employees had. We knew the unions would balk, and they did. They told us, 'We're not in the business of running Alaska Airlines. We're in the business of looking out for our members.' "

Gray wasn't surprised at the negative reaction. It is part of the pre-bargaining dance. Management goes into every contract negotiation resigned to the fact that the existing contract became obnoxious and unfair to the union the day after it was signed. Unions go into every contract negotiation convinced that the company is determined to get as much as it can and give as little as possible.

According to Gray, the IAM local negotiating committee actually accepted a B-scale, but the union's international rejected it. The local, after refusing Gray's plea to submit the B-scale plan to the entire membership, did a complete turnaround and also unanimously rejected the two-tier scale. It was back to the bargaining table, and Gray began to get some decidedly negative vibes.

He was convinced, and never changed his mind, that if the local negotiating committee had submitted the B-scale proposal to a membership vote, it would have passed. But, of course, that would have caused a fatal collision with the IAM's national policy.

The company, desperate to get costs down, reacted to this impasse by hardening its own position. Bob Gray attended an officers' meeting called to discuss the situation, listened to one colleague after another voice the opinion that the airline had to take a strike, and finally was asked how he felt. He stood up and gave everyone, including Bruce Kennedy, his honest "for whom the bell tolls" assessment.

"Gentlemen, with the position we're taking, we'll probably have a strike," Gray said. "Frankly, it's going to be a long one and a difficult one, so you'd better start getting ready."

In recalling the atmosphere around the airline during those tense days, Gray conceded that it wasn't a difficult prophecy to make. "The B-scale issue was important but not the only reason they walked out," he related. "I think the union people felt they had been settling for less than they deserved during a series of profitable years and had fallen behind their peers at other carriers. They figured '85 was the time to go in and get theirs, and never mind anything else. Anyone in my position could have seen a strike coming."

And come it did, starting with the final bargaining session, when Gray rose and announced that further negotiations were futile. As he and Neufeld left the room, one of the IAM committee members yelled, "We're going to bring this company to its knees!"

The ensuing strike began at midnight on March 3, 1985, and didn't end until June 4. Those 93 days saw angry acts and bitter internal strife within the union itself, creating grudges that lasted for years.

Inside the IAM, there was a growing numerical disparity between the mechanics and the ramp workers. The second IAM group, the clerical, office, and passenger service personnel (COPS), tended to side with the ramp people. Together, they outnumbered the mechanics, who were used to being at the top of the union heap because of their technical skills.

Traditionally, airline mechanics have always considered themselves a breed apart, a rather elite group with a great deal of pride that at times seemed curiously out of tune with the IAM's fierce militancy. It created divided loyalties that affected some of Alaska's veteran mechanics in particular, men and women who had mixed feelings about the strike. They were caught in the middle, trying to be loyal union members, although many would rather have been working on airplanes than walking a picket line.

The classic example of a skilled mechanic, enormously proud of his job and emotionally torn apart by the strike, was Carsten C. Nelson, otherwise known as C.C. This dedicated airplane maintenance professional went far beyond merely qualifying as a veteran. He joined Alaska Airlines in 1950 as a mechanic's helper at Paine Field and, after achieving the high rank of aircraft inspector, didn't retire until 2003, 53 years later.

He was the first employee in the company's history to receive a 50-year pin, and during that time he also won the FAA's coveted Charles E. Taylor Master Mechanic Award, named for the mechanic who built the engine for Orville and Wilbur Wright's famed *Flyer*. This was the highest honor in Nelson's profession, and it was easy to understand his soul-wrenching ambivalence toward the strike and his deploring the few random incidents of violence.

One random target of such hardball tactics was Lou Cancelmi, the airline's new head of corporate communications and eventually a vice president.

He hadn't been with the airline very long when the strike began. Coming out to the parking lot after work one day, he found a bullet hole in a rear fender. A second officer later discovered a bullet hole in his car.

Bob Handley drew the unusual task of walking through the parking lot every day with a huge magnet picking up nails that had been strewn all over the pavement in front of the corporate headquarters building.

Another longtime mechanic, Smokey Schnee, was in management in 1985 and didn't have to worry about divided loyalties. But even as an IAM member, he always resented intimidation tactics directed against less militant mechanics like himself. These tactics were tried once against Schnee after some fellow union members advised him not to work overtime because of a slowdown strategy. Schnee was miffed.

"You guys don't pay my rent, and you don't pay my bills," he retorted. "So if I wanna work overtime, I'll do it."

The next day, Smokey found that someone had painted SCAB on his locker in large letters. "They did that several times," he said, "and they did it to other mechanics that went against a slowdown."

Management had heeded Gray's advice to get ready. Its strategy was simple: keep the airline running even if it was necessary to hire replacements for the striking workers. The AFA complicated matters by ordering flight attendants not to cross IAM picket lines.

That tactic failed for three reasons: (1) Before the strike, a number of management people and nonunion office workers had received flight-attendant training and were ready to work flights if the AFA, in effect, also walked out by honoring the picket lines. (2) The flight attendants' union was counting on pilot support that didn't materialize. And (3) there were plenty of willing replacements available, mostly former Wien flight attendants who had recently lost their jobs when Wien floundered.

Almost with the appearance of the first picket signs, the airline began hiring replacements for the striking mechanics, ramp workers, and COPS members. In the first week of the strike, Alaska operated only 10 percent of its scheduled flights. But the percentages grew daily: first 20 percent, then 50, and long before the strike ended in early June, the airline's flight schedules were back to normal. The flight attendants began drifting back to work within two weeks, only too aware that the company was hiring replacements.

Bob Gray had given fair warning. Just before the IAM struck, he was having lunch with a couple of AFA officers, and one of them remarked, "You know,

Bob, the flight attendants are going to stand united behind the mechanics."

"So we'll have to replace the flight attendants who refuse to report for work," Gray warned in turn.

Knott said the difference between labor's victory in the 1976 flight attendants' action and its loss in 1985 was that the courts during the interim had ruled that replacement workers had to be provided permanent jobs following a strike. "This is a card the airlines always had held, but never tried to use before," said Knott. Frank Lorenzo of Texas International Air and Continental Airlines gained fame — or infamy, depending on your perspective — as the first to employ it successfully. It then became a hammer in the toolbox of airline managements.

For the strikers, especially the mechanics, it had to be demoralizing to see Alaska's operations gradually but steadily return to normal. It also was difficult for employees because of the divisiveness within the company. Remember, many striking workers, union loyalties notwithstanding, still regarded the airline as a kind of family.

Ultimately, the union underestimated the effectiveness of Alaska's replacement strategy. It wouldn't have worked for a large carrier with thousands of unionized employees because the replacement supply would have been too limited. For a small airline like Alaska, however, replacement was a viable response. So, in a practical sense, the strike had been broken and the IAM local retreated.

Yet throughout most of the 93-day strike, Bob Gray continued to hold talks with the union through Chuck Easley, general chairman of District 143, who represented IAM unions in the northwest region. It was a common, almost daily occurrence for Gray to tell Gail Neufeld, "I'm going over to the Hyatt to talk to Chuck."

Those talks were going on seven days a week, as they kept trying to reach mutually satisfactory terms. Neufeld recalled that Gray and Easley actually hammered out a new contract agreement just a few weeks after the strike began. But when Easley reported the agreement to the IAM international, he was refused permission to submit it to his members for a vote. So the strike continued more than two months longer than it should have. It was a decision that would come back to haunt the IAM.

In compliance with the Railway Labor Act, the company was then free to unilaterally impose the terms of the Gray-Easley agreement on the IAM, which was duly notified that a new contract was in effect. Yet the IAM was not required to call off the strike and didn't until June 4, when the new contract was finally signed. By then, the unnecessarily prolonged strike had inflicted untold damage on the lives of hundreds of employees.

"I do know that a lot of families were torn apart," Neufeld said, "and some employees lost their homes. Everyone eventually got their jobs back, but there were quite a few mechanics, ramp workers, customer-service agents, and flight attendants who found themselves transferred out of Seattle to stations elsewhere, including Alaska, because the replacement hires had been promised they wouldn't be relocated even when the strikers came back to work."

Bea Knott could speak about this from firsthand experience. Because she had chosen to honor the mechanics' picket line, Knott had to move to Portland at the end of the strike and, at least initially, take part-time work to get back on the payroll at Alaska Airlines. Ultimately it took more than a year for her to regain a position at the Seattle ticket counter. Only then was she able to come home, and it left her feeling, in her own understated words, "a little bit bitter." However, she said, "the experience made me stronger, better, and a more committed negotiator. After the strike was over, my incentive to return was the people who work here."

Others found themselves in similar circumstances. In some cases, transfers were ordered by overzealous supervisors motivated by revenge. Eventually this resulted in some lawsuits that charged unfair treatment and cost the company money.

It is often said that there are no winners in a strike, and that is true. But the end result of this strike was far more onerous for the IAM. As the strike dragged on, the international's continued assurances that they would bring the airline to its knees and win a new contract began to alienate the majority of the airline's mechanics. The seeds of defection had taken root and would sprout in years to come. What was especially disheartening to the union local was that not only was the airline able to open two new stations during the strike — Los Angeles and Phoenix — but in addition, passenger traffic increased by nearly 4 percent and the airline earned a respectable profit for the year.

Thirteen years later, in 1998, the IAM still had the ramp workers and COPS on its roster, of course, but it was ousted from representing the mechanics by the Aircraft Mechanics Fraternal Association (AMFA). The mechanics may not have been as numerically strong as the other two groups, but they were the highest paid of the three, and the IAM took a bath in the form of drastically reduced income from dues.

Whether the company or the IAM came out ahead in the 1985 strike is debatable. Perhaps the verdict depends on "the eye of the beholder." But the mechanics did accept a modified, less odious B-scale plan, and Gray felt that it was equally or even more important that the company won changes in work rules. Ramp people were now allowed to move airplanes, a task formerly assigned exclusively to mechanics. In addition, ground services at smaller stations could be performed by personnel from other carriers, thus eliminating the old IAM rule that at least one Alaska Airlines mechanic had to be on duty every time an Alaska flight landed. This was especially costly at smaller stations where flights not only were less frequent but also were spread out over a 24-hour period. "That meant you had to have a mechanic available 24 hours a day, sometimes when there were only one or two inbounds all night," Gray pointed out. "And that's why work rules are more important than wages in determining labor costs."

Bea Knott described the union's position as one seeking fairness and equity. "No one went out on strike intending to kill the company," she said. "For us this was a dispute over issues, and our object was to reach a reasonable compromise. I believe, however, that Bruce Kennedy, for whatever reason, harbored ill will toward the unions. A lot of us felt that he wanted to bust the unions at Alaska. And so, because of his position as CEO, he naturally became the target of our ire, and we did personalize things. One of our mechanics, for example, named his horse that he raced locally Brucebuster. There were other various Brucebuster signs and pins. Kennedy kept one of them in his desk, and one day, while a couple of customer-service agents were visiting him, he pulled out one of them. The agents advised him that it was time to get over it, but he seemed always more emotionally dug in than we were."

Knott said that Gray persuaded the IAM to yield even more ground a year later. She described the COPS negotiations held in the fall of 1986 as one big one-sided 24 percent wage and benefits concession. The people affected "were all the people who had crossed the picket line and had kept the company operating," said Knott. "So I said to Bob, 'You said you would never forget [referring to COPS employees who had crossed the picket line]. Is this how you are going to remember them?' He said, 'You bet it is.' So I said, 'Well, I'll be sure to tell them.' So that became my little theme as Joanne Robitaille, a colleague of mine from the Juneau station, and I traveled around the system to talk to our work group. Joanne had crossed the line; I had not." Knott said that fact made the impact of their retelling of Gray's comments to union audiences much more powerful.

Only in a technical sense were the 1985 labor wars over, for they left a residue of scars that would fester and erupt years later. But no one was looking that far ahead, not when over the immediate horizon were two significant developments. One was a different kind of conflict: a contentious relationship with a relatively new Alaskan rival that started out as a supposed ally and ended up a dangerous enemy. The other was a far happier relationship: a merger with a California-based carrier whose highly motivated workforce was as service-oriented as Alaska's.

The first was MarkAir, owned by a colorful wheeling-and-dealing ex-bush pilot named Neil Bergt. The latter was Jet America.

CHAPTER TWELVE

War and Peace

For Alaska Airlines, Neil Bergt was a tough competitor. The onetime Fairbanks milkman, bush pilot, and founder of MarkAir may not have been one of Alaska's legendary bush pilots, but there is no doubt he was one of the most interesting. A self-made man, Bergt was born in Tacoma, raised in Anchorage, and as a young man, accumulated enough money to take flying lessons. When he qualified for a pilot's license, he began flying for Jim Magoffin, the bush pilot and founder of Interior Airways.

Always colorful and known for his piloting skill, Bergt did have one nonfatal accident while working for Magoffin. He was piloting a Beech 18, a small twin-engine aircraft with a twin tail and the first retractable landing gear ever installed on a transport aircraft of that size. Because a retractable gear was unfamiliar to many pilots back then, Beech provided a warning horn that sounded if the aircraft reduced power for landing with the gear still raised. When Bergt flew it for the first time, he tried to land with the wheels up and was lucky to walk away unhurt. Magoffin naturally asked him why he tried to land with the gear still up.

"I was so distracted by a f-----g horn going off," he explained, "that I forgot to lower the damn gear."

Magoffin eventually named him chief pilot because Bergt actually was an excellent instructor. "He could really teach you how to fly an airplane," fellow bush pilot Gary Lintner conceded. "He was a damned good pilot. He gave me some advice that I later passed on to every student I taught to fly. He'd ask us, 'What's the difference in airspeed between a flying airplane and a stalled airplane?'

"We'd all guess a figure that was way too high, and Bergt would warn us, 'The difference is less than *one* knot, and the point I'm trying to make is that if you get into a stall, you don't have much time to recover while taking off or landing.' "

Going into management didn't change Bergt one iota. Like the majority of veteran bush pilots, he often flew by the seat of his pants and was proud of it. Neil Bergt was simply a charter member of this fiercely independent breed. This, in turn, dictated his relationships with his pilots; they either swore by him or at him, but they all followed.

In person, Bergt was about five feet nine, rather stocky, with reddish-blond hair and an ingratiating smile that made most people instinctively like and trust him. And he was ambitious. He bought Interior Airways from Magoffin when the economic bread and butter of the little enterprise was flying freight and backcountry charters. Soon afterward, Bergt renamed the flying service Alaska International Air, and formed a holding company, Alaska International Industries (AII).

Much to the amazement of his bush-pilot brothers, he began to acquire an expensive fleet of Lockheed Hercs, and Alaska International began to deliver cargo around the world, including Bangladesh, Pakistan, and Libya. He also positioned his enterprise to take advantage of the huge airfreight demands associated with the construction of the trans-Alaska pipeline. Interestingly, one of AII's employees during that period, albeit briefly, was George W. Bush, later to become the nation's 43rd president. Bush worked for Bergt's company as a summer hire in the mid-1970s while pursuing a graduate degree in business from Harvard.

In the early 1980s, Bergt took time away from his Alaskan air-cargo company to assume control of Western Airlines as chairman and CEO. The month before becoming Western's chairman, he led an effort by Eagle International, a start-up company with $50 million, to acquire Wien. The intention was to merge Wien into Western.

A June 1982 Reuters article reported that an administrative-law judge had recommended approval of the Wien purchase: "The recommendation also called for allowing the merged carrier and Alaska International Air to come under the common control of Neil G. Bergt, Western's chairman, owner of Alaska International, and president of Wien." Not bad for an Alaskan bush pilot, but the pieces didn't fit together and the plan was scrapped. A short time later, Bergt was replaced at Western by Jerry Grinstein, which eventually led to Western's merger with Delta.

As an airline owner, Bergt never commanded the fierce loyalty that so many Alaskans, employees and customers alike, bestowed on Art Woodley, although he was not unlike Art in his aversion to government authority. The other characteristic he shared with Woodley, although not with the same unforgiving intensity, was a dislike of Alaska Airlines.

In 1984, Bergt changed Alaska International Air's name to MarkAir, acquired Boeing 737-300s, and switched from air cargo to scheduled passenger service. It wasn't long before MarkAir was competing head-on with Alaska Airlines. At that time, relations between Bergt and Alaska Airlines' Bruce Kennedy were amicable, but a code-sharing arrangement that had been crafted by the two carriers was a time bomb. Alaska agreed to code-share with MarkAir in Alaska markets it didn't serve, and also in some markets where the two carriers would be competing. There would be a wall between them in some places, and a head-to-head brawl in others.

Ray Vecci honestly believed that the five-year pact, initiated in 1985, would work to Alaska's advantage. MarkAir, having already replaced the collapsing Wien at Prudhoe Bay, was also flying in competition with Alaska at Bethel. But it announced plans to serve Dutch Harbor, and was serving King Salmon and Dillingham, all of which were not on Alaska's routes.

When Vecci brought the deal before an officers' meeting, however, there was less than unanimous support. Among the opponents were Ken Skidds and his young protégé, a refugee from Wien named Marvin Van Horn.

Van Horn had come to Alaska before the pipeline boom, when Anchorage was still a small town with a frontier atmosphere. After working briefly in physical therapy and as a ski-lift operator at the Alyeska Ski Resort, he eventually landed a job with Wien. There he quickly established himself as a self-trained expert on bush-station operations.

Ken Skidds heard about this young whiz who would go into an inefficient Wien bush station, clean it up, and install modern ticketing and accounting procedures, and had thereby built a reputation as a skilled troubleshooter. When Alaska inaugurated service at Kotzebue in 1980, Skidds made a point of inviting then-competitor Van Horn to see the first flight arrive, and Van Horn still remembered the eye-opening experience years later. "Bruce Kennedy, John Kelly, and Jim Johnson were among the officers who came," he related, "and the way Alaska marched into that little station with all the bigwigs really got to me. I found out that Skidds had gone into town looking for me to make sure I'd be present so I could meet everybody. I even felt a little awkward, as if I didn't belong there, and frankly, I was blown over.

"They had a brand-new terminal, everyone was nice to me, and Bruce Kennedy came over to shake my hand. I remember thinking, 'If this is what the competition looks like, Wien's not gonna survive,' and that night I told my wife I'd better hitch my wagon to Alaska."

Van Horn heard that Alaska was going back into Prudhoe Bay and was building a new terminal at Deadhorse. So he called Skidds. "I know Dead-horse," he said, "so how about hiring me as the station manager there?"

Skidds agreed and soon discovered he had hired someone with a mind of his own. Van Horn had been station manager in Deadhorse for only a few days when he realized that Alaska's flights in and out of the airport were run-ning almost empty.

"Alaska thought Deadhorse was going to be like Kotzebue, where all the airline had to do was show up," Van Horn said. "I knew better. The trouble was that Wien already had five flights a day at Deadhorse; we had two, and that was too much capacity.

"After about 10 days of almost zero load factors, I figured I'd better hit the streets and drum up some business. Almost everything was done on credit then, so I beat the bushes lining up charge accounts. I immediately ran afoul of Dave Hall, our regional sales manager, who summoned me to Anchorage and read me the riot act."

"Drumming up sales is not your job," Hall scolded.

"Well," Van Horn retorted, "then somebody better do it because our flights are operating empty."

Van Horn had made his point, and Hall hired a sales rep named Rexanne Forbes to handle Deadhorse. She eventually became Van Horn's alternate manager at the station, and they formed a compatible team. They already knew each other from the days when Van Horn worked for Wien and Forbes was an innkeeper in Kotzebue.

Van Horn's incursion into sales territory hadn't done him any harm in

Ken Skidds's eyes. The two of them quickly forged a lasting friendship.

"It wasn't enough just to say that Ken Skidds was involved with all of Alaska's stations," Van Horn related. "*Involved* was an understatement. He looked at how furniture was placed, what kinds of pictures were on walls, and how carpets were laid out. He gave you the feeling that Alaska was *his* airline, and that its airplanes were *his* airplanes.

"I loved Ken and really respected him, but he was a very difficult man to work for. Yet, ironically, he also was one of the easiest. He expected a lot from you and he made high demands on your time. But if he trusted you, he'd leave you alone. He'd call at all hours of the day and night, and sometimes go into orbit over anything that was really bothering him. Ken was also always one step ahead of you, bringing up something you hadn't quite thought through yourself."

Both Skidds and Van Horn served on a so-called "Commuter Committee," established to put together a code-sharing network of small Alaskan carriers. Vecci chaired the committee, which included Lane Kemper, a bright young woman from accounting who later would become director of reservations.

Van Horn and his cohorts worked out the first code-sharing deals with three carriers: Era, Air Pac, and Bering. Then Vecci got the idea that MarkAir would make a good additional partner.

It was no wonder that Skidds's and Van Horn's voices were among the loudest raised against doing any kind of business with Neil Bergt. Both were old Alaska hands and were only too well aware of Bergt's reputation.

Vecci, on the other hand, had met Bergt when the code-sharing arrangement was first discussed and thought he was very likeable. This was not so surprising, because Bergt could charm the skin off a 20-foot python.

Yet both Skidds and Van Horn understood why Vecci believed that code-sharing with MarkAir made sense. "Ray was a strategic thinker," Van Horn pointed out. "We had a flaky arrangement with Air Pac [a small Alaskan regional carrier], and Wien was going out of the picture fast. Ray was anxious to find ways to serve the whole state, and he honestly thought code-sharing with MarkAir would be to our advantage."

Vecci did ask Van Horn, "Do you think it will work?"

"Ray," he replied, "it's going to be tough, as you'll find out."

"Can we do it?"

Van Horn hesitated, then said, "Well, *technically* we can find a way." He had deliberately hung on that word *technically*, but Vecci either missed or ignored the implication and began negotiations with the likeable Mr. Bergt.

Van Horn worked closely with Irv Bertram on all code-sharing contracts and especially hard on the one with MarkAir. Weeks after the deal was put into effect, however, Skidds's suspicions about Bergt kept surfacing with alarming frequency. He would call Van Horn in the middle of the night with a fresh complaint about Alaska's new code-sharing partner. "What the hell's going on with that damn MarkAir?" he'd bellow. "They're screwing us!"

"Settle down, Ken," Van Horn would say soothingly. "I'll look into it."

The truth was that the Alaska Airlines–MarkAir relationship was built on the flimsy sands of mutual distrust. In the beginning, however, it was at least friendly if somewhat wary, like a couple of pugnacious dogs circling each other while deciding whether to play or fight.

Van Horn had been afraid of inevitable hostility when he and Bertram worked out the code-sharing contract. He knew that MarkAir used American's computerized reservations system called Sabre, which was different from the one Alaska was operating. So Van Horn insisted that Bertram include provisions delineating how much computer information each airline was willing to share and exactly what information they would agree not to share.

"We didn't want them to have full access to our computer system to operate those code-sharing flights," Van Horn explained. "I kept worrying about how to control access to make sure they wouldn't take advantage of it. How were we going to keep them from picking up our passengers at places where we were competitive if they could tap into our reservations data?"

Van Horn informed MarkAir that if they could access Alaska Airlines' computer system, Alaska should have access to theirs. So Bertram added a clause to the contract that required MarkAir to furnish Alaska with a Sabre-accessible computer set, and Alaska would provide them with one linked to its own reservations system. It sounded fair, at least in theory. MarkAir didn't want Alaska to access Sabre any more than Alaska wanted them snooping around its own reservations data. So at first it was a kind of checkmate; yet it was only a matter of time before somebody threw the first punch.

Both airlines pointed accusing fingers at each other. Marvin Van Horn swore that it was MarkAir. "At the beginning, I don't think we ever went into their Sabre system," he insisted. "The threat was there, however, and for a while it kept them from accessing ours." It was an agreement destined to fail.

The shaky alliance with MarkAir was to culminate in a full-fledged war, even as Alaska was engrossed in some other momentous events such as repulsing an uninvited takeover attempt and successfully engineering a merger with a carrier much like itself. All of which coincided with the formation of a new corporate structure known as Alaska Air Group, Inc.

Alaska was at a financial zenith, and along with new routes, it studied what acquisition opportunities might offer for expansion. Kennedy was looking for synergy, something that could increase its profitable north-south service, especially to its markets in the state of Alaska.

In 1985 the board of directors of Alaska Airlines, with the approval of its shareholders and with an eye toward the future, established the afore-mentioned Alaska Air Group, Inc., as a holding company for Alaska Airlines and future acquisitions. Bruce Kennedy was looking ahead to forging more permanent alliances, and that meant mergers and/or acquisitions.

Such aspirations may have seemed a bit pretentious, considering the airline's expanding size but limited route structure. Yet Kennedy had evidence that Alaska's financial comeback during the 1980s was attracting industry-wide attention for its enviable brand of service. It was not generally known that both Bob Crandall of American and Dick Ferris of United had sounded Kennedy out on the possibility of acquiring Alaska.

"I know you're not interested in a merger at this time," Crandall told Kennedy, "but if you ever are, call me."

Ferris said the same thing, and Don Carty, who succeeded Crandall, repeated American's offer to John Kelly a few years later, after Kelly had become Alaska's CEO. Northwest was another carrier that expressed interest in merging with Alaska.

Along about the time Northwest was first fluttering its eyelashes in Alaska's direction and the 1985 strike was petering out, finance vice president Ray Vingo phoned Kennedy one morning. "Marvin Davis has been trying to get in touch with you," Vingo reported. He went on to identify Davis as an extremely wealthy oilman from Denver, now living in Los Angeles, whose many investments included films. "I think you might as well talk to him," Vingo advised.

Kennedy did call Davis, who insisted he had to see him as soon as possible.

"Well, I'm going on a two-week vacation tomorrow," Kennedy said. "We can meet when I get back."

"What are you doing this afternoon?" Davis pressed.

Four hours later, Davis arrived in Seattle aboard his own 727 executive jet accompanied by Steve Gray, his financial officer. Kennedy sent his assistant, Vicki Johnson, to fetch the Davis party and chauffeur them to Alaska's headquarters, where Kennedy and Vingo were waiting.

One glance at the towering, massive Davis, and Kennedy could read in Vicki's discreet smile that she had had a carload. After introductions, Davis lowered himself into a barrel chair, which seemed to compress to the floor.

In less than an hour's discussion, billionaire Davis, whose reputation as a hostile acquirer preceded him, made it clear that he was set upon acquiring Alaska Air Group, that his son would be running it, and that there was little reason to resist the proposal. Davis, a former wildcatter, had recently acquired 20th Century Fox. There was, according to Davis, "only the matter of determining the price."

Kennedy and Vingo teamed to telegraph genuine reluctance to each other without provoking hostility. As a cordial offer, Davis invited them to tour his personal jet, and Kennedy and Vingo drove their guests back to the Davis jet, which was parked in Alaska's hangar. While touring the impressive aircraft, Vingo risked a faux pas by asking Davis if he could really get into the circular glass shower in the forward stateroom.

Talking softly, Gray assured Kennedy that he would be well taken care of for delivering the airline to Davis. Gray appeared puzzled when Kennedy responded that there was "no sum of money that would motivate him to acquiesce to Davis."

Neither Gray nor Davis realized it, but they had offended probably the last man in the airline industry to be even remotely interested in any personal gain that might be derived from a merger, especially an unwelcome one. But still confident, Davis himself turned to Kennedy, gave him a bear hug, and assured him that everything could be worked out satisfactorily.

Kennedy and Vingo returned to the office and immediately placed a call to one of the foremost anti-takeover law firms in the country. Their office turned out to be only a floor or two removed from Marvin Davis's offices in Beverly Hills. The lawyers advised Kennedy not to enter into any further discussion with Davis, and not to return what the lawyers knew would be a barrage of calls from the Davis enterprise. After a few weeks of bluff and bluster, the assault ceased.

Shortly thereafter, Davis took a significant equity position in Northwest Airlines, from which he soon profited nicely when California businessmen and investors Al Checci and Gary Wilson made their successful acquisition of the Minneapolis-based airline.

Kennedy's eyes were fixed on a small, terminally ill carrier based in Long Beach that Ray Vingo and others had been investigating. So had other airlines fishing around for possible new destinations, and seeking to establish a presence on the West Coast. One of them was the powerful Delta. The object of all this attention was Jet America.

At the time Alaska's courtship began, Jet America was less than five years old. Yet in that short span of time, it had achieved a reputation for offering superb service at low fares. Moreover, it boasted one of the most highly motivated, loyal workforces in the entire industry.

Born in the aftermath of airline deregulation, it had begun operations in November 1981. Its prime bread-and-butter route was Long Beach-Chicago, where it competed against a pair of powerhouses: American and TWA. Within two years, it had run TWA completely out of the market. And this success story had been written largely by a small group of California businessmen, including former Air California vice president of marketing Skip Kenison, who played a leading role in Jet America's founding and became its president.

While at Air Cal, Kenison had done a route study that showed that the population center of Orange County had shifted north of Anaheim and that if an airline put service into Long Beach, it would have a tremendous impact. Kenison never had a chance to capitalize on the study's findings while at Air Cal, but instead he organized a group composed mostly of former associates at Air Cal that raised about a million dollars in initial seed money to found Jet America. He and his cohorts hired an underwriter to raise the $40 million they needed to start operations with a stock issue, but the stock sale fell short by about half.

"That left us tremendously undercapitalized," Kenison related. "But by the fall of 1981 we had all our people in place, and we were getting ready to fly when the city of Long Beach got tied up with a noise-abatement lawsuit and we couldn't get into the airport."

Kenison had a small cadre of about 25 employees already on full salary. He called them all into a meeting that was held in an airport parking lot — the airline had no offices yet — and laid out the gloomy facts. "You're going to be taking a 50 percent wage cut," he began. "It might even be more than 50 percent because we don't have enough money and we can't begin service without an airport. So, if anyone wants to pull out now, I'll try to find them another job and write a good letter of recommendation." Not a single person left.

"Undercapitalized" was the right word for Jet America. Kenison did not want to start an airline with a fleet of worn-out, secondhand airplanes, yet without much cash, leasing was the only way to obtain new equipment.

He chose the MD-80 because they were built in Long Beach and McDonnell Douglas had the training facilities — flight simulators and cabin mockups — that Jet America couldn't afford yet.

The infant company leased four MD-80s to begin with and added more as traffic increased. At the time of the merger with Alaska, its MD-80 fleet numbered eight plus two delivery positions. Because of Jet America's financial problems, however, McDonnell Douglas and the International Lease Finance Corporation (ILFC) required stiff lease payments, and these were to eat away at the airline's cash reserves.

When the city had settled the lawsuit brought by homeowners in the airport area, Jet America received its FAA certificate and began offering nonstop service between Long Beach and Chicago. Jet America settled on an introductory fare of $99, but the underfunded airline didn't have enough money to advertise its promotional bargain.

When Kenison confided the problem to a Delta vice president he knew, he received some sound advice: "Just do a little public relations work. Publicity doesn't cost anything."

So out went a few judiciously placed news releases announcing the $99 introductory fare from Long Beach to Chicago, and only $44.50 for the return Chicago-Long Beach flight. The response was successful beyond what anyone expected, and actually was *too* successful. On November 16, 1981, approximately 3,700 people swamped the Long Beach Airport for the inaugural flight, and word came from Chicago that there were another 1,200 waiting there for the return flight. The crowd at Long Beach was so large that the city sent a squad of policemen to set up crowd-control barriers. It was commanded by a Sergeant Dave Bowers, and in gratitude the airline named its first airplane tug *Sgt. Bowers.*

Only two of Jet America's first four leased MD-80s had been delivered, and even using both of them on the round-trip inaugurals took care of fewer than 300 of the nearly 5,000 customers who had purchased tickets at the special introductory fare. Kenison knew the bargain-basement tickets had to be honored, so for about a month the two MD-80s were losing money on every Long Beach-Chicago round-trip.

But at least the new airline was finally off the ground, a carrier the size of a mosquito with the spirit of an eagle. It had to increase fares, of course, but it remained a low-cost carrier even though only Alaska could come close to matching its in-flight service. Jet America's coach meals were the equivalent of what major carriers such as United served its first-class passengers.

Jet America was using Marriott as its caterer, but a lot of the planning for in-flight service was done by a young woman who happened to have been the 19th employee that Jet America hired, originally as a flight attendant. She eventually became Kenison's wife, and as Mary Kenison she was to contribute much to Jet America's flight-attendant corps because she had an instinct for hiring motivated people.

Jet America was nonunion, and that included its pilots and flight attendants. Mary Kenison gradually acquired more responsibility, hiring not only flight attendants but also such frontline employees as ticket agents. She recruited well even though the airline's nonunion pay scales were markedly low.

Kevin Finan, a former Navy airman, was the airline's first and only chief pilot. Finan interviewed all the pilot applicants, most of them ex-Navy like himself. The interviews took place in the same large room where Mary Kenison was screening flight-attendant hopefuls.

"I kept sneaking looks at Kevin's group to see which of my applicants were drawing the most attention from his," she admitted, "and those were the ones I was hiring."

No one joined Jet America for the money. Captains started out at $50 an hour, copilots at $25. Initial pay for a flight attendant was only $11.50 an hour, they flew 80 hours a month, and they never reached a salary higher than $35,000 a year, one of the industry's lowest figures.

On the other hand, the airline's senior management made every effort to compensate employees for their low salaries. The company paid 100 percent of health insurance, and crew-layover hotels had to be first-class establishments.

Come June of 1982, the airline's underwriter suggested the need for another stock offering, but warned that Jet America would have to show a profit that summer. As he had during Jet America's birth pains, Skip Kenison went to his employees.

When they had come through the first time, and operations had been launched successfully, he gave back every bit of the 50 percent cut he had asked them to take, plus the equivalent amount in stock. Now he asked them to take a 10 percent wage cut across the board and promised to pay them back if the summer was profitable. He kept his word, but this was the last thing he was able to do for them.

Another company that Skip Kenison was associated with had become embroiled in a savage legal fight. To protect Jet America from any involvement, Kenison resigned from the airline he had helped found. His wife, Mary, stayed on, however, and was an enormous help to Jet America's new president, Don Rhoads, who had been on the airline's board from its inception and was a former high-ranking executive at Sears and its Allstate insurance subsidiary. Under his leadership, the airline enjoyed more than 20 consecutive profitable months. Then the combination of heavy competitive pressure from American Airlines and cash-draining lease payments took their toll.

Another negative factor was a decision to serve Dallas, American's backyard, which was like waving a red flag in front of a bull. Yet it no longer made any difference where Jet America went, for by the fall of 1986, the airline was out of cash and out of hope that it could survive.

"It was not just on the brink of Chapter 11," Alaska's Ray Vingo recalled. "It was on the brink of Chapter 7 and total liquidation. They were trying to interest buyers, but all their prospective buyers took one look at those high aircraft-leasing costs and backed away."

Alaska didn't back away. Vingo was the point man in the negotiations, while Bruce Kennedy stayed in the background. Kennedy's concern was that if a merger was consummated, the transition would probably be painful for Jet America's dedicated employees. He knew that some trauma was inevitable. Instead, Kennedy envisioned two separate airlines, one union and the other nonunion. While Jet America's culture was similar to Alaska's, the differences between a unionized company and a nonunion one are significant. Kennedy understood the perspective of each and the possible incompatibilities that might result. He also pondered the possibilities of expanding Jet America in the Lower 48.

Alaska's first tender offer was to acquire controlling shares of Jet America stock for $20 million, not a very high offer but generous inasmuch as the stock was virtually worthless by then. The offer was contingent on negotiating new lease terms with McDonnell Douglas and ILFC. Vingo figured it was a done deal until Delta unexpectedly came in with a higher tender offer. Alaska upped the ante, and Delta abandoned the battle for Jet America when it decided to pursue and ultimately acquire Western Airlines.

So for a sum of slightly over $30 million, Alaska Airlines had acquired eight almost-new MD-80s and nearly 800 skilled employees, including several destined to become important contributors to their new employer.

"The real reason we bought Jet America," recalled John Kelly, "was precisely because it was nonunion and they were going to be our growth vehicle in the Lower 48. It was a very deliberate strategy to get around our high costs and inability to get competitive wages and work rules from existing work groups, even after the 1985 strike enabled us to get a B-scale and other concessions."

So initially, Jet America was operated as a separate airline, retaining its east-west route structure. By mid-1987, however, less than a year after the acquisition, it was evident that Jet America's east-west flying could not be made economically viable. Unforeseen competition, depressed yields, and low load factors took their toll. Union carriers simply would not provide feed to the low-cost, nonunion Jet America flights. Kennedy and his Alaska team decided the wisest course was to merge Jet America's people and equipment into Alaska Airlines and redeploy them on the West Coast. Alaska's employees, especially its pilots, felt threatened. The pilots didn't stop work, but by "working to book," they stalled departures.

The slowdown culminated in an all-employee meeting chaired by Kennedy. "The employees were unmerciful, yet Bruce hung in there and answered questions for hours," remembered Kelly. "The plan to operate Jet America as a separate carrier was not going to work. That's when Alaska changed course."

Alaska kept the California carrier's valuable Orange County, San Francisco, and Long Beach markets and discontinued service to all Midwest and East Coast destinations on the former Jet America system. These included Dallas, Chicago, and Washington, D.C. — all would be added to Alaska's system later — and Minneapolis/St. Paul, St. Louis, and Detroit, previously passed over by Alaska because of stiff competition from Northwest Airlines.

The mid-1980s saw an epidemic of mergers affecting smaller California-based carriers struggling to stay alive in the rough-and-tumble environment of the fare wars caused by deregulation. One by one, they succumbed to economic pressures and invited acquisition by carriers seeking a foothold on the West Coast. Delta acquired Western, US Air gobbled up Pacific Southwest, and American swallowed Air California.

Some of the Jet America alumni to leave their imprint on Alaska Airlines were Mary Kenison; Kevin Finan, who would eventually become Alaska's vice president of flight operations and then executive vice president of operations; and Kit Cooper, who had been with Skip Kenison at Air California. Cooper would be instrumental in the operational success of Alaska's expansion into Mexico and even back into Russia.

"I saw it all happen," Cooper remembered. "I had a lot of friends at both Air Cal and PSA, and the day after their mergers took place, you didn't know their airlines had ever existed.

"These were people who had taken a lot of pride in their old companies, but they couldn't transfer that pride over to a strange new corporate entity that suddenly owned them. That's one reason why all these attempts by Delta, American, and US Air to move in on West Coast markets never really succeeded for any of them.

"I was Air Cal's station manager at Oakland when American took us over. They sent over their San Francisco general manager, who informed me that American's dress code for station managers called for business suits with white shirts, and that we were never again to wear sports jackets in the office.

"Striped shirts were absolutely forbidden. I came into work one day wearing a striped shirt, and the guy told me I looked like a Mississippi riverboat gambler," said Cooper. Things like that illustrated the cultural differences between conservative American and informal Air Cal, just as PSA's flamboyant style disappeared when US Air took it over.

"When Delta was courting Jet America, they sent some management people over to talk to us," Cooper continued. "We were told that while we'd be guaranteed a job, it might not be where we were working now. Alaska came in and told us we were not only guaranteed a job, but it would be on the West Coast. That made all the difference in the world.

"Most of Jet America's employees favored Alaska over Delta, figuring they'd get a better deal than if they were shuffled into one of Delta's massive hub operations in Atlanta or Dallas."

This was true. Still, for practically everyone at Jet America, it was more a case of choosing the lesser of two evils than really welcoming any merger. Going with either Alaska or Delta generally was simply the bitter pill that had to be swallowed as the only alternative to bankruptcy.

The unanswered question was which airline would treat them better, and according to Mary Kenison, the flight attendants were more concerned than any other employee group. "There was a lot of apprehension," she recalled, "so much so that when the merger took effect, we already had lost between 10 and 15 percent of them. Then later, when they tried to get back in and found they couldn't, they were sorry.

"Yet I must add that after the merger, it was a nightmare for our flight attendants for at least two years. They weren't used to the union guidelines that suddenly began ruling their lives. I had some of them coming into my office sobbing.

"I was apprehensive, too," she added. "At Jet America, as director of in-flight I was Queen Bee and I was used to doing things my way. If I thought the flight attendants needed something, I just went to the president of the airline and got it for them. Suddenly, I was in a new environment where I really had little say. And I was used to talking frankly to my people without having a third party between us."

One contentious issue was typical. Jet America flight attendants had been taught a "handshake" ritual. This required flight attendants to shake the hand of every first-class passenger boarding a flight, call the person by name, and introduce themselves. But at Alaska, they were soon informed by the AFA that the handshake would no longer be allowed because of concern that it could spread germs. That didn't stop the personal gesture, and some of Jet America's flight attendants now flying for Alaska continue their practice of introducing themselves personally to first-class passengers.

One former Jet America flight attendant was Carmen Jones, whom Mary Kenison considered the best she had ever seen. Jones actually had resigned from Jet America before the merger to become a physician's assistant, but she missed flying and asked Kenison to intercede with Alaska on her behalf.

"Alaska was smart enough to hire her on my recommendation," Kenison related. "As of 2005, Carmen [now Carmen Poloni] was based in Anchorage, still flying, and as far as I know, still shaking hands. She had a smile that would light up a coal mine, and she not only loved her job but also was very creative. When she worked first class, she'd bring her own linens aboard the airplane because she didn't think Jet America's were nice enough."

Carmen Jones was part of what Mary Kenison used to call her A team, a quarter of the flight attendants who stood out even on an airline loaded with above-average cabin crews. The others, all of whom eventually found a receptive home at Alaska, were Sue Romero, Helene Erickson, and Sue McGinley.

At first, Mary Kenison supervised in-flight operations in Long Beach. Later she moved to Seattle and became the airline's assistant vice president of in-flight services. During the transition, she tried her best to help the California-based flight attendants cope with their new culture. They paid her the ultimate tribute by asking her to represent them in negotiating a variety of issues with the AFA union.

"She not only did," Skip Kenison said proudly, "but she won them full seniority rights, not a small achievement."

"Most of the Alaska flight attendants were friendly right from the start," Mary Kenison recalled, "while others took some time before they came around. Some, I believe, thought we were going to come in and tell them how they should be doing their job and showed some resentment, even though that never happened."

Dealing with the flight-attendant corps was blissful in comparison to merging the two mutually hostile pilot groups. Integration of pilot-seniority lists has always been one of the stickiest issues of every airline merger. It was especially difficult after the decision to merge Jet America into Alaska because the integration process pitted Alaska's ALPA members against Jet America's nonunion pilots.

Long before the merger, Bruce Kennedy dispatched a team of Alaska officers, with Bob Gray as the chief coordinator, to Long Beach with the goal of making the whole process as painless as possible for Jet America's personnel. The decision to operate Jet America temporarily as a separate airline helped the integration process. The strategy was humane, reflecting a rare sensitivity atypical of the usual airline merger, in which the acquired carrier often is treated like a conquered nation suddenly occupied by an invading army. Yet the touchy seniority issues remained. During the early merger talks between the two companies, some of Alaska's ALPA pilots served notice that Jet America's nonunion pilots would not be welcome aboard Alaska's airplanes.

Gray, as vice president of industrial relations, was handed the job of negotiating an integration agreement that would be fair to both sides, an assignment that made Solomon's biblical "Who gets the baby?" decision look easy. Gray would retire in another three years, and settling the pilots' seniority flap would be his toughest negotiating effort.

In talking to the Jet America pilots from the earliest days of Alaska's acquisition, Gray had discovered that the Long Beach airline's pilots were a staunchly independent group that never had any intention of joining the Air Line Pilots Association. "They didn't want to affiliate with ALPA when Jet America first got off the ground for a very simple reason," Gray explained. "They knew that if their airline had to live with union work rules and pay scales, a low-cost fledgling airline like Jet America couldn't survive."

Gray had talked to the Alaska pilot group and was informed that if the two airlines merged, Jet America's pilots were going to the bottom of the seniority list.

"I know you can do whatever you please to those guys," he commented, "but they're a godsend to us, and I wish you wouldn't."

That was the post-merger impasse that Gray faced. He could understand the strong fraternalism of Alaska's unionized airmen, just as he could understand the equally strong independent attitude of Jet America's. Over a period of several months, not even his patient *modus operandi* could bridge a gap that was more of a chasm dividing the two parties. Not until both sides agreed to binding arbitration was a compromise reached, the arbitrator's award basically integrating the seniority lists according to date of hire.

There was a final hitch because of some language problems in the award. When that was resolved, both Gray and Jet America chief pilot Kevin Finan agreed it was the fairest deal that could have been expected, although each side insisted they were gypped.

"I'm sure the Jet America pilots wanted more and the Alaska pilots thought they had given up too much," Gray said, "but at least we got an agreement that stuck."

Finan agreed with that assessment, adding this commentary on the merger from the viewpoints of people from both carriers:

"There was something of a culture shock when it happened. Every airline has its own personality or culture, whatever you want to call it. That was true of Jet America. Its pilots, flight attendants, and mechanics were a very close-knit bunch. We were a family because we were very small. We had suffered together through all our problems as well as the merger trauma, and we had a lot of pride.

"Of course, Alaska itself had gone through some very tough times, too. In 1985 they had the IAM strike, and there was still a lot of tension within the workforce. I think the fact that Alaska had bought Jet America was viewed negatively by some employees who felt it would have been better for their company to grow by itself instead of buying another airline. And at the same time, we were invited into a company that was strange to us, a company that had a lot of things going on below the surface in which we had no background or experience.

"So even though there were a lot of similarities between the two companies, there also were cultural divisions. But I'm also convinced that the same differences brought out the best in both cultures and ultimately brought us together.

"Alaska benefited from Jet America's strong customer-service commitment, its spirit and job attitude. Jet America certainly benefited from Alaska's strong historical traditions and deep roots."

No one who worked for Jet America can ever forget that brave little airline. Some 500 people showed up for its 25-year reunion, and an annual golf tournament raises $40,000 a year for a scholarship foundation established by the Kenisons.

Today it would be impossible to tell which Alaska Airlines pilot, flight attendant, mechanic, ticket agent, customer-service agent, or anyone else had ever worked for Jet America. Time, the forging of new friendships, the sharing of common interests and setbacks, healed all differences.

This was especially true of the merger's most contentious principals: the pilots. They eventually staged their own kind of merger, one based on mutual respect, love of flying, and that innate feeling of brotherhood that bonds all airmen.

Reflecting years later, John Kelly cited the wisdom of Kennedy's team in merging Jet America into Alaska's north-south service as critical to making it one of the most successful and efficient airline combinations to come from the merger mania of the mid-1980s. Unlike the other acquisition of the period, it was Alaska's north-south system that was ultimately strengthened by its Jet America acquisition.

"All the other acquiring carriers had east-west operating hub systems that simply didn't — and still don't — work with north-south flying on the West Coast, or the East Coast for that matter," said Kelly. "The timing of aircraft flows and number of hours per day to cover the distance don't allow a carrier to do it with a single aircraft. And once you need two aircraft to do it, you've lost the power of the hub systems and are left with the north-south operating separately from the east-west."

More than a decade after the merger, Alaska was able to return to some of the cities once served by Jet America as well as expand to others on the East Coast. That new chapter of Alaska's expansion would be written not because of its north-south route system, but because of the development of a new generation of long-range aircraft supported by the power of solid market strength and customer loyalty in the Pacific Northwest and in the state of Alaska.

The Jet America merger was one of the most outstanding accomplishments of Bruce Kennedy's regime. Yet in that same eventful year of 1986, he also could have said, "You ain't seen nothin' yet."

On the last day of that year, Horizon Air became part of Alaska Air Group.

By 1990, MarkAir's route expansion had become a threat to Alaska Airlines. MarkAir served 130 rural Alaska communities, its routes extending 15,000 miles, and it had become the largest intrastate carrier in Alaska. But the cost of continuous expansion also had exhausted Bergt's financial resources. In

1991 he proposed that Alaska Airlines acquire MarkAir.

By then Ray Vecci was the airline's chairman and CEO. He asked Ray Vingo and his staff to review MarkAir's financials and provide advice for the board's consideration of a possible acquisition.

"A lot of work went into evaluating whether we should acquire MarkAir," recalled Vecci. "We were also trying to meet Neil Bergt's deadline for making a decision because he stated he could not hold off much longer with investment bankers to raise capital for the airline. Somewhere along the line I met with Neil, and he stated his view that it would be cheaper to buy him out than compete with him."

After Vingo's evaluation had been completed, Vecci called a special board meeting to review the material and to argue his position not to acquire MarkAir. "Although everyone agreed, I'm not sure they did so with a great deal of conviction. After the board meeting, I called Neil to let him know the conclusion."

Vecci described Neil Bergt as a prominent businessman/entrepreneur in Alaska who had "a long-standing relationship with both Ron and Bruce as well as the other directors." Several weeks or even months after what had become a competitive battle with MarkAir, Kennedy came to Vecci's office and told him that he had had a telephone conversation with Bergt. "Bruce," said Vecci, "you can't do this. All it does is encourage him that he will ultimately prevail in his desire for an acquisition."

After that meeting, Kennedy's communication with Bergt stopped, but what had been a low-volume feud between the two airlines over code-sharing violations and route encroachment heated up. In an effort to gain a greater market share, MarkAir inaugurated service between Seattle and Anchorage, and the war that broke out between the two airlines was ultimately fatal for Bergt's overleveraged company.

Bergt wanted more business, and he knew that the Seattle-Anchorage route was lucrative for Alaska Airlines. MarkAir acquired a dozen Boeing 737s and for a time became Alaska's worst nightmare, a discount carrier serving Alaska Airlines' principal markets.

The MarkAir assault on Alaska's markets had become costly, and that's when Bergt called Frank Lorenzo, a friend he had made during the short period that Bergt ran Western Airlines in 1981. Lorenzo was a Wall Street-savvy corporate raider who had taken over Continental Airlines in the 1980s by merging it with Texas International. By the late 1980s, he was out of Continental and running the Houston-based consulting firm Savoy Capital.

Lorenzo was not interested in investing in MarkAir, but he did introduce Bergt to Wall Streeters and told potential investors that in Alaska, MarkAir was the lifeblood to countless small communities. Lorenzo introduced Bergt to the Wall Street investment firm Kidder, Peabody & Company, and it at first agreed to underwrite an initial public offering of $35 million, but the IPO never took off.

Whatever his faults, Bergt had a flair for creating good marketing ideas. One of the best was his State of Alaska Permanent Fund Dividend promotion. In an effort to share the oil wealth with all its citizens, the state of Alaska had created a permanent fund where 25 percent of the revenue generated by its assorted mineral-related income would be placed. Out of the earnings of this fund, half would be distributed to the state's residents — every man, woman, and child.

Bergt conceived the idea of exchanging airline tickets for the dividend checks. In other words, if you, as a state resident, endorsed your dividend check over to MarkAir, and say it was for $1,000, you'd receive at least $1,000 worth of air-travel tickets. It was one of the few successful sales gimmicks that hadn't originated in John Kelly's precedent-setting and prolific marketing factory. Yet it was so good that Alaska unabashedly copied it. MarkAir's cash flow temporarily boomed because of the popular promotion, and this probably helped the airline stay in business a while longer.

MarkAir's short-term ascent eventually stalled, however, and it began selling off its assets, including two Hercs. It later sold three hangars to the state of Alaska pension fund for $5.8 million, and then leased them back. By then, MarkAir had nearly bled out.

Defiantly, Bergt taunted Alaska Airlines, referring to it as an old dinosaur. "They let their costs run amok," he said, but that was really the pot calling the kettle black. At the same time, he likened MarkAir to low-cost Southwest Airlines.

In the face of cutthroat competition in 1991, Alaska Airlines' stock fell 18 percent, and investment-research firms were downgrading it. Prudential Securities projected that Alaska would lose money for the first time in 19 years. Its assets were being depleted in its fight for survival.

MarkAir's service had deteriorated, passenger complaints mounted, and traffic melted away. It enticed passengers by offering half-price fares between Anchorage and Seattle, but that merely turned what had been a profitable route into a money-loser.

Bergt also filed a $150 million lawsuit against Alaska Airlines, charging

that the larger carrier had terminated its code-sharing contract and coop-
erative frequent-flier arrangements illegally, and had moved to destroy
MarkAir because it had invaded Alaska's lucrative markets in Southeast
Alaska and Seattle.

In 1992, six months after the hangar transaction, MarkAir filed for
Chapter 11 bankruptcy, but Bergt was no quitter, even when he was broke.
With the protection provided by bankruptcy, Bergt began moving more of the
airline's jet operations out of Alaska beyond Seattle and into large markets in
the West, the Midwest, and the East, usually over the objections of its creditors and competitors alike.

In 1994, MarkAir, in bankruptcy, went back to the state of Alaska, this
time seeking a $40 million loan to keep flying and for continued expansion.
By some accounts, MarkAir was then $100 million in debt.

Strongly supported by the entire officer corps and a dozen or so other
Alaskan carriers, many of them code-sharing partners, Vecci decided to
oppose the loan on the grounds that MarkAir had already squandered the
state's original support, and that giving it another $40 million was throw-
ing good money after bad. Neil Bergt, on the other hand, was preparing an
impassioned plea to save the jobs of his employees and allow MarkAir to
compete against the arrogant and greedy Alaska Airlines. He claimed that
MarkAir's low fares were saving Alaskans some $75 million a year, so the
loan was as much for the public's benefit as for his airline's.

The somewhat ironic battle lines had been drawn. For the first time in
more than six decades, Alaska was cast in the role of a giant Goliath threatening to exterminate a tiny but courageous David.

The Anchorage hearings began in early 1995 before a blue-ribbon
commission composed of nine members selected by state officials. Bergt's
case was based largely on the David-vs.-Goliath theme, claiming that Alaska
Airlines wanted to put him out of business because it was afraid of MarkAir's
low-fare competition.

"Our competitors have painted MarkAir as a basket case," Bergt said at
one point. "Nothing could be further from the truth, and they know it. We
have become the most efficient airline in America, flying our routes cheaper
than anyone else in the nation."

Bergt's explanation for the huge debt was at least partially true. He
admitted that MarkAir's financial troubles dated back to 1991, when it overexpanded service in the Lower 48 and was unprepared to handle it.

But overall, Bergt's case was weak, and the commission knew it. The bottom line was that if MarkAir was as great as Bergt tried to paint it, why did it so badly need a $40 million handout?

Throughout the entire war with Alaska, Bergt never stopped insisting he was fighting on behalf of his employees, not himself. One of Alaska's rebuttal arguments was to disclose Bergt's total compensation for 1991. It was $926,608, only a third of it representing salary. The rest was a bonus, which made him the third-highest-paid CEO in the U.S. airline industry. (Vecci's salary that year was less than a third of Bergt's compensation.) Yet 1991 had been cited in his lawsuit as the year in which MarkAir was forced into bankruptcy.

Alaska's and the other Alaskan air carriers' chief witness in opposition to the loan request by MarkAir was Arlon Tussing. A prominent Northwest economist long associated with the University of Alaska's Institute of Social and Economic Research, Tussing had solid Alaskan credentials. He was hired by the dissenting carriers to review the economics of MarkAir's proposal and to testify at the commission's meeting. At the hearing, Tussing proceeded to dissect, dismember, and destroy Bergt's arguments and pleas.

After listening to all the arguments, the nine panelists went into a closed-door session and emerged only 15 minutes later with their unanimous decision: the loan application was denied. MarkAir folded before the end of 1995.

Bergt encountered open skepticism from the majority of Alaska's media, but the most unexpected development that helped sink him was a widely circulated series of spoofs of Bergt and MarkAir perpetrated by an unidentified writer who created a fictitious airline called Colorado Air. (Before it sank into Chapter 7 bankruptcy, MarkAir's headquarters had been moved from Anchorage to Denver.) It was no coincidence that the masthead logo on its fake news releases closely resembled that of MarkAir. Most of the releases, which chronicled Colorado Air's supposed attempt to raid the state's treasury not once but twice, quoted a "Ben Dover," identified as the ersatz airline's vice president of finance.

Included in the barrage of spoof literature were several cartoons featuring unflattering caricatures of Bergt. Evidently the mysterious prankster was also an artist, or had some artistic help.

The author also timed the public appearance of his work perfectly. Bergt, who had good political connections in the state legislature, went to Juneau just before the hearings began with an elaborate dog-and-pony show aimed at convincing the lawmakers that MarkAir's survival was important to the state's economy, the airline's own employees, and the traveling public. Unfortunately for him, the same audience he was planning to impress was hit with "vice president of finance" Ben Dover's news releases, along with the cartoons ridiculing Bergt. Even legislators friendly to Bergt and MarkAir were laughing. And laughter used against the most impassioned argument can be more destructive than outright confrontation.

It would be going way too far to credit the Colorado Air caper with destroying Bergt's hoped-for political support. There is no doubt, however, that he was counting on that support, and obviously it failed to emerge at the hearing itself. But Bergt had too much going against him anyway.

One thing that could be said about him is reminiscent of Charlie Willis: Bergt was a fighter who never stopped insisting that Alaska Airlines had wronged not only him but also MarkAir's employees.

The most difficult aspect of a man's character to judge fairly is his sincerity. So fast-forward to July 22, 1998 . . .

On that date, the $150 million lawsuit that Neil Bergt had filed against Alaska Airlines eight years earlier was settled out of court with MarkAir's trustees for $19 million, the amount approved by a bankruptcy judge. By then John Kelly was Alaska's CEO, and the legal team convinced him that any continued legal wrangling made no business sense and would be a waste of time.

The bankruptcy judge served as an intermediary between MarkAir's creditors' committee and Alaska Airlines at a settlement meeting held in Anchorage. The judge very fairly went from room to room, back and forth, working both sides to get a settlement. Each side was reminded what the outcome "could be," and that a settlement was a better course of action.

The committee of creditors finally settled on a sum of $19 million. "I was loath to pay the sum," said Kelly, "but I was convinced by our legal team and the judge that it made good business sense. And it did." The money was eventually paid to bankrupt MarkAir's creditors.

Bergt said in a statement released to the press that he had won only a moral victory because $19 million was far too inadequate to cover the damages inflicted on MarkAir. "Our research indicated that a jury award in excess of $60 million was probable," he declared. "Quite frankly, I was looking forward to telling our story in open court and winning full restitution and vindication for our 1,800 loyal employees . . . and I wanted our creditors paid in full."

He professed no regrets on his own behalf, only for MarkAir's people —

some of whom, incidentally, were welcomed into the Alaska Airlines family, which now included not only the merged Jet America but also the acquired Horizon Air.

CHAPTER THIRTEEN

Horizon Air — The Little Giant

Horizon Air owes its birth to at least three people, and all of them are named Milton Kuolt. This biographical and historical phenomenon can easily be explained by anyone who knows something about the airline industry and its most colorful tycoons. If it were possible to x-ray a man's personality, Kuolt's would reflect three different individuals: Eddie Rickenbacker of goliath Eastern, Bob Six of midsize Continental, and Bob Peach of tiny Mohawk.

Each ruled his airline with what amounted to one-man authority. In varying degrees they were benevolent dictators, Six the most reasonable and Rickenbacker the most autocratic.

Peach, like Six, was a maverick with an instinct for the unconventional that was uncommon for a small regional carrier such as Mohawk. Remodeling the interiors of his obsolete DC-3s, he gave them a Gay '90s decor, with appropriate flight-attendant uniforms, and beer on tap. These "Gaslight Flights" actually predated the Willis-Giersdorf Gold Rush theme. Peach also was the audacious character who once sued the government's mighty FAA, claiming that its inefficient air traffic control system was responsible for delays that had cost his little airline a lot of money. He lost, but the entire industry silently cheered his effort.

Put all these personality traits — rebellious and resourceful Peach, dictatorial Rickenbacker, and competitive Six — into a single person and you'd be looking at Milt Kuolt. Only up to a point, however. Milt also was an original. He may have blended the personas of these aviation titans, but on the other hand, there was no one else like him in the industry.

His bluntness could carve a stuffed shirt like a Benihana chef slicing beef. His opinions, usually voiced in the saltiest language possible, left no doubt whatsoever as to where he stood on any issue, especially those involving Horizon. He had nicknames for everybody, most of them unflattering.

He professed to be as tough-skinned as a fire hydrant, an unsentimental cynic, and no one would have been surprised if Kuolt's Christmas cards had featured an unrepentant Scrooge bemoaning the fact that he had reformed prematurely. All this was camouflage for a heart as soft as Jell-O.

He loved to dress like a western gunslinger, including a long duster coat and fancy cowboy boots. When he generously volunteered to help out on a busy ticket counter, he still looked like Jesse James eyeing an unprotected stagecoach. It took a lot of courage for employees to finally suggest that customers might feel less intimidated if he was wearing a regular agent's uniform.

When aviation historian Jon Proctor was editor-in-chief of *Airliners* magazine, he wrote a very favorable article about Horizon Air in its July-August 1998 issue, years after Kuolt had left Horizon. Proctor was and still is one of the most respected and knowledgeable aviation writers in the country, and most airline executives have been grateful when he expressed interest in their carriers. Yet even Proctor was curious and a little apprehensive about Kuolt's reaction to the *Airliners* article. So he called Kuolt's secretary.

"I was wondering if Milt has seen our story," he inquired politely.

"Yes," she said, then added ominously, "I think he wants to talk to you."

Proctor held his breath until the voice from Mount Sinai boomed into his receiver. "Proctor," Kuolt bellowed, "I just read your goddamned article. The trouble with it is that it's partially true!"

It was typical of Milt, however, that after having almost punctured Proctor's eardrums, he called him back and ordered 20 copies.

Kuolt had his share of prejudices, and among his pet peeves were corporate annual reports. He argued, and with considerable justification, that they were so dull and stereotyped that nobody read them. So he ordered Horizon's 1985 annual report to be printed in the format of a breezy newspaper, with news stories replacing the usual stilted language of accountants and statisticians. The headline on the front page had nothing to do with 1985's financial results or 1986's outlook. It read:

Horizon's Chairman Says Let's Print an

Annual Report People Will Pick Up and Read

Kuolt was dictatorial, obstinate, irreverent, brutally frank, painfully honest, and hopelessly opinionated. He also was a natural leader who attracted both talent and loyalty in impressive proportions.

The bottom line was that not only did Milt Kuolt care about his people, but he also ran one hell of an airline from the day it began: September 1, 1981, with a single minuscule route between Seattle and Yakima, Washington.

The airline had fewer than 100 employees. In the beginning, its "fleet" consisted of two well-worn 40-passenger F-27 propjets purchased from Quebec Air, so beat-up that the refurbishing and overhaul costs, which included new leather seats and carpeting, almost equaled their purchase price. They were acquired through aircraft broker Scott Kidwell, who later sold a third ex-Quebec Air F-27 to Horizon that was in almost the same sorry state as the first two. Kuolt didn't have the cash to pay the broker's commission, so he gave him stock in Horizon. That turned out to be a better deal than what he would have earned in commissions.

When the first plane arrived in Seattle, Kuolt's face had the look of a man who had just been handed a dead fish left in the sun for five days. He glared at the broker. "My God!" he roared. "You call *that* an airplane? Is that piece of junk what we paid money for?"

It took Dick Heaton, his recently appointed vice president of maintenance, to calm him down. Heaton was afraid that Kuolt was going to inflict bodily harm on the aircraft broker. "Don't worry, Milt," Heaton promised. "When we get through refurbishing it, you won't even recognize it." And Heaton kept his word. The airplane looked pretty good when it took off from Sea-Tac on Horizon's inaugural flight, a proud occasion marred only by Captain Tom Cufley's first announcement from the cockpit.

Cufley had been hired away from Cascade Airways and was considered to be one of the finest F-27 jockeys who ever flew that airplane, just as Dick Heaton was an expert in maintaining them. But when Horizon's inaugural flight was ready to pull away from the gate, Cufley was overwhelmed by the drama of this magic moment.

"Ladies and gentlemen," he intoned, "welcome aboard Cascade flight 100 . . . "

On such an inauspicious note was an airline born — with a single airplane and a cabin public-address blooper. Twenty-five years later, Horizon Air and its 4,000 employees were operating a fleet of 68 modern jets and propjets, making nearly 500 daily departures over a route system serving 46 cities in seven U.S. states and Canada.

Milt Kuolt must have been doing something right.

Milton Kuolt II, the son of missionaries, was a successful businessman in the Pacific Northwest. By the time he founded Horizon with two fellow entrepreneurs, Joe Clark and Bruce McCaw, he had already been bitten by the aviation bug. Kuolt had spent more than 20 years at Boeing, where he advanced to business planning manager for the 737 program, working under Ben Wheat, who ran the program in its earliest stages.

It was only natural that Kuolt and Wheat would become fast friends. Ben, in fact, was Milt's role model when it came to blunt, well-salted language and a fondness for self-deprecating humor. When a reporter once called Kuolt "brusque," Milt claimed he had to look up the word in a dictionary to make sure he hadn't been insulted. Wheat professed to have the same trouble when someone complimented him on his "verve."

It was easy to understand why Kuolt both admired and emulated Wheat, whose antics at Boeing were legendary. There was the time Wheat became convinced that Boeing's security guards never really looked at employee ID badges. To prove his point, he began coming to work with fake badges that identified him variously as Superman, Batman, and serial killer Ted Bundy. No one ever challenged him. Corrective measures were taken before Wheat chanced to show up as Greta Garbo.

Kuolt left Boeing to launch Thousand Trails, a network of membership campsites throughout Washington State. They proved so successful that he was able to put $2 million of his own money into the airline he started.

His battle plan was simple — to provide air service to the state's smaller communities — and the industry's deregulation in 1978 was the door through which he planted his snakeskin cowboy boot. Horizon's only rival at the time was Cascade Airways, already more than a decade old and well established. But Kuolt thrived on the competition.

He believed that every customer deserved more than merely a ride from Point A to Point B, and that meant superior service even on Horizon, a puddle-jumping little airline at the time. When it came to comparative size, Horizon and Cascade were like David and Goliath, except that Kuolt's slingshot was a brand of service unusual for such a small carrier. It began with complimentary wine, then blossomed into other little but much-appreciated amenities such as free newspapers handed out at the gate, complimentary coffee, and baskets on board filled with munching snacks that included all kinds of goodies.

Thus was created a culture, a way of life, and a state of mind that may have lacked Alaska Airlines' rich historical heritage, yet was just as firmly embedded in the work ethic and attitude of every Horizon employee. It was not dissimilar to what had existed at Jet America.

Kuolt encouraged this spirit like a gardener nursing fragile plants and flowers. One of his proudest accomplishments at Horizon was the creation of what was known as the Horizon Air Academy, actually a program for hiring and training new employees, especially those whose jobs would bring them into direct contact with the public.

"We had a guy from Disney come in and organize it," Kuolt related. "My idea was to indoctrinate people in the culture we had established at the airline's very inception: To have a passion for serving customers and to have a passion for excellence.

"For example, say we had 12 potential flight attendants in a class and we could only hire two. We'd find jobs at other airlines for the 10 we couldn't hire.

"The people we hired at Horizon didn't work for a paycheck. They worked because they loved what they did. You may think that's corny, but it was true," said Kuolt.

Horizon was still flying that original pair of F-27s at the time of its acquisition by Alaska Airlines, although by then Kuolt had acquired some decent airplanes. The fleet had been judiciously enlarged in coordination with route expansion. Only one year after inaugurating Seattle-Yakima service, Horizon was flying to 11 other cities in Washington, Oregon, and Nevada, and was providing seasonal service to Sun Valley, Idaho. Much of the early route expansion was made possible by the acquisition of Air Oregon, which turned its fleet of Swearingen Metroliners (an 18-passenger twin-engine transport) over to Horizon.

Horizon's first brand-new airplane was the de Havilland Dash 8, a beautifully designed twin-engine propjet. The plane was built by de Havilland Canada (DHC), whose British parent company had been designing airplanes since before World War I. The Dash 8 resembled the F-27 in that both were high-wing, twin-engine propjet aircraft, but the resemblance was almost entirely visual and superficial. The F-27s were slow and had poor altitude capability. From the more important standpoint of engineering, the Dash 8 was a far superior aircraft. Even though its 37 seats were three fewer than the F-27's, its operating costs were much lower. Not by accident was the Dash 8 DHC's best-selling airplane.

Milt Kuolt conducted the negotiations early in 1986 with de Havilland, and he played the manufacturer like a violin, first whetting their appetite with a bold announcement. "We're going to buy 10 Dash 8's with an option for 10 more," he told de Havilland's chairman, who, figuratively speaking, was licking his chops. He knew that Horizon had been talking to Brasilia and Aérospatiale, two other manufacturers of small regional transports. Now the competition apparently had been eliminated. At the established price of about $5 million per aircraft plus spare parts (roughly the price tag of a single 707 or DC-8 at the start of the jet age), a firm order for 10 Dash 8's added up to a $60 million contract.

Then Kuolt dropped the other shoe. "There are a couple more things I have to tell you," he smiled. "First, we don't have any money."

"Well, we can finance part of the 60 million," the chairman assured him.

"I'm afraid you're gonna have to finance *all* of the 60 million," Kuolt confessed. "And there's one more thing. As part of the deal, de Havilland must take our F-27s in trade as part of the financing."

"And what would you be expecting as a trade-in allowance?" the chairman asked cautiously. He knew by now that he was walking through a minefield.

"Oh, about $500,000 per airplane," Kuolt replied airily.

When Milt left the room, he had the deal he wanted. And it also marked the beginning of a long and fruitful relationship between Horizon and de Havilland of Canada. Years later, after Kuolt retired and Boeing had bought DHC, Horizon ordered a stretched version of the Dash 8, the Q-400, seating 70 passengers, which at this writing remains an important member of Horizon's modern fleet.

Horizon's first pure jetliner was the Dutch-designed, Dutch-built Fokker F-28, which in Horizon's configuration carried 70 passengers. This was good capacity for a short-haul route system, but it was largely offset by the airplane's poor fuel economy and lack of range.

Nevertheless, it was still a real jetliner. Kuolt obtained the first three, used, from an Ivory Coast airline and eventually Horizon wound up with a dozen F-28s, most obtained from US Air. Ordinarily, Kuolt probably wouldn't have bought the airplane, but he heard that Cascade was going to start operating jets, and he reacted defensively. He also acted wisely, resisting the temptation to buy brand-new jetliners that he knew Horizon couldn't afford.

Kuolt was, of course, the ultimate hands-on CEO in virtually every phase of the airline's operations. A delayed or canceled flight would send him up the wall, and he insisted on knowing the reason for every failure to meet schedule.

When Horizon was operating out of Eastern's Sea-Tac gate, the only one available in 1981, the arrangement also called for Eastern to handle baggage loading and unloading. Kuolt went down to the baggage area one day and saw Eastern's ramp workers goofing off while a departing Horizon flight was waiting for its baggage to be loaded. His temper blew every one of its short fuses. His four-letter epithets would have made a longshoreman blush, but the startled Eastern employees began loading Horizon baggage.

Strong leaders like Kuolt often are known for inconsistencies, starting with the love-hate relationships they develop with both employees and managers. Kuolt, blessed with good people at Horizon, never looked for yes-men or sycophants when it came to hiring management personnel. This was true from the very start of Horizon's existence. The airline began life with a small, strong, extremely capable cadre of management talent: people such as Dick Heaton, along with partners Joe Clark and Bruce McCaw, already mentioned.

There also was Dianna "Dee Dee" Maul, a no-nonsense, competent former Cascade employee who was quite possibly the only person at Horizon Air of whom Milt might have been slightly afraid. There certainly was no doubt that he respected her and that she stood up to him when she thought he was wrong. She had been with Cascade for 10 years, most of them in customer service, and came over to Horizon with Tom Cufley when Kuolt's airline consisted of a second-floor office at Boeing Field.

Maul was the one who made sure that Horizon had all the ticketing codes, without which it would not have been able to interline with other carriers. She also arranged for the airline to use Eastern's gate at Sea-Tac. In fact, she was horrified when she heard of Milt's tirade in the baggage area, fearing that Eastern's local manager might cancel the gate-sharing deal.

Kathy Anderson, a former flight attendant who had known Kuolt when he was running Thousand Trails, was another early employee who made an impact at Horizon. She was particularly adept at hiring motivated flight attendants and customer-service agents. She later became Kathy Kuolt, but died of breast cancer several years later, at age 40. Milt, hit hard, never remarried.

There also was Alan Zanouzoski, Horizon's first chief pilot; H. A. "Andy"

Anderson, a former Air Oregon board member whose financial acumen was of enormous help; and John Kuolt, Milt's brother, who steered Horizon skillfully through the requirements of its early sales and marketing efforts when there wasn't much to market.

This list could go on and on, but two individuals in particular must be mentioned because both were to become important contributors to Alaska after leaving Horizon. One was George Bagley. The other was a brash youngster named Bill Ayer.

George Bagley was a former Army paratrooper who took flying lessons, then got a job flying for the Lycoming aircraft engine company in Williamsport, Pennsylvania, his hometown. He joined the Air National Guard, learned to fly jets, quit both the Guard and Lycoming, and enrolled at Utah State University to earn a degree in economics. A professor he knew at the university had become involved with Trans Western, a small regional carrier flying mostly out of Salt Lake City to Jackson Hole, Wyoming, and Sun Valley, Idaho Falls, Twin Falls, and Pocatello, all in Idaho. Bagley not only joined Trans Western as a pilot, but in a short time became its president.

"We were operating Swearingen/Fairchild Metros," Bagley said, "and I heard that Horizon wanted to sell some that they had acquired when they bought Air Oregon. That's how I met Milt Kuolt, who then got interested in Trans Western as a merger partner."

Kuolt not only offered to buy Trans Western, but he also offered Bagley a job as vice president of operations. "I couldn't resist the guy," Bagley recalled. "He was larger than life, a high-intensity character. I never had a hard time working for him. He could be difficult at times. His level of attention was much higher than average, and if you didn't want to play that game with him, he gave up on you very quickly."

But Kuolt never gave up on George Bagley, who fit in immediately with Horizon's culture. He sold Trans Western to Kuolt in 1983, exchanging his Trans Western stock for shares in Horizon. At the time, however, he wondered whether it was a wise move. He had joined Horizon when it was going through a very tough period.

"The airline was losing money while trying to get established competitively," Bagley remembered, "and this was at a time when Cascade was dominating the Northwest commuter market. But Milt had built a good company with a good route system. And he did it with inferior airplanes.

"When I joined Horizon," he remembered, "those obsolete F-27s and the little Metroliners it had obtained from Air Oregon made up the fleet. The

F-27 was rugged, but we used to call it a 'low and slow' airplane. In those days Horizon was a lot like Alaska used to be — our service was better than our flight equipment, and several notches above our competition's."

Bagley's career at Horizon had been at a higher level of authority and responsibility than that of the other Horizon alumnus who was headed for greatness at Alaska. In fact, Milt Kuolt fought against even hiring Bill Ayer.

When it came to versatility, William Ayer was a modern-day Leonardo da Vinci. He was a fully qualified commercial pilot, and he held a degree in economics from Stanford and a master's degree in business administration from the University of Washington. He had founded and operated his own airline. While still in his twenties, he had evolved his own theory about why so many small airline ventures ultimately fail: they are launched by entrepreneurs who know a lot about flying but very little about business. He personally had to learn that lesson the hard way. But once this was accomplished, Bill Ayer possessed such a broad range of experience in so many phases of aviation that it would have been hard to find any airline president or CEO to surpass him.

In 1980, armed with his MBA and all his commercial pilot ratings, he started a small carrier called Air Olympia, of which he was both the president and one of its pilots. The airline operated scheduled flights from Olympia, the Washington state capital, to Yakima and Spokane.

Air Olympia consisted of two 10-passenger, twin-engine Piper Chieftains, president/pilot Ayer, another full-time pilot, and about six other part-time employees. Everyone shared in handling reservations, sales, and bookkeeping tasks during the two years that Air Olympia operated. But as Ayer would put it later, establishing the airline "wasn't the smartest decision I ever made."

"Our flights ran pretty full," he reminisced, "and we didn't do badly, but the economics of a 10-seat airplane are very difficult. We still needed two pilots, and we didn't have high utilization. We operated only one trip over in the morning and back at night. I'd fly the airplane in the morning, make sales calls during the day, and fly the trip back at night. Nor was there any demand for midday service.

"But we did try to give good in-flight service. We even served small meals, which the copilot handed out, doing double duty as a flight attendant. [This was an interesting throwback to the late 1920s and early '30s, when 'second pilots' on single-engine transport aircraft handled in-flight service.]

"We lost money, though nothing astronomical, and it was a great learning environment. Yet we knew we couldn't go on losing money indefinitely, so in 1982 we shut down. Our timing was good because Horizon was started only a few months before we folded. I tried to sell Air Olympia to Kuolt, but he was too smart for that."

Actually, not only did Milt Kuolt want no part of Air Olympia, but he didn't want to have anything to do with its young president either. Milt's brother John was the one who knew him, liked him, and suggested that Ayer would be a good addition to Horizon's management corps.

"We don't need the guy," Milt argued.

"He has great potential," John insisted, and Milt finally gave in.

"Aw, okay," he growled. "Give the little SOB a thousand bucks a month and let him hang around the office until he grows up."

One of Milt Kuolt's many virtues was his willingness to admit mistakes, a rare quality in a man with such a dominating personality. More than two decades after trying to keep Ayer out of Horizon, he confessed that he had been wrong. "In the very first job he had at Horizon," Kuolt said, "I realized he had great scope and vision."

Ayer started out in Horizon's sales and marketing department as manager of charter service, a brand-new assignment stemming from the realization that Horizon had too many F-27s. The airline was operating five, and the scheduled route system needed only two. So Ayer was asked to put a charter operation together.

"I hooked up with a guy in Lake Tahoe," Ayer recalled, "and we started flying casino junkets from Seattle, Portland, and other cities. Eventually our scheduled service grew to the point where we didn't need the charters anymore, and I moved into regular operations."

Ayer became involved with integrating flight equipment into routes and coordinating aircraft with scheduling needs, a job that expanded dramatically when Horizon acquired Trans Western, with its routes into Utah and Idaho. With surprising speed, Kuolt's little airline had become a very comprehensive carrier and a serious challenger to the Northwest's commuter champ, Cascade.

"Looking back," Ayer remembered, "these were among the most fun times I've ever had in the airline business. We were small, everybody knew everybody, and we could turn on a dime. We moved into and out of markets very quickly."

There was one kind of fun, however, for which Alaska's future leader was solely responsible, one that may not have always produced unrestrained general laughter. It seems that Bill Ayer was a skilled mimic whose imitations of certain Horizon officers were uncomfortably realistic. His impersonations included an obvious target: Milt Kuolt himself.

"Ayer was the company clown," Kuolt recounted. "At marketing staff meetings, he'd get up and mimic me, Bruce McCaw, Dick Heaton, and all of the other senior officers. *Impish* is a good word to describe what he was like at Horizon."

Kuolt, as might be expected, ran very loose staff meetings. He invited arguments, discussions, and debates, and when things became too heated he'd bellow, "Let's knock off all this bullshit and have a few snorts." Then he'd open up his cache of whiskey, rum, vodka, and gin and assume one of his favorite roles: bartender to his friends and associates.

"We didn't have any real giants at Horizon at the time," he reminisced wistfully, "except for Bagley and later Ayer. I knew Bagley was good, but I didn't realize that Ayer was so smart.

"But what we did have was a great team of people who had a passion for their work and for everything they did. I don't know if that kind of passion comes from the top, but I do know I've been lucky. Maybe you'd call that leadership, but truthfully, my management skills aren't that great, at least the technical part of management.

"That's why I think I kind of lost it at the end, and decided the company needed more discipline, more structure. Hell, maybe it takes a good leader to recognize that."

Read over those last two paragraphs. They explain why the people of Horizon Air loved Milt Kuolt, including those who thought he could be unreasonable, autocratic, bull-headed, and almost as often wrong as he was right. Reportedly, as Horizon grew and prospered, many of his officers began to chafe under his one-man rule. There were undercurrents of rebellion stirring before Milt himself decided to sell out.

But that is exactly what made Kuolt so refreshingly different from, say, a dictator like Rickenbacker, who had to be forced out of power and until his dying day refused to admit he had ever been wrong. Not Milt Kuolt. First and foremost, he lacked the enormous ego typical of so many old airline tycoons, who left behind a litany of alibis and self-serving rationalizations. Kuolt left a legacy of solid achievement but a weak balance sheet, as Alaska was soon to find out, but it was a service-oriented carrier that already had replaced Cascade as the Northwest's dominant commuter airline.

The acquisition itself was unique in U.S. airline history because even in comparison to Alaska's relatively benign purchase of Jet America, its arrangement with Horizon was more like the forging of a friendly partnership.

There had been earlier merger overtures from Alaska, the first being a visit by Gus Robinson to Kuolt, who said flatly he wasn't interested. Later, Ray Vecci talked to him, although they had different recollections of what transpired. After Alaska acquired Horizon and they had become good friends, Vecci claimed that Kuolt had thrown him out of his office at their first meeting.

Kuolt denied it. "I never threw anyone out of my office," he declared, "although I may have used a few harsh words."

Merger proposals lay dormant for a while, as Horizon grew and prospered. Cascade, meanwhile, cut its own throat by buying new jetliners that were beyond its ability to finance and operate.

One of Kuolt's techniques for buying new airplanes was rather unconventional. He sometimes bought when he *needed* cash. "I'd go to Swearingen/Fairchild, say, and tell them I was short of dough," he related. "So they agreed to sell me an airplane and pay me a hundred thousand in what manufacturers call a fleet-integration fee. So I'd get a new airplane and some cash, and then defer payments on the airplane until we could afford it. But we never reneged."

Before filing for Chapter 7, Cascade's president tried to borrow money from Horizon, but Kuolt turned him down. Cascade retaliated for the rebuff by getting the state attorney general to sue Horizon for unfair competitive practices, an instant replay of Neil Bergt's strategy to save MarkAir by instigating litigation. Kuolt angrily pointed out that Horizon was the little guy in the dispute, and Cascade the big guy that had been in business for more than a decade before Horizon came on the scene. He pointed out that predatory pricing was a weapon that large airlines used, not small ones.

Even after Cascade went into Chapter 7, its bankruptcy trustees vigorously pursued their case against Horizon. Their claim was based on their contention that Horizon had allegedly conspired to put Cascade out of business, and the trustees asked for triple damages. The case never went to trial. "We were able to get the federal district court judge in Spokane to dismiss the case on a summary judgment motion," recalled Alaska's legal affairs chief, Keith Loveless. "The trustees appealed the decision to the Ninth Circuit Court of Appeals, which upheld the lower court's decision."

Inevitably, there was some pre-merger apprehension among Horizon's officers. They feared that their airline, like so many others acquired by larger companies, would be obliterated. Both Kuolt and George Bagley were well aware of those fears.

"They had seen too many examples of larger airlines taking over smaller ones and rearranging them in a way that seemed to wipe out all but a few memories," Bagley pointed out. "But the purchase by Alaska of Horizon turned out to be much different than what most people had anticipated."

Bagley himself admitted to being surprised. He remembered talking with Bill Ayer and predicting that Alaska would send someone over the minute the deal was finalized to take charge and tell everyone what to do and how to do it. But it didn't happen that way.

The sale of Horizon was officially completed at midnight on December 31, 1986 (to give Kuolt a tax advantage), but it was another six months before anyone from Alaska actually came over to replace Milt.

"Alaska kept everything separate, including the work groups," Bagley emphasized, "which avoided a lot of conflict." (Horizon's pilots remained nonunion for 13 years, until the Teamsters, which had an airline division, won a bargaining election.)

Kuolt's reaction to the way Alaska handled the acquisition was even more pronounced than Bagley's. "Horizon, unlike virtually all of today's carriers," he pointed out with considerable feeling, "still has the culture that is part of its heritage. Normally, when a big company absorbs a smaller one, that doesn't happen. Like when Boeing bought de Havilland, only to find out that the number of hours it took to build a Dash 8 was twice what the company had expected. The company did everything possible to whittle that number down, but that was a difficult task in the Canadian labor environment. In the end, Boeing recognized that de Havilland, and the manufacture of small commercial aircraft, really had no place in its long-term plan and it was sold.

"That's what big companies do. They try to make the smaller one fit their own mold, and it's the worst, the most terrible thing you can do, especially if the smaller one has a well-developed culture of its own.

"But this didn't happen when Alaska took over Horizon, and I give Bruce Kennedy full credit for that. He told his people to leave Horizon alone. Provide help if they need it, but let them keep running their own airline."

And that is exactly what took place. Kennedy's pre-merger pledge — "We're here if you need us" — is still in effect, and Horizon retains its independence as a valued partner in Alaska Air Group. The one thing Alaska did provide was a new CEO to replace Kuolt. Kennedy, eager to preserve Horizon's reputation for high-level in-flight and customer service, dispatched an officer whose imagination, creativity, and originality had already helped lift Alaska's in-flight service toward the top of the nation's domestic airlines. And just as Horizon's employees were people-minded, so was their new CEO.

Kennedy had another motive in making his choice. He was eyeing this particular officer as a potential CEO for Alaska. Thus did the charismatic John Kelly succeed the cantankerous Milt Kuolt.

Kelly heard that when Kuolt agreed to bringing in a new CEO from Alaska, he had added, "Anyone but that pretty boy" — meaning Kelly. This may have been just a typical sarcastic Kuolt put-down, for the only thing he seems to have had against Kelly was John's reputation for always being well-dressed and immaculately groomed. This, of course, was in stark contrast to Kuolt, who at times dressed like an unmade bed. With his penchant for assigning irreverent nicknames, he subsequently referred to Kelly as Hairspray, and he called the deeply religious Kennedy the Hallelujah Kid.

Kuolt's reported opposition failed to deter Kelly. He wrote Kennedy a confidential letter openly seeking the Horizon position, pointing out that he had an extensive operational background and adding "I'm the right guy for the job."

Kennedy agreed, and even Kuolt came around to admitting that Kelly was an ideal choice to run Horizon. This acceptance came in the form of a *mea culpa* typical of Kuolt's willingness to admit his own shortcomings. He never believed in the corporate adage "If at first you don't succeed, pitch the blame back to someone else."

"All Horizon needed was a little more discipline in management, and Kelly gave it just that," Kuolt said. "Hell, I sure was undisciplined myself. Our officers, including yours truly, used to call ourselves the Wild Bunch. And, believe me, we were — a lot of partying and drinking. I never got to know Kelly real well, but he did one hell of a job at Horizon."

Kuolt revealed that he came razor-close to making a deal with United before deciding to merge with Alaska. "Actually, I had negotiated a pretty sweet arrangement with United," he related. "In addition to sharing ticket revenues from Seattle to Chicago, I insisted on getting a 10-dollar fee for every Horizon passenger we put on United, and they agreed. Then I also asked for a 10-dollar fee for every returning Horizon passenger they flew from Chicago to Seattle, and they agreed to that, too.

"The day before I sold Horizon to Alaska, United called me and asked me not to sign anything because they were sending a guy to Seattle with another offer. He never showed up, so I said the hell with them and closed the deal with Kennedy. But even if that guy had shown up, I don't believe it would have made any difference. In the end, I think the problem with United was that it was too small a deal for them to really fight for it, but it was a huge deal for Alaska."

In the last stages of negotiations with Alaska, Kuolt made a point of advising Kennedy, "There are two guys in our company you should keep your eye on."

"Who are they?" Kennedy asked.

"George Bagley and Bill Ayer," Kuolt replied. "They can really do you a lot of good."

Kennedy invited Kuolt to serve on Alaska's board of directors. Milt hesitated, but agreed to attend a meeting to see if he really belonged in this august group. What happened at the meeting can only be described adequately in Kuolt's own words.

"So the meeting started, and after a few minutes I took a look at one of the outside directors, a prominent local businessman, and the guy's sound asleep. I poked Kennedy and suggested he wake him up. Bruce said, 'Aw, let him sleep.' After the meeting, I told Bruce, 'I'm not sure you'd ever want me as a director, because I'm not one of those guys who sleeps at board meetings.' "

And true to his word, Kuolt never served as an Alaska director, which may have been the board's loss, not Milt's. He always kept himself informed about events at Horizon and the performance of latter-day leaders Bagley and Jeff Pinneo. He did no coaching from the sidelines, although he did try, unsuccessfully, to talk Bill Ayer into letting Horizon shift operations from crowded Sea-Tac to little-used Boeing Field. Ayer considered it, but decided that it would require millions of dollars in new terminal facilities such as ticket counters and expanded baggage areas and would hamper connections with Sea-Tac flights.

Utilizing Boeing Field was one of Kuolt's unfulfilled dreams for the airline he had fathered. Another was a Mexico City route, which Alaska itself began operating in 2005. The third dream was to buy a Boeing 737, although Kuolt conceded that the airplane was too large and expensive for Horizon. "This was all passion and heart, but no head," he added. "Hell, we couldn't have afforded one of the engines, let alone a whole airplane. Today, I would have figured out how to do it, but not when I was running Horizon."

His stint at Boeing ranked second to the years he spent guiding Horizon to its status as one of the leaders in the regional airline industry. "I often thought how great it would be to go back to that company and buy one of their airplanes," Kuolt said. "It would have been like the prodigal son finally coming home as a success."

His idiosyncrasies and abrasiveness aside, not one person who remembers Milt Kuolt from his days at Horizon can speak of him without eyes twinkling with warm memories. He truly was a character, his own unique brand. Milt Kuolt may have launched only a small airline, but in determination, basic honesty, and dynamic personality, he belongs up there with history's airline giants.

CHAPTER FOURTEEN

Of Food, Fun, and the Eskimo's Face

Bruce Kennedy's final half-decade as Alaska Airlines' leader may have qualified as some of the happiest five years any airline has ever enjoyed. It was a
period marked by unprecedented profit, labor peace, route-system growth,
and the start of a magical relationship with Disney. It was also the calm
before the storm.

Important technical developments in both communications and flying
contributed to the company's efficiency. Alaska took its first major steps into
the information age with the installation of two huge mainframe units and
computer peripherals for faster storing and processing of data. And its pilots
began enjoying the enhanced safety of a new device for bad-weather landings
called Heads-Up Display (HUD).

To the traveling public, however, the airline's most noticeable achievement involved Alaska's in-flight food service. A tradition of exceptional cuisine
launched in the 1970s became a cornerstone of the airline's marketing image.
Over the ensuing years, that tradition and the reputation surrounding it
would be maintained and even enhanced by Mike Ryan's successors. In
terms of bang-for-the-buck, it culminated with the hiring of Carl Baber years

later as the new director of food service, and his discovery of a top-notch executive chef, Wolfgang Erbe, who could make a mouthwatering presentation out of a boiled egg.

The title of Ernest Hemingway's memoir *A Moveable Feast* could have described Baber and Erbe's culinary achievements, one of the reasons why the airline was recognized 12 times by the prestigious *Condé Nast Traveler* magazine for outstanding customer service. Baber himself, however, would be the first to point out that neither of them joined Alaska Airlines until the late eighties, he in mid-1988 and Erbe a few months later when Marriott's airline-catering subsidiary assigned him to the Alaska account.

While Mike Ryan was at the marketing helm at Alaska, the airline's cabin service — including the hiring and supervision of flight attendants and the quality of the total in-flight service experience — was his concern. John Kelly, his protégé, focused on sales and the company's advertising.

Kelly, who looked upon Ryan as a mentor as well as a boss, tried to curb his cavalier attitude toward budget restrictions. "He wouldn't listen," Kelly said. "The result was great food service, but he didn't seem to care how much it cost."

One of Ryan's spending sprees finally drew the attention of the airline's legal department and ended up in the unwilling lap of Irv Bertram. It seems that Ryan had decided the domestic wines served on Alaska's flights were inferior to French wines. So he flew to Paris, investigated the French wine market, and selected a top-grade brand.

Ryan planned to give away a split of wine to every passenger, first class and coach, over the age of 21. He ordered 40,000 cases (960,000 splits) that were to be shipped to Seattle. Then he flew back to Seattle and walked into Irv Bertram's office to discuss the purchase. "By the way, Irv," he added casually, "I'm wondering if we're gonna have any trouble getting all that wine into the country."

Bertram did some fast and alarming research, then gave Ryan the bad news. "For starters," Bertram said dryly, "to get any imported wine into the United States, you have to be a licensed importer, which we are not. Second, every bottle in those 40,000 cases has to bear the importer's name printed on every label.

"Now, the first thing we have to do is get someone to import the wine. The second thing is to get the required labels on every bottle, including the importer's name in print."

Alaska's can-do tradition saved Ryan and his 40,000 cases of very expensive French wine. As an importer, the airline used its regular liquor distributor in Alaska, so the wine was shipped to him. Getting the requisite labels on every split was achieved by a method whose details remain murky. Suffice it to say, the shipment cleared all customs inspections.

It took eight months to consume the 40,000 cases of splits. Bertram never faulted Ryan for the purchase, either. "He got a great deal buying it in bulk like that," Bertram acknowledged, "and I must say it was a hell of a good wine."

Along with improved food service came the airline's association with one of the advertising industry's most colorful characters, a man known as the Mel Brooks of television commercials. His name was Joe Sedelmaier, and he specialized in devilish satire that usually poked fun at a client's competition.

Sedelmaier had been an art director at such prestigious ad agencies as Young & Rubicam and J. Walter Thompson. But he chafed under their conservatism and in 1967 formed his own film-production company that specialized in TV commercials. The creative Sedelmaier soon established a reputation for producing zany but effective television ads. His masterpiece was the famous Wendy's "Where's the beef?" campaign, which dared to poke fun at McDonald's, the giant of the fast-food industry. "Where's the beef?" didn't put McDonald's out of business, but Wendy's sales vaulted into the stratosphere.

Sedelmaier was just the kind of unconventional advertising maverick that Alaska's imaginative marketing crew was looking for. "We wanted to get across the idea that Alaska Airlines was different from any other carrier," John Kelly reminisced. "Roger Livingston, then with the Chiat/Day advertising agency and later principal of his own firm, Livingston & Company, came up with the idea for what became known as the 'atrocity campaign.' Sedelmaier understood Roger's concept and executed it perfectly."

A key element was the creation of a fictitious airline called SkyHigh Airlines, a name that came from the agency's Jim Copacino. He even composed a little jingle that was supposed to be its advertising theme song. The majority of the commercials depicted SkyHigh subjecting its passengers to every annoying, frustrating, and unpleasant experience known to the air-travel industry. Then he compared this airborne torture chamber with Alaska's in-flight service.

A few examples:

Narrator's voice proclaims: "It's nice to start the day with a good hearty breakfast. On some airlines . . . [camera then shows an unhappy SkyHigh passenger looking hopelessly at a skimpy roll]. Fortunately, on Alaska Airlines you can look forward to a full hot meal."

Another Alaska campaign promoting the airline's food service asked, "Do you occasionally wonder if airline executives ever eat the same food they serve to you? At Alaska Airlines our top executives eat our food at least twice a week because we would never serve you a meal we didn't enjoy ourselves."

Poking fun at the service being offered by low-cost airlines, the narrator said, "Many airlines offer you reduced fares. Unfortunately, that's not all they reduce. At Alaska Airlines we have low fares, too, but you'd never know it by the way we treat you." One commercial's punch line was "At Alaska Airlines we try to treat baggage with as much care as we treat passengers, because we want to see you and your baggage again."

"One of the best and most humorous," Kelly remembered, "was the pay toilet on one of SkyHigh's airplanes. Back then we had no idea that one day some airlines would charge passengers for the use of pillows and blankets."

The campaign was a bell-ringing success, and "SkyHigh Airlines" joined "Where's the beef?" as one of Sedelmaier's finest and funniest efforts. Yet the SkyHigh caper would have backfired if Alaska Airlines itself hadn't delivered what those audacious commercials were promising: superior service that stamped it as a truly different air carrier.

After Ryan left and Kelly took over marketing, the quality of Alaska's in-flight service remained the envy of the industry. Alaska's per-passenger expenditure on food was the highest of any U.S. carrier. When Kelly left for Horizon, his replacement as vice president of marketing was Bill McKnight, hired away from United. McKnight, in turn, was well acquainted with Carl Baber, himself a 21-year UAL veteran.

United at one time was the only major U.S. carrier that operated its own food kitchens, which Baber supervised as director of the airline's food service. A graduate of Michigan State's hotel management school, Baber was no chef himself, but he knew chefs and how to work with them. He was happy at United, where he had autonomy to go with great responsibility. Working for another airline was about as far from his mind as joining the U.S. Marines.

In late February of 1988, McKnight called him from Seattle and told him that Alaska Airlines had a job open as director of food service. Baber had trouble taking him seriously. "Bill, I'm already director of food service for the largest airline in the free world," Baber pointed out. "Why would I want to go to work for little Alaska Airlines? Thank you, but no thanks."

McKnight persisted. "I know what you're making at United, Carl," he said meaningfully. "I think you should at least come out here and talk to me. You really don't know what Alaska Airlines is all about."

Baber, a dedicated basketball fan, happened to have two tickets for himself and his son to the NCAA quarterfinals in Seattle that year. He figured that as he was planning to go there anyway, he might as well say hello to McKnight.

He picked an alluring time to visit corporate headquarters. The building's new west wing, with its beautiful lobby pool and graceful staircase leading to the executive offices on the second floor, had just been opened. Baber was impressed with everything he saw and everyone he met, and the following June moved his family to the Pacific Northwest.

Somewhat surprisingly, he experienced no culture shock going from a large airline that operated its own food kitchens to a smaller one that, as did virtually all other carriers, used outside caterers such as Sky Chefs and Marriott. "I didn't treat my job differently," Baber recalled. "The outside catering chefs still reported to me. We had the same control over quality that I had at United. And there was one significant improvement I didn't expect at Alaska — things got done faster."

He hadn't been in Seattle long when, at one of his staff meetings, someone suggested a menu change that Baber liked. At United, that same suggestion would have had to climb through several levels of management until someone close to the top passed the word that it had been approved, a process that invariably took at least a month and often longer.

Less than two weeks after Baber indicated that he liked what he thought was just an idle suggestion, the caterer called and informed him that his menu change was going into effect. Baber asked one of his staff members what was going on. He replied, "Carl, you said you liked that menu change, so we went ahead and did it."

That really hit home: an airline that moved fast. He later recalled his nearly 20 years at Alaska in one succinct sentence: "I have never once looked back and asked myself, 'Why did I do it?'"

The other half of the company's dietary duo, Wolfgang Erbe, technically was never an Alaska Airlines employee, although he was always identified as its executive chef. This was Baber's idea; he thought an executive chef added professionalism and prestige to an airline's in-flight service.

His choice had credentials that were impressive and even incredible.

Erbe was a German by birth, and his father was a colonel in the Luftwaffe (German air force) who spent the last years of World War II in a Soviet gulag, or prison camp. Wolfgang grew up not knowing whether his father was alive or dead and didn't see him until after the war.

Erbe became a chef at two of the finest hotels in Europe before immigrating to the United States. He then worked as catering director for Time-Life publisher Henry Luce's private dining room and operated his own first-class restaurant in Washington, D.C., for 12 years. The restaurant was within walking distance of the White House, and famous presidential chef Henry Haller was one of his frequent patrons and also a good friend

Erbe finally sold the restaurant, explaining, "I was working too hard and drinking too much." He moved out to the West Coast and found a job as a chef in the Marriott hotel chain's airline-catering subsidiary. Marriott hired him after one of the shortest job interviews on record.

An assistant vice president, a big crusty Swiss, opened the interview by growling, "I don't want to see any résumé or references; just tell me where you learned the chef business."

"First, the Four Seasons Hotel in Hamburg," Erbe replied.

"Then where?"

"At the Dolder Hotel in Zurich."

These were two of the finest hotels in Europe. The Marriott vice president stared at him and snapped, "Good — you're hired."

Erbe proved himself quickly, drawing the attention of chairman J. W. Marriott when he went to Tokyo and nailed a lucrative Japan Airlines account. JAL had previously turned Marriott down, a defeat that Erbe blamed on his own inadequate presentation to a JAL delegation that visited Seattle.

"I couldn't understand how we could have blown that contract," Erbe said. "But after I went to Japan and saw JAL's huge, spotless kitchen facilities in Tokyo — they even had a separate kitchen for their 747 flights — I realized I had made the most common mistake in the food business. We had never made any attempt to find out what *they* were looking for. We showed them what *we* thought they should have, not what *they* wanted."

Then one day in late fall 1988, Carl Baber walked into Erbe's kitchen in the Marriott catering facility at Sea-Tac and introduced himself. "Mr. Erbe," he began, "I'm Carl Baber from Alaska Airlines. I've got some food here that I want you to taste and tell me honestly what you think of it."

"I don't remember what he showed me," Erbe related, "except that it was something with tomatoes on it. It wasn't very good and I told him so.

Carl just grunted, said thanks, and left. Then I heard that Marriott was going to be Alaska's caterer and that I was to work exclusively on their account."

It was, of course, a lucrative deal for Marriott and one that pleased J.W., a friend of Bruce Kennedy. But it also was a great deal for Alaska Airlines because Erbe's services came with the package. He already was a seasoned veteran in the unique requirements of airline food service, one of the least understood and most frequently criticized — even ridiculed — segments of air-travel operations.

By necessity, his observations on airline food now have a nostalgic quality, for decent airborne meals have been perhaps the most symbolic casualty of the September 11 disaster. Yet his views on the subject are still appropriate because Alaska is one of the few carriers that made a real post-9/11 effort to serve good food, albeit not in the quantity and style that was once its trademark.

"It's far more difficult to prepare food for an airline than for a restaurant or hotel," Erbe pointed out. "They're totally different animals. First, the logistics and nature of airline meals prevent you from doing the things you can do at a hotel or restaurant. And there are certain things you tend to stay away from in airline menus, such as soups.

"In airplanes you have a large scale of food service, where flight attendants push a button when it comes time to heat everything up. Sometimes they have different ideas on when to do that, depending on their workload. And then there are certain items that stand up to the environment of an aircraft and others that don't. Money too, of course, is always an issue. But in spite of budget constraints, Alaska always had the attitude of 'we can do it better.' "

The 1990s were the glory years for Alaska's food service, for no other airline had a team like Alaska's Baber-Erbe duet. They admired and complemented each other, sharing their areas of expertise with absolutely no clash of egos in a profession that has its share of temperamental prima donnas and martinets.

The more extroverted Erbe drew the most attention and publicity, but he was quick to acknowledge Baber's contributions to the airline's food-service dominance. "I always admired Carl for his great knowledge and his management and budget skills," Erbe stressed. "He admitted he couldn't cook, but he knew what he wanted and what would work. And that's the sign of a good manager.

"We served great meals because we had the money to spend on food services. Back then we used to get several hundred dollars each way between

Seattle and San Francisco. These days the airline is lucky to get half that.
But the difference between other airlines and Alaska was that other carriers
never put profits back into food service. Alaska reinvested a lot in the form of
better food service to its customers.

"I remember when we were offering fresh shellfish dishes in first class
and a lot of salmon in coach. We weren't afraid to introduce new entrées like
halibut, and once we even tried reindeer steak. Yet when things got tough
and our food budget was cut drastically, we still had better food service than
anyone else."

Erbe will always be remembered for the days he spent riding on Alaska
Airlines flights, wearing his chef's uniform with the traditional tall white
hat along with his medals won over a career of culinary craftsmanship. He
would walk up and down cabin aisles asking passengers how they liked the
meal they had just been served, and whether they had any suggestions for
improvements.

These widely publicized and universally enjoyed "our executive chef is
with us today" flights began in the summer of 1990 after Carl Baber suggested the idea. Erbe, who balked at first, thought it was a crazy idea and a
waste of time that could be better spent in his beloved kitchen. Yet he trusted
Baber's judgment, and he knew that the head of corporate communications,
Lou Cancelmi, considered it a great publicity opportunity.

The script called for Erbe to board a flight and, while the meal service
was under way, go into the rear galley and put on his white chef's jacket and
hat. Then a flight attendant would announce on the aircraft intercom system
that Executive Chef Wolfgang Erbe was on board and would be talking to the
passengers individually about the meal service.

It turned out to be better entertainment than a lot of in-flight movies, a
good subject for subsequent commercials, and a memorable experience for
Wolfgang, who, like many great chefs, was part thespian. "Some people were
so speechless, they'd just nod when I asked about the meal," Erbe recalled,
"yet others were effusive. No one ever gave me a really hard time.

"I remember one man who told me, 'Usually your rolls are lousy, but the
ones I had today were very good.' That pleased me because we *had* been serving terrible rolls, and we had just replaced them with rolls from the Oroweat
bakery in Seattle.

"What negative comments I got, not unexpectedly, came almost entirely
from coach passengers. The most important thing was that almost every
passenger was impressed by the fact that Alaska had put a guy out there in the

open to listen to their opinions. It not only gave us some helpful feedback, but it made our customers feel important, and everyone likes to feel important."

In addition to the benefit of face-to-face time with customers, there was a real public relations value associated with Erbe's trips. "We unabashedly took advantage of Wolfgang's planned flights to gain media attention," said Cancelmi. "Our media relations manager, Greg Witter, and I knew from the start that having the chef on board would be a publicity gold mine. But even we cynical PR types were taken aback by all the coverage Chef Erbe commanded."

The chef flights lasted about two years. Sometimes Erbe would take three of them a week, occasionally only one a week. The word around the airline was that Wolfgang was having so much fun that it might be necessary to eventually drag him off airplanes.

Erbe summed up his airborne assignment as a case of mixed blessings. "All this time I was still going to my regular work," he joked, "but they never paid me for providing the in-flight entertainment."

Forced into painful decisions early in the 1990s, Vecci began to pare down the budget for in-flight food. "I had to continue to pare it down when I took over in 1995," said Kelly. "But the amazing thing was that, with the Baber-Erbe team, we continued to get new, exciting, and high-quality food — just for less money. For example, they came up with some of the best sandwiches ever served."

Erbe retired after the impact of the post-9/11 carnage and subsequent fuel-cost crunch devastated food service on all carriers. Baber retired in 2005, after staying long enough to tenaciously maintain Alaska's food-service traditions by insisting that what *was* served had to be of high quality and sufficient quantity, and as tasty as possible. In that sense, it may have been Alaska's finest in-flight food-service performance.

The airline's interest in the Northern Tier route had no more than cooled when Alaska expanded its service into California, as well as to the Southwest. Burbank and Ontario were added to the route system in 1981, Phoenix in 1985, and San Diego a year later. By the end of 1986, the airline had also initiated service to all points in Alaska that were of immediate strategic importance to the expansion blueprint Bruce Kennedy had drawn up. Its goal was to serve most if not all of the important West Coast cities.

"Still characteristic of our business model, though less extreme than before deregulation, was the problem of seasonality," explained Kennedy. "We were unique among our competitors in that we lacked a true winter resort destination. We touted Phoenix and San Diego as best we could, but for Alaskans and Pacific Northwesterners, and Californians for that matter, we lacked a subtropical beach destination.

"Alaskans in particular," Kennedy added, "were hooked on Hawaii, partly the result of those hugely annoying Western Airlines 'Triangle Fares' that included a Hawaii leg on an Anchorage/West Coast trip at little additional cost."

To counter, Alaska promoted Disneyland.

Disneyland was a huge draw across the nation, especially along the West Coast. When the Magic Kingdom opened in 1955, 28,000 people attended, 11,000 by invitation and the rest by party crashing. The Kingdom was successful beyond anybody's wildest dreams, except perhaps those of Walt Disney himself.

The airline's marketers began waking up to Disneyland's potential in 1981, after Alaska inaugurated service to Ontario and Burbank. Customer-service agents in Anchorage, Seattle, and Portland noticed increasing numbers of excited children boarding the southbound flights to those two California cities. And flight attendants working northbound trips from Ontario and Burbank began seeing even more vivid evidence of the Magic Kingdom's attraction. More and more of their passengers were sunburned, tired, but still excited kids wearing mouse ears or Donald Duck beaks. What had started as a trickle turned into a torrent in 1987, when Alaska opened a station at the John Wayne Airport in Orange County.

The market was enormous. During the 1990s, Disneyland recorded as many as 15 million visitors a year, and by the end of 2000, its total ticket sales neared 450 million.

Disneyland travel was difficult for Alaska to promote at first. The Magic Kingdom's brand was guarded by a phalanx of attorneys. Mouse ears used in an Alaska Airlines ad for Southern California could draw legal fire. But relations between Alaska's Eskimo and Mickey's keepers warmed during one salmon season in the late 1990s.

Dave Palmer, then Alaska's assistant vice president of marketing, described the change between the two companies. "We invited one of Disney's vice presidents, Mark Feure, to Waterfall Resort, near Ketchikan, to go fishing. During an otherwise casual conversation, I said to him, 'You know, we would really like to work more closely with Disney.'

"He asked, 'Why can't we?'

" 'Well, you have this deal with Delta Airlines,' I responded.

" 'Well, that deal is going to go away,' Feure replied.

"During the trip he got to know us, and some of our customers," Palmer said. "That was the turning point, when the relationship between Alaska and Disney changed. Mark said that he thought he could work with us. He did have a great time fishing."

When the fishing party was over, Palmer continued to nurture the relationship. The agreement with Delta ended, but Disney didn't select another airline partner immediately. Meanwhile, Alaska came up with a promotion where kids flew for free. The Disney organization loved it.

Disney officials also got behind a promotional idea in 2002 that resulted in a 140-foot flying billboard: an Alaska Airlines 737-400 painted with Disney characters from nose to tail. For the first time in more than 25 years, the Eskimo came off the tail and was replaced by Mickey Mouse.

To this day, no one at either the airline or at Disney remembers exactly who came up with the idea, but the name of the creator is unimportant in comparison to the creation itself. It took a team of 68 Disney artists 15 days to paint the airplane, using 68,000 feet of masking tape and 50 gallons of top-coat to seal the drawings; the normal time to paint a 737-400 is only six days.

Christened *The Spirit of Disneyland*, the gleaming blue jetliner went into service early in 2003 and was followed by a second 737-400 featuring a Tinker Bell motif. A third livery was unveiled in 2006. It featured the grinning, wish-granting genie of Disney's *Aladdin* to promote the Make-A-Wish Foundation. Artistically, these aircraft were just as eye-catching, but nothing could match the impact of the first one.

Kelly still recalls his excitement upon first seeing the newly painted airplane. "I went up to Paine Field and opened up the hangar door. I don't think I've ever seen a more beautiful aircraft in my life. That color of blue they chose was perfect."

While Alaska painted airplanes, Disney brought new business to the airline, including the California theme park side of the vacation business. The relationship expanded still further when Alaska began flying to Orlando, Florida, the home of Walt Disney World and Epcot Center.

If replacing the Eskimo with the world's most recognizable mouse on just one Alaska jet generated this much excitement, imagine the stir that followed a report in 1988 that Alaska Airlines was planning to remove the smiling Eskimo from *all* its aircraft tails in favor of a different symbol.

Alaska's marketing department had engaged a San Francisco design firm to take an objective look at whether the airline's logo and brand identity needed updating. The firm did a thorough review of the company's brand and came up with an eye-catching stylized mountain. The designers felt that the proposed new look would appeal not only to Alaska's existing customers but also to its rapidly expanding passenger base along the West Coast.

Somehow the idea was leaked to the media, and all hell broke loose. Though only a proposal, it was taken seriously by most of the airline's workforce and the entire state of Alaska. In fact, the Alaska state legislature ended up passing a resolution denouncing the idea.

Media opposition stretched from Nome all the way down the West Coast to Los Angeles. Editorials urged the airline to retain the Eskimo. Also among the objectors was Livingston, the airline's Seattle advertising agency, whose staff always referred to the Eskimo as "Elmo," after the famed *Sesame Street* character.

As State Senator Tim Kelly, sponsor of the State of Alaska's "Don't Touch the Eskimo" resolution, put it, "It may not be the best representation of an Eskimo, but it's our Eskimo, and Alaskans feel it's their airline."

Marketing, which had innocently dropped a match into a barrel of high-octane fuel, was initially surprised, but then realized the value of all the additional publicity that the controversy was generating. Instead of immediately scotching the design rumor, it allowed the hubbub to play out for a little while longer, with Kennedy's blessing.

The truth is that the fierce defense of what so many in the 49th state itself considered an almost sacred symbol should not have surprised anyone familiar with the affinity the people of the state of Alaska have had with the airline. While some of the marketing people liked the new design and thought it was a fresh approach, no one liked it well enough to justify retiring the Eskimo. (Even if they had, they might as well have proposed removing the entire tail along with the face.)

After enjoying a week or two of additional notoriety and free advertising, the airline finally made a definitive announcement that the Eskimo was staying on the tail of its aircraft — and peace returned to Alaska's route system.

Another example of that special relationship with Alaskans occurred up in the far north region of the state. Alaska's pilots used to execute a traditional little ritual on flights between Nome and Kotzebue, a route that took the aircraft over the Arctic Circle. As they approached that point, the captain would announce that the flight would be crossing the Arctic Circle and ask passengers to make sure their seat belts were fastened. At the appointed time, the pilot would pull up and then depress the yoke without comment. Neophyte passengers were usually taken by surprise, but immediately got the joke and broke out in laughter and applause. But there was a humorless passenger on one flight who didn't think the ceremony was funny and filed a petition to stop the practice.

The complainant never knew what hit him. Kotzebue citizens organized an SOB Committee — "Save Our Bump" — and the protestor's petition suffered a quick demise.

Like the state of Alaska, Seattle experienced an economic boom as a result of the pipeline construction. Its business climate bounced back from the deep recession of the early 1980s, and air traffic increased from all parts of the country. In fact, Seattle-Tacoma International Airport has been on a nonstop building spree ever since. From Seattle, Alaska Airlines would face competition no matter which way it flew. However, Alaska was still by far the airline's biggest market, and it was essential to have enough capacity to meet summer demand, or it would risk losing passengers to competitors that were less dependent on travel to the 49th state.

Kennedy and everyone else at the executive level knew that the airline's main strength was its dominance in Alaska. But conversely, they also considered it a weakness. Alaska had to commit much of its still-limited aircraft resources to serving a market that teemed with traffic in the summer and went into virtual hibernation in the winter.

Better fleet utilization was the challenge that Bruce Kennedy and his staff faced in the last few years of his leadership. Increased service to California destinations was one obvious solution, but not a definitive one. The answer, as Kennedy saw it, was to point the Eskimo's nose toward Mexico. For better or for worse, it was now going to be "Amigo Elmo."

CHAPTER FIFTEEN

The Eskimo Goes International

When Bruce Kennedy was elected Alaska's president in 1978, the airline's August revenue passenger miles (RPMs) that year were double its February RPMs, an enormous passenger-traffic imbalance that created aircraft and staffing complications. It meant schedule adjustments; layoffs in the fall and rehirings in the spring; chartering, parking, or selling unneeded aircraft as winter approached; and sometimes purchasing used planes and refurbishing them before the busy summer tourist traffic to Alaska. Heavy maintenance took an aircraft out of service for months. Clearly, Alaska needed a plan to make more efficient use of its fleet through growth, particularly growth that featured counter-seasonal routes.

Over most of Kennedy's tenure at the airline's helm, the need to grow steadily and rationally was tempered by his early experience during the late 1970s, when he was handed the reins of the company just as deregulation untethered the industry and expansion became rampant. Airlines were spreading their wings and expanding their route systems, proliferating like mosquitoes during a wet summer. Some, like Braniff, expanded too rapidly and failed, while Alaska's growth was steady, and very deliberate.

Kennedy's planning sessions were informal. After asking in general terms where the airline should go next and why, Kennedy would sit back and listen to the views of various officers. Vecci provided input based on his expertise as a planner, Kelly offered the marketing point of view, Vingo described financial scenarios, and others added their various professional outlooks. The group weighed the opportunities for expansion, particularly counter-seasonal expansion into markets with limited competition.

"It wasn't as if we had a chart on a board showing how the next route decision should be executed," John Kelly recalled. "That didn't happen until we had taken stock of our strengths, and could see what we could do well and why. Then we could make strategic decisions that took advantage of particular situations and opportunities in line with our resources."

Resources was a key word. When Kennedy first took command, the airline's fleet consisted of less than a dozen aircraft: 727-200s connecting Seattle with Alaska and 737-200 combis assigned primarily to providing Alaskan communities with year-round passenger and freight service. The carrier's MD-80 aircraft would begin to join the fleet in the mid-1980s, but both the 727-200s and MD-80s were still shorter-range aircraft incapable of serving far-off beach destinations such as Hawaii. However, either one could serve "sun-and-sand" points in Mexico, plus warm-weather spots in Southern California and Arizona.

By the mid-1980s, Alaska had developed a route network south of Seattle that included most major destinations on the West Coast. And Kennedy saw an opportunity to stretch beyond that even farther south. Scheduled service into Mexico may have seemed a bit of a reach for such a small airline, but it represented a logical extension of its existing north-south traffic flow, and that compass heading had served Alaska well in the past.

Discussion of Mexico as a potential counter-seasonal market was at first cautious. "Perhaps during the off-season," so the discussion went, "parked aircraft could be pressed into the charter business."

In 1988, Carlos Salinas de Gortari, a 40-year-old Harvard graduate, became president of Mexico. Recognized as a strong advocate for private enterprise, he believed in his country's tourist resources. He encouraged the development of Cancún, on Mexico's Caribbean coast, and the expansion of vacation facilities along the country's West Coast, including Puerto Vallarta, Mazatlán, and Cabo San Lucas.

During the mid-1980s, Alaska had assigned Dick Grissom to study Mexico regarding possible destinations for Alaska charter flights. As part of his assignment, Grissom went looking for a consultant, someone with airline experience in Mexico. The person he found — the result of Grissom's many years of airline savvy, his gut instinct for people, plus a dose of good luck — was Julian Acosta, a 20-year veteran of the industry in Mexico.

Acosta was only 18 when he entered the business in 1958 as a sales rep for what is now known as AeroMexico. Later he worked for Alitalia, Varig, and eventually in Europe with Braniff.

When Grissom offered him a consulting contract to help Alaska Airlines with its Mexican charters, Acosta quickly proved his worth. He informed Grissom that a new bilateral agreement was about to be signed between Mexico and the United States and that under the agreement Alaska could likely enter the scheduled airline business in Mexico.

Acosta flew to Seattle, where he met with three of Alaska's senior executives — Harry Lehr, Ray Vingo, and Ray Vecci. After briefings with them on the probable implications of a bilateral air agreement, Acosta was ushered into Bruce Kennedy's office, where a similar briefing became a job interview.

When Acosta left Seattle, he was no longer a consultant but a full-time employee, one destined to become the airline's Mr. Mexico. He also left behind a "do-we-or-don't-we" dilemma for Kennedy and his officers, some of them eager to get into Mexico on a scheduled basis, others dubious.

Kennedy recalled, "Ray Vecci and Bill McKnight were incredulous that I would give even a thought to missing what appeared to them to be the chance of a lifetime. And they were right. Others, like John Kelly, who at the time worked across the street as Horizon's CEO, were dead set against it because of what they perceived as a wide spectrum of problems, from health to politics."

Mexico was essentially a regulated market for airlines, and that appealed to Vecci. It had two national airlines, Mexicana and AeroMexico. But the bilateral agreement then in the process of being renewed would permit each nation to designate one additional carrier to serve specific markets.

Once the decision was made and then approved by the authorities of each country, nobody, with the possible exception of Julian Acosta, was more committed to establishing Alaska's successful presence in Mexico than Bruce Kennedy.

Alaska's executives had watched Continental enter and exit the Mexican market. They had also witnessed PSA's brief expedition south of the border and learned from the mistakes of others.

"We looked at the differences between those carriers and us," said Dave Palmer. "We had an established feeder system to Mexico from Alaska,

Seattle, and other parts of the Pacific Northwest through San Francisco as a gateway. We also had good relations with tour operators and cruise lines going to Mexico. They were the same lines that served Alaska, and we felt we could get immediate support from them. This gave us the will to try."

Alaska's approach to these and other new markets differed from its competitors'. It was friendly, not flamboyant, and it resembled the relationships long established with small Alaskan communities from Ketchikan to Nome. These were bonds built more with personal diplomacy than political clout.

Inaugural flights were important promotional opportunities for Alaska, and the guest lists for those events were carefully compiled. Kennedy made a personal commitment to be on each of the inaugural flights to Mexico, a practice that had been a tradition at Alaska since its earliest days to introduce itself to its newest communities.

A classic example of the Alaska style came after it filed with the Department of Transportation for authority to serve Mexico. The airline sent a delegation to meet with the governor of each affected state, the purpose being to introduce the company and explain Alaska's objectives and the benefits of the proposed service. In addition to government officials, the delegation met with hotel and convention associations in each city.

In advance of starting service to Mexico, Alaska participated in a large research project to better understand North American tourists' attitude toward travel in Mexico. Perceived health issues associated with travel there inevitably included unflattering references to Montezuma's Revenge, not a minor deterrent to travel in Mexico.

"We heard about the food, water, and language differences that could make travel to Mexico difficult," Palmer said, "and all of the drawbacks were cited in the study. Yet the same study showed that American tourists who had been to the coastal resorts were very likely to return."

In the end, the solution for success in Mexico was basic. "God bless bottled water," said Palmer. "I think bottled water did as much to develop markets in Mexico as any of our 'brilliant' marketing."

Because service to the west coast of Mexico from the west coast of the United States was limited, Alaska had immediate strong support from both government and industry leaders. "Before we started service to Mexico, we had our bases covered," recalled Kennedy.

Acosta reported to Marvin Van Horn, and when Alaska Airlines Mexico

S.A. was formed, Acosta became its titular head.

The manager put in charge of opening Puerto Vallarta and Mazatlán was a seasoned airline veteran who had joined Alaska after stints at Golden West, Air California, and Jet America. His name was Charles Cooper, but everyone called him Kit. He came to Alaska from Jet America, where his competent performance as station manager in Oakland plus 20 years of air-carrier experience attracted the attention of Alaska's brass. After the Jet America merger, he was Alaska's customer-service manager at the Orange County airport until he was asked to help Van Horn establish Alaska's operations in Mexico.

Van Horn was working 18 hours a day opening up the Mexican destinations when he sent Cooper to Puerto Vallarta. "We've hired away a good guy from Mexicana Airlines, Antonio Alvarado, as our station manager," Van Horn told Cooper. "But he's swamped and could use your help."

Cooper got along famously with Alvarado, who was still running that station well into the 21st century. He taught Alvarado Alaska's business procedures and various administrative duties. Then Van Horn dispatched Cooper to help local managers open up Mazatlán, Puerto Vallarta, Guadalajara, and Acapulco.

A little later, service from Ontario, California, to Mexico City was added, but the airline soon realized that Los Angeles International Airport (LAX) was the preferred portal to Mexico from Southern California. Alaska soon abandoned its Ontario-Mexico City route and didn't resume service to Mexico's capital until 2005, when it could provide nonstop flights to and from LAX.

When Van Horn left for an extended vacation in Australia, Cooper succeeded him as manager of Alaska's Mexico operations. He found that he had been bequeathed an able Mexican colleague in the person of Julian Acosta.

Van Horn had considered Acosta invaluable, and Cooper, too, came to rely on and admire him. Cooper, who knew that bribery was not uncommon in Mexico, was always proud that the airline refused to play that game in all its years of Mexican service. That made him appreciate Acosta, a big, jovial man with a dominating personality, even more. Acosta somehow managed to still get things done, cutting through red tape and navigating the labyrinth of bureaucratic government regulations.

Acosta's efficiency was legendary, and Alaska's first foray into Mexico City from Ontario proved it. Cooper, who was in the United States at the time, was ordered back to Mexico immediately because the airline had just filed for Mexico City authority. When he arrived, Acosta greeted him with a wide grin. "We can be ready to start operating in Mexico City by tomorrow," he announced, to Cooper's complete surprise. He had already arranged for ticket-counter space, communication facilities, and gate space at the Mexico City airport — all within 48 hours.

Cooper himself recalled that his biggest problem in Mexico was communication. "Not in language," he added, "but in basic equipment like fax machines. For the first six months I was there, we didn't have a fax because there weren't any to buy. I think we finally purchased the first one in the whole country. There were no computers, either, and the amount of paperwork the Mexican government was generating was unbelievable.

"For example, various forms relating to routine airline business required seven copies for each form. Marvin once discovered a building where one particular tourist document was being stored. There were stacks and stacks of them piled up. Today they're storing information in computers, but as far as I know, they still keep all that paper around.

"Why so many copies? Because the government required a detailed report with multiple copies from every airline station in Mexico. How many people were on each flight. How much freight was boarded, and so on," explained Cooper.

To help introduce Alaska Airlines to the Mexican tourist industry, the airline chose Tianguis Turistico, Mexico's largest travel industry trade show. Held annually, it was more akin to a fiesta than business, a perfect venue for creating buzz about a new product or service. For a moment Alaska forgot the budget, created a handsome nine-projector presentation, and mailed out invitations.

Kennedy wrote and rehearsed a well-thought-out speech that he intended to deliver personally at a special event scheduled for this gathering of tourism giants. On the morning of the presentation, he met with Mexico's secretary of tourism, then returned to work on his speech. As he rehearsed, Kennedy fell prey to "Montezuma" and almost passed out.

Palmer remembered thinking, "Our guy is going to go down."

To the amazement of his associates, Kennedy rallied, and against all odds he walked on stage that night and delivered what Palmer and others collectively agreed was one of his best performances ever.

Language differences created early complications for the new scheduled service into Mexico. Staffing flights with Spanish-speaking cabin crews initially conflicted with the company's labor agreement with the Association of Flight Attendants. The AFA contract required that all trip assignments be on a bid basis, with the determining factor being seniority, not language skills.

At the time, Alaska didn't have many bilingual flight attendants, and only a few of them had much seniority. The company's temporary solution was to use Spanish-speaking management personnel to accompany the flights and assist the flight attendants. Since then the airline has launched system-wide Spanish-language initiatives that cover not only in-flight but also reservations, check-in, and access to the company's website. Today even the chairman's comments in the airline's monthly award-winning onboard magazine, *Alaska Airlines Magazine*, appear in Spanish as well as English.

In the company's 1988 annual report, the most significant news to share-holders was Alaska's first regularly scheduled international flights from San Francisco to the Mexican resorts of Puerto Vallarta and Mazatlán. The company also announced that it was planning to add service to nine additional destinations in Mexico, including flights to Acapulco and Guadalajara starting in April 1989.

Acapulco was an active cruise-ship port, and aside from Mexicana, Alaska would be the only air carrier to serve that market from San Francisco and Seattle. But service to Acapulco and the airline's initial foray into Guadalajara proved to be a bust. Most of the cruise-ship business to Acapulco was generated through Los Angeles, not San Francisco. Although the airline was able to funnel some passengers to Mexico through San Francisco from Alaska and the Pacific Northwest, passengers ticketed in the Bay Area were mostly migrants headed home. There was virtually no business travel. "So, not too long after we started, we pulled out of both the Guadalajara and Acapulco markets," said Brad Walker, Alaska's director of leisure marketing.

There was more to the story, however, and it demonstrated the character of the airline perhaps even better than its success. "After we decided to shut down Alaska's service to Acapulco," recalled Acosta, "Bruce Kennedy told me, 'We have to find out why we failed there.' He also asked me to meet with the secretary of tourism and talk frankly with him about Alaska's decision. I gave the secretary the results of our study, which pinpointed a number of reasons, including poor security.

"The secretary told me, 'This is the first time any airline has gone to the trouble of explaining why they were pulling out of a Mexican destination.

Usually, they just leave without explanation, and I really appreciate what Bruce Kennedy did. I want you to set up a meeting with all the hotel people in Acapulco and let them know why you are leaving.' "

Acosta recalled, "We had the meeting about three weeks after we stopped our Acapulco service. I think about 85 percent of the people there expressed their gratitude for our letting them know why we pulled out, and they promised to find out what could be done to entice Alaska into returning to the legendary seaside resort town. The other 15 percent didn't understand our decision. But the meeting itself was a class act, typical of Kennedy and Alaska Airlines."

Two years after inaugurating its service south of the border, as a sign of Alaska Airlines' regard for Mexico, it scheduled a board meeting in Mexico City. Kennedy wanted the meeting to include a fiesta where the company's directors and officers could meet senior government and tourism officials to discuss their mutual interests over a celebratory dinner. Again, Julian Acosta was instrumental in organizing what Kennedy hoped would be a memorable gathering.

But on the night scheduled for the Alaska celebration, U.S. Secretary of Transportation Samuel K. Skinner had also planned a dinner that included top Mexican government dignitaries. For a time, Kennedy thought he and his officers might just have a quiet dinner alone, but then Acosta received an invitation too good to refuse. It was from the office of Mexico's President Carlos Salinas. Kennedy, Ray Vecci, and Acosta were invited to meet with President Salinas on the presidential plane during a flight to Acapulco.

At the airport, Kennedy and Acosta ran into Secretary Skinner, who less than gracefully asked, "What are you doing here?"

Kennedy replied, "Well, you ruined my party for tomorrow night, so this is my only chance to meet with President Salinas."

After the president's brief meeting with Secretary Skinner, Kennedy and others were invited to meet with the president in the conference center of a gleaming new Boeing 757, his personal aircraft. Kennedy brought up his concern about Mexico's addition of navigation charges to its already especially high landing fees. President Salinas countered, pointing out that "Alaska wouldn't be entering these markets unless it expected to make a fair profit." Kennedy had to agree, and the matter was dropped. "For sure he was no sympathetic pushover," Kennedy recalled.

Not long after they arrived in Acapulco, the Mexican minister of finance's plane also landed, and Kennedy, Vecci, and Acosta were invited to fly back to Mexico City with him, where Kennedy again had an opportunity to express the airline's interests.

For Kennedy, the best part of the trip surfaced a few days later. Alaska's Washington, D.C., counsel, Marshall S. "Sandy" Sinick, received a call from Secretary Skinner. As Kennedy later recalled, the gist of Sinick's conversation with the secretary was that "Skinner was frosted when he learned that while he got a brief audience with the president, the entourage representing Alaska Airlines had a private audience aboard the presidential airplane."

Entering new markets can be expensive, and Mexico was no exception. To attract new air service and reduce a carrier's financial risk, the principal beneficiaries, such as hotels and the Mexican Department of Tourism, would sometimes guarantee a portion of the costs associated with development of a new market. Establishing such relationships was an area where Acosta shone.

"He was very well connected. He was well known in the tourism and airline travel industry. He was able to open a lot of doors on behalf of Alaska Airlines," recalled Palmer. "He brought Manzanillo and other opportunities to us."

As large luxury hotels began to spring up along the west coast of Mexico, Alaska added more flights to keep pace with the growing new business. Then the landscape changed. "When I started seeing people with little kids traveling to Mexico, I knew things had changed for the better," said Palmer. "All of a sudden it became a family destination. When that happened, all the old fears went away."

By 2006 there were more than 3,000 hotel rooms in Southern Baja alone, and booking one during spring break became about as likely as seeing Elvis on the beach. A corresponding explosion of activity was evident north of the border, too. During the same year, Alaska operated more international flights out of Los Angeles International than any other airline, thanks to its service to Mexico.

One of Alaska's other major marketing efforts targeted not just Mexico, but a whole new travel spectrum: tour and vacation packages, opening new vistas for the young eager beavers in marketing.

That part of the business really began in the 1970s with a shoe box filled with football tickets, a unique garden in which to plant the seeds of a new marketing venture. And in this case, the one holding the watering can was

Dave Palmer.

He had heard by way of the grapevine that CSAs and flight attendants were noticing that some Seattle-bound passengers in the fall were a little rowdier than usual. They found that these groups of regular customers were traveling south to attend pro football games. The National Football League had expanded in 1976 with the debut of the Seattle Seahawks, whose home was the new 66,000-seat Kingdome. Season ticket holders came from as far away as Nome, Alaska.

Palmer made the connection between accommodations, airfare, and sports. "We started to see all of these people flying from Alaska for Seattle Seahawks home games. We reasoned that there might be others in Alaska who would like to come to Seattle for a game that didn't have season tickets. And we were right."

Palmer instinctively saw the potential to fill seats on airplanes using football tickets as bait. He began with a shoe box full of Seahawks tickets, enough to melt down his company credit card, and a loose business plan that was based more on hunch than on fact. It was pretty much a one-man show. "We went to the Mileage Plan people and asked if anyone might be available to take calls and book hotel rooms. We had to work out the logistics of getting the tickets to the package buyers. We tried will-call desks, but it took a while to work out the kinks," recalled Palmer. "Mike Ryan might have done it differently."

That was the start of Alaska Airlines Vacations. "We didn't ask anybody for permission," said Palmer. "We just started offering the packages. This was in the 1970s. It started to be pretty successful, so we looked for other destinations, like Disneyland. We were already flying to LA. At that point we went to John Kelly, then vice president of marketing, and said, 'We need some help, a budget, and some computers.'

"He said, 'For what?'

"We explained that we had a plan to offer vacation packages. We threw some numbers around. We got a couple of people and an old computer to work with. I think we started doing Disneyland and went back to John and asked for a bigger house. The numbers were there to support the new enterprise.

"We ended up with a computer system that did real-time inventory management. That was the start of Alaska Airlines Vacations. It just started out as a low-cost opportunity and grew from there.

"Another thing Alaska Airlines Vacations did was keep the other tour operators honest. They were always threatening to take their business elsewhere if we didn't support them. But once we had our own tour company, we were less vulnerable to others. We represented competition, but really we were creating markets that others didn't already serve."

John Kelly remembered Palmer's early interest in tour packaging and his arguments for its success. "Dave always wanted this to happen. He saw it as an opportunity, but I saw it as a jumbled bunch of facts. It was more a dream than a plan. Once he got some help, he was able to really start that business. He then developed a plan where the company could track the returns generated. It ultimately became very successful and has grown into a great business."

If the opposition to going to Mexico was considerable, it was a mild breeze in comparison to the tornado stirred up by Bruce Kennedy's news-making decision in the waning years of his leadership to introduce scheduled service to the Soviet Far East. It was a mission dictated as much by his heart as his head.

But this wasn't Alaska's first foray into Russia. Much marketing hay but ultimately precious few dollars were made with the airline's "Golden Samovar" charter service to the Soviet Far East during the colorful reign of Charlie Willis and promoter extraordinaire Bob Giersdorf. Despite its unceremonious end when Cosgrave seized the reins of the company, the idea of service to Alaska's hulking neighbor to the west was not dead.

Although the Cold War was still on, there were signs of thawing, and *détente, glasnost,* and *perestroika* were making their way into the Western vernacular. Kennedy had been touched by stories of Eskimo families in the Soviet Union sending messages to relatives in Alaska using balloons, the only means of communicating under a communist government that discouraged contact with the West. He now saw his chance to make a small gesture of friendship through flying between the United States and the Soviet Union.

This coincided with the same interest being expressed by the airline's Community Advisory Board members, a group of Alaskan community leaders who worked closely with the carrier on issues and problems affecting its service to, from, and within the 49th state. One future advisory board member in particular, Jim Stimple, had been communicating with Eskimo people in the Russian Far East and had learned of the balloon network between the Soviet city of Provideniya and Nome. After World War II, both borders were closed. Eskimos could no longer travel between Alaska and the Soviet Union, and some hadn't seen their families for years. This was the situation that Stimple eventually brought to Kennedy's attention and also to Alaska's small but energetic congressional delegation.

Kennedy presented the idea of flying to Russia at a Horizon planning session in San Diego. Among those in attendance were John Kelly, CEO of Horizon; Ray Vecci, Alaska's COO; and Bill McKnight, Alaska's vice president of marketing. They all respected Kennedy's vision, yet they had a collective gut feeling that such a route would be more trouble than it was worth. But McKnight spoke up, "If the chairman wants to go there . . ." And that's how the airline eventually established seasonal, scheduled service to Russia's Far East.

The wheels of bureaucracy began to turn, albeit with excruciating slowness, in both Washington and Moscow. First there were talks between the mayor of Provideniya and a National Geodetic Survey team. Then Kennedy asked the airline's attorneys in Washington, D.C., to get the State Department's help in obtaining authorization to provide scheduled air service between Anchorage/Nome and Provideniya.

Service would be preceded by a survey flight carrying a small technical delegation to inspect airport facilities in Provideniya. As with any communication with the Soviet government, it took forever to hear from Moscow.

"I think we wrote to them early in 1987," Jim Johnson recalled. "We asked for authority to fly into Provideniya, provided it had adequate facilities. We didn't hear anything until later that year, around Memorial Day, when our attorney phoned me from Washington and said he had just gotten a call from the Soviet Embassy. 'They want you to call them and they'll confirm the authorization,' he added.

"At that point," Johnson said, "we didn't know if Provideniya even had an airport, let alone an adequate one. I phoned the Soviet Embassy and told them we needed authorization to fly a small survey team into Provideniya, so we could obtain information on such items as runway length, available navigation aids, radio frequencies, and so on. This they furnished us, but our troubles with the Soviet bureaucracy weren't over."

In May 1988, Alaska chartered a small twin-engine Piper from Bering Air, a code-share partner, to fly an inspection team from Nome to Provideniya, a 225-mile hop that didn't require a large airplane. Aboard the little aircraft were Bruce Kennedy, Jim Johnson, Bill Boser of flight operations, and Elisa Miller, a language specialist from the University of Washington who spoke fluent Russian. Alaska captains Terry Smith and Steve Day were passenger/observers seated directly behind the Bering Air pilots.

Nearing Provideniya, the plane was unable to contact the airport control tower because, as they learned later, they didn't have the right radio frequency. They landed anyway and were met by annoyed airport officials who discovered belatedly that Moscow's landing authorization had somehow gotten lost in a bureaucratic shuffle. The Alaska inspection team received apologies and a warm greeting. Publicly the Alaska team genuinely returned their hosts' warmth in kind. But their private reaction was dismay — not because of the landing snafu, but at what they saw of the airport itself. The only paved area was in front of a dingy terminal. The one runway was 5,000 feet long, adequate for jets but all gravel.

The town itself seemed way too small to be any kind of tourist attraction, and hotel accommodations were skimpy at best. So the team flew back to the United States and reported that although they had been received with hospitality in Provideniya, some other city would have to serve as the destination terminus. Kennedy knew that serving Provideniya was high on Jim Stimple's agenda because of its proximity to a sizable number of Alaskan Eskimo families. This led to a second flight to Provideniya, which was publicized as a combined goodwill gesture and suitability test. In response to the inspection team's warning about gravel ingestion, one of Alaska's two 737-200 combis equipped with gravel kits was assigned to the historic trip. Alaska Senator Frank Murkowski, who later became the state's governor, was especially helpful in facilitating the event, cutting through considerable governmental red tape.

The departure board at the Nome Airport on June 14, 1988, read:

Flight 6059 Nome - Provideniya Departs 7:50

Unofficially, it went down in history as "The Friendship Flight."

Commanding the 737 were captains Terry Smith and Steve Day, obvious choices because in addition to being highly skilled airmen, they had previously experienced landing in Provideniya as members of the inspection team. Kennedy again headed Alaska's delegation, one documented in the October 1988 issue of *National Geographic*. Jim Johnson and his "Mr. Alaska" successor, Bill MacKay, acted as unofficial hosts for the party. Governor Steve Cowper and his vivacious wife were prominent passengers. Kennedy noted, "Governor Cowper, through his Office of International Trade, and specially assigned staff member Ginna Brelsford did a remarkable job to support and advance the historic Friendship Flight."

Guests included media reporters from Seattle, New York, Los Angeles, San Francisco, and Alaska, plus state dignitaries and other VIPs. The most important passengers among the 82 aboard, however, were a group of Eskimo people on their way to reunite with relatives they hadn't seen or talked to since 1948, when the border was closed. These Eskimos from Northwest Alaska were the real center of attention when the plane landed in Provideniya, where they were met by a cheering delegation of their Siberian brothers.

A big banner hung across the terminal entrance:

PEACE & FRIENDSHIP BETWEEN ALASKA AND CHUKOTKA

(Chukotka is the province in which Provideniya is located.)

After everyone had deplaned, carnations were handed out to the visitors and then the two Eskimo groups converged. "The formalities," David Foster of the Associated Press wrote later, "soon gave way to hugs, handshakes, and exchanges of gifts."

The airline had brought along several bushels of Washington State apples, and these were distributed to children at the Provideniya schools that the group visited when they toured the city.

The Friendship Flight had achieved one of its main goals with the Eskimo reunion. It also proved to be a publicist's dream, newsworthy enough to generate media attention, including a six-page spread in *National Geographic*, front-page coverage in *The Wall Street Journal*, and a lengthy segment on the *CBS Evening News*. In fact, the late Terry Drinkwater, son of a former Western Air Lines chairman and a television journalist who loved Alaska, did the reporting for CBS.

The entire visit lasted only a day, a sliver of time in which the Cold War was temporarily forgotten. Yet despite the warm hospitality of Provideniya's officials and populace, there was unanimous agreement that using it as a destination city would not attract enough tourist traffic to justify regular service.

As a businessman, Kennedy was profit-minded, but his humanitarian interests could influence some of his decisions. "Our involvement, while a departure from our usual business activities, has been gratifying. We welcome the chance to play even a small role in promoting understanding and goodwill between the people of our two countries," he wrote in his 1988 chairman's letter.

The Friendship Flight had whetted Kennedy's interest in pioneering scheduled service to the Russian Far East. Ray Vecci was not enthusiastic about the Russian initiative, so Kennedy appointed Doug Versteeg to oversee what became a difficult, complex three-year-long venture. Versteeg was vice president of administration, not an operations manager, but Kennedy had confidence in him and knew he could be trusted "to go directly to and confront reluctant souls." Vecci was not alone in his opposition. In fact, among the senior officers, only Jim Johnson and Versteeg supported Kennedy's plan.

The itinerary that Versteeg outlined simply to get to Magadan and Khabarovsk for exploratory meetings gave fair warning that providing the service might not be so easy. The group had to fly from Seattle to Tokyo, take a train to Niigata, and then fly to Magadan or Khabarovsk. The team included representatives from appropriate departments such as flight operations, maintenance, and marketing. Carl Baber went along to check out food-supply availability and kitchen facilities, and there were two Russian-speaking interpreters. No one had ever been to Russia before, and all were warned to take along a lot of essentials.

"None of us could understand such advice," Kit Cooper related. "The Soviet Union was supposed to be an industrial powerhouse, so we figured it couldn't be that bad. So my first impression, and that of most of us, was that the Russians had pulled a gigantic hoax. From what I was able to see, there was no way those guys could have waged war against the United States.

"In Magadan, for example, we found out the airport was on one side of the city and the major hotels were on the other side, and if you wanted to call one of the hotels from the airport, you had to go through an operator because there was no direct dialing. And if you wanted to call the United States, you had to make a reservation hours or even days in advance. I inspected the local major telephone switching station there with our communications expert from the airline. He just threw up his hands. It was what we had back in the 1920s and 1930s.

"Khabarovsk, the second-largest city in the Russian Far East, wasn't much better. This was despite being an industrial center where most Japanese firms did business. [The largest city in the region was Vladivostok, which Alaska Airlines would later serve, beginning in 1993. It initially remained closed to foreigners because of its military and naval installations.]

"When our party checked in at one of the best hotels in Khabarovsk, I discovered my room had no heat. I complained to the desk and was told their maintenance man had gone home for the night. Their solution was to send up a second blanket.

"Everything was totally backward, including their navigation aids, at the Far East airports. They had a form of ILS [instrument landing system] that wasn't used anywhere else in the world. It wasn't even close to the efficiency of our navigation aids. We ended up with only three airplanes equipped to receive their ILS signal, and that's how we got around when we started service."

Carl Baber experienced the same shock when he inspected kitchens and food markets in the two cities, especially Khabarovsk. "I went to markets and a couple of kitchens," he related, "and it was scary. You couldn't buy a chicken breast or a chicken thigh; you had to buy the whole chicken. Of the couple of kitchens I visited, only one had hot water. So I decided to plan very simple menus for the return trips, capitalizing on the few things they could do best, such as salads. We brought in our own major provisions like beef and chicken, and boarded meals in Anchorage so they'd be available for the turnaround flight. On one occasion I asked Wolfgang Erbe if he had ever cooked a moose. He said, 'No, but let's get some and I'll try it.'

"Well, Wolfgang happened to be a wild-game expert, so we went with it, serving moose steaks and red cabbage in first class on the Russian flights. It was a terrific meal."

Later, after the flights began, Baber sent Erbe over to train Russian cooks. In the course of that mission, Wolfgang got a look at the challenges of catering flights out of Khabarovsk. "I didn't think much of Russian food," he reported, "but then again, they didn't have much to work with. One of our officers, Lou Cancelmi, spoke a little Russian, and he did some food shopping in the local markets there. He shared with me that the best stuff was in their privately run markets, and that the food sold in the state-operated markets cost a lot less, but was awful.

"Ironically, the scarcest commodity," said Erbe, "was ice. But all those problems notwithstanding, the people I worked with in Russia were extremely courteous and helpful. No one ever bucked me or made things difficult for me."

The original plan called for a maximum of three flights a week between June and September, although frequency naturally would depend on traffic. The initial round-trip Anchorage-Magadan coach fare was set at $1,000, and $2,500 for Anchorage-Khabarovsk, a thousand miles south of Magadan.

Five-, six-, and eight-day tour packages were priced from $1,145 to $1,795 per person. Assembled under the direction of Wendy Kettering in marketing, the packages ranged from tours of sites in Khabarovsk and Magadan to those that included more exotic locales. One favorite tour was a combination air/rail package to the Eastern Siberian city of Irkutsk and nearby Lake Baikal, a World Heritage Site and the world's deepest and oldest freshwater lake. Transportation to those destinations — 1,370 miles east of Khabarovsk — was provided by a combination of Aeroflot, the Soviet national airline, and the Trans-Siberian Railroad.

Magadan was selected more as a refueling stop than a tourist attraction. It was a seaport city of 150,000 people and, like many other Russian communities during the communist rule, was colorless and uninviting.

"Everything is gray," an American visitor once remarked about Moscow, and it was an apt description of most Russian cities, including Magadan, which was especially unappealing. It had been a gateway to one of Stalin's notorious gulags, the same prison camp where Wolfgang Erbe's father was incarcerated during the war. The roads around the city had been built by German prisoners of war. The bones of the hundreds who died of starvation and disease during the construction still line those roads, for they were buried wherever they fell while trying to work.

Khabarovsk, with a population of 600,000, was no Paris or London, but it was a far more attractive tourist destination than Magadan. Kit Cooper faced one of the most challenging job environments of his airline career when he opened up Alaska's station there. The culture shock began with his first encounter with Soviet bureaucracy.

The Russians had provided Alaska Airlines with an office at the Khabarovsk airport, but when Cooper was ready to move in, he was informed that the office was going to be repainted for its new occupants.

"That's fine," Cooper said gratefully.

"However," the official added, "once it's painted, you must stay out of the office for another 48 hours because the paint is full of toxic materials."

Cooper then found himself with a squad of Alaska Airlines employees, all on full salary, ready to train Russian ticket agents and ramp-service personnel, but without a space to conduct business. This went on for another five days. Each morning, Cooper would ask some airport official when the paint would be safe. For five days he got the same answer: "Tomorrow."

Then Cooper got a break when he was invited to a reception celebrating Japan Airlines' inaugural flight into Khabarovsk. He was introduced to the city's mayor, they hit it off, and Cooper unburdened himself. "We haven't been able to get into our office for almost a week," he told the mayor. "We can't begin operating until we do, and all I'm getting is a daily runaround."

The mayor promised to look into the matter. The next day the airport manager came to see Cooper and asked what the problem was.

"The problem," Cooper said tartly, "is that I've got eight people here doing absolutely nothing and I'm paying for it."

The airport director smiled. "Don't worry about it," he assured Cooper. "You know, we've got a whole country of people sitting around doing nothing and getting paid for it."

The office was opened the next day. But the incident gave Cooper an understanding of communist Russia. "At a certain point," he theorized, "maybe in the mid-1950s or '60s, the country just stopped progressing. Yes, their space program was an exception, but the only one. You could see the decay everywhere.

"They had a new terminal at Khabarovsk, and it took them 15 years to build it. When we started service there, it was only a year old and looked as if it had been built 20 years before. Incidentally, the military operated all the airports, too. I think the airport director who helped me was a brigadier general."

Cooper said he found it hard to cope with the Russians' suspicious, distrustful, almost paranoid nature. It dominated business relationships. "When they got to know you, they were great," Cooper added. "But until then, their attitude was, 'How are you going to screw us?' They'd look at a contract and ask, 'Where's the clause that says we're going to get cheated?' "

The irony was that American companies such as Alaska, even after communist rule ended, often faced a double standard: the Russians demanded concessions that they refused to grant themselves.

After its first scheduled service to two cities (Khabarovsk and Magadan) began in the summer of 1991, Alaska added three more cities to its network of destinations within the Russian Far East. It even eventually offered year-round service. Flights began to Vladivostok (1993), a city whose natural beauty is often compared to San Francisco's; to Petropavlovsk (1994), on the Kamchatka Peninsula, renowned as an outdoorsman's paradise; and, finally, to Yuzhno-Sakhalinsk (1997), site of one of Russia's major offshore oil and gas developments.

Alaska officially inaugurated scheduled service on June 17, 1991, when Flight 29 took off from Anchorage International Airport at 6:35 p.m. with 137 passengers and seven crew members, bound for Magadan. The aircraft was a Boeing 727-200; later, MD-83s would be used on the route. Among the passengers were the obligatory VIPs, media, and other guests, including 60 members of the Alaska State Chamber of Commerce and the US-USSR Trade and Economic Council.

Ray Vecci, who became Alaska's chairman in May 1991, continued the Kennedy tradition of being a passenger on inaugural flights, including the first scheduled service between Anchorage and the Russian Far East. Vecci commented, "The start-up required tremendous effort throughout the airline. Aircraft had to be equipped with extra fuel capacity and avionics; weather and operations data were gathered and digested; two stations were created and provisioned half a world away; and extensive training and technical support were provided."

Flight 29 did not mark the first scheduled air service between the United States and the Soviet Union. That honor went to Pan Am when it began New York-Moscow flights in 1968. Nevertheless, Alaska's precedent-setting scheduled service to the Russian Far East was still a major-league endeavor.

In due time, after the excitement of the first service began to dissipate, the reality of serving Russia began to sink in. Alaska encountered problems that never would have been tolerated at a U.S. airport. The runways, for instance, were long but of block construction. In freezing weather, the blocks would heave so that a landing would be like running over speed bumps. The summers brought a different headache. The Russians were constantly sealing the slab edges with tar, which rendered a runway inoperable until the tar dried.

On one occasion, the Khabarovsk control tower assigned takeoff clearance to an Alaska MD-83 without advising the crew that their assigned runway had just been sealed. The MD-83's engines were slanted at an angle that sucked up runway debris like a vacuum cleaner. The jet started down the runway and both engines began ingesting the fresh wet tar. The takeoff was aborted, and a new engine had to be flown in — an airport mistake that cost the airline about $250,000.

Aeroflot, the airport's controlling entity, flatly refused to pay for the damage. The Russians did agree to hold a hearing, which somehow determined that air-traffic control in Moscow had been at fault. But, Cooper ruefully remembered, "because air-traffic control in Moscow was run by a government agency, the government absolved itself of all liability, and we were stuck with the bill."

Then there was the famous "vodka on the rocks" incident at Magadan, when an MD-83 picked up a load of ice while parked next to the terminal in 70-degree weather. A peculiar trait of the MD-83s, ice accumulations would sometimes occur under certain temperature and humidity conditions when fuel, super-cooled during flight, would chill the aircraft's upper wing surfaces in spite of above-freezing temperatures. On this occasion, one wing had iced up, and in such mild weather the Magadan airport had no de-icing fluid available.

Captain Zip Trower suggested a solution, an aviation first that may not rank with what the Wright brothers accomplished at Kitty Hawk, but certainly placed high in the annals of Alaska Airlines and its can-do tradition. "How about trying vodka?" Trower suggested.

After a brief discussion, Alaska mechanic Mike Saporito, who was stationed in Magadan during the summer, went to the nearest liquor store. He returned with 25 bottles of 100-proof vodka, which not only swiftly de-iced the MD-83 wing, but at 100 proof quite possibly could have caused shrinkage in an Alaskan glacier.

Trower was one of a handful of Alaska pilots who flew the Russian route and established a perfect safety record under conditions reminiscent of the hazardous days of wintertime bush flying. Bear in mind that both the 727-200 and MD-83 had limited range, and there were no alternates within reach if weather closed down a destination airport.

Kit Cooper explained why this left little margin for error. "Getting updated Russian weather information could take nearly two hours, and we needed to get weather information to Anchorage four hours before departure so we could start planning the trip.

"One of the reasons we were to have a lot of trouble with our Russian service later was that we never had a Julian Acosta there," observed Cooper.

Even in the operation of tour packages, Aeroflot provided an interesting contrast to Alaska's way of doing business. Aeroflot's aircraft were designed more for military use than comfort, and its schedules were conditional. One morning Brad Walker, who then managed Alaska's tour business to Soviet Siberia, received a call at six o'clock from his agent Kathleen McClure. McClure, who spoke Russian, was stranded along with a group of 32 American tourists in Irkutsk. The Aeroflot aircraft did not have enough fuel to return the party from Irkutsk, and nobody seemed to know when some might arrive by truck.

To make matters worse, McClure explained to Walker, "a tour group from Moscow arrived in the city today and every hotel room in town is booked."

Walker asked, "What are our options?"

"Well," McClure said, "they built a new hospital here. It is the nicest place in town, and they can accommodate our people."

"I just couldn't see putting our customers up for a night or two in a hospital, but Kathleen assured me it was the best and only option." The unexpected stay lasted two days, and when the fuel arrived, the airplane's captain had to pay for it in cash.

Early on in the Russian venture, Vecci had asked his senior officers to review the company's services to the Far East. "We came to the conclusion," recalled Kelly, "that we could continue to offer scheduled service to Russia, but operationally we would have to add some extra pieces of equipment, which was authorized."

A subsequent meeting included Brad Walker. "All our vice presidents," said Walker, "were at the meeting. They asked how the tour packages with Aeroflot were going.

"I told them that our customers liked the tours. They complained a little about the food and the toilet paper, but they seemed to like the tours, and they supported our flights.

"The vice presidents asked about how we got our customers back from Irkutsk. I told them Aeroflot.

"They asked about Aeroflot. 'Do they have all the necessary insurance?'

"I told them that Aeroflot had hull insurance.

" 'What about passenger insurance?' they asked.

"No, no passenger insurance, I replied.

"There was a risk-management person in the meeting. She said that if the aircraft carried 40 passengers, it could mean upward of $50 to $75 million in liability.

"Vecci said, 'What? Are you kidding me?'

"I was a manager and I was more than a little uncomfortable.

"Ray then said, 'We are shutting those goddamn things down now.'

"That was the end of that tour package."

Despite its best efforts to build the Russian market, by the late 1990s Alaska had started to sour on what had begun so nobly and hopefully. The increasing influence of the Russian mafia after the fall of the Soviet regime was one negative factor. Another was a sharp downturn in the Russian economy.

The bottom line, however, was simply declining traffic. As the allure of visiting the Soviet Union began to fade, traffic flow started to shrink. There were other factors as well, such as unsatisfactory profitability and safety issues like the wet tar incident. Ultimately the decision to discontinue service to Russia followed government approval of nonstop service between the Russian Far East and Seattle, something that state-owned Aeroflot long-range aircraft could do but Alaska's MD-80s, without the range, simply couldn't.

In 1998, Cooper got the word from Seattle to shut down the Russian service. He was not surprised and in many ways was relieved. He liked the Russian people as individuals and had made many friends, but doing business with them was difficult and sometimes impossible.

Although he retired in 1991, Bruce Kennedy saw his dream of scheduled service to the Soviet Union fulfilled. He was chairman emeritus when service to the Russian Far East ended.

Though still on the board, Kennedy had severed most of his other connections with the airline in order to concentrate on church and personal activities. These included teaching English in China and later serving as chairman of Mission Aviation Fellowship, an organization dedicated to providing aviation, communications, missionary, and other support to developing countries and isolated areas worldwide. In more recent years, he was involved in the creation of a new single-engine airplane that could fly medical and food supplies into remote areas of impoverished Third World countries. Designed and built by Quest Aircraft Company, it would be an aircraft capable of landing and taking off almost anywhere, even on dirt strips not much longer than a football field. Profits from commercial sales would fund the purchase and operation of airplanes for missionary flying, and help finance flying "mercy missions." Kennedy served as Quest's board chairman.

Acquisitions, holding companies, domestic and international route expansion, consistent profitability, and a "mountain" of publicity associated with the airline's in-flight product, its service to Mexico, and its return to Russia were just some of the dramatic symbols of growth and progress made on Bruce Kennedy's watch. During his tenure, Alaska maintained an outstanding safety record. Revenue grew from less than $100 million to more than $1 billion, and company assets increased more than tenfold to $1 billion. In his years as Alaska's chief executive, Kennedy delivered unequaled, consistent profits while paying out more than $19 million to the company's stockholders in dividends, and acquiring both Jet America and Horizon Air. The stock market acknowledged these results, and during his tenure, shares in what had become Alaska Air Group increased in value from $4 to $30 per share.

Also during the Kennedy era, Alaska had pushed its borders west into the Soviet Far East and south along the Pacific coast of Mexico. To be sure, there had been challenges, occasional setbacks, and unfinished business as well. In particular, there was an underlying festering of difficult labor issues that had been settled but not really put to rest. Despite that, on balance, the airline and its employees made significant strides forward under Kennedy.

Yet in the turbulent, unpredictable world of the airline industry, where sunny skies so often are replaced by menacing thunderheads, attaching permanency to success is about as elusive as getting mercury into a bottle. For in departing, Kennedy left a legacy of not only success but also controversy so bitter that the only thing that didn't boil over was the water in the pool that adorned the lobby of the corporate office building.

CHAPTER SIXTEEN

The DaVecci Code

While he was still chairman and CEO, Bruce Kennedy began making notes in a journal. Among the entries was a rating system he had devised for selecting his eventual successor, and the names of the people he considered qualified to assume the top leadership positions within the company.

"The Book," as Kennedy referred to it, was a black 8½-by-11-inch loose-leaf notebook that he kept locked in his desk. He had begun using it in the mid-1980s, when he started to think about retiring. Kennedy carefully guarded his precise rating formula, but he revealed later that his system embraced such factors as experience, past performance, intelligence, personality, and tenure at Alaska.

The task of selecting a new CEO fell largely to the company's board of directors, but they relied on Kennedy's input — his general assessment of the company's current strengths and weaknesses, and the challenges the airline was likely to face in the future. Without revealing the existence of his personal rating blueprints, Kennedy established a succession committee within the board of directors, and in early 1990 he and the committee began the process of naming his successor. Two top candidates emerged. They were Ray Vecci and John Kelly.

Years later, when Kelly himself was considering retirement, Kennedy confided about The Book. He offered to show him its detailed plan of succession, and then brought it to Kelly's office. "I was dumbfounded at its impressive scope and how well it was laid out," Kelly remembered. "It even took into consideration such factors as revenue-projection accuracy, and included an elaborate rating system for various candidates."

The scoring system for each category was one to five, five being the highest. "John outscored Ray by two or three points overall, but in most categories they were even," Kennedy related. "However, I had to take into account other factors besides the scoring system."

These were considerations that in his own mind tipped the scales in favor of Vecci. Kennedy cited them when he brought his recommendation to the succession committee. He argued that Kelly had reported to Vecci, who had more seniority and thus was ahead in the line of succession. He said there wasn't enough difference between the two men to justify ignoring this narrow margin, determined by an evaluation system that, in effect, had established an orderly succession process.

He added that if Vecci were chosen, Kelly would be a good team member willing to work with Ray, but that if the committee picked Kelly, Vecci probably would leave.

In the fall of 1990 the board named Vecci as Alaska Air Group's president and chief executive officer, and chairman, president, and chief executive officer of Alaska Airlines. At the same time, Kelly was named chairman, president, and chief executive officer of Horizon Air Industries.

Vecci was asked by Kennedy to recommend his replacement as the company's chief operating officer. The leading candidates were Ken Skidds and Pat Glenn. Vecci discussed the position with both of them, and they individually suggested to him that the position should be senior vice president of operations rather than chief operating officer, excluding marketing and planning from the position's responsibilities. Vecci chose not to consider the new title, and he recommended Pat Glenn for that job.

Raymond J. Vecci was a tough-minded, blunt-talking product of the Bronx. He entered the airline industry in 1961 when he took a job with the International Air Transport Association (IATA), and during that time, he went to night school at City College of New York, where in 1965 he received a bachelor's degree in business administration. A year later he left the IATA and worked part-time in the *New York Times* customer-service department taking complaints from customers whose ads had been placed incorrectly or simply not printed at all. During this time he earned an MBA from New York University. He was hired by United Airlines in 1967 and began his career in its economic and fleet planning department. Before completing a year in his new position he was drafted, and on New Year's Day 1969, he was sent to Vietnam as an infantryman. He rejoined United Airlines a year later.

Vecci spent a total of seven years with United, later serving as a senior analyst and project manager. He was hired by Cosgrave in 1975 and for much of his career at Alaska Airlines served as the company's chief planner. He had a very logical mind, with an uncanny ability to project the potential viability of proposed new markets. It was said that he could mine information from numbers on a printed report like a skilled pianist coaxing beautiful music out of a keyboard.

Of the many people who knew him and provided their insights into this complex, controversial character, perhaps the fairest was Bill O'Dwyer, a director in the finance department, who accepted Ray's trigger-tempered and abrasive personality as part of the job. "To get along with Vecci," O'Dwyer explained, "you had to remember one thing: he was a New Yorker. Once you remembered that, you would be okay."

There was a lot of truth to that analysis. Ray's background was like that of Ron Cosgrave — middle-class with a strong work ethic, although in many respects he and Cosgrave were as different as night and day. And Vecci's demeanor was a departure from that of the quiet, sometimes secretive Kennedy.

As president and CEO, Vecci became responsible for all aspects of Alaska Air Group, with the notable exceptions of finance, legal, and the operations of the corporate secretary's office, which still reported to the chairman. "This did not trouble me," said Vecci, "because the company was never managed according to strict organizational lines." He saw dual reporting as "in the nature of the way the company ran."

Kennedy retained his position as chairman of Alaska Air Group, Inc., and the relationship that developed over the next several months grew out of what might be best described as a clash of styles between the company's top two officers. Kennedy played his cards close to the vest, while Vecci preferred a more open dialogue. Lines of communication between them became tangled, a frustrating issue for Vecci. "On several occasions when I was addressing a particular problem, I would later learn that the same matter was also being addressed by Bruce. I became disturbed about being left unaware of important matters, especially since I would frequently be in Bruce's office to brief him on my activities, sometimes more than once a day."

Vecci feared that this was typical of what he could expect in the future. "I felt that despite Bruce's expressed desire to reduce his level of organization responsibilities, in fact his heart was not in it."

After much soul searching, Vecci wrote a concise letter to him. Kennedy had just returned from an early fall board meeting when Vecci walked into the chairman's office. There was uncommon tension in the air as the two men sat down in comfortable armchairs, face to face. There was no small talk. Vecci handed his letter to Kennedy. Vecci described its contents as "a one-sentence letter of resignation."

The two men had worked well and successfully together for 15 years, but at this meeting they struggled to be understood. "Words did not come easy for either of us," recalled Vecci. "It was my feeling that we had a truly unique and productive relationship over the years, and for me this meeting was very emotional, and in retrospect, traumatic.

"I think Bruce fully understood the problem I was trying to address," explained Vecci. "My letter was intended to lead to an uncomplicated plan for my leaving Alaska with a minimum of disruption.

"I had thought my position through for some time, and I fully expected that my meeting with Bruce would produce a plan that we both could follow." Vecci could not have been more surprised by what transpired.

"After I finished explaining my position, there was a long pause. That's when Bruce told me that he would be stepping down as chairman at the next shareholders' meeting and that I would assume his title and responsibilities. Then he handed the letter back to me." Vecci was stunned.

"Overwhelmed and obviously grateful" was the way Kennedy described Vecci's reaction.

Kennedy bequeathed a list of challenges to Vecci. The first Gulf War was about to cause fuel shortages and, subsequently, soaring Jet A prices. And that was just the beginning. There were a growing number of start-up, low-cost competitors, and the challenge of a soon-to-be-bankrupt MarkAir, wreaking havoc with its lowball pricing, particularly in the 49th state. Even in its death throes, MarkAir would attempt to invade many of Alaska's traditional routes.

Over the waning months of 1991, "the overriding driver behind our management actions and sense of urgency," recalled Vecci, "was not the recession, fuel prices, or even the challenge of MarkAir. The driver was our conviction that ticket prices would always be lower than needed to support our cost structure, and this would be a permanent situation. It made no difference whether low fares were the result of new entrants or financially distressed carriers. One or all would be there indefinitely, and we had to tailor our cost structure in recognition of that reality."

Vecci's conviction was not shared by everyone because, in the past, business had eventually returned to normal. "When we started to make progress in reducing costs," Vecci recalled, "I actually became concerned as ticket prices began to increase. I feared that the increases would be embraced by management and employees as a sign that better times were just ahead, and we would then lose momentum in our cost-reduction efforts. As it turned out, the ticket-price improvements during the spring of 1992 were short-lived."

MarkAir invaded Alaska's lucrative Seattle-Anchorage route in 1991, offering two-for-one discount fares, 50 percent below the standard $400 ticket price. As competition quickly heated up, nearly a third of Alaska Airlines' revenue came from routes being challenged by MarkAir.

Alaska discontinued its code-sharing and marketing agreements with MarkAir and formed new partnerships to serve several Alaska markets with PenAir, Era Aviation, and Reeve Aleutian Airways. The airline expanded its service within Alaska. It opened service to Barrow, in the state's Far North, and celebrated the station's opening with a Mexican fiesta for the entire town of 2,500.

By the end of 1992, MarkAir had filed for bankruptcy protection. Contrary to more conventional views, Vecci saw the MarkAir feud as having a positive effect on Alaska Airlines. "I'm not sure we could have mustered the determination to get out of some of our aircraft, or to restructure our leases to the extent that we did, without the costly impact of MarkAir."

Vecci saw MarkAir as only one of several bankrupt carriers the company had to contend with, and thought the next wave of price-cutting might have its nexus in a seemingly unrelated part of the country. "One of the characteristics of airline ticket pricing," Vecci lectured to his managers, "is that a pricing action somewhere in the domestic system has a tendency to spread to many markets, even sometimes including the Alaska marketplace."

The figures spoke for themselves. In 1991, Alaska Air Group earned a $10.3 million profit, but this was a drop of nearly 40 percent from the previous year's results. Investors, sensing that the possible effects of MarkAir's challenge were not over, pulled away from Alaska Airlines, and its stock price tanked. Prudential Securities predicted that Alaska would post a loss for 1992, and in the airline's 60th-anniversary year, the bottom fell out of the bucket. Alaska Airlines posted its worst financial deficits in nearly two decades. Traffic was up, but revenue fell. Kennedy's legacy, and 19 consecutive years of profits, stood in stark contrast to the company's whopping $85 million loss in 1992.

Starting in the flight kitchen and proceeding through the company's annual $1 billion budget, Vecci moved to rein in Alaska's elaborate and expensive service. This was not a popular decision among the company's employees or its passengers, and it was counter to the company's culture. The airline eliminated hot meals on some flights and complimentary wine in the main cabin, among other cost-saving measures.

Yet there remained nearly unanimous agreement among officers and employees alike that the hard-boiled, sometimes ruthless Ray Vecci was probably the right man to be CEO at that particular time. "Ray was the kind of general you'd want in a war," commented one of Alaska's veteran officers. "John Kelly was the kind of general you'd want in peacetime."

Vecci was decisive. He conveyed a sense of urgency, and he was not always interested in establishing a consensus among company management. He appeared at times to cut costs with an ax instead of a scalpel, and this was to forever tag him — perhaps not always fairly — with the reputation of an executioner rather than a surgeon. He was not willing to scrape away a wart when an amputation was necessary, and his role as the airline's *de facto* savior was often overlooked.

Vecci canceled or delayed aircraft orders valued in excess of $600 million. This alone lessened the company's list of capital commitments by $350 million. He also nixed plans to build two maintenance centers, and that reduced its capital commitments by another $150 million. This was still not enough to show a profit to the airline's stockholders, but it did buy the company time.

Under Vecci, Alaska was rated the best U.S. airline for the fifth consecutive year by *Condé Nast Traveler*. But as *BusinessWeek* reported in 1993, "Raymond J. Vecci had little time to celebrate." The company's blood continued to spill, in part because Southwest entered the Pacific Northwest market by acquiring the low-cost regional carrier Morris Air. At the same time, United Airlines began offering inexpensive shuttle flights between Seattle, Portland, and San Francisco. And if that weren't enough, Alaska's flight attendants were poised to strike.

No one ever questioned Ray Vecci's intelligence or ability. What *was* in question was the confrontational way he sometimes dealt with people. That, in essence, was the Da Vecci code, and its priorities did not include winning popularity contests. At officers' meetings, he could tongue-lash a vice president like a five-star general chewing out a buck private.

His toughest questions were sometimes reserved for veteran officers he thought were too set in their ways to accept new ideas for greater efficiency, or those who instinctively tried to keep their departments immune from economy measures he believed were absolutely necessary. Despite the remarkably productive debates that Vecci and the company's other officers took part in before Ray became CEO, times and the balance of power had changed, and so had the nature of disagreement among the airline's senior managers.

All during the Kennedy years, the airline had thrived by attracting business travelers willing to pay for top-notch service, gourmet meals, and fine wine, but a plethora of low-cost carriers put an end to the little luxuries of flying. No-frills competitors such as the expanding Southwest Airlines were able to provide a degree of service for 7 cents per available seat-mile. Alaska's luxuries cost the airline 11.5 cents per seat-mile, and at times exceeded 16 cents per available seat-mile.

Vecci appeared one day at Marriott's Alaska Airlines kitchen facility, where Wolfgang Erbe, Carl Baber, and two assistant chefs showed him some of the new menus they were planning. Not only was Ray unimpressed, but he also seemed annoyed. He called all of them aside.

"I want to tell you something," he said in a tone that wasn't angry but was definitely stern. He held out his palms, placing one about two feet higher than the other.

"We don't need our in-flight food to be this much higher than everyone else's," he declared.

Then he lowered his upper palm until his hands were only two inches apart. "You just have to be here," he added. "I want to be higher than the rest but not too high."

He departed. Lecture over. Message received.

That brief scene in the Marriott kitchen provided instant confirmation of Ray Vecci's simple brilliance. Sooner than most other airline executives, he had unerringly grasped the harsh realities of the changing air-travel market, a market that had been turned upside down and was going to stay that way for a long time, maybe permanently.

To address the pressures of cost and competition, Vecci established a group of senior officers consisting of himself, Kelly, Pat Glenn, vice president of planning Harry Lehr, and vice president of finance Ray Vingo. Basically this top-level quintet was Alaska Air Group's informal think tank, trying to find ways to climb out of the financial swamp into which the company was sinking.

The group began calling in various department heads, who were asked to detail what economy measures they were taking to help solve this crisis. Vecci could be merciless in those sessions, especially if he suspected that any officers were dragging their feet, and some of them undoubtedly were.

Kelly remembered one excruciating incident involving Bill McKnight, vice president of marketing. McKnight waffled about the measures he was taking to contain costs, and even Kelly, who loved marketing, knew that McKnight hadn't really put much effort into reducing costs.

Vecci and McKnight got into an argument about one sales representative whom McKnight thought essential and Vecci considered excess baggage. Vecci finally lost his temper. "Tell you what, Bill," he said coldly. "We'll just cut half your sales force arbitrarily, and later we'll hire some of them back if we have to."

Which was exactly what he did. Desperate measures for desperate times.

"That was pure Vecci," Kelly said. "In my opinion, the cuts had to be made, but they were too deep in some areas, and Ray's approach wasn't team-driven. So people had a tendency to grit their teeth and follow the famous adage: Don't get mad, get even."

The new bottom line for established carriers like Alaska was starkly evident. Gone were the days when the airlines could depend on businesspeople willing to pay any first-class fare for plush service and more comfortable seats. Confined to the dusty shelves of nostalgia were memories of the early jetliners with first-class and coach seats divided equally. Retired to obscurity was the kind of opulent service that on one carrier meant 12 napkins provided for each passenger during flights between New York and Paris.

Now the public was interested solely in low fares, and the lower the better. To an analytical mind like Vecci's, high-cost service and low fares were totally incompatible. That little visual demonstration in the Marriott commissary reflected his absolute conviction that Alaska had to become a low-cost carrier even if it meant providing only modestly better rather than vastly superior in-flight amenities.

Besides, he knew that "service" wasn't simply the food. It was the overall experience, and in that sense, the ace in the hole that Alaska had over other airlines was its top-notch flight attendants and customer-service agents. In fact, emphasis on "customer service" as the real point of differentiation between Alaska and its competitors would be a mantra that Vecci would invoke many times during the course of the changes he was about to make.

In the company's 1992 annual report, Vecci described the situation: "A failed effort last spring to restore rationality to the fare structure was sobering affirmation that fare levels cannot be established by the strongest carriers when the financially distressed attempt to satisfy cash requirements by deep discount pricing."

At the same time, Vecci reassured shareholders that he had no intention of standing pat in the midst of the mess in the industry. He told them, "We've mapped a course that enables us to return to profitability over the long term while competing with an array of different carriers: financially distressed, healthy, full-service, and new, low-cost carriers."

Vecci also noted that both Alaska and Horizon had dropped marginal or unprofitable flying; that nearly 1,000 flight attendants, customer-service agents, and other personnel had been furloughed; that Alaska's service to Bellingham, Toronto, Boise, and Tucson had been eliminated; that, instead, lower-cost Horizon Air would continue to serve Bellingham, Boise, and Spokane, providing feed traffic to Alaska; that seasonal suspension to some markets within Alaska, such as Kodiak, Dillingham, and King Salmon, would be implemented; and that an ongoing analysis of operations would continue questioning all basic assumptions and identifying ways, large and small, to reduce costs long term.

A year later Vecci would note that "we redefined customer service, emphasizing the value of treating customers with genuine concern and personal attention. We streamlined management layers and staffing and ended 1993 with 416 fewer employees."

While Vecci was shrinking amenities and personnel on the one hand, he was increasing utilization of his aircraft on the other. In the last half of 1993, for example, he increased aircraft use by 10 percent over the prior year, and utilization jumped by more than 20 percent in 1994.

One of the more visible areas that received its share of attention from Vecci was in-flight services. A few cost-cutting measures taken included revamping menus, changing from heavier fare to light meals, and discontinuing meals entirely on short flights and those outside traditional meal times. Though this represented a departure from the 1980s philosophy at Alaska, when value meant continually adding amenities, Vecci felt, and rightly so, that the real essence of Alaska's in-flight product remained its flight attendants.

Bill Cox had joined Alaska in 1987 as its staff vice president of in-flight services after being manager of United's in-flight services department at Chicago's O'Hare. This was United's corporate headquarters base and the largest in its system, and Cox supervised more flight attendants at that single location than there were on Alaska's entire roster. But he loved the contrast between a giant airline and a much smaller one, especially a carrier with a tradition of well-motivated personnel and a reputation for good in-flight service.

"It was a great opportunity to be responsible for something that already was outstanding," Cox said. "I guess my biggest job was not to screw it up. I was impressed with the quality of Alaska's food and the airline's willingness to invest in more innovative menus. This was award-winning service that was due, in my opinion, to the flight attendants and the quality of the meals they served."

It was a minuscule, almost inconsequential item in the food service that put Bill Cox in Vecci's well-populated doghouse, and reaffirmed Vecci's competitive direction for the airline. Cox's offense didn't even involve food. It concerned a single serving utensil. Spoons.

Ironically, it was Ray Vecci's own cost-reduction orders to all departments, including in-flight services, that led to the spoon incident. Bill Cox got the message in the Marriott kitchen. He knew that in-flight services could not be exempt from the economy measures being undertaken and that Vecci's pointed demonstration had made sense. A good team player, Cox began casting about for additional ways to save money and eventually zeroed in on stainless-steel spoons placed on meal trays in coach.

"It didn't become a big issue with the traveling public," Cox said. "We took the spoons off because there weren't many meals being served in coach that required spoons. It also was an effective cost-cutting measure that made a lot of sense. Spoon theft was always a problem, and we were about to order a large new supply when I made the decision to eliminate them in coach entirely. Furthermore, the spoons were heavy, so removing them reduced weight and saved fuel."

But Vecci brought up the spoons issue at an officers' staff meeting a short time later. "This spoon thing is really bothering me," he complained. "I'd like to go around this room and find out how everyone here feels about the spoons."

The consensus, according to Cox, was in support of his removal decision. There was also, with the exception of Vecci, a unanimous feeling that had nothing to do with the pros and cons of eliminating spoons in coach. Most were wondering why so much time was being spent on such a trivial subject. The issue of spoons, however, was not a trivial topic to Ray Vecci.

"At the next few officers' luncheons," Cox related, "when we were trying out whatever new menus would be served on our flights, Vecci would remark, 'I see there are still no spoons on the coach meal trays.' " Cox sensed that he now resided in Ray Vecci's escape-proof doghouse. He didn't expect a medal for the cost savings associated with the removal of spoons from Alaska's food service, but he didn't expect to be eventually fired, at least in part, because of it. Cox's error, however, had less to do with saving money than with what he proposed for the savings.

Nominees for Vecci's doghouse were those who impeded his efforts to streamline the company, including its in-flight services. To Cox it was about a spoon. To Vecci it was more. In reference to Cox, Vecci recalled, "He informed me on how he managed to save a significant amount of money with some particular change and then turned around and said he used that savings to add or enhance some other service feature. He truly believed and stated that it was his mission to provide the best possible service in the form of amenities, spending up to the budgeted amounts.

"This was typical of very large organizations, such as companies the size of United, or government agencies where a budget was viewed as a bank account with actual funds in it. A feeling grew for me that he [Cox] did not understand or accept what we were trying to do."

In any objective appraisal and analysis of Ray Vecci as a man and a leader, it must be emphasized that he definitely was complex, demanding, and even at times dictatorial. But such traits were not uncommon among the management characters that populated the airline's first 75 years, including some who earned the adjective *beloved* but also could often be arbitrary.

The real Ray Vecci also could be a kind, caring man with a sense of humor that occasionally peeked out from under his tough exterior. The irrepressible Dave Palmer caught him at such a moment when he went into his office one day to discuss some marketing problem.

It was not a subject that Palmer particularly enjoyed talking about with him because Vecci, coming from conservative United, was not a great fan of airline marketing in general. In fact, he tended to regard it with some disdain. The minute Palmer sat down that day, Vecci began denouncing airline marketing practices. The more he talked, the madder he became, until he noticed that Palmer was staring at him.

Palmer knew he was about to be on the receiving end of a Vecci tirade, but it so happened that he held a trump card. "I knew that Ray loved movies," Palmer related, "and one of his all-time favorites was *The Caine Mutiny*. I had heard him talk about it several times, especially the scene where Captain Queeg turns the destroyer upside down trying to find out who stole a quart of strawberries from the officers' mess."

This bit of knowledge saved the day. Vecci finished his litany of marketing sins, glared at Palmer, and growled, "Well, what do *you* think?"

"Ray, I think somebody stole your strawberries," Dave said with a straight face.

Vecci's complexion faded from florid to normal as he digested that answer. And when he suddenly grasped the reference, he burst out laughing.

"He could be a funny guy at times," Palmer recalled, "and he could laugh at himself."

Lou Cancelmi was also someone who, at times, saw Vecci at his best and worst. "I'd wince when I'd hear and see him lay into somebody," Cancelmi said.

Yet he could testify personally that Vecci was also a kind, thoughtful, and warm-hearted man. One morning, Cancelmi's wife, a teacher, had to work while their young son had the day off from his school. Not wanting to leave the boy home alone and being unable to find a sitter, Cancelmi, with some misgivings, took him to work.

"I didn't know exactly what the reaction would be to a nine-year-old hanging around the corporate offices," he recalled, "but I had no choice. Michael was a well-behaved kid, so I just hoped for the best."

He got the best — Vecci's best. Ray spotted the boy, sitting quietly in the corner of Cancelmi's office.

"Who's this?" Vecci asked gruffly.

"My son, Michael. We couldn't get a sitter at the last minute so I had to . . ."

"No matter," Vecci interrupted. "Michael, come with me."

"I'll never forget that morning," Cancelmi related. "Ray took him to his office for upwards of an hour. They talked, and I seem to recall they watched television together. Ray would do stuff like that. He'd handwrite someone a personal note of congratulations. If he knew you were dealing with some type of personal issue in your family — say, an illness — he'd ask how things were going. Anyway, if you can measure a man by the way he treats a child, then Ray Vecci stood awfully tall in my mind, and in Michael's."

The softer side of that dual personality could confound those who believed he was always irascible. Not many CEOs in American industry, for example, played a larger role than Ray Vecci in setting an example for the hiring of people with disabilities. He made sure the airline gave equal consideration to visually impaired applicants when interviewing prospective reservations agents, and once they were hired, invested in the proper tools, such as Braille keyboards, so they could succeed at their jobs. Many of them have gone on to long careers with Alaska Airlines. Vecci himself was named to the board of advisers of the Resource Center for the Handicapped, a Seattle-area organization dedicated to helping the disabled secure meaningful employment.

Vecci once told an interviewer that his management style was very informal, and when it came to dress code, it certainly was. Not long after he became CEO, he passed the word that wearing coats and ties to work in the corporate offices was no longer necessary and that women were free to wear slacks. Such informality, which actually began first at Horizon under Kelly, was much appreciated and remains in effect to this day, long after his departure.

The airline industry was not known as a friendly choice for either career-minded women or minorities, but Vecci was unlike other industry CEOs of his time. He sought out and advanced women and minorities he considered good potential executives. One was Marjorie Laws.

Laws, who rose to be vice president of corporate affairs and corporate secretary, was the first woman to attain that rank in the airline's history, under Kennedy. She was smart, efficient, well-liked, respected by her peers, and — once you had earned her trust — the most loyal of friends. She bestowed that loyalty on Ray Vecci.

Laws began to work directly for Vecci when he became CEO. Aside from that formal role, she was a friend, an adviser, a confidante, and his personal wordsmith. She used to help him with his speeches, some of his correspondence, and his editorials for the in-flight magazine. She was a stickler for accuracy and had instinctive good judgment, both of which Vecci valued greatly.

Above all, she remained Ray's friend throughout his tumultuous years as CEO, for she had a different interpretation of what others perceived as the dark side of his character. "Yes, I know he liked to butt heads," she recounted. "His philosophy was to have a full and vigorous debate on every issue because he felt in that way that he'd be able to look at the subject from all sides, identify any weaknesses, and end up with a better decision or better product."

Vecci was a master at seeking out countervailing arguments no matter which side he was on. And he loved a good debate, especially between his cadre of officers. Their wrangling provided Ray with conflicting views that in the end were the grounds for making informed decisions.

"It's wonderful to debate that way if you're confident enough to debate the top guy," said Laws. "But when *you're the guy* at the top, as Ray was, it wasn't going to happen the way he intended. He never seemed to realize that when he began an aggressive debate, people from all areas of the company, people whose livelihoods depended on him, weren't going to be as aggressive as he was.

"Ray never got it. And it infuriated him. The very thing he tried so hard to get, namely aggressive action, was exactly what he failed to get because of his own aggressive personality."

Laws believed that while Vecci was brusque and tough on the outside, he was a man who simply loved a good fight that could end with no hard feelings. "He could get into a bloody argument with someone," Laws recalled, "and afterward, while walking out of the room, turn to the guy and say to him, 'Hey, let's go have a beer.' "

He had that kind of relationship with Gus Robinson, who also had the exterior smoothness of brand-new sandpaper. Laws remembered them at planning sessions going at each other in angry exchanges so studded with profanity that she thought they were about to start throwing punches. "Then they'd leave the room practically arm in arm," she marveled. "They were both volatile people, and yet they were always good friends."

Laws also defended, or at least tried to explain, some of Vecci's often-criticized firings of veteran department managers, directors, and even vice presidents. She emphasized that the majority of his manpower cuts affected managerial personnel and relatively few rank-and-file employees. Yet she conceded that while some of his dismissals, or mandatory early retirements for people who didn't want to retire yet, were justified, others may not have been.

"We would often talk about certain personnel cuts beforehand," Laws said. "Some of them seemed reasonable and some of them seemed capricious. Ray would become convinced that someone was not equal to the job, and more often than not, this was the case. Anyway, that was his rationale, his reason for swinging the ax. Or we might have a whole layer of people he'd want to get rid of, and he'd argue that in such situations, we couldn't afford to look at individuals."

In his eyes, Vecci's targets were functions, not people. Laws recounted: "He told me we had to do it by their function, and if the function wasn't necessary, then each individual position wasn't necessary. Inevitably, a lot of people felt that if this meant firing or prematurely retiring someone who had been with Alaska for 25 years, there should be an attempt to find them some other job to do, and let someone who had been with the company only six months go first. But Ray didn't always do that. In fact, he seldom did. This was one of the most uncomfortable things I saw him do."

According to some former colleagues, Vecci was impulsive, and yet at times could be surprisingly indecisive and uncertain.

Whatever the merits of the observations about him, two nearly unanimous opinions of Ray Vecci emerge. First, outwardly he was not perceived as a "people person," cast in the mold of, say, a John Kelly. Second, only a man with Vecci's will would have had the resolve to take the cost-cutting measures that kept Alaska Airlines from going over the brink in the first half of the 1990s. From 1993 to 1994, the number of employees per flight declined 12 percent; seat capacity per employee increased 22 percent; and customers per employee increased 33 percent. And daily utilization of aircraft increased substantially.

There was no doubt whatsoever that Vecci turned Alaska around financially, and with amazing speed. That horrendous 1992 net loss of more than $84 million was reduced by nearly $54 million the following year, and turned into a $30.9 million profit in 1994, his last year in office. Vecci and his executive team accomplished this primarily by examining in detail whether a program, activity, or function would be instituted if it did not currently exist. If not, it was eliminated. If the answer was unclear, it was also eliminated unless the action was irreversible and the long-term consequences of being wrong were unacceptable. As a result, about $100 million in permanent cost reductions were implemented in less than three years.

Interestingly, Alaska's dramatic turnaround was achieved without the massive payroll cuts normally associated with major cost-cutting campaigns. The total Alaska Air Group payroll in 1992 numbered 8,979 employees. It dropped slightly to 8,733 the following year, then jumped to 9,852 in 1994.

So, almost incredibly, what permanent downsizing there was affected various levels of management, but very few rank-and-file employees. The vast majority of the latter did not have to take salary cuts, but their productivity increased as a result of changes in new labor contracts. Those furloughed early on found themselves called back.

Ray Vecci earned praise and pillory alike for his role in the comeback, while unsung hero Ray Vingo helped the airline's credit rating and investor relations survive the economic bloodshed of the early 1990s. "All that Ray Vingo did in the 1980s," Kelly emphasized, "we needed in the 1990s. Thanks to him, we got respect on Wall Street, in the banks, and with financial analysts." That respect was needed when market expansion necessitated major fleet expansion. Alaska Airlines was to make good in virtually every new market it entered throughout the 1990s and into the 21st century.

If Vingo's most important contribution was earning respect in financial circles, Vecci's strong point was judging the potential viability of new markets he thought would work for Alaska in the dog-eat-dog environment of deregulation. And this talent would pay important dividends several years later, when the airline's fleet plan included ordering future aircraft with transcontinental range, making nonstop service to major East Coast cities and Florida possible.

It was the "other Ray," chief financial officer Vingo, who played a pivotal role in dealing with fears of a possible unfriendly takeover, a fate that would have doomed this fiercely independent airline. The Marvin Davis overtures, although quickly rebuffed by Kennedy, raised some red flags. "This was the time of corporate raiders trying to take over airlines," Vingo pointed out. "And our stock was undervalued, which made us an especially vulnerable merger target."

To prevent the kind of unfriendly takeover that already had occurred at TWA, where raider Carl Icahn had seized control, the airline persuaded International Lease Finance Corporation to buy a large chunk of a special Alaska Airlines stock issue, enough to block any Icahn-style invasion. "One way for companies to defend themselves," Vingo explained, "is to have an additional base of voting shares. So our investment bankers and lawyers helped us create something we called a convertible preferred stock that initially was held only by ILFC. Basically, it meant that no raider would stage a successful takeover because the value of convertible preferred stock exceeded the market rate, and thus no tender offer could outbid it."

In return for this safeguard, Alaska signed a long-term lease agreement — 20 to 22 years — for 20 Boeing 737-400s. ILFC actually was buying the first 100 airplanes off Boeing's 737-400 assembly line, so that gave Alaska a leg up on delivery positions. The long lease period meant the airline was really buying the 20 jets for more than what ILFC had paid for them, but it still was a good deal for both parties and solidified the positive relations that had existed between the two companies.

Another milestone during Vecci's regime was a major promotion that occurred in flight operations. It was precedent-setting and gutsy, and it would make the recipient an Alaska Airlines legend. The promotion came at a time when the airline found itself up to its corporate chin in hot water with the FAA. And it took an unusual man to empty the tub.

His name was Mike Swanigan, and he was the first African-American ever to become chief pilot of a major U.S. airline. Swanigan was the second African-American pilot Alaska hired. Jim Wiley was the first, but his career was cut short by early retirement.

Swanigan's full name was Michel Antoine Swanigan. "My mother was a French-language nut," he explained. He had wanted to be an Alaska Airlines pilot since he was a 15-year-old kid growing up in Anchorage. He took his first airplane ride in an Alaska Boeing 727 at a time when the airline had only two of them. Mike remembered their aircraft numbers, 797 and 766, and years later he was to fly both of them as a captain.

"Swannie," as everyone called him, started out in the banking business, first as a loan officer with a credit union and later as a vice president of the National Bank of Alaska. But he got his first flight training by enlisting in the Alaska Air National Guard and ended up flying C-130s, the famed Hercs.

He gave up his banking career in 1980 and applied to Alaska Airlines. He qualified as a 727 flight engineer, and then earned successive promotions to first officer, captain, and then check captain. In the fall of 1993, while on a layover in Anchorage, Swanigan received a call from Bill Boser, at the time an assistant vice president in the flight operations department.

"Mike, we need a new chief pilot here in a hurry," Swanigan recalled

Boser saying without preamble. "We're in one hell of a mess with the FAA.
It may be only a temporary assignment, but can you get down here fast and
help us out?"

Swanigan knew why he was being offered such a job, even though he
had relatively low seniority. His previous status as a bank vice president, he
believed, had tagged him as having managerial potential.

He found out quickly why the feds were ready to lower a few booms on
the airline. The current chief pilot, along with several senior captains and
check pilots, had been skipping mandatory ground-school training before
transitioning to different equipment. Their pilot licenses were now in jeop-
ardy and so were their jobs, and Alaska could ill afford to lose their services.

"The FAA position," Mike explained, "was that we had these check
pilots who were unqualified to monitor all our other pilots who also were
transitioning to new equipment because, not having taken the required
ground-school training, they weren't qualified themselves. The mess involved
mostly transitioning to 737s from 727 cockpits, and we were facing a possible
shutdown of operations."

Swanigan's subsequent negotiations with the FAA were complicated and
somewhat convoluted, but the end result was a compromise that satisfied the
feds and kept the airline and its pilots flying. Basically, Swanigan successfully
argued that while the airmen *were* technically illegal, they had been flying
737s in perfect safety, which in a practical sense demonstrated that they were
qualified on these aircraft even without ground school. His strongest point
was that all the line pilots involved, along with the accused check captains,
had successfully passed what are called "PT" rides: proficiency training flights,
which, he pointed out, were just as stiff as a regular check ride.

"I can show you documentation," he told the FAA, "that we've sent
pilots who failed a PT back for additional training. So in my view, there's no
difference between a PT and a check ride. They've got a different name and
a different regulatory status, but to a pilot they're the same. So here's what
I propose: let all our guys take another PT, but this time under a check pilot
who's clean."

The FAA chief operations officer in charge of the inquiry agreed. Swanigan,
figuring that this kind of audit was going to take five or six days, enlisted
Boser's help in lining up as many pilots as possible for the crucial PT rides.

Swanigan's next task was to enlist the cooperation of the Sea-Tac tower
chief, who had to approve the numerous touch-and-go landings that usually
are part of check and PT rides, all of them at night when traffic is light.

"We're in a jam here," Swanigan pleaded, and explained the situation.

"We'll work with you," the tower chief replied.

Whatever touch-and-go operations were needed went on for the next few days. The entire FAA audit, which included line checks between two city pairs, was conducted over a period of three weeks, with pilots shuttling back and forth between Seattle and Portland.

"By that time," Swanigan related, "we had qualified every pilot who had been potentially tainted, and we were able to keep our operation going."

Boser was happy to inform Vecci that the airline had itself an ideal chief pilot, one who blended protection of his airmen with discipline. And Swanigan's temporary position was made permanent. He proved his worth yet again after a scary incident involving an Alaska 737-200 while departing Juneau. The aircraft encountered severe wind shear — a sudden collision between two strong air masses at low altitude — and flipped over on its back. The aircraft fortunately was just high enough for the pilot to regain control.

Swanigan was informed of the aircraft's whisker-thin escape from disaster and called in the flight's captain. After hearing his account, Mike remarked that it must have been a terrifying, traumatic experience. "How are you handling it?" he asked.

The captain hesitated, then replied, "Well, we're talking among ourselves."

"Who's 'we'?"

"Myself, my copilot, and the flight attendants," the captain reported. Then he admitted that the entire crew had been calling each other almost daily since the Juneau incident. They were suffering from post-traumatic stress and yet had been flying regular trips since that day.

That was all the chief pilot needed to hear. He grounded the entire crew and then arranged for them to get professional counseling before restoring them to duty.

John Nance, the ex-Braniff pilot who had become an Alaska captain by the time the Juneau incident occurred, heard how Swanigan had handled the aftermath from the 737's captain himself. "The reason that story was so important to me," Nance commented later, "was that it demonstrated how the wonderful people of this airline learn from experience, and they learn very well."

Mike Swanigan's concern and compassion for that crew was the first step in what eventually became a formal program. Lou Cancelmi saw Swanigan's handling of the Juneau flight mishap as the genesis of an in-house program called CIRP (Critical Incident Response Program), for training people to help each other in a major crisis. "This would be extremely important a few years later, when we suffered our first catastrophic accident in three decades."

Flight operations was one area that largely escaped Vecci's pruning shears. Not so for some key managerial personnel in flight operations' sister department, in-flight services. This, Vecci suspected, was one area where he could gain control of Alaska's high cost per seat-mile, which at the time exceeded 14 cents per available seat-mile, when low-cost carriers' were below 7 cents per available seat-mile.

As Bill Cox, vice president of in-flight services, had feared, his days at Alaska were numbered. His relations with Vecci had been deteriorating ever since the spoon incident.

It was during Cox's tenure that Alaska began hiring older women as flight attendants, and Bill's defenders gave him at least partial credit for this enlightened policy. The decision to hire more mature flight attendants, including married women with families, was not his exclusive idea. Martha Minter, an ex-Flying Tiger flight attendant who joined Alaska in 1978 and became manager of flight-attendant training, was one of the policy's first advocates. The impetus would also come from Maggi Hanson, whom we shall meet later. She was the one who hired the redoubtable Bambi Coons, another legendary character who'll be described in a later chapter.

Alaska led the industry in this age-is-no-longer-a-hiring-factor decision. It was phased in so gradually that Ray Vecci's opinion of the change was never clear, but in view of his general policy toward the promotion of women, it is likely that he supported the change. However, he definitely was involved in the issue of flight-attendant health, which had become not just a problem but a mystery, one that Vecci was determined to solve.

The issue was air quality on Alaska's jets, specifically the MD-80s, where reports began to surface of some flight attendants on some flights suddenly becoming ill. This began in Bruce Kennedy's last years as chairman and continued through Ray Vecci's time at the helm. The symptoms were alarming enough: dizziness, nausea, light-headedness, even disorientation. The company's immediate reaction was concern for the individuals but skepticism about the cause.

Admittedly, there was some precedent. In the early days of jet operations, the airlines began getting claims from some flight attendants that working high-altitude jet flights was causing everything from varicose veins to irregular menstrual periods and even sterility. The claims proved to be groundless and were generally dismissed as attempts by some to get more pay for supposedly "hazardous" working conditions.

The Alaska incidents involved unexplainable yet legitimate health issues, and continued to occur. Sometimes there would be a cluster of multiple complaints, then long gaps between incidents. Eventually they spread through the entire MD-80 fleet, and affected flight attendants were sent to medical facilities for tests and evaluations, which turned out negative. Meanwhile, similar incidents were reported on a few 737 flights. One of the most puzzling elements was the fact that no other airline operating MD-80s was experiencing the same incidents.

Vecci established a task force to help solve the mystery. It included not only Vecci himself but also AFA representative Ronda Ruderman of the union's safety committee; Terry Taylor, an AFA officer; and Debby Horton, a supervisor of workers' compensation. Over a period of several months, the task force, with the help of the airline's maintenance department and human resources group, tried everything, including dismantling an MD-80's entire ventilation system, looking in vain for something that might be the root of the trouble. Theories abounded; evidence and proof remained elusive.

Even experts from the Centers for Disease Control were brought in. Cox and Terry Taylor flew to the Ohio headquarters of the National Institute for Occupational Safety and Health, and the federal agency agreed to investigate. Ultimately, NIOSH issued its own report, which simply added to the mystery. In summary, the institute couldn't find anything wrong.

Eventually, the incidents dwindled and then ended, which in itself simply created another mystery. To this day, the source of the illnesses of what ultimately were a small number of flight attendants remains unknown.

While the air-quality flap ended peacefully if not conclusively, in some ways it seemed to symbolize the hot-and-cold relations Vecci appears to have had with flight attendants. For instance, he was viewed as *persona non grata* as the principal architect of the strategy to train nonunion replacements to counter any flight-attendant walkout. Yet with colossal irony, the greatest favor that Ray Vecci could have possibly done for the flight attendants' union was one of the major contributors to his eventual fall from grace.

CHAPTER SEVENTEEN

Vecci vs. The Board

When it comes to an impartial summation of Raymond J. Vecci's career as Alaska's chairman, CEO, and president, it might be best measured against his own expectations. "Throughout my career," he wrote in a post-Alaska Airlines résumé, "I've led team efforts in formulating strategies and, more importantly, turning plans and intentions into reality. My strengths lie in leading top management to clearly identify challenges, ensuring everyone shares the same aims, and executing coordinated actions to achieve them."

As Alaska's chairman, CEO, and president, Ray Vecci was more of a scrapper than a consensus-builder, but arguably he saved the airline's bacon. The human toll was substantial, but in many cases necessary. His Achilles' heel was an uncompromising personality, combined with brilliance and undeniable determination. In the end, he was fired.

In Vecci's mind, while boards have every right to fire a CEO who's making too many mistakes, they have no right to interfere with the way a chief runs the tribe, and he told John Kelly just that. "They [the board] can fire me if they don't like the way I'm running the company."

Just as aircraft accidents seldom if ever have a single cause, Vecci's eventual ouster was merely the culmination of several contributing factors all coming together at what was for him precisely the wrong time. His demise was based more on style than substance. When he became Alaska's chief executive, he swiftly identified the challenges, but not everyone liked the way he handled them. Yet few would deny that he was always honest.

In fact, during one executive session with his board of directors after becoming chairman and CEO, he raised the issue of his hold-nothing-back personality. He told them that his "approach and personality traits were not the best. But," he added, "I am who I am." The comment was made not in defiance, but rather to explain that it would be difficult for him to be anyone other than himself.

There was a lengthy pause before Ron Cosgrave responded, "Ray, we knew your personality when you were selected." For a time, that was that.

Vecci knew himself well. He had taken several psychological-evaluation tests while at United. "The person reviewing the results with me said, among other things, 'You want to control things,' " recalled Vecci.

A Myers-Briggs test, a survey questionnaire designed to help identify personality indicators, had been administered at Alaska to a group of officers during Kennedy's reign. Vecci was tagged as an INTP, a personality type that engages in, among other things, hairsplitting logic. "I doubt that anyone who knew me would dispute these characterizations," added Vecci.

By its very nature, taking the reins of a company whose previous chairman sits as a member of the board can be precarious, regardless of the issue. The relationship between Vecci and Kennedy came under some strain from the start, even after Kennedy stepped down as the board's chairman. And communication, or the lack of it, between them continued to puzzle both men long after Vecci assumed the board chairmanship.

"When Bruce first briefed me about being selected to succeed him as chairman," said Vecci, "he mentioned that the board wanted him to stay on for a while as chairman of the Executive Committee, but he added that he would not likely hold this position for long. He also said the board wished to have monthly meetings of the Executive Committee to keep it briefed on the management of the airline."

Vecci viewed this as interference between the board's chairman and the board. "Bruce would stop by for briefings, and at least on a monthly basis, I would have lunch with him, usually just prior to the Executive Committee meetings. Then I would participate in the meeting.

"I felt very strongly that all board members should have the same information and briefings, so for a time, I would provide the accumulated information at the quarterly meetings to them for their review. At first it seemed unwieldy, but I got accustomed to it.

"At one particular lunch with Bruce, we were not only reviewing what was going on with the airline, but I was also exploring with him my relationship with the board. He smiled and in a matter-of-fact way said, 'This is my board.' I understood he had played the leading role in nominating most of them, establishing relationships that went back many years. But I did wonder about the need that prompted the remark."

Vecci's first nominee to the board was former cell-phone executive and onetime Horizon Air shareholder Bruce McCaw. Ironically, McCaw's first board meeting would be Vecci's last.

Vecci was more challenging than tactful when he requested the board's approval of salary increases and incentives for the company's officers. By some estimates, Alaska Airlines' officers were paid 40 percent less than their peers within the airline industry.

Directors felt that Vecci was exceeding his authority by refusing to acknowledge theirs. The sensitive subject of officer compensation in virtually all publicly held companies is within the jurisdiction of a corporate board's compensation committee. Alaska Airlines was no exception, and on its compensation committee were such respected directors as Bobby Parker Jr., Richard Wien, Mark Langland, and Mary Jane Fate; the latter two were a bank president and the general manager of a family business, respectively. This was the group that collided head-on with Vecci, who thought they were picking salary scales out of their hats instead of researching what other carriers were paying their equivalent management personnel.

The catchphrase for determining salaries in the airline industry, for management and employees alike, is "market rate." In other words, to retain good people in management and also just to be fair, it's best to follow general market-rate guidelines. This was a very personal matter to Vecci, who honestly thought Alaska's management was grossly underpaid, and that the directors didn't seem to appreciate all they were doing to pull the airline back to profitability.

Marjorie Laws, his only real confidante, knew exactly how Vecci felt about the compensation issue, and that he was putting his own job on the line by confronting the board's compensation committee. "There had been a previous compensation study done under Bruce Kennedy," she remembered, "and its conclusion was that officer salaries at Alaska were quite low compared with other airlines, but also that the big salaries some carriers were paying top executives were almost obscene."

As Laws put it: "Ray didn't want to do this at Alaska, and I certainly agreed with him that when times are tough and you can't give employees a raise, it's not fair to give officers big increases. Bruce himself refused increases for several years running.

"Ray's approach was a little different. He believed it was one thing to claim we were paying market-rate salaries, but another matter if we didn't really know what the actual market rates were. So he went out and looked, and I mean *looked*. Then he went back to the compensation committee with his recommendations for revised officer scales."

The committee members were unimpressed. Although they generally followed Vecci's recommendations for the officer group (and those increases were modest), they fell far short of accepting the substantial boost Ray had proposed for himself. Vecci later refused the salary increase the board approved for him. There is no written record of what he told the compensation committee, but Laws knew him well enough to paraphrase his remarks. He said he had given the committee a logical, detailed compensation program, which it proceeded to ignore in favor of random numbers.

John Kelly personally warned Vecci against butting heads with the board, although not on the compensation issue specifically. "Ray, don't do it," he advised. "You're going to get fired."

Vecci's answer was the same he had given others who had voiced similar concerns: he was running Alaska Airlines, not the directors. On the pay issue, however, Kelly acknowledged that Vecci had made a logical case and proved it. "Officer pay scales were definitely lagging behind the rest of the industry," Kelly pointed out. Later, "Ray finally got the directors to approve a new Management Incentive Plan, a bonus program based on performance."

But this proved to be a Pyrrhic victory. Vecci continued to make unilateral decisions regarding policies and personnel. In many cases his decisions were clearly within the purview of the chairman, and those that backfired simply hammered more nails into the corporate coffin he was fashioning for himself.

He did not lack friends and supporters within the airline. Many of them tried to warn him that his repeated insistence on taking unilateral action, especially senior personnel assignments and terminations, without consulting or even informing the board of directors was going to get him fired. Vecci ignored all such warnings.

Incidents of flouting or ignoring board authority piled up, and inevitably some of his firings of well-liked managerial people began raising eyebrows among concerned directors, especially Bruce Kennedy. One case in particular seemed indefensible because the victim was none other than Mary Kenison, who'd had a primary role in integrating the former Jet America flight attendants into Alaska's cabin corps. Kenison's contributions to her new airline had gone beyond that integration process, and included valuable input at the start of scheduled service to the Soviet Far East. It had been her idea to help get the Soviet service up and running by using former Jet America flight attendants still based at Long Beach, primarily because they were already qualified on emergency over-water evacuation procedures. This was special training required for extended over-water flights, and because Alaska had no such routes, it had not provided that training for its flight crews.

Vecci was well aware of her competence and value to the airline. The puzzling aspect was that Vecci didn't seem to have any case against her except a suspicion that she had misled him. Their confrontation took place after Bill Cox had left the company, a time when intensely acrimonious contract talks between the airline and the Association of Flight Attendants had reached an impasse and a strike appeared inevitable. There were rumors that a walkout might occur at any time, and Vecci was under considerable strain.

This, of course, may have explained Vecci's short-fused reaction to what could have been a simple misunderstanding over a rather minor matter. Rightly or wrongly, he believed that Kenison had provided vague and contradictory information about an incident involving the head of the flight attendants' union. Kenison flatly denied Vecci's interpretation then and denies it today. But none of that mattered. Kenison was gone.

Many years later, Vecci revealed that the Kenison dismissal had been gut-wrenching. "It was the most difficult termination for me in 20 years at Alaska. She was a great manager, set an impeccable example for the flight attendants, and truly did a great job," he acknowledged.

John Kelly tried to make amends in Mary Kenison's case. After he became Alaska's CEO, he offered her what she considered a very reasonable severance package or, as an alternative, the opportunity to return as the airline's base manager in Long Beach.

"I decided against returning," Kenison said. "It had been a great life and a great experience, but I didn't want to do it all over again."

The Kenison incident was only one of many points of contention that found their way to the boardroom. It is possible that some or perhaps even many of those who were "downsized" were really incompetent or ineffective, but quite a few terminated employees had supporters who complained to an increasingly receptive board.

Among them was Tom Dezutter, who had been staff vice president of stations before the ax fell. His position represented an obsolete function, and it was eliminated. Vecci acknowledged that Dezutter had done nothing wrong. Years later Vecci remembered Tom as "always cheerful, energetic, and in many ways he demonstrated a pleasantly feisty management approach."

Vecci had directed each department head to review functions that could be eliminated, and Dezutter's position was considered expendable. "I pressed, but I always relied on the recommendations of others, especially in operational areas," said Vecci, "and our strict adherence to a functional approach to workforce reductions was meant to avoid the 'likeability' factor in decisions.

"There was no systematic approach to find a job for the best people and displace someone else within the company," he lamented. "I don't know how to interpret the fact that in the largest division in the company, where there were always some openings, none could ever be found for Tom Dezutter, given his extensive operating experience."

Vecci did make an effort to meet with people who had been terminated. "I felt it was my responsibility to give them a chance to meet with me face-to-face. I don't think I had much to say other than I deeply wished it could have been different, but I do remember having difficulty getting the words out."

Dezutter was more fortunate than some others who were forced to leave Alaska. A few years afterward, Bruce Kennedy reviewed his file, decided that Dezutter had been treated unfairly, and arranged for an improved retirement package.

Comparatively speaking, the terminations were only a small coffin nail, whereas Vecci's approach to labor relations was deemed, by some, to be the size of a railroad spike. It had been a long and acrimonious conflict between the Association of Flight Attendants and the company, with marathon negotiations dating back to October 1990. It would take more than three years to produce an amicable peace agreement, exactly 1,239 days of mutual name-calling and distrust.

That 1990 date stemmed from a provision in Alaska's 1987 contract with the AFA, which allowed both parties to amend the original agreement after it had been in effect for three years. Both company and union were panting to make changes; AFA came to the bargaining table with 195 desired revisions in the original contract, and the company submitted 151. This triggered the initial round of name-calling exchanges, the first major broadside being fired by Gail Bigelow, president of the union's Master Executive Council (MEC). She told reporters that the company's chief negotiator was "arrogant and condescending."

Bob Gray had retired and Nick McCudden, assistant vice president of labor relations, was one of the company's three principal negotiators, along with Tim Metcalf, staff vice president of human resources, and Gail Neufeld, Gray's former assistant. McCudden got along reasonably well with Bigelow. So did Neufeld. But there was no love lost between the MEC chief and Metcalf; he was the one at whom her unflattering remarks had been aimed.

After a year of talks, the union and the airline each had whittled about 50 items from their shopping lists of contractual changes, which represented some progress but was far short of a real agreement. So negotiations continued. By the fall of 1992, their differences had been narrowed down to about two dozen major issues, but these were the biggest bones of contention, defying compromise.

AFA was demanding wage increases and expensive adjustments in scheduling rules. The company dug in its heels, arguing that such goodies were impossible at a time when Alaska was trying to compete against low-cost carriers. And Vecci, with his cost-cutting crusade, was a natural target. At one point, AFA set up "informational picketing" at both Sea-Tac and the Long Beach airport. The signs that the pickets carried pointed to Vecci as the bad guy and accused him of refusing to bargain in good faith. The company line, of course, was that AFA was being shortsighted and unreasonable at a time when the company was trying to compete in a vicious, competitive market.

Such mutual hyperbole goes with the territory of contract talks, yet the behind-the-scenes negotiating sessions were just as acrimonious. Mediators were called in, but by May 1993, some 30 mediated sessions had failed to make much progress, and the union requested arbitration. The company refused, for Vecci took the position that an arbitrator, unfamiliar with what was happening in the beleaguered airline industry and its suicidal price wars, might award the union more than the airline could afford.

So the stage was set for a strike, yet it would be a kind of walkout never seen before.

AFA was acutely aware that the airline, as it had done before, was training replacements in case the union called a strike. So the union devised an ingenious tactic to counter this management strategy. It was called CHAOS, an acronym for Create Havoc Around Our System, and its intent was to disrupt normal operations by staging surprise walkouts by one or two flight attendants just before a plane was scheduled to pull away from the gate.

The idea was that each departing flight attendant would simply walk off the job in a legally protected "mini-strike," and before a nonunion substitute could be found, the flight would have been badly delayed, with a planeload of unhappy passengers. Originating with Alaska Airlines' AFA unit, the technique was later adopted at other carriers and was well named. Delaying just a handful of flights without warning would be enough to almost completely dismantle normal schedules. The airline then would have not just two or three planeloads of disgruntled passengers but scores, most of them blaming not the flight attendants but the carrier.

This was the union's intent, but the company's counterattack would be just as ingenious as CHAOS itself. The goal was to blunt the surprise element that made CHAOS so potentially effective. No one knew whether a flight attendant would walk off a plane in Mexico, San Diego, or some other place where it would take a long time to get a replacement on the scene. The answer was to assign two newly trained contingency flight attendants (CFAs) to every trip, so that if an AFA member or two suddenly walked off an airplane, CFAs would be immediately available to work the flight.

Martha Minter, director of flight-attendant training, became a key figure in the company's plan to effectively negate CHAOS. Minter trained hundreds of CFAs, not merely to serve drinks and meals, but also to qualify in all phases of emergency procedures. More than 500 generally reluctant candidates from various departments, including mostly middle- and lower-echelon management personnel, went through the two-week course. Only department heads and those who couldn't qualify — by not knowing how to swim, for example — could ask to be exempted.

Minter recalled that unwilling trainees were in the majority by a wide margin. "A lot of them didn't want to be in those classes and made no bones about it," she related. "In the long run, however, it was the best thing we could have done for the regular flight attendants because most of those 500 managers found out that a flight attendant's job wasn't as easy as they had imagined. For instance, we had a couple of management guys from maintenance who couldn't believe how extensive the training was. 'You mean I have to learn *all* this stuff?' one of them grumbled."

Minter insisted on establishing the same pass-fail standard she did in regular training. One manager from maintenance actually looked pleased when she broke this news to him. "You mean if I flunk, I can go back to my regular job?" he chirped.

"Yep," Minter said dryly. "Then you also can go back and tell your boss you flunked stewardess school."

"That remark got around in a hurry," she chuckled, "and we never had anybody flunk."

If anyone tried to get out of taking the course, Minter required them to bring a letter from their department vice president excusing them from training. Those tagged for CFA duty also learned, usually to their dismay, that their tour wouldn't be over even when the regular cabin crews went back to work. The FAA required that all qualified flight attendants on U.S. carriers go through annual recurrent training. This didn't sit well with a lot of CFAs, who figured they had already done their duty. That, plus the strain of separation from family and regular job, took a toll on morale. This may have been a factor in what happened to bring about a new contract.

Technically, CHAOS went into effect on July 20, 1993, the day that AFA members were authorized to strike. All mediation and negotiating efforts had failed. AFA members voted to strike if no agreement had been reached by June 10, and this triggered a mandatory cooling-off period of 30 days, effective June 20.

The company had fair warning that CHAOS would be put into effect as an alternative to a mass walkout, and this may have been a mistake on the part of the union, which literally telegraphed its new strategy well in advance of its actual implementation. It gave the airline a little more time in which to devise and perfect the CFA countermeasures, and train more people. The advance warning was couched in deliberately generalized language, informing the media that CHAOS would feature unannounced, intermittent work stoppages and slowdowns rather than a full-blown strike. "A guerilla-like campaign" was one newspaper's interpretation.

But CHAOS was challenged. The airline's operations were barely affected at all, and only a small handful of AFA members actually walked off airplanes. Gail Neufeld theorized that either the very presence of CFAs on all flights — they were known as "ghost riders" — discouraged the regulars from walking off, or most AFA members weren't that enthusiastic about CHAOS to begin with.

In another respect, however, CHAOS indirectly contributed to a settlement that gave the union even more than it had asked for. In the eyes of Gail

Bigelow and her flight attendants, Ray Vecci was transformed overnight from a Frankenstein monster into Cary Grant.

Lou Cancelmi, of the airline's corporate communications department, remembered the day it happened. CHAOS was still on, there was no sign of an agreement, and Vecci had just learned of a remark attributed to Gail Bigelow. "It's too bad," she reportedly said, "we don't have a company with a Herb Kelleher at its head, someone who cares about people, and who'd give them a contract like Southwest's flight attendants have." Kelleher was Southwest's charismatic and very funny CEO, whose paternalism toward his employees was legendary.

Vecci had been aware of discussions that had taken place among flight attendants either in favor of or opposed to the Southwest contract. Quietly he had assembled a small group of senior advisers to analyze Southwest's contract with its flight attendants and consider the possibility of its adoption at Alaska. A consensus emerged that many provisions of the contract would not work easily for the company, or for the flight attendants. But while pay rates would rise and with them costs, the airline could also see very significant savings from productivity improvements related to work-rule changes. In the end, Vecci's recollection was that everyone involved in the analysis agreed that the idea should be advanced.

Up to that point, the company's evaluation of the Southwest contract had been kept extremely confidential. To avoid a premature leak, Vecci decided to communicate the offer publicly. Appearing in Cancelmi's office, he asked, "Can you get a reporter in here fast? And be sure the reporter asks me about the flight-attendant references to Southwest and its contract."

Cancelmi, unaware of the analysis that had preceded this, stared at Vecci in disbelief. "Are you sure you want to do that?" he asked incredulously.

"Yes!" Vecci snapped.

Cancelmi contacted Sean Griffin, a business and aviation reporter at the Tacoma *News Tribune* who had always treated the airline fairly. He suggested that Griffin come over for an exclusive, one guaranteed to make headlines. And it did, the first one appearing in the Tacoma paper the next day under the banner headline:

ALASKA WILLING TO SETTLE ON
SOUTHWEST ATTENDANTS' TERMS

The accompanying story quoted Vecci as saying that if the flight attendants wanted the same contract as Southwest, all they had to do was just substitute "Alaska Airlines" for "Southwest" and "Association of Flight Attendants" for "Transport Workers Union."

"Do that, and we could have an agreement in 24 hours," he declared. Vecci would later recall that the key comment he made was that there be "no cherry picking" of the Southwest contract — that is, neither side could selectively accept or reject specific provisions. It was all or nothing.

This was more important to the union than was apparent to most people at the time. After the mandatory cooling-off period ended and CHAOS ensued, Alaska had imposed a unilateral contract. An important element of that imposed contract was inclusion of an "open" shop, a provision that allowed individual flight attendants to either opt in or opt out of the union. Vecci's "no cherry picking" comment was designed to communicate to the union and its leaders, without explicitly saying so, that a "closed" shop — part of the existing Southwest contract and a provision mandating that all flight attendants be dues-paying members — would become part of Alaska's new contract.

Within a few days, Gail Bigelow, the head of the flight-attendant union, wrote Vecci a friendly letter suggesting that they adopt the Southwest contract verbatim except for changing the names of the companies and the unions involved, as Vecci had already proposed. "It is my sincere hope . . . that this agreement will represent the beginning of a new era in labor relations," she wrote. "If this agreement bolsters the competitiveness and profitability of the company, we will all benefit."

Vecci said, "I felt the contract was one of the most significant actions I had taken to the benefit of the company, and right after the contract was announced I received a call congratulating me on the settlement from Ron Cosgrave. When I presented the positives and negatives of the agreement to the board, the contract received prompt approval."

Company-wide the contract was not unanimously supported. Many worried as much about what was in the contract as what had been overlooked in the attempt to convert a contract that served the needs of a low-cost carrier, Southwest, into something that could benefit a full-service carrier like Alaska Airlines. Was it a truck full of landmines on a bumpy road? Time would tell.

Long before the contract would run its course and prove or disprove Vecci's wisdom, he was fired. The primary thing it achieved for the next five years was labor peace. Unfortunately, during that time the airline was also saddled with a contract difficult to live with, simply because Alaska Airlines was not

Southwest, and vice versa.

Gail Neufeld recalled that the negotiating team was "stunned" by the Vecci decision. She summed it up from the company's standpoint as objectively as she could. "It was mind-boggling," she remembered. "Here we had spent about four years of our lives trying to achieve a contract that was fair to both sides, and it was useless. We felt that our legs had been cut out from under us. For starters, the Southwest contract had no negotiating history. In most negotiations, often you look at a contract for the history behind certain provisions. There are reasons behind this or that clause, but in this case we had nothing to go on.

"So we were stuck with a contract tailored for an entirely different kind of airline, and it was imposed *in toto* on Alaska. This all happened in January of 1994, and we finally signed the contract the following May. Even after the contract was implemented, we ended up with years of arbitration over provisions that simply didn't work at Alaska."

The obvious question everyone was asking: Why did Ray Vecci do it? It was apparent that CHAOS hadn't created the extensive havoc that its name so strongly implied.

Cancelmi offered this logical explanation: "I think Ray got a lot of pressure from management people because there was real concern that the airline was going to have trouble retaining personnel if CHAOS continued for any extended period. There was lots of grumbling everywhere about this CFA business keeping them away from their jobs and families."

This made sense. Most of the drafted CFAs had been unhappy campers to begin with, and they got unhappier as months passed with no sign of a settlement.

Greg Witter, a director of corporate communications, was a CFA and admitted that he got fed up just riding around on airplanes waiting for something to happen that never did. He didn't quit, but he later wrote a fascinating thesis for his master's degree on CHAOS and the events that led up to it. In his thesis, appropriately titled "Chill in the Air," he wrote about being impressed by one of Vecci's post-settlement statements. Ray was trying to explain why negotiations had finally reached the stage where relations between management and the union were "bordering somewhere between hostile and venomous," as Witter phrased it.

"As time goes by," Vecci said in a rare conciliatory tone, "there's a tendency to develop rigid views and suspicions, and maybe you're still hearing, but you've stopped listening. It took a long time, but we listened to recent messages and responded." Witter pointed to those two sentences as "summing up the roots of this long and ugly ordeal." They also supported the theory that Vecci had become worried about the effect that CFA duties were having on management morale at almost every level, and decided to act. Given the fact that patience was not necessarily his strong suit, it is very likely that he simply got tired of the whole stalemate and decided to end it as quickly as possible.

Vecci's explanation to the media for the sudden settlement was that he just wanted to get on with the real business of keeping Alaska Airlines healthy and competitive. The most significant statement he made, however, was that he was glad the "agonizing" process was over.

By the end of 1993, the airline was showing promise in the face of a $22.5 million loss, but Vecci's cost reductions had not been implemented until late in the year. In the annual report that year, he reiterated what had become his mantra: "First, low-price competition is here to stay. Second, customers will always gravitate to the lowest price in the market. And, finally, our future success depends upon our efforts, not outside forces." The optimism that that year's annual report suggested for 1994 was based on the vastly more efficient airline Vecci had crafted since he took over in 1991.

Terminations were mostly a matter of reconstructing the company's cost structure, but equally critical were key promotions, and one of the most important was that of John Kelly, and it very nearly didn't happen.

Because of his success at Horizon, Kelly's management talents had become increasingly apparent inside and outside the company, and in 1994 he was contacted by an executive headhunter who asked him if he would be interested in interviewing for the top job at Aloha Airlines. Kelly expressed a willingness to talk with the regional carrier, but first he told Vecci. During that conversation, Kelly mentioned that Kennedy had given the recruiter his name. "I never felt that there was anything improper about giving John's name out," recalled Vecci, "but I was surprised that Bruce kept it to himself."

At the next board meeting, without inside directors present, Kennedy asked Vecci what was going on between John Kelly and Aloha. "I was surprised and paused to gather my thoughts because it seemed Bruce knew more about the matter than I did. I then explained to the board that John was planning to interview with Aloha."

Board members Richard Wien and Bill Clapp urged Vecci to offer Kelly

the position of president and COO. Vecci agreed, but wanted to complete
a formal evaluation. Ultimately, he preempted any Aloha proposal with an
informal offer to Kelly to become Alaska's executive vice president and chief
operating officer. However, Kelly refused to make any commitment until
he had met with Aloha. Following his return from the Aloha interview, and
despite the fact that he was Aloha's first choice to be their new CEO, Kelly
accepted Vecci's offer and became the airline's second in command in
November 1994.

"John, hands down, was not only the leading candidate, but probably
the only one for the job," said Vecci.

Then came the task of selecting a replacement for Kelly as Horizon's
chief. Vecci and Kelly discussed the merits of a savvy woman named Kathy
Iskra, who had worked her way up the corporate ladder to become Alaska's
highly regarded staff vice president of finance.

"We both conveniently ignored her lack of operational experience,"
recalled Kelly, "figuring she had proved herself a good financial officer and
that we already had very capable operations people at Horizon.

"A short time after this discussion, the board held a meeting in Mexico,
and there were rumors that Vecci was not only going to make me chief
operating officer, replacing me with Iskra, but also make Harry Lehr the new
chief financial officer, and that would be a more controversial appointment.

"Vecci wasn't there for the dinner meeting the first night, but Bruce
Kennedy questioned me repeatedly about what was going on — not specifically, but about rumors of changes Vecci was going to announce. I told him
if he really wanted to know, I'd tell him — but only on direct orders — and he
chose not to pursue the matter.

"Later I was called before the board and informed that the directors had
accepted Vecci's three new appointments, including mine, but it was clear
from their questions that they had doubts about Lehr and Iskra."

At the same meeting the directors named Vecci chairman of the board's
Executive Committee. Vecci had argued with the board for this position, and
in the end he won. With this appointment he would no longer have to report
to Kennedy in any way, and he could brief the board directly.

Kelly himself called it "a fatal mistake." It may have bolstered Ray's
conviction that in a practical sense, he outranked the directors, but it put him
in an unfavorable light, magnifying all the other problems of the past years.
So it wasn't surprising that within three months he was gone.

Iskra's promotion turned out to be like throwing a defenseless swimmer

into a pool of sharks. Iskra was an extremely competent finance officer, but
she had no experience in other phases of airline operations. She quickly found
herself mired in the quicksand of inexperience.

In effect, Vecci had done her a terrible disservice. For almost a year,
Iskra served in a frustrating situation that she had never sought in the first
place. She ultimately decided to resign, and moved on to resume her successful career outside the industry. George Bagley was sent back over to Horizon
as her replacement.

In 1994, the airline began to show the promise suggested to the board in
the later months of the previous year, but Vecci was exhausted and short on
patience. Then he ran head-on into another group whose own patience had
been exhausted. On February 9, 1995, a year and one month after he offered
AFA the Southwest contract, Alaska's board of directors dropped the termination ax on Raymond J. Vecci himself.

His supporters, his critics, and those who had ambivalent feelings
about him all shared a common reaction to his dismissal. It sent shock waves
throughout the airline. There was no single reason why the directors fired
him. It simply boiled down to too many sins of commission and omission
that the board regarded as insubordination and usurpation of its authority.

Eddie Rickenbacker of Eastern and, more recently, Harry Stonecipher
of Boeing were two exceptionally strong CEOs booted out by their respective
boards. Both had personalities that could only be described as domineering,
an adjective frequently applied to Vecci.

Alaska's board of directors, if not individually then certainly as a
group, outranked Ray Vecci. The "sins of commission and omission" that
formed the board's indictment of him combined both those elements: he
would take a controversial action (commission), often without consulting
anyone (omission).

Ron Cosgrave and Bruce Kennedy, former chairmen and CEOs who were
respected by employees and trusted by directors, had received numerous calls
from Vecci detractors asking, "Do you know what's going on?" The general
discontent finally reached the point where it couldn't be ignored. Nor was it.

Perhaps the fairest and most pertinent observation came from the
board member who had the most overall aviation experience: Richard Wien,
son of the legendary Noel Wien of Wien Alaska and a former airline pilot, as
well as the founder and CEO of his own company in Fairbanks. He was one of
seven outside directors. Wien felt no personal animosity toward Vecci, but he

had watched in dismay as Ray's disregard for the board's authority continued unabated. Wien's account of the events that led up to that black day of February 9, 1995, gave Vecci full credit for his accomplishments, but . . . it was a very large "but."

"What happened with Ray in my estimation," Wien recounted, "is that as soon as he became chairman and CEO, he immediately took the position that he was czar of the airline. The entire board had a great deal of respect for his abilities, but you never know someone's true personality until you put him in charge.

"In my opinion, he probably would have been a very valuable man in a number two or number three position, but as number one, he did have a personality change. There were senior officers under him who became unhappy, and, gradually, so did the board. Admittedly, times were tough, and Ray did an excellent job of finding ways to operate more efficiently. Yet he seemed to ignore the fact that, at the same time, Alaska also had a board of directors with former CEOs like Cosgrave and Kennedy, and directors who had their own businesses. All of us knew about the corporate relationship that must exist between a chief executive officer and the board of directors, and that the CEO needs to collectively poll the board as well as his senior staff before making major decisions.

"Vecci, on the contrary, had nothing but disdain for the board. As far as he was concerned, the directors were a necessary evil and an impediment to his operations. His management style was dictatorial."

Wien also felt that Vecci's abrasive attitude toward the airline's partner carriers in Alaska itself threatened to damage the important friendly relationships that people such as Cosgrave, Kennedy, Jim Johnson, and Bill MacKay had worked so hard to develop. It had been Vecci who recommended against the acquisition of MarkAir.

"Those relations with other Alaskan carriers were deteriorating," Wien said. "Vecci had been dictatorial with them, too. They didn't like it, and we began getting some disturbing feedback from them.

"We actually had several meetings with Vecci, and they all ended up with him telling us that he was going to run the airline his way, and he didn't care what the board thought."

And it was at this point, Wien added, that he himself began asking other directors, "What are we doing?" He did not remember either Kennedy or Cosgrave instigating the board's "impeachment" of Vecci. "Bruce was very reluctant to take any aggressive action against Ray," Wien recalled. "Kennedy felt that he himself already had served his time, and he wasn't the kind of person who wanted to seize control in some kind of a coup. Neither did Ron.

"Nobody on the board, including myself, got any enjoyment out of doing what we did. But the bottom line was that even considering what Ray had accomplished, we felt that internally as well as externally, he was bringing the airline down around our ears."

Wien personally held out a last-ditch olive branch, trying to make Vecci realize he was leaving the board with no choice other than to fire him. In a face-to-face meeting well in advance of the fateful morning of February 9, Wien asked him to talk things over with the board. "We've got some problems here between you and the directors, Ray, and we've got to get them solved," Wien said in as friendly a tone as he could muster.

"I don't care how the board feels, or what the board does," Vecci retorted.

"Ray, this isn't good," the director warned.

Vecci just shrugged, thus slamming the door on his future with Alaska Airlines. The eventual February 9 vote, Wien emphasized, was unanimous.

The whole Vecci affair had been a painful experience for all the directors, but probably more so for Richard Wien. His association with Alaska Airlines, because of his own extensive aviation background, was probably the closest in a sentimental or even emotional sense.

At first he had harbored serious doubts about being on Alaska's board and serving an airline that had once been his father's bitter competitor. "Then I came to realize that the work Ron Cosgrave and Bruce Kennedy did in developing this airline was textbook," Wien said. "It was just like what you would learn in a college business-management course. That's what so impressed me about Alaska Airlines, and it was the reason I agreed to serve as a director."

According to Wien, it was Cosgrave who insisted that Vecci be treated fairly in his severance package and that it reflect the company's gratitude for his many accomplishments. "Ron liked Vecci," Wien said. "He told us that even though we weren't happy with the events of the past year, Ray still deserved to be rewarded for the good things he had done. Bruce agreed with Ron, too."

Cosgrave stressed that "during Vecci's turbulent tenure as CEO, he had cut $100 million out of the company's cost structure, positioning it to become competitive in the industry's changing environment." Cosgrave also pointed to the restructuring of aircraft costs and orders as one of Vecci's major contributions.

"And for that matter," said Wein, "none of us felt any bitterness toward Ray, least of all Cosgrave and Kennedy. They were the only board members who really had a soft spot for him in their hearts."

The atmosphere around headquarters was somber on that traumatic morning, most fitting for a day of a corporate execution. For Marjorie Laws, being the closest to Vecci, "somber" was an inadequate description of her own feelings. Everyone else was losing a chief executive officer who, for better or worse, had dominated their lives for four years. She was losing a treasured friend.

The actual "firing squad" consisted of three respected directors: Ron Cosgrave, Bobby Parker Jr. of Parker Drilling, and Bill Clapp, chairman of the Matthew G. Norton Company and a scion of the Weyerhaeuser family. They had the unpleasant task of informing Vecci that he was through at Alaska Airlines. Probably because he had been expecting this, Ray took the news quietly.

"I think he already knew that something significant was going to happen," Cosgrave related. "He had told me not very long before that he was running the airline the way it had to be run, to get it out of its financial problems, and that if the board didn't agree with this, it might as well fire him."

As soon as the trio of directors was in Vecci's office, Cosgrave wasted no time. "Ray," he began, "do you remember telling me that if the board of directors didn't like the way you were running the airline, it could fire you?"

"Yes," Vecci said.

"Well, it's happened."

"It was just as simple and quick as that," Cosgrave said later. "Ray showed no sign of anger or resentment."

"He has taken the company through some difficult times," Cosgrave pointed out to the board, "and we should realize that Ray was so intense about getting the job done, he didn't care how he was doing it. There's no doubt he hurt a lot of people in the process, but he has done a tremendous job for Alaska Airlines for some 20 years and deserves to be treated fairly."

Many of the people of Alaska Airlines eventually came to have a similar view of his chaotic and controversial record as their commander: grudging gratitude for his good deeds; lingering resentment over many of his actions; and relief from the tension now that his aggressive style of management was gone.

The day of Vecci's dismissal was a hectic one for the corporate communications staff. "I remember sitting in my office wondering what the hell was going on," Lou Cancelmi recalled. "Then Marjorie Laws came in and told me I'd better be ready to issue a news release. She had been tipped off the night before when one of the directors, probably Ron Cosgrave, called her at home."

"What's going on?" Lou asked.

"Ray's gone."

"Gone where?"

"He's been fired."

Cancelmi was shocked yet not surprised, for the discord between Vecci and the board had been building for a long time.

The news release that went out that day said Vecci had "resigned at the request of Alaska Air Group's board of directors" and that the resignation was due to "a growing difference in management style between Vecci and the board." Vecci had insisted that the release be worded without any nonsense about "personal reasons" or "other opportunities."

Defenders viewed Vecci as a decisive leader; detractors said he was frequently arbitrary. A prime example of the latter occurred only a week before his dismissal, when he abruptly canceled service to the Russian Far East in a dispute with the company's pilots over what he felt were uneconomic demands. Subsequently reinstated after Vecci's departure and continued until 1998, the airline's Russian adventure had been fraught with risk and lean on profit. However, it began as Bruce Kennedy's visionary and almost philanthropic plan to connect two Cold War adversaries with direct air service, and it was a continuing source of pride within the organization, and good press.

Many years later, when discussing Vecci's firing, John Kelly mentioned that his cancellation of the airline's service to Russia did not sit well with Kennedy and the board. Although never mentioned directly and even denied by a company spokesman at the time, some suspected that this action may have been one of the final straws that contributed to Vecci's demise.

There was no immediate mention of John Kelly becoming chairman. That would be announced later.

Marjorie Laws could not remember exactly when she first talked to Vecci himself after the news broke, but she did recall seeing him two days later, on Saturday, when he came in to clean out his office. His security key card had already been deactivated, and it was Laws who had to open the door for him.

No one could have blamed her for feeling real sorrow when she saw Vecci as he was about to leave the big room where he had ruled for the past four turbulent years. After Vecci had finished packing up some personal papers and possessions, Laws had a chance to talk briefly with him, but she was so upset that her memories of those few moments were hazy.

"He was trying to make me feel better," she said. "He was making an effort to sound philosophical, like 'Don't worry, we'll go on from here.' I just can't remember his exact words, but what I do remember is that there was no profanity, no outburst of temper, and he wasn't blaming anybody. That he had no regrets because at least he did it his way, just like the lyrics in that Frank Sinatra song 'My Way.' "

John Kelly, too, remembered talking briefly with Vecci on Ray's last morning in his office, the same office that Kelly himself would be occupying the next day. "He had a lot of integrity, and he left with dignity," Kelly added feelingly.

Milt Kuolt surprised Vecci when he flew in to town and asked Ray to dinner. "It was more than just a kind gesture, and one that I will never forget, because his company was just what I needed," Vecci recalled.

Vecci's firing was the result of his ongoing difficult relationship with the members of the board of directors. But it generally was also about his hard-driving style, difficult at times and one undeniably different from that of his predecessor. Still, that same style helped propel the single-minded compulsion he felt to quickly convert high-cost Alaska into an airline that could compete with Southwest and other low-cost newcomers to the marketplace. This, most would agree, he accomplished.

Vecci didn't stay unemployed for long. After leaving Alaska, he went on to senior executive positions at Carnival Air and Tower Air, and in 1997 Northwest Airlines hired him as an executive vice president with responsibility for ground and cargo operations.

"I did it my way" is an appropriate requiem for an extremely capable, well-meaning man whose strong-willed character is still admired by those who long ago forgave him for his forceful personality. Raymond J. Vecci was, indeed, the right man for the job at that particular time.

And so was the man who succeeded him.

CHAPTER EIGHTEEN

Charisma and Confidence

The change in command was like going from rawhide to flannel, yet not many at Alaska Airlines realized how close the airline had come to losing John Kelly before he succeeded Ray Vecci.

"The history of Alaska Airlines and Alaska Air Group," Bruce Kennedy was to comment years later, "would have been dramatically different if John had taken the Aloha job. I don't know where we would have gone.

"Some people had been asking me to come back if Vecci left. I confided this once to John, and he said if I had come back, I would have spent all my time looking for a successor. Which," added Kennedy, "was probably the truth."

So, upon Vecci's departure, Kelly became the airline's new chairman and CEO, at age 50, a well-liked, personable, and articulate man with a personality that could defrost the inside of a meat processor's locker. He also had impressive credentials as an airline veteran, experienced not only in marketing but also in virtually all phases of air-carrier operations. What he hadn't learned at Alaska he had picked up and honed as Horizon's CEO. However, despite his appealing personality and obvious operational chops, Kelly's penchant for always presenting an immaculate appearance gave some people the greatly erroneous impression of superficiality, with no real depth or focus.

Thankfully, Kelly was blessed with an Irish sense of humor. He thought Milt Kuolt's nickname for him, Hairspray, was funny, and he always had the grace to laugh at himself. Yet he also realized that some doubt may have existed among a few officers about whether he might be too nice, too easy-going, too unwilling to take strong measures without worrying about whether they'd be popular.

So the problem Kelly faced as Alaska's new CEO was one of perception. Both his personality and his management style were so completely different from his predecessor's that it was easy to mistake a natural charisma, a genuine concern for people, as being indicative of weak resolve.

Marjorie Laws was one of the early doubters. Kelly knew that she had told another officer she didn't think he was big enough to handle the CEO's job. Kelly never said anything to her, and Marjorie later not only admitted she had been wrong, but also gave Kelly the same loyalty she had given Vecci.

In truth, he invited loyalty, because he always tried to return it in equal measure.

John Kelly was a native of the Seattle-Tacoma area, where his father was executive vice president of a large insurance company. He was proud of his father and inherited much of his innate business sense. From his mother he inherited a sense of humor, a joy of living, and a resilience to fate's bad breaks.

Lillian Kelly, his mother, was a funny, feisty, self-reliant dynamo, a woman with such an uninhibited personality that after Kelly became CEO, he was talked into using her in Alaska Airlines radio commercials. She loved the idea. There was nothing shy or clinging about Lillian. Her on-air personality was reminiscent of Columbia Sportswear's chairman "Ma" Gert Boyle and her iconic promotion of her company's outdoor clothing during the late 1990s.

Lillian also proved to be a smash hit, delivering her lines with perfect inflection and timing. If anything, her radio commercials were as effective as the famous Sedelmaier television campaign.

The first radio spots were built around a single theme: Lillian's stubborn refusal to say what a spokesman for Alaska Airlines wanted her to say. A few samples, starting with the opening skit . . .

Announcer: Why do people think Alaska's fares are still higher than those of discount airlines? Let's ask the mother of Alaska Airlines' president. Here are two identical fares, one from Alaska and the other from a no-frills airline. *Same price, right?*

Lillian Kelly: Of course. But I would say Alaska's prices are higher than those of other airlines.

Ann.: But you just admitted that the prices are the same.

LK: Yes, I did. But Alaska gives you so much more for your money.

Ann. (trying desperately to repair the damage): So even the mother of Alaska Airlines' president can't convince people that Alaska's prices are just as low as the other guys'.

In later commercials, Lillian remained as stubborn as ever and even administered such motherly admonitions as "sit up straight, young man," and "stop that fidgeting." Then came the two funniest spots in the series:

Sound of telephone.

LK: Hello?

Ann.: Hi, it's me!

LK: I hope you're not calling again to convince me that Alaska's fares are the same as those discount airlines'.

Ann.: Not today.

LK: No?

Ann.: Absolutely.

LK: Oh, you've lost it now, young man.

Ann.: Allow me to explain. Right now, kids can fly free with an Alaska Airlines Southern California vacation package.

LK: So now my son can fly with me free?

Ann.: Yes . . . uh, wait a minute. Your son is chairman of Alaska Airlines.

LK: So he doesn't qualify for a free trip?

Ann.: No, because he's not 11 or under.

LK: Of course he's not! A 10-year-old running an airline? Don't be ridiculous!

The final chapter:

Sound of doorbell.

LK: Oh, it's you again.

Ann.: I have some news. And if I can't convince you that Alaska Airlines' fares are just as low as those no-frills guys', I will never bother you again.

LK: Wow! This is too good to pass up. What's your news?

Ann.: Well, American, Continental, and Canadian Airlines have joined Northwest, TWA, KLM, British Airways, and Qantas as travel partners in Alaska's Mileage Plan!

LK: Look, my son doesn't have time to run nine airlines. He's busy enough being chairman of Alaska Airlines.

    Ann.: But your son isn't running nine airlines.

    LK: Well, why not? He's perfectly capable of doing anything he sets his mind to.

    Ann.: Of course, but now members of Alaska's Mileage Plan can earn mileage on all those other airlines and . . .

    LK: Are you saying that my son is not qualified to run nine airlines?

    Ann. (sighing in a tone of utter defeat): You really enjoy this, don't you?

It was no wonder that people found it easy to fall in love with Lillian Kelly.

John Kelly earned a degree in business administration from the University of Puget Sound in 1967, and decided on an airline career. Despite having a college education and a father with a high-ranking job in the insurance industry, he willingly started out on the front lines as a ticket agent with Continental. Well, maybe "reluctantly" would be a better adverb. With the typical brashness of an Irishman, Kelly wrote to three airlines just before he graduated offering his services as a *vice president*. Continental was so impressed with this unprecedented audacity that it hired him, albeit *not* as a vice president.

After he joined Alaska in 1976 and began his rise up the executive ladder, he hired Barb Johnson, who became his secretary, friend, and confidante. Barb joined Alaska in 1976 after graduating from the University of Washington. She was assigned to Kelly when he was assistant vice president of marketing and stayed with him as his administrative assistant until he retired 25 years later. She was typical of the airline's administrative assistants, combining the qualities of diplomat, chief organizer, and mother hen. All of the above, of course, explained why John Kelly took Johnson with him when he became Horizon's CEO. He had come to trust and depend on her. They both had to adjust to the environment of a smaller, less-formal airline.

Kelly went there with Bruce Kennedy's marching orders still ringing in his ears. "John, don't feel that what you had to do at Alaska, you also must do at Horizon," Kennedy cautioned. "Horizon has its own culture."

"I already knew that," Kelly said, "but to have the CEO himself, who lived in a certain world at Alaska, take time to tell me that made a lot of difference. He absolutely supported me in everything I did at Horizon. For one thing, unlike Alaska, Horizon was primarily a nonunion company with a nonunion environment. It was entrepreneurial in spirit, not a 50-year-old airline with 50-year-old traditions.

"Bruce gave me the freedom to do what I wanted to do at Horizon, while still respecting its traditions and culture. This was a relief to Milt Kuolt, who once called Alaska a 'boutique airline.' Milt was full of colorful axioms. He told me once, 'Never trust a guy who wears loafers with tassels.' I always wondered if he was referring to me."

"The transition from Alaska to Horizon," Barb Johnson recalled, "was a change for both of us." The real culture shock was the airline's more informal, more personal atmosphere, and fewer meetings. But in what counted most — service oriented attitude, work ethic, and pride — Kelly and Johnson both found the people of Horizon to be major leaguers.

Some of Kelly's earlier innovations at Horizon were cosmetic, such as ordering new uniforms for the flight attendants and customer-service agents (CSAs). His major contributions, however, were in the areas of modernization, efficiency, and fiscal discipline, adding to Horizon's existing culture without changing it.

"Horizon had problems typical of an entrepreneurial company when I went over there," Kelly remembered. "For example, accounting procedures truly needed help. My strategy was to keep the airline entrepreneurial, while implementing new systems and procedures that were simple, yet efficient."

It was impossible for him to travel throughout Horizon's route system right away, so that all employees could meet him personally. Instead, to supplement his personal visits and to reach as many employees as possible, he produced a series of videos in which he explained what he wanted to do for the airline. In effect, he was eager to assure everyone at Horizon that while he was no "Uncle Miltie," so to speak, he was a stand-up guy who admired their airline, which he wanted to make even better with their help.

Kelly held a weekly officers' meeting at Horizon, and as the airline began seriously discussing recommended changes, especially those involving policy and procedures, he would ask the group: "Guys, do we actually need to do this much, or should we back off?"

"Purposely," Kelly related, "we did only the things that had to be done, without becoming overly bureaucratic and losing the verve and spirit that Milt had forged into the company, and I think we accomplished that goal."

Some years later, after Jeff Pinneo had taken over from George Bagley as Horizon's CEO, he invited Kelly to write a guest column for the airline's in-flight magazine. This 2006 occasion was Horizon's 25th anniversary, and John wrote a love letter to the scrappy little company that had been his home for seven years. Seven *happy* years, Kelly stressed in the column that began

"Dear Horizon" and went on to thank the airline for giving him the training and confidence he needed when he went on to become Alaska Airlines' and AAG's number one officer.

What John left out of the article, because everyone at the company already knew all about it, was another kind of love story. It was while he was at Horizon that he met Maggi Hanson.

Barb Johnson did more than merely observe the course of their romance; she sort of nudged Cupid. She had known Cheri Kelly, John's late wife, as "a wonderful person" and had tremendous admiration for the way Kelly doggedly tried to carry out his normal duties even though he had known for some time that Cheri's cancer was very likely terminal. Not everyone was aware of the strain he was under, because he told only a few officers confidentially that there was little hope for his wife.

"After she died," Barb recounted, "he didn't date and did hardly any socializing because he was spending all his time with his daughter, who was a junior in high school when her mother died."

He was at Horizon and his wife was still alive when Alaska recruited Maggi Hanson as director of in-flight services. Kelly had heard about her work there, along with reports that she resembled actress Angie Dickinson. So when they first met, at a reception for Bob Gray, his first words upon spotting her were, "You must be Maggi."

They shook hands and chatted briefly, and Kelly forgot all about their encounter until many months after Cheri had passed away. They happened to see each other in a corridor at corporate headquarters. Again, they chatted about business matters, but when John returned to his office, Maggi phoned him and asked if he wanted to have a drink with her after work.

Kelly mentioned the unexpected invitation to Barb Johnson. "She probably wants some advice about her department," he theorized in a masterpiece of naiveté.

Barb gave him one of those pitying men-are-so-dumb looks. "John," she said softly, "I don't think so," thus handing Cupid an arrow.

Kelly himself related the sequence of future developments. "We went out to dinner," he recalled, "and it was a wonderful evening. I wore her out asking questions about her work and her life in general. The next day she called to thank me. I said we ought to go out again, and that's how our romance started."

Barb noticed that he seemed to be increasingly cheerful. "I think you're smitten," she remarked one day.

"Smitten? I am *not* smitten!"

"John, you're definitely smitten."

"No, I'm not," he muttered with considerably less emphasis, and retreated red-faced into his office, followed by the sound of her knowing laughter.

John and Maggi were married in April 1993. After Kelly became Alaska's chairman and CEO, however, his romance with his airline's supervisors and managers began on an entirely different note — with unexpected shock treatment directed at management.

In his very first meeting with Alaska's managers, Kelly greeted everyone with the announcement that he wanted to get rid of management. The ensuing clap of thunder was the sound of jaws dropping. Then Kelly went on to explain that he thought managers should *lead*, not manage, and that meant learning to manage yourself before you could lead others.

A lot of people in the room were exchanging glances of genuine interest, if not instant approval. This was in sharp contrast to the previous CEO's style. Yet even as Kelly began selling and then implementing his own brand of leadership, he had the class and decency to pay public tribute to his predecessor, who was often unfairly maligned.

Annual reports are not usually regarded as popular reading matter, but there was more than the usual prepublication interest in the 1994 report, prepared early in 1995 and Kelly's first as CEO. There was much curiosity as to what it would say about Vecci's firing. Yet Ray himself could not have had any objection to what the annual report *did* say.

His departure was mentioned briefly in John Kelly's breezily informal introduction to the year's official facts and figures. It was covered in one simple sentence that said, "I recently succeeded Ray Vecci as chairman, president, and chief executive officer of Alaska Air Group and Alaska Airlines." Kelly could have stopped right there, but he insisted on adding a not very subtle plea that shareholders, employees, and officers not judge Vecci harshly. In noting the dramatic financial turnaround in 1994, Kelly emphasized that the majority of it was due to what Vecci had accomplished during his time in office.

"I know I speak for the entire company," John added, "in thanking him for successfully leading us through a changing competitive environment."

A few paragraphs later came another tribute, indirect yet by implication even more significant than the earlier commendation: "A complete analysis of where we are today and what we accomplished in 1994 must reference the dynamic, sometimes painful preceding years. The foundation was laid from 1991-93 when we determined that our future must be framed around three guiding principles: low prices aren't temporary; customers always seek the lowest fare; and we must continue to deliver service that is perceptibly better than our competitors'."

Sound familiar? It should, for the entire paragraph was paraphrasing Ray Vecci's prescription for addressing the headaches of bargain-basement fares. In 1994 alone, the average price of an airline ticket had dropped 14 percent over the previous year, the fourth consecutive year of declining fares.

At any rate, Kelly's graceful and generous acknowledgment of the debt the airline owed to Vecci was typical of Alaska's new chief. He was a leader who preferred communication over confrontation, and he gave credit where it was due.

Kelly's past actions, and those he would take over the ensuing months, demonstrated that he himself led by example. Years earlier when he was the head of marketing, for instance, he introduced a new method of screening applicants for frontline positions such as flight attendant. "We're hiring attitude" was the way he described it at the time to John Berlan of the *Investor's Business Daily*.

Kelly's major contribution as Alaska's new top dog was perhaps his determination to combine Alaska's tradition of superior service — the "human touch" — with new technology to make it even better. John Kelly had always been what is known as a gadget freak, fascinated by practically every new device that came on the market. He preferred things that could be applied to the airline business, but he didn't limit his interest to that area. If anyone had invented something like an electric potato peeler for home kitchens, John would have been the first one standing in line to buy one.

Barb Johnson used to shake her head with amusement at his enthusiasm for any new gadget that caught his attention. "He was inquisitive about everything," she recounted. "If he saw someone with, say, a new PalmPilot, or a new kind of tape recorder, he had to know how it worked and try it himself. And if he thought any new development, electronic or otherwise, meant things could be done more efficiently, you could bet he'd tell his officers about it.

"I remember he was fascinated with the Franklin planning system. It is a system that helps you organize the day's work and helps you to identify values and priorities you have for your job. Then you plan each day's work to best meet those values and priorities."

Johnson was impressed by the way Kelly faithfully adapted the Franklin managerial organizer system to his own work schedule, and urged all officers to try it. Each morning he'd decide what to do and in what order to attain his overall goals in as short a time and as efficiently as possible. To prioritize them, he used the Franklin rating system. He assigned A, B, and C ratings to each item on his daily schedule, and the numbers 1 through 5 to each of those letters. The most important projects, for example, would be A-1, and the least important on the day's schedule would be C-5.

Kelly didn't necessarily expect every officer to use this organizational tool, though most did. Looking back, however, it might be considered a smaller, symbolic component that was helping him and the company to draw a blueprint for Alaska's future. That blueprint included an unprecedented degree of route expansion.

In the early 1990s, Boeing had presented new airplane concepts to Vecci. Boeing described them as a new generation of 737 models priced well below any of the big, long-range widebody aircraft. This major purchase fell into the hands of Kelly after Vecci's departure. Although attractive, the proposed aircraft increased the 737's capacity by only 16 seats over the 400, already the mainstay of Alaska's fleet, and even the small increase would require adding a flight attendant to the cabin's crew.

Kelly sat down with Boeing Commercial Airplane chief Rod Woodard and described the problem. Woodard mentioned a concept aircraft that Boeing had been evaluating, the 737-900, and Kelly immediately saw its potential. So the Alaska order was amended to include the 900 and the efficient, smaller-capacity 700 for use in developing markets. It was Alaska that persuaded Boeing to build the 737-900.

The 737-900 and its smaller brother, the 737-700, had range capability of 3,100 miles to 3,700 miles, respectively, and were among the most fuel-efficient aircraft in the 737 family. The version of the 900 that Alaska would launch could carry 172 passengers, 16 in first class and 156 in coach, a configuration that the airline's planners believed could support a variety of new and existing markets more profitably.

The decision to buy longer-range airplanes stemmed from a study made during Vecci's tenure, but the order wasn't placed until November 10, 1997. Alaska ordered 10 of the new 900s along with several 737-700s. The airline's CEO could never stop operating in the promotion-minded mode he had inherited from Mike Ryan, and Kelly made the delivery of the first 900, on May 16, 2001, not merely an occasion, but also a fund-raising event to benefit four charities whose work involved children: Ronald McDonald House Charities, Make-A-Wish Foundation, Shriners Burn Center, and AirLifeLine.

Airliners magazine editor Jon Proctor, one of the guests invited to ride on a special delivery flight, was impressed by the new 737-900, yet was equally impressed by the ingenuity the airline's marketing crew had put into what could have been just another traditional, rather routine delivery ceremony. "To raise funds for those charities," Proctor recalled, "they invited members of Alaska's frequent-flier Mileage Plan to bid for 50 seats on the special delivery flight, with the proceeds going to the four children's charities. The gimmick was that they were bidding air mileage instead of cash."

Sixteen Mileage Plan members were the top bidders, offering at least 100,000 miles each, and the total mileage raised topped 2.5 million. Proctor estimated this to equal 125 round-trips for the four charities to provide to children with medical needs.

Boeing sweetened the pot by contributing $5,000 in cash to each of the four charities. The generous Mileage Plan donors were guests, along with a few youngsters representing the charities, on the nearly two-hour delivery flight from Boeing Field around the Seattle area.

Kelly couldn't stop there. He invited his friend astronaut Buzz Aldrin, as well as the voice of the Seattle Mariners, Dave Niehaus, and motorcycle daredevil Robbie Knievel along as guests. And unlike the delivery of the airline's first MD-80, the ride was sweet and the press coverage positive and extensive.

The 737-900s, along with the smaller 700s, were purchased to serve the carrier's north-south route structure with aircraft perfectly sized to accommodate the various-sized markets, but they also became crucial to attaining Alaska's dream of one day breaking out of its mold as primarily a West Coast carrier. Ultimately, the 700 was to prove far more versatile than the larger 900.

Between 2001 and mid-2003, when Kelly retired, the airline inaugurated nonstop service between Seattle and five major East Coast destinations: Washington, D.C. (both Reagan and Dulles) in 2001; Boston, Miami, and Newark in 2002; and Orlando in 2003.

But John Kelly's focus on aircraft was not confined to ordering the right models to improve profitability and support expansion. He was equally interested in bringing technological advances into the cockpit if they could achieve significantly greater safety and efficiency. He was no pilot himself,

For a time, Alaska Airlines had nearly as many logos as jets. Both
Cosgrave and Kennedy credited Ryan with choosing the Eskimo logo
over the other three designs: the miner, the Russian cupola, and the
totem.

Ronald F. Cosgrave, on left, with Bruce R. Kennedy, who became
Alaska Airlines' president in 1978.

The Eskimo logo on 727 tails in Seattle during the mid-1970s.

Corporate headquarters, 1976.

Bill MacKay, who became known as "Mr. Alaska," with Paul Rosenthal, a violinist bound for the Sitka Summer Music Festival.

Alaska Airlines augmented its fleet with twin-engine McDonnell Douglas MD-83s and deliveries began in 1985.

Shown with the company's first MD-83 are, from right, Gus Robinson, Ed Bollinger, Ken Skidds, Ray Vecci, Jim Johnson, Ben Benecke, Doug Versteeg, and an unidentified McDonnell Douglas representative.

Jet America flight attendants, 1985.

Milt Kuolt, Horizon Air's founder and a legendary character.
A Horizon F-27 and Mount Rainier.

Bruce Kennedy in Mexico, 1988. Inaugural flights were important promotional opportunities, and Kennedy made a personal commitment to be on each of the inaugural flights to Mexico, a practice that had been a tradition at Alaska Airlines since its earliest days to introduce itself to its newest communities.

Russia, 1990. Shown is the flight crew, including, second from right, Captain Mike Swanigan.

Ray Vecci became Alaska Airlines' and Alaska Air Group's president and chief executive officer in 1990 and chairman in 1991. Shown are, from left, Ray Vecci, Bruce Kennedy, and Pat Glenn.

Alaska signed a long-term lease agreement — 20 to 22 years — with International Lease Finance Corporation for 20 Boeing 737-400s, which were 60 percent more fuel-efficient than the previous fleet of 727s.

A 1992 advertisement illustrates the variety of aircraft operated by
Alaska Airlines during its first 60 years.

John F. Kelly abruptly became
Alaska's CEO in February 1995.

A 737-400 with Alaskaair.com livery after the company's
first Internet address went live in 1995.

(Photograph by Mark Abbott.)

In 2002, Disney artists created artwork for an Alaska Airlines 737-400.
Called "Spirit of Disneyland," the work represented a comprehensive,
multi-year partnership agreement between Disney and Alaska Airlines.

(Disney characters © Disney Enterprises, Inc. Used by permission from Disney Enterprises, Inc.)

Pilot's view of Runway 7R into Anchorage from the flight deck of a Boeing 737-200C. Image by Bob Shane.

Alaska Airlines' 2006 senior officers, from left: Bradley D. Tilden, executive vice president, finance, and chief financial officer; Captain Kevin P. Finan, executive vice president, operations; Gregg A. Saretsky, executive vice president, marketing and planning; and William S. "Bill" Ayer, chairman, president, and chief executive officer, Alaska Air Group.

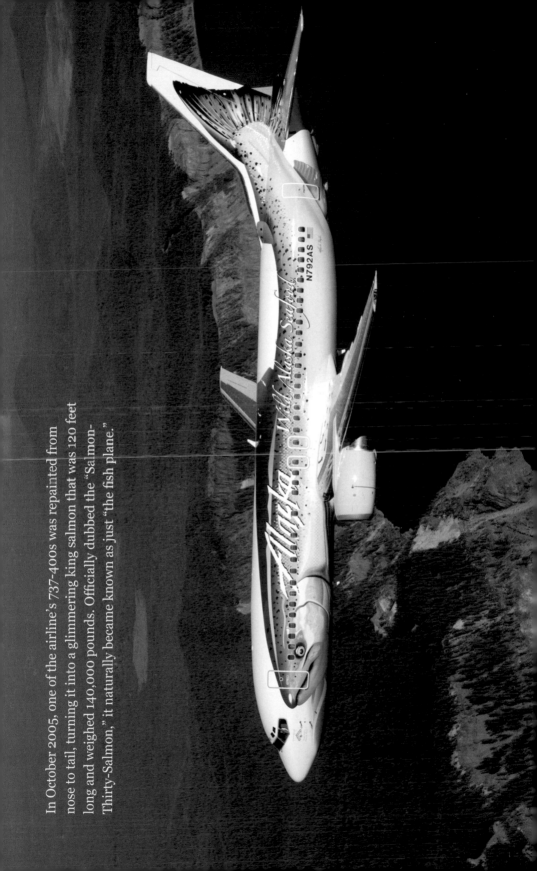

In October 2005, one of the airline's 737-400s was repainted from nose to tail, turning it into a glimmering king salmon that was 120 feet long and weighed 140,000 pounds. Officially dubbed the "Salmon-Thirty-Salmon," it naturally became known as just "the fish plane."

A 737-800 with winglets over Mount Rainier.

but he admired and respected Alaska's airmen, and one of his favorites was Mike Swanigan.

Swanigan wasn't really all that happy being chief pilot. He preferred flying 737s to "flying a desk," the pilots' derisive term for being confined to office duty. Kelly unexpectedly walked into Swanigan's office in flight operations one day, shortly after being named CEO, and shut the door behind him. An ominous sign, Swanigan thought, figuring he was going to be fired as chief pilot.

Kelly sat down in front of Swanigan's desk. His opening remark confirmed Swanigan's suspicion. "Mike, I've got something to tell you," Kelly said.

Here it comes, thought Swanigan. "Okay, John, go ahead and say it."

"Swannie, I'm sending George Bagley over to Horizon as its new CEO, and I want you to succeed him as vice president of flight operations."

Swanigan was overwhelmed. Having started out as a rookie flight engineer only 15 years before, he felt tremendous pride that he was now being asked to be a vice president of a major airline. Yet he also was disappointed at the prospect of merely getting a bigger desk instead of going back to the cockpit.

"John, I'm not quite sure I'm ready for that kind of responsibility," he said cautiously.

Kelly shook his head. "Swannie, I like the way you work. I like the way you handled that pilot-qualification mess. You're the man I want."

"Okay," Swanigan agreed. "I'll give you four years."

"No deal. I need you until you retire."

"Four years, John. That's all."

Kelly rose, started out the door, and turned around. "Okay!" he snapped.

One of the few African-Americans to hold such a senior role at a major airline at the time, Swanigan ended up staying on the job four and a half years before finally resigning and going back to flight duties as a captain. But he remained long enough to encourage and to see the adoption of a new navigation device of incredible accuracy whose introduction into airline service was pioneered by Alaska Airlines.

Required Navigation Performance, more commonly referred to inside the industry as RNP, ranks as perhaps the most significant air-safety advance since the airlines began equipping their fleets with airborne weather radar in the mid-1950s. Kim Kaiser and Mike Adams, two of the airline's most technically astute captains, in conjunction with avionics equipment manufacturers and the airframe manufacturer, helped to design, develop, and pioneer the system on behalf of Alaska. After Kaiser left to become 737-400 fleet captain, Kim Rackley, another highly skilled technical captain, joined Adams to work on approval of the system's initial installation on the airline's 737-400 fleet in 1996.

RNP was especially welcome in Alaskan operations, where tough terrain and extremes of weather can be extraordinarily difficult for aviators. The RNP system uses onboard computers linked to global positioning system (GPS) satellites to guide aircraft along a precisely defined flight path. A technical wonder, RNP has a practical side from a customer's perspective, because it reduces cancellations, delays, and diversions. Even more important, RNP increases the margin of safety at locations that require absolutely precise positioning, are susceptible to adverse weather, or are surrounded by challenging terrain. It allows pilots to follow a consistent course through what would otherwise be unflyable conditions. Currently, RNP is used in such diverse cities as Juneau and six other towns in Alaska, Palm Springs, Portland, and Washington, D.C.

At Alaskan airports such as Juneau and Cordova that are so frequently vulnerable to bad weather, RNP lowers the minimums for a standard approach to only one-mile visibility and a ceiling of less than 400 feet. In 2006 alone, the airline recorded some 1,200 instances when its aircraft could land safely under weather conditions that formerly would have resulted in delays, diversions, or even cancellations.

Kelly did not hesitate to ask for the board's approval for RNP's $10 million initial cost, nor did he hesitate to acquire another new safety device known as an Enhanced Ground Proximity Warning System (EGPWS). EGPWS provides visual and aural warning of nearby terrain obstructions with pinpoint accuracy and not only is invaluable in mountainous areas but also prevents prematurely low approach descents, one of the leading causes of accidents. The double visual/audible alert feature of EGPWS is far more effective than the audible-only warnings of earlier terrain warning devices. By the time Alaska entered the 21st century, RNP/EGPWS had been installed on every aircraft in the fleet, with the exception of Alaska's remaining 737-200s and MD-80s, and this, too, was an industry first.

Behind this alphabet-soup nomenclature for new cockpit-safety hardware was Kelly's determination to apply new technology to service and safety alike. Overall technology was at the core of his competitive strategy to beat the competition in the air as well as on the ground.

Immediately before Kelly's ascension to the chairmanship, Alaska had finished 1994 on a high note, not merely with its financial turnaround but also through further expansion into California markets, acquisition of new aircraft, and the renegotiation of 737-400 lease terms with International Lease Finance Corporation (ILFC), a major cost-cutting move. These encouraging developments, however, were offset somewhat by Southwest's invasion of several of Alaska's markets on the West Coast and United's transfer of its West Coast routes to a low-cost regional carrier operating as the United Shuttle in 1993.

To the new chairman, this was more of a minor headache than a painful migraine. He met the challenge by utilizing computers in new ways and picking good people who shared his own grasp of high-tech potential.

One of those people was Gregg Saretsky, a Canadian who began his airline career as a flight attendant with Canadian Airlines and who later became Alaska's executive vice president of flight and marketing. No one, including Saretsky himself, could have predicted that kind of success story. He was born in Montreal and raised in Quebec, the son of a Canadian mother and a German-immigrant father. His intention had been to become a doctor.

A brilliant student, he earned a bachelor of science degree, majoring in microbiology and biochemistry. But while in school he worked three summers as a flight attendant, and like so many other young men who had never considered making the airline business a career, he was hooked. He returned to school, got a master's degree in business administration, and in 1985 joined Canadian Airlines, where he eventually became vice president of strategy implementation. By then he had acquired impressive experience in several phases of the airline business, including pricing, marketing, airport relations, and revenue management.

When Canadian Airlines fell on hard times and was merged into Air Canada, Saretsky decided he was ready to make a career move, and that's when Alaska began recruiting him. Several interviews in Seattle, including a key one with John Kelly, convinced him that his future lay with this aggressive, innovative company.

One of Saretsky's most important contributions, in the midst of all the exciting technical achievements, was to expand the airline's alliances with other carriers, not only in the United States but also throughout the world. Saretsky would take marketing into hitherto untapped territories, just as others would take the company into uncharted areas of technology.

When Saretsky joined Alaska in 1996, its only code-share partner outside the state of Alaska was Northwest. He and his marketing team wound up adding Continental, Lan Chile, Qantas, American, Hawaiian, Cathay Pacific, and Delta to the code-share roster. By 2005, Alaska could boast 15 U.S. and foreign carriers as either code-share or frequent-flier Mileage Plan partners.

Saretsky's chief lieutenant in developing more code-share partners was Craig Battison, who had worked with Kelly, Dave Palmer, and Bill MacKay in marketing during the days of the famous gold ingot campaign, when Mike Ryan headed that department. Battison created a promotion program called "Alaska Aeronaut," which marked the airline's first step toward developing what eventually would become its award-winning Mileage Plan.

"Craig came up with the idea of recognizing customers who flew Alaska frequently," said Dave Hall, then a junior member of the marketing group. "At first, the program consisted of a wall-mounted plaque that recognized the number of trips a frequent passenger took. There were spaces for eight brass medallions at the base of the plaque, each one featuring a scene from the state's history and heritage, such as an oil rig or a caribou. The customer got a new medallion after flying so many trips."

Battison's forte, however, was not promotion but interline sales. He had almost a decade of experience at TWA behind him when he took a gamble and joined Alaska, where his knowledge of domestic and international markets was put to good use. In fact, he was the key person who got Alaska together with United in a pre-code-sharing arrangement, where each other's flights provided applicable and convenient connections for their respective passengers.

When Battison was hired in the mid-1970s, Alaska was more than 12 times smaller than what it eventually became. So code-sharing with much larger carriers, both here and abroad, turned out to be the fastest and easiest way to broaden travel opportunities for customers and to control traffic for the airline.

"The primary advantage of code-sharing alliances for customers," Battison pointed out, "is a much larger air-travel network that provides such compatible services as getting all the necessary boarding passes and baggage-checking done at a single carrier."

Northwest did not want Alaska to add any new partners, and at Alaska itself, some officers worried that any expansion of alliances might be at the expense of losing Northwest's participation. Horizon established a code-share relationship with Northwest Airlines when Kelly was at Horizon, with Alaska's blessing. As Kelly recalled the genesis of the relationship, "I tried to convince Ray to do the same with Northwest at Alaska, but he just wouldn't do it. After I took over as CEO, however, I met with John Dasberg and we agreed to move ahead."

But when Saretsky and Battison began hammering out new alliances beginning in 1998, Northwest didn't bolt. By then the industry had accepted the fact that code-sharing created mutual benefits for all partners. It offered an economical way to expand a carrier's own route system without having to buy new airplanes or to spend a lot of money opening and staffing new stations.

One thing Kelly did early in his tenure at the top was to strip himself of the presidential title. He split his position into two functions, allowing him as CEO to concentrate on major current problems and long-range planning while the president attended to the airline's day-to-day operations. This move also continued the unofficial tradition established by Cosgrave and Kennedy of choosing their own successors. For by vacating the presidency, as he did in 1997, Kelly created a combined training and proving ground for a future CEO.

The result was another significant crossroads in Alaska's history. On Kelly's strong recommendation, the directors named William S. Ayer as the airline's new president. Bill Ayer by that time had come over from Horizon and had risen to the post of Alaska's senior vice president of marketing and planning. These happened to have been, perhaps by coincidence, the two separate departments that Kelly and Vecci had once respectively headed.

If the last five years of Bruce Kennedy's regime had been a happy and productive period, the same could be said of John Kelly's first full five years as CEO. The accounting ledgers dripped black ink, and there was a feel-good atmosphere around the entire airline.

From 1995 through 1999, the airline amassed net profits totaling some $400 million, a sum that included a record $134.2 million in 1999. Obviously, the combination of dramatic, customer-friendly technological advances, Kelly's dynamic people-friendly leadership, and the outstanding service delivered by employees on the front lines was the right formula.

Not the whole story, however. What Kelly also had going for him was something that neither he nor Kennedy ever forgot and always relied on: something that grew out of Alaska's resourceful roots in the nation's 49th state. For if it were possible to print out an airline's DNA, Alaska's would be a 10-letter word: *Innovation*.

CHAPTER NINETEEN

Revolution dot-com

Two of the chief players who implemented John Kelly's vision of what technology could do for the customer — and the airline — had certain qualities in common, yet ironically, neither could be classed as a computer geek. Bob Reeder's specialty was not so much pure computer technology as it was its application to business. In that sense he was another John Kelly, albeit with a more technical background. Steve Jarvis would prove to be a crackerjack engineer and marketer who also understood the computer's potential.

A native of California, Reeder earned a bachelor's degree in business administration from Idaho State University and, after graduating, spent 18 years at John Deere, the world's largest manufacturer of farm equipment, in various positions as diverse as data processing and customer service. Essentially, his expertise was in information management, which at Alaska and elsewhere at the time was simply called data processing. But under Reeder, it became known as information technology, then shortened to "IT."

When Alaska hired Reeder, Bruce Kennedy was still CEO and Ray Vecci was chief operating officer. Years later, Reeder remembered Vecci's farsightedness as a CEO more vividly than his perceived take-no-prisoners personality. Reeder firmly believed that Vecci, too, embraced computer technology when it was in its earliest stages at Alaska. "He was for anything that worked," Reeder pointed out. "For example, he became very interested in a proposed solution that would be a great help to our ticket agents." This eventually became a computer system called Image.

Image was envisioned by John Kelly, who intended to hire a software contractor to develop a system for Horizon that would simplify computer commands that airport agents used so they could pay greater attention to the customer across the counter. "We made a preliminary presentation to Alaska, and Reeder made it clear that we didn't need outside help, and that his team could create what we needed," recalled Kelly. "Reeder's work led to everything else we did, including our eventual use of visual displays and touch-screen passenger check-in at kiosks."

"In the beginning," Reeder recalled, "some of the older officers at Alaska resisted the new technology. There had been a long history of dissatisfaction with the ponderous old data-processing system, and lots of friction between its supporters and opponents.

"When I got here," said Reeder, "there was open warfare between the data-processing people and the people who handled communications technology. In fact, I told someone that if I had been CEO, I would have fired all of them. We were trying to run an airline, and these technical people kept sniping at each other. To make matters worse, because of the reporting structure, issues couldn't get resolved until they got to Ray, who didn't have any patience with that sort of thing."

A stubborn resistance to change may well have been Vecci's reason for firing or retiring certain veterans, although Reeder didn't venture an opinion on that theory. Doug Versteeg, vice president of administration, who already had data processing reporting to him, assumed responsibility for the communication technology department. He then arranged a shotgun marriage between the two feuding groups. "We're going to get one organization out of this, and we're all going to work together," Versteeg decreed. And by the time he retired in early 1995, he had set the stage for Reeder to take the reins of a new technology team.

This take-it-or-else armistice achieved two important results. It was the first step in changing the focus of computer technology toward customer service, and it began delivering more value to the nonaccounting aspects of data processing.

"The Image system was the turning point for us," Reeder emphasized.

"It showed everyone we could do something else besides payroll.

"Kelly's early advocacy of technology was focused on making the computer system easy to use for agents," Reeder added. "He wanted to get away from a process that required so much intensity that we had to hire intense people to use it. He believed that Image could provide something far simpler. If we could do that, we could focus on hiring customer-service agents with personality who, in turn, would relate more to our customers than to their computer terminal. It was just as much a marketing decision as one motivated by technology."

To fully grasp the impact of the computer revolution and the role it played in Alaska's achieving technology leadership, flash back to the mid-1980s, when there was only one personal computer in the entire corporate headquarters building: Ed White's Osborne, produced by a very early and short-lived company in the emerging personal-computer industry. In 1984 Kelly bought a Macintosh for home use. That early experience anchored his belief that every computer system should be just as easy to use. Later, to facilitate electronic communications, Livingston & Company, the company's ad agency at the time, provided John with a Mac for his use at Alaska. People would drift into Kelly's office to see this "unique computer," and before long everyone became familiar with Macintosh capabilities. Eventually most managers were provided Macintosh computers, before the company's systems were converted to Microsoft-based personal computers. By 2005, the airline had progressed from two museum pieces — an antique Osborne and an early Mac — to 7,000 PCs.

In 1990, the year Bob Reeder joined the airline, Alaska had two major computer systems in use. One was its own mainframe system, which handled everything except reservations and airport operations. The other was the central reservation system, which was used by customer-service agents in the airports and at the company's reservation call centers. Alaska, like most airlines, used a central reservation system provided by an outside vendor.

There were two big challenges to advancing the company's computer technology. First, the two systems were not interconnected. Most of the airline's employees who had direct contact with customers used the central reservation system. The rest of the company used Alaska's internal system.

The second challenge was the central reservation system itself. It required agents to memorize hundreds of cryptic codes, and that required a lot of training. It worked, but it was cumbersome at best.

The problems were solved by taking two major steps. First, technicians interconnected the two systems and replaced single-purpose terminals, often called "dumb terminals," with personal computers that were all connected by a communication network. That enabled the second solution, which was to install Image at all customer-contact locations. While Image did simplify a lot of the agent processes, its real innovation was to integrate other systems behind the scenes so agents could work from a customer perspective instead of strictly an airline-reservations point of view.

These two things were fundamental to all the innovations that followed. "I know John didn't want to know the details of how we did this, but he certainly saw the possibilities, and we had his unwavering support," recalled Reeder.

Those early decisions have stood the test of time. "We now run our business on probably 600 central computers, some big, like the central reservation system, and some small, but all interconnected," said Reeder. "We process transactions in our data centers in Seattle as well as in London, Boston, Tulsa, Milwaukee, and Portland. You can't run an airline for very long today without computers." Besides reservations, Reeder said, today virtually all aspects of the business rely on the computer, most prominently and importantly in the areas of flight planning, dispatch, and maintenance.

Kelly, with his instincts for the potential of computer technology, had formed a task force in 1994, shortly after he returned to Alaska as its COO, to move to electronic tickets. The answer he got back was that it couldn't be done and that frequent travelers weren't interested in it anyway.

"Some of our own people were telling us that customers want tickets, they have always had tickets — heck, that's why we have ticket counters," Reeder recalled. The doubters, scoffers, and outright opponents argued that business travelers in particular rely on a piece of paper with specific guarantees and a printed record of fares paid and passenger itinerary. The airline's lawyers were concerned about all the legal obligations printed on the back of conventional tickets. Reeder's reply was simple: "Who reads them anyway?"

With Kelly's support and the technical foundation in place, Alaska became a very early adopter of electronic ticketing. The real pioneer in electronic ticketing itself was ValuJet, one of the numerous new low-cost carriers that sprang up after deregulation. ValuJet later became AirTran, and electronic ticketing technology spread to other airlines, including Morris Air, and later Southwest and United.

By 1995 the World Wide Web was starting to establish a commercial presence. Here again, Alaska's technology task force was not quick to recognize its potential. To describe Kelly as frustrated with the task force's verdict would be a major understatement. He had to grip his chair to keep from exploding, but settled for unveiled sarcasm. "Have any of you guys ever used an ATM?" he inquired. "Do you think a survey would show that most people would rather see a teller than use a machine?"

Kelly continued, "I tried to calmly explain that we didn't have a choice. As the smallest of the major carriers, our distribution costs for travel-agent commissions and global distribution system (GDS) fees on top of that were soaring. We needed a way to reduce and ultimately control this cost."

Kelly then enlisted the help of the one person who had demonstrated any real interest in the project, and that was Bob Reeder. Reeder's team took electronic ticketing one step further and began writing the program that would allow Alaska to go online and sell tickets.

Yet this was still easier said than done. "A number of key people didn't want to deal with these new concepts of computer utilization, and the World Wide Web was one of them," Reeder said. "There were those who considered it a threat. Nobody was really trying to move it anywhere. In fact, there was a lot of sandbagging going on until Kelly provided some muscle."

Kelly's motivation for wanting to sell tickets online was reducing costs, but, said Reeder, Alaska also knew that Southwest was developing the capability as well, so the immediate goal was to be first to market.

"We got on to the World Wide Web because John was early in recognizing this emerging technology as the dramatic business shift it turned out to be," said Reeder. "We didn't study it very long, and we didn't try to do an economic analysis. The potential was obvious. John just said, 'Make it happen,' and that was all we needed to hear."

Alaskaair.com, the airline's first Internet "address," went live in 1995. That modest initial website followed the introduction of electronic ticketing earlier in the year. Reeder gave John Kelly full credit for pushing the vital development of *alaskaair.com,* the visual features of which had Kelly's stamp all over them.

That input reflected his gut instinct for judging whatever visual effect was needed. Reeder once described Kelly as someone who refused to accept anything unless he could visualize it first. In fact, it was Kelly who insisted that one of Alaska's 737s be painted a distinct dark blue with *alaskaair.com* reversed out along the aircraft's side, replacing the standard Alaska Airlines script from the plane's nose to its tail.

"My only regret is that we didn't do 10 of them instead of one," Kelly said. "It was a beautiful design. I loved the blue and the way the type reversed out of it. And this is what we were selling. That's where we were hot."

Kelly used his innate visual instinct for judging value. He sensed that if something looked right, it was going to be more efficient, and if it was efficient, in the end it would save money.

"When I communicated with John," Reeder said, "I wouldn't go in and try to talk to him because he wasn't a very good listener. But he would always read something I sent him, and the most effective way to present an idea was to show him a picture or drawing.

"He is an extremely visual guy, with a great eye for design and style. In the early days, accountants controlled computers, judging their value solely on how much money they could save. John didn't ignore that aspect, but his vision went way beyond that," Reeder stressed. "John believed, as we did, that our goal was to make things more effective for the customer, and if we achieved it, efficiency would follow."

One other technology innovation positioned Alaska to compete successfully in the jungle warfare launched by low-cost carriers. It was the development of kiosks, introduced as a key element in Alaska's effort to speed up the check-in process.

One or two other airlines had tried to introduce airport kiosks, but something kept them from being successful. Alaska suspected that it was because of the actual size of the kiosk and perhaps the way it was programmed. They also knew that the successful introduction of check-in kiosks was going to require changes in both customer and agent behavior. Alaska was the first airline to successfully introduce check-in kiosks. "The big contributor to Alaska's success with the kiosk," said Reeder, "was the small machine we selected, which is now ubiquitous throughout the industry. The first kiosks we studied were large and expensive."

Bob Reeder clearly recalled the day when Kelly set up a demonstration by a kiosk vendor. The vendor was pitching a model that was mostly a variation of the ATMs used by banks, and it carried a price tag of $10,000 for a single unit.

"John asked me what I thought, and I said it was the right idea but the wrong product," said Reeder. "He said, 'Then go get the right one.' We had been working with another company that was developing a small machine specifically for the airlines. It was about the size of a breadbox and was less costly. The other big plus was that we could take some of the investment we had made in Image and program it ourselves."

Reeder brought a mockup of the smaller kiosk to an officers' lunch and held it up so everyone could see how compact it was. "This is what we're going to have at airports for self-check-ins," he announced. Then he put the hollow mockup over his head and added, 'If it doesn't work, I'll be inside.' "

But it did work. The computer unit itself was small enough to allow the airline to experiment with various locations for its installation. "The first place we put them was the airport lobby, but customers would walk right past them and go to the ticket counter," Reeder explained. "Ultimately we ended up putting them on the ticket counter, and it didn't take long for customers to accept them. The key to our success turned out to be the placement of kiosks, so machine size and our ability to adapt the software to customer behavior was our true innovation," he added.

It was Kelly who suggested assigning agents to the kiosk operation to help any passengers who weren't sure how to operate one. This was especially reassuring not only to customers daunted by the very sight of an unfamiliar computer, but also to Alaska's ticket-counter personnel, who naturally feared that this latest technology development, coming on the heels of the website, might cost them their jobs.

It was true that after the kiosks went into full operation, Alaska didn't hire anyone for what would have been the next class of new counter agents. But the new technology didn't affect anyone who was already with the company. "That," Reeder stressed, "was Kelly's decision, and he made it very clear right from the start that no employees would lose their jobs because of our technology initiatives."

The company's continuing focus on technology to be more efficient, differentiate its products, and improve the passenger's airline experience culminated in yet one other original innovation. Initially dubbed the "Airport of the Future," it involved a check-in and bag-drop process utilizing homegrown and fine-tuned technologies. It combined technology with a whole new way of thinking about how to move passengers through airports from curbside to aircraft cabin. The objective was simple: Speed up passenger flow and eliminate one of the most annoying and time-consuming aspects of modern travel, the lengthy check-in lines that create anxiety for customers and add an extra burden for employees.

What was at first a dream became a reality in 2004, when Alaska inaugurated a brand-new wing and concourse at the Anchorage International Airport. Standing traditional airport design on its head, Alaska jettisoned the long, linear ticket counter that typically fronts a shallow passenger reception area and jams people into long, snaking lines. In its place, the airline, working closely with airport officials, designed a deep, large, open lobby-like area for its new wing. It installed an array of kiosks to allow passengers to check themselves in and built special baggage stations where passengers could tag and place their bags onto conveyor belts.

This new process alters the role of the passenger as well as the customer-service agent during check-in. Instead of doing the check-in for passengers, agents monitor boarding passes acquired at the kiosks or on the Web, check personal identification, tag bags, and are liberated to interact more personally with the customer. Meanwhile, their colleagues, known as lobby coordinators, help unfamiliar passengers with the new process. At the same time, most passengers get the psychological lift of feeling less anxious and more in control.

The Airport of the Future opened to great fanfare in Anchorage. Passenger wait times were cut in half, check-ins were quick, and lines were relatively short. So successful was the Anchorage model that more versions were rolled out or planned for other cities. And other carriers, seeing the benefits, began to copy Alaska's system. In 2006, Alaska Airlines was awarded a U.S. patent for the process.

Punch *pause* for a moment before going on to the next step in Alaska's technology evolution. For after the airline's establishment of a steadily expanding website and high-tech tools to improve the airport experience, an aeronautical-engineer-turned-Internet-marketer marched onto center stage and fired a massive broadside at Alaska's competitors.

Steve Jarvis was an unusual young man with unusual parents. It would have been extremely hard to find anyone else in the entire airline industry whose father and mother were both psychiatrists. They produced a son who, fortunately for Alaska Airlines, never had any interest in pursuing their profession. In fact, Steve spent an inordinate amount of time deciding exactly what he *did* want to do and where he wanted to do it.

He was born in Northern California but raised in Seattle, and remembered that as a youth he watched Alaska's television commercials, including the famous Joe Sedelmaier "atrocity" episodes. At that point, however, he wouldn't have bet five cents that he eventually would become a vice president at that same airline, with an impressive talent for steering website functions into new and lucrative fields.

Jarvis graduated in 1990 from the University of Washington with a degree in aeronautical engineering and an MBA, and spent the next three years as a design engineer on two top-secret military aircraft projects — the B-2 bomber and the F-22, an all-purpose fighter. He wasn't happy at Boeing, although he admitted this wasn't Boeing's fault; he simply had not yet found a career niche that he would fit into and also enjoy.

He resigned and began taking support calls for Autodesk, the world leader in designing computer software for engineers. While at Boeing, Jarvis had become familiar with Autodesk's flagship product, AutoCAD, which engineers used to make drawings. AutoCAD, for example, was the software that Boeing used for the wide-bodied 777, the first airliner to be designed on a computer instead of with conventional drawings.

"Supporting Autodesk products provided a transition from engineering to software for me," Jarvis related, "because I could speak to design engineers and knew how they needed to use software. Over time I became less of an engineer and more of a software businessperson. At Autodesk, if you were bright, aggressive, and ambitious, you could really move forward, whereas in engineering it was all about seniority and tenure."

So Jarvis's transient career took him from Autodesk to a succession of other firms that added to his expertise, not only in software but also in its application to the Internet. The latter included Destinations.com, a travel marketing firm that hired Jarvis to run its business development and to secure new website marketing accounts. He spent a year doing this without realizing that he was opening a door to an opportunity he never dreamed would come along.

Just as Jarvis was getting bored with the travel destination company, John Kelly was talking to Bob Reeder about moving *alaskaair.com* into hitherto unexplored territory. What he was looking for, Kelly subsequently told an officers' planning session, was someone with sales experience as well as technical knowledge, specifically to market a more versatile website.

The job requirements might as well have been Steve Jarvis's résumé, and when Jarvis was recruited he immediately became staff vice president of a new department called E-Commerce. That very title reflected the belief of both Kelly and Reeder that the website had commercial possibilities that would supplement its customer convenience value. In effect, the website became a new channel for travel distribution business that had been the almost exclusive territory of travel agencies.

Jarvis recalled that Kelly used to rib him about his use of Internet jargon. "The other officers don't understand all this high-tech language," Kelly complained. "You might as well be speaking Greek."

"You think *you're* having trouble?" Jarvis thought. "You have no idea what *I'm* going through. The airline industry has more unfamiliar terms and acronyms than the computer industry."

"My first job at Alaska," Jarvis recalled, "was to rattle the cage of the traditional travel distribution business. I had skills that didn't make sense to a lot of companies, but they sure made sense to Alaska. So-called travel distribution is simply how you sell airline seats. I believe Alaska's leadership liked the fact that I would break old industry norms without even knowing I was doing it."

When Jarvis came on board, there were three ways to sell those seats: two of them traditional, the third a brand-new channel that Jarvis was directed to take way beyond its current state of development. Kelly had specific percentage goals for travel booked using the Internet for the near future, and it was Jarvis who was tasked with meeting those goals.

The first way to sell seats was through travel agents. The second was via an 800 number that reached more than a thousand reservations agents in the carrier's Seattle and Phoenix call centers. The third and newest way was through the Internet. Jarvis's job was to devise and manage the distribution strategy for all three channels. The goal was to generate the most revenue at the lowest cost, while achieving the maximum customer convenience. And the Internet provided both cost savings and the best customer interface.

"What Bob Reeder and his people did," Jarvis recounted, "was to develop the technology that allowed customers who were browsing on the Internet to connect with our inventory. His team did the code work, and my job was to market it."

Cost effective? Efficient? Successful? In 1999, the year Jarvis joined Alaska and when *alaskaair.com* was just four years old, the Internet produced about $90 million, amounting to only 5 percent of the airline's revenues that year. By October 2007, annual revenue from the Internet exceeded $1 billion, and accounted for one-half of its total revenues.

Throughout the website's functional growth and mushrooming viability, no one in the officer ranks, from John Kelly on down, ever lost sight of its potential impact on employees who feared that computer technology would threaten their jobs. Jarvis recalled discussing further expansion plans with a group of call-center employees on the occasion of the website's fifth anniversary. One remarked, with open concern, "You have to understand that *we're* the big revenue producers for the company, so you guys should be looking to us as the place to grow revenue."

"That's not actually true," Jarvis replied. "In five years *alaskaair.com* has gone from generating 5 percent of our revenue to 35 percent and now outbooks the call centers by three to one. Have we furloughed any reservations agents over that time? No, we haven't. Without the Internet, Alaska would not have had the capacity to grow efficiently in the last decade. In addition, the job of the reservations agent has changed from one primarily of sales to one of customer service, one of supporting customers who are shopping on *alaskaair.com*."

Any resentment on the part of call-center and airport-counter employees paled in comparison to how travel agents viewed Alaska's increasing reliance on the Internet. Traditionally, passengers had been the customers of travel agents, not of the airlines themselves, because most bookings were made through travel agencies. For a brief time, Reeder said, the travel agencies retaliated by refusing to book clients on Alaska. But this form of revenge lost its steam when all carriers adopted Internet ticket sales.

Then came the even more menacing *alaskaair.com* innovation that incorporated the sales tool that allowed the website to become its own travel agency. The Reeder/Jarvis team expanded the website's services by adding the capability of making hotel and car-rental reservations. Customers could now book passage on cruise ships as part of a vacation package, and even check the weather at their destinations.

To paraphrase that old Oldsmobile advertising slogan, "This is not your father's website." It was really an invasion of what was once the almost exclusive province of travel agencies, and the resentment swelled from grumbling to angry protests.

Yet Alaska did not want to sever relations with an industry that was still a valued partner. Its answer to the understandable storm of complaints was, to quote Jarvis: "We told them, in effect, your major job has always been to aggregate and provide travel information to customers. This was the principal value you brought to your client relationships. But, thanks to the Internet, customers can now do that for themselves. Now your job goes beyond simply providing information to providing expertise, such as where to stay or what to do at a destination.

"The really good travel agencies understood this," Jarvis said, and pointed out that Alaska had no intention of flying solo, ignoring travel agencies completely. "We work very closely with corporate travel agencies and the clients they serve, such as companies like Microsoft, Starbucks, and Boeing."

There were some at the officer level, though, who were concerned that face-to-face contact with customers might suffer from these high-tech innovations. John Kelly didn't share their concern, for the simple reason that he thought those innovations enhanced the airline's traditional rapport with the public, rather than damaging it. Besides, as Jarvis himself pointed out, no officer with a negative attitude toward computers and/or the Internet was likely to keep bucking Kelly on the subject.

"Over the years," Jarvis said, "he gave me a lesson on how to get support from the top for a new initiative, and how important that support is if you want it to succeed."

So, from Image to electronic ticketing to *alaskaair.com* to e-commerce, the Reeder/Jarvis communications juggernaut rolled on toward two more key projects.

One is Customer Relationship Management (or CRM), which at this writing still has years of development ahead. Its goal is to create a customer information infrastructure that enables Alaska to know its customers better, to market and serve them more personally and individually.

Another project was originally called Voice Recognition, a name later changed to Natural Language (NL), which more properly describes its function. NL, which went into operation in 2006, is aimed at helping customers who lack either immediate or any access whatsoever to a computer. Natural Language allows them to use the telephone to obtain the same services provided by the website. In effect, the human voice takes over the role of a computer keyboard, with voice commands replacing the keys.

Yet even this latest project doesn't render obsolete what has been far more important than any magical new technology: the human beings who created and maintain the Alaska Airlines Spirit, with its tradition of superior customer service. Even a high-tech advocate like Steve Jarvis not only freely admits this but also emphasizes its importance.

"There are still customers out there who need personal assistance, and they get it from very special people," Jarvis said. He cited complicated itineraries or irregular circumstances such as weather problems that result in last-minute cancellations or missed connections. "That's when customer service

can save the day as no computer can. The Internet and kiosks allow our own
very special people to be more readily available in situations where personal
assistance is needed. More and more, the call centers and airport agents have
been supporting the Internet instead of fighting it."

And because history is written by people, not historians, it is time
to meet some of Alaska's special people, from customer-service and
reservations agents to maintenance technicians. From the unseen world
of dispatchers to a baggage handler who invented a new in-flight movie
system. From those unheralded folk who run the cargo side of the airline to
one of Alaska's early female pilots. From a flight attendant who could be a
professional entertainer to a woman who taught the entire company how to
handle grief. They are the heart of the airline.

CHAPTER TWENTY

A Few Characters
with Character

Alaska Airlines by the end of 2006 employed more than 9,500 people who moved more than 17 million passengers and 75 thousand tons of freight between such distant locations as Boston, Nome, Mexico City, and Seattle. That, most would say, is all in a day's work, but not just anyone can warm a baby's bottle, calm a first-time flier during turbulence, serve meals at 35,000 feet, coax an escaped cat back into a travel container, or fly Copper River salmon from Alaska to Newark and have it arrive fresh. Alaska has always sought, hired, and trained uniquely qualified people for all aspects of its operations, from selling tickets to fixing and flying airplanes.

To get some sense of their special brand of dedication and service, one only needs to listen to some of the stories told by the airline's frontline troops. Meet Jacquie Witherrite, the quintessential customer-service agent (CSA): personable, unfailingly friendly, always helpful, and unflappable even in the face of the most daunting crisis or the angriest customer.

Probably the most uninhibited of the more than 120 people interviewed for this book, only the indomitable Jacquie would have freely admitted the unusual circumstances under which she was hired in 1972, launching more than three decades of exemplary service to Alaska Airlines. Having applied to what was then the personnel department, she was told that someone would call if anything opened up. When the call came, however, her seven-year-old son answered the phone and asked who was calling.

"This is Mr. Sykes of Alaska Airlines," he told the child.

"Mommy can't talk to you right now," the little boy solemnly informed Sykes. "She's in the shower with Daddy and the bathroom door is locked. They probably won't be out for a while."

A few minutes later, Jacquie emerged from the bathroom and asked her son who had called.

"Some man from Alaska Airlines, but I forgot his name. Anyway, I told him you were taking a shower with Daddy."

She remembered the name only too well. With a face the color of an overripe tomato, she called Sykes and started to apologize, but never finished the first sentence.

"You're hired," he interrupted. "Want to know why?"

"Yes," she answered feebly.

"Two reasons. First, you've got your kid well trained. Second, you've got your priorities straight."

On that note of a little boy's honesty and a mother's acute embarrassment, Witherrite began working for Alaska. She was initially hired on a temporary basis for only six weeks to replace a woman undergoing kidney surgery. Those six weeks, of course, turned into a career of unusual longevity, marked by her refusal to ever get stale or cynical about her job or to alter her can-do attitude toward her multi-faceted mission as a CSA. That mission over time would include damage control, extra effort as a matter of course, occasional improvisation, and a consistently exemplary form of customer service that in the military would be called "above and beyond the call of duty."

Witherrite could be blunt without offending, and was ever patient with even the most demanding customers, often by simply making them laugh or smile at the situation. One such encounter took place at Sea-Tac, when a passenger insisted that he sit next to a friend on a flight on which the only empty seats were in the lavatories. "I don't see why you can't seat us together," he argued.

"Well, sir," Jacquie chirped, "this flight is absolutely full. So I'll make an announcement asking all the passengers to move so you can sit with your friend."

The passenger blushed and mumbled, "Aw, that's okay — don't bother."

Among Jacquie's many counterparts was Lenore Small, an agent in Alaska's Lost and Found office at Sea-Tac. She was confronted one night with three lost items of an unusual nature: three nuns in traditional habit, looking tired, desperate, and lost. Small got their story from the Mother Superior, who had arrived with the other two nuns on an Alaska Airlines flight from San Francisco that same morning. They had been assigned to a convent in the Seattle area, and were supposed to have been met by someone from their new residence. But their ride never showed up, it was now past the dinner hour, and to make matters worse, none of the trio could remember the name of the convent.

Lenore sent for Jacquie, and the two of them called every Catholic church in the area before finally finding the right one, the Palisades Retreat. One problem: the nuns by mistake had arrived a day early, and it was now too late for anyone to come get them. It was at this point that Lenore performed above and beyond. "My shift is over now," she told Jacquie. "I'll call the retreat back, get directions, and drive them there myself." She proceeded to do that, although the trip was interrupted by another act of mercy when she learned that they hadn't eaten all day. Small pulled into Salty's, a popular Seattle-area seafood restaurant, only to be told by the hostess that the kitchen was closed for the night.

"Look," Lenore said desperately, "I'm with Alaska Airlines, I've got three starving nuns in my car, they haven't had anything to eat all day, and isn't there something you can find to feed them?"

The hostess took one look at those three tired faces and surrendered. "Tell you what," she said. "The main dining room is closed, but if they're willing to sit in the bar, I'll have the cook warm up some clam chowder."

Small not only paid for the soup, but also ordered up some sherry, and watched — with great satisfaction mixed with awe — as the three nuns kept lacing the steaming chowder with generous portions of sherry. When they finally arrived at the convent, the Mother Superior thanked Lenore profusely, then added with a shy smile, "You know, my dear, I haven't had so much fun since I entered the convent 16 years ago."

Incidents like that were instrumental in helping Alaska Airlines build an amazingly loyal customer base that has survived even the most trying times and cutbacks. Jeff Cacy, introduced earlier, found that out as a young sales agent in Fairbanks when Alaska Airlines launched an early version of its Mileage Plan, called the Gold and Travel program. Cacy received a call one day from an elderly woman who introduced herself as a resident of Cordova. Her voice was calm, yet Cacy sensed she was trying hard to keep her composure.

"I'm in Seattle right now," she informed him. "I brought my husband to a hospital here. He's always flown on Alaska."

"Is there some problem with your account?" Cacy inquired.

"Oh, no. You see, he just died and I have to take his body back to Cordova. He loved your airline and I . . . I was wondering if I could get mileage credit for his last flight on Alaska. I mean from . . . from Seattle to Cordova."

Cacy didn't wait to check with any higher authority on this unusual request. "Absolutely," he said instantly, and then helped the widow make the necessary arrangements. He told the story later to Bill McKnight, then vice president of marketing, who referred to the incident on the occasion of the airline receiving a *Condé Nast Traveler* magazine award. Several newspapers picked up the story, which spread quickly throughout Alaska and the nation.

Often it has been touching things, such as a pilot taking the time to help a child, that have distinguished so many Alaska Airlines employees. At other times, it has been a truly poignant action, like Sandy Robertson, a CSA in Anchorage, providing aid to a customer beset by tragedy.

Robertson was checking in a sad-faced Eskimo woman who asked for a seat next to her daughter. Sandy asked where her daughter was, and she murmured, "She is already on the plane."

This didn't make sense, as Robertson knew that no one had boarded the flight yet. Then, as she noticed that the woman's eyes were filled with tears, she realized the truth. The daughter *was* on the plane, because she had died, and her body was being transported home.

Sandy assigned her a seat, and blocked out the seat next to her. "I gave you an aisle seat, and the seat next to you is for your daughter," she said softly. Then she added, "I want you to know how sorry I am."

The woman nodded, then whispered, "Thank you for what you just did."

Gus Webb had been a ground operations agent with Alaska Airlines in Anchorage for almost 30 years when, shortly after he retired, he was stricken with brain cancer. He ended up at a special cancer center hospital in Georgia, where every form of treatment failed to halt the malignancy. As his powers of speech gradually faded, he began whispering, over and over, the only five words he seemed capable of uttering: *"I want to go home . . . I want to go home."*

His wife, Marie, confided this desperate request to friends, and a delegation of his old comrades in ground operations flew down to Georgia to see Gus. They included manager Steve Carlisle, Jerry Holliman, Bill Gould, and Sonny Carlisle. They, too, were moved by Gus's barely audible plea and talked to Marie Webb about it. They all knew that Gus was too sick to fly home on any airline and would require a special medical evacuation (medevac) airplane, which seemed out of the question. A medical charter flight from Georgia to Anchorage would cost thousands of dollars.

But it wasn't out of the question for Steve Carlisle. Without saying anything to Marie Webb, he called Rexanne Forbes, then Alaska's assistant vice president of customer service, and explained the situation. "If we can find a medevac plane," he continued, "could Alaska Airlines advance us the money to charter it? Then we'll organize some fund-raisers to pay the company back."

The wheels of collaboration began to turn. Forbes was confident that Bill MacKay, Alaska's vice president of public affairs, would support the plan. He was always sympathetic and willing to lend a hand, if at all possible.

Next, Forbes went straight to a source she figured might provide the most reasonable deal for transportation: Jim Vande Voort, president of Era Aviation, one of Alaska's most reliable alliance partners within the state. Yes, Vande Voort told her, Era Aviation had a top-notch medevac aircraft, a fast Learjet. Yes, the airline would charter it to Alaska for what amounted to peanuts; Alaska would have to pay only fuel and crew costs. The airplane, however, was under lease to Providence Hospital's LifeGuard program in Anchorage.

"I'll call them and see what I can do," Vande Voort promised.

Within hours, Rexanne Forbes was on the phone to Steve Carlisle with the news: not only was Era Aviation donating the airplane, but Providence LifeGuard was going to furnish the medical personnel to accompany the flight as well. That left only the fuel and crew costs to be covered, and Ed White, vice president of customer service, informed Carlisle that he had talked to Bill MacKay and the airline would pay those expenses.

Only then did Carlisle tell Marie Webb about the plan. The doctors in Roswell warned her that Gus was not likely to survive the flight, but she didn't care. Gus was going home. All the way to Anchorage, as he drifted in and out of consciousness, "Hang in there, Gus" messages kept pouring into the Learjet's radio.

The medevac flight landed in Anchorage on May 29, 2000. Gus was awake, and with Marie and Carlisle by his side, he looked out and saw who was welcoming him home: scores of Alaska Airlines pilots, flight attendants, and ground personnel.

Gus Webb defied the odds not only by surviving the trip home, but also by staying alive long enough to fill his remaining days with amazing bursts of energy and clarity. For the next three weeks, he received visits from more than a hundred friends and relatives, many of whom flew in from distant cities, and scores who couldn't come sent cards.

Gus Webb died on June 19, 2000, not surrounded by faceless and nameless doctors and nurses in a far-off Georgia hospital, but in his beloved Alaska.

Marie Webb remarked that she didn't know how to show her gratitude for what the people of two airlines had done to bring Gus home. She got her answer from something that Jacquie Witherrite wrote for "Wing Tips," a customer-service newsletter column: "You see, Marie, Gus gave all of *us* a gift — the chance to help. Slogans like Caring, Alaska Spirit, Can Do, and Doing the Right Thing took on a little more meaning."

Captain Al Brunelle came from Braniff in 1992 with experience in and out of the cockpit that would benefit both Alaska Airlines and its employees. At Alaska he noticed that company employees were always passing a hat or holding bake sales to raise money to assist employees faced, like the Webbs, with calamities.

At Braniff, employees had established a 501(c)(3) nonprofit organization so that they could directly aid less fortunate fellow employees struck by unexpected and catastrophic expenses. Brunelle presented the idea to Alaska Airlines. Keep in mind that this was 1992 and Ray Vecci was looking for savings, not additional expenses. Vecci, however, shared Brunelle's enthusiasm for an employee fund and appropriated $10,000 as seed money to form the new organization, the Alaska Airlines Employee Assistance Fund (EAF).

The EAF was established as an independent organization, separate from the airline. Brunelle became head of the 12-member board, which solicits donations from employees and manages the fund's expenses and operation. Since its inception, funding has come from employees who have agreed to contribute at least $1 from each paycheck. The fund has become a model, garnering attention from several other airlines and the City of Seattle, which have requested help in establishing similar organizations for the benefit of their employees.

While the EAF provides money to employees in need, one employee's contribution was actually priceless. It was a kidney that would save a coworker's life. Carolyn Jenkins, a longtime reservations agent, made this extraordinary donation to a fellow employee.

Reservations agent Hetty Gaeb was on an organ-donor list and had been receiving dialysis treatments three times a week for several years. Jenkins watched as her colleague lost ground and grew weaker. "I just kept thinking somebody should do something," said Jenkins, "and I decided it had to be me."

Jenkins had two critical and very personal things she could offer her colleague: a matching blood type and the will to do something selfless. After a conversation with her husband, Jenkins approached Gaeb and offered her a kidney.

"I just screamed," recalled Gaeb. "It was a miracle. I had an angel at my table."

Following exhaustive testing, the two entered the hospital. Several days later they were released. Gaeb was thrilled. "I've gained 17 hours each week just not having to be hooked up to the dialysis machine." In fact, she gained a whole new lease on life.

Jenkins later retired from the airline, but has left an unmatched living legacy, Hetty Gaeb.

Dispatchers are the unsung untanglers of airline traffic. They schedule crews, airplanes, and gates, and when a flight is delayed or canceled, it is the dispatcher who is charged with making a silk purse out of a sow's ear. The average passenger hardly knows they exist, but pilots listen to them and almost invariably bow to their judgment.

They belie the old Mark Twain saying that "everybody talks about the weather, but nobody does anything about it." Dispatchers can't really do one blessed thing about the weather, but they are enormously skilled at trying hard to compensate for weather-caused disruptions to airline schedules. They can juggle like a circus performer, shift direction like an all-pro halfback, and somehow turn chaos into reasonable order like a magician pulling rabbits out of a supposedly empty hat. Significantly — and this is no joke — many dispatchers love to do jigsaw puzzles, and some of them gave up chess because they found that it was getting too easy.

The public often associates dispatch with air traffic control, yet while ATC work is hectic and tough, dispatch in some ways can be just as hard.

ATC centers deal with traffic in one specific area; dispatchers deal with their airline's nationwide traffic. This was less significant at Alaska when it was small, but it grew in importance as the airline expanded into a major transcontinental carrier, dispatching hundreds of flights a day at Sea-Tac International alone.

Flight schedules being the most vulnerable component of airline operations, dispatchers don't always succeed. Not, as we have already pointed out, when a couple of delayed flights can cause a chain reaction whose effects are felt for an entire day or even longer.

Jerry Cutler was an Alaska dispatcher for more than a quarter of a century and a veteran of some of the worst operational crises in the airline's history. His nomadic early years with Alaska were typical of young rookie employees in that era, starting out at Skagway and then moving to Ketchikan, learning almost every facet of airline operations along the way. Although hired as a weather observer, he also worked in freight, customer service, and baggage handling. This was not unusual for employees at a small Alaska station. Cutler was still a long way from finding his eventual niche in dispatch, but he got plenty of exposure to the weather problems that surfaced frequently in Southeast Alaska.

Cutler became a certified dispatcher in 1981, joining six other dispatchers at a time when the airline was operating only 14 airplanes. "There was one other dispatcher my age," he recalled, "but the other five were veterans with years of experience. Everything we did was manual. We were making out flight plans by hand, a very laborious process, and we began pushing for computerizing the dispatch procedure, along with getting more timely control of flights. Gradually we established the airline's first operations control system, which is known today as System Operations Control."

The major difficulty that dispatchers encountered during the 1980s, however, was that the airline's growth outstripped the development of the technical tools they needed to keep up with such growth. Cutler cited as an example the 1989 San Francisco earthquake, the second major challenge he had to face as a dispatcher. "We were still doing everything on paper," he related, "and when some calamity like an earthquake or prolonged fog or snow disrupted your flight operations, you had to keep track of everything in your head because there was no screen display to do it for you.

"When that earthquake hit San Francisco, I ended up dealing with about 50 airplanes, each flying a half-dozen segments every day, and somehow they all had to connect tomorrow and the next day. In addition, there was the complexity of operating different types of aircraft, some of them completely wrong for a segment, and requiring another type of airplane that may or may not have been quickly available."

Cutler would never forget that fall day in 1989. He had been promoted to director of flight control (DFC), supervising dispatching, crew scheduling, and maintenance control. He shared that position with a colleague, John Gracie, because at the time, flight control was under two DFCs, each working a four-days-on, four-days-off shift. That meant being on call for 96 consecutive hours.

Cutler was working the swing shift when the earthquake hit San Francisco, just before the start of the 1989 San Francisco-Oakland World Series. Maintenance control had requested permission to bring a television set into flight operations, and Cutler gave his permission but warned, "Keep it out of sight — this is a workplace."

That was the luckiest decision he ever made. The quake cut off all communication with San Francisco International Airport (SFO). No one in dispatch was even aware that it had happened until someone in maintenance control who had been watching the TV set rushed out and yelled to Cutler, "Jerry, you'd better come take a look. There's been a big earthquake at Candlestick Park!"

Cutler raced into maintenance control, took one hasty look, and began pushing figurative panic buttons. He was still trying to reach someone in SFO operations when Joyce Silvano, one of his own dispatchers, interrupted his efforts to tell him she had made contact with SFO through a San Francisco airport pay phone.

Cutler's first order was to keep someone on that SFO pay phone all night if necessary, because it was vital to maintain communication. His second order was for Silvano to pass the word to Alaska's station personnel in the stricken city: "If you can get flights out, do it." His third order was to keep crew scheduling and maintenance control in both the Bay Area and Seattle staffed as long as required.

The situation was critical and actually worsened when the weather turned marginal throughout Northern California, putting pressure on the alternate Bay Area airports, Oakland and San Jose. Cutler, Gracie, and their team went into an expert juggling act, diverting flights destined for San Francisco temporarily north to Portland and, later, even to Seattle. Alaska was the first airline to resume normal operations in the Bay Area.

Cutler also recalled that Portland was often a life-saving haven on various occasions when Sea-Tac was closed by fog or snow. In fact, in December 1985, fog essentially shut down Sea-Tac for *two weeks*. Because it is virtually at sea level, Sea-Tac is especially vulnerable to fog, and dealing with that prolonged '85 mess amounted to a dress rehearsal for handling the effects of the later San Francisco quake. Seattle's prolonged fog problem had forced Portland to close one of its runways and use it as a parking lot to accommodate the armada of airplanes diverted from Seattle.

Alaska's Head-Up Guidance Systems (HGS) — fondly referred to as the "Fog Buster" by airline employees and customers alike — as well as Required Navigation Performance (RNP) and Enhanced Ground Proximity Warning System (EGPWS), were heartily welcomed by the dispatchers, for those high-tech innovations dramatically reduced the frequency of diverted flights. Somewhat less publicized, yet also welcomed, was the improved communications system between Alaska's flights and dispatch, first developed by Dave Zehrung (Chapter 6) when he was an electronics expert in Alaska's flight operations group. Alaska continually enhanced this system over the years.

That network, giving dispatchers immediate voice contact with any en route Alaska Airlines flight, was of enormous help when Mount Redoubt, south of Anchorage, erupted in 1989, sending volcanic ash thousands of feet into the atmosphere. Such ash is an infrequent yet potentially deadly menace to jet aircraft because it can be sucked into turbine engines and instantly clog them, causing a shutdown. In 1982, a British Airways 747 flew into an unreported cloud of volcanic ash at an altitude of 37,000 feet over the Indian Ocean and all four engines failed. The big jet dropped more than 25,000 feet before the crew miraculously got the engines restarted in time to avoid disaster. The incident taught civil aviation a lesson, and when Mount Redoubt erupted, all carriers except one either diverted or canceled Anchorage flights. The exception was Alaska. Through innovative communications, its pilots kept advising dispatch of the exact location, altitude, and drift direction of the ash cloud, so flights going in and out of Anchorage could simply avoid it.

At one point, the Anchorage ticket counter had more than 400 standbys from other carriers trying to get on Alaska flights. And Alaska's ticket counters in Seattle also were jammed with people trying to get back to Anchorage. Once again, the airline's people had stamped that "can do" slogan with an emphatic "we did it."

Alaska Airlines is well populated with flight attendants possessing very special qualities. Like CSAs, flight attendants enjoy the company of people.

Many have a sense of humor that captivates even the most travel-weary customer. Others simply transmit to every passenger an obvious love of job and pride in their profession and their airline.

A Roman poet named Horace, who lived in the first century B.C., had a definition of humor that could be applied to flight attendants of the 21st century. "A jest," he wrote, "often decides matters of importance more effectually and happily than seriousness." Uninhibited natural comedians such as Bambi Coons and Marty Calhoun fit that definition to a T. They loved to make passengers laugh, but also to make them listen. Obviously, few can match their talents, but even cabin announcements that somehow impart friendliness and a touch of informality do a better job than safety briefings rattled off like boredom being poured out of a can.

Bambi Coons was senior flight attendant on one Seattle-San Francisco trip, and her spiel from pre-takeoff to landing was so remarkable that an Alaska Airlines employee who had never flown with Bambi before wrote down her tongue-in-cheek announcements almost verbatim. In abbreviated form, here's what came over the public address system, starting with her announcement as the airplane left the gate:

"Hello and welcome aboard Alaska Airlines Flight 468. If you're going to San Francisco, you're in the right place. If you're *not* going to San Francisco, you're in for an awfully long evening.

"We'd like to tell you about the important safety features on this MD-83. The most important features are . . . (long, dramatic pause) the flight attendants. So please pay attention to them.

"In the event of loss of cabin pressure, those baggy things now being demonstrated will drop down over your head. You stick it over your nose and mouth like the flight attendants are demonstrating. The bag won't inflate, but there's oxygen there, I promise you.

"If you're sitting next to a small child, or someone who's acting like a small child, please do us all a favor and put *your* mask on first. If you're traveling with two or more small children, please take a moment to decide which one is your favorite, help that one first, and then work your way down.

"There is no smoking in the cabin on this flight. There also is no smoking in the lavatories. If we see smoke coming out of a lavatory, we'll assume you're on fire and put you out. This is a free service Alaska provides.

"But there *are* two smoking sections on the airplane, one outside each wing exit. We show movies on those sections, and let's see — the movie tonight is . . . just a moment . . . oh, here it is. *Gone with the Wind.*"

Marty Calhoun earned his own measure of fame as the airline's own version of Dana Carvey or Rich Little, the great comic impressionists. Calhoun was self-taught and could imitate celebrity voices so skillfully that he could have been a professional entertainer himself.

He had a counterpart at Southwest, Jeff Simpson, another skilled impressionist who was once called "America's funniest flight attendant." Their repertoire is similar.

Yet it would be hard to find anyone, including the talented Simpson, who had a more varied routine than Calhoun's. His subjects have included Arnold Schwarzenegger, Jimmy Stewart, John Wayne, cooking guru Julia Child, Cary Grant, Ronald Reagan, Bill Clinton, Liberace, Alfred Hitchcock, CBS commentator Andy Rooney, and Mickey Mouse, along with most of his Disney friends.

Calhoun began imitating voices when he was only 10 years old, starting when he watched Ed Sullivan's variety show on television. He used to call it "Sullivision," and drove his parents crazy with 'We've got a great, *great* show for you tonight, folks,' Sullivan's standard opening line.

He never met Dana Carvey or Rich Little, but he did meet Mel Blanc, the "man of a thousand voices" and the voice of Bugs Bunny and many other Looney Tunes characters. "Mel Blanc was my idol and role model," Calhoun admitted. "I met him just before he died, and right after I joined Alaska in 1985."

Calhoun's earlier background was non-aeronautical. He had worked for two cruise lines, Holland America and Carnival, selling shore tours to cruise-ship passengers. When crew members provided the entertainment on one night of every cruise, Marty began contributing his impressionist act.

A friend of his in Miami, a National Airlines flight attendant, got him interested in an airline career, and Calhoun worked briefly for two British carriers serving the Caribbean area before applying to Alaska.

"I thought I was going to be hired as a ticket agent," Marty related, "but after one interview with John Kelly when he was vice president of marketing, I became a flight attendant.

"He asked me about my cruise-ship experience, and I mentioned how the crew members occasionally provided the entertainment and that I had participated with my celebrity imitations. I did a couple for him, and he hired me on the spot."

Calhoun went beyond mere imitations. He scripted each routine, combining amazing mimicry with the humor of an expert comedy writer; it was not just the uncanny sound-alike voice, but *what* the voice was saying.

A few samples . . .

He had Jimmy Stewart, one of his favorites, doing the safety briefings. While funny, they never made light of the importance of the message. Calhoun was proud of the fact that a number of passengers told him, "You know, I laughed, but that was the first time I ever really *listened* to those messages."

Another Calhoun favorite has been California Governor Arnold Schwarzenegger. In that famous Teutonic accent, Calhoun informed everyone on board, "Alaska Airways is going through some bad financial times, just like California. So ven ve land, everyone must give the pilot vun dollar so ve can go back to fiscal responsibility and into the green."

Calhoun built his imitation of Bill Clinton around the former president's flurry of pardons just before he left the White House. Marty had him pardoning everyone on the airplane, then added, in Clinton's familiar Arkansas drawl: "I am issuing pardon number one hundred and seven to the crew of this airplane, excusing them for causing our delayed departure."

There are a few celebrities Calhoun has tried to do but didn't feel he had their voices down pat. He tried Rod Serling of *Twilight Zone* fame, but couldn't get that distinctive voice quite right, either. "Probably just as well," Calhoun concluded. "I don't know what would have happened if I'd told everyone, 'Hope you didn't make any special plans for after arrival, because this airplane is going into . . . the Twilight Zone.' "

Only once did he get a complaint from a passenger who objected to his imitations as "unprofessional." He sent the complaint to John Kelly, who told Calhoun to forget it. "Marty," Kelly said, "there's always going to be someone like that, so just keep up the good work."

That lone complaint didn't bother Calhoun as much as the time he imitated a celebrity he didn't realize was on the same flight. It happened to be Liberace, and as soon as another flight attendant told Calhoun the pianist was aboard, Marty rushed over and apologized. "No apology is necessary," Liberace assured him. "You sounded just like me. You were great."

In other words, personality counts just as much as humor. Personifying this was Alaska Airlines flight attendant Tanya Roberts. Like Bambi Coons, Roberts considered every passenger a personal guest. Born in Atlantic City but raised in Fairbanks, Tanya became known among her coworkers for having taken part in an unusual crew-scheduling crisis, unusual because you could count the number of times it has happened since the jet age began on the fingers of one hand.

The 1958 introduction of aircraft carrying more than 100 passengers and larger cabin crews also dictated the necessity of never staffing the jets with an inordinate number of rookie flight attendants. Flight-attendant training on jets was harder than on the piston-powered aircraft, with far more emphasis on safety. So the universally adopted industry policy was to never have more than two first-timers on the same airplane, and preferably not more than one.

But Roberts and three of her classmates were summoned to crew scheduling only a few hours after their graduation ceremony in 1978. They were informed that they would all be working the same flight the very next morning, a 12-hour puddle-jumping 727-100 trip from Seattle through Southeast Alaska via Juneau and Ketchikan.

It seems the regular crew had arrived in Seattle the night before so late that they could not legally fly the next morning. There would be no senior flight attendant to help them, not even one, although a supervisor tried in vain to find one. Alaska didn't have that many flight attendants in those days, so reserves were not readily available.

Roberts never forgot that first flight. Her classmates became her flight crew — Kelly Milan, Laura Gillette, and Bruce Catano. Gillette was the only one who had any previous airline experience, having worked for Wien, so she did the announcements.

The unlucky quartet didn't have their uniforms yet, so they had to borrow odds and ends from sympathetic off-duty colleagues. Tanya was wearing a blue and orange outfit, Kelly tan and orange, and Laura had to settle for a skirt that was two sizes too large.

The captain, Chuck Bates, took pity on the four rookies. After takeoff, he kept in contact with a flight-attendant supervisor in Seattle, who told him what the rookies were supposed to do and what kind of service was offered on the flight. This was fine for their normal routine, but it didn't take into account an unexpected crisis. Bruce, who had been a bartender, took over the beverage service and was doing fine until he spilled tomato juice on a passenger's jacket.

No problem. They had been taught in training to rub off such spots with soda water. This wiped away the spot but left the jacket wet, so one of the gallant rookies — and for charity's sake, we shall not reveal the name — suggested putting the jacket in the galley oven so it would dry faster, a solution that was *not* taught in training. The oven *did* dry it faster. It also burned the jacket.

Thus did Tanya Roberts's flying career, which at this writing has lasted almost 30 years, get off to an interesting start. Since then, Roberts has earned not only the respect of colleagues and customers alike, but also the appreciation of her counterparts on all U.S. carriers for her involvement with the Black Flight Attendants Association (BFAA). An African-American, she has encountered some prejudice along the way, not from fellow employees but from a few passengers, and there were times when she would return home from a trip in tears because of racial slurs. "Never from Alaskans themselves, however," she added. "They always have been tolerant. But now and then you meet somebody who's a little too condescending. I had a woman once remark, 'You know, 25 years ago you wouldn't have had this job.' I replied, 'Twenty-five years ago I was too young to have this job.' "

"You have to expect prejudice," Roberts said, "and try to turn it around, which is one of the BFAA's goals."

Proving that an airline career can take many turns was another flight attendant, Lin Jauhola, who decided to try a flying career after accumulating 23 years in three other jobs with the airline. Jauhola started out as a secretary in 1976, when Bruce Kennedy was still vice president of properties and Ron Cosgrave was running the airline. When Kennedy's secretary left, Lin became his secretary, and later went to work for Ray Vecci.

While she enjoyed being secretary to those two future CEOs, Jauhola tired of office work and became a CSA and close colleague of Jacquie Witherrite. When Jacquie began holding classes for new CSAs, Lin joined her as a fellow instructor. Starting a special school to train CSAs was Witherrite's idea. She had suggested it to Ray Vecci when he was CEO. Vecci told her he'd approve it if she invited him to attend a class so he could see for himself whether the school was worthwhile. He came to one of the first classes, and when it was over he told Jacquie, "I want you to take this show on the road. I want you to travel around the entire system and teach all our CSAs, veterans as well as rookies, what customer service is all about."

The CSA experience led to Jauhola's decision to become a flight attendant, and it is safe to say that she didn't need much training when it came to the do's and don'ts of handling airline customers. "The only difference is that you're either dealing with passengers on an airplane or on the ground," she pointed out. "The important thing is to remember that people don't get mad at you personally; they get angry at a situation."

Like all the more senior Alaska flight attendants, Jauhola mourned the post-9/11 decline in cabin meal service that had once won so many awards.

Yet to those who remembered the glory years, the necessity of reduced in-flight food and beverage service was merely a challenge to excel in other areas, such as simply making passengers feel welcome and comfortable.

On one flight she was working, Jauhola had a couple from Juneau who had been flying with Alaska since 1964. They still remembered the opulent Samovar Service with the Cossack hats and the Gay Nineties uniforms that were part of Golden Nugget Service.

"We felt real bad when you dropped meal service out of Juneau," the wife remarked. "But we're still going to the East Coast on Alaska, because we wouldn't go any other way."

Loyalty, it goes without saying, is something an airline earns. People like Lin Jauhola not only learned this, but also taught it.

Another flight attendant, Bob Hudson, shared with Bambi Coons the unusual background of having once worked as a cabin crew member on fire-fighting aircraft. He had another unusual quality: everyone at Alaska Airlines called him solely by his last name, Hudson. A great many flight attendants never knew his first name. He was also different in that he was something over six feet five inches in height.

His first flying job was with Evergreen, a charter airline that also operated a 727 firefighting airplane. After two years with Evergreen, he tried to land a flight-attendant job with scheduled carriers but was turned down because he was considered too tall. Ironically, the only airline that would hire him was one operating aircraft with small cabins, none other than Horizon. He spent five years there, three as a flight attendant and two as a supervisor, before Mary Kenison had him transferred over to Alaska as a supervisor. Which, in turn, gave him an interesting perspective from both points of view: that of the flight attendant, and that of the flight attendant's immediate superior.

When Hudson became a supervisor, he discovered there still was an atmosphere of animosity between a number of Alaska's flight attendants and management, much of it a residue of the bitter CHAOS dispute. Yet to his surprise, he found no evidence whatsoever that any ill feelings were carried over into job performance. "I've said for years," he emphasized, "that I have never known an Alaska Airlines flight attendant to take his or her anger, or their own personal troubles, out on our passengers."

As of 2005, shortly before Hudson left the company, each Alaska Airlines flight-attendant supervisor had an average of 212 people under his or her jurisdiction, a fairly high ratio by traditional industry standards.

So, generally speaking, Alaska's some 1,200 flight attendants are largely a self-disciplining, self-motivating group of people trying to maintain tradition and reputation. Their reward is invisible, yet powerfully tangible. It comes in the form of customer loyalty.

Do not think for one moment that Ray Prentice has had the worst job at Alaska Airlines, although many may well consider handling customer complaints to be aviation's equivalent of following a parade of circus elephants with a shovel and a plastic bag. Prentice, who was hired in 1988 to work in the airline's frequent-flier program, subsequently held positions in several departments. But through a succession of job changes and promotions, his most interesting and memorable experience has been in customer relations. He will never forget the up-and-down, feast-or-famine nature of this consumer-sensitive department, ranging from "I love Alaska Airlines" to "I'll never fly your crummy airline again."

The art of responding to angry airline customer complaints and/or unreasonable restitutional demands would frustrate the entire U.S. diplomatic corps. Prentice learned quickly that surviving in this frequently adversarial climate requires most of all a sense of humor, possibly the only effective way to avoid spending six months on a psychiatrist's couch.

This is why Prentice, like most people in airline customer relations, treasured a serious and totally justified gripe presented so humorously that corrective action was taken more eagerly than usual. So it is no wonder that he nominated the following complaint letter as the funniest and most effective of his career.

It was a one-sentence letter, with a photograph enclosed. It read:

Dear Alaska Airlines:

Where is my luggage?

The photograph was a snapshot of a woman passenger sitting forlornly in her underwear.

"When someone is that creative," Prentice said, "I want to talk to the customer as quickly as possible. I did in this case, found out that her husband had taken the picture, and she told me she really did love flying with us, but this time we had goofed. Her sense of humor made it easier for us to deal with her and rectify everything to her satisfaction." Prentice never did say if he was able to find her bag.

Prentice's associate in customer relations, Michelle Minor, compiled her own share of unforgettable letters, especially when they were kudos instead of complaints. One of her favorites came from a son whose father and mother were on an Alaska Airlines flight from Spokane to Phoenix. The father suffered a heart attack after the airplane left Spokane, and the captain made an emergency landing in Portland, Oregon.

Unfortunately, the father died before they landed, but the son's letter praised the flight attendants and the pilot for what they tried to do to keep him alive until professional medical help was available. Then he went on to voice his heartfelt thanks to the flight attendants and the ground crews at Portland who stayed with his mother during the crisis, keeping her occupied while others were trying to resuscitate her husband.

Then after customer relations was advised of the tragedy, Prentice sent a huge Harry and David gift basket to the family on behalf of the entire airline, and the flight's captain expressed his condolences with a card.

Later the son wrote to Prentice's office thanking everyone for the basket, and adding these words: "I have been in the travel industry for over 29 years, operating my own travel agency for 12 of those years. Although agencies and airlines have had their differences in recent years, our common ground has always been our customers. Alaska Airlines performed under pressure with compassion and class, and for that I shall be eternally grateful."

"I would say it's part of our culture that we don't publicize performances like that," Prentice commented. "I know for a fact that the flight attendants and pilots involved in similar incidents all asked us to keep them informed of the outcome because they wanted to send appropriate cards.

"Carrying a million passengers a month, with different backgrounds and a variety of medical conditions, we probably encounter in-flight health situations requiring us to go out of our way to help people a couple of times a month." This can entail an unscheduled landing, something done at the discretion of the captain.

Another Michelle Minor favorite letter: "My son-in-law is a six-foot-four gunnery sergeant in the U.S. Marines who was accompanying the body of a Marine buddy who had died in combat in Iraq. He was bringing him home on an Alaska Airlines flight to his parents in San Francisco for burial. Your crew moved him from coach to first class and did everything possible to make his difficult journey home easier."

Children can be the most surprising category of passengers, sometimes displaying maturity and judgment beyond their years. Prentice's sister, Laura, an Alaska Airlines flight attendant, witnessed this quality on a flight from

Seattle to Orlando, and it was an incident that also got parents involved.

A male coach passenger was sitting next to a pair of unaccompanied minors, two boys aged 7 and 12. He was carrying a small bag, and about an hour and a half after takeoff he asked the children, "How would you kids like to see my fireworks?"

The older boy took a look and recognized the contents for what they were: *real* fireworks. How the man had smuggled them past security was never disclosed. With great presence of mind, the 12-year-old said, "Excuse me, I gotta go to the bathroom," and headed for the rear lavatories, where he told a flight attendant about the fireworks.

Meanwhile, the passenger asked the seven-year-old if he wanted to smoke a cigarette with him. The younger boy announced he also had to go to the bathroom and informed a flight attendant that the man was going to smoke a cigarette with a bag of explosives on his lap.

A deadheading male flight attendant trained in martial arts happened to be on the plane, and he quickly put the bag owner under restraints. The flight was diverted to Tulsa, where police took charge of the passenger, but the diversion and subsequent arrest delayed the flight for so long that the breakfast eggs had spoiled.

Now the flight attendants had a planeload of about 150 hungry passengers and no airline caterer was available. American, which was handling the diverted flight at the airport, had a maintenance base at Tulsa, but there was no food-service facility other than an airport restaurant.

Laura called her brother, Ray, who gave her an emergency flight operations credit card number that she and the captain used to buy as many sandwiches as they could. They fell far short of the required 150 they needed, so Laura explained the situation on the cabin public-address system. "We were able to buy only 50 sandwiches," she explained, "so we're going to cut each sub into four sandwiches so everyone will at least get something to eat."

Only one passenger objected, a man in first class who loudly complained that he had paid for first-class service and insisted on a whole sub. He got it, along with contemptuous glares from about 149 other passengers.

Prentice also arranged for the two youngsters to fly first class on their royally treated return trip to Seattle, and he mailed their parents the tape of a television interview they had given on their long-delayed arrival in Orlando. The 12-year-old was particularly effective in front of a battery of cameras and microphones. Chewing gum nonchalantly, he described the experience as "pretty cool" and added a modest disclaimer that could have come from someone twice his age: "We did what every good citizen should do."

Cargo has always been a mainstay of Alaska Airlines. As we already have chronicled, there were times in the airline's earlier years, especially during the Willis era, that airfreight revenues were all that kept the company flying. Nor should the importance of reliable, adequate air cargo service to isolated, thinly populated areas such as Alaska ever be underestimated.

Such reliance even dictated the airline's eventual choice of flight equipment: i.e., its gradual transformation into an all-Boeing fleet. On a typical 737-900 nonstop flight from Seattle to Boston, with a full load of 172 passengers and their luggage, the airplane can routinely carry four tons of cargo, including restaurant-bound wild salmon from Alaska. On a shorter nonstop, say from Los Angeles to Seattle with a full passenger load, the 900 can carry as much as seven tons of freight. And the unique configuration of a 737-400 combi is capable of carrying 72 passengers and about eight tons of cargo.

More than a few veterans who succeeded in positions related mostly to passenger operations got their start in cargo. An outstanding example was Ron Suttell, who became something of a legend around the airline for his encyclopedic knowledge of its history and his impressive collection of company memorabilia. If Alaska Air Group ever wanted to establish its own museum, Ron would be an odds-on choice as its first curator.

Suttell was hired in 1971 as a kid fresh out of college and was assigned to cargo for the first two years of a career that saw him eventually promoted to director of facilities. So his memories of Alaska Airlines go back to the final year of the Willis regime and the trauma of the 727 crash at Juneau. His first assignment, in fact, was to the airfreight facility in Juneau, where his supervisor, Phil Martin, had been working 30 straight days without relief because of the accident. So Ron had to learn all about airfreight in a hurry, and among the things he learned was how bad the airline's undermanned cargo service was.

"I was always dealing with irate customers," Suttell recalled. "Shipments were late, we didn't always have enough cargo space, and we had problems if we were using different types of equipment. The few 720s we picked up from Western, for example, were in all-passenger configurations and didn't have as much cargo space as the 727-100C.

"The Juneau grocery stores used to put signs in their windows reading: 'Our fresh produce didn't arrive today because Alaska Airlines lost our freight shipment.' "

As of mid-2004, cargo represented only 5 percent of Alaska's annual revenues. It had reached a whopping 40 percent when the airline was much smaller and promoters like Charlie Willis and Jim Wooten had to rely on cargo contracts to keep it from sinking into bankruptcy. But factor in what airfreight has always meant to the state of Alaska, and one gets a different slant on cargo's financial role. In certain markets, especially in the 49th state, cargo revenues equal passenger revenues. Even that 5 percent figure, which may seem like an insignificant contribution, is higher than at most other U.S. passenger carriers.

No wonder. Alaska Airlines and the Alaska fishing industry are mutually dependent partners, welded together in a relationship that goes back to the days of bush pilots who made more money carrying a load of fresh fish than they did passengers.

Schedule reliability is as important to the airfreight business as it is to passenger operations. This is because so many restaurants in such cities as Boston, New York, and Washington, D.C., rely heavily on punctual shipments of seafood from the waters of Alaska.

"We have scheduled freight service just as we have scheduled passenger service," emphasized Keola Pang-Ching, former head of cargo services for Alaska. "What I always tried to explain to our employees was that each igloo [container] of freight could have as many as a couple hundred customers.

"For instance, take the Legal Sea Foods chain, which has about 30 restaurants on the East Coast. We worked with them to promote wild salmon and its high protein values.

"Actually, the state of Alaska is not the only source of fresh seafood. We also ship oysters out of North Bend and Coos Bay in Oregon, and Penn Cove on Washington's Whidbey Island." Oysters, mussels, crab, and all sorts of cold-water fish are shipped from the Pacific Northwest.

Nor are the seafood shipments a one-way deal, with all such cargo heading east. Alaska does a brisk business flying lobsters from Boston to Seattle, and from there to other West Coast cities and up to Anchorage. One of the airline's big advantages is its dominance in the state of Alaska, combined with its transformation into a transcontinental carrier.

"In the old days," Pang-Ching explained, "say you were a cargo customer in Sitka and you wanted to ship a load of seafood to Boston. Alaska could only fly it to Seattle, where it had to be transferred to another carrier with nonstops to the East Coast. So we lost most of the revenue."

The ability to provide one-carrier transcontinental cargo service is one more reason why the Eskimo stays on the tails of Alaska's aircraft. Another vital factor is the versatility of the 737-400C passenger/cargo aircraft. They can fly passengers and freight into small fishing communities such as Bethel, Cordova, Kodiak, Bristol Bay, and King Salmon in the afternoon and fly out that same night with 15 tons of seafood.

Mickey Mouse and Tinker Bell may have marked the first two times the Eskimo came off the tails of any Alaska jets, but significantly, it took a fish to accomplish it a third time. In October 2005, one of the airline's 737-400s had its fuselage repainted from nose to tail into a glimmering king salmon 120 feet long and weighing 140,000 pounds, creating what officially was dubbed the "Salmon-Thirty-Salmon" but naturally became known as just "the fish plane." The project, which took Seattle artist Mark Boyle 24 days to complete, was funded by the Alaska Fisheries Marketing Board to promote the state's wild seafood.

The fish plane also proved to be a morale-booster at a time when Alaska Airlines was trying to come out of the worst financial crunch since the fare wars of the early 1990s. Contentious labor-management relations were threatening to wreck a precious tradition that proclaimed, "No matter what, we're still a family."

Yet when that newly painted 737-400, complete with a tail and dorsal fin, almost seemed to swim out of the hangar for its first showing, more than 4,000 employees and guests burst into delighted applause. One could almost sense that all the setbacks and strife hadn't quelled another special tradition: Alaska was still an airline a little different, and always trying to be a few notches better than anyone else.

The "fish" also reminded old-timers of an event that occurred on March 30, 1987, when Alaska Airlines Flight 61, taking off from Juneau, collided with a large fish, probably a salmon. It turned out that an eagle had just plucked the fish out of the water and flew right into the path of an oncoming 737-200C. Startled, the bird dropped its catch, which hit just behind the last cockpit window on the captain's side and bounced off. Captain Bill Morin's radio report raised a lot of eyebrows: "We just collided with a fish at 500 feet."

Alaska Airlines committed far more to the state's fishing industry and its fishing communities than just agreeing to repaint one of its airplanes as a flying billboard. In June 2006, it took delivery of the first of at least five 737-400s uniquely configured and modified to haul as much as 16,000 pounds of freight along with 72 passengers. The conversion program represented a $100 million investment in airfreight as an essential component of the airline's plans for a more financially secure future. By the beginning of 2006, after Pang-Ching had retired and had been replaced by Matt Yerbic, managing director of cargo, freight and mail revenue had increased by 12 percent in the previous two years, reaching the $100 million mark in annual revenues for the first time in the company's history.

At a time when most carriers discourage shipping live animals by air, Alaska has welcomed everything from pet dogs and cats to such varied representatives of the animal world as musk oxen, bears ranging from cubs to full-grown adults, zoo animals, and horses.

The airline equipped one of its now-retired 737-200 freighters with a special horse stall, and provided a handler to accompany the equine passenger. Alaska also routinely carries sled dogs, including those competing in the annual Iditarod race from Anchorage to Nome.

The bulk of the animal passengers, however, are pet cats and dogs. Baggage handlers in Fairbanks a few years ago opened up the cargo compartment of a jet that had just landed and found themselves staring at a very happy and friendly tail-wagging large dog of undetermined breed. Supposedly, it had been shipped in a securely closed crate. Except that he was not in the crate. He had chewed off the crate's metal gate latch and then found his exit from the crate blocked by three big suitcases. So he chewed his way through all three suitcases and opened a pathway to the cargo bin door.

"We had a hell of a hard time explaining the suitcase damage to the owners," Ray Prentice recalled ruefully.

Smart cats as well as high-IQ dogs have a mysterious ability to escape confinement. Some years ago, a supposedly well-crated cat jumped out of the cargo compartment of an Alaska plane at Sea-Tac when baggage handlers opened the cargo door. The owner was visiting relatives in Seattle and had brought the cat with her.

"We really care about animals entrusted to us," Prentice said, "and we told the cat's owner we were going to keep looking for her pet."

Former communications chief Lou Cancelmi remembered the incident only too vividly. "We turned the airport upside down trying to find that cat," he recounted. "He was last seen entering one of the airport buildings, and we had a small army in there looking for him, with no success. The story got out and the press clobbered us, the gist being that Alaska Airlines was irresponsibly careless about the safety of animals.

"About a week later, a ramp-service agent heard a funny sound that turned out to be a meow. The cat had somehow gotten into a belt loader, and had been hiding inside the machine. We literally had to take that belt loader apart to extricate the animal. That part of the story was never printed.

"Then we flew the owner back to Seattle to pick up her cat, and she was delighted. The point is that despite what the newspapers were saying, we never gave up trying to find that cat."

Obviously, one never knows what a baggage handler is going to find when he opens up a cargo door. Which brings us to another group of unsung heroes.

Baggage handling is a cardiovascular workout. Alaska's flights sometimes pull away from the gate within 30 minutes of their arrival. One hundred bags off, one hundred on, can be all in a half-hour's work.

Mark Ramstad joined Alaska in 1974, and 29 years later he was serving as passenger service coordinator, with baggage handling as his specialty. Ramstad's exposure to baggage handling was preceded by assignments first to cargo and later working in customer service at the Sea-Tac terminal. But the most important event in his long career was participating in a revolutionary new program introduced in 1999 that shot Alaska Airlines toward the top of the industry with the fewest complaints involving mishandled baggage. It was called the RAC Room, the acronym standing for Ramp Action Center, and it was created by Jeff Schultz, who was head of baggage processing at the time.

"We went from ranking about 15th in the nation in baggage handling to number one," Ramstad reported, "and we had other carriers coming to Jeff begging to know how RAC worked.

"The whole industry has been plagued with baggage foul-ups usually caused by irregular operations, which is a euphemism for delayed flights that cause passenger luggage to miss connecting flights. It's a sorry situation for a passenger who barely makes the connection himself and then has to wait two days for his luggage to catch up to him.

"With RAC, we didn't let a lost bag turn into a 36- or 72-hour problem. We squelched the problem immediately. Suppose a passenger arrived on a late inbound Alaska flight with no way to make his connection. We would get him booked on another connecting flight. RAC software would then match the luggage with the passenger, and as we like to say, 'It keeps the buck and the bag together.' Once we know that a passenger is going to miss his connection, a CSA will meet him at the gate to inform him of his new booking, and that his luggage is being transferred to the same flight."

Increased security after 9/11 threatened to disrupt RAC until, according to Ramstad, "the federal government came in and started really looking at our operation and agreed that with our new system, we actually had better control over passenger luggage."

Admittedly, subsequent even tighter security measures, including increased adoption of high-tech devices for detecting explosives, can adversely affect even systems like RAC. Yet what Jeff Schultz developed remains among the best cures for mishandled-luggage problems yet devised.

So we now leave that area of dealing with freight and move to the front of the airplane and the cockpit that is the workplace of people with great skills, split-second reflexes, and vast aeronautical knowledge.

Behind well-protected doors, amid a sea of switches, gauges, computers, monitors, and radios, pilots earn their keep. Time for passenger contact is usually limited to a brief greeting and flight information. But because Gary Ellington occupied the right seat as the first officer on a Seattle flight to Los Angeles, it became truly a flight to remember for one passenger and a symbol of the caring nature of Alaska employees to the passenger's family, as the following letter described:

Dear Alaska Airlines:

When my husband and I boarded our flight from Seattle to Los Angeles, a very nice pilot [First Officer Gary "Duke" Ellington] invited our son to the cockpit. Christopher, who had Duchenne muscular dystrophy, was 15. His face just lit up, and he told us that when he got well he wanted to be a pilot. The flight was wonderful and the entire crew was just great to Chris. When we landed, the pilot asked for our address. Several weeks later, Chris received a beautiful card and a pair of wings the pilot had earned in the service. Chris just did not want to take those wings off. About three months later, Chris had his 16th birthday. There came a knock on the door and it was the pilot. He wanted to see how Chris was doing and had a surprise — one of his old pilot jackets he wore in the service. Chris was beside himself. Six months after that, Chris passed away. We still have the jacket and the card. The generosity, kindness, and thoughtfulness of the employees of your airline are overwhelming. We are so grateful to you for treating our son with such respect and dignity, and making his final days so happy.

Flying is a career choice that usually begins with a dream. Katsie

Hirsh's dream of becoming a commercial pilot started when she took her first airplane ride on an Alaska Airlines 727 at the age of eight.

Hirsh was a native of Seattle, but used to spend summers in Alaska, where her father operated a fishing camp at Dry Bay, about 60 miles south of Yakutat. Salmon were plentiful there, but to get the catch to market, he had to clean the fish, put them on ice, and ship them out either by truck or, if available, preferably in an airplane. When Hirsh eventually got her pilot's license, her first flying job was transporting fish for her father.

She took her first flying lesson at age 16, then soloed and got her private pilot's license at 18 after training at Boeing Field. One of her earlier instructors was Russ Rathbone, who later became an Alaska Airlines captain.

Once she earned her instrument and commercial ratings, she began flying for a series of employers ranging from a word-processor manufacturer to small Alaskan carriers. One firm hired her only because she had a degree in finance as well as a pilot's license; Hirsh had to promise to work on its books as well as fly the company airplane.

She became engaged to a pilot who went to work for Northwest in Minneapolis, but she refused to give up her own dream of becoming an airline pilot. After knocking on every door in the Twin Cities, trying in vain to get a flying job, she went back to Alaska and was flying a Cessna Citation business jet when Alaska Airlines, which had her application on file, contacted her.

Hirsh was hired as a 727 flight engineer in May 1984, but was not even close to being the first female cockpit crew member to fly the line; at least seven women had been hired ahead of her. One of her predecessors was terminated for poor performance, although she claimed she was picked on because she was a woman. "When I went on the flight line after I qualified as a flight engineer," Katsie recalled, "every time I walked into a cockpit I could sense the captain thinking, 'Oh God, here's another one.' I just tried to work harder to gain respect.

"And I must add that there wasn't a pilot at Alaska Airlines who didn't give me a fair chance. No matter what their attitude was outside the cockpit or inside their heads, it was never conveyed to me on the job. Their attitude was completely professional."

She transitioned to first officer in 1986, and later qualified on the new MD-83s, although like most Alaska pilots, she never lost her love of the old "three-holer" 727. "It climbed like a fighter," she remembered, "although it guzzled fuel and was hard to land." The latter was because with the wing flaps extended, the 727 had an extremely high sink rate, like a runaway elevator whose cables had snapped.

Hirsh married her Northwest pilot in 1984, the same year she qualified as a flight engineer. Somehow they continued to make the marriage work, even though she was based in Seattle and he continued to fly all over the map for Northwest as a 747 captain. They had two daughters and a son, and Hirsh eventually became concerned that she wasn't spending enough time with them.

She finally decided to see Mike Swanigan, who had become chief pilot, and ask for an unprecedented five-year leave of absence. Hirsh had no idea what his reaction would be, but she laid it on the line, knowing it might very well be a permanent instead of a temporary farewell to her job. All she had going for her was her husband's total support, but that meant little without Swanigan's approval.

She requested the five-year leave and explained, "Mike, I love my job, but I need time with my kids. In five years I'll have been with the company for 18 years, but I need this time *now*, while they're still young."

Swanigan nodded understandingly. "Katsie," he said, "my kids are the most important things in my own life, so we're going to make this five-year leave happen for you. You just have to promise me you'll come back."

She gave him that promise and kept it. She admitted having pangs of anxiety when the five years was up and she had to requalify, enduring the same ordeal a brand-new pilot hire must face. Before going back into training, she told her family, "You guys are still number one, but for the next three months what I'm doing has to be a family effort, and you have to support me 100 percent."

There were times when the three months felt like five years. Hirsh had been warned that no Alaska Airlines pilot had ever taken five years off and still managed to return to flying. Skills can deteriorate during such a long layoff.

The climax was an extremely stiff FAA check ride in a 727, and there were three first-officer trainees scheduled to fly ahead of her. The check ride included touch-and-go landings and mock emergency procedures. There hadn't been time for introductions.

While Hirsh was waiting her turn, they broke for lunch. She went out and brought back some sandwiches and soft drinks that she shared with the pilots on the airplane.

"Boy, this is cool," the FAA pilot remarked. "I've never had a flight attendant on a check flight before."

Still smiling to herself, Hirsh aced the check ride and resumed her flying career, graduating to MD-83s first as a copilot and later as a captain. She was proud of the fact that when she flew with an all-woman MD-83 cockpit crew for the first time — Joan McIntosh was the copilot — it already had become such a common occurrence that no one made any fuss about it.

A few carriers used to have an unwritten, unofficial, and for obvious reasons unpublicized policy of discouraging women pilots from making public-address announcements, because it was feared that a feminine voice coming from the cockpit might make too many passengers nervous. To have women airline pilots accepted not only by their male peers but also by the public as routine was the ultimate achievement for this particular captain, who had once been a little girl with an apparently impossible dream.

Thomas Edison would have respected the work of another inventor, Bill Boyer. Boyer's credentials as an inventor were dubious at best. He was a college dropout. If he *had* graduated, his college yearbook probably would have listed him as "the most unlikely to succeed."

When he quit school in 1988, he was hired by Alaska Airlines as a baggage handler. There was nothing to indicate he was destined to become one of the most successful baggage handlers in the history of the airline industry.

Born in Germany, Boyer shared a God-given talent with another school dropout, Thomas Alva Edison, who was insatiably curious, a quality that usually begins with tinkering and eventually matures into inventing. That certainly described Boyer, who was fascinated with industrial technology and learning what new products or innovations industries need. He inherited this interest from his father, who had once worked for Boeing.

"As soon as I joined the airline," Boyer confessed, "I started thinking about ways to make baggage handling more efficient." This resulted in his first practical invention. He designed and then built a protective plastic bumper that tilted on the end of the portable luggage conveyor belt that the airline used to load baggage. In designing the bumper, he began in the same way he approached every idea for some new gadget: he first built a mockup out of cardboard and glue, then a small working model, and finally a full-size prototype.

Boyer hit the proverbial jackpot when Alaska began operating nonstops between Seattle and the East Coast. The new long-range routes, with five-and-a-half-hour flights serving New York, Boston, and Washington, D.C., created a need for providing in-flight entertainment.

Dave Palmer, the airline's managing director of marketing, revealed in *Alaska's World*, the airline's employee newspaper, that the company was looking for some kind of in-flight movie system for the 737-900s. He pointed out, however, that all the existing systems used by other transcontinental as well as transoceanic airlines created weight and cost problems, and added some 2,000 pounds of extra weight that increased fuel consumption.

That was all the incentive Boyer needed. He started with a drawing of a lightweight digital player whose screen was even smaller than those on most laptop computers. He showed the sketch to Palmer, who not only was intrigued but also remembered Boyer's bumper invention. Palmer did warn Boyer, however, that eventually he would have to work out some kind of deal with film distributors.

Boyer cobbled together an actual unit, a prototype that became the production model. Dubbed the digEplayer, the unit weighed less than two and a half pounds, ran on a 10-hour battery, could be set up on seatback trays, and did not require expensive installation because each player not only was self-contained but also provided up to 64 full-length digitized feature movie choices plus other forms of entertainment.

Deals with major film production companies, starting with 20th Century Fox, followed the development phase, and while Alaska was the first airline to offer digEplayers, Boyer was free to sell the system to other carriers. Yet, until 2005, Boyer continued to handle baggage at Sea-Tac on weekends, even though he had become CEO of his own company. Not until his innovation demanded his full-time attention did Boyer leave the airline.

An airline's hangar may be filled with parts, maintenance manuals, and sophisticated tools, but its most important assets are its mechanics. And Tada Yotsuuye has been an exceptional asset for Alaska Airlines by any measure for more than 40 years. At 78, Yotsuuye is Alaska Airlines' most senior maintenance employee. Soft-spoken and modest, he has an uncanny ability to help his coworkers when they need it most.

Yotsuuye learned his trade in the Air Force, worked for West Coast Airlines, and then joined Alaska Airlines in 1965, when the company owned two jets and Charlie Willis was president. During his tenure with Alaska he has worked on C-130 Hercs, Super Constellations, Convair 990s, MD-80s, and all of Alaska's Boeing commercial aircraft from the 720 to the most recent 737s — all the time sharing his knowledge freely and mentoring scores of coworkers.

A Japanese-American who grew up on his family's vegetable farm in Fife, Washington, he has known hard work as a way of life. At age 14, he was uprooted from his home and sent to an internment camp in Idaho to await the outcome of World War II. After the war, he graduated from high school, joined the Air Force, and obtained his flight engineer and airframe and powerplant licenses.

In 2006, Tada Yotsuuye received the Charles Taylor "Master Mechanic" Award. (Taylor earned his place in history by building the engine for the Wright brothers' aircraft.) The award is presented annually in recognition of the lifetime accomplishments of senior maintenance personnel.

Yotsuuye was the sixth Alaska Airlines mechanic to receive the distinguished award, and his name was added to the FAA's Roll of Honor at its headquarters in Washington, D.C. The same year, his peers recognized Yotsuuye with the Alaska Airlines Legend Award, the highest recognition an employee can receive.

One might ask Yotsuuye when he planned to retire. His response, at age 78: "I have no plans to put away my tools."

Making a plan to deal with disaster is done with the hope of never having to follow the plan. Sue Warner-Bean's official job title was something new and unusual at Alaska Airlines: she was its first director of emergency response.

The position had been created largely because of the Family Assistance Act, passed by Congress in 1996, which required airlines to provide competent counseling personnel to help the families of air-crash victims deal with the trauma of unexpected tragedy. Most carriers, including Alaska, already offered aid, but those informal programs were usually staffed by amateurs, volunteers with little or no professional training. Yet they were dealing with extremely sensitive and complex psychological reactions: uncertainty, disbelief, depression, intense grief, anger, and bewilderment, to name the most frequent manifestations.

When Warner-Bean joined Horizon Air in 1985, she had no inkling she would play a major role in establishing such a complicated program at the airline. She started out as a payroll clerk simply because she wanted to work for an airline, and didn't care what kind of starting job it was. In college she had majored in Russian literature and cultural history, both about five galaxies away from either aviation or post-accident trauma.

Eventually, however, she amassed experience and knowledge in more appropriate areas than payroll. Public affairs and customer relations became key assignments in learning how to work with people faced with difficult situations.

When the 1996 legislation was passed, George Bagley handed Sue the job of implementing a family-assistance plan at Horizon. Then both Bagley and John Kelly agreed that it made no sense to have two separate programs, and Warner-Bean was given the task of creating one program for both carriers.

She gathered information from other carriers, principally American and US Air, as well as the Air Transport Association, the Regional Airline Association, and the FBI. Her major ally in the job was Scott Lautman, manager of employee relations. Warner-Bean also received considerable help from Dr. Carolyn Coarsey-Rader, one of the pioneer researchers in the field of post-accident trauma; she had written her Ph.D. thesis on the subject and established her own consulting firm.

The emergency-response group that Warner-Bean formed and managed drew input from all these sources. It has evolved into one of the industry's most comprehensive and effective. It consists of several response units, ranging in size from several hundred members to about 30, each with specific areas of responsibility.

One group, known as CARE (Compassionate Assistance Relief Effort), the largest group, deals directly with the families of crash victims, providing support services, information, and whatever other assistance is needed as required by the Family Assistance Act. Another group, the Site Support Group, arranges ground transportation, hotel accommodations, meals, and so on for victims' families who are able to come to crash sites.

In addition, subteams have narrower, more sharply defined responsibilities. One small, technically oriented team of about 30 people assists with the accident investigation by cooperating and coordinating with the National Transportation Safety Board, FAA, FBI, local police, and any involved military authorities such as the Navy and Coast Guard.

A critical incident response team includes people trained to provide peer support to employees who may be having their own problems dealing with the aftermath of an accident. Alaska's entire emergency-response organization began with about 500 volunteers, growing to more than 700 by the start of the 21st century. Warner-Bean and her fellow organizers, such as Lautman and also Craig Battison of sales and marketing, had no difficulty in signing up people willing to undergo very intense specialized training and pledge their availability in the event of an accident.

Warner-Bean, for one, was pleasantly surprised by the response. "To get such a large number of people to participate," she emphasized, "showed the kind of people we have at Alaska and Horizon Airlines. If I had to characterize the difference between what everybody else was doing and what we did, I'd have to say it was in the quality of our leadership and the quality of our people, and not in any magic in our program."

An interview with Sue Warner-Bean appeared in the April 30, 1999, issue of the company newspaper, a month and a half after she had been appointed director of the new emergency-response program and already had begun training volunteers. "The likelihood of ever using this program is minimal," she predicted. "Hopefully, I will never know if I did a good job."

On January 31, 2000, only nine months later almost to the day, at approximately 4:21 p.m. PST, the "minimal likelihood" turned into a nightmare of reality.

It was Flight 261.

CHAPTER TWENTY-ONE

Flight 261

"At 4:21 p.m., January 31, 2000, the world as we knew it changed. Forever."
Those somber words from Chairman and CEO John Kelly introduced Alaska
Air Group's annual report for the first year of the 21st century.

Although it couldn't be foreseen at the time, Alaska's world did change.
It changed by lessons learned. It changed in painfully honest, introspective
reforms. It changed in the determination, if at all humanly possible, to never
let anything like Flight 261 happen again. Most of all, it changed in the way it
brought an airline together as one grieving family.

Before chronicling the most traumatic event in the airline's history,
this author finds it mandatory to share a very personal observation: I have
covered air-carrier accidents since 1947. Yet in all those six decades, I have
never seen any airline so emotionally affected by a fatal crash as Alaska was
by Flight 261 — and to such an extent that the traumatic effects seemed to be
as imperishable as words carved into granite.

Every single person interviewed about the Flight 261 disaster — from
CEOs and other senior officers to employees at all levels — broke into tears in
the middle of the taping session and asked that the tape recorder be stopped
so they could compose themselves. I had never witnessed such long-lasting

trauma. It was as if my tape recorder was an x-ray machine providing an uninvited glimpse into minds and hearts, exposing a depth of sorrow and an inability to believe that 261 could have ever happened.

Yet it did happen, because like virtually every other airline crash, it was an accident in which a number of factors intersected at precisely the wrong moment. A coincidental series of mistakes, erroneous assumptions, false confidence, and just plain bad luck converged on a timetable apparently dictated by fate itself.

A lot of people don't believe in fate. They're convinced that the flawed actions and attitudes of human beings cause bad things to happen, and sometimes they may be right. In the case of Flight 261, however, there were seemingly unrelated decisions and developments that were to play major roles in what happened to Alaska's MD-83 on Monday, January 31, 2000, off the Southern California coast.

In retrospect, perhaps the most important decision involved the original design of the nation's first twin-engine jetliner, the Douglas DC-9, launched in 1965. Because its engines were mounted on the rear fuselage, the airplane had a horizontal stabilizer with flap-like elevators to control lift and descent of the nose and tail. The horizontal stabilizer sat atop a vertical stabilizer that contained the rudder section to control the aircraft's movement to the left or right. The combination of both stabilizers formed a large T at the rear of the airplane.

The mechanism that moved the stabilizer up or down was a massive component called the jackscrew. And this was where transport aircraft design philosophy became an issue in the fate of Flight 261. Boeing's policy was to build "redundancy" into its airplanes, in other words a backup part or system for every component crucial to safe flight. This was the same design philosophy followed by Convair, but not so stringently at Douglas, nor at McDonnell Douglas after Douglas Aircraft was merged into the McDonnell Company in 1967. Thirty years later, in 1997, Boeing acquired McDonnell Douglas and the technology and liabilities that came with the merger.

A related development was Alaska's seeking and then accepting a decision by Boeing that it had "no technical objection" to the use of a different lubricant on the jackscrew, one that no other MD-80 operator had adopted. Another was the FAA's formal acceptance of longer inspection and lubrication intervals that was ultimately approved by regulators on the basis of past performance backed by mountains of technical data and hundreds of millions of miles of experience.

One would have to be clairvoyant to foresee how these and a multitude of other seemingly unconnected decisions and actions might become contributing factors. Indeed, jetliners like the MD-83 were stretched versions of the original DC-9 with the same basic jackscrew design that had been successfully operated for over 40 years, with one of the best safety records in the industry. The jackscrew on the MD-80 series was considered very sturdy, built so strong that no one could conceive of its failing.

But the unit on Flight 261 did fail. And that was when the nightmare began.

There were 88 people aboard Flight 261, a scheduled nonstop from Puerto Vallarta, Mexico, to San Francisco: five crew members and 83 passengers. It was a light load. Beyond the five working crew members, there were seven off-duty Alaska and Horizon employees and 32 others who were family and/or friends of Alaska Air Group people. Inevitably, this unusually high percentage of airline-connected victims — half of the people on the plane — increased the sense of personal loss that swept through both Alaska and Horizon. It seemed as if everybody at Alaska knew somebody personally who died in that crash.

Captain Ted Thompson and First Officer Bill Tansky, occupying 261's cockpit, were former Jet America pilots with impressive reputations for airmanship and judgment. Thompson, in fact, had been a check pilot at Jet America and was so demanding that his nickname was Chainsaw.

Kevin Finan, who had been Jet America's chief pilot before coming over to Alaska, used to be base manager at LAX and knew Thompson especially well. "His nickname reflected his toughness," Finan recalled, "but also his integrity. Ted had unwavering standards when it came to check flights. It didn't matter if a pilot was Charles Lindbergh himself. If he was taking a check ride with Thompson, he knew that Ted wouldn't bend from those high standards."

This was most definitely true. A former astronaut applied for a job as a Jet America pilot, and Thompson gave him a check ride. After they landed, Thompson informed him he had flunked and to go get a flying job elsewhere.

"How could you flunk a former astronaut?" Thompson was asked.

"The guy may be able to fly a rocket," Thompson retorted, "but he's not gonna fly one of my airplanes."

Kevin Finan led a long list of experts from both the airline and investigative agencies who agreed that there wasn't a pilot on earth who could have saved Flight 261 from disaster, nor any emergency procedure that could have overcome the malignancy that destroyed the aircraft's control system.

After departure from Puerto Vallarta that fateful day, Thompson and Tansky experienced so-called "trim" problems with the airplane. There was no reason for immediate concern, but as the airplane headed north along the Southern California coast, the pilots radioed company dispatch about the issue and discussed landing in Los Angeles to have the aircraft checked.

By the time Flight 261 neared Los Angeles, however, communications between the plane and the air traffic control center at Los Angeles International Airport pointed to some kind of control failure, but no solid clue as to its source. The fate of Flight 261 was decided in only 11 terrifying minutes, from 4:10 p.m., when the Alaska crew first reported a serious control problem, to 4:21 p.m., when the crippled MD-83 hit the water nose down, at high speed, off the coast of Ventura County, north of Los Angeles.

The transcript of radio communications during those final 11 minutes, released by the Federal Aviation Administration four months later, is chilling:

261: "Center, Alaska 261. We're in a dive here."

LAX: "Alaska 261, uh, say again."

261: "Yeah, we're out of 26,000 feet, we're in a vertical dive — not a dive yet — but, uh, we've lost vertical control of our airplane."

LAX: "Alaska 261, roger."

261: "We're at twenty-three-seven, uh, yeah we've got it back under control there — no we don't . . ." (voice becomes garbled)

At 19 seconds past 4:15 p.m., the cockpit transmissions resumed.

261: "LA, Alaska 261. Uh, we're with you, we're at twenty-two-five, we have a jammed stabilizer and we're maintaining altitude with difficulty, uh, but, uh, we can maintain altitude, we think, and our intention is to land at Los Angeles."

LAX: "Alaska 261, roger, uh, you are cleared, uh, to Los Angeles airport via present position then direct Santa Monica, direct Los Angeles, and, uh, you want to lower now or what do you want to do, sir?"

261: "Center, Alaska 261. I need to, uh, get down about 10, change my configuration, make sure I can control the jet, and I'd like to do that over the bay if I may."

Meanwhile, the LAX Center had established contact with two other aircraft in the vicinity, a private pilot and a SkyWest Airlines flight, asking them to keep an eye on the MD-83. At 4:19 p.m., the private pilot passed the word that the Alaska pilots apparently had lost vertical control again:

Private pilot: "Five-zero delta x-ray. That plane has just started a big huge plunge."

LAX: "A big huge plunge, ah, thank you. SkyWest 5154, the MD-80 is, ah, one becoming about two o'clock about 10 miles now. Another pilot reports he's really looking pretty bad there ahead and to your right. Do you see him?"

SkyWest 5154: "Yes, sir, ah, I concur he is, uh, definitely in a nose-down, uh, position descending quite rapidly."

LAX: "OK, very good. Keep your eye on him. Alaska 261, are you here with us yet, sir?"

261 did not respond.

4:20:59.

Private pilot: "And he's just hit the water."

SkyWest 5154: "Ah, yes sir, he, ah, he, ah, hit the water. Ah, he's down."

4:22 p.m.

The agony for the 88 passengers and crew aboard 261 was over.

The agony for their families, friends, and the nearly 15,000 people of Alaska Airlines and Horizon Air was just beginning.

The weather in the Seattle area late in the afternoon of January 31 was gloomy, with heavy rain and that damp chill so typical of the Northwest's "Emerald City" at that time of year. It also seemed darker than usual for that time of day. Many were to associate the miserable weather with their memories of Flight 261. It matched the mood of the entire airline when early hopes of a successful ditching were eradicated by confirmed "no survivors" reports.

Hope was John Kelly's initial reaction when he heard the first sketchy reports that 261 had come down over water. He was talking with chief financial officer Brad Tilden when Barb Johnson, Kelly's administrative assistant, walked in.

"There's a problem, John," she interrupted. "I think you'd better get back to your office."

Kelly didn't even bother to ask her what the problem was. He knew from the expression on her face that it was something serious, and with a worried glance at Tilden, he accompanied Johnson back to his office.

Kelly learned from the airline's corporate communications staff what they knew thus far: an "all-white jetliner" believed to be an Alaska Airlines plane was "in the water" off the coast near Los Angeles. Kelly admitted later that he assumed the aircraft must have ditched — meaning a controlled landing, wheels up, in the water — which presumably meant there could be survivors. He was not alone in that assumption, but as further details trickled in, mostly from televised newscasts from the crash site, any initial hope quickly gave way to the grim reality, and the mood became as gloomy as the weather outside.

Ironically, only a few days before Flight 261 disappeared from radar's all-seeing eye, Sue Warner-Bean, head of the airline's emergency-response team, which was almost but not entirely in place, had staged a mock drill built around a fictitious ditching. The scenario had an Alaska Airlines MD-83 en route from San Francisco to Seattle go down in the ocean off the coast of Oregon.

Some officers and employees at first thought the January 31st alarm bells were just another drill. Kelly could only wish it *were* all make-believe, something strictly for training purposes. Instead, it wasn't long before he knew he had to get to the crash site as quickly as possible to lead his company through an event that every airline official prays will never happen.

Bill Ayer, the airline's president and chief operating officer, also was an emergency team member, but he was in Juneau, meeting with government officials along with Bill MacKay, senior vice president of public affairs. Kelly was advised that both Ayer and MacKay already were on their way back to Seattle.

That was good news for CEO Kelly. He especially needed Ayer now to run the shaken airline while he headed the company's response from Los Angeles, near the accident site. During the same time frame, he got a call from Boeing, offering one of the company's private jets to take him and other members of his initial response team to Los Angeles.

It was a welcome gesture, one reflecting the aerospace company's concern for a hometown neighbor and acceptance of its technical responsibility inherited along with the MD-83's manufacturer. All MD-80s had legally become Boeing airplanes after the two aerospace companies merged in 1997. The MD-90, the improved MD-80 variant that Alaska almost bought before it decided to standardize its fleet with the 737, in fact, was renamed the Boeing 717.

For John Kelly, this was the second accident he'd had to deal with as an airline CEO. The first was at Horizon in 1987, when a Dash 8 developed a fuel leak, caught fire, and ran into the Sea-Tac terminal. Thankfully, on that occasion there were no fatalities, but for Kelly it still was an experience that shook him to the core. Afterward, he became acutely aware of a CEO's responsibilities in the event of an air disaster, and began to run realistic "just-in-case" drills at Horizon for everyone involved, including himself.

As soon as he realized that 261 was far more serious than the successful ditching he had hoped for, he told Barb Johnson, "Call Maggi. Tell her to pack my bag with enough changes of clothing for a week and bring it here as soon as possible."

Greg Witter, Lou Cancelmi's second-in-command in corporate communications, was getting ready to leave the office a bit early that Monday afternoon so he could take his daughter to a swimming lesson. He had put on his jacket and was picking up his briefcase when he overheard colleague Jack Evans, Alaska's media relations manager, handling a call. There was a reference to a "white plane down in the water," and that stopped Witter in his tracks.

Cancelmi was out of the office at an appointment elsewhere, and Witter found himself temporarily in charge as the company's public relations point man. After listening to Evans as he tried to get more information, Witter put down his briefcase and quickly walked over to Donna Hartman's desk. Hartman was not only Bill MacKay's administrative assistant at the time but also the logistical head of an important task for the airline's media response team procedures: setting up two rooms for team personnel to use to take calls on special dedicated phone lines designed for emergencies.

"Donna," Greg said quietly, "I think we've got a serious incident on our hands. Just to be on the safe side, better get those rooms ready."

The response plan also included an extensive "phone tree," a priority list of corporate communications people and volunteers who needed to be mobilized in the event of an accident to gather, process, and distribute information. Witter knew that the phones would start ringing off the hook if things turned out to be as bad as he feared. So he gave his next order to Jeanne Gessitz, Cancelmi's administrative assistant.

"Jeannie, I'm afraid we may have a plane down. Start the phone tree and tell everyone to stand by in case we need them and that if we do, we'll need them damn quick. And call Lou on his cell phone. He'll want to get back here fast." Gessitz didn't waste time asking a lot of questions but merely nodded and started making the calls.

Witter then talked to John Fowler, executive vice president of technical operations and system control, and chief pilot Paul Majer. Fowler's title was relatively new and underscored his growing influence within Alaska's executive ranks. Originally vice president of maintenance, Fowler had been promoted over time and put in charge of all maintenance as well as flight operations. That, in turn, made Mike Swanigan subordinate to him. Friction developed between the "hard-charging" Fowler and the easier-going Swanigan, resulting in the latter's resignation prior to the accident. That friction reflected a broader attitude within Fowler's organization that was to play an indirect role in the tragic story of 261.

While Witter was talking to Fowler and Majer, neither of whom at that point really knew a lot more than he did, another member of the airline's media response team arrived at corporate headquarters, namely Dave Marriott, partner in a Seattle-based public affairs firm. For the past 15 years, Marriott had worked frequently for the airline as a respected and trusted consultant. He and Cancelmi, in fact, had drafted the airline's first comprehensive media response plan in 1985. Marriott had even taken part a few days earlier in the eerie mock drill so similar to what was now a reality off the coast of Southern California.

Marriott and his wife had planned on having an early dinner that Monday evening so they could attend a jazz session in which their two sons were playing. They were just getting ready to leave their home when Witter phoned and told Marriott that his help would be needed at corporate headquarters.

Marriott arrived just ahead of Cancelmi. By then everyone knew that the company was facing a potential catastrophe for the first time since the Juneau crash in 1971. There remained some hope that the airplane had ditched, but the televised shots of the crash site taken from hovering helicopters were discouraging. There was no sign of wreckage, let alone survivors. Just an eerie sheen on the water.

After Cancelmi arrived, he huddled with Witter and Marriott, and the decision was made that he would accompany Kelly to Los Angeles. For the next several days — almost a week in some cases — Witter, Evans, Marriott, and staff in Seattle would spend their days and nights debunking speculation, informing the media, and dealing with a wide range of other public aspects of the tragedy.

Cancelmi later said that the combined effort of the members of his media response team far exceeded anything that one should reasonably expect. "They worked round the clock, getting little or no sleep, putting everything else aside to help the airline get through an absolutely crushing experience," Cancelmi remembered. "I can't begin to describe how important their performance was to the airline, and to me personally. It was about concern for one another and about our mutual concern for the airline."

Meanwhile, the contingent that boarded Boeing's company jet that cold, rain-sodden night included Ed White, vice president of services. White had just returned from Atlanta and the Tennessee-St. Louis Super Bowl XXXIV game with his wife. They had planned to spend the evening with their children until White was informed about Flight 261 and that he would be going to Los Angeles with Kelly, Cancelmi, vice president of maintenance Bill Weaver, and an MD-80 pilot from flight operations, Dugan Blechschmidt.

The occupants of the tiny jet for the most part sat quietly throughout the flight, alone with their own thoughts and fears. White kept dozing off and thinking that the crash had been just a bad dream until he awoke and realized he was on an airplane speeding to the scene of a real-life tragedy. He could not help worrying about the grim-faced John Kelly, who he knew was about to endure an ordeal that few airline CEOs ever have to deal with in such a personal manner. At one point during the flight south that night, White, a man of deep faith, asked Kelly if he would mind if he prayed for him. Kelly said he would welcome it, and the two men stood in the aisle of the small jet as White prayed that Kelly would be given the strength to handle whatever the days ahead might bring.

Kelly inevitably would have to face the families of Flight 261's victims and a demanding media with no immediate answers to the question "Why?" White talked briefly with Kelly about what both of them might encounter when the families began to arrive on the scene. Despite planning and preparation, neither was sure how he would cope with the real thing.

At the same time, Cancelmi was concerned about Kelly's interaction with the media that he would have to face for several days beginning that night. In particular, Cancelmi was aware of the potentially adversarial atmosphere of a news conference — the pack mentality — especially when there are few facts and no answers.

This first company news conference would be no drill, and in truth, no amount of preparation could have completely prepared Kelly for it. He was about to undergo a freewheeling, no-holds-barred onslaught of questions from an army of international, national, and local media with their battery of microphones, cameras, and glaring lights. How Kelly conducted himself under these incredibly difficult circumstances could have staggering consequences, and Cancelmi knew it. But he also knew that Kelly was articulate, composed, and media savvy, despite being untested.

When Kelly's jet landed at LAX, he received a quick update and then was escorted to an airport auditorium for the news conference. It was around 11 p.m., just in time for local stations' late news. The place was packed with media and equipment. Kelly was personally in shock, already tired, even haggard, with eyes that resembled two burned holes in a blanket, yet he answered every question honestly if, at times, guardedly. Facts related to 261 were still limited, but Kelly kept his cool and made his airline comrades proud.

Kelly went out of his way to praise the veteran crew aboard 261, the pilots in particular. Word had already leaked out that Thompson and Tansky had reported control problems, but Kelly avoided either confirming or denying any speculation. He emphasized that the NTSB was in charge of the accident investigation, and that the airline would cooperate with the agency in every respect. It was not enough, but at the time it was all there was.

His overall conduct, given the dearth of solid information, conveyed what Cancelmi had hoped for: Alaska Airlines would not duck its responsibilities, and its most immediate concern was for the 88 people aboard that airplane, and their families and friends.

Over the next several days, Kelly was booked on as many live national network and cable interviews as possible. He and Cancelmi felt that it was in the company's interest — and simply the right thing to do — to make sure the victims' families and friends, the general public, and the news media heard *early and often* from the head of the airline.

Meanwhile, if Kelly was to be tested by the media in Los Angeles, so was Alaska's "Man in Mexico," Julian Acosta. Flight 261 had originated in Puerto Vallarta, so Acosta became involved nearly from the start. He had been in his Mexico City office that day, and had listened to music while driving home that evening. When he arrived, his wife said, "I'm afraid you are going to be very busy tonight."

"Why?" Acosta asked.

"Because an Alaska Airlines plane flying from Puerto Vallarta has crashed in the Pacific near Los Angeles."

Acosta, like Kelly, was about to be confronted by a tragedy that would test his professionalism. He lacked the advantage of having received media training, and he didn't have a public relations person by his side. His reaction would have to be guided by good judgment and executive instinct.

Later, Acosta recalled getting more than 120 calls that night, mostly from Mexican government officials and people wanting to know if there were Mexican nationals aboard 261. There was only one, as it turned out, although that fact didn't lessen Acosta's involvement, nor pain.

The news media, both American and Mexican, descended on him after he flew to Puerto Vallarta to represent Alaska Airlines as its lead person in the city. He handled the media as best he could, limiting reporters to twice-daily briefings where he passed on whatever new information had come to him from corporate headquarters.

Media central, however, was in Seattle. There, Jack Evans conducted marathon briefings for the media with the support of Witter and Marriott. While Evans did the briefings, Witter and Marriott gathered information and wrote and released a stream of news releases, one after another after another.

Almost from the moment the news broke, satellite trucks crammed the company's Seattle corporate parking lot, and dozens of reporters and cameramen jammed the main reception area. Evans was peppered with questions at his hourly briefings, and his sincerity and responsiveness demonstrated the airline's compassion, caring, and concern — an impression that exactly matched reality.

Whether in Los Angeles, Puerto Vallarta, or Seattle, the company's media response was built on the belief that doing everything possible to be accessible would help to preclude at least some misinformation, fill information vacuums, and most important, serve everybody's interests. This approach also went a long way, together with the work of the company's assistance teams, toward confirming the authenticity of the organization's stated corporate values: caring, professionalism, resourcefulness, integrity, and Alaska Spirit. Interestingly, these values had been identified years earlier by employees in a company-wide exercise initiated by Kelly.

After the Los Angeles news conference, Kelly and Cancelmi checked into a Marriott hotel near the airport. There they huddled to discuss their next steps with Dave Bean, a longtime public relations consultant for the airline who had dropped the business he was doing for another company in Arizona on the night of the accident and flown immediately to Los Angeles to lend assistance. That's when the decision was made to secure and accept any invitations to speak on live network and cable shows to make sure information from the airline reached the broadest possible audience.

Meanwhile, another hotel nearby would become the company's headquarters for media and local family briefings, family support by the airline's CARE team, and meetings with NTSB and FAA officials. The hotel itself was about 60 miles south of the Naval and Coast Guard facilities at Port Hueneme, California, that had become the nerve center for the massive search-and-rescue operation then in progress. Ironically, the name of the city, not far from the accident site, comes from the language of the coastal Chumash Indians and means "resting place."

At the hotel in Los Angeles, Ed White was the designated senior CARE officer on-site, with the specific responsibility of overseeing the family-support team that tended to the practical needs of families, including information and referrals to other services such as counseling. Like the other CARE team members, he was anxious and feared that he might not be up to the job. The first family arrived early Tuesday morning, and it was decided that he should establish the first contact.

White was to become the focal point of the close relationship that would develop between the families and the airline; to most of them, Ed White *was* Alaska Airlines. He became someone they felt they could trust, someone who could relate to *their* feelings, whether of sorrow or anger.

His account of that first encounter movingly demonstrated that no training, however efficient, nor any drill, however realistic, could quite prepare anyone for coping with the initial impact of sudden death on a victim's loved ones. "It was a couple," White related. "They came into the room we had set aside for the families and sat across a table from me. They were just in total shock. I remember thinking, this is *really* shock. They're not sad, they're not angry, they just can't react.

"I remember introducing myself, but I've never been able to recall exactly what else I said to them. I know I apologized to them for their loss, and I guess when you're talking to people torn apart by what had happened, you instinctively start making what you say sound humane.

"What I *do* remember is getting tears in my eyes as I talked to them, and I talked a lot longer than I intended because I didn't know what to say, and they were too much in shock to say anything."

The turning point for everyone, including the increasing number of arriving families, came on the second day, when a Coast Guard officer, with regret etched into every line of his windblown face, announced that the "search and rescue" phase of the operation was over and that "search and recovery" efforts were under way. Up to that moment, there had been hope, no matter how tenuous, that there could have been survivors on rafts that the airplane carried, or maybe swimmers wearing lifejackets who had been carried away by ocean currents and could still be alive while drifting unnoticed by searching helicopters and vessels. There had been an infant aboard 261, and one family insisted the baby might still be alive.

But almost all speculation and hope vanished with the Coast Guard announcement. "Search and recovery" meant only one thing: the Coast Guard and Navy were now looking only for bodies and wreckage, because there were no survivors.

"It didn't sink in right away for the families," Ed White recalled. "The officer had to go over it a couple of times, and even then people were asking him if he was sure they had looked far enough. Maybe the tides had carried some survivors quite a distance. And I was thinking, you poor, poor people — you just don't understand — and it tore me up."

As the bitter truth finally dawned on everyone, the focus of the families shifted to wanting the remains of loved ones recovered as quickly as possible. They needed closure.

Sue Warner-Bean, head of Alaska's emergency planning, had arrived the morning after the crash, a welcome sight to Ed White. She had been attending a relative's funeral in Portland, Oregon, on the day of the accident when she got a message to call Steve Cunningham, director of systems operations control. After Cunningham gave her the bad news, she caught the first available flight to Seattle and left the following day for Los Angeles, where she was to spend the next 10 days.

While she was in Portland, the emergency response procedures already had been initiated by Fritz King, manager of emergency response systems and logistics. Warner-Bean was able to start her own work as soon as she arrived in California, where about 20 or 30 families already had begun gathering by early Tuesday afternoon.

She found that Ed White had taken over by the time she arrived on the scene. He had recovered from his numbing, emotional session with the first arriving couple and was handling subsequent arrivals with amazing professionalism.

"It was inspiring to watch Ed greet every family that came into the room," Warner-Bean recalled. "He'd sit down with them, talk to them, and get them to talk about their loved ones. By the manner in which he did this, I think he gave everyone on the CARE team the courage to do what they had to do."

Sue herself had little direct interaction with the families. Her job was to keep the CARE team functioning, especially when word of "no survivors" finally sank in and the mood of many families changed from shock and grief to anger.

"The realization that loved ones would never be coming home again, would never be seen again, created new challenges for our CARE workers," Warner-Bean pointed out. "There were some awkward situations that some of our volunteers had trouble handling. They'd take me, or someone like Ed White, aside and ask our advice. Fortunately it didn't happen very often, and many times they'd report how they had dealt with a particularly difficult problem with some family, and I'd assure them they had done exactly right.

"Not one team member left because the experience was too traumatic. Many told me it had been rough, but they'd be willing to go through it again. We had some really good people out there."

They presented the facts with honesty, but also with personal compassion. Considering that their training had consisted of only two days, these men and women volunteers from practically every work group at Alaska Airlines and Horizon Air proved remarkably effective. This was not only the perspective of Warner-Bean, but also the opinion of the overwhelming number of family members themselves.

Later, when as much wreckage as possible had been fished out of the water and body-recovery attempts ended, NTSB chairman Jim Hall gave family members a final briefing. Hall mentioned the fine work done by the Coast Guard and Navy, then unexpectedly praised the Alaska Airlines CARE team for what it had done to ease the pain and grief of the victims' families.

Every family member rose and gave the team a standing ovation. Subsequently, the NTSB was to single out Ed White for special recognition. Both the ovation at the briefing and the later honor were unprecedented. It was obvious that John Kelly's frank acceptance of corporate responsibility, coupled with the compassion of CARE's personnel and Ed White's forthrightness, helped counter what was to become another unprecedented development: an unrelenting post-accident media blitz. Much of it was driven by good reporters with a thirst for facts, but the amount of misinformation was unexpected and unjustified.

Like White, John Kelly personally met and stayed engaged with most of the family members, either one-on-one or in group meetings. Their grief and pain moved both Kelly and White.

Next came the understandable but nonetheless unpleasant task of compensation. The airline's insurance underwriters recommended that Alaska voluntarily send a reasonable upfront cash payment to the families of 261's victims, in recognition that the loss the families suffered might cause immediate financial difficulties that could not await liability-insurance payments. At the time, this represented an unprecedented gesture in the context of airline disasters. Kelly instantly agreed. When someone asked the CEO why he had accepted the insurance companies' suggestion so quickly, he responded, "Because it's the right thing to do."

Kelly decided that $25,000 per family was a fair immediate sum. He authorized sending a check for that amount to each of the 88 families, along with a personal letter emphasizing that this was not to be considered in any way a final settlement. It was intended as an immediate gesture that reflected compassion and represented part of a pattern that had begun to take shape in that Los Angeles hotel and would solidify at the edge of the water that was the grave site of Flight 261. It was one example of the carrier's corporate character in the face of the kind of trauma feared most by those in the airline business — the loss of life.

How the airline dealt with 88 sudden deaths advanced the bonding of the victims' families with the airline's on-site people, with officers such as Kelly and White, and with every member of the CARE team. Throughout the Alaska Airlines system, however, individuals were trying to deal with disaster in their own way. They had all lost friends. Flight 261 had impacted nearly 15,000 employees and their own families in one way or another, and post-accident trauma was not confined to a few meeting rooms in a California hotel. Many employees accepted counseling help from the critical incident response team created to help employees deal with events generating unusual stress.

Many, of course, handled 261 in their own way, as reflected in these few examples.

For Kevin Finan, the sense of personal loss ran deep. Ted Thompson and Bill Tansky had been his friends, and beyond that, there was the sudden cloud of suspicion that had enveloped the MD-83.

Finan, like virtually every other MD-80 pilot, liked the airplane. It was easy to fly and reliable. Yet the early reports of control problems worried him. In particular, that first message from 261: "We've lost vertical control" . . . and then the eyewitness transmission from SkyWest minutes later . . . "definitely in a nose-down position, descending quite rapidly."

Finan could not understand how there could have been a catastrophic failure of the entire control system, nor could any other pilot flying the twin-engine jet. "Jammed stabilizer," the 261 crew had reported, but what could have jammed it?

Katsie Hirsh was another MD-83 pilot who refused to lose faith in the airplane. But she had another problem dealing with 261: the possible effects on her children. "I didn't know how they would react to a crash if the airplane involved was the same type I flew," she admitted. "I was sick when I heard about it. My oldest was 10, the next one eight, and the youngest three. My husband was watching our eight-year-old daughter playing in a basketball game when I called and told him about the accident. I said, 'You have to talk to her about it.' "

He did. The little girl asked him only one question: "Daddy, did the pilots have kids?"

Hirsh said that affected her as much as anything, and she got tears in her eyes every time she thought about Flight 261 and her daughter's simple yet moving reaction.

"I tried to talk to all three children," she added. "I told them that more kids die every year falling out of trees than the number of people who died on 261. I said the difference was that kids don't fall out of trees all at the same time. I stressed that we have excellent planes, excellent pilots, and excellent training, and that if I didn't think flying was safe, I wouldn't be an airline pilot."

The crash of Flight 261, however, brought a sense of *déjà vu* to Captain Hirsh because her father was supposed to have been on the 727 that crashed at Juneau and decided at the last minute not to go. "My parents personally knew a lot of people who were on that airplane," she remembered. "So when 261 went down, it brought back memories of Juneau, and I had to deal with that."

Katsie was fortunate in that she didn't go back to flying until after the cause of the crash had been determined and corrective actions taken. Other MD-83 pilots, however, privately confessed to being briefly wary of the airplane, acutely aware that both 261 pilots had done everything right and still crashed.

Marty Calhoun, senior flight attendant and comedic impersonator, had a special reason for being traumatized by 261. Allison Shanks, one of the three flight attendants on the lost aircraft, was a good friend of both Marty and his wife. Allison had a four-year-old daughter, Hailey, who had gone trick-or-treating with the Calhouns' two young sons the previous Halloween.

Marty had to check in for a trip about 6:30 that night, only a few hours after the crash, and was still numb. Later he did remember that he was deadheading to some city in California where he was supposed to pick up his own trip.

He sat by himself on the deadheading leg. He began writing down all his thoughts about Allison, and what a wonderful person she was, in a letter he would mail to her mother, asking her to show it to Hailey when she was old enough to understand.

While he had difficulty remembering much about that deadhead-ing flight, he did recall — vividly — that while he was waiting to board the airplane, employees from other airlines kept coming up to him and the other Alaska flight attendants, expressing their sympathy. "Some of them," Calhoun added, "even gave us their phone numbers and urged us to call if there was anything they could do." (After 9/11, by the way, the same thing happened. People from every carrier serving Sea-Tac, including Alaska, were going over to the American and United ticket counters, offering to help in any way.)

Marty felt fortunate that his own youngsters weren't particularly disturbed about the accident. "I think little boys are more naive than little girls," he theorized. "I guess they hadn't really thought that I might be killed in a crash myself. The oldest one did ask me if I had been on the 261 plane, but I didn't talk about it much because I could see they really didn't understand what had happened."

Calhoun stopped doing his impressionist routines for weeks after 261 and also repeated this hiatus after 9/11. "I just didn't feel like doing them anymore," he explained, "and I didn't resume until I felt like it."

Calhoun's own religious faith sustained him through the painful ordeal of losing a good friend. He did mail that letter to Allison's mother and felt better for having done it.

The families needed even more inner strength after one particular briefing. The NTSB, with good intentions, invited someone from the local coroner's office to discuss the extremely delicate and sensitive subject of victim identification.

No one faulted the NTSB for what happened; the families themselves had been pressing for word on body identification, and it was a natural assumption that a medical examiner could offer some information. The problem was that the examiner provided more gruesome details and information than anyone wanted or needed to hear. He might as well have been lecturing an audience of fellow coroners totally familiar with the residue of violent death.

It took a long time before Ed White, normally a peaceful, tolerant man, could talk about the examiner's insensitivity without anger boiling from every pore. "It was," he would comment later in a masterpiece of understatement, "a huge mistake."

Some families wanted to visit the actual crash site, and the CARE team arranged for transportation to a beach park fairly close to the area where 261 had crashed. CARE also had arranged for boats to take them out to the actual crash site, but the NTSB rejected the entire visitation plan. It didn't want any unauthorized persons wandering around in an area where wreckage was still being recovered and examined, and White had to agree with its decision.

"They kind of protected us from ourselves," he admitted.

One more thing remained on the agenda, however. The families had requested that some kind of memorial service be held at the actual crash site, and they also wanted someone from Alaska Airlines to speak at a private memorial ceremony set for February 5 on the grounds of Pepperdine University, in Malibu.

John Kelly was the first name to come to mind, but White asked him if he'd mind letting him make a few remarks on behalf of the company at the ceremony. Kelly, cognizant that Ed White had been the closest to all the families, readily agreed.

At that ceremony, Kelly committed the company to finance the creation of a permanent memorial that would be erected on the beach near the crash site and dedicated on 261's first anniversary. The families themselves formed an advisory committee to work with a sculptor on an appropriate design concept.

As for the memorial service, Kelly gave White carte blanche to say whatever he felt was appropriate from someone representing the entire airline.

On Saturday, February 5, White addressed the solemn-faced families:

Last Monday, I returned home from an early dinner with my family to a phone call I never wanted to receive.

Last Monday, many of you received an even more difficult phone call regarding your loved ones.

Last Monday, our lives were forever changed.

I asked our chairman, John Kelly, to give me the opportunity to speak at your memorial today, not just to represent our airline but to speak to you from my heart, because of the time we have been together.

This last Thursday, I traveled to Point Mugu Naval Air Station to review preparations for your visit. Having additional time before you arrived, I took a walk on the beach to reflect on this loss that has hurt us all so deeply.

That was a difficult time for me. Standing there alone, looking out over the Santa Barbara channel, I thought of Flight 261 — our crew members and passengers — the precious people you would soon be here to remember.

I cried until tears could no longer come.

A short time later, your buses arrived.

The wonderful people of the U.S. Coast Guard, U.S. Navy,

Ventura County Sheriff's Department, California Highway Patrol, and numerous other agencies were there to honor your loved ones. The Coast Guard officers were there to collect your flowers to be taken to sea and deposited at the site.

I, too, brought a flower. As I remembered those lost, I kissed my rose, said good-bye, and set it among the countless beautiful flowers you had already placed.

Following that, I walked along the beach. I was deeply touched by your many expressions of love and loss. Among the flowers, pictures, prayers, and tears, I felt the tremendous compassion within each family, and the *collective* feeling of love was simply overwhelming.

I have cried many times since then, and still our loss cannot be replaced.

But we do have memories and memorials. My memories of Thursday and today will be with me for the rest of my life. And it is comforting for me to know that we all have other beautiful memories of our friends and loved ones. Memories last forever.

You have my heartfelt sympathy for the tremendous loss you have endured.

Please be assured that you have the thoughts and prayers, not just from me, but from the thousands of caring and loving people at Alaska Airlines and Horizon Air.

Good-bye.

But it was not good-bye. Ed White was to remain in close contact with the families for another year, during which time he held monthly meetings with the memorial design group. It was at one of these meetings, some weeks after the crash, that White walked into the room where the family committee had gathered and sensed immediately that there was something wrong.

He began discussing the business at hand, then stopped. "Okay," he said, "what's wrong? Something's gone wrong here. So let's get it out in the open."

Something *was* wrong, and Ed found out quickly what had obviously upset everyone in that room. The families had been made aware of the first of what was to be a drumbeat of negative stories accusing the airline of shoddy maintenance practices, of alleged sins of omission and commission that seemed to spell unforgivable negligence. The good, still-grieving people in that room were only human, and they were being told that their loved ones and friends had died needlessly, the innocent victims of somebody else's carelessness.

One woman finally stood up and faced White. "Ed, I can't speak for everyone," she said with admirable calmness. "But I've seen the inflammatory stories, and I've been hit by a troublesome dichotomy. We've worked with you from the beginning. We like you. We trust you, and we can't thank you enough for that. When you come in to talk to us, you *are* Alaska Airlines. I know you and I've worked with you, but our relationship with you is diametrically opposed to what I've been reading and hearing, and I don't know how to deal with it."

White remembered that everyone then began talking, and when they had vented similar feelings, almost akin to betrayal, he expressed exactly how *he* felt. "I understand what you're saying," he told them. "I've been in the same position as you. I don't take your hard negative feelings personally. We've worked on a lot of things together, and nothing can erase that."

The emotionally charged exchange seemed to be a turning point for the group and symptomatic of the unusual relationship that developed between the airline and the families. Considering what the accident investigation itself was to disclose, and the accompanying negative media coverage, that relationship was even more remarkable.

The story of Flight 261 was far from finished. Months and even years of bitter controversy, recriminations, accusations, and turmoil still lay ahead.

At the center of the ensuing controversy, amid the twisted, torn remnants of Flight 261 strewn all over the floor of a Naval Air Station hangar, lay the MD-83's supposedly indestructible, foolproof jackscrew. The jackscrew on an MD-83 — a metal shaft two feet long — turns inside a stationary large nut, called a gimbal nut, and moves the stabilizer. But when the jackscrew assembly from Flight 261 was retrieved from the water, investigators found that the jackscrew was worn and had stripped the threads from the gimbal nut, like a worn-out automobile clutch that won't grab anymore. It was so worn that when the pilots tried to regain control, the jackscrew moved beyond the limits of its design.

There were only minimal traces of lubrication on the jackscrew and what was left of the nut. Something supposedly fail-safe had, in fact, failed.

Lubrication? Design? Maintenance? Hanging in the air like a choking fog was an unanswered question: How could this have happened?

CHAPTER TWENTY-TWO

Fingers of Blame, Hands of Healing

In many ways, John Fowler was the quintessential airline maintenance man, hired by Alaska Airlines as vice president of maintenance and engineering in 1991 with impressive credentials. Fowler had spent 25 years at Pan American World Airways, starting as an aircraft cleaner and retiring as vice president of maintenance and engineering. But his roots at Pan Am were much deeper. His father had been a mechanic and then a maintenance manager with Juan Trippe's airline for more than 40 years, dating to the days of historic flying boats such as the legendary Boeing 314 Clipper, the luxurious 747 of its time.

So Fowler was weaned on airplane engines and systems. He also was terribly conscious of Pan Am's ignominious decline from the world's greatest air carrier, one that pioneered so many global transoceanic routes, into a flabby, uncompetitive loser that eventually perished.

When he expressed interest in joining Alaska, then-chairman and CEO Ray Vecci interviewed Fowler. After responding to a number of Vecci's questions, he asked Ray one. "I was wondering what you think will be the direction of the company over the next five years," Fowler said. "Is there any kind of a five-year plan or strategy?"

Vecci, congenitally allergic to telling the slightest fib, shook his head.

"No, we don't have one," he replied. "We handle things as they come along."

This was uncomfortable for someone like John Fowler, who had so sadly witnessed Pan Am's failure to recognize that it had no real plan to cut its operating costs and adjust to the new realities of the industry.

Fowler and Vecci shared several qualities. Both were New Yorkers, still retaining a strong trace of that distinctive accent. Both were tough, blunt, and sometimes painfully honest. Neither suffered fools lightly, each gave his own personal popularity an extremely low priority, and each was strong-willed.

"Though they were infrequent, I had some tough discussions with Ray," Fowler confessed. "Many nights I'd come home and tell my wife I couldn't take dealing with him too much more. Yet I still have respect and admiration for what he did for the airline."

Fowler was another officer who thought Ray was a man who really cared about people but often didn't know how to show it, and thus was subject to the misimpressions of others. Ironically, there was some of that quality in John Fowler himself. He was a demanding individual, one obsessed with a need to tell the truth as he saw it even when he knew that it often alienated others.

Above all else, he hated to be lied to, and passed the word throughout his entire maintenance and engineering (M&E) organization that this was *the* unforgivable sin. He was not happy with what he found at Alaska Airlines when he took over the M&E department, and just like Vecci, he made enemies while making changes.

When he began as the company's maintenance and engineering chief, there had been three predecessors in that position in little more than five years. Each had a different style of management, and the turnover added up to a lack of stability in the department, with a lot of problems and issues going unresolved.

Among those issues and problems was an undercurrent of still-lingering resentment within the frontline mechanics' ranks, like hidden termites eating away at a structure. This was a residue of the 1985 mechanics' strike that still affected a small but intensely disgruntled core of people who angrily remembered how some had been transferred out of Seattle after the strike ended as a kind of punishment.

Fowler alleged that his immediate predecessor had been a knowledgeable maintenance man who wanted to be friends with everyone, and acknowledged that he, as the successor in a potentially volatile, feud-infested atmosphere, was someone with exactly the opposite view of management responsibility. John Fowler's perspective on management leadership was simple and direct. "I'm not here to make friends," he once said, "but I'm not here to make enemies, either. I'm just here to do a job and to do it the best way I can."

Fowler got permission from executive vice president and chief operating officer Pat Glenn, to whom he initially reported, to run an independent audit of the whole department by outside experts. In effect, it would duplicate the stiffest of all FAA safety checks, known as a NASIP, an acronym for National Aviation Safety Inspection Program.

According to Fowler, the audit, which took three weeks and cost $16,000, uncovered at least a hundred items that the FAA probably would have considered safety violations. "Many were irregularities wherein certain tasks were being performed differently than the way they were described in our own manuals," Fowler said, "or they were not adequately covered in our manuals at all. In either case, the FAA would have tagged them as violations."

John Fowler began sweeping a stiff-bristled broom in every corner of the maintenance department. "Six months after I came," he said, "there were a lot of unhappy M&E management people. And there was a pretty large exodus from the department. Some of them left because they were unhappy, and some of them left because they saw the handwriting on the wall and realized they weren't going to last very long anyway.

"I never asked or told anyone to leave, with two exceptions: I fired someone from management ranks for lying to me, and I fired a secretary who was spending several hours a day outside smoking."

To those with whom he worked, Fowler exuded a no-nonsense demeanor. "Folks always knew where John stood," said one former colleague.

That straightforward attitude was never more evident than during one of his very first employee meetings with frontline mechanics. "One mechanic commented that he had seen people like me [vice presidents] come and go," said Fowler, "so he wondered why they [the mechanics] should believe I would be around long enough to make the changes in the relationships between frontline supervisors and mechanics I discussed during our meeting. My response was direct. I said, 'I plan to be around for a long time.' "

Sometime after that meeting, Tom Gibbs, then the International Association of Machinists (IAM) local president, gave him the moniker "John I-plan-on-being-here-a-long-time Fowler." A few of the mechanics reportedly referred to Fowler by that nickname. No doubt some meant it as a good-natured description of their intensely focused boss; for others, it may not have been so good-natured.

Yet despite some tension and dissatisfaction, the M&E department made changes and achieved goals under Fowler's leadership. Costs were cut and budget controls were instituted. Departmental performance helped the airline improve operational and schedule reliability. Supervisors at all levels began to maintain mandated monthly communication and briefing meetings and, just as important, obtain answers to employee questions and follow through with them. Fowler even hired a consultant to conduct focus groups with his employees to obtain baseline data that influenced the department's subsequent business plans and objectives.

The company rewarded him with two successive important promotions that actually stamped him among some as a long-shot future CEO. Still, Fowler himself admitted that his major drawback was a lack of marketing experience, and that made Bill Ayer the better candidate.

In fact, in early 1997, Fowler became senior vice president of technical operations on the same day that Ayer became senior vice president of customer service, marketing and planning. Both reported to Kelly. Later that year, the board elected Ayer president, and Fowler began reporting to him. Although still ultimately responsible for the airline's maintenance organization, Fowler relinquished direct day-to-day oversight of M&E to a subordinate in 1998, when the board elected him executive vice president of technical operations and systems control, a position he would continue to hold as the tragedy of Flight 261 engulfed the airline.

The flurry of negative media coverage in 261's aftermath included attacks that began even while the NTSB was still trying to determine why the control system had failed. And resentment toward maintenance management personnel, many of them perceived as bullies or martinets, had the effect of confirming some of these media attacks on Alaska's maintenance.

Did negative press coverage affect the investigation itself? While it had no impact on passenger traffic, some within the airline believed it was a very important factor in the behavior of the NTSB, FBI, and FAA. There is almost nothing bureaucrats hate more than to have the newspapers say they aren't doing their job. No doubt that placed added pressure on the agencies. Still, the most significant, undebatable conclusion to emerge from the tragedy of 261 was that excessive wear and inadequate lubrication of the all-important jackscrew *were* the direct cause of the component's catastrophic failure.

What was never made completely clear was *why* there was excessive wear and insufficient lubrication. This became an area of continued speculation, unproven theories, and unresolved issues that have never entirely disappeared. An atmosphere of such uncertainty inevitably attracted aggressive, sometimes unfair and hostile reporting that at times resembled the feeding frenzy of blood-sensing sharks.

The first negative story appeared on the front page of the *Seattle Times* on February 2, two days after the crash, and was picked up by wire services and radio and TV stations nationwide. Its impact could be measured by the fact that the story carried the bylines of the paper's investigative reporter Steve Miletich and two of its staffers, Chuck Taylor and David Postman.

Quoting an unnamed Alaska mechanic, the story claimed that the MD-83 operating as Flight 261 had reported having some kind of stabilizer trouble after leaving the gate on the southbound trip out of San Francisco, and had been forced to return to the terminal. The obvious implication was that whatever constituted the trouble, it evidently had not been fixed. Alaska officials and the NTSB immediately interviewed the pilots of the southbound flight, both of whom denied encountering any kind of mechanical difficulty, including a stabilizer problem. Yes, they had returned to the gate, but it was only to pick up a passenger who had arrived late and missed the flight. Three days later, the *Times* had to "clarify" the erroneous report.

Miletich had a good reputation as a dogged, hard-nosed investigative reporter. If he did have a conscious or perhaps subconscious bias against Alaska Airlines, as some have speculated, it may conceivably have stemmed from the fact that a friend and colleague of his, the *Times*'s highly respected wine columnist, Thomas Stockley, and his wife, Margaret, were passengers on Flight 261.

It also must be pointed out that Miletich's interest in Alaska Airlines and its maintenance practices had begun a year before the Flight 261 tragedy, when a grand jury probe was launched into alleged unsafe practices at Alaska's Oakland maintenance hangar. The allegations were thoroughly investigated by then U.S. Attorney for San Francisco Robert Mueller, who was later appointed director of the FBI by President George W. Bush. No grand jury action was ever taken.

Nevertheless, like any good reporter, Miletich became interested in the airline's safety standards. The Oakland situation was still under the U.S.

Attorney's review when 261 went down, and though initially unrelated to the accident, the investigation quickly expanded to include the maintenance of the jackscrew that had failed. And it became part of the media onslaught on Alaska Airlines afterward.

Meanwhile, even as the NTSB was focusing its attention on the jackscrew as 261's probable culprit, 64 mechanics from the airline's heavy maintenance base in Seattle sent a letter to Kelly, with a copy to Fowler. It was just coincidentally leaked simultaneously to the *Seattle Times*. The letter alleged that the manager of Alaska's Seattle heavy maintenance base was incompetent, and it raised questions about the safety and airworthiness of aircraft released into service following major checks done at the base. The fact that the newspaper received the letter as quickly as Kelly did appeared to confirm that, in addition to real or perceived concerns, there was a certain amount of animosity and distrust simmering in the mechanics' ranks.

The airline at once formally notified the FAA, the NTSB, and the U.S. Attorney in San Francisco of the allegations and ordered an immediate internal investigation into the charges. Kelly also called a news conference to answer questions and announce that he was going to implement an investigation of the airline's operations by outside experts and immediately hire a safety officer who would report directly to him.

Then, after a "white glove" inspection of the airline in April, the FAA announced in June that it might prohibit the airline from authorization to perform so-called "heavy" or major aircraft maintenance. It gave the airline 30 days to shape up or else.

John Fowler told John Kelly and Bill Ayer that if this happened, the airline would have to shut down. At that point, it was unclear what was supposed to be fixed within 30 days, but the FAA chose to make public its threatened action. The effect, intended or otherwise, was to pronounce the airline guilty before any trial.

The subsequent FAA inspection of Alaska's maintenance found that the company was not always abiding by its procedures, that the top safety position at the airline was not filled, and that there were some failures to properly record completed maintenance work. In response, Fowler oversaw the development of an Airworthiness and Operations Action Plan, a 60-point operational program to address every issue raised by the FAA, most of which was implemented by the end of 2000. But all that would come too late to prevent an avalanche of damaging publicity.

"Evidence of Irresponsibility Mounts at Alaska Airlines" read a headline in *USA Today*.

"FAA Threatens Action That Could Shut Airline" proclaimed the *New York Times*.

"FAA Says It May Ground Alaska Airlines Planes — Agency Targets Maintenance Practices" declared the *Washington Post*.

It is only too true that both Miletich and another *Times* staff reporter, Byron Acohido, found employees willing to criticize the airline. It is equally true that in the case of 261, there were grounds for legitimate criticism: that crucial jackscrew did fail, and because it failed, 88 people died. Yet for the few Alaska Airlines employees who thought it necessary to leak allegations, there were also at least a thousand other employees whose first reactions were bewilderment and concern, but later became resentment of coverage they saw as slanted and biased.

What is far more important and even unusual is that throughout all the sustained barrage of bad publicity, the airline's load factors remained high, an incredible demonstration of customer loyalty.

Significantly, only one family member ever challenged the final monetary awards that Keith Loveless, Tom O'Grady, and the airline's insurance underwriters offered in settling liability claims, and that case too was eventually resolved.

The almost total absence of adversarial litigation with the families in so controversial an accident was unusual, and so was the absence of depressed load factors. Still, there was a great deal of adversarial litigation with Boeing, which ultimately led to an agreement that Alaska would assume 60 percent of the liability and Boeing 40 percent. In the grand jury matter, well over a dozen Alaska employees were called to testify, and many more were subjected to FBI interviews.

Issued in December 2002, almost three years after the accident, the NTSB verdict on what caused the crash primarily faulted Alaska's maintenance. The report said, "The probable cause of this accident was a loss of airline pitch control resulting from the in-flight failure of the horizontal stabilizer trim system jackscrew assembly's acme nut threads. The thread failure was caused by excessive wear resulting from Alaska Airlines' insufficient lubrication of the jackscrew assembly." This was *the* bottom line in responsibility.

When it came to contributing factors, the Board discounted a new grease that Alaska had sought to use and that Boeing had approved without technical objection. It did cite the fact that the MD-80 series was not designed with a fail-safe mechanism to prevent catastrophic control failure, an indirect reference to the airplane's lack of redundancy in a component so crucial to flight control.

The Board also acknowledged the confusion caused by two McDonnell Douglas maintenance manuals, each calling for different inspection and lubrication intervals. It noted that the FAA itself had approved Alaska's request for less-frequent intervals based on the airline's operating experience.

In acknowledging this, the NTSB actually made more than 20 safety recommendations that were not addressed to the airline but to other aviation entities such as airframe manufacturers. Included as a *contributing* factor, but not a causal factor, was the agency's comment that the manufacturer's design of the jackscrew on the MD-80 lacked a fail-safe mechanism.

The NTSB attached no blame to the crew, but indulged in what might have been construed by many pilots as some second-guessing. It said Captain Thompson may have made a mistake when, after lowering the wing flaps because he intended to land at LAX, he then ordered them retracted. The Board said that action increased the speed of the dive.

Maybe, but wing flaps and braking slats on jetliners are not designed to withstand high speeds. Lowering them in a nose-down, accelerating dive position probably would have torn them off during the uncontrollable 26,000-foot descent, long before impact.

Why had the jackscrew failed? Why did the very device that was supposed to prevent catastrophic loss of control fail to do its job? Why did the jackscrew and its associated gimbal nut show little evidence of having been lubricated?

The jackscrew on the 261 aircraft had been inspected for wear during a heavy maintenance check at Alaska Airlines' Oakland base in 1997. The initial measurement taken showed that thread wear on the jackscrew was at the allowable limit prescribed by Boeing. Boeing's instructions were for mechanics performing the measurement to check that "limits are between .003 and .040 inch. Readings in excess are cause for replacement of the acme jackscrew and nut."

Even though the result of the initial measurement, .040 inch, was satisfactory, the measurement appeared to one line mechanic to recommend replacement of the jackscrew. A lead mechanic, however, later overruled that recommendation, a decision based on five subsequent tolerance tests to determine if the wear was extensive enough to warrant replacement. All subsequent measurements, like the initial measurement, were within the manufacturer's service limits.

Some believed that was the key that opened a Pandora's box of tragedy, wrecked professional careers, and stained the reputation of a proud company. As it turned out, the mechanic who had originally ordered the replacement was the same mechanic who had previously raised issues that had given rise to the original grand jury investigation of alleged impropriety at the Oakland maintenance base.

Alaska never contested the NTSB findings, although there was a general feeling that the Board had unfairly ignored the potential role played by Alaska's decision to use an alternate grease to lubricate its MD-80 jackscrews. When Alaska asked for Boeing's approval to use the product, a more expensive grease but one already being used on its 737s, the latter replied that it had no technical objection. The company's two legal point men, Loveless and O'Grady, as well as John Kelly and some metallurgical and grease experts, remained convinced that switching grease types, something the government considered immaterial, had had a corrosive effect.

Was the disagreement between a lead mechanic and a line mechanic over the jackscrew replacement an example of morale-destroying friction between mechanics and some supervisory personnel? If so, did that contribute to 261?

The NTSB did not delve into that issue, nor could there be any definitive answer, but there certainly was an unhealthy atmosphere that had permeated maintenance dating back to at least the 1985 strike. It was also apparent there were still some supervisors who couldn't relate to frontline mechanics, despite Fowler's attempts to promote communication within the department.

The NTSB was critical of some of Alaska's past maintenance practices, but rejected a recommendation by its staff investigators that the FAA should perform a new thorough inspection of the airline. The Board pointed out that the airline already had cleaned up its own house.

And indeed it had, including the departures of its two top maintenance officers and a number of lower management personnel. One of those casualties, in fact, was executive vice president John Fowler.

Less than six months after the accident and long before the NTSB hearings, where he testified on behalf of the company, Fowler said, he offered himself up as a "sacrificial lamb" after a routine officers' luncheon meeting. This was

right after the FAA announced its intention to rescind the airline's authorization to perform major maintenance, a potential death sentence that had the
airline in a state of shock.

The FAA announcement came at the worst possible time for a company
whose officers and employees were still trying to cope with the trauma of
261. Word about the jackscrew findings already had leaked out, and many
employees' confidence in their own company and its leaders was shaken.
Internal tensions had reached the point where Bill Ayer had gone into
damage-control mode, conducting a series of meetings with employees
aimed at strengthening lines of communication. Morale had been fragile,
ready to shatter with the first indication of more bad news. And the meetings
were producing more acrimonious doubts than reassurance.

Bill Ayer had a brand of charisma all his own, as effective as John
Kelly's and yet subtly different. Kelly projected a dynamic, larger-than-life
image of leadership, Ayer one of earnestness and sincerity, quieter yet just as
powerful. The FAA shutdown threat, however, was something that no one
could have possibly expected nor easily handled.

"I think a lot of employees who were starting to recover from the crash
trauma," Fowler remembered, "were pushed right back into it. So they
became very much concerned and irate. Bill was taking a lot of heat at these
employee meetings, with people demanding to know whether he himself was
still behind the maintenance and engineering organization.

"He wasn't giving them direct answers because at that stage he didn't
have any. So at this officers' luncheon, he had been telling us about a particularly ugly meeting he had just held with employees, about the typical questions being asked, and the issues involved. The main topic at the luncheon
was the FAA threat, and Bill obviously was upset."

When the meeting ended, according to Fowler, the only officers left in
the room were himself and the company's general counsel, Keith Loveless,
both sitting in a glum silence finally broken by Fowler.

"Keith," he said, "this company needs a scapegoat. And nobody makes
sense except me or somebody higher."

"Come on, John," Loveless scoffed. "You can't possibly mean that."

"I mean every word of it. A man does what he has to do. Without a scapegoat, someone specific to blame, the employees aren't going to move on."

Nothing more was said, but Loveless naturally reported the conversation
to Ayer and Kelly. Two days later, late in the afternoon, Ayer called Fowler.

"I've got an employee meeting in a few minutes," he said, "but would you mind meeting me at corporate at six o'clock?"

Fowler agreed. However, because of the irregular hour of the meeting and his luncheon conversation with Keith Loveless two days earlier, he was certain of the meeting's purpose. He called his wife, Diana, and calmly said, "I will be fired this evening."

At six that evening, he met with Kelly and Ayer. The former pulled a severance agreement out of a desk drawer and handed it to Fowler, who glanced at it only long enough to see what it was.

"You know that I have done nothing wrong," Fowler said.

"This is not about right or wrong," said Kelly. "It's about moving on."

Fowler didn't believe him then, nor thereafter. Five years later, he admitted still feeling bitterness toward both Kelly and Ayer. "Not because of what they said, but because of what they didn't say," said Fowler. The airline's CEO and its president had lowered the boom without also assuring him they believed he really had done nothing wrong.

And above all else, John Fowler, in a professional sense another 261 victim, sincerely believed there was nothing basically wrong with his leadership of the maintenance and engineering department. He felt he had been betrayed by a set of unusual circumstances reflecting bad luck.

In his own words: "If I could have ruled that conversation with Keith out of my mind, I would have sat there and assumed I was being fired for doing something wrong. And, you know, no one nor any agency ever said that I did."

When asked if he believed he was a scapegoat, Fowler replied, "Certainly. My conversation with Keith only days prior, and the total lack of any discussions — ever — with my superiors involving any negative sentiments about my job performance left no other conclusion. But that's what I stepped up for." Others within the organization claim that Fowler sensed that the handwriting was on the wall and that he was, in effect, going to be fired even if he had not raised the possibility of his leaving in the first place.

Fowler's departure was described officially as his decision to take early retirement. He was only 52, and the face-saving announcement didn't fool anyone, least of all Fowler.

Other heads rolled in the aftermath of 261, mostly involving a gradual but abnormally high turnover in certain maintenance positions. Yet there also were important additions: the appointment of the airline's first vice president of safety, and the creation of a safety committee within the AAG board of directors long before the NTSB hearings were even held.

Dave Prewitt, hired to fill the vice president of safety role, was a veteran of accident prevention and investigation work, most of it gained in the military but also at TWA, where he had served as staff vice president of safety after flying the line as a DC-9 pilot. He had been at TWA for five years when he received a call from Jackie Williams of Alaska's human resources department, who told him the airline was planning to hire a vice president of safety and invited him to Seattle for interviews.

He talked to John Kelly, Bill Ayer, and John Fowler, and also Jack Enders, who had been president of the Flight Safety Foundation and was a former FAA official. Enders, who then headed a safety consulting firm, already had begun a private safety audit of all the airline's operations at Kelly's invitation.

Prewitt accepted the job and reported for work on June 1, 2000, which happened to coincide with the FAA-threatened shutdown. Prewitt was getting his ID card at corporate when John Kelly came in and noticed he was dressed informally in slacks and a sweater with no tie.

"When you're finished here," Kelly said, "Bill Ayer wants to see you. And by the way, do you have a suit?"

"Sure," Prewitt replied. "At TWA we were required to wear them."

"Good. Wear it tomorrow because we're meeting with the FAA."

So Prewitt's first assignment as Alaska's brand-new vice president of safety was to help the airline deal with the FAA edict handed to Kelly, Ayer, Fowler, and himself the next day: Alaska Airlines had exactly nine days to come up with the detailed action plan to correct any deficiencies in heavy maintenance.

The quartet returned to corporate headquarters to discuss how they were going to comply with this order, and Ayer suggested going beyond the heavy maintenance issue generated by 261. "While we're at it," he suggested, "let's look at everything."

The proposed plan they and a lot of other dedicated people fashioned in eight days had nearly 30 major sections and hundreds of individual items.

"Everyone worked around the clock," Prewitt recalled, "and submitted it to the FAA on June 9th. They had it in Washington for about a month while their Flight Standards people studied it, and finally accepted what we proposed to do."

The FAA assigned a team to monitor the plan's implementation, a group consisting of its own technical people plus FAA representatives from Delta Air Lines to provide balance.

"We met with the oversight team every quarter to report on our activities and progress," Prewitt related. "Over a period of about 18 months, we had four such sessions before the FAA agreed we had met all our obligations under the action plan the agency had approved."

But that wasn't all. The airline actually had two major safety-assurance projects going on almost simultaneously: the FAA-approved action plan and the separate audit being conducted by the Enders organization. To have two such sweeping tell-us-what-we're-doing-wrong internal corrective projects going on was unprecedented and, in the long run, would be the best response to the post-261 accusations and allegations.

Furthermore, Alaska didn't merely collect a bunch of recommendations and then sit on them with deliberate inactivity. It implemented them down to the letter. "With both the Enders recommendations and the FAA action plan," Prewitt remembered, "we were probably managing three or four hundred individual tasks. One of them, for example, was standardizing all cockpit checklists for the entire fleet. Safety became the tracking organization for all these major changes throughout the airline."

The new, permanent safety organization, originally consisting of Dave Prewitt and 10 staff members, began by assigning the highest priority to three areas: flight safety, ground safety, and maintenance safety. Small groups were set up to coordinate with these three major departments.

"We gave them a new philosophy, a kind of new attitude toward safety," Prewitt related. "We told them that safety is no accident — that if you don't manage it, it won't happen. You can assume it's there, but if you're not visibly working on it and it doesn't become part of your strategic planning, you're really just counting on luck."

To detail everything the new safety organization accomplished, all the changes, reforms, revisions, new approaches, and additional safeguards, would fill the pages of a full-length book. One interesting example: quality assurance was taken out of maintenance's jurisdiction and put into the safety department, to reassure everyone of the independence of this safeguarding program.

By 2005, the safety department had expanded to 58 full-time people. Major emphasis was put on improving communication between all levels of employees in all departments and the safety department. Everyone was encouraged to report any and all incidents and/or concerns relating to existing or potential safety problems. Safety department staffers were available 24 hours a day, seven days a week. Prewitt himself passed the word that he didn't mind getting phone calls at 3 a.m. if someone wanted to report a possible hazardous incident or condition.

It took time and salesmanship to build confidence in the new department. Many pilots, for example, initially viewed with suspicion the policy of reporting any problem immediately — even if the employee himself might have caused the problem. "They were afraid it was a kind of 'Big Daddy is watching and will spank you if you admit making a mistake,' " Prewitt acknowledged. "It took a while to convince them that we weren't out to punish anybody — that maybe there was a reason for their mistake that could be corrected.

"For example, how many aborted takeoffs did we have in the last quarter, and how many block returns [when an airplane returns to the gate after pulling out] were occurring? Do such incidents reflect possible deficiencies in maintenance reliability? What are we finding from audits? Are on-the-job injury rates going up or down, and why?"

The safety department reported directly to the CEO and to the board of directors' safety committee, whose first chairman was airline-savvy Richard Wien. Prewitt established lines of communication between employees and the department that stretched into areas not traditionally monitored for safety problems. Example: keeping track of high overtime figures to determine if that might lead to fatigue-caused injuries.

Prewitt also suggested that Horizon Air have its own safety department, staffed by its own people and reporting to Alaska Air Group's board of directors.

In general, the safety department employed the nonpunitive system established by the FAA and the airline industry several years earlier. Called ASAP (Aviation Safety Action Program), it was an agreement between three parties: the FAA, the airline, and the unions. It created a policy that called for the self-reporting of all incidents or conditions involving a threat to safety, regardless of who or what created the hazard, without fear of being punished.

ASAP became a natural and important component in Alaska's acceptance of what 261 taught: it really *was* a tragedy that should not have happened, and the company faced up to all the implications and obligations of that fact. Alaska really *had* considered itself to be a completely safe airline, but when 261 demolished that overconfident assumption, it wasn't afraid to take the drastic corrective measures required to restore its proud image, even though those measures were in effect an indirect admission of some serious shortcomings.

At least some measure of closure was achieved on January 31, 2003, when family members of the victims and Alaska Airlines unveiled the permanent memorial erected on the shore that bordered the actual crash site. The design was the choice of the family memorial committee, which considered at least 25 proposed concepts before selecting the finalist.

The winning sculptor used two themes: the time of the accident and the incongruous yet touching scene at the crash site witnessed by a small group of family members who had gone there in a boat. They could never forget seeing dolphins, scores of them, frolicking directly over the point of impact. Then, almost mysteriously, when the boat left, all the dolphins suddenly disappeared.

The memorial features a large, working sundial almost 20 feet across. On the base, in bronze lettering, are the Roman numerals for 4:21, the established time of the accident, and around the rim of the sundial are 88 frolicking dolphins, representing the 88 victims. A plaque reads: "We Will Remember Them with Love for All Time."

That night, Ed White attended a dinner hosted by about a dozen family members, who presented him with a miniature replica of the actual monument. It was inscribed: "To Ed White, Alaska Airlines. Thank You for Always Caring. Alaska Airlines Flight 261 Monument, January 31st, 2003."

Another kind of memorial had been created at the instigation of John Kelly in August 2002 next to the company's flight operations and training center building at Sea-Tac. The names of every Alaska Airlines employee who "died on duty" are engraved there, including the names of those who perished on 261, and at Juneau in 1971 on Flight 1866. The area became known as Reflection Park.

Recognition for the airline's post-261 performance in working with victims' families came in May 2000, hardly drawing much public attention but vastly appreciated by Kelly, Sue Warner-Bean, and all the volunteer counselors who had tried to help the families deal with the tragedy. The airline was honored by the International Grief Survivors Foundation, whose president and founder presented to Kelly and Warner-Bean its International Award for Corporate Humanitarian Conduct.

Over time there have been other accolades as well. Indeed, by most accounts the team performed virtually without flaw and, even more important, with heartfelt compassion. Somewhat ironically, it was John Fowler years earlier who had been a catalyst for instituting a more formal emergency response unit at Alaska in order to comply with the federal government's then newly enacted Family Assistance Plan. Looking for the right person to lead the function, he interviewed all the candidates and made the right choice: he handpicked Sue Warner-Bean.

In time, history will be the final judge of the crash of Flight 261. As with all accidents, a series of unfortunate occurrences, facts, and circumstances came together, lined up one to the other, and in so doing perhaps made a tragedy inevitable. But the difference here was that when the unthinkable did happen, Alaska Airlines displayed character, the kind of character that has made it and its people unique over the course of a proud history.

CHAPTER TWENTY-THREE

A Time of Transition

The last transmission between Boston Air Traffic Control and American Airlines Flight 11 was logged at 8:13 a.m. Eastern Daylight Time, and 33 minutes later it was flown into the North Tower of the World Trade Center.

At 8:14 a.m. United Flight 175 lifted off the runway from Boston's Logan International Airport, and 49 minutes later it was steered into the World Trade Center's South Tower.

American Airlines Flight 77 was guided into the west side of the Pentagon, and by 10:07 a.m., United Airlines Flight 93 had flown into the ground near Shanksville, Pennsylvania. The unthinkable had become reality.

As the East Coast watched peace give way to terror, those on the West Coast woke to clear skies and the promise of a beautiful late-summer day, but soon their peace, too, was shattered. Later that morning, John Kelly assembled Alaska Airlines' employees in the corporate headquarters' central rotunda, where, short on words, he began by saying, "This day, everything changed forever."

Bill Ayer was stationed in Alaska's command center. "My most vivid recollection on September 11," he recalled later, "was sitting in the Alaska command center, where we gathered to find out where our airplanes were being sent after the FAA shut down the airspace, and to begin formulating a plan to restart the airline whenever that was allowed. There's a radar plot of the entire country across the hall in our control center that shows air traffic across the country, and I started looking at it every 10 minutes or so, and watched in amazement as every single dot dropped off the map. What followed was a conference call with the other airlines and with our trade organization, the Air Transport Association. The mood on the call was mostly stunned silence.

"When the order to land was issued at 9:30 a.m. Eastern time [6:30 a.m. Pacific time]," recalled Ayer, "most of our aircraft were at their regular departure or destination gates and positioned to leave sooner than airplanes stranded at unfamiliar airports once the order was lifted."

One exception was Alaska's Chicago-Seattle nonstop. It had been ordered to land at Madison, Wisconsin, shortly after taking off from O'Hare. Both O'Hare and Midway were already clogged with diverted airplanes.

Flight attendant Tanya Roberts was on that flight. "At first we didn't know why we had been diverted," she recalled. "We thought it was a bomb scare. We didn't know what had just happened in New York. We sent all our passengers into the terminal, and I used my cell phone to call my parents, who were watching TV and had seen the first plane hit the World Trade Center."

Tanya started to tell them her flight had been diverted to Madison because of a bomb scare, when her mother cried, "Oh my God — there goes another one!"

Yet not until their aircraft finally returned to Seattle did Roberts grasp the enormity of those mass attacks. "I was driving away from Sea-Tac when I felt fear for the first time," she recounted. "I saw a plane coming in for a landing and for some reason that's when it hit me — how vulnerable we were to terrorists."

Like all flight attendants, she could not avoid thinking about her counterparts on the doomed American and United aircraft, and what everyone in the cabins must have gone through. As it did for so many at Alaska and Horizon, it brought back memories of Flight 261.

Greg Perry, an MD-80 captain at Alaska, could only imagine the helplessness of his fellow pilots in the aircraft taken down that day. "I knew those [American and United] pilots could not have been in control," he said. "What those crew members were going through is something we all think about now."

The effects on the company's Alaskan operations were far more serious than in other parts of its system. Airspace in the 49th state also was closed, and this affected scores of communities that relied on regular airfreight shipments of food and medicine for survival.

Cargo director Keola Pang-Ching remembered being in the system command center that first day and being confronted by a concerned Bill Ayer, who had been advised that people in Alaska, especially those in remote areas where roads were virtually nonexistent, had been cleaning out grocery stores since air service was halted.

"Everyone's worrying about passenger service," Ayer pointed out, "but people in Alaska are panicking over suspension of cargo shipments. They're running out of food in some places, so find out what's needed up there, and give it priority when we can fly again."

Pang-Ching's cargo department sent seven 737-200 freighters to Nome and other Alaskan destinations within a few hours after the government reopened the nation's airspace. Passenger flights were crammed with priority cargo.

Inconvenience was widespread, but Adrienne Porter, a representative from the airline's marketing department, found herself in a real fix, marooned in Katmai National Park. Porter was a product development supervisor who spent weeks every summer experiencing every tour offered by Alaska Airlines, and on Monday, September 10, she had flown along with several Alaska Airlines Vacation sales agents to King Salmon, in Southwest Alaska, for a tour the next day into Katmai National Park.

After a comfortable night at the Quinnat Landing Hotel, the party boarded a 40-foot boat for the hourlong cruise up Naknek Lake to Brooks Camp. Porter's mission was to familiarize the airline's sales agents with one of the park's principal attractions, brown bears feeding on the fall salmon run up the Brooks River.

The group had heard only an initial report earlier that morning that an airplane had flown into the North Tower of the World Trade Center. Upon their arrival at the Brooks Camp ranger station, they took note of the flag flying at half-mast, but information was sketchy. There was no cell-phone service or television reception at the camp. They knew little about the world-shaping event as they waited for their "bear etiquette" class, a mandatory lecture before hiking in the park.

When the group reached the first of several viewing stands, they found the salmon running and the bears, some estimated to be near 900 pounds, feeding voraciously. They spent the day amid the splendor of the Katmai, hiking between viewing stands along the river to Brooks Falls. When they returned to the dock later that afternoon, they found their return launch inoperable.

"The boat's crew tried to get the engine started for over an hour," recalled Porter. "They finally off-loaded us and moved the boat into the calmer waters of Deadman's Cove. When it finally did start, the skipper decided not to risk the engine dying again and returned to King Salmon without us." Porter's contingency plan relied on a floatplane, but by then all aircraft had been grounded.

Meanwhile, hunters and other tourists returning from the wilderness filled Brooks Camp. "Some were stranded like us," recalled Porter. "The few cabins at the camp were already taken, and due to the large number of unexpected guests, food had to be rationed."

Porter, the sales agents, and other stranded tourists were offered emergency accommodations in a Park Service yurt. It was surrounded by an electric fence to keep the bears out. Inside, its walls were lined with bunk beds, and rubber sheets and wool blankets were provided.

Porter described that night: "Nobody in the yurt slept a wink. When the bears pushed on the electric fence, it sounded like a bug zapper."

Brad Walker, director of leisure marketing, described Porter as "about as far from a camping type as you can imagine. And here she was with a group of hunters in a yurt."

Her husband, who frantically tried to contact her by phone, was incredulous when the Quinnat Landing Hotel manager told him that Adrienne was at Brooks Camp. "You don't understand," he told the manager. "My wife doesn't camp."

Late the next morning, the boat returned for Porter and her party, but before they reached King Salmon, the engine quit again. "We waited five hours in very turbulent water for another boat," said Porter. "Finally a mid-water transfer was somehow orchestrated, and we were returned to our hotel, hot water, a full bar, and comfortable beds."

During their protracted stay at the hotel, they came to know what the rest of the nation already knew, and the group began to feel the gravity of the events in the Lower 48. They were not able to fly out of King Salmon until Friday evening.

She called Walker after the group's rescue. "I hate you!" she said. She had been on the list to handle a Disneyland trip before Walker switched her to Alaska. Who knew? At least her group had an experience they will likely never forget.

Alaska's stranded passengers in Mexico fared better than those in Porter's group. They found the nation's innkeepers most gracious. "Our flights were shut down for three days," acknowledged Walker. "Hotels in Mexico were not getting anyone in, so they really didn't need to get people out. Goodwill was rampant. Some hotels provided rooms at discounted rates, while others simply provided rooms free of any charge."

With its fleet on the ground and a start-up plan in place, Alaska Airlines' senior officers turned their attention to another effect of the shutdown. "In Alaska's command center," recalled Ayer, "there was discussion about the daily financial drain with no or minimal revenue, and how many days of cash carriers had remaining. John and I looked at each other and without saying a word knew that there were some big decisions ahead.

"We were very fortunate in having a decent balance sheet — not too much debt compared to most everyone else, and we had a very strong cash position. I'll always be thankful to our conservative financial folks who insisted on not running things close to the edge. But it was clear that our industry was moving into a horrible time.

"The industry had already started to decline prior to 9/11, so we reasoned it wouldn't take much for most of the others to become really stretched. We didn't have to react immediately. We were burning cash like everyone else, but had time to develop a strategy."

The grounding lasted two days, and planning the start-up schedule was commanded by Brad Timboe, Systems Operations Control (SOC) director. It wasn't easy rescheduling and launching hundreds of interrupted flights. On the first day after the FAA reopened U.S. airspace, Alaska completed only 41 segments out of a typical 530. Timboe himself gave a lot of credit to pilots and flight attendants who tossed seniority bidding privileges out the window and volunteered to work whatever flights needed immediate staffing.

Within three weeks of 9/11's mass murders, America's air carriers had furloughed more than 82,000 employees, the layoffs ranging from 440 at Frontier to 20,000 at both United and American. Alaska reduced its flight schedule by 13 percent, but out of all the established airlines, only Alaska and Southwest bucked the epidemic of panic buttons.

Ayer reflected on the effects of 9/11. "There was no denying that customer demand dropped following 9/11, so there were only two choices: park airplanes and furlough employees or take some existing airplanes and fly to some new places. Everybody except Southwest and us did the former. We settled on the second path."

Kelly announced to company employees, "With a strong balance sheet, $661 million in cash and short-term investments on hand, and much stronger demand than in other parts of the country, we made a key decision: to return to a full schedule by the first quarter of 2002."

Alaska held its annual officers' planning session a few weeks after the attacks, and used that session to further develop the strategy. "Our goal was to take advantage of our relatively strong financial position and to add some large Seattle point-of-origin markets like Boston, New York, and Florida," said Ayer.

"We had long been interested in those markets, but feared a severe competitive retaliation if we had tried to expand eastward in earlier years. I heard little debate at that planning session. The officers thought this was the right approach, and I think they were motivated by both the opportunity and the fact that we would be doing something different than the rest of the industry."

Named the "Seattle Strategy," the plan was for Alaska and Horizon to become a more significant airline for passengers who lived in the Pacific Northwest. Proposed new routes would also benefit the company's Alaska-based passengers by providing better connections from Seattle to the nation's capital and to other popular East Coast destinations such as Florida. This decision, he assured employees, "enabled us to make another critical decision, which was to not furlough any Alaska employees and keep Horizon reductions to a bare minimum."

The idea worked well from a marketing standpoint, and as Ayer pointed out, "the most significant immediate effect was the pride that it instilled in our employees. This was the 'Alaska Spirit' in action — taking an innovative approach to an almost impossible situation and giving it a try.

"If it didn't work, we could always fall back and be like everyone else, but it seemed like a decent shot. Many employees that I talked with had friends at other airlines who were now out of work. I heard people say that they appreciated our plan to both improve our financial and market position for the long term, and do what we could to keep jobs intact so long as the new routes made a positive contribution. I sensed that people really gave it their all to make these routes succeed."

Kelly's letter in the company's 2001 annual report also assured its loyal base of passengers that Alaska was not abandoning its traditional West Coast markets, but rather expanding its hubs in Anchorage, Seattle, and Los Angeles. Its new fleet of 737-700s and 737-900s had greater range than the models they replaced, and new routes included Seattle to Boston and Denver, and Los Angeles to Cancún and Calgary. Horizon also inaugurated new service from Portland to Denver, and from Boise to Denver, San Diego, and San Francisco.

After normal operations were restored, Horizon temporarily lost more than 40 percent of its short-haul traffic. Its Portland-Seattle shuttle, for example, was a prime business market that collapsed. Why battle long lines and two hours or more at the airport even before boarding a 60-minute flight when you could drive between Seattle and Portland in three hours?

The pall that was 9/11 hung over every department at both Alaska and Horizon. The latter, heavily dependent on business travelers, saw one of its crucial sources of revenue decimated as recession-affected companies cut back on business travel. Telephones, e-mail, and even driving were a lot cheaper and less hassle than flying.

Post-9/11 recommended check-in times became uncomfortably stretched to accommodate the cumbersome, unfamiliar, but necessary new security measures. Before the end of the year, the federal government enacted the Aviation and Transportation Security Act. It provided for the establishment of the Transportation Security Administration (TSA) within the Department of Transportation. This new agency was charged with aviation security. Fees for passenger screening were added to the price of tickets. Terrorism rose to the top of the list of business risks to be assumed by the airlines.

Horizon quickly developed a plan that was approved by the TSA that shortened the security check lines. It added an express lane that cut the security processing time from 60 to often less than 20 minutes.

Economic carnage within the industry included airline bankruptcies, mergers, deterioration of domestic in-flight service, and hardship for thousands of airline employees. The federal government, recognizing the economic consequences of 9/11 for an already ailing industry, provided millions of dollars in emergency aid. Alaska and Horizon combined received $79 million, yet Alaska Air Group as a whole still suffered a $39.5 million loss in 2001. Even with the financial boost from the federal government, John Kelly was staring unhappily at income statements printed in bright red ink. And, with equal distaste, he also was facing the reality of having to cut costs even if this included emasculating Alaska's vaunted in-flight service.

Food service director Carl Baber's department already had navigated the shoals of a major cutback during the Gulf War recession. His budget for 1993 had been slashed by $15 million, enough to make an innovative perfectionist like Wolfgang Erbe weep. Yet Baber, whose greatest talent was in managing food service resources judiciously, had coped with that crisis while still maintaining the quality of in-flight food service.

He had instituted a number of seemingly inconsequential changes, yet their sum total added up to achieving the $15 million mandated cut. He reduced menu changes from twice monthly to monthly. He limited entrée choices in coach. He bought peanuts for a cent less per package, which saved up to $750,000 a year. He boarded enough meals for at least a round-trip and maybe more of a day's flights. He offered food service only at normal breakfast, lunch, or dinner hours and even then with vastly truncated menus. And he did dozens of other things, large and small, to trim costs while at the same time keeping the customer in mind.

Warm turkey or roast beef sandwiches, for example, became a standard lunch or dinner entrée, cold cereal and sweet rolls for breakfast. On a few routes Alaska experimented with selling simple snack boxes to coach passengers, a procedure adopted reluctantly after other carriers tried it successfully. Baber made sure that such items as turkey and beef sandwiches were of the highest quality and reasonably sized, but *Condé Nast* didn't give out awards for effort.

First-class meal service took a severe hit, too, for one of the revenue-depressing consequences of 9/11 was the virtual disappearance of the few remaining passengers paying full first-class fares. First-class seats, once occupied mostly by business travelers on company expense accounts, were increasingly filled with customers enjoying Mileage Plan upgrades.

As long as possible, John Kelly clung to the hope that advances in technology, translated into greater efficiency, would achieve sufficient reductions in operating costs so that wholesale furloughing of employees could be avoided. Bill Ayer had that hope, too. The hemorrhaging flowed unabated in 2002, Kelly's last full year in office. Alaska Air Group ended the year with a net loss of more than $67 million. And that figure did not include one-time "goodwill" charges reflecting accounting changes that brought the net loss to $118.6 million.

Ever the practical optimist, Kelly pointed out that, in spite of this unprofitable performance, Alaska had the second-best balance sheet of all the major carriers. And instead of following the industry's general expedient of reducing costs by mass layoffs, Kelly — as he had throughout his airline career — disdained the conventional solution for deficits. He announced a multi-pronged attack on operating losses that stressed aggressive yet careful market expansion, returning to full schedules as soon as possible, planning ahead for future strategic growth, keeping costs down "while keeping people in mind," as he put it, increasing aircraft utilization, and accelerating the growth of Internet sales through *alaskaair.com*.

This was the ambitious agenda he handed to Bill Ayer, whom the board officially elected as his successor, to take effect at the annual shareholders' meeting in May 2003. Another major change in command had taken place when Kelly moved Horizon CEO George Bagley back to Alaska Airlines as executive vice president of operations.

A time of transitions had begun. New emphasis was given to the potential of the company's website. Its goal was to sell more than a quarter of its tickets online by the end of 2003, and increase that number to 50 percent by 2005.

An increase in aircraft utilization was an integral part of route expansion. In 1998, Alaska's fleet sat on the ground nearly half the day (11.5 hours). During 2002, the company's fleet utilization fell to 10.6 hours, and that contributed to significant losses. During that year, equipment was switched between routes, and routes were in some cases redesignated from Alaska to Horizon, and Horizon to Alaska, and that provided more seats on heavily traveled routes. Smaller aircraft were assigned to short-run, less traveled routes.

Costs were reduced by consolidating heavy maintenance operations in Oakland, and refocusing Seattle's facility on aircraft modification and manufacturer service bulletin fulfillment.

The company's top-10 list also identified possible savings from improved boarding processes, an initiative that would lead to Alaska Airlines' "Airport of the Future." The list also stressed better utilization of technology for staff scheduling and streamlining the company's annual $1 billion supply chain. The cost of everything from fuel to soft drinks went under every manager's microscope. Insurance costs skyrocketed after 9/11, and the company set an objective of reducing those costs to pre-2000 levels during the following year. Fares were also adjusted, where possible, and if something was tried that didn't work, managers were encouraged to keep trying.

Bagley's successor at Horizon was an airline veteran who looked a lot younger than his extensive experience indicated.

His name was Jeff Pinneo, and his career had begun at Continental, where John Kelly hired him as a flight attendant. Though he enjoyed the operational side of the business, his heart was more in sales. He had majored in marketing at the University of Washington, so he left Continental to work briefly for a charter carrier and then a charter marketing company in Bellevue.

Pinneo joined Alaska in 1981. His first assignment, in fact, was a flying job as a passenger service coordinator (PSC), a position that Mike Ryan had brought with him from Continental. PSCs were a kind of purser, helping flight attendants when necessary, but really serving as airborne salespersons mainly to book passengers on future Alaska flights. This was ideal training for someone like Pinneo because it provided both the experience he still needed on the operational side and the opportunity to hone his marketing skills. Eventually he was promoted into a special marketing group that was developing the first stages of the airline's early frequent-flier program. The program was based on awarding gold ingots whose value increased with accumulated mileage.

After Ryan left, John Kelly took over marketing. He promoted Pinneo to director of advertising, an expression of trust since advertising was Kelly's first love and unending passion.

Pinneo always remembered the day in June 1987 when Kelly came into a meeting at the Livingston ad agency, which at the time was handling Alaska's advertising account. "He was wearing a big smile on his face and a Horizon baseball cap on his head," Pinneo related. "Then he announced he was leaving Alaska to take over as the new CEO at Horizon. I had a wide range of reactions. On one hand, I was just getting my feet wet in advertising, and I felt this was like Disneyland, and Mickey Mouse had just announced he was leaving. Kelly was my role model and mentor.

"On the other hand, and this realization came with the benefit of hindsight, John's leaving allowed me a personal and professional growth opportunity to operate more independently. I had to adapt to a new boss, Bill McKnight, a good guy, but totally different from Kelly."

In 1990, Pinneo got a surprise call from Kelly, who offered to move him over to Horizon with the title of vice president of stations. Stations? Pinneo had been around Alaska long enough to associate that job with the legendary

Ken Skidds, whose style of leadership was a rather unique combination of kindly grandfather and unforgiving monarch.

Pinneo assumed that Kelly, too, had a mind-set on how stations should be run, although he assumed it would be different from Skidds's *modus operandi*. But it didn't take Pinneo very long to realize that Kelly had an interesting experiment in mind, one that made the Horizon job seem not only more appealing but also challenging.

"We've got a lot of technically smart people at Horizon, people who know how to run an airline," Kelly told Pinneo. "What we're lacking is a leader who sees the travel experience through the customer's eyes, who understands what customers are interested in."

Any misgivings that Pinneo had about his new job faded and disappeared completely as Kelly continued: "So, Jeff, I want to hire people with a little different focus into our culture, and I think you're the kind of guy who can make it happen."

"If you think I can handle it," Pinneo replied, "I'll give it my best shot."

And that was how Jeff Pinneo ended up at Horizon, at 33 already an airline veteran, but one with little managerial experience and a lot of self-questioning about his ability to do the job. His first staff meeting at Horizon was more like a third-degree interrogation in which he was the suspect.

One Horizon employee at that meeting in particular wore his skepticism like a suit of clothes, asking the new vice president of stations: "What do you think you can bring to this department that we don't already have?"

An appropriate answer would have been "How the hell do I know? I just got here." But Pinneo, carefully feeling his way among these strange faces, answered truthfully, "Well, at this point I'm not sure. I have to get to know all of you."

But Jeff Pinneo had enough pride and determination to justify the faith that both Kelly and Bruce Kennedy had expressed in him. He went on to contribute to an even better Horizon Air, building on traditions and establishing some new ones in his post as vice president of stations. It might be called modernizing without messing up the underlying foundation.

His work was recognized. Jeffrey D. Pinneo became Horizon's president and CEO in 2002. Along the way to the top job, Pinneo also served as vice president of passenger services and then vice president of customer services.

Like others who moved "across the street" from Alaska to Horizon, Pinneo had to adjust his attitude and perceptions about a smaller airline. For one thing, he had to come to grips with what appeared to be extremely high costs. While Alaska in 1991 was desperately trying to reduce its costs below 11 cents per available seat-mile (ASM), Horizon was well over 24 cents/ASM. This was the reality of small aircraft and short routes.

A smaller organizational structure was another adjustment hurdle to be faced when going from Alaska to Horizon. The latter had only eight officers in the entire company, with a relatively small layer of supervisors, managers, and directors. Only five management tiers separated frontline employees from the CEO.

"I think a lot of us at Alaska believed that a small airline with small airplanes had to be small in many other respects, such as being minor league operationally," Pinneo admitted.

"Well, I learned very quickly this simply wasn't true. Horizon was every bit as top-notch and sophisticated as Alaska, and in many ways even more so in terms of the short-haul, high-cycle type of operation Horizon was running.

"And the reverse was true. I think I was able to help Horizon's people recognize that Alaska's people also really cared about their own traditions and culture. My job was to bring that story to Horizon, just as John Kelly did a great job of selling Horizon to Alaska's people."

The 9/11 volcano erupted just as Horizon was about to celebrate its 20th anniversary, and the planned observances had to be canceled. It also occurred while the airline was getting used to the change of command at the top, and Pinneo remembered how the carnage forged a new relationship between Alaska and Horizon. "9/11 was like a bomb hitting the same neighborhood where we both lived," he recalled, "and the effect was to bring all the neighbors together. We came out of that disaster with a much higher level of collaboration, mutual respect, and understanding than ever before."

As a matter of fact, Pinneo turned Horizon around with surprising speed, considering the effects of 9/11 on short-haul business travel. Horizon lost $43 million in 2001, another $20 million in 2002, and then finished the next two years in the black, with a $17 million profit in 2004.

After Pinneo took the reins at Horizon, it helped immeasurably that he, Kelly, and Ayer formed a kind of triumvirate, an executive subgroup of cohesion and coordination within Alaska Air Group's structure that positioned both carriers to best weather the post-9/11 storms.

Meanwhile, it was no secret that John Kelly was facing burnout. Flight 261 and 9/11 had taken their toll emotionally and physically. Nor was it any surprise when Kelly announced his retirement and was succeeded by Bill Ayer in May 2003.

Jeff Pinneo's admiration for Ayer was boundless. In fact, Pinneo never forgot a little-known incident that occurred in 1994 while Kathy Iskra served as Horizon's CEO. She had named Ayer senior vice president of operations, but she needed him in Portland, where so much of Horizon's operations were centered.

"Bill hated to leave Seattle," Pinneo related, "but he was a good soldier. He sold his Seattle home and went down to Portland. We gave him a big farewell party at my house, he bought a home in Portland, and within days after he settled on that house, Kelly announced he was bringing him back to Seattle to assume the role of vice president of marketing and planning at Alaska. We never heard him utter one word of complaint."

Just as Kelly had been Pinneo's mentor in marketing, ex-airline owner/ pilot Ayer became Pinneo's role model in developing better relationships between historically incompatible groups. Ayer, for example, had brought flight operations and maintenance together at Horizon. Horizon benefited greatly from the acquisition of two new aircraft during the late 1990s and the first years of the new century. The airline was the launch customer for both the Bombardier Q400, a twin-engine propjet, and the Bombardier CRJ700, a 70-passenger twin-engine pure jet. The latter was ideally sized and ranged for the longer-haul markets, and the 74-passenger Q400 was a larger version of the popular Q200, extremely reliable and economical for shorter-haul markets. These additions gave Horizon an all-Bombardier fleet. Gone were the fuel-thirsty F-28 jets and the unreliable Dornier 328s, the 30-seat prop-jets that Horizon had acquired in the early 1990s.

The CRJ700 became the new queen of Horizon's fleet, an extremely fuel-efficient jetliner equipped with drag-reducing winglets, small vertical fins attached to the wingtips. The CRJ700 was not only one of the fastest jets flying, but it also had a 1,900-mile range.

Pinneo also managed to get Horizon's foot in the door of a supposedly inaccessible regional commuter market: Denver, a hub that offered an especially inviting fit with Horizon's own route structure and a market that was dominated mostly by United and Frontier. Both Alaska and Horizon had entered that market early in 2002, Alaska operating three round-trips daily between Seattle and Denver, and Horizon operating twice-daily Portland-Denver round-trips and one daily Denver-Boise round-trip.

Horizon further mined that market early in the fall of 2003 by forging an alliance with a carrier already well established at Denver, namely Frontier. The timing was perfect, for Frontier's alliance with Mesa Air was about to expire.

Historically, the first Gulf War, with its accompanying recession and booming fuel costs, changed the way small regional airlines operated. Most of them started out with an independent business model identical to the Horizon of Milt Kuolt. They usually operated on a prorated basis with major airlines. For example, if Horizon carried a passenger from Yakima to Seattle, where she would connect with an Alaska flight to Los Angeles, the two carriers would split the fare. Yields were high enough and costs low enough so the regional could make money.

But in the early 1990s, the combination of rising costs and excess capacity sliced into the profits of the majors. Yet they didn't want to give up market share, and that coincided with the emergence of the new regional jetliners that Bombardier and Embraer were producing — modern airplanes with high price tags but low operating costs.

So these two factors prompted the majors to tell the regionals: "Look, if we buy these new airplanes, we'll let you operate them because your costs are lower than ours. And yet we can still keep our presence in these markets. We'll buy the jets, paint them in our colors, we'll schedule them for you, and this takes all the risk off your shoulders. Furthermore, we'll pay you on a cost-plus basis, and you don't even have to worry about how many people are on the airplane."

The result was that some of these regionals that got what amounted to a free ride grew explosively. Horizon, however, wasn't one of them because, as Pinneo put it, "we were parochially focused on just doing things for Alaska.

"We weren't a part of what fueled the growth of regional carriers," Pinneo pointed out. "But after 9/11 we thought that by having a foot in this business, we would be diversifying our operations. We explored several options, and aggressively pursued one prospect, Frontier, which seemed aligned with our culture and operational capabilities as well as allowing us a return on capital investment."

This wasn't the original Frontier Airlines, however. It was a fairly new carrier using the same name as the one that had sunk into bankruptcy earlier, unable to compete in the savage post-deregulation environment.

The Horizon-Frontier deal, consummated in September 2003, was assigned nine Horizon CRJ jets. Staffed by Horizon cockpit and cabin crews, the nine aircraft were painted in Frontier's livery and each carried a small plaque reading: *Proudly operated by Horizon Air.*

Frontier officials assured Pinneo right from the start that they were very much aware of Horizon's special culture. "We're concerned about losing that culture," they told him. "We know you guys have a very special thing going on over there, so how are you going to manage this arrangement in a way that your own people will still feel connected to Horizon?"

It was a good question, and the answer was to add several provisions to the alliance agreement. For example, Horizon flight attendants assigned to Frontier still wore their Horizon uniforms. The public-address announcements informed passengers, "This is Frontier Jet Express Flight so-and-so, proudly operated by Horizon Air." Passenger comment cards in the seatbacks were addressed to Horizon, not Frontier. These and a few other steps were taken to assure everyone that they were walking into a Horizon environment.

Some 200 Horizon employees were assigned to the Frontier operation. Two years after the 12-year alliance pact was signed, the operation represented 20 percent of Horizon's capacity and about 10 percent of its revenues.

By taking nine jets out of its own schedules, Horizon achieved better fleet utilization. Four of them, in fact, were unproductive at the time anyway, serving markets that didn't warrant 70-passenger jetliners.

"Moving the nine airplanes to Denver had a domino scheduling effect," Pinneo explained. "It tailored our capacity to each market and made our whole system healthier. Within two years, we were posting record load factors in each market and also expanding the system with new service to Albuquerque, Dayton, and Fresno — all supporting our Frontier network in Denver."

The alliance achieved more efficient aircraft utilization for Frontier as well. It was operating a fleet of narrow-body Airbuses, which had about the same seating capacity as Alaska's 737-900s, and using them uneconomically in markets ideally suited to CRJs.

The Horizon-Frontier marriage ended in a premature yet amicable "divorce" in 2006, when both carriers agreed that the arrangement had outlived its usefulness. On Horizon's part, one of the main motives behind the Frontier alliance was too much capacity at the time on some long-haul routes, and the alliance had solved that by shifting the nine CRJs to Denver.

But by 2006, Horizon no longer had an overcapacity problem. Its own steady route expansion had increased the need for CRJs, and the airline found it needed the nine jets allocated to Frontier Express. The alternative was to let Frontier keep the nine and buy new airplanes, but with fuel prices soaring, that was economically unfeasible.

Frontier actually wanted to add more of those fuel-efficient airplanes to the commuter schedules, but to its credit, it understood that conditions had changed somewhat for both carriers. It agreed to line up a new alliance partner while phasing out its pact with Horizon.

Jeff Pinneo had served as Horizon's CEO for five years when the Horizon-Frontier relationship ended, and any disappointment was tempered by the practical acceptance of its inevitability. Horizon, like its older and bigger sister, was growing in spite of the post-9/11 havoc, carefully moving into markets either underserved or vacated by industry-wide contractions.

If Pinneo had any disappointment during a half-decade at the helm, it was the departure of Kelly and the dissolution of that informal, unofficial Kelly/Ayer/Pinneo triumvirate that had worked so well, fueled by the mutual respect existing among the three men.

No one wanted Kelly to leave, but there wasn't an employee or officer who didn't understand why he had decided to retire at the relatively young age of 58. The fatigue lines were etched into his face, and those pouches under tired eyes were the painful legacy of leadership during the 261 and 9/11 ordeals.

"When John announced he was leaving, I was glad for him," Pinneo reflected. "I knew those two traumatic events had taken a lot out of him. But I was grateful that he had laid out the whole game plan for me, and I looked forward to working with Bill Ayer, for whom I had tremendous respect. I was amazed at the leadership gifts Bill had that I didn't."

Kelly had spent 27 years with the company, seven of them as chairman and CEO of Alaska Air Group. He left behind a record of solid accomplishments and warm memories of his larger-than-life, charismatic personality. One of those accomplishments, sometimes forgotten, was his very first one: the healing process he provided after the turbulent, challenging reign of Ray Vecci, whose bottom line was regaining profitability, not winning popularity.

Among the many major achievements of the Kelly years, include industry-leading Required Navigation Performance (RNP) and other safety enhancements, airport check-in kiosks, online ticketing, the Airport of the Future concept, the most profitable year in the history of the airline, the massive safety reforms instituted after Flight 261, refusal to engage in the wholesale layoff of thousands of employees as other carriers had done after 9/11, and the carefully plotted route expansion undertaken at a time when most of the industry was cutting and contracting.

Nor could anyone forget his on-site presence in Los Angeles after the Flight 261 crash, the way he handled the media with frankness and simple honesty, and what it had meant to the victims' families to have the airline's CEO face them and so visibly share their grief. That took more than mere charisma. It took guts.

John Kelly also contributed something far less tangible than kiosks and cockpit hardware, yet in some respects just as important. His was a "feel good" leadership. Like Charlie Willis, Kelly tried to make flying fun, but unlike Charlie, Kelly insisted that the airline be run at a profit.

Kelly and Bill Ayer actually were progressing toward their goal of transforming Alaska Airlines into a low-cost carrier that still offered superior service. But the double whammy of another Middle East conflict following on the heels of 9/11 changed the very definition of "low cost."

Ayer himself accurately summed up the situation in the 2003 AAG annual report, the first issued under his name. "A quarter of our industry is now comprised of low-cost carriers," he wrote, "and another 45 percent of restructured majors. So 70 percent of the industry has or soon will have a low cost structure. As a result, despite two years of cost improvement, we've seen our position as a carrier whose cost structure was comfortably in the middle of the pack in the late '90s become uncomfortably close to the higher end of the group."

He wrote those words in the spring of 2004, and things were to get worse. For suddenly, all previous economy measures, past or planned, were rendered inadequate. As of the beginning of 2007, the lowest price Alaska was paying per gallon of fuel was $1.97 — the same fuel that at the start of the jet age in 1958 cost 10 cents a gallon. In some of the remote areas of Alaska, jet fuel was selling for as much as $5 per gallon.

The total fuel capacity of the 737-400, a jet that makes up about 40 percent of Alaska's fleet, is 5,300 gallons, and to "fill 'er up" costs at least $10,440 at $1.97 a gallon. Calculated by the amount of fuel being used in the 2003-2005 period, just a one-cent-per-gallon increase cost Alaska about $4 million.

This was massive inflation of an item representing a huge chunk of Alaska's total operating expenses: 15 percent in 2003, 19 percent in '04, and a backbreaking 24 percent in '05. And it was accompanied by a nose dive in fares; the lowest price became the dominant factor in customer choice, superseding service and even schedule convenience.

Between 1978, the year of deregulation, and 2003, industry-wide ticket prices, adjusted for inflation, fell by more than 50 percent. Combine that steady, unending free-fall with skyrocketing fuel costs, and it's easy to see how the old-line, established carriers wedded to high-cost labor contracts could never compete against the newer low-cost carriers, not when they were often losing money on flights that had every seat filled with a paying passenger.

Alaska was no exception, desperately needing some formula to compete against such low-fare carriers. So this was the can of worms that fate handed Kelly's successor, a very large can with one side labeled "Fuel Prices" and the other side "Labor Costs."

William S. Ayer, with a stubborn resolve that matched his brand of quiet charisma, never flinched. In the hostile climate of this new century, he saw only two choices: *Cut costs or cut jobs.*

And the latter was what he fervently wished to avoid.

CHAPTER TWENTY-FOUR

Biting the Bullet

"Fasten your seat belts; it's going to be a bumpy ride." That memorable line, spoken by Bette Davis in the film *All About Eve*, could have been applied to the warning Bill Ayer was forced to give Alaska/Horizon officers and employees in his first full year as chairman and CEO of Alaska Air Group.

A fact to remember: few in the airline industry had been better prepared and more thoroughly trained to assume the top leadership of a corporation than Bill Ayer. And he was the first to give John Kelly full credit for a grooming job that taught, honed, and fine-tuned him to handle the awesome challenges of airline life at the worst time in the history of modern commercial aviation.

After Kelly promoted Ayer to the presidency in 1997, he brought up the subject of succession. As Bruce Kennedy had before him, Kelly wanted to make sure he had the right person ready to take over when he retired. Originally, the directors had six potential CEO candidates in mind to take Kelly's place, and Ayer was one of them. Kelly let him know he was being seriously considered by the board, but also advised him that he needed seasoning in areas where he was relatively inexperienced, a point with which Bill Ayer was in complete agreement.

"He recognized early on that I didn't have all the necessary background to be a good CEO," Ayer admitted. "He knew I had experience in marketing and planning. What he gave me over time were additional jobs and responsibilities, especially in customer service, where I had savvy people reporting to me. Later came maintenance and engineering, and flight operations. John was making sure I was being exposed to every element of the business. During the learning process, I was vice president of marketing and planning, then senior vice president of marketing and planning as well as customer service, and eventually, president and chief operating officer.

"John was really smart in laying all this out, and coordinating it with the plans he had for his own retirement. He gave me all the time I needed and made sure I spent a lot of time with directors at board meetings giving various presentations. He wanted me to have the chance to put forth and defend my own ideas, and to let the directors get to know me better."

The outgoing CEO and the soon-to-be CEO didn't always agree on everything, but they were never reluctant to talk over any disagreements. And they were 100 percent convinced that, however Alaska and Horizon mapped the future, any plan had to be based on adherence to a prescribed set of values.

Under Kelly's leadership, those values were distilled to five from a long list of suggestions identified and offered at meetings of employees, both relative newcomers and veterans, conducted over a period of months. These were labeled Alaska Spirit, Integrity, Professionalism, Caring, and Resourcefulness. Concurrently, five corresponding attributes were also identified as keys to the airline's long-term prosperity. Known as "critical success factors," they were Safety, Continual Improvement, Quality People, Profitability, and Quality Service.

Ayer included the values and critical success factors in the foundation of his own blueprint for the future. Yet those 10 pillars, important as broad guidelines to follow, were not enough by themselves to withstand the economic battering that followed.

Nor was all of John Kelly's careful tutoring of his protégé sufficient to arm Ayer with easy answers, quick solutions, or warmly received corrective measures. Mass furloughing, the course taken by so many larger carriers, was anathema to Ayer, as it had been to Kelly. He was convinced that reducing labor costs was the key to survival, and while painful, it was less so than losing one's job entirely. It still was a tough message to communicate to a workforce that was about 80 percent unionized. The cardinal rule in management-labor relations, enunciated years earlier by Bob Gray, was never try to take away what a union already has won.

But this collided head-on with the chilling statistics and grim realities of the reeling industry. In 2003 alone, the 11 major domestic carriers had suffered a staggering combined loss of $6 *billion*, the fourth consecutive year of red ink. Only four had earned any pretax profit, three carriers remained in bankruptcy, and 123,000 employees had lost their jobs.

Ayer was trying to appeal to a workforce almost three-quarters of which was traditionally skeptical of any management cost-cutting proposal. Yet he coupled his belt-tightening pitch with a specific plan for a better future based on some necessary sacrifices in the present. It was called "Alaska 2010," a long-range blueprint not only for attaining future profitability but also for positioning the company to avoid the economic feast-or-famine cycles so typical of the airline industry.

What he was trying to achieve, Ayer explained, was a restructured airline in which 2010 would be the year when "we can look back with great pride on how we transformed ourselves, how we took control and willed ourselves to be one of the preeminent airlines in the United States." But, he stressed, achieving this by 2010 depended entirely on actions taken now or in the immediate future, and a large proportion of those actions involved salary reductions, benefit adjustments, and work-rule changes. This was like asking someone expecting Band-Aids to undergo major surgery.

The most immediate goal of "Alaska 2010" was to cut annual nonfuel costs by $307 million, of which $112 million would come from union employees in the form of wage reductions, adjustments in some benefits, and changes in work rules. Having organized labor contribute about a third of the projected savings obviously was going to be Ayer's toughest selling job. In effect, he was selling sacrifices.

The company attacked the problem of volatile fuel prices by what is known as "hedging." In simplest terms, Alaska was betting that fuel prices were going to climb even higher, and contracted with suppliers to buy in advance a certain percentage of its future fuel needs. It was a gamble, but one designed to smooth out and remove the volatility of huge price swings. Between 2003 and 2005, Alaska bought about 50 percent of its fuel in advance. Hedging saved Alaska a considerable amount of money, and, significantly, at that time Alaska and Southwest were the only established carriers with enough cash to buy hedge contracts.

Another effective cost-saving strategy implemented by the Ayer regime was to restructure the fleet, starting with a modest but significant addition of the most fuel-efficient airplane Alaska had ever operated: the Boeing 737-800, an aircraft equipped with drag-reducing winglets, like Horizon's CRJs. Winglets, which extend vertically from the wingtips of a plane, are actually small airfoils that reduce drag and provide extra lift. They also reduce fuel consumption and improve cruising range.

The airline initially ordered only three 800s, and they were planned for the prime long-haul transcontinental routes, especially the Seattle-Florida route. The new Boeings were smaller than the 737-900s, with a capacity for 157 passengers compared to 172, but with greater range for serving the long-haul flights to and from Orlando and Miami.

Not only did the 737-800s have greater range than the bigger 900s, but so did the airline's 22 even smaller Boeing 737-700s. This freed the 900s to be available for the heavy demand for Mexico service in the winter and the summer tourism season in Alaska. It was all about sizing the right plane to the right market.

At the same time Ayer announced the 800 order, he also disclosed plans to retrofit the 737-700 fleet with winglets. Would those rather innocuous fins really save fuel? Emphatically, yes. In fact, they have reduced fuel consumption between 3 and 5 percent, which translates into a reduction of 130,000 gallons per year for a single aircraft.

The 737-800 order and the decision to retrofit the 700s pushed Alaska closer to another eventual goal: an all-Boeing fleet. By March 2005, as the airline took delivery of its first 737-800, the phase-out of the entire MD-83 fleet was well under way. By then, Alaska was operating only 26 MD-80s, a dozen fewer than were flying at the start of the 21st century. A year later Ayer announced the airline's plan to accelerate its conversion to an all-Boeing fleet.

During 2004, Ayer's first full year at the helm, two scarcely publicized recognitions took place. One was the FAA's Diamond Award to Alaska and Horizon jointly for excellence in maintenance training. The other was the Shield Carrier Award, presented by the Medallion Foundation, an FAA-supported organization established to promote aviation safety in Alaska. U.S. Senator Ted Stevens presented a plaque to safety vice president Dave Prewitt, and a few months later, a similar honor went to PenAir, one of Alaska's valued alliance partners in the 49th state.

So the stains and scars of Flight 261 were at last beginning to fade, although not entirely, because even nonthreatening incidents drew an inordinate amount of attention from the Seattle media. In late October 2005, reports, sourced anonymously, surfaced that mechanics had discovered two Alaska Airlines MD-83s with inadequately lubricated jackscrews. The FAA, quite naturally, promised a thorough investigation of the airline's jackscrew-inspection procedures. Ayer ordered an immediate fleetwide inspection of all the airline's MD-83s as a precaution and also welcomed any FAA investigation, promising complete cooperation. But he also pointed out that the status of the lubrication conditions on both airplanes had been uncovered by the very procedures that had been instituted after 261.

Then came a very interesting turn of events. The two unions representing Alaska's pilots and mechanics joined two company officials in a joint statement strongly denying that the safety of either aircraft was ever imperiled in any way whatsoever. Their allegedly dry jackscrews had been tested, as were the measurements of vertical-stabilizer movement. Both were found to be well within proper specifications.

The statement was signed by John Pollom, safety and standards chairman of the Aircraft Mechanics Fraternal Association; Captain Jack Wilkes, central safety chairman of the Air Line Pilots Association; Fred Mohr, vice president of maintenance and engineering; and Dave Prewitt, vice president of safety and security.

Three months later, after some in the Seattle media had resurrected the pain of Flight 261, the FAA laid it to rest once more. The FAA said its investigation of Alaska's jackscrew-maintenance practices confirmed that the airline had met or exceeded all requirements.

Every air carrier CEO is beholden to three individual constituencies, each with somewhat differing and sometimes conflicting agendas: customers, shareholders, and employees.

Customers, of course, rate high priority for obvious reasons — passenger and freight revenues are every carrier's lifeblood. One industry-leading, customer-oriented move taken in 2003, for example, was to simplify Alaska's version of the industry's bloated fare structure. It eliminated about 10,000 different fares, removing the universally hated weekend-stay requirement and narrowing the gap between first-class and coach tariffs.

While there was little that Ayer or anyone else could do about the industry's trend toward truncated in-flight meal service, he preached that preserving Alaska's traditions of extra courtesy and effort cost absolutely nothing. But it meant a lot to customers. Though meals in coach on most Alaska flights would be replaced with meals available for purchase, Alaska's traditional first-class service remained first class.

No top executive, not even Kelly, had tried harder to stay in touch with frontline employees than Bill Ayer. What the two men had in common was a desire to relate to the workforces, to understand their problems and ambitions without being paternalistic.

Ayer was often seen prowling Sea-Tac terminal talking to customer-service agents, visiting with flight attendants who were coming and going, or poking his head into the cockpit of flights he boarded, to better learn about employee concerns even as he hoped they could understand his.

He probably held as many and perhaps even more meetings with employee groups than any previous chairman. He was always striving to get across his main theme: the need for all to accept the concept of competitive costs in order to remain viable and to secure jobs.

During Ayer's first full year at the helm, the need for the airline to maintain a strict focus on cost management loomed larger and larger. Growing revenue per available seat-mile (RASM), reducing cost per available seat-mile (CASM), and achieving "market rates" for labor became Ayer's mantras. The specific goal of his "Alaska 2010" program was to achieve a CASM excluding fuel costs of 7.25 cents in order to remain competitive while also being profitable. At the time, Alaska's CASM stood closer to 8 cents, with many routes performing unprofitably. By late summer 2004, it was more and more evident that Ayer and Alaska needed to take action and that difficult decisions would be impossible to avoid. In September of that year, the airline announced a major and painful change. The airline's Oakland maintenance center would be closed and its work contracted out. Up to that time, Oakland had been responsible for about 40 percent of the airline's so-called "heavy" maintenance, extensive stem-to-stern checks of aircraft done over weeks, as opposed to "line" maintenance, done on an as-needed, overnight basis or over short periods. The other 60 percent of the airline's heavy maintenance had already been contracted out.

During the process of closing the Oakland base, mechanics there would have the opportunity to "bump" fellow mechanics with lower seniority at other locations or bid on open maintenance positions within the company. But as a practical matter, with the vast majority of remaining jobs in Seattle and other line maintenance locations, most of the base's 340 mechanics would be leaving the company.

As part of the same announcement, the airline said it would contract out all remaining in-house fleet service functions — the cleaning of aircraft interiors between flights. Also contracted out would be ground support equipment operations, and the airline would close its remaining city ticket offices.

Combined with a previously announced 150 jobs in management either voluntarily or involuntarily eliminated, a total of 900 people would be departing the company.

The news was stunning and shattering. Despite the fact that Ayer and his senior officers had laid the foundation for his actions by continuously communicating the need for this type of change, it still came as a shock to the entire organization. To soften the blow, the airline offered generous and attractive voluntary severance incentives for high-seniority employees in affected work groups in the hope that involuntary departures could be minimized.

Alaska wasn't alone. The entire industry remained in the doldrums. After the upheaval of 9/11, the industry racked up losses of $32.3 billion from 2001 through 2004. High fuel prices, high labor rates, ongoing downward pressure on fare levels due to torrid competition, particularly from new low-cost carriers, all continued to take a toll. United, in bankruptcy since 2002, was joined in 2005 by Delta and Northwest.

In May 2005, Ayer, after 20 months of unsuccessful negotiation with the IAM, addressed the cost of another major function: Seattle's ramp-service operation. The airline's decision to "outsource" ramp-service work at its largest station came only after a lengthy evaluation in which numerous options were considered in an effort to find ways to save money and improve efficiency. While entertaining proposals from outside providers, the airline continued contract talks with the IAM. In the end, after more than a year and a half of negotiations, the parties were unable to reach an accord.

Ayer was later to regard this decision as the hardest he ever had to make. "I knew only too well it hit longtime, dedicated people," he admitted. "But the bottom line was that at the bargaining table, we couldn't make a deal with the IAM that made economic sense in the environment we found ourselves."

The company's efforts to temper the pain of the changes failed to quell the inevitable union bitterness toward such draconian actions as outsourcing. The 475 ramp-service people who lost their jobs received a total of $16.1 million in severance packages that averaged nearly $34,000 per person, plus accumulated pensions.

Ayer's frequent meetings with employee groups included frank question-and-answer exchanges that exposed him to large doses of cynicism, skepticism, and often open hostility. Yet he never ducked a question. Most important, he really understood the perspective of unhappy employees. A question asked more than once challenged one of the core values that Ayer, and Kelly before him, had always stressed. The value the employees cited was "caring."

"Okay, Bill," one said, "how can you talk about caring being one of the company's values when you've just laid off nearly 500 people in Seattle ramp service?"

It was a tough but fair question, and one asked at several meetings. Ayer answered it with the earnestness that so delineates his personality. "First, we have to worry about the viability of this company for the vast majority of our employees, for the 95 percent who are going forward," he explained. "Second, if you have to take such drastic action affecting good people who have had long careers here, then you have to treat them in as caring a fashion as possible. So we hope people leave here not with a bitter taste in their mouths, but feeling that the company did everything it could to care about them, given the economic circumstances. I know there are people out there who are bitter. But I don't think in the course of things that we're changing our fundamental values."

This was about as honest an answer as any CEO of an ailing company could provide. It also was in contrast to the way many airlines handled much larger furloughing than Alaska. Most of the industry's 130,000 employees who were laid off in this black period were not given the same extensive personal briefings, painful explanations, and factual economic justifications and generous severance packages from highest-level management that Alaska's people got from Ayer.

Just as John Kelly had the inner courage to face grieving and potentially angry victims' families, Ayer displayed the same moxie in facing employee groups that in some cases were bristling with resentment. Ayer would listen to them take strong issue with most of his cost-cutting actions, and then bluntly say: "You know what's been happening in the industry with airlines like United, Northwest, and Delta. You know about the brutally competitive nature of our business, where customers are much more price-sensitive than ever. And finally, you know about our own cost-structure and the fact that we've suffered more than $200 million in direct operating losses over the past four years.

"So let me ask you something. What would *you* do? You tell *me*. I'm open to ideas. I don't like doing stuff that impacts our people. Nobody has ever said, 'I've got a better idea, so do this instead.' You just say, 'I don't like that particular part of what you're doing.' Well, I don't like it either, and I wish it were different."

The backdrop to the ongoing broader conversation Ayer was having with employees was the multiple discussions the airline had going on with its unions. Of the six separate union contracts that cover the airline's organized employees, five were amendable in 2005. And because the stakes were enormous, Ayer became personally involved. He tried hard to communicate to Alaska's union members his attitude about organized labor. "I think the unions have done a lot of good in our industry," he said. "The issue I have with labor is whether unions are really concerned about the interests of their members in one company; or are they more concerned about their position in the industry across the country?

"What I tell our people is to get in there and be active in their union. Make sure *your* views are represented at the bargaining table. Over time, I think management gets the kind of labor relations it deserves. If management is a bunch of rotten buggers, they end up with rotten buggers on the other side. We have made progress with our labor leaders because of a management team that's been respectful of the process of trying to work together."

Between 2005 and 2006, four of the five amendable contracts were ratified, including new four-year agreements with the Association of Flight Attendants, the Aircraft Mechanics Fraternal Association, and the International Association of Machinists. A contract extension with the company's smallest labor group, the Transport Workers Union, also was ratified.

However, negotiations with the pilots fell apart and went into arbitration a year earlier. This came as a huge disappointment to Ayer. When an arbitrator decreed an annual pay cut averaging a stunning 26.5 percent, Ayer orchestrated a new negotiation to trade off productivity improvements in exchange for a lesser pay cut of around 20 percent. Union members voted down the 20 percent offer and accepted the arbitrator's more drastic cut in return for a contract with a two-year term instead of the five-year agreement for which Ayer had hoped.

So in the end, the labor peace achieved in 2005 and 2006 was like a stretch of highway patched with necessary haste, leaving some big potholes to be fixed later. The arbitrator's decision did, however, achieve the savings the airline needed to turn the corner. Alaska Air Group ended 2005 with a $55 million profit, a turnaround in which employee sacrifices, to be sure, contributed a large share. Hedging, record load factors, higher revenue yields, and that precious commodity known as customer loyalty also were vital contributions to the dramatic comeback.

The latter could not be underestimated, for just as customers had demonstrated their unique allegiance during the Flight 261 crisis, they did it again in the summer of 2005, when Alaska's schedule reliability went into a steep dive. Ayer's frequent trips to the teeming ticket counters and through the corridors and gate areas at Sea-Tac gave him firsthand evidence of disappointment bordering on disillusionment not only from customers but also from frontline employees. He kept encountering good Mileage Plan passengers and loyal Board Room members asking him bluntly, "What's happening to our favorite airline?"

And he kept getting the same worried queries from veteran frontline employees, whose morale had dropped almost as sharply as on-time arrivals and departures. There was no single reason for the schedule-reliability decline, but there was no question that employee morale had suffered.

Ever mindful of the need to listen as well as communicate, Ayer decided he needed additional eyes and ears for a fresh outlook on employee thinking and morale by others besides himself. He first targeted the sagging morale he had personally witnessed at Sea-Tac and gave a special assignment to Glenn Johnson, vice president of customer service/airports, who like Ayer himself was a Horizon alumnus.

"I want you to look at our overall operations," he told Johnson. "Find out how we can re-engage with our people. I'm not talking about technical things. It's about whether we can get people to feel good again about working here."

Among the suggestions that came from Johnson's research was to hold a few open-house receptions for fairly large groups of employees. These would be hosted by Ayer at corporate headquarters so the "troops" and their families could meet and interact with him and other officers and managers.

The first one, in July 2005, was a success. Attendance topped a surprising and very satisfying 500, packing the breezeway between the east and west wings of the corporate headquarters building. Subsequent meetings at headquarters and major stations elsewhere in Alaska's system attracted large turnouts and provided one more avenue of dialogue between employees and their leaders.

But Ayer also realized that he needed to explore more objective ways to judge employee attitudes. The receptions had been a positive step in the right direction, yet he knew that, while polite, important, and a good first step, these social gatherings had not been occasions for venting strong opinions.

So the next step was to hire an outside firm and give it an unusual assignment: interview a cross section of employees, from new ones to the most senior. Talk to customers, too. Find out what it would take to reinvigorate the airline's special brand, namely its can-do image. Ayer needed a top officer to work with the consultant, and his choice was quiet, level-headed Gregg Saretsky, executive vice president of marketing and planning, whose department was focused on brand identity.

The project involved several hundred completely frank "get-it-off-your-chest" interviews with a broad cross section of management at all levels and frontline employees from all work groups. Seniority ranged from those who had been with Alaska for at least 20 years to people who had six months' service with the company. After the first hundred or so, Ayer and Saretsky already had some interesting observations.

Ayer, for example, noticed that people who had been with Alaska the longest were the most concerned about the drastic changes, notably the elimination of the entire ramp-service workforce in Seattle, which was cited frequently. Coming on the heels of similar outsourcing of fleet service, the ramp-service ouster had really upset more people than just those terminated.

Saretsky found that one of the survey's most fascinating, yet in some ways most disturbing, revelations was the large number of people, especially long-term employees, who thought Alaska had lost its "we're not just a company, we're a family" tradition. That was an understandable concern of many veterans, yet Saretsky himself thought this didn't necessarily have to be a bad development. Moreover, it probably was inevitable as the airline's workforce grew to keep pace with an expanding system.

"So we began thinking now more in terms of being a close-knit community rather than a family," Saretsky said. "Community is not as strong a designation as family, but family also can denote a kind of parent-child dependent relationship. A company can't be a parent to employees, the one who makes all the tough decisions for a child too immature to make them for himself. But we haven't yet made that long leap to where we can regard ourselves as a cohesive community."

Saretsky was encouraged by one common thread in the interviews. "The survey results showed that the employees' foundation had been rocked and, yes, they viewed the future somewhat more skeptically. But we also found that employees hadn't given up. That conclusion, significantly, was very different from how employees felt at many other airlines throughout the country."

Inevitably, the interviews disclosed considerable resentment that employees were being asked to take wage cuts while management salaries weren't affected. "That's always a challenge," Saretsky conceded. "We had told everyone we were going to pay market-based wages, and what they replied was 'Isn't it convenient that management salaries are already market-based so they don't have to take cuts?'

"What they don't understand is that we can and do lose a lot of excellent management talent not only to better jobs at other airlines, but also to profitable companies like Microsoft, Nordstrom, Starbucks, Paccar, and Boeing. We have to pay competitive salaries to get and keep top management people."

Despite this reality, senior management did lead the way by taking voluntary 15 to 20 percent pay cuts in 2003, something forgotten by many in the ensuing years of contentious contract negotiations. And management employees had their pay frozen in 2003 and 2005, while union employees continued to receive step increases guaranteed by their contracts. The company's 2005 proxy statement reported that, even with a base salary lower than that of 75 percent of his airline peers, Bill Ayer chose to forgo an additional performance award worth several hundred thousand dollars because of "the ongoing transformation of the company and recent sacrifices by frontline employees." Probably only employees who read the fine print in this lengthy financial filing were aware of their CEO's shared sacrifice.

Perhaps the most important conclusion to emerge from this extensive, deep-probing public-opinion survey was a need to get employees more involved in the policy-making process, assuring that their views and feelings are taken into consideration. The framework was already in place for such participation. The airline's senior leadership and the Alaska Airlines Labor Coalition held joint meetings, definitely a positive step forward in labor/management relations. But these good intentions had been simply overwhelmed by the devastating current events of that period: 261, oil, war, 9/11, and economic calamity for the airline industry. Ayer resolved to revitalize these quarterly sessions to once again encourage candid dialogue and foster a more cooperative relationship between labor and management.

As history closed the books on 2005, Bill Ayer could point with pride to the accomplishments of that pivotal year: an adjusted profit of $55 million; aggressive route expansion, especially in Mexico; and fleet restructuring that included buying new airplanes and converting older ones into revenue-earning freighters. In other words, Alaska was like an army in retreat that suddenly began waging well-timed offensives. Ayer was betting that by spending wisely in carefully selected areas, the airline would end up not only saving money but also generating incremental revenue and making money to reinvest in itself and to benefit its employees and its shareholders.

Between mid-2005 and mid-2006, the airline's route expansion included new service to Dallas/Fort Worth, seasonal Phoenix-Anchorage nonstops, and additional service to Mexico: Los Angeles-Mexico City, Seattle-Cancún, and Portland-Los Cabos/Puerto Vallarta.

In June 2005, the airline ordered 35 of Boeing's so-called "Next-Generation" 737-800s, with deliveries to be phased in over six years. Included in the deal were purchase rights to an additional sixty-five 737-800s. It was the largest commitment for new jets since Alaska signed for twenty 737-400s in the early 1990s. The addition of these fuel-efficient, long-range aircraft was designed to open up even more opportunities for transcontinental nonstop service. As of February 2008, 31 of the 737-800s had been delivered, and Alaska now truly had the ideal airplanes for many more service opportunities.

Taking advantage of the capability of the new equipment, Alaska announced in the spring of 2007 a fall flight schedule that included nonstops from Seattle to the Hawaiian islands of Kauai and Oahu. The decision to enter this competitive, albeit desirable market was based primarily on the range and economy of the new 737-800s. Two weeks after the service was announced, 70 percent of Alaska's capacity through January between Seattle and Hawaii had been booked, and reservations were being received at an unprecedented rate.

Earlier, in 2006, Ayer had formed a special task force headed by Kevin Finan, executive vice president of operations, to coordinate Alaska's transition out of the MD-80s and into a single fleet type. By retiring all the remaining MD-80 aircraft earlier than originally planned, the airline would have to pay off remaining leases, but that would be offset by lower maintenance costs on a newer, fuel-efficient fleet. Not only would the new 800s save fuel, but they would also accommodate 17 more passengers than the aging, fuel-thirsty MD-80s.

By late June 2007, Finan's task force had been successful, and the carrier announced an agreement to sell 20 of its 24 remaining MD-80s to an aviation holding company in Chicago. The transaction was completed in 2007, but 16 of the 20 planes were leased back by Alaska until final retirement from the airline's fleet in December 2008. Intentions also were to sublease the carrier's remaining four MD-80s or park them in storage until their leases expired in 2012.

With this development, Alaska was well on its way to completing its transition to a single fleet type, long a goal and accomplished five years earlier than originally planned. By retiring the MD-80s early, Alaska figured to save about $130 million a year in maintenance, fuel, pilot training, and other costs. And later decisions upped the original June 2005 firm order for 737-800s from 35 to 55, with options for another 45.

Meanwhile, cargo was not the forgotten stepchild amidst all this fleet restructuring, for no one from Ayer on down ever lost sight of the airline's commitment to what that Eskimo on the tail stood for: Alaska was the isolated 49th state's flagship carrier, and serving its unique needs was not only a priority but also a sacred pledge.

In June 2006, Alaska took re-delivery of one of its 737-400s converted from an all-passenger aircraft into an all-cargo freighter. This was part of a $100 million commitment to modernize and expand the airline's cargo services, long one of its strengths and so vital to the Great Land. Five other 737-400s were to be converted into "combis," aircraft with a fixed bulkhead on the main deck capable of carrying 72 passengers in the rear along with four cargo pallets up front. These six "converts" would enable the airline to replace its older nine 737-200Cs that had served the airline and the state of Alaska so well for the previous 26 years. By 2007 the 200Cs, or "mud hens," as they were so fondly referred to by their adoring Alaska crews, had been phased out by the more modern equipment with greater cargo capacity.

While improvements in fleet composition were in progress, yet another task force was established in 2006, this one devoted to operations and an offshoot of Ayer's strong belief in generating more joint-employee/management involvement in projects beyond specific job duties. The core group consisted of 23 people, 14 of them frontline employees such as customer-service agents, reservationists, and flight attendants, plus ramp, dispatch, and maintenance. There were also eight department directors or managers and one vice president, Steve Jarvis. The overall goal: to make flying easier for the customer by identifying and resolving issues and situations that make flying so difficult. The 23 troubleshooters were to address five general areas of concern:

Simplifying the time-consuming process of changing and reissuing tickets
Ensuring more thorough cleaning of aircraft interiors
Providing more consistent, accurate, and timely flight information
Assuring sufficient staffing of customer-service and reservations agents,

even if this might require hiring additional personnel

Enabling frontline employees to resolve customer problems on the spot, without having to go through several management layers for decisions

At this writing, the group is well on its way to completing its immediate goals, with many of the aforementioned five problem areas already or in the process of being resolved. As an example, with the endorsement of the group, the company rolled out a tool on *alaskaair.com* allowing customers to make most itinerary changes themselves, even after travel has begun.

An achievement of equal importance, probably more so as significant symbolism, was that these 23 people had proved that management and labor *could* work together if armed with mutual respect.

Alaska Air Group ended 2006 with an adjusted net income of nearly $138 million. Once again, the company that Linious McGee had founded with a single little airplane had conquered adversity thanks to that special spirit that enabled it to overcome every obstacle from poor management to man-made disasters, from flawed human judgment to technical mistakes, and many times just a bum deal from fate.

There was no magic formula. No outstanding policy. No single individual leader. Nor any one specific work group.

It took all of the above to contribute to the making of Alaska Airlines. All, indeed, vital factors in Alaska's success. Yet they do not tell the whole story of this airline. For what really has made it so special is a state of mind of its people, born in 1932 and somehow sustained throughout its three-quarters of a century.

It was, still is, and hopefully always will be . . .

The Alaska Spirit.

On Guts and Glory

I'm an aviation writer with a love of the past and a respect for the present, but when it comes to Alaska Airlines' future, that story is better told by someone with more at stake, someone who honors the character and characters of the airline's past, but one destined to play a significant role in the company's future. That person is the airline's current chairman and CEO, Bill Ayer, and the concluding words to my story are his words, his view of the company's strengths and his vision of Alaska Airlines' future.

Bob Serling

You don't spend 75 years serving the people and communities of the great state of Alaska and not have a few tales to tell. Robert Service made a career of it. And as you've read, we've spun a few ourselves. From former airline president Charlie Willis rolling beer kegs onto the plane in the 1950s, to the hundred-dollar paychecks of the '70s, to the salmon that hit one of our 737s in midair (dropped by an eagle) in the '80s, we've seen some "strange things done in the midnight sun," as the bard Service so aptly put it.

But beer kegs and flying fish aside, Alaska Airlines' real story is about people. It's people who have made us what we are today. People like Jim Johnson, Ken Skidds, Ed White, Jacquie Witherrite, Martin Calhoun, Tada Yotsuuye, Ray Prentice . . . I could go on and on. Some are still here and some have long since moved on, but together they made this airline great.

Our employees are the rare "spice" not present in any other organization that I've seen. And like good seasoning, they are subtle, but remarkable. It's the flight attendant's smile and the mechanic personally delivering the part to the aircraft. It's the customer-service agent calling you by first name and the ramp agent who hustles a late bag onto the aircraft. It's the pilot who offers his "wings" to a critically ill child and the administrative assistant who tutors at a local school on her lunch hour. It's the reservations agent who donates her kidney to a coworker to give her a new lease on life.

That dedication and caring is the glue that holds us together as an airline and drives what we do day in and day out. It's the reason for our relentless optimism, even as we remain realistic about the challenges of the day. And it's how an obscure little airline in America's hinterland has continued to survive and thrive for 75 years while once-proud giants disappeared.

How did we do it? With sheer guts, grit, and determination. And the fact that our roots are firmly planted in the permafrost of the state of Alaska. Alaska Airlines is more than just an airline to the people and communities of Alaska. We're a lifeline. Because of the absence of roads, everything and everybody flies. With special combination passenger/cargo airplanes, we fly everything from eggs and milk to mining equipment, snowmobiles, and live walrus — literally. And with challenging weather eight months out of the year, our pilots and ground crews battle Arctic conditions and sometimes-ferocious winds, at the same time keeping an eye out for any stray polar bear or caribou that may have wandered onto the airfield.

You don't handle experiences like that every day in Alaska and take other challenges lying down. A little air-traffic congestion in Newark or being put into another holding pattern over Chicago doesn't seem so bad in comparison.

And while Alaskans have depended on us, we've depended on them as well. Our solid foundation in the state of Alaska has allowed us to grow into new markets. Our more recent success in the Lower 48 has come from our ability to translate what we do in Alaska to the unique needs of other travelers. We long ago recognized that understanding the needs of every community and providing a personalized, engaging experience for every customer on every flight was paramount. This service philosophy is still at the heart of all we do and has been our formula for success whether we're serving Nome or Newark.

Keeping the customer at the top of our mind has given us a window into the future. And with our smaller size and "get-er-done" attitude, we've been able to act quickly, well ahead of our competitors.

Our "Airport of the Future" project is an example of how we're continuing to use technology to make the travel experience easier. We've removed barriers, creating a more flowing, natural pathway for customers to get from curbside to planeside quickly. And we've gone high-tech without losing that all-important human touch. You can see this in action at airports such as Ted Stevens Anchorage International Airport and Seattle-Tacoma International Airport daily. Following in the footsteps of legendary Alaska Airlines "greeter" Ron Crouteau, our customer-contact employees make it their business to spot tech-wary customers and gently teach them how to use the self-service check-in kiosks, so the next time they can do it themselves.

We've also made adjustments in our in-flight service offerings. Chef Erbe and the roast pork loin and free chardonnay of our legendary "Gold Coast Service" are long gone. But we've differentiated our airline in other ways that matter more to today's customers — newer, more fuel-efficient airplanes, leather seats, ample legroom, assigned seating, a selection of modestly priced snacks or hot meals, and above all else, competitive airfares.

Looking ahead, this laser-sharp focus on the customer will continue to drive us, because the bottom line is that customers vote with their wallets and it's money that makes airplanes fly. That's why we will continue to work on lowering our costs and increasing our revenue. And by staying profit-able, we will continue to offer secure jobs and retirements for our employees who deliver the brand of service that sets us apart. Achieving these things should result in a virtuous cycle, where good performance in one area leads to improved performance in another, and they all add up to being the best in customer service.

We are beginning to see this cycle of improvement take hold, and our results are encouraging. With an assumption of continued profitability, we've committed to a long-term fleet and growth plan, including an order for up to 100 new Boeing 737s and a plan to accelerate the retirement of our MD-80s to achieve an all-737 fleet by the end of 2008. Thanks to our conviction about maintaining a strong balance sheet, we've contributed to our employees' retirement accounts, giving us the best-funded plans in the industry. And that same balance-sheet strength provided the opportunity to actually expand our network following the dark day of September 11. While soaring fuel prices and economic pressures continue to buffet the industry, our service focus and financial discipline put us in a better position than most to weather those storms.

This gives you a glimpse into what I feel the Alaska Airlines of the future will look like. It'll be profitable, with fuel-efficient airplanes that allow you to fly in safety and comfort while respecting the environment. It'll be efficient and easy, using technology and streamlined processes to get you where you want to go with the least hassles. And it'll be warm and friendly, with service provided by impassioned employees who make the difference.

In all, our future looks promising, and we have our early leaders to thank for making the tough choices they did. Looking back, despite their differing personas and styles, Charlie Willis, Ron Cosgrave, Bruce Kennedy, Ray Vecci, and John Kelly were the right leaders at the right time for what the airline needed to achieve. Charlie set the tone for a fun and brash airline that could take on the world. Ron and Bruce righted the ship, getting the books in order and growing the company during the exciting time following deregulation of the airline industry. Ray's planning prowess and vigorous cost-cutting set the stage for the advances and opportunities the airline was presented with in the '90s, and the charismatic and customer-savvy John made them happen in spades.

If Alaska's founders could see it today, they would be in awe of what this airline has accomplished. Serving 92 cities across three countries with our sister airline Horizon Air, a modern fleet of jets, and more than 10,000 employees — indeed, Alaska Airlines has grown up. But what is perhaps more remarkable is the fact that, in doing so, we haven't lost our youthful spirit.

This spirit — a can-do attitude that we call the "Alaska Spirit" — is embodied in the hearts and minds of the men and women of Alaska Airlines, and has been for years. It's what drove Mac McGee to climb into his three-seat Stinson 75 years ago and launch this airline. It's what propelled the airline's expansion into the Lower 48 to take on the Goliaths of the industry. It's what put the fire in our belly to move eastward into previously uncharted markets while still providing dedicated service to the small communities in rural Alaska. And it's what has made us one of the most successful U.S. airlines today.

For this we have a circle of lifelong customers and our dedicated employees — both past and present — to thank. They have made this airline what it is today, and their collective Alaska Spirit will weave the tales of the airline's history for the next 75 years.

Bruce Roger Kennedy
1938 – 2007

Ron Cosgrave . . . Bruce Kennedy . . . Ray Vecci . . . John Kelly . . . Bill Ayer. Of these five individuals who have captained Alaska Airlines from the post-Willis days to well into the 21st century, it is ironic that the one who looked too young to be running an airline was the first to "fly west" — the synonym for death used by the old bush and airmail pilots.

Kennedy was killed around 7 p.m. on Thursday, June 28, 2007. He was piloting his single-engine Cessna 182 when he crashed while landing at Cashmere, in north-central Washington. On his final approach to the small town's 1,800-foot runway, heading west into a bright, late afternoon sun, Kennedy's aircraft hit the top of a tree, then fell to the ground and burst into flames just short of his destination.

In one of the beautiful eulogies delivered by his children at the memorial service a week later, his son, Kevin, said, "There is no doubt he died doing something he loved, and that his last minutes on this earth were spent enjoying life, and that his untimely death spared him a future that he did not desire."

Kevin went on to explain: "It was not widely known that he [Bruce] had been diagnosed with a form of blood cancer almost two years ago, and was just reaching the point where he would soon need to make some decisions regarding treatment, and let's just say my dad wouldn't have been the best patient in the world. He closely guarded the news of his condition and would not have liked the attention that his cancer might have ultimately brought." This news took most of the 600 people at the service by surprise.

Kennedy practiced his faith throughout much of his life, and the Kennedy family demonstrated how the strength of faith can console, comfort, and heal grief.

Karin Hejmanowski, Kennedy's daughter and a Presbyterian minister, also spoke of her father at the service. "Dad's opinions and decisions in the workplace were not always the most popular," she said. "His was a prophetic voice. He was committed to hearing the opinions of others, taking them into account, and then doing what he thought was right."

Some myths surrounding Kennedy's faith persisted, but Kevin debunked one of them at the service. It was the long-held belief by many associated with Alaska Airlines that it had been Kennedy's idea to put printed prayer cards on the airline's food-service trays. Actually Kennedy's predecessor Ben Benecke, by way of Mike Ryan, who brought the idea with him from Continental Airlines, authorized what was to become a distinct, if not controversial, difference between Alaska Airlines and its competitors.

And Kevin reminded those assembled of Kennedy's love for the state of Alaska. He described Kennedy's connection to the Great Land this way: "My dad was an Alaskan at heart, and he was determined that the airline that bore the name of the state he loved would remain as unique and independent as the people it served."

Obituaries were plentiful. One article printed in *The Wenatchee World* several weeks after Kennedy's death was written by Kevin Swanson, CEO of Mission Aviation Fellowship, one of Kennedy's post-Alaska Airlines interests. Swanson described Kennedy's life as "undivided," suggesting that Kennedy didn't separate his faith from his professional, civic, or personal life. "His spirituality and the rest of his life were integrated, not compartmentalized."

Swanson also wrote of Kennedy's reply when he was once asked by a fund-raiser to approach some of his wealthy friends. "What you don't understand," said Kennedy, "is that my friends are the kind of people who leave oil stains in your driveway."

In his final comment at the service, Kevin Kennedy left no doubt that his father was ready to meet his Maker; pointing out the symbolism of the accident at sunset, these were his words: "It was as if God reached down and said, 'Well done, good and faithful servant. . . . Come and share your Master's happiness.' "

Listening intently, along with more than 600 others, were the four surviving CEOs who had been invited to attend the memorial, Ron Cosgrave, Bill Ayer, John Kelly, and Ray Vecci. Together for the first time in years, they were bound by the history they shared, and the respect they had for the man.

Thus did family, friends, and former colleagues bid farewell to The Kid.

ACKNOWLEDGMENTS

My thanks and a few thoughts on what you've read.

No historian ever boards a time machine for a trip into the past and then flies solo. A great many people accompanied me on this voyage of 75 years, including the more than 100 individuals who submitted to interviews and those who helped in countless other ways.

I am indebted to all of them, but I owe enormous thanks in particular to certain individuals without whose knowledge and unselfish cooperation this project would have suffered from my own shortcomings. I must first single out two former officers of Alaska Airlines. Throughout the four years this endeavor required, I depended heavily on crucial guidance from Lou Cancelmi, retired staff vice president of corporate communications, and Jim Johnson, retired senior vice president of public affairs. They served not as censors but as editors, making sure I did not wander off in the direction of inaccuracy and/or unfairness.

My gratitude to former CEOs Ron Cosgrave, Bruce Kennedy, and John Kelly and current CEO Bill Ayer, all of whom graciously allowed me to interview them more than once, simply because their input was too valuable and extensive to be covered in any single session.

And thanks as well to these other special persons:

Barry Provorse of Documentary Media, the most cooperative and helpful publisher I've ever encountered in a career that has produced 25 published books.

My old friend and colleague Jon Proctor, former editor-in-chief of *Airliners* magazine, whose encyclopedic knowledge of airline history saved me hours of drudging research and whose several articles on Alaska and Horizon were invaluable sources.

Within my own family, thanks to my daughter Jennifer for assisting her klutz father with his iMac computer, my son Jeff for helping me with a special area of research, and my wife, Dr. Patricia Hoyer, who not only corrected my frequent typing errors but also supported me in every way possible. Patty proved that my father, for once in his life, was wrong when he told me many years ago, "Never marry a woman who's a lot smarter than you are."

Among the many treasured friendships I made in the course of research were those cemented with that noble breed known as administrative assistants, so unfailingly helpful and efficient. I refer specifically to Jeanne Gessitz, Maria Koenig, Donna Hartman, and Barb Johnson. Jeanne earned an additional medal for helping me transcribe several long interviews when I was drowning under sheer volume.

A low bow to Sarah Dalton, director of training and technology at flight operations, and Captain Mike Adams, who navigated me through the technicalities of RNP cockpit instrumentation and procedures.

Greg Witter and Don Conrard, consummate professionals and veterans of the corporate communications staff, stood out among the people to whom I am beholden for their frequent and most valuable help.

Some individuals went beyond what I learned from their interviews and endured my pestering them for additional information and background. I refer to Captains Kevin Finan and Mike Swanigan of flight operations; Keith Loveless, Tom O'Grady, and Irv Bertram from legal; Gregg Saretsky of marketing and planning; Richard Wien of Alaska's board of directors; Milt Kuolt, Horizon's founder; Marvin Van Horn, who provided much insight into the Alaska vs. MarkAir fight; Jeff Pinneo, Horizon's CEO; Ed White, who was of tremendous help with the story of Flight 261; Dave Palmer of marketing; Susan "Ms. Alaska" Bramstedt; and CSA Jacquie Witherrite, who turned out to be the best-prepared subject I've ever interviewed. She even wrote out many of her anecdotes in advance, which saved me hours of transcribing.

It is an accepted fact that the most inept, hopelessly thin-skinned, and biased editors are not those who read manuscript drafts, but the authors themselves. We fall in love with the sound of our own words. We deeply resent any changes, we bristle if someone challenges our opinions, and we associate even minor rewriting suggestions with such unpleasantries as the Spanish Inquisition and Asian water torture. I am no exception.

So I must emphasize with much gratitude that throughout this long project, in the course of which I wore out two tape recorders and a printer, I was encouraged to express my own conclusions about controversial events described in this history and the often-controversial individuals involved in those events.

There will be some, perhaps many, readers who will take issue with what I've written. There will be, I expect, some unfavorable reviews by those critics who automatically assume that because the company itself has commissioned a corporate history, it has to be a complete whitewash job, an account sanitized, cleansed, and stripped of all faults, flaws, and foibles personal as well as corporate.

Yes, Alaska Airlines did commission this work. No, they did not dictate its contents. The marching orders I received from CEO Bill Ayer and retired CEOs Bruce Kennedy and John Kelly were simple: "Write an honest and accurate history of our first 75 years, warts and all." That I have tried to do. Any errors of commission or omission are mine.

I relied to a great extent on the personal recollections of those who actually participated in the major events of those 75 years. Admittedly, this is one of literary nonfiction's largest minefields, lined with booby traps that can blow fact into unintended inaccuracies.

Author Ralph Keyes, in a recent book titled *The Quote Verifier* (St. Martin's Griffin), summed up this hazard with an extremely astute observation. "Memory may be a terrible librarian," he wrote, "but it's a great editor." He was referring to the fact that many of history's most famous quotations either were never uttered or have been attributed to the wrong person. Apply that conclusion to the memories of, say, four people who witnessed the same event — they not only describe it in four different ways, but each person sincerely believes that his or her version tells what really happened.

The job of the historian is to judge these four varying views by (1) whatever documented evidence is available, such as annual reports, official meeting minutes, or hopefully reliable newspaper coverage; (2) which account seems the most logical considering the overall evidence; (3) which version is supported by a majority of witnesses; and (4) chronological accuracy — innocently placing an event in the wrong time context or in the wrong sequence is a frequent source of inaccuracy.

Add the natural tendency of people to embellish, to exaggerate one's role, to have memory tarnished by bias, or to be victimized simply by a frequent human failing: faulty memory. In other words, while truth is in the eye of the beholder, the historian still must base his own judgment on the predominant evidence. I hope that the reader will do likewise.

I fear that some, if not many, of those I interviewed will be disappointed that I did not use more of the information they provided. Believe me, in some instances it was tempting to include virtually entire transcripts, as the voluminous material was that interesting and important. The same was true of the stories submitted by those responding to a request in *Alaska's World* for such material. (That well-edited and well-written company newspaper, incidentally, was of great value.)

But judicious cuts and careful selections had to be made to keep the book's length within reason. As it was, its original projected length of 350 pages had to be stretched to more than 500. In one sense, writing a history is no different from writing a film script; inevitably some great stuff must wind up on the proverbial cutting-room floor.

All of which is a preamble to expressing my gratitude to the following individuals who either were interviewed at least once or submitted written material. Saying thanks is inadequate. The book could not have been written without its real authors: the people who lived and are still living this story. They are listed alphabetically; all were or are associated with AAG except where indicated.

Julian Acosta, Mike Adams, Shannon Alberts, Tom Allee (Frontier), Bill Ayer.

Carl Baber, George Bagley, Sandi Baker (Boeing), Craig Battison, Irv Bertram, Roger Blair, Caroline Boren, Bill Boyer, Susan Bramstedt, Marcia Broyles, Sheri Buggins.

Jeff Cacy, Marty Calhoun, Lou Cancelmi, Don Conrard, Bambi Coons, Kit Cooper, Ron Cosgrave, Jo Coughlin, Bill Cox, Debi Crawford (Livingston ad agency), Jerry Cutler.

Tom Dezutter, Bob Dodd, Jim Doman.

Wolfgang Erbe.

Kevin Finan, Barb Foster, John Fowler.

Dick Garvin, Pat Glenn, Bob Gray.

Bob Handley, Katsie Hirsh, Tom Holmes, Bob Hudson.

Kristen Jarman (FBI), Steve Jarvis, Lin Jauhola, Barb Johnson, Jim Johnson.

Dennis Kelley, John Kelly, Maggi Kelly, John Kelsey, Mary Kenison, Skip Kenison, Bruce Kennedy, George Knuckey, Bob Koslick, Milt Kuolt.

Paul Landis (Era), Greg Latimer, Wes Laubscher, Marjorie Laws, Jennifer Lee, Marianne Lindsey, Helen Loudenback, Keith Loveless.

Bill MacKay, Danna Maros-Siverts, Dave Marriott, Mike McMillen, Irene McSorley, Warren Metzger, Michelle Minor, Martha Minter.

John Nance, C.C. Nelson, Gail Neufeld.

Bill O'Dwyer, Tom O'Grady.

Dave Palmer, Keola Pang-Ching, Stan Patty (writer), Ron Peck, Art Peterson, LeRoy Peterson, Jeff Pinneo, Ray Prentice, Dave Prewitt, Jon Proctor (*Airliners*).

Mark Ramstad, Bob Reeder, Kay Reeves, Scott Ridge, Kim Roberts (Air Transport Association), Tanya Roberts, Gus Robinson, Barbara Roehl.

Gregg Saretsky, Smokey Schnee, Paul Schneider, Orrin Seybert (PenAir), Ken Skidds, Ray Silvius (Western), Ken Smith, Gail Spaeth, Ron Suttell, Mike Swanigan.

Walter Turner.

Marvin Van Horn, Ray Vecci, Ray Vingo, Chris Von Imhoff.

Sue Warner-Bean, Ed White, Richard Wien, Clancy Wilde (Boeing), Jacquie Witherrite, Greg Witter.

Dave Zehrung.

BIBLIOGRAPHY

The following is a partial list of factual sources. It does not include all of my own published aviation-history works, nor such standard references as *The World Almanac*. Articles published in *Airliners* magazine are credited in the author's acknowledgments.

America's Fascinating Indian Heritage.
Pleasantville, NY: Reader's Digest Books, 1978.

Bean, Barbara. *Of Magic Sails: A Photographic History of Air Travel, 1926–1976*. Chicago: Graphic Alliance, 1975.

The Bush Pilots. Alexandria, VA: Time-Life Books, 1983.

Davies, R. E. G. *Airlines of the United States Since 1914*.
London: Putnam, 1972.

Davis, Burke. *The Billy Mitchell Affair*. New York: Random House, 1967.

Endicott, Bill. *Remember the Magic: The Story of Horizon Air*.
Paducah, KY: Turner Publishing, 2001.

Felleman, Hazel, comp. *The Best Loved Poems of the American People*.
New York: Doubleday, 1936.

Great Disasters. Pleasantville, NY: Reader's Digest Books, 1989.

Green, William. *The Macdonald Aircraft Handbook*.
New York: Doubleday, 1964.

Gunston, Bill. *The Illustrated Encyclopedia of Commercial Aircraft*.
New York: Exeter Books, 1980.

Gunston, Bill. *The Illustrated Encyclopedia of Propeller Airliners*.
New York: Exeter Books, 1980.

Harkey, Ira. *Noel Wien: Alaska Pioneer Bush Pilot*. Fairbanks:
University of Alaska Press, 1974.

Helmericks, Harmon. *The Last of the Bush Pilots*. New York: Bantam, 1969.

Job, Macarthur. *Air Disaster*, Volumes II and III. Sydney:
Aerospace Publications, 1996.

Nance, John J. *Splash of Colors: The Self-Destruction of
Braniff International*. New York: William Morrow & Co., 1984.

Proctor, Jon. *Convair 880 & 990*. Miami: World Transport Press, 1996.

Satterfield, Archie. *The Alaska Airlines Story*.
Anchorage: Alaska Northwest Publishing, 1981.

Serling, Robert. *Birth of an Industry*.
Chicago: Reuben Donnelley Corporation, 1969.

Solberg, Carl. *Conquest of the Skies*. Boston: Little, Brown, 1979.

These United States. Pleasantville, NY: Reader's Digest Books, 1968.

INDEX